Open Door

NATO and Euro-Atlantic Security After the Cold War

Daniel S. Hamilton and Kristina Spohr
Editors

Paul H. Nitze School of Advanced International Studies
Johns Hopkins University

Daniel S. Hamilton and Kristina Spohr, eds., *Open Door: NATO and Euro-Atlantic Security After the Cold War.*

Washington, DC: Foreign Policy Institute/Henry A. Kissinger Center for Global Affairs, Johns Hopkins University SAIS 2019.

Supported by

DAAD Deutscher Akademischer Austauschdienst
German Academic Exchange Service

Funded by

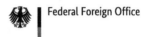 Federal Foreign Office

Distributed by Brookings Institution Press.

Foreign Policy Institute and Henry A. Kissinger Center for Global Affairs
Paul H. Nitze School of Advanced International Studies
Johns Hopkins University
1717 Massachusetts Ave., NW
Washington, DC 20036
Tel: (202) 663-5882
Email: transatlantic@jhu.edu
http://transatlanticrelations.org
https://www.fpi.sais-jhu.edu/
https://www.kissinger.sais-jhu.edu

ISBN: 978-1-7337339-2-2

Contents

Acknowledgments

NATO's decision to open its doors to new members after the end of the Cold War and the collapse of the Soviet Union was one of the most momentous—and controversial—choices in recent history. It was rooted in efforts by the North Atlantic Alliance to revise its missions for a new era of challenges and to respond to Eastern European desires to join the "institutional West." More generally, NATO's enlargement grew from the process of an overall reshaping of the "architecture" of institutions and mechanisms binding North America and Europe for the post-Cold War world. The causes and consequences of these decisions have been the subject of intense scrutiny and fierce debate.

In this book, senior officials and opinion leaders from the United States, Russia, Western and Eastern Europe who were directly involved in the decisions of that time describe their considerations, concerns, and pressures. They are joined by scholars who have been able to draw on newly declassified archival sources to revisit NATO's evolving role in the 1990s. All were able to exchange perspectives and offer comments at an authors' workshop at Johns Hopkins SAIS on March 12, 2019—the 20th anniversary of Czech, Hungarian and Polish accession to the Alliance.

This project has been conducted by the Foreign Policy Institute and the Henry A. Kissinger Center for Global Affairs of Johns Hopkins University's School of Advanced International Studies (SAIS), specifically our program on The United States, Europe and World Order.

We are particularly grateful to the German Academic Exchange Service (DAAD) and the German Federal Foreign Office for their support of our postdoctoral program and related activities, including this project.

We would also like to thank our colleagues Francis Gavin and Christopher Crosbie, Director and Associate Director, respectively, of the Henry A. Kissinger Center for Global Affairs at Johns Hopkins SAIS, and Carla Freeman and Christine Kunkel, Director and Associate Director, respectively, of the SAIS Foreign Policy Institute.

A special note of thanks goes to our Program Coordinator Jason Moyer, who has been tireless in his support of us and our postdoctoral fellows and made countless efforts to ensure the success of this project. We express particular gratitude to Margaret Irvine—the cover designer—and our copyeditor Peter Lindeman for converting the manuscript so quickly into this book.

The views and opinions expressed are those of the authors, and do not necessarily reflect those of any institution or government.

Daniel S. Hamilton
Kristina Spohr
April 2019

Foreword

In 1949, Secretary of State Dean Acheson transmitted to President Truman the original North Atlantic Treaty. In doing so, Acheson pointed out that in order for the Alliance to be "fully effective" it had to be open to "as many countries as are in a position to further the democratic principles upon which the Treaty was based, to contribute to the security of the North Atlantic area, and ... to undertake the necessary responsibilities."

Within a decade, the Alliance's twelve founding members began adding to their ranks. They brought Germany and Spain, two formerly fascist countries, into the family of European democracies. They welcomed Greece and Turkey, helping stabilize relations between those two countries. Each of these enlargement decisions helped the Alliance become stronger, overcome old divisions, and anchor more nations in the community of democracies that NATO was designed to unite and protect.

The strength, vitality and resolve of NATO helped tear down the Berlin Wall without firing a shot. But when the Cold War ended, and the Warsaw Pact dissolved, it left a security vacuum. Europe's new democracies, after being forced by the Soviet Union to live behind an Iron Curtain for forty years, wanted control of their future and wanted to belong to Europe's economic and security institutions. The Alliance therefore faced a dual challenge: first, how to preserve a favorable strategic environment into the next century; and second, how to seize the opportunity to build a Europe whole and free.

In meeting that challenge, NATO faced a blunt choice. Would it be the last institution in Europe to continue to treat the Iron Curtain as something meaningful, or would it aid in Europe's reunification and renewal? Would NATO exclude from its ranks a whole group of qualified democracies simply because they had been subjugated in the past, or would it be open to those free nations that were willing and able to meet the responsibilities of membership and contribute to the Alliance's security?

I believe Allied leaders made the right choice. They saw an opportunity to do for Europe's East what NATO and the Marshall Plan had done for Europe's West. Their goal was to create a sphere of common interest in which every nation could live in security. To this end, they established linkages through the Partnership for Peace between NATO and other European democracies. They transformed the Organization for Security and Cooperation in Europe into an arena for supporting democracy and human rights. And as chronicled in the ensuing pages, they undertook a gradual and deliberate process for enlarging NATO.

Many of the contributors to this edited volume played a critical role in that process. Their accounts greatly enrich the historical record, at a time when the legacy of NATO enlargement deserves to be revisited and better understood.

For my part, I was serving as President Clinton's Ambassador to the United Nations when many of the key decisions about NATO expansion were made. Although I was in favor of bringing new members into the Alliance, I had kept my counsel when the prospect was first raised. I did not want anyone to suspect me, a Czechoslovak by birth, of special pleading on behalf of the Czech Republic, Slovakia, or other potential NATO candidates. I was also focused on my portfolio in New York. But as the debate gathered momentum and I took office as Secretary of State, I became a vigorous advocate for expansion.

One did not have to be a native of the region to see the logic of NATO opening its doors again to new members. After four decades of Communist subjugation, the nations of Central and Eastern Europe were eager to join an enlarged NATO. If they were denied NATO protection, they would be left in political limbo and might well seek security through other means, resulting in unpredictable alliances, efforts at rearmament, and the possible use of force to settle disputes.

All this seemed obvious, but many in the U.S. foreign policy establishment took a different view. One can easily forget how strong the opposition was. George Kennan, the ageless icon of U.S. diplomacy, denounced NATO enlargement as "the greatest mistake in Western policy in the entire post-Cold War era" (few recall that he had opposed NATO's creation in 1949). More than 50 prominent political and academic figures accused the Clinton Administration of "making an error of historic proportions." And an informal Council on Foreign Relations poll showed experts opposing NATO expansion two to one.

The Clinton Administration was determined to overcome these critics by making the case that a larger NATO—with the Czech Republic, Hungary and Poland as the first new members—would serve American interests.

We argued, first and foremost, that enlargement would make America safer by expanding the area of Europe where wars did not happen. By making it clear that America would fight to defend its new Allies, we believed it would be less likely that we would ever be called upon to do so.

We also pointed out that the prospect of a larger NATO had given the nations of Central and Eastern Europe an incentive to strengthen their democratic institutions, improve respect for minority rights, establish civilian control over their militaries, and peacefully resolve border and ethnic disputes. This progress would help ensure that outside powers were never again dragged into a conflict at the heart of Europe.

A final reason why enlargement passed the test of national interest, we argued, was that it would make NATO itself stronger and more cohesive. The prospective allies were passionately committed to NATO, and had risked their lives alongside U.S. troops in the Gulf War and in Bosnia. They saw membership not as a burden, but as an opportunity to show the world that they were able to give something back to the community of freedom that stood by them in their years of darkness.

Still, we also had to address concerns about Russia. President Boris Yeltsin and his countrymen were strongly opposed to enlargement, seeing it as a strategy for exploiting their vulnerability and moving Europe's dividing line to the east, leaving them isolated.

I spent much time while in office talking through these objections with my Russian counterparts and NATO leaders, eventually reaching an agreement—the NATO-Russia Founding Act. This document provided an institutional means for Russia to participate in transatlantic security deliberations, without giving them a veto over Alliance decisions.

Perhaps no aspect of NATO enlargement has proven as controversial as the impact on Russia. As of this writing, there are still legions of critics who argue that it poisoned the relationship with Russia, and is therefore to blame for all of the geopolitical problems facing the world in 2019.

This is ludicrous. It is a huge mistake to think that every time Russia does something we do not like, it is to "punish" us for bringing Hungary or Poland or the Baltic states into NATO.

Our disagreements with Russia in the Middle East or in Ukraine have come about because of the manner in which Russia defines its national interests in those parts of the world. These differences existed long before NATO decided to open its doors to new members. If we had kept NATO a closed shop, we still would not have resolved those differences with Russia. We would, however, have turned our backs on nations that stood with us on a range of security issues that mattered to the Alliance.

History will show that the United States and its Allies did seek a true partnership with Russia. But we did not want that partnership to be purchased by denying a dozen European countries the right to seek membership in NATO. A partnership built on an illegitimate moral compromise would not be genuine and it would not last.

For all these reasons and more, the story of NATO opening its doors to new members and new missions—the story told in these pages—involved much, much more than the immediate future of the countries in question. It involved the future security of the United States; the future of an undivided Europe; the future of Russia and the character of NATO's relationship with it.

While it is impossible to prove a counterfactual, it is clear to me that the world would be far more dangerous, and Europe far less prosperous and stable, had NATO not helped in erasing the continent's old, artificial divisions.

That makes this a story worth telling. So I am grateful to the editors of this volume for capturing this moment and for teaching a new generation about the importance of the decisions that we made.

Madeleine K. Albright
Washington, DC
April 2019

Introduction

Daniel S. Hamilton and Kristina Spohr

This book is a highly unusual blend of memoir and scholarship that takes us back to the decade when "post-Wall Europe" was made. Drawing on newly-released archival material, each scholar offers his interpretations. Drawing on memory, experience, and personal notes, each protagonist retraces his or her original impressions, choices and contributions to how NATO, in its exit from the Cold War, came to reaffirm its purpose while revising its missions, opening its door to new members, building new relations with other institutions and partner countries, and attempting cooperation with Russia.

On April 4, 2019 the North Atlantic Treaty Organization (NATO) celebrated its 70th anniversary. Few would have expected this when the Alliance was born. In 1951, when General Dwight D. Eisenhower assumed command of NATO forces in Europe as the first Supreme Allied Commander Europe (SACEUR), he mused that "if in 10 years, all American troops stationed in Europe for national defense purposes have not been returned to the United States, then this whole project will have failed." The U.S. commitment was intended to get war-torn Western Europe on its feet and off America's back. But the Allies hung together, for fear that otherwise they might hang separately.

NATO saw off the Cold War and the demise of the Soviet Union. Yet when the East-West conflict ended, the United States did not reduce its commitment to Europe, it extended it. 40 years after Eisenhower's prophecy, some 150,000 American troops remained in Europe.[1] On NATO's 50th birthday in 1999, its leaders not only welcomed three new members (Poland, Hungary and the Czech Republic), they approved the blueprint for a larger, more flexible Alliance that would remain committed to collective defense but be capable of meeting a wider range of threats to common Alliance interests.[2]

This mixture of solidarity and flexibility proved to be an essential combination in helping NATO see out the Cold War. There were times when the Alliance had seemed under impossible strains, for instance when trying to respond to the Soviet deployment of SS-20 missiles. But the Alliance managed to craft the so-called 'Dual Track' policy in 1979 that ultimately led to the withdrawal of all intermediate-range missiles in Europe. NATO was also an essential factor in the process of German unification. The insistence by U.S. President George H.W. Bush and German Chancellor Helmut Kohl that unified Germany must remain a member of the Alliance assured Moscow against German revanchism and also justified the continuing presence of U.S. military forces in post-Cold War Europe.[3]

But what would NATO look like in post-Wall Europe? In their London Declaration of July 6, 1990 NATO leaders stressed their intent to "remain a defensive alliance" while espousing the goal of becoming a more "political" community, so that members of the disintegrating Warsaw Pact could "establish regular diplomatic liaison with NATO." The aim was to "work with all the countries of Europe" in order "to create enduring peace" on the continent.[4] In the fall of 1991 they created the North Atlantic Cooperation Council (NACC). NACC was intended to represent the Euro-Atlantic Community at large—from Vancouver to Vladivostok—and symbolize NATO's stretched-out "hand of friendship" to the formerly antagonistic East—the Warsaw Pact states including the USSR.[5]

Ironically, however, the Cooperation Council's very first meeting on December 20, 1991 coincided with the Soviet Union's dissolution into "sovereign states." NACC suddenly found itself dealing with a multitude of separate entities in the post-Soviet space. The question quickly became whether NACC would "remain the embodiment of the liaison program" or become "a way station on the road to Alliance membership."[6] How should NATO differentiate between the new democracies in Central and Eastern Europe eagerly looking to join the West and former Soviet states still in the orbit of Moscow's "Near Abroad"?[7]

As America and its Allies worked to design and build a post-Cold War Euro-Atlantic security architecture, their biggest challenge in this chaotic situation was forging a partnership with the new post-Soviet Russia und President Boris Yeltsin. How would such a partnership look? How could Russia's transformation be supported—both economically and politically? Could that now highly volatile country be engaged in a cooperative relationship? How could stability and security be secured in Central Europe after the Balkan powderkeg exploded anew with the disintegration of Yugoslavia?

Various options for the new architecture were gradually ruled out. French President François Mitterrand's vague model of a "European Confederation"[8] (excluding the United States) quickly fell by the wayside because American power clearly remained a crucial element in the security equation. The eastern enlargement of the European Union (EU) was still far off, and it lacked a hard security component. It was increasingly clear why Eastern European eyes, including those of the Baltic trio—at the interface of Europe and Russia—turned towards NATO and the United States.[9] George H. W. Bush could not solve that conundrum in 1992. It was left to the Clinton Administration from 1993 to move from loose ideas about "liaison" to offer a concrete response to the growing desire of Eastern Europe to formally join the Western Alliance.

Opening the Alliance's door and enlarging its territory were crucial for the "new" NATO. But more was at stake. In the post-Wall world, NATO needed to redefine its mission if it wanted to stay in business.[10] Although it remained the politico-military institution that integrated the armed forces of much of Europe and provided the United States and its Allies with a unique capacity to influence each other's policies, the NATO Alliance would have to modify its modus operandi. That meant being able to engage militarily "out of area," manage crises, consider peace enforcement missions and even undertake humanitarian interventions. Through all of this America remained the leading "ordering power."

*   *   *

NATO's decision to open itself to new members and new missions is one of the most contentious and least understood issues of the post-Wall world. It has now been twenty years since the Czech Republic, Hungary and Poland entered the Alliance in 1999, yet controversy surrounding the motives and choices of that time continues to accompany contemporary debates about the bonds between Europe and the United States, the future of East Central Europe, and relations between Russia and the West. Seen from our point of view—one of us a protagonist and the other an historian of that period—many of those debates have become narrow, one-dimensional caricatures of a more complex story. In this volume we have sought to present that story in a richer, multi-dimensional perspective—not least to counter the abuses of this history that are increasingly undertaken by politicians as they seek to "rewrite" the past to serve their current political purposes.

Rashomon (羅生門 Rashōmon), the classic Japanese film directed by Akira Kurosawa, has become synonymous with the struggle to uncover "objective" truth. The film is known for a plot device that involves various characters providing substantially different yet equally plausible accounts of the same incident. The film shows how the same events can be viewed in completely different ways by different people with different backgrounds, expectations, and experiences. The "Rashomon effect" is a term used by scholars, journalists and film critics to refer to contradictory interpretations of the same events by different persons. It highlights the subjective effect of perception on recollection.[11]

A number of the officials who participated in this project, including at our Washington workshop, told us they felt like a character from *Rashomon*. The analogy is helpful yet somewhat dangerous, because at the end of *Rashomon* it actually turns out each of the characters was lying, and the film intentionally fails to offer any accompanying evidence to elevate or disqualify any version of the truth.

Nonetheless, *Rashomon* underscores how individual interpretations of events can be deeply intertwined with subjective personal memories and perceptions at the time. It also highlights the need to supplement personal narrative with evidence, as we have done by including contributions drawing on newly-released archival materials.

A related guide is the ancient fable of the blind men who each feels a different part of an elephant:

> My friends and I can't seem to figure out what this thing in front of us is. One of us thinks it's a wall; one thinks it's a snake; one thinks it's a rope, and one thinks it's four tree trunks. How can one thing seem so different to five different people?"
>
> "Well," said the zoo-keeper. "You are all right. This elephant seems like something different to each one of you. And the only way to know what this thing really is, is to do exactly what you have

done. Only by sharing what each of you knows can you possibly reach a true understanding.[12]

The fable teaches a lesson about the limits of individual perspective. One person's view of an ultimate truth may not tell the whole story. Perception is influenced by the truth each individual is able to touch. Each protagonist creates his own version of reality from a limited personal perspective. He may be tempted to believe he has a better handle on the truth than others. Yet only when each protagonist shares his individual perspective does a fuller picture come into view.

The problem, of course, is that the men in the fable were blind. Our authors, in contrast, were key decision makers at the time. Each saw a part of the elephant—their personal role and that of their country/government—and can tell that part of the story. By asking them to share their observations with each other and us in our intense one-day parley and then combining them in essay form into one volume, we are able to offer a fuller view of the whole elephant. This is important because NATO's post-Wall enlargement and the decisions of the 1990s are still the elephant in the room when it comes to current debates about the future of NATO and relations with Russia.[13]

The final context for our collection of articles is what cinematographers call the Reveal Shot. When a camera focuses narrowly on a particular actor or actors, viewers can't see the whole set. When the camera pans out, or cuts to a wider view, the audience can see other aspects that can entirely change their understanding of the story. By delineating specific details and documents while putting them in larger context, our authors offer the broader perspective that is necessary to a clearer understanding of the security dynamics of post-Wall Europe.

Perhaps the most useful contribution this book can make is as a cautionary tale for those who seek to promote absolute truth, ascribe malevolent intent to others, or overreach in their interpretations. Different actors have different impressions of the same issue, depending on their individual mental maps, vantage points and national interests. As a result, their outlooks and goals, perceptions and experiences differ. By seeing through their eyes, looking over their shoulders, and studying meticulously the contemporary written and spoken record, we are able to re-examine and explore:

- how leaders and their administrations across the Euro-Atlantic space reacted to the upheavals of 1989–1991;

- how they imagined the future and what realities they were up against—in the domestic arena and international politics at large;

- why NATO survived the Cold War;

- why its strength—collective defense, rather CSCE-style collective security—mattered to members and aspirant countries;

- why and how the Alliance was revived and reinvented as a central pillar of the Euro-Atlantic security framework; and

- how key protagonists sought to find a place for Russia.

Together, these essays help us understand the origins of today's transatlantic relationship and can inform debates about its future.

Notes

1. Eugene Carroll and Pat Schroeder, "The Soviet Union dissolved and common concern at getting that transition right," *Chicago Tribune* September 2, 1994.

2. "The Washington Declaration"—signed and issued by the Heads of State and Government participating in the meeting of the North Atlantic Council in Washington D.C. on April 23-24, 1999, https://clintonwhitehouse2.archives.gov/WH/New/NATO/statement2.html. See also Wade Boese, "NATO Unveils 'Strategic Concept' at 50th Anniversary Summit," April 1, 1999, https://www.armscontrol.org/act/1999_04-05/natam99. Cf. "NATO takes measures to reinforce collective defence, agrees on support for Ukraine," April 1, 2014, https://www.nato.int/cps/en/natolive/news_108508.htm.

3. This is discussed more fully in Kristina Spohr, *Post Wall, Post Square. Rebuilding the World after 1989* (London: HarperCollins, 2019; New Haven, CT: Yale University Press, 2020), Chapters 3 and 4.

4. The London Declaration on a Transformed North Atlantic Alliance, July 6, 1990, https://www.cvce.eu/en/obj/the_london_declaration_on_a_transformed_north_atlantic_alliance_6_july_1990-en-9c5fa86b-12a0-4f59-ad90-e69503ef6036.html.

5. Thomas L. Friedman, "Soviet Disarray: Yeltsin Says Russia Seeks to Join NATO," *New York Times*, Dec. 21, 1991; North Atlantic Cooperation Council (NACC), https://www.nato.int/cps/en/natolive/topics_69344.htm.

6. George H.W. Bush Presidential Library, College Station, TX (*hereafter* GHWBPL), NSC, Barry Lowenkron Files, European Strategy Steering Group (ESSG): ESSG Meeting—February 3, 1992, NATO and the East: Key Issues, no author (likely NSC) undated. See also The National Archives UK, Kew Surrey (*hereafter* TNA UK), PREM 19/4329, Memo, Weston to Goulden (confidential)—The Future of NATO—The Question of Enlargement, 3 March 1992, pp. 1-7. On the NACC meeting and Soviet disintegration, see Friedman, op cit.

7. GHWBPL, NSC David Gompert Files, ESSG (CF01301), U.S. Security and Institutional Interests in Europe and Eurasia in the Post-Cold War Era, undated, enclosed with David Gompert to Robert Zoellick et al., "February 21, 1992 ESSG Meeting, Situation Room, 10:00-11:00 A.M. February 19, 1992. "Given the large number of NACC members, how do we implement a policy of differentiation toward the new democracies in Eastern and Central Europe? What steps can we take bilaterally to reinforce our desire to have these countries drawn closer to NATO? How do we respond to requests from these, and other NACC members, for NATO membership?" p. 3.

8. Jean Musitelli, "François Mitterrand, architecte de la Grande Europe: Le projet de Confédération européenne (1990-1991)," *Revue Internationale et*

Stratégique no. 82 (2011/2), pp.18-28. Frédéric Bozo, "The Failure of a Grand Design: Mitterrand's European Confederation, 1989–1991," *Contemporary European History* 17, no. 3 (2008), pp. 391-412. Cf. Julie M. Newton, *Russia, France, and the Idea of Europe* (Basingstoke: Palgrave Macmillan, 2003). See also Benoît d'Aboville's chapter in this volume.

9. Kristina Spohr, *Germany and the Baltic Problem after the Cold War: The Development of a New Ostpolitik 1989–2000* (London/New York: Routledge 2004), Chapters 3 and 5. Note: In late fall 1991, ahead of the first NACC meeting, NATO Secretary General Manfred Wörner highlighted that at this "decisive moment in European history" it was the United States which found itself "in a position to lead in this endeavor" of forging a new, post-Cold War Euro-Atlantic Community around NATO. GHWBPL, NSC, Barry Lowenkron Files, NATO: Wörner (CF01526-021), Memo by Scowcroft for Bush—re: President's 11 Oct. Meeting with Wörner, Oct. 9, 1991, p. 2. Cf. in the same file, Memcon of Bush-Wörner talks, Oct. 11, 1991, 11:30am-12:00noon, The Oval Office, pp. 1-5.

10. See endnote 6 and 7 above: "Nato and the East" as well as "U.S. Security and Institutional Interests in Europe and Eurasia in the Post-Cold War Era."

11. The 1950 film was based on Ryūnosuke Akutagawa's 1922 short story "In a Grove." For more on the Rashomon effect, see Robert Anderson, "The Rashomon Effect and Communication," *Canadian Journal of Communication*, Vol. 41 (2016), pp. 249–269. An earlier example of such a plot device is Robert Browning's long poem, originally published in 1868, *The ring and the book* (Peterborough, Ontario: Broadview Press, 2001). The 1999 film *Run Lola Run* also offers alternate narratives and outcomes, but as Anderson notes, *Lola* is not, like *Rashomon*, about distinct versions of the same incident, but three similar but slightly different sequences, each with different outcomes.

12. "The Story of the Six Blind Men," https://www.his.com/~pshapiro/elephant.story.html.

13. For a related approach, see Hans Binnendijk and Richard L. Kugler, *Seeing the Elephant: The U.S. Role in Global Security* (Washington, DC: National Defense University Press and Potomac Books, 2006), p. xi. On the "NATO enlargement question" and subsequent political controversy, see Christopher Clark and Kristina Spohr, "Moscow's account of Nato expansion is a case of false memory syndrome," *The Guardian*, May 24, 2015; Kristina Spohr, "Precluded or Precedent-Setting? The 'NATO Enlargement Question' in the Triangular Bonn-Washington-Moscow Diplomacy of 1990–1991," *Journal of Cold War Studies* 14, no. 4 (2012), pp. 4-54.

Part I

The Cold War Endgame
and NATO Transformed

Chapter 1

Piece of the Puzzle:
NATO and Euro-Atlantic Architecture
After the Cold War

Daniel S. Hamilton

Much debate about NATO's post-Cold War enlargement has suffered from three weaknesses.

The first has been a tendency to view NATO and its enlargement exclusively through a Russian prism. Russia-firsters worried that NATO enlargement would exacerbate Russian insecurities and further divide the continent; Russia skeptics supported enlargement because they believed NATO needed to capitalize on a period of Russian weakness and disorientation by expanding its frontiers. What united the two camps was the view that NATO was a threat-based institution whose sole purpose was to deter, and if necessary, repulse, an attack on Western Europe by the Soviet Union and its satellites in the Warsaw Pact.[1] Now that the threat that had given rise to NATO's creation was gone, many Russia-firsters asked why the Alliance would even continue to exist, much less expand. Russia skeptics, in turn, asked why the Alliance didn't expand as quickly as possible; just because the Soviet Union had collapsed didn't mean that the Russian bear wouldn't be back.[2]

These views were short-sighted in many ways. The Russia skeptics only exacerbated the very Russian insecurities the Russia-firsters highlighted. Many Russia-firsters, in turn, treated as secondary the security concerns of hundreds of millions of non-Russian Europeans who lived outside the institutionalized order in which Western societies were free, largely prosperous, and secure. Both camps' Soviet/Russia-centric, threat-based view of NATO blinded them to the fact that the end of the Cold War did not solve Europe's security issues. Europe and the United States faced a host of other security challenges for which NATO could be extremely relevant. Some of those challenges did not stem from or even have much to do with Russia; some were not even in

Europe; and some were such that NATO-Russia cooperation could be of considerable value.[3]

This one-dimensional, Russia-centric caricature of NATO also ignored the Alliance's various purposes. Three days after the North Atlantic Treaty gave life to NATO in 1949, the great political commentator Walter Lippman wrote that it would be

> remembered long after the conditions that provoked it are no longer the main business of mankind. For the treaty recognizes and proclaims a community of interest which is much older than the conflict with the Soviet Union and, come what may, will survive it...[This community] would be a reality if we were at peace with the Soviet government and it will still be the reality when at long last we are again at peace with the Russian people and their government.[4]

Since its inception the Alliance not only provided for the collective defense of its members, it institutionalized the transatlantic link, offered a preeminent framework for managing relations between Allies on issues of security and strategy, and provided an umbrella of reassurance under which European countries could focus their security concerns on common challenges rather than on each other. In the aftermath of two World Wars and throughout a half-century-long Cold War, that latter purpose, so often underplayed or misunderstood, was critical to Europe's recovery, prosperity and security. As U.S. Secretary of State Madeleine Albright commented at the time, "Certainly, NATO's cold-war task was to contain the Soviet threat. But that is not all it did. It provided the confidence and security shattered economies needed to rebuild themselves. It helped France and Germany become reconciled, making European integration possible. With other institutions, it brought Italy, then Germany and eventually Spain back into the family of European democracies. It denationalized allied defense policies. It stabilized relations between Greece and Turkey. All without firing a shot."[5] These functions of the Alliance—reconciling adversaries and reassuring allies in a frame of common security—was as relevant at the end of the Cold War as it was at the beginning.[6] "The security NATO provides," Albright notes, "has always been essential to the prosperity the EU promises."[7]

Even today it is difficult to go to any conference on NATO without someone lazily parroting the simplistic—and incorrect—bromide attributed to Lord Ismay, NATO's first Secretary General from 1952-1957, that the goal of NATO was to keep the Russians out, the Americans in and the Germans down.[8] While the first two purposes were essentially correct, the third evolved to such an extent that by 1989 it was no longer apt. NATO's role, together with other institutions, had been to embed West Germany within mutually reassuring structures that assuaged doubts by neighbors—and many Germans—about West Germany's growing weight. Far from keeping the Germans down, NATO, the European Communities and other institutions helped the new Germany stand back up. If this were not true, Germany would never have unified with the support of the four former allies who vanquished Hitler. While much credit must go to the Germans, without the security provided by the embedded framework, neither the Germans nor their neighbors are likely to have had the confidence to reconcile, to integrate, and to reach across European divides.[9]

Over the decades the Alliance proved that it could adapt its purposes in response to changing strategic circumstances. In the late 1960s NATO's original strategy of deterrence and defense evolved to complement the emergence of political détente. In 1991 the George H.W. Bush Administration and all Allies agreed in NATO's new Strategic Concept that "risks to allied security are less likely to result from calculated aggression against the territory of the allies, but rather from the adverse consequences of instabilities that may arise from the serious economic, social and political difficulties" arising from ethnic and territorial disputes in central Europe."[10] The Alliance looked to such new missions as peacekeeping, peace-enforcing, crisis management, and humanitarian assistance. By the end of the Bush Administration, NATO's static defense posture, anchored by heavy armored divisions, was giving way to lighter, more mobile forces for projection into areas beyond NATO borders.[11]

These evolutionary changes underscore that alliances do not necessarily exist solely to wage or deter war, they can also manage relations among member states. Over decades NATO followed in this tradition; the end of the Cold War afforded it the opportunity to extend its management function to neutral and non-aligned states as well as former members of the Warsaw Pact, including Russia. By reaching out to

Moscow with a range of partnership initiatives, the Clinton Administration and European Allies worked to temper the other third of Lord Ismay's witticism: keeping the Russians out.[12]

This relates to a third weakness of the debate: the tendency to focus on NATO alone rather than on the Alliance's role within a broader framework of European and Euro-Atlantic architecture. Critics who believed the Atlantic Community was nothing more than a creature of the Cold War ignored the fact that at the end of WWII the United States and its partners set forth a vision based not only on the need to contain Soviet power and communism in the east, but also to draw together allies and partners in the West. They were as much focused on the continent's overall instabilities as on the Soviet threat.

During the Cold War, attention focused naturally on the first goal—containing the East. But the second part—reordering and adapting the West after two world wars, depression and the rise of fascism—was equally important, and in fact preceded the Cold War and the creation of NATO. The vision for this political order was articulated in such statements as the Atlantic Charter of 1941, the Bretton Woods agreements of 1944, and the Marshall Plan speech of 1947. The founding of such institutions as the World Bank, the International Monetary Fund (IMF), the General Agreement on Tariffs and Trade (GATT), the Organization for European Economic Cooperation (OEEC), and its successor, the Organization for Economic Cooperation and Development (OECD)—helped to stabilize and liberalize postwar market economies, structure cooperative relations within Europe and across the Atlantic, and promote unprecedented peace and prosperity. Western Europe's own integrative mechanisms, starting with the European Coal and Steel Community and leading to the European Communities, both reinforced and gave deeper meaning to these efforts. Even the North Atlantic Treaty of 1949 was aimed as much at generating confidence among Western European peoples that they could tame their conflicts by binding democracies together as it was an alliance created to balance Soviet power.[13]

The leaders of the Atlantic Community realized that Europe's security could not be based solely on external guarantees; it had to be built from within societies. They knew they would be able to deal with the external challenge from the East only if they could draw effectively on the inner resources of the West. The two goals were mutually reinforcing; the strategic vision was enormously successful. The Atlantic Alliance created an umbrella under which European unity could develop, and together these institutions helped produce unparalleled peace and prosperity for half a century—even if for only half a continent.

This context is important to understand because the decision to enlarge the Alliance was not taken in isolation; it was part and parcel of the Clinton Administration's broader efforts to update and realign the entire "architecture" of relations between the United States and Europe. The goal was to put to rest residual problems not just of one war, but of all the European wars and instabilities of the 20th century.[14] For President Clinton and his team, opening NATO's door was not a threat-driven or Russia-centric decision, it was part of a broader strategy of projecting stability, unifying Europe, and positioning the U.S.-European relationship for the opportunities and challenges of a new and uncertain era.[15]

Bush, Clinton and Europe

In a number of ways neither former Clinton or Bush Administration officials are probably wont to acknowledge, the Clinton Administration's efforts built on those of the Bush Administration. Both sought to operationalize President Bush's vision of a "Europe whole and free."[16] Both were convinced that U.S. engagement on the continent remained essential. So did the Europeans—certainly during the German unification debate. The Germans themselves, as well as their French and British partners, but also other neighbors in East and West, saw NATO as a stabilizer on the European continent. All understood that a single "overarching structure" could not deal with the great variety of security challenges facing such a diverse continent, and so sought to construct an integrated Euro-Atlantic security architecture in which existing institutions such as NATO, the European Union (EU), and the CSCE/OSCE could be adapted and transformed to play complementary and mutually supporting roles across a wider European space. All worked intensively with Moscow to dampen, and where possible, eliminate the most dangerous legacies of Cold War competition and to support Russia's own democratic reforms.[17]

While both administrations had a general sense of where they wanted to go, neither operated from a pre-set playbook. William H. Hill characterizes Bush Administration actions as "a set of apparently ad hoc reactions to unforeseen and unprecedented events and opportunities, in particular responses to sudden conflicts and emergencies."[18] Ronald D. Asmus acknowledges that the Clinton strategy "was not the product of a single decision or a sudden epiphany. Instead, it evolved over the course of President Clinton's two terms in office into an increasingly coherent policy in response to events on the ground and as the Administration's own views matured."[19]

President Clinton was guided by his political instincts rather than a detailed blueprint. He admired Franklin Roosevelt and Harry Truman for intuitively understanding what their world required of them; neither had grand strategies but were guided by "powerful instincts about what had to be done." Strategic coherence, he said, was largely imposed after the fact.[20] In each administration, even those engaged in one element of the "architecture" often had little time for, or awareness of, how other potentially complementary elements were proceeding. That is how the sausage is made.

Of course, differences were also significant. The Bush Administration was overwhelmingly focused on peacefully managing the Cold War's denouement and moving to design a "new Europe and new Atlanticism" (as Secretary of State James Baker put it); the Clinton Administration faced the task of peacefully managing the emergence of the post-Cold War world. By the time the Bush Administration came to an end, two states—the Soviet Union and Yugoslavia—had dissolved into no less than twenty new countries in Eurasia. The future of violent conflict in Europe seemed likely to stem more from the disintegration of states rather than from disagreements between them.[21] The Bush Administration, together with its Allies, especially the Germans as "partners in leadership," had begun the process of updating and reorienting Euro-Atlantic architecture, but the relationship between the various institutions was left unclear, as was the process of potential membership.

The violent breakup of Yugoslavia and a series of conflicts between and within some of the new states on the periphery of the USSR presented an especially daunting challenge for peace and stability in the rest of Europe. Post-Wall Europe's remade institutions were untried. It soon became apparent that the EU and the CSCE lacked the mechanisms and institutional capabilities to prevent, suppress or mediate the conflicts arising in this broad area. NATO alone had the structures and forces for engage in such tasks, but many of its members did not have the will do to so.[22] With nations at odds and America initially leaving the ball in "Europe's" court, NATO appeared to have turned into a bystander, more misalliance than alliance.[23]

Crucially, the Bush and Clinton administrations differed about what all of this meant for U.S. interests. Watching the Yugoslav tragedy unfold, Secretary of State James Baker famously declared "we ain't got no dog in that fight," a stance Richard Holbrooke decried as "the greatest failure of the West since the 1930s."[24] Serbian President Slobodan Milošević later told U.S. diplomat John Kornblum that Baker's words had electrified him: "That was my go-ahead to start a war."[25]

The changing domestic context in the United States was also crucial. Despite President Bush's masterful orchestration of the unification of Germany, the peaceful end of the Cold War, and victory in the Persian Gulf war, enough voters believed he had taken his eye off the ball on problems at home to elect a new President committed to domestic renewal and "the economy, stupid." The mood was decidedly inward-looking; there was talk of a peace dividend and retrenchment from global exertions.[26] A new case would have to be made for continued U.S. engagement in Europe. This was the context in which the Clinton Administration came into office in January 1993.

Euro-Atlantic Architecture

Behind the twists and turns of politics, underlying continuities were visible in the U.S. approach to Europe. A relatively coherent strategic vision was emerging of how the various pieces of Euro-Atlantic architecture had to transform and adapt. That included but went far beyond NATO. The question was as much how NATO should fit as what it should do.

This focus on "architecture" does not necessarily come naturally to Americans, who by tradition and instinct are often inclined to want to solve foreign policy problems rather than manage them. From the end

Euro-Atlantic Architecture in 2000

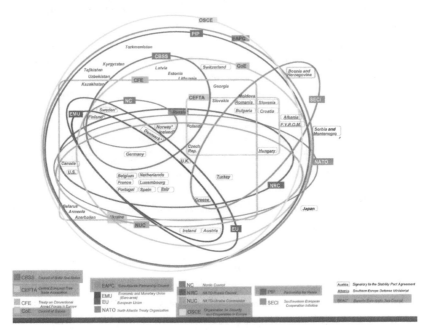

For additional details about this diagram, see Strobe Talbott, *The Great Experiment: The Story of Ancient Empires, Modern States, and the Quest for a Global Nation*, Simon & Schuster Paperback (New York, N.Y.: Simon & Schuster, 2009), pp. 319-321.

ropean security problems, or a U.S. politician, in good Yankee jargon, proclaiming Europe 'fixed.' The implication of these pronouncements, of course, was that NATO, mission accomplished, could be dissolved.

This view not only ignored the fact that Europe's security issues were not "solved" by the Cold War's end; it underestimated the continuing relevance of institutions to Europe's security. Europe's diversity and historic rivalries remain a determining aspect of efforts to maintain stability. Maintaining peace in Europe has traditionally depended on a complicated set of structures that balanced often-conflicting interests. From the European perspective, the many contradictions and strains in European power relations have become more manageable largely as a result of institutional devices, none more imaginative or successful than NATO, the European Union, and the OSCE.

At one point along the way Deputy Secretary of State Strobe Talbott asked for a visual depiction of the emerging architecture. I worked with colleagues to craft a solar system of 13 colored overlapping circles, with the names of countries grouped according to the institutions to which they belonged. It was complicated. Secretary of State Madeleine Albright joked that "you have to be either a genius or French to keep it all straight." [27]

Despite its complications, this dense web of interlocking institutions and mechanisms was essential to Euro-Atlantic and European security and prosperity. It was how Europeans built their security. Albright said the Euro-chart reminded her of an inscrutable comment a French diplomat actually made once in response to an American proposal: "It will work in practice, yes. But will it work in theory?" [28]

Strobe Talbott later said that "I saw NATO enlargement as an objective that not only made sense in theory but might work in practice—as long as we could avoid causing a train wreck (a phrase common in the predictions of the policy's opponents) in our relations with Russia."[29]

This story is how decision-makers sought to align practice with theory.

Distractions and Divisions

Bill Clinton came into office in January 1993 focused on his domestic agenda. When it came to foreign policy, the President's priorities were to ramp up U.S. support for democratic reform in Russia and to raise the profile of economic themes in U.S. engagement abroad by ratifying the North Atlantic Free Trade Agreement (NAFTA), finalizing the Uruguay Round of multilateral trade negotiations, and jumpstarting Asia-Pacific Economic Cooperation (APEC). The Administration's attention was further diverted by crises in Somalia and Haiti.

When it came to Europe, the administration was beset by a welter of discrete challenges, most left on the Bush Administration's plate when it walked out the door. Bosnia preoccupied attention, but there was little appetite for U.S. engagement—in spite of Clinton's emotive rhetoric and accusation during the election campaign that Bush was doing too little to address the humanitarian crisis in Yugoslavia.

Debates over the appropriate role for post-Cold War NATO were inconclusive; at a cabinet meeting on October 18, 1993 the Administration decided, in Strobe Talbott's words, to "kick the can" down the road.[30]

Clinton was more preoccupied with growing instability in Russia. Meeting in March of that year, Clinton and German Chancellor Helmut Kohl declared that ensuring Russian democracy was a "paramount challenge" and that "the rest of the G7 countries must cooperate with us and each other to vigorously produce a program of support for Russia."[31] Both worried that Boris Yeltsin could be toppled if economic and political transformation did not soon take root. A failed coup attempt in September heightened those fears. "This guy's in the fight of his life," Clinton exclaimed.[32] He was intent on doing what he could to help Yeltsin. He managed to secure Congressional support of $2.5 billion for the post-Soviet nations, two-thirds of which would go to Russia. Kohl urged Clinton to include Yeltsin as a full participant in the G-7; objections by the U.S. Treasury Department, however, convinced the President to distinguish between a G7 without Russia on financial issues and a G8 with Russia on political issues.

Other challenges revolved around defusing potential tensions remaining from Soviet era. One was to persuade Russia to withdraw troops from Estonia and Latvia, which it did in 1994.[33] The other was to continue the Bush Administration's efforts to reduce Cold War arsenals of weapons of mass destruction, including dismantling nuclear weapons stockpiles with the former Soviet Union.

These issues were not easily subsumed under some grand vision for transatlantic partnership, nor was that the President's inclination. A first effort to define an overarching "Clinton Doctrine" came when President Clinton's National Security Advisor Tony Lake set forth a strategy of enlargement of the community of democracies and market economies in a speech at Johns Hopkins University's School of Advanced International Studies in September 1993. The Central and Eastern European region, located adjacent to the transatlantic community and showing prospects for success, was a perfect place to demonstrate that the Clinton Administration could implement that vision.[34]

Nonetheless, despite entreaties earlier that year by German Defense Minister Volker Rühe as well as Václav Havel, Lech Wałęsa, József Antall and other Central and Eastern European leaders, given the Clinton Administration's other priorities it was unclear how committed it was to having the United States integrally involved in European affairs overall, not to mention the particular concerns of Central Europeans.[35]

Nor had the Clinton Administration translated Lake's broad doctrine of enlargement into an operational European strategy. While Clinton later said that he had already contemplated the enlargement of NATO as a way to secure the gains for freedom and democracy in Central and Eastern Europe during his election campaign in 1992,[36] Tony Lake described the President's position as "not so much a policy as an attitude."[37]

It was within this context that divisions became apparent within the Clinton Administration, as other authors in this volume explain. Differences turned on interpretations of the Partnership for Peace (PfP), which became a temporizing compromise—construed as a first step to NATO enlargement by those who were inclined to support it, or as a holding station of undetermined duration by those who were not. The divisions within the administration were reflected by similar divisions within the Alliance.[38]

The action-forcing event was President Clinton's first trip to Europe in January 1994. The President set the tone. On the eve of his trip he said that he did not want to give the impression that the United States was creating another dividing line in Europe after it had worked for decades to get rid of the one that existed before. He added, however, that PfP would "permit the expansion of NATO, and I fully expect that it will lead to that at some point."[39]

Each side of the debate thought the President had sided with them. Those opposing enlargement focused on the part of his statement about no more dividing lines. Those favoring enlargement focused on the President's clear expectation that NATO enlargement would happen.

At the January NATO Summit, the President declared that PfP "sets in motion a process that leads to the enlargement of NATO." And then two days later in Prague, he said "the question is no longer whether NATO will take on new members but when and how." Clinton also raised the issue of what he called the architecture of European security with Yeltsin in Moscow, but did not set forth a systematic view of what that could be. [40] The Brussels NATO Summit had made clear that NATO "plainly contemplated an expansion," he said, but that was for an unspecified future, and PfP was "the real thing now."[41]

For several months after Clinton's pronouncements in January, the issue of NATO enlargement had dropped down the Administration's priority list. The Pentagon and the State Department had more pressing concerns, including continued denuclearization efforts in the former Soviet Union and the need to get the Partnership for Peace up and running. [42] Attention of senior officials remained on Bosnia after the horrific February bombing of the Sarajevo marketplace. As Christopher writes, "Not only did this conflict occupy much of our time and energy, but psychologically we found it exceedingly difficult to focus on expansion while NATO groped for a way to stop the bloodshed in southern Europe."[43]

America and the Berlin Republic

"They've asked me to be Ambassador to Germany. You have to come with me."

Richard Holbrooke was on the line. I had worked closely with him when I coordinated two U.S. national commissions on the future of U.S. foreign policy at the Carnegie Endowment for International Peace. Holbrooke had been a member of the first commission, chaired by Winston Lord and Stephen Bosworth, which in June 1992 issued a report *Changing Our Ways*, intended as a bipartisan blueprint for a post-Cold U.S. foreign policy. Mort Abramowitz, the Endowment's president, then asked Holbrooke to chair, and me to coordinate, a follow-on effort to propose ways to restructure the U.S. government's foreign policy apparatus for a new age. Our proposals were instrumental to the Clinton's Administration's creation of the National Economic Council in the White House, the position of Undersecretary for Global Affairs in the State Department, and a variety of other innovations.[44]

Following the 1992 election, Holbrooke and I parted ways—he the Asianist, I the Europeanist. Holbrooke was angling for a senior position in the new Administration—preferably U.S. Ambassador to Japan. In the end, Walter Mondale expressed interest in the job. The next country on the list was Germany—not Holbrooke's first choice. As he considered, he called me to say that if he took the job, given his own relative inexperience with Germany he would need someone as his own personal policy advisor on German affairs (Mondale had done the same on Japan). I agreed, but told him that my wife and I were about to have a baby who would most likely need to undergo a bone marrow transplant. I could not come right away. We discussed asking Fritz Stern, an eminent scholar of Germany, to join Holbrooke for the fall of 1993; I would come in early 1994.

We also agreed that I would use my remaining time at the Endowment to chart how the United States should reframe its relations with a united Germany in the post-Cold War era. I asked a number of senior Democratic and Republican opinion leaders, including a few Clinton Administration officials (in their personal capacity) to join the project.[45] Our deliberations informed a short book I finished in the fall of 1993. Holbrooke, now in Bonn, received my drafts, providing comments and urging policy-relevant recommendations.

In the book I suggested a variety of ways Americans might approach a Germany undergoing a significant transformation. I coined the term "Berlin Republic" to explain that while deep continuities bound united Germany to the West German "Bonn Republic" to which U.S. decision-makers had grown accustomed, it found itself in a profoundly different situation. The "Berlin Republic," I argued, would not simply be the "Bonn Republic" writ large. It was likely to be a more open yet less settled society, more volatile politically, more pressured economically, and less circumspect internationally than the west German "Bonn Republic" to which Germany's neighbors and allies—and the Germans themselves—had grown accustomed over forty years. The United States and Germany would remain pivotal partners, but would now need to harness their relationship to shape a new transatlantic architecture.[46]

The first objective would need to be a German-American strategic partnership toward Central and Eastern Europe and the Soviet successor states. This would be needed to revamp Europe's collective defense and security organizations, which in turn would hinge on active U.S. engagement in Europe and a German commitment to establish the political and operational preconditions to fulfill its part of a new security bargain. Germany would need to "transform itself from an importer to an exporter of security and stability." I argued that there was a vital strategic convergence between the United States and Germany with regard to the east. "This can and should be translated into a strategic partnership that acts as the drivewheel of progress to export democratic structures, assist market-oriented reforms, secure arms reductions, develop habits of military cooperation and promote civilian control of the military throughout eastern Europe and the Soviet successor states, while facilitating their association and eventual integration into western structures." Other Allies and partners would of course be included, but the bilateral relationship would be the essential fulcrum of change. The strategy would need to embrace a panoply of security, economic and political instruments, and seek to reshape and reorient the primary institutions of NATO, the U.S.-EU partnership, and the CSCE to these ends.

While NATO's core purpose of collective defense had to be maintained, "to it must now be added the purposes of collective crisis management, force projection "out of area" and export of stability to the east...NATO will be unable to guarantee security in the West unless it is able to operate with non-NATO members in the east." While supporting the principle of NATO enlargement, I argued that "precipitous" enlargement "could undermine rather than enhance prospects for greater peace and stability in Europe." That phrasing captured the prevailing thinking within the Clinton Administration at the time, with Holbrooke parsing the language as I was writing and with other senior officials (and RAND analyst Ron Asmus) participating in the study group deliberations. The "practical reality," I argued, was that east European nations are not ready to become NATO members overnight. Moving NATO suddenly to the Russian border could easily be misunderstood: It could create a Russian threat where there is not one today."

At the time, the Partnership for Peace appeared to be a pragmatic effort to navigate these shoals. Joseph Kruzel, Deputy Assistant Secretary of Defense for NATO and a member of my study group, argued strongly for its relevance. Ultimately, however, I wrote that the PfP could only be "a station along the way to a fundamentally new relationship between east and west that will require the United States to clarify whether the consolidation of democracy in the region is of sufficient national interest to extend a security guarantee...It may well be in the U.S national interest to commit men and women from Montana, Wisconsin and Virginia to defend the eastern borders of Poland, Slovenia and Hungary—but not without a major national debate." The possibility for enlargement was there, but I argued at the time that such a commitment would be hollow unless anchored by a bipartisan consensus in the United States.

If NATO's new outreach to the East was to work, it had to be coupled with a rebalancing within the West. "The United States must be willing to allow Europeans to deal with crises on their doorstep should the United States be unwilling or unable. I welcomed the idea of Combined Joint Task Forces and with them the premise that Europe's emerging defense identity should be "separable but not separate from NATO."

Meanwhile, Richard Holbrooke arrived in Germany in September 1993 with two notions. He was quickly disabused of both.

The first was that as Ambassador to newly unified Germany he should devote priority attention reaching out to the 16 million East Germans whose views of the United States had been shaped by life in the Soviet bloc. He soon understood, however, that it was the West Germans who needed tending. West German elites were deeply unnerved by the prospect that the United States might disengage from Europe, which might also mean that NATO could also eventually disappear and with it the very foundation of Germany's security. Holbrooke spent a good deal of his time reassuring primarily West Germans that the U.S. remained committed to Europe and would not abandon Europe for home or for a Pacific vocation. The Germans no longer feared a massive invasion across the Central European plain. But they were concerned that the aftershocks of the political and economic earthquakes that had shaken Europe's East threatened to spill over into its West in the form of mass migration, xenophobia, economic dislocation, secessionist movements and regional instabilities. German officials became increasingly concerned that their Western partners, including Washington, did not share their sense of urgency.

Holbrooke did share this urgency, especially with regard to the unfolding tragedy in the Balkans, which he often called the greatest failure of the West since the 1930s. Yet his second notion was that EU membership was the most important and quickest potential bond for East Europeans who had freed themselves from the Soviet empire yet found themselves in a grey zone—no longer "East," but not yet "West." NATO membership would come later. He was again disabused of this notion:

> What turned me around was the realization that the EU, mired in its own Euro-mess (the common currency, the endless arguments about process, its inner-directedness, and its failure on Bosnia), was not going to invite any of these countries in, at the earliest, before 2003. They had lived through a terrible century, and were still plagued by instability, insecurity, and immaturity. In short, they were vulnerable to a number of different scenarios that would have sent them back into new darkness.
>
> I concluded it would be irresponsible and potentially dangerous to leave these countries outside the "West" for so long after the fall of communism. Close association with the West seemed the best inoculation against such an outcome—but only if it could be accomplished without a setback to Washington's efforts to forge a productive relationship with Russia, the administration's most impressive and sustained foreign policy achievement. In short, could we have our cake and eat it too?[47]

Holbrooke's considerations had been shaped by his conversations with German leaders, particularly Chancellor Helmut Kohl and Defense Minister Volker Rühe. Rühe had come out publicly to support NATO's opening to the east. Kohl was more cautious, believing that such efforts had to be balanced with attention to Russian insecurities. Nonetheless, Holbrooke often cited Kohl's powerful phrase that Germany "cannot remain indefinitely Europe's eastern border," straddling a new front line between stability and instability, as an important consideration.

On Track ... and Then Off the Rails

During the winter and spring of 1994, as the crisis in Bosnia continued to deteriorate, the Partnership for Peace was announced, and President Clinton issued his famous statement that the question of NATO enlargement was no longer "whether, but when," there was a growing sense among the President's senior advisors, principally Tony Lake and

Strobe Talbott, that the Administration's Russia policy and its Europe policy were coming unstuck.

Talbott had been appointed Deputy Secretary of State in February 1994 and so now needed to focus on how to make his Russia portfolio align with overall U.S. foreign policy goals, particularly regarding Europe. He and Lake convinced the President that Holbrooke needed to come back to Washington as Assistant Secretary of State for European Affairs. As Holbrooke told me upon breaking the news, "Dan, we've got two jobs to do: Bring peace to Bosnia and enlarge NATO." He asked me to come back to Washington with him, as his policy advisor, to direct the European Bureau's office of policy and public outreach.

Holbrooke and Talbott agreed that they would need to reach a common position on NATO enlargement and its relationship to Russia policy and other elements of Europe's security landscape before Holbrooke arrived back in Washington. As Holbrooke recalled, they agreed that "Central Europe needed the reassurance of an American commitment to their security; the issue was whether or not this could be accomplished without wrecking the emerging U.S.-Russian relationship."[48]

Meanwhile, Lake was frustrated that at such an historic moment for the U.S.-European relationship the Administration was not showing how various U.S. initiatives fit together into a coherent vision.[49] He wanted to use the President's visit to France on June 8, 1994 to move the ball forward. Speaking before the French National Assembly, the President alluded to the need to adapt the broad range of Europe's security institutions "to meet new imperatives." He expressed understanding for "the historical anxieties" of Central and Eastern Europe. He then declared that "The security of those states is important to our own security. And we are committed to NATO's expansion."[50]

The President had again publicly expressed his support for enlargement of the Alliance. Those statements, however, had yet to be translated into operational policy. With the interagency debate at a standstill, Lake asked his own staff for a blueprint, which he received and sent to the President in late June. Talbott had commented and supported. It argued that the Administration had to make the case that expansion was not a threat to any other country, would be stabilizing and reduce the security vacuum in central Europe. It argued that the President had to take the ball forward on his July trip to Europe, which he did in Warsaw on July 1 when he said "in my view, NATO will be expanded, that it should be expanded." He characterized the Partnership for Peace as a "first step toward expansion of NATO," and "now what we have to do is to get the NATO partners together and to discuss what the next steps should be."[51] He reiterated his stance a few days later again in Berlin, meeting with Kohl and with Holbrooke at his side.

As Alexander Vershbow recounts in this volume, he and his NSC colleagues then moved the ball forward again with a memo to Lake on July 15 entitled "NATO Expansion—Next Steps." He proposed launching exploratory discussions in September with key Allies on the issues of criteria and a timetable to be followed by a broader discussion in the Alliance as a whole. He suggested using the December meeting of NATO Foreign Ministers to launch a NATO enlargement study to start spelling out in greater detail U.S. and allied thinking on a NATO-Russia relationship. Lake agreed.[52]

Holbrooke was also concerned that the foreign affairs and defense bureaucracy was bucking the President's wishes when it came to enlargement. By the time he returned to Washington, he and Talbott had reached a common position: "it was possible to bring new members into NATO, slower than the Kissingers and the Brzezinskis wanted but faster than the Pentagon and some others desired." [53]

The first job was to tame the bureaucracy and get it pointed in the direction of the President's policy. The first occasion came on Labor Day weekend in early September. Vice President Gore was to give the keynote speech on the occasion of the departure of the storied Berlin Brigade, which had safeguarded the city's safety during the Cold War. Holbrooke wanted to ensure that Gore would reaffirm President Clinton's statements that year in Brussels, Prague, Paris, Warsaw and Berlin that NATO enlargement was moving forward. I worked with John Kornblum, now the Principal Deputy of the European Bureau, to craft strong language.[54] The Pentagon wasn't buying it, as Wesley Clark recounts in this volume. Drafts kept flying back and forth to Holbrooke, who was in Berlin for the speech. I was in Berlin with Holbrooke, who asked me to work with Kornblum and Tom Malinowski, a talented member of the Policy Planning Staff, to make sure the language remained robust. In the end, Holbrooke prevailed. Gore tore his Achilles tendon and did not make the trip, but he still gave the speech via video link. The key sentence was Gore's public statement that "We will begin our discussions" on NATO enlargement "this fall." [55]

The next opportunity came with the interagency grouping Holbrooke was now leading in Washington. At the group's dramatic first meeting, I watched as Holbrooke asserted clear control, as described by Wesley Clark and other authors in this volume. "When Holbrooke sat down with his colleagues in September and October 1994," James Goldgeier recounts, "he was not reopening a discussion of the issue; rather, he was presenting his counterparts with a fait accompli."[56]

Meanwhile, the President continued to define the policy. At a private lunch in the White House on September 27, Clinton told Yeltsin directly that "there will be an expansion of NATO." He sought to reassure Yeltsin that the issue was about addressing Central European fears "of being left in a grey area or purgatory," and it was about maximizing the chances of "a truly united, undivided, integrated Europe" in which Russia would be included. Clinton emphasized that there was no timetable, and that U.S. policy would be guided by "three no's": no surprises, no rush, and no exclusion of Russia.[57]

Holbrooke was now accelerating NATO expansion discussions. When General Clark, Joseph Kruzel and other Pentagon officials expressed concern at the difficulties of enlargement because new members would have to fulfill over 1000 standardization agreements, Holbrooke asked them to prepare a study on the "how" of enlargement, which they presented to the interagency group in October 1994, and which served as an initial framing document for NATO's own 1995 enlargement study.

Meanwhile, as Alexander Vershbow recounts in his chapter, the NSC staff had prepared a strategy paper for NATO enlargement in which a timeline would be announced during Clinton's first term and enlargement accomplished early in the second term.[58] The paper listed five objectives for the end of the year: launching a formal Alliance review on a framework for expansion; an initial sketch of benchmarks for potential new members; an expanded PfP program for future members and non-members alike; an expanded NATO-Russia relationship; and a strengthened OSCE to underscore Western interest to include Russia in a new European security architecture.[59]

The next step was to build what Holbrooke called the "two-year plan" for the remainder of Clinton's first term to upgrade and recast Euro-Atlantic architecture. The effort would be built on multiple pillars: a new NATO, a revamped U.S.-EU relationship, and transformation of the CSCE into the OSCE. Russia policy and European policy needed to move along parallel tracks, with the realization that in the end they were also intertwined. And Bosnia, if untamed, would cause all of it to crumble. The core rationale for an integrated approach would turn on Central and Eastern Europe.

In November Holbrooke asked me to work with Bureau colleagues to articulate the Administration's comprehensive approach to a transformed Euro-Atlantic architecture for a speech Secretary Christopher was slated to give on November 28.[60] The timing was important. Russia was teed up to join the Partnership for Peace at the NATO Foreign Ministers meeting on December 1, and on December 5 Boris Yeltsin would join President Clinton and the leaders of the CSCE states to herald its transformation into the Organization for Security and Cooperation in Europe—another pillar in the updated concept. It was important to signal to the Russians—as well as to Allies and other European countries—how the Administration was approaching the various pieces of the puzzle.

Things did not go as planned. In the end, Christopher did not give his speech due to other conflicts. The Russians had learned of the interagency group's work and the Pentagon's study on what it would take to actually enlarge the Alliance. On November 29 Yeltsin complained in a letter to Clinton about what he called U.S. efforts intent on "speeding up the broadening of NATO."[61] Three days later Foreign Minister Kozyrev unexpectedly refused to sign up for the Partnership of Peace, as he recounts in his own personal recollection in this volume. On December 5 in Budapest, Yeltsin lashed out publicly at a surprised and none-to-happy Clinton, accusing him of "sowing the seeds of mistrust" and plunging Europe into a "cold peace."[62]

Vice President Al Gore tried to patch things up with Yeltsin and other Russian leaders on a visit to Moscow December 16, underscoring that Washington was not subordinating relations with Russia to NATO expansion. Gore stressed that the two processes would move forward in tandem, with no surprises, and that no new countries would enter

NATO in 1995.[63] Talbott and Christopher followed with their own conversations with Russian interlocuters in January 1995, but with little progress.[64] The only bright spot had been the December 1994 Budapest Memorandum, signed by the United States, the United Kingdom, and the Russian Federation, containing security assurances for Ukraine in return for renouncing its status as a nuclear weapons state.[65]

The situation was not good. NATO Allies wondered what was happening, Central Europeans were worried about abandonment, and Russian suspicions were high. The Republicans had taken control of Congress in the November 1994 elections, in part on the basis of their "Contract with America," which included robust support for NATO enlargement. Pundits were also starting to shape the public debate. Former U.S. National Security Adviser Zbigniew Brzezinski commented in *Foreign Affairs* on the need to eliminate "any potentially disruptive geopolitical vacuum between Europe and the new Russia.[66] In Europe, Kohl confidante Michael Mertes joined with French commentator Dominique Moïsi to urge Western governments to focus on "the security vacuum" between Germany and Russia, the area where European wars have historically started,[67] a region described by Henry Kissinger as a strategic "no-man's land between the German and Russian peoples.[68]

These dynamics rendered more urgent the effort to articulate and operationalize President Clinton's "predisposition" to enlargement and square it with his commitment to support Russian reforms within a recast architecture for U.S. engagement in, and with, Europe. The draft speech now needed to be recast into an article, which was finished in January and published in the next issue of *Foreign Affairs*. It became the road map for U.S. European policy. Subsequent statements by the President and senior officials throughout the remaining six years of the Clinton Administration hewed closely to and expanded upon the rationale set forth in the article.

The emerging architecture was based on six cornerstones.

America, a European Power

The core premise of the article, as reflected in the title, was that America was a European power. "Should we add a question mark?"

Holbrooke asked me. The answer was a resolute no. The question mark had been the problem.

For decades the United States had been a European power. By that we meant it had been integral to the continental balances, coalitions and institutions that maintained stability, protected democracy, and expanded prosperity for half the continent. Now, with Cold War divides disappearing, Europeans across the continent were asking themselves whether the United States would remain as deeply committed and involved in Europe's security as it had been in the past.[69] It was also not immediately obvious to Americans that the United States should be so engaged. With the Cold War over, it was tempting to say that it was time for the Europeans to work this out themselves, while Americans focused on problems at home.

The Administration itself had not decided whether Europe was a priority. The United States was in danger of drifting from being a European power to a power in Europe—selectively engaged, distracted by other challenges, and less intuitively convinced of the link between European order and global order.

It was time to erase the question mark with a strong justification of American engagement in the post-Cold War era.[70] After two world wars and a forty-year Cold War there was an enormous historic opportunity to build down Europe's divisions. But dangers abounded. Europe was not yet there. It remained turbulent und unfinished. Without America's active and comprehensive engagement, the continent was in danger of succumbing to new instabilities: "In the 21st century, Europe will still need the active American involvement that has been a necessary component of the continental balance for half a century. Conversely, an unstable Europe would still threaten essential national security interests of the United States."[71]

The assertion that the United States remained a European power became a standard refrain of the President and other senior officials throughout the remainder of the Clinton Presidency.[72]

Shaping a New Architecture

Second, understanding its role as a European power meant that the United States had to affirm its role as stakeholder and shaper of the post-Cold War architecture. "As far back as we can remember, questions of war and peace in Europe—with their vast effect on the rest of the world—have been decided by architecture—the architecture of security." [73] Holbrooke cited Jean Monnet, the great architect of European unity, who had said that "nothing is possible without men, but nothing is lasting without institutions." The efforts of Monnet, Marshall, and others, Holbrooke wrote, "produced unparalleled peace and prosperity for half a century—but only for half a continent." [74] Now it was time for the United States to reach beyond old divides and to lead in the creation of a security architecture "that includes and thereby stabilizes all of Europe—the West, the former Soviet satellites of central Europe, and, most critically, Russia and the former republics of the Soviet Union." [75]

Cold War architecture was static; it reflected the nature of the East-West stalemate. The new architecture, in contrast, had to be dynamic; it needed to address the open nature of the new Europe. While NATO was the "central security pillar of the new architecture," [76] others were also essential, including the EU and the OSCE. Each, however, would need to transform internally and be open externally.

John Kornblum elaborated on the architectural metaphor:

> The history of Europe, the relationships among the countries of Europe, and in fact the relationships between the United States and Europe—at least in this century—have tended to be organized around structures of one sort or another...By architecture we mean relationships among peoples, among countries, among organizations which give both the sense and the substance of cooperation, or maintenance of stability, or maintenance of predictability...Since 1991, '92, with the end of the communist regimes in Central Europe and the collapse of the Soviet Union, Europe has been without a clearly defined security architecture. It has been in a period of considerable transition and this has led both to conflicts—many of which were papered over under the old security architecture—and to a good deal of uncertainty among peoples, both East and West, as to what, in fact the future security rela-

tionships in Europe are to be.....building a security architecture in Europe really is the essential question of building democracy, building stable societies, and ultimately building a stable and just peace across the continent....

I want to stress that the approach of the United States is not to define NATO as the only aspect of the security architecture. It's an important one, a very important one, but it's not the only one. And we would never argue that you can have any kind of stable peace in Europe if you just base it on NATO.[77]

Strobe Talbott often used the architectural metaphor. "The goal," he said, was to "help build a Europe that is whole and free and at peace for the first time in its history":

The means, as we see it, are largely institutional—or, as is often said, architectural. We are building a structure in which we and our children and our grandchildren will make our homes. The foundation of that structure is a shared commitment to democratic governance, to civil society, to sustainable development through the dynamism of the free market, to the rule of law and human rights, to the principles of mutual respect, and to the peaceful settlement of disputes...The task of constructing a new Europe requires us to adapt existing structures where possible and build new ones where necessary...The size, the scope, the job descriptions, and the membership lists of these institutions are different, but their missions and their compositions are often overlapping. In some key respects, they are mutually reinforcing. Together, they make up the superstructure of the new Europe.[78]

In 1991 James Baker had already set forth a U.S. vision for future European security structures based on an interlocking series of institutions based on NATO, the European Community and the CSCE grounded in common values of democracy and human rights. The Clinton Administration, however, had to put in place the operational strategy to realize that vision.[79] As then-U.S. Ambassador to NATO Robert Hunter later recalled, "one reason that NATO took three and a half years from the moment of deciding to enlarge to the naming of the first invitees: it was essential to build a broad, encompassing architecture that could include all countries engaged in European security."[80]

The Challenge of Central Europe

Third, to be effective, the new architecture needed to address what Holbrooke called Europe's "greatest threat," which was no longer Soviet expansionism but "local conflicts, internal political and economic instability and the return of historical grievances...Any blueprint for the new security architecture of Europe must focus first on central Europe, the seedbed of more turmoil and tragedy in this century than any other area on the continent." [81] Failed efforts of the past, from Versailles and Trianon to Yalta and Potsdam, and the collapse of the Soviet empire had "left throughout central Europe a legacy of unresolved and often conflicting historical resentments, ambitions, and, most dangerous, territorial and ethnic disputes. Without democracy, stability, and free-market economics, these lands remain vulnerable to the same problems, often exacerbated by an obsession with righting historical wrongs, real or mythical. If any of these malignancies spread—as they have already in parts of the Balkans and Transcaucasus—general European stability is again at risk." [82]

The dangers were apparent. "East-Central Europe is littered with potential mini-Weimar republics," RAND analysts Ronald D. Asmus, Steven Larrabee and Richard Kugler had written some months earlier, "each capable of inflicting immense violence on the others."[83]

The opportunity, however, was historic. The wild mélange of posters and placards borne by the many thousands of people who in the late 1980s and early 1990s had jumped into their Trabants, Skodas and Ladas and taken to the streets of Budapest, Gdansk, Prague, Leipzig, Bucharest and other central and eastern European cities essentially carried one message: "We want to return to Europe"—to be part of a Europe to which they had always belonged, and yet had been prevented from joining because of where the Red Army stopped in the summer of 1945. Their message had unleashed an earthquake that was shaking the continent and its institutions. Their message was both opportunity and obligation: the opportunity to build a continent that was truly whole, free, and at peace with itself, and the obligation to see it through. "For the first time in history" the nations of central Europe have the chance simultaneously "to enjoy stability, freedom and independence based on another first: the adoption of Western democratic ideals as a foundation for all of Europe." [84] It was imperative that Western Europe and the United States "jointly ensure that tolerant democracies become rooted throughout all of Europe and that the seething, angry, unresolved legacies of the past are contained and solved." [85]

Holbrooke underscored the urgency of action. "It would be a tragedy if, through delay or indecision, the West helped create conditions that brought about the very problems it fears the most. The West must expand to central Europe as fast as possible in fact as well as in spirit... Stability in central Europe is essential to general European security, and it is still far from assured." [86]

The Administration had come to understood both opportunity and obligation. It realized it would need to balance its message that the doors to the West stood open with a "tough love" message that only those countries who could consolidate democracy, build market economies, control their militaries, and reconcile with their neighbors had any chance of walking through those doors.

The opportunity to develop the Central Europe theme came when Karsten Voigt, President of the North Atlantic Assembly, asked Holbrooke to join German Defense Minister Volker Rühe at the Assembly's spring meeting in Budapest on May 29. Holbrooke asked me to prepare his speech with a strong emphasis on the significance of Central Europe, but with a strong "tough love" message.[87] We went through successive drafts; he was very focused on the importance of this talk. In many ways this speech was a bookend to the *Foreign Affairs* article.

The United States, Holbrooke declared, would "support the entry of the nations of Central Europe into the institutions of Europe—the European Union, NATO, the OECD, and the Council of Europe." [88] Then came the tough love message. "The people of Central and Eastern Europe now have a real opportunity to create a lasting peace," he said. "But to do so, they must be prepared for one final act of liberation—this time from the unresolved legacies of their own tragic, violent, and angry past."

> For the peoples of this region, the words Versailles, Trianon, Munich, Yalta, or Potsdam are not just names on the map; they are living legacies of conflicting historical resentments, ambitions, and, most dangerous, unresolved territorial or tribal quarrels—quarrels that allowed the false ideologies of fascism and communism to

prosper, and that now threaten progress toward integrating Central Europe into an undivided Europe.

Even as democracy and free markets sweep the continent, armed conflict and political instability are more pervasive and severe than at any time during the past half century. They are concentrated in Southeastern Europe, extending to the region beyond our NATO allies, Greece and Turkey. I submit to you that this vast region—including its neighbors in the Transcaucasus, and Syria, Iraq, and Iran—has become the most explosive region on earth. Ottomans and Habsburgs, czars and commissars have left behind them unresolved legacies that continue to roil the entire area. Some, such as Bosnia, Croatia, Moldova, Nagorno-Karabakh, and Chechnya, have already exploded. Others continue to fester, such as tensions over Cyprus or those between Athens and Tirana, Athens and Skopje, Bratislava and Budapest, Budapest and Bucharest, Bucharest and Kiev, Kiev and Moscow, even Rome and Ljubljana.

These forces, if not contained, risk holding the new Europe hostage to its own history.

Every country in this region, no matter what the current state of its economy, can aspire to join in time this rich tapestry of nations. But joining the core institutions of the West is not the same as joining a country club. Countries aspiring to enjoy the benefits of membership also have the responsibility to meet its obligations.

Holbrooke laid out the terms. Stability did not come solely from external guarantees; it must be built from within. Democratic structures were important. So was a vibrant civil society, independent institutions, a free press, respect for human rights and fundamental freedoms, including the free expression of ethnic, linguistic and cultural identities in an area in which peoples and borders do not match. No one country should seek to join the European mainstream by leaving its neighbors behind. Democratic pluralism demands regional cooperation. Borders must not be changed by force. Holbrooke cited a host of examples where Central European countries were engaged in reconciliation and cooperation; he also admonished his Hungarian hosts and others for areas where such reconciliation had yet to take place. The message: The United States would stand with those ready to make the changes needed to truly "return to Europe"—but they would have to lead the way.

Secretary of Defense William Perry echoed these sentiments in a February 5 speech to the *Wehrkunde* Munich Security Conference. Perry set forth what became known as the "Perry Principles," the criteria by which NATO would judge the new members eligible: they had to make commitments to democracy and markets, to the sovereignty of others, to NATO's consensus decision-making, to developing interoperability in doctrine and equipment, and to the defense of the other allies. [89]

Holbrooke's "tough love" message, together with the "Perry principles," gave the Administration leverage and helped it to define a timetable for deeper integration that would enable it to build support within the Alliance and align the Central European track with its efforts with Russia. It became a became a standard refrain for Administration officials. Kornblum brought home the point: "The most important security architecture is to be found inside countries. It is democratic development, democratic systems, free market economies." [90]

A Place for Russia?

The next piece of the architectural puzzle was Russia. Holbrooke, Talbott and other senior officials were consistently clear that the dynamic of integration was not directed at Russia, in fact it could help define the role of Russia which, in Holbrooke's terms, "has been outside the European security structure since 1917." In Budapest he argued that this dynamism presented "the opportunity—indeed, the necessity—to extend this Europe of the institutions to the Europe of the map."[91] As Talbott later commented, "Over the long term, pan-European integration depended both on the Central Europeans joining the major structures of the West, including NATO, and on Russia's remaining on a reformist track internally and a cooperative track in its foreign and defense policies. These goals were in tension but not necessarily irreconcilable."[92]

The Administration and its partners would need to move along parallel tracks. Moving too fast along the central European track could upset delicate developments in Russia. Moving too slow could mean losing the momentum for reform and opening oneself to the charge of sacrificing central European security in the face of Russian pressure.

Sandy Berger said the Administration had to navigate between "Scylla and Charybdis;"[93] Talbott called it a Sisyphean task.[94]

Political concerns over the U.S. budget deficit and Cold War legacies had left Clinton unwilling or unable to explicitly propose a Marshall Plan for Russia. However, his administration came up with $4.5 billion in bilateral assistance to Yeltsin's government from 1993 to 1996. This aid helped facilitate economic reform in Russia by curbing inflation and stabilizing the ruble. As a result, by 1996 more than 60 percent of Russia's gross domestic product was generated by its private sector. In fact, the Clinton Administration's assistance helped Russia privatize more property in less time than any other foreign development venture in history. By September 1996 more than 120,000 Russian enterprises had been transferred to private hands, with foreign trade up 65 percent since 1993. Meanwhile, the United States became Russia's largest foreign investor, with the Export-Import Bank of the United States, the Overseas Private Investment Corporation, and the Trade and Development Agency supporting commercial transactions with Moscow valued at more than $4 billion.[95]

The President was also keen to help Russia become part of the institutional architecture, not only the G-8 but the WTO, the Paris Club and the OECD. He favored a cooperative relationship with NATO, and never deviated from his view that should the day ever come, NATO's door also had to be open to Russia. As Talbott has noted, "Clinton's concept of NATO enlargement always included—for reasons that were strategic, not cosmetic or palliative—the idea of Russia's eventual eligibility and indeed its entry." Talbott adds: "He knew that the idea was, as he sometimes said, "blue-sky stuff." If the day ever came when Russia entered NATO, it would obviously be a different Russia, a different NATO, and a different Europe. But, anticipating—and, better yet, inducing—transformation was what strategic policymaking was supposed to be all about."[96]

In a letter to Congressman Benjamin Gilman on May 9, 1996, President Clinton reiterated the premise that it was essential "to place NATO enlargement in the context of a broad, balanced and integrated approach to increasing stability and security throughout the transatlantic area by building a cooperative security structure in Europe. This includes a revitalized NATO, support for enlargement of the European

Union, strengthening the OSCE and enhanced cooperation with other states not immediately aspiring to NATO membership of who may not be in the initial group of states invited to begin accession talks with the Alliance. It also includes a strong and productive relationship between the Alliance and Russia, given the key role Russia can play in shaping a stable and secure Europe."[97]

"The problem," Talbott noted at the time, "is that, historically, Russia has tended to define security in zero-sum terms—win/lose, or, as Lenin famously put it: *kto/kogo*. The Soviet Union seemed unable to feel totally secure unless everyone else felt totally insecure. Its pursuit of *bezopasnost'*, or absence of danger, posed a clear and present danger to others, especially small countries on its periphery. The issue on all our minds is whether post-Soviet Russia, as it goes about redefining its political system through elections, will redefine its concept of state security as well."[98]

Commenting on a report that Boris Yeltsin told Helmut Kohl that Europeans surely realized that "the security of all European countries depends on Russia feeling secure," Talbott wrote that in "that one statement, Yeltsin had captured the nub not just of the immediate problem but of much trouble in the century coming to an end: Russia had habitually defined its own security at the expense of others'; many Russians seemed incapable of feeling secure unless others felt insecure.[99]

Upgrading U.S.–EU Relations

A fifth puzzle piece in the emerging architecture, one often overlooked in many debates about NATO enlargement, was the need to make the transatlantic partnership more effective in addressing global challenges. A more secure, prosperous and confident Europe was potentially our primary partner when it came to a range of issues that even a superpower could not address effectively alone. An unstable Europe, in contrast, would look inward and be less of the partner that the United States needed. This reinforced the U.S. stake in extending the space of democratic stability in Europe where age-old conflicts had healed and war simply did not happen. Moreover, those European areas that were not integrated into the European and Euro-Atlantic mainstream were themselves becoming focal points for many of the transnational issues we needed to address—organized crime, human trafficking, critical energy flows, environmental degradation, terrorism and nuclear smuggling. And because this new partnership would be tied to clear transatlantic interests around the world, it would give the U.S. role in Europe new meaning and staying power. In that sense, the issue of new members in Europe and new missions beyond it were linked."[100]

The emerging architecture needed to give us the means to address those challenges more effectively together. For decades, NATO had been the institutional expression of the transatlantic link. There was no equivalent U.S. link, however, with the European Union (EU), even though the EU was the most important organization in the world to which the U.S. did not belong. The EU was increasingly the institution that European governments used to coordinate their policies and actions. It would be America's essential partner in many strategic areas that were beyond NATO's purview and capacities. If we were to advance a more effective transatlantic partnership, including a reformed NATO, we realized we had to build a stronger, more strategic U.S.-EU relationship.[101]

"The Problem from Hell"

Finally, it was clear that this grand architectural effort would fail if we were unable to contain the fire spreading from Europe's southeastern corner. Secretary Christopher called the Bosnian conflict "the problem from hell."[102] Christopher recalls, "As long as Bosnia was unresolved," he recalled, "it was a cloud that hung over our heads… if NATO could not find a solution for Bosnia, then why think about enlarging it? Did NATO have a mission worth enlarging for if it could not solve Bosnia?"[103]

In his article, Holbrooke made the challenge clear. "Bosnia is a brutal reminder of the power of ethnic and nationalist hatreds, how dangerous this power is to the peace not just of a particular part of Europe, but to Europe as a whole, and how important it is to defuse ethnic grievances before they explode…The tragedy of Bosnia does not diminish the responsibility to build a new comprehensive structure of relationships to form a new security architecture. On the contrary, Bosnia, the greatest collective security failure of the West since the 1930s, only underscores the urgency of the task." [104]

Bosnia would be the litmus test of Holbrooke's assertion that the United States would continue as a European power, and would occupy most of his energies throughout 1995.

Meanwhile, other pieces of architecture needed to fit into place.

A New Transatlantic Agenda

Having set forth the interlocking elements of its European policy, during 1995 the Clinton Administration sought to advance each track in mutually reinforcing ways. Progress on NATO enlargement had been set for the year by the December 1994 NATO foreign ministers' decision to use 1995 to address the "why" and "how" of enlargement; NATO's study on the matter was completed in September. It reflected in large part the Perry Principles.[105] Its conclusions were communicated to PfP members through the fall. Significant U.S. diplomatic effort was expended on engaging directly with central European countries with regard to political, economic and military reform and reconciliation with neighbors. Russia overcame its earlier hesitations and joined the Partnership for Peace in May. The OSCE was fully engaged in its transformation into a full-fledged organization following the December 1994 Budapest Summit. Holbrooke began his intense focus on Bosnia that was to lead to the Dayton Peace Accords that fall.

The missing piece of the architecture was an upgraded U.S.-EU relationship. Just as Russia policy had threatened to get ahead of European policy during the first two years of the Administration, NATO and OSCE policy now threatened to get ahead of an updated U.S. approach to its relations with the European Union.

With Holbrooke fully immersed in Bosnia and the other architectural pieces on track, I turned attention to this theme, together with European Bureau colleagues, Ambassador to the EU Stuart Eizenstat and his key deputies E. Anthony "Tony" Wayne and Charles Ries, and Secretary Christopher's Policy Planning Staff.

We quickly agreed that it was increasingly urgent to upgrade the U.S.-EU relationship for a combination of positive and negative reasons. Trends in Europe were clearly unnerving political leaderships. The lagging pace of progress within the EU and a growing sense of insecurity in Europe as a whole were raising doubts about the prospects for further integration and uncertainty how the task of EU construction fit within the broader context of European and transatlantic change. The results of the November midterm elections in the United States reinforced European doubts about the steadfastness and durability of the Atlantic partnership. Western European doubts and Russian grumpiness, in turn, were raising anxieties among East Central Europeans who were almost desperate to establish a tight bond to the United States. We were concerned that the positive proposals being set forth by the United States could shift to a defensive debate over how to stave off the erosion of the transatlantic partnership.

The best way to counter such fears, we believed, was to give further evidence of dynamism and cooperation. We also understood that the EU was embarking on a series of decisions—regarding its own future enlargement, a nascent economic and monetary union, defense and other issues—in which the United States had a stake but not a seat at the table. We were concerned that the multiple challenges of deeper and wider EU integration could turn many of our key Allies inward at a time when the United States increasingly needed an outward-looking partner who could deliver on a broad range of subjects of common concern. Finally, through an enhanced U.S.-EU economic and political partnership we could equip ourselves with a wider range of tools to address the varied sources of instability now afflicting the continent. We needed a mechanism to engage the EU in ways that went beyond the 1990 U.S.-EU Transatlantic Declaration.

As we intensified our work, the public spark for an upgraded U.S.-EU partnership came initially from Europe. In April in Chicago, German Foreign Minister Klaus Kinkel called for a Transatlantic Free Trade Agreement, or TAFTA, as a logical follow-on from the recently concluded NAFTA and Uruguay Round negotiations, and as a new binding glue between Europe and North America. Kinkel embraced President Clinton's theme of integration as a binding force, and took it one step further. TAFTA, Kinkel said, should be part of "a trans-Atlantic zone of close political, economic and military cooperation (that) is the logic of our common history."

The idea gained force. That same month, British Prime Minister John Major pitched the idea to President Clinton. Spanish, Swedish, Italian and other European leaders signed on, as did business leaders and Lane Kirkland, the long-time head of the AFL-CIO labor union. In its May 27th issue, *The Economist* endorsed the idea, noting that "economics and security go hand in hand" and calling it potentially a first step toward a "shared foreign and security policy...a new NATO of tomorrow." French politicians were notably silent.

The idea had supporters within the Clinton Administration. A TAFTA could complement NATO as a second anchor to the transatlantic partnership. There were also skeptics. Some argued that since the United States and the EU accounted for such a large part of the global economy, a transatlantic deal would be "too big," meaning it could subvert multilateral trade negotiations under the WTO. Others argued it would be "too small," meaning that the EU and the United States enjoyed such low tariffs that they were essentially already engaged in free trade, so that the benefits of a deal would be marginal, and that precious time and energy would be better spent tackling high trade barriers imposed by others.[106] Holbrooke asked me to bring together experts for one of his "Saturday seminars." But distracted by Bosnia and ambivalent in his own mind, Holbrooke concluded that TAFTA was "an idea whose time has not yet come."[107]

Nonetheless, the idea of reinvigorated transatlantic economic leadership struck a chord with an administration committed to raising the profile of economic issues in U.S. diplomacy. It also resonated with those of us who were arguing that the U.S.-EU piece of the "architecture" could complement and reinforce the other tracks of our policy and equip our partnership with more than military means to address "out of area" issues. We could build on the 1990 Transatlantic Declaration to offer a comprehensive partnership that included but went beyond economic issues.

This approach resonated with Secretary Christopher, who asked our team to be ambitious in our new vision for the U.S.-EU relationship. He unveiled the approach in Madrid on June 2, 1995. In his speech Christopher explained U.S. goals for a comprehensive partnership with the EU within the context of the emerging European architecture that Holbrooke had articulated in his *Foreign Affairs* article. He declared

U.S. support for EU and NATO enlargement, citing President Truman's Under Secretary of State Robert Lovett, who in 1948 said that the objective "should continue to be the progressively closer integration, both economic and political, of presently free Europe, and eventually of as much of Europe as becomes free." [108]

Christopher also framed the need for closer U.S.-EU cooperation within the context of the global economic architecture design the Clinton Administration had been advancing. The United States was implementing NAFTA, working to complete negotiations on a free trade area in the Americas by the year 2005; and advancing APEC's decision to achieve free and open trade and investment in the Asia-Pacific region by 2020. "Our vision for the economic relationship between Europe and the United States must be no less ambitious…Our long-term objective," he said, "is the integration of the economies of North America and Europe," consistent with the principles of the WTO. [109]

He proposed a comprehensive investment regime, innovation cooperation, aligning standards, opening skies, liberalizing financial services and telecommunications. He went further to call for greater cooperation politically to fight the proliferation of weapons of mass destruction, international crime, terrorism and narcotics trafficking, to coordinate humanitarian and development assistance, to promote human rights, and to address regional challenges, particularly in the Middle East and Mediterranean.

EU leaders responded enthusiastically. Intense negotiations began immediately. They led to the formation of the New Transatlantic Agenda, signed by President Clinton and EU leaders in December 1995.

The 1990 U.S.-EU Transatlantic Declaration had primarily sought to ensure that the transatlantic relationship kept pace with accelerating European integration and the dramatic political changes unfolding in central and eastern Europe as the Cold War ended. It stressed the desirability of close consultation, but focused more on identifying the beliefs and values that united the United States and Europe than on actual policy cooperation.

The 1995 New Transatlantic Agenda (NTA) moved U.S.-EU relations from consultation to cooperation in four broad areas: promoting peace and stability, democracy and development; responding to global challenges; expanding world trade and promoting closer economic relations; and building people-to-people bridges across the Atlantic. A Joint Action Plan identified some 150 measures to be advanced. Together, these agreements amounted to a framework for dialogue consisting of bilateral summits (initially twice per year) biannual dialogue at the level of EU Foreign Ministers/U.S. Secretary of State; a Senior Level Group at the level of U.S. Undersecretary of State and EU Commission Director General to oversee implementation of the NTA; and an NTA Task Force at Director level to facilitate exchange at the operational level. The NTA also gave rise to a variety of other dialogue structures, most notably varying economic innovations in the guise of the 1998 Transatlantic Economic Partnership and the current Transatlantic Economic Council; a series of stakeholder dialogues, the most durable of which proved to be the Transatlantic Business Dialogue (TABD) and Transatlantic Consumer Dialogue (TACD); and a Transatlantic Legislators Dialogue (TLD), which built on existing regular exchanges between the European Parliament and the U.S. House of Representatives.

At the time, the NTA framework went considerably beyond other frameworks for bilateral cooperation—in terms of ambition, formality, and institutional procedures—than either partner had with other parties. Nonetheless, Christopher's ambitious goal for the integration of the European and North American economies encountered considerable headwinds on each side of the Atlantic. Even though the economic pillar of the agenda was to be a Transatlantic Marketplace, to be achieved by "progressively reducing or eliminating barriers that hinder the flow of goods, services, and capital," there were few specifics, no commitment to comprehensive coverage, and no deadlines for achievement of such a goal. The U.S. Trade Representative's office and the European Commission's Directorate General for Trade agreed simply to conduct a "joint study" of trade liberalization possibilities, and the TAFTA boomlet subsided.

Tragedy and Triumph in Bosnia

Meanwhile, after further tragedies, the intensive efforts of Holbrooke and his team to find a solution to the war in Bosnia bore fruit. The U.S. success in concluding the peace accords signed in Dayton,

Ohio, in fall 1995 gave U.S. and NATO officials more confidence to speak about how the emerging architecture, including NATO enlargement, could prevent future conflicts.[110] NATO had gone out of area to end the Bosnian war. France had drawn closer to the Alliance and Germany was taking part in Allied military operations out of area. The NATO-led Implementation Force (IFOR) validated both the CJTFs and the PfP, which now provided an ideal framework to bring together allies and non-allies into an Implementation Force (IFOR). Of the initial 60,000 IFOR troops deployed in early 1996, one in six were from non-NATO countries. Aspirant countries took to heart NATO's message that closer integration into Western structures was also likely to be accelerated to the extent a country "acts like a member" even before it becomes a member. Hungary, Poland, the Czech Republic and other aspirants joined the peace implementation process.

IFOR also demonstrated that NATO and Russia could work together. NATO ground troops were deploying—for the first time in Alliance history—with Russian soldiers at their side as partners, not enemies.[111] NATO, the EU, and the OSCE were working in mutually reinforcing ways to implement the peace.

Holbrooke recounted that "three main pillars of American foreign policy in Europe—U.S.-Russian relations, NATO enlargement into Central Europe, and Bosnia—had often worked against each other. Now they reinforced each other."[112] Ian Davidson wrote in the *Financial Times* that Dayton was "having an electric effect on NATO" and ended the debate over whether NATO had a post-Cold War purpose. As French Foreign Minister Herve de Charette put it: "America was back."[113]

NATO Enlargement: On Track

After Dayton Holbrooke signaled that he was leaving the Administration. James Steinberg asked me to succeed Steven Flanagan as Associate Director of Secretary Christopher's Policy Planning Staff, where we continued work on NATO's enlargement and adaptation as part of the evolution of the broader security architecture.

On January 26, 1996 the U.S. Senate gave its advice and consent to ratification of the START II Treaty. Through the rest of the year we continued to pursue the timetable that President Clinton had given to Boris Yeltsin. There would be no surprises, no rush, but we also needed to demonstrate our determination to open NATO's door to the strongest candidates. The decision on "who" was for the second term; for the last year of the first term the key was to weather the Russian elections and to put other building blocks of the emerging architecture into place.

As we did so, it was important to affirm our continued momentum. East Central Europeans were anxious that the process was slowing down; they needed continual reassurance that things truly were on course. The Russians, in turn, were proving difficult; they needed to hear that they could not derail NATO enlargement and that it would proceed following the Russian elections. I worked with Tom Malinowski, James Steinberg and John Kornblum to craft a clear statement for Secretary Christopher to deliver in Prague on March 20. At Prague's storied Cernin Palace, Christopher again reviewed the different elements of the overall architecture, emphasizing that "NATO enlargement is on track and will happen." As Christopher later recounted, "The speech marked a turning point in our policy: after it there was no doubt in Central Europe, among our allies, or in Russia that NATO expansion would take place."[114]

After Yeltsin's reelection on July 3, 1996, the U.S. Congress signalled its support for enlargement of the Alliance. On July 23 the House passed the NATO Enlargement Facilitation Act by 353-65, and the Senate followed two days later, 81-16.[115]

The European Pillar

Meanwhile, three more pieces of the puzzle needed to fit. The first was to demonstrate that we were not just enlarging the Cold War Alliance, we were creating a new NATO for a new era. The second was to give the PfP a political dimension. The third was how to address Baltic fears of abandonment.

The redesign of Euro-Atlantic architecture needed to adapt NATO to new challenges. Collective defense remained an essential anchor of the Alliance. But Bosnia underscored that NATO might be called on to perform new missions related to conflict prevention and peacekeeping, most of which were likely to be beyond Alliance territory. NATO would need to streamline its planning and force preparations, simplify and speed up its decision-making, provide for greater European responsibilities and capabilities, and be able to operate with a wide range of partners, including the European Union.

Bolstering the Europeans' capacity to defend their interests in instances where the United States might not be involved had been a related puzzle piece. France in particular sought to bolster the Western European Union (WEU) as the defense arm of the European Union. When it became apparent that there was no consensus within the EU for this approach, and as budget strictures began to weigh on French capabilities, President Chirac became more amenable to reintegrating France into Alliance structures if the Alliance could lift European leadership of key commands and if the Alliance could adapt to new missions outside of Alliance territory.

U.S. officials remained ambivalent about efforts to build a European defense profile. U.S. political leaders routinely expressed rhetorical support for a more cohesive Europe that could act, effectively and confidently, as America's partner on the European continent and in the wider world. Yet when Europeans actually moved to establish truly "common" foreign security and defense policies, they were often faced with U.S. concerns that such coherence could become inward-looking and exclusive, or based on lowest-common-denominator consensus-building within the EU, and thus weaken the primacy of NATO or impede U.S. leadership and freedom of maneuver. The Clinton Administration's initial view had been summarized by Holbrooke in the *Foreign Affairs* article: "It would be self-defeating for the WEU to create military structures to duplicate the successful European integration achieved in NATO. But a stronger European pillar of the alliance can be an important contribution to European stability and transatlantic burden-sharing, provided it does not dilute NATO." He then foreshadowed the growing interest of the second-term Clinton Administration in more effective European capabilities to address out-of-area challenges: "The WEU establishes a new premise of collective defense: the United States should not be the only NATO member that can protect vital common interests outside Europe."[116]

The effort to balance these differing approaches was reflected at the June 1996 NATO ministerial, when Allies agreed that under certain circumstances, NATO could make available to the ten members of the WEU specific assets that would enable the WEU to be militarily effective. This included the provision of CJTF headquarters for WEU use, the double-hatting of some NATO officers, the identification of specific military assets that could be released to WEU, and the designation of the Deputy Supreme Allied Commander Europe (filled by a European) as the potential WEU strategic commander. Assets to be released to the WEU, subject to decision by the North Atlantic Council, could even include elements of the U.S. military, such as large transport aircraft, satellite-based communications, and sophisticated intelligence capabilities. NATO support for an effective ESDI would enable the European Allies to take greater responsibility for meeting some security challenges on the continent—if the political will to do so could be created and sustained.

These reforms enabled the full integration of Spain into NATO's military command. France inched closer, although in the end Chirac was not prepared to agree to full reintegration.[117]

The Baltic Action Plan

The Baltic states were another piece to the architectural puzzle. As the Bosnian peace began to be implemented and prospects for concrete progress on NATO enlargement loomed, Tony Lake was adamant that the Administration had to move beyond its internal deadlock over the goals of U.S. Baltic policy and align its approach with broader European strategy. The Baltic states were nervous that their security would be undercut if they were not among the first new members of NATO. We needed to devise an approach that would ensure this would not be the case, while working with the Baltic republics to facilitate their integration into the European and Euro-Atlantic mainstream, including walking through NATO's door at some point. NSC Senior Director Dan Fried asked me and Carol van Voorst, the European Bureau's Director of the Office for Nordic/Baltic Affairs, to move beyond the bureaucratic stalemate. We set to work.

By spring 1996 we had crafted a "Baltic Action Plan" to foster the integration of the Baltic republics into the European and transatlantic mainstream. The plan consisted of three tracks.

The first track sought to strengthen Baltic sovereignty and promote internal reforms by integrating the three republics into European and Euro-Atlantic institutions. This would include U.S.-Nordic cooperation in support of Baltic efforts to integrate. Denmark, for example, had been instrumental already since 1994 in supporting the formation of the Baltic Battalion (BALTBAT), a peacekeeping battalion and training program of the three Baltic states, and had some of their forces participating with the Nordic Battalion in Bosnia.

The second track promoted the use of bilateral and multilateral efforts to encourage the development of good relations with Russia. This meant, for example, providing additional resources to the Baltic nations to encourage regional cooperation between the Baltic states and Russia in the areas of crime prevention, energy use, commercial cooperation, and education, and encouraging Estonia and Latvia to resolve their border disputes with Russia and to integrate their Russian minorities more fully into their nations' political and social communities. The goal was to convince Russia to see the Baltic Sea region not as a zone of influence or a buffer against nonexistent enemies, but as a gateway outward to the new Europe, of which Russia could be an active participant.[118]

The third track expanded U.S. efforts to demonstrate its commitment to the Baltic states by developing a regional economic and commercial strategy to bolster U.S. investment and to highlight the potential role of the three Baltic states as an economic platform from which companies could access markets in the European Union, the Baltic states, and in Northwestern Russia. The Baltic-American Enterprise Fund, for instance, provided an average of $1 million a month in loans and investments throughout the Baltic states.

Our ideas overlapped in some ways with those set forth by Ron Asmus and Robert Nurick in an article in *Survival* that summer. While Asmus and Nurick used NATO enlargement as the pivot for their article, proposing a U.S.-Nordic alliance to mute negative fallout from an initial round of NATO enlargement that would not include the Baltic republics, the Baltic Action Plan had a positive agenda that was focused on fostering Baltic integration overall. It included the issue of NATO enlargement but was less defensive and did not make it the centerpiece of the approach. Nonetheless, since our thinking coincided in many ways, Talbott was able to distribute this public document around as something worth reading.

Meanwhile, Baltic leaders were increasingly concerned that they might be excluded from NATO. In late May President Clinton received a letter from the three Baltic Presidents Algirdas Brazauskas, Lennart Meri, and Guntis Ulmanis asking him to publicly affirm U.S. commitment to eventual Baltic membership in NATO. When he met with the three Presidents on June 28, he reassured them that the United States wanted to see the full integration of the Baltic states into the West. NATO's door would remain open after the first round of enlargement, the President said. "Unfortunately," he went on, "I cannot say to you today what you want me to say": that the Baltic states would be in the first wave of new members to NATO. In a separate meeting, Republican Presidential candidate Bob Dole also did not give the Baltic Presidents that reassurance.

The Baltic Action Plan, not yet released, had framed U.S. preparations for the meeting of the President. That meeting helped us put together some finishing touches to the plan. On August 28 Strobe Talbott shared the Baltic Action Plan with the three Baltic ambassadors to the United States. Their reaction was muted. Their single-minded focus on getting into the Alliance in the first wave caused them to assign less importance to this comprehensive approach to their deeper integration into the architecture. Ojars Kalnins, the Latvian Ambassador, described the Baltic Action Plan as the American's "best shot," but then described "best shot" as "being one that does not provide security guarantees, no hard promises on NATO but a complex of programs and assistance wherein the hope is that the whole will appear to exceed the sum of the parts and convey the impression of security."[119]

Secretary of Defense Bill Perry made it clear in October that the Baltic states were "not yet ready to take on the Article V responsibilities of NATO membership," but that "we should all work to hasten the day that they will be ready for membership." NATO's position for countries that would not be accepted in the first wave," he said, "is not 'no,' it is 'not yet.'"[120]

Despite initial Baltic disgruntlement, we moved ahead with the Baltic Action Plan, which energized U.S. diplomacy in Northern Europe.

An Atlantic Partnership Council

The next piece of the puzzle was to give the Partnership for Peace a political dimension. That opportunity came April 22-23, 1996, when I attended a meeting of the Atlantic Policy Advisory Group, which brought together policy planners from across the Alliance and now from partner countries as well. Such a grouping could offer a useful testing ground for policy. The Romanians had offered to host the meeting in Sinaia, a former casino resort town favored by Ceausescu. We were treated to freezing bedrooms, army blankets and bedbugs. Nonetheless, the atmosphere was collegial and the discussions substantive and open.

At Sinaia I presented a "non-paper" entitled "Europe's Security Architecture: The next phase," in which I "test marketed" a new element in the security architecture. PfP had offered Partners an important military link to the Alliance, I argued, but it did not provide an equivalent political link. NACC was moribund. Its original intent was as a forum for sharing information between now non-existent military blocs, not as a forum for political-military consultations on shared challenges and objectives. In addition, PfP was a hub-and-spokes arrangement; partners were linked to the Alliance but not necessarily to one another. If we were to realize our goal of establishing an architecture that could project stability across the continent, we needed a mechanism that would enable strategic discussions among Allies and partners as well as among partners on their own. If NATO Allies and non-NATO partners were to engage on military-security activities together, they also needed a mechanism that provided for political discussion and decision-making. I suggested retiring NACC and establishing a political counterpart to the PfP that I called an "Atlantic Partnership Council."

As soon as I had presented the idea, Mariot Leslie, head of the Policy Planning Staff in the UK Foreign and Commonwealth Office (and later UK Ambassador to NATO) asked me, "Are you serious about this? If so, we should act on it right away." Other colleagues were equally enthused. Momentum quickly built to implement the idea.

The opportunity to propose the Atlantic Partnership Council publicly, as well as to move forward other key elements of the architecture, came in September 1996. Secretary Christopher had been invited by German Foreign Minister Klaus Kinkel to speak in Stuttgart to commemorate the 50th anniversary of a landmark speech by former Secretary of State James Byrnes that repudiated U.S. postwar policy toward Germany in favor of a policy of economic revival and democratic renewal, including support for German unity, that set the stage for the Marshall Plan and eventual U.S. support for German integration into Western structures.[121] Christopher, Steinberg and Kornblum wanted the speech to reinforce the architectural design and chart a roadmap for advancing each element for Clinton's second term. John Kornblum contributed building blocks; Tom Malinowski and I worked through a draft.

The Stuttgart speech updated and expanded upon the architectural framework first introduced by Richard Holbrooke in his *Foreign Affairs* article almost two years earlier. "The vision that President Clinton and I have for the United States and Europe in the next century," Christopher began, "is a vision for a New Atlantic Community. This community will build on the institutions our predecessors created, but it will transcend the artificial boundaries of Cold War Europe. It will give North America a deeper partnership with a broader, more integrated Europe on this continent and around the world."[122] Christopher affirmed the Administration's core premise that the United States was a European power and mentioned each pillar of the architectural construct, including strong support for EU enlargement. He then previewed the Clinton Administration's second term agenda by making six major architectural proposals.

First, he recommended that NATO should hold a summit in early 1997 "to agree on NATO's internal reforms, launch enlargement negotiations for NATO, and deepen NATO's partnership with Russia and other European states." At the summit, Christopher said, "we should invite several partners to begin accession negotiations." He reiterated that NATO's door "will stay open for all of those who demonstrated that they are willing and able to shoulder the responsibilities of membership."

Second, he said it was time to "expand the scope of NATO's Partnership for Peace…beyond its current missions. We should involve our partners in the Partnership for Peace in the planning as well as the execution of NATO's missions. We should give them a stronger voice by forming an Atlantic Partnership Council."

Third, Christopher urged leaders at the OSCE Lisbon Summit in December to launch negotiations to adapt the CFE treaty and complete the Forum for Security Cooperation.

Fourth, he proposed developing an enhanced partnership between Ukraine and NATO.

Finally, he proposed "the next logical step" in "Russia's cooperation with NATO": "a formal Charter" that "should create standing arrangements for consultation and joint action between Russia and the Alliance."

Finally, he proposed moving "toward a free and open Transatlantic Marketplace," saying that "We are already at a stage when we can realistically discuss the true integration of the economies of Europe and North America. We should now pursue practical steps" to advance that goal.

Christopher also highlighted a rationale for the new architecture that was to become ever more prominent during President Clinton's second term, at which Holbrooke in his article had merely hinted. A more stable Europe was not only important to the United States in its own right; a more stable Europe could also become America's partner to address other global and regional challenges, particularly terrorism and the environment. "Our New Atlantic Community will only be secure if we also work together to meet the threats that transcend our frontiers—threats like terrorism, nuclear proliferation, crime, drugs, disease and damage to the environment." The danger posed by these threats, he argued, were as great as any that we had faced during the Cold War.

As American voters went to the polls in November 1996, the Clinton Administration had put together the edifice of a new Euro-Atlantic architecture. Yet much still needed to be done.[123]

Notes

1. Strobe Talbott, *The Russia Hand: A Memoir of Presidential Diplomacy* (New York: Random House, 2002), pp. 92-93.

2. Ibid.

3. Ibid., pp. 92-93.

4. Cited by President Clinton at his remarks for the North Atlantic Council Summit, NATO Headquarters, Brussels, Belgium, January 10, 1994.

5. Madeleine K. Albright, "Why bigger is better," *The Economist*, February 15, 1997.

6. See G. John Ikenberry, "America's Alliances in the Age of Unipolarity," January 14, 2003.

7. Albright, "Why bigger is better," op. cit.

8. Instead of citing a quote attributed to Lord Ismay, those fond of him may prefer to cite a quote actually sourced to him: "On NATO I am convinced that the present solution is only a partial one, aimed at guarding the heart. It must grow until the whole free world gets under one umbrella." Robert Smith, *The NATO International Staff/Secretariat, 1952-1957* (London: Oxford University Press, 1967), p. 65.

9. I had the uncomfortable opportunity to challenge Helmut Schmidt on this issue on *ABC Nightline*, March 18, 1990, the night of East Germany's first—and only—free parliamentary elections. For a Clinton Administration statement on this point, see Strobe Talbott, "The United States, Germany and the Idea of Europe," Address at the New Traditions Conference "Intellectual Leadership for the New Century," American Academy Berlin, March 20, 1998.

10. "The Alliance's Strategic Concept," in *NATO Handbook* (Brussels, 1995), p. 235.

11. See U.S. Department Of State, *Report to Congress on the Enlargement of the North Atlantic Treaty Organization*, February 24, 1997, p. 10.; Paul E. Gallis, "NATO: Congress Addresses Expansion of the Alliance," Issue Brief 95076, Congressional Research Service, Library of Congress; and Paul E. Gallis, "NATO Enlargement and Russia," CRS Report 97-477, Congressional Research Service, Library of Congress.

12. See Strobe Talbott, "Why NATO Should Grow," *The New York Review of Books*, August 10, 1995; Strobe Talbott, "Russia Has Nothing to Fear," *New York Times*, February 18, 1997, p. A25.

13. See Mary N. Hampton, "NATO at the Creation: U.S. Foreign Policy, West Germany, and the Wilsonian Impulse," *Security Studies*, Vol. 4, No. 3, Spring 1995, pp. 610-656; Mary N. Hampton, *The Wilsonian Impulse: U.S. Foreign Policy, the Alliance, and German Unification* (Westport, Conn.: Praeger, 1996); Ikenberry, op. cit.

14. Robert E. Hunter, "NATO in the 21st Century: A Strategic Vision," *Parameters*, Summer 1998, pp. 15-29.

15. http://www.worldaffairsjournal.org/article/search-allies-vaclav-havel-and-expansion-nato.

16. "A Europe Whole and Free," Remarks by President George H.W. Bush to the Citizens in Mainz, Federal Republic of Germany, May 31, 1989, https://usa.usembassy.de/etexts/ga6-890531.htm.While there was a natural tendency in the early years of a Democratic administration not to use Republican phrases, by Clinton's second term Administration officials working on Europe used the term freely. See Secretary of State Madeleine Albright's commencement address at Harvard University, June 5, 1997, http://gos.sbc.edu/a/albright3.html; Secretary of State Madeleine K. Albright, Remarks before the New Atlantic Initiative Conference, The Mayflower Hotel, Washington, D.C., February 9, 1998 https://1997-2001.state.gov/statements/1998/980209.html; Strobe Talbott in Helsinki 1998: https://1997-2001.state.gov/policy_remarks/1998/980121_talbott_eursecurity.html.

17. Warren Christopher, "Charting a Transatlantic Agenda for the 21st Century," Address at the Casa de America, Madrid, Spain, June 2, 1995; William H. Hill, *No Place for Russia: European Security Institutions Since 1989* (New York: Columbia Univ. Press, 2019).

18. Ibid.

19. Ronald D. Asmus, *Opening NATO's Door* (Columbia University Press, 2002), p. 291.

20. Cited in Talbott, *The Russia Hand*, op. cit., p. 133.

21. See Hill, op. cit., p. 67.

22. Ibid., p. 68.

23. Hill p. 68.

24. Richard C. Holbrooke and Michael E. Mandelbaum, "Expanding NATO: Will it Weaken the Alliance?" Great Debates Series, Council on Foreign Relations, December 9, 1996, http://www.bits.de/NRANEU/docs/ExpandingNATO.htm

25. John Christian Kornblum, "The United States and Europe: Toward a Global Atlantic," *Foreign Service Journal*, April 2017, p.37.

26. The mood at the time was captured in *Changing Our Ways*, a national commission on U.S. foreign policy sponsored by the Carnegie Endowment for International Peace, in which Holbrooke and I were involved: "there has been no Victory-over-Communism Day, no confetti, no strangers kissing in the street. Indeed, it has been a long time since America has been so uneasy about itself and so uncertain of where to go next...After decades of global exertion, Americans seem in the mood for retrenchment."

27. U.S. Secretary of State Madeleine K. Albright, Remarks before the New Atlantic Initiative Conference, The Mayflower Hotel, Washington, D.C., February 9, 1998, https://1997-2001.state.gov/statements/1998/980209.html.

28. Ibid.

29. Talbott, *The Russia Hand*, op. cit., p. 99.

30. Ibid., p. 100.

31. "Ensuring Russian Democracy is "Paramount Challenge""—Trancript: Clinton Kohl newsconference, 26.3.1993, in USPIT, no. 33/1993 (March 30, 1993), pp. 3-12, here p. 4.

32. Ibid., p. 87.

33. Clinton used that gesture of including Yeltsin in the G7 political meetings to extract from the Russian President a formal, categorical announcement that Russia was proceeding with the withdrawal of the seven thousand Russian troops still in the Baltic states to meet their August 31 agreed deadline. Ibid., p. 125.

34. James M. Goldgeier, *Not Whether But When: The U.S. Decision to Enlarge NATO* (Washington: Brookings Institution, 1999), p. 9.

35. Asmus, op. cit. p. 19.

36. http://www.worldaffairsjournal.org/article/search-allies-vaclav-havel-and-expansion-nato.

37. Cited in Asmus, op. cit. p. 25; see also Douglas Brinkley, "Democratic Enlargement: The Clinton Doctrine," *Foreign Policy*, 106 (Spring 1997), pp. 111-127.

38. http://www.worldaffairsjournal.org/article/search-allies-vaclav-havel-and-expansion-nato; Asmus, op. cit., p. 19.

39. Talbott, *The Russia Hand*, op. cit. p. 110

40. Cited in Asmus, op. cit., p. 57.

41. Talbott, *The Russia Hand*, op. cit., p. 115

42. Ibid., pp. 114-115; Douglas Brinkley, "Clinton and Democratic Enlargement," https://erenow.net/modern/risetoglobalismdouglasbrinkley/19.php;

43. Warren Christopher, *In the Stream of History: Shaping Foreign Policy for a New Era* (Palo Alto: Stanford University Press, 1998), p. 227; Ashton B. Carter and William J. Perry, *Preventive Defense: A New Security Strategy for America* (Brookings, 1999), pp. 1ff.

44. A summary of the Commission's recommendations were published in a special report entitled "Policymaking for a new Era," *Foreign Affairs*, Winter 1992/1993.

45. Including, for example, Ron Asmus, Fred Bergsten, Jeffrey Garten, Robert M. Kimmitt, Joe Kruzel, Col. Bruce Scott, James Steinberg, and Robert Zoellick.

46. Daniel S. Hamilton, *Beyond Bonn: America and the Berlin Republic* (Washington, DC: Carnegie Endowment for International Peace, 1994); German version published as *Jenseits von Bonn: Amerika und die Berliner Republik* (Berlin: Ullstein, 1994). A summary of the book was published as a special edition of Germany's *Der Spiegel* weekly newsmagazine on the eve of President Clinton's visit to Germany in June 1994.

47. "Marooned In the Cold War: An Exchange between Mark Danner and Richard C. Holbrooke," http://www.markdanner.com/articles/marooned-in-the-cold-war-an-exchange-between-mark-danner-and-richard-c-holbrooke.

48. Ibid.

49. Cited in Asmus, op. cit., p. 57.

50. "Remarks to the French National Assembly in Paris June 7, 1994," Public Papers of the Presidents of the United States: William J. Clinton (1994, Book I), June 7, 1994, pp. 1051-1055. U.S. Government Publishing Office, https://www.govinfo.gov/content/pkg/PPP-1994-book1/html/PPP-1994-book1-doc-pg1051.htm.

51. Asmus, op. cit., pp. 78-79; "Remarks by President Clinton, Chancellor Kohl, and President Delors in Press Availability," East Hall, Reichstag, Berlin, Germany, July 12, 1994; Goldgeier, op. cit., pp. 67-69; William Clinton, "Remarks Following Discussions with President Lech Walesa of Poland and an Exchange with Reporters in Warsaw," July 19, 1994, *Public Papers, 1994*, Book 1, pp. 1205-1206; William Clinton, "Interview with Thomas Lis of Polish Television," July 1, 1994, *Public Papers, 1994*, Book 1, p. 1187.

52. See Alexander Vershbow's account in this volume. Also Asmus, op. cit., p. 79.

53. "Marooned In the Cold War," op. cit.

54. Various iterations of the Gore speech are in the author's files.

55. Department of State Dispatch, September 12, 1994, vol. 5, pp. 597-98; Goldgeier, op. cit., pp. 71-72; Gen. Wesley Clark, "Richard Holbrooke: The pragmatist," December 14, 2010, https://www.greatertalent.com/press/general-wesley-clark-reflects-on-the-life-of-richard-holbrooke/; Richard Holbrooke's Brilliant Drive, https://www.care2.com/news/member/451276626/2675200

56. Goldgeier, op. cit., p. 155.

57. Cited in Talbott, *The Russia Hand*, op. cit., p. 136.

58. Goldgeier, op. cit., p. 71.

59. Asmus, op. cit., p. 92; NSC Paper, "Moving Toward NATO Expansion," October 12, 1994.

60. Author's notes; United States Information Agency Television and Film Service, "U.S.-European Relations," Guest: Ambassador Richard Holbrooke, Assistant Secretary of State for European and Canadian Affairs, November 17, 1994. Transcript in author's files.

61. For the text of the letter, National Security Archive, Document 13, Official informal No. 248 "Boris-Bill Letter."

1994-12-06, Source: U.S. Department of State. Date/Case ID: 07 JUL 2004 200000983, https://nsarchive2.gwu.edu//dc.html?doc=4390827-Document-13-Official-informal-No-248-Boris-Bill.

62. See Elaine Sciolino, "Yeltsin Says NATO Is Trying to Split Continent Again," *The New York Times*, December 6, 1994;

63. National Security Archive, "What Yeltsin Heard," Document 13, 14, 16 and 17, https://nsarchive.gwu.edu/briefing-book/russia-programs/2018-03-16/nato-expansion-what-yeltsin-heard.

64. Asmus, op. cit., p. 106-109; Talbott, *The Russia Hand*, op. cit.

65. Hill, op. cit., p. 106.

66. Zbigniew Brzezinski, "A Plan for Europe," *Foreign Affairs*, vol. 73, no.1, (Jan/Feb 1995), p. 30.

67. Dominique Moisi and Michael Mertes, "Europe's Map, Compass and Horizon," *Foreign Affairs*, vol. 73, no. 1, (Jan/Feb 1995), p. 125.

68. Henry Kissinger, "Not This Partnership," *Washington Post*, November 24, 1993, p. A-17.

69. Hill, op. cit., p. 14.

70. This became a fundamental starting point for subsequent U.S. policy statements on Europe. See, for instance, President Bill Clinton's speech in Aachen upon

receiving the Charlemagne Prize in 2000, https://www.karlspreis.de/en/laureates/
william-jefferson-bill-clinton-2000/speech-by-bill-clinton; Albright, New Atlantic Initiative Conference, op. cit.; Assistant Secretary for European and Canadian Affairs Marc Grossman, Statement submitted for the record, as prepared for a
hearing before the Senate Foreign Relations Committee (canceled), October 1997,
https://1997-2001.state.gov/regions/eur/971000grossman.html; Thomas R. Pickering, Under Secretary of State for Political Affairs, "Shores of Peace: Advancing
Security and Cooperation in the Baltic Sea Region," Keynote address at the Conference on Baltic Sea Security and Cooperation, Stockholm, Sweden, October 19,
2000, https://1997-2001.state.gov/policy_remarks/2000/001019_pickering_bssc.
html.

71. Richard Holbrooke, "America, A European Power," *Foreign Affairs*, March/
April 1995.

72. It was a term also used by President George H.W. Bush and senior officials
in his administration.

73. Draft Remarks for Richard C. Holbrooke, December 16, 1994, in author's
files.

74. Holbrooke, "America, A European Power," op. cit.

75. Ibid.

76. Ibid.

77. John Kornblum, "New European Security Architecture," USIA Foreign
Press Center Briefing, January 24, 1995.

78. U.S. Deputy Secretary of State Strobe Talbott, "Opening Doors and Building Bridges in the New Europe," Address to the Paasikivi Society, Helsinki, Finland, January 21, 1998, https://1997-2001.state.gov/policy_remarks/1998/980121_
talbott_eursecurity.html

79. See James A. Baker, "The Euro-Atlantic Architecture: From West to East,"
Address Before the CSCE Council of Foreign Ministers in Berlin (June 18, 1991).

80. Robert E. Hunter, "NATO in the 21st Century," op. cit., pp. 15-29.

81. Holbrooke, op. cit.

82. Ibid.

83. Hill, op. cit., p. 111.

84. Holbrooke, op. cit.

85. Ibid.

86. Ibid.

87. "Europe Must Avoid Being Held Prisoner By Its History," Richard C. Holbrooke, Assistant Secretary for European and Canadian Affairs, Remarks before the North Atlantic Assembly, Budapest, Hungary, May 29, 1995.

88. Ibid.

89. Goldgeier, op. cit., pp. 94-95; Perry remarks at the *Wehrkunde* Munich Conference on Security Policy, February 5, 1995, "The Enduring Dynamic Relationship That Is NATO," Defense Viewpoint, Vol. 10, http://www.defenselink.mil/speeches/1995/s19950205-perry-html. NATO, *Study on NATO Enlargement*, September 1995, http://www.fas.org/man/nato/natodocs/enl-9502.htm.

90. John Kornblum, "New European Security Architecture," op. cit.

91. "Europe Must Avoid Being Held Prisoner By Its History," Holbrooke, op. cit.

92. Talbott, *The Russia Hand*, op. cit., p. 94.

93. https://apps.dtic.mil/dtic/tr/fulltext/u2/a394506.pdf

94. Talbott, *The Russia Hand*, op. cit., p. 224.

95. Brinkley, "Clinton and Democratic Enlargement," op. cit.

96. Talbott, *The Russia Hand*, op. cit., p. 132.

97. Copy in author's possession.

98. Strobe Talbott, "A Baltic Home-Coming: Robert C. Frasure Memorial Lecture," Tallinn, Estonia, January 24, 2000.

99. Talbott, *The Russia Hand*, op. cit., p. 225.

100. Ronald D. Asmus and Richard C. Holbrooke, "Re-Reinventing NATO," Riga Papers, German Marshall Fund of the United States, 2006.

101. Ibid.

102. Elaine Sciolino, "U.S. Declines to Back Peace Plan as the Balkan Talks Shift to UN," *The New York Times*, February 2, 1993.

103. Cited in Goldgeier, op. cit., p. 98.

104. Holbrooke, "America, A European Power," op. cit.; Roger Cohen, "Richard Holbrooke: A European Power," in Derek Chollet and Samantha Power, eds., *The Unquiet American: Richard Holbrooke in the World*, pp. 165-166.

105. These five principles are based on the NATO Enlargement Study of 1995 and were subsequently laid out by former Secretary of Defense Perry in a speech in Norfolk, Virginia in June 1996. They are: commitment to democratic reform; commitment to a free market economy; good neighborly relations; civilian con-

trol of the military; and military capability to operate effectively with the Alliance. https://1997-2001.state.gov/regions/eur/971000grossman.html.

106. See Charles P. Ries, "Is it Time to (Re) Consider a TAFTA?" in Daniel S. Hamilton, ed., *Shoulder to Shoulder: Forging a Strategic U.S.–EU Partnership* (Washington, DC: Center for Transatlantic Relations, 2010).

107. R.C. Longworth, "Trade Pact with U.S. Tantalizing Europeans," *Chicago Tribune*, May 21, 1995, https://www.chicagotribune.com/news/ct-xpm-1995-05-21-9505210532-story.html.

108. Warren Christopher, "Charting a Transatlantic Agenda for the 21st Century," Address at the Casa de America, Madrid, Spain, June 2, 1995.

109. Ibid.

110. Goldgeier, op. cit., p. 96;

111. Asmus, op. cit., p. 125.

112. Richard Holbrooke, *To End a War* (New York: Modern Library, 1998), p. 359. Goldgeier, op. cit., pp. 96-97. Carter and Perry, *Preventive Defense*, op. cit., p. 38. Even before accession negotiations began, in June 1993, during a meeting of the European Council in Copenhagen, EU member states officially confirmed that the countries of Central and Eastern Europe, currently affiliated with the EC, would join the EU after fulfilling economic and political criteria. On April 8,1994, the Government of the Republic of Poland made a formal request, in Athens, for membership in the European Union. During the European Council summit held in Essen on December 9–10 1994, EU member states adopted a pre-accession strategy, defining the areas and forms of cooperation recognized by the EU as essential to speed up integration. This process also confirmed that the EU was willing to go through with enlargement to associated countries. Formal confirmation of the strategy as outlined in a White Paper on the alignment of countries with the requirements of the internal free market was adopted at the European Council Summit in Cannes in June 1995.

113. Cited in Asmus, op. cit., p. 125.

114. U.S. Secretary of State Warren Christopher, "A Democratic and Undivided Europe in Our Time," Cernin Palace, Prague, March 20, 1996; Christopher, *In the Stream of History*, op. cit., p. 399; Asmus, op. cit., pp. 144-145.

115. Goldgeier, op. cit., p. 104.

116. Holbrooke, "America, A European Power," op. cit.

117. U.S. Ambassador to NATO Robert Hunter declared French reintegration into NATO at that time "about 95 percent done." Hunter, "NATO in the 21st Century," op. cit., pp. 15-29.

118. Estonia, Latvia and Lithuania and United States Baltic Policy. Hearing before the Subcommittee on European Affairs of the Committee on Foreign Relations, U.S. Senate, Second Session, July 15, 1998, https://www.govinfo.gov/content/pkg/CHRG-105shrg50539/html/CHRG-105shrg50539.htm.

119. Asmus, op. cit., pp. 161-163.

120. Ibid., p. 163.

121. Speech by J.F. Byrnes, United States Secretary of State, "Restatement of Policy on Germany," Stuttgart, September 6, 1946, https://usa.usembassy.de/etexts/ga4-460906.htm.

122. "A New Atlantic Community For the 21st Century," Speech in Commemoration of Secretary of State James Byrnes' 1946 Speech of Hope, Secretary of State Warren Christopher, September 6, 1996, https://usa.usembassy.de/etexts/ga7-960906.htm.

123. As other authors recount in this volume, President Clinton then made an important speech on NATO enlargement on October 22, 1996, in Hamtramck, the site of a Bush address on Eastern Europe in 1989, in which he declared "America's goal" to be to admit the "first group" of aspirants to NATO membership "by 1999, NATO's 50th anniversary." He went on to urge Russia to reconsider its opposition to NATO expansion on the grounds that it would "advance the security of everyone." "Remarks by the President to the People of Detroit," The White House, Office of the Press Secretary, October 22, 1996. See also Goldgeier, op. cit. p. 104.

Chapter 2

Opening NATO and Engaging Russia: NATO's Two Tracks and the Establishment of the North Atlantic Cooperation Council

Stephan Kieninger

In the second half of the 1990s, when NATO was preparing to extend its membership eastward, Russian officials began to claim that the entry of former Warsaw Pact countries would violate a solemn "pledge"—made in the context of German unification diplomacy—not to include any former Communist countries into the alliance. Over the past decade or so a debate has been raging over the question whether or not Western policymakers made any legally binding commitment never to move NATO's borders eastward.[1]

As Philipp Zelikow and Mark Kramer have pointed out, the declassification of documents from all sides bear out that neither the United States nor any other Western country pledged not to expand NATO beyond Germany.[2] Joshua Itzkowitz Shifrinson has claimed that the United States was playing a double game, leading Gorbachev to believe that NATO would be subsumed in a new European security structure, while in truth working to ensure hegemony in Europe and the maintenance of NATO.[3]

In this chapter I emphasize that the West did not play a double game. I argue that NATO itself pursued a policy of two tracks.

First, the aim was to open up NATO, but slowly, cautiously and combined with an expanded effort to engage Russia. NATO's gradual approach was the means to secure Central and Eastern Europe and to support Mikhail Gorbachev's and Boris Yeltsin's reforms.

Second, by working gradually, NATO hoped to buy time and to work out a cooperative relationship with Russia. The emergence of the North Atlantic Cooperation Council (NACC) in November 1991 reflected NATO's gradual but also inclusive approach.

The initiative was designed to give the Central and East European countries a perspective for closer association and eventual NATO membership.[4] At the same time, the endeavor was intended to include Russia in the future European security system.

In Search of Security:
The Countries of Central and Eastern Europe

The countries of Central and Eastern Europe had always been looking West even when Europe was divided. Ronald Asmus pointed out that "rejoining the West had been an important leitmotif of the revolutions of 1989."[5] The events of 1989 and Germany's unification transformed Europe. The Warsaw Pact dissolved in 1991.[6] The question now was, what would come next?

NATO's opening was not a predetermined affair. First of all, it was imperative for NATO to adapt itself and to change its doctrine. The process of NATO's transformation was initiated at the London Summit in June 1990. U.S. President George Bush emphasized that we "must build a transformed alliance for the new Europe of the 21st century." In the same vein, British Prime Minister Margaret Thatcher said that "our signal from this meeting must continue to be one of resolve in defence, resolve and unity in defence coupled with willingness to extend the hand of friendship to Eastern Europe and the Soviet Union."[7] At London, NATO extended a "hand of friendship" to the Warsaw Pact countries, inviting them to form a new relationship with NATO and to establish regular diplomatic liaison with NATO in an effort to think aloud with each other during a historic period of change. This involved meetings between the Ambassadors of the Central and East European countries in Brussels and visits by NATO Secretary General Manfred Wörner and his staff to Eastern Europe and the Soviet Union.[8]

Initially, the Central and Eastern European countries sought only closer ties with NATO, not membership. However, given the crisis in Yugoslavia and the aborted coup against Mikhail Gorbachev in August 1991, the political leaderships of the Central and Eastern European countries were afraid of a security vacuum developing in their region. Starting in 1990, Czechoslovakian President Václav Havel, Polish President Lech Wałęsa and Hungarian Prime Minister József Antall articulated their desire to develop the closest possible relations with NATO.

Equal security was a precondition for them also in their endeavor to join the European Community. But from their vantage point, only NATO was able to provide the kind of hard security they were seeking. In September 1990, Poland's Prime Minister Tadeusz Mazowiecki told George H.W. Bush that "no one doubts the direction of change—toward the market—is irreversible, but Poland needs some signs that their economic problems are appreciated by the Western world."[9] In October 1990, in a conversation with Bush, Antall made the point that "economic problems can create social problems. I don't know if we can control the situation. If we don't, that would be a huge propaganda victory for conservatives in the Soviet Union and China."[10] In November 1990, Havel emphasized that "with the collapse of communism in Czechoslovakia, Poland, Hungary and other countries, we may be facing a temporary vacuum as all the old links cease to exist. It could be breeding ground for chaos and instability. Our democracies are just emerging. To fill this vacuum is not just our problem; it is also an obligation of the West."[11] Therefore, the reformers in the East were seeking Western assistance to transform their economies.

Western policymakers were meanwhile confronted with a multitude of challenges. In late 1990 and early 1991, Saddam Hussein's invasion of Kuwait and the ensuring war in Iraq somewhat diverted the Bush Administration's attention from Eastern Europe. The formation and the maintenance of the global coalition against Hussein took up most of Bush's time.[12] Against this background, in March 1991, Germany's Foreign Minister Hans-Dietrich Genscher reminded Bush that "with regards to Eastern Europe, this is critically important too. They badly need our economic help and we are prepared to work with you. [..] Also there is a security vacuum now in Eastern Europe. We need to give these countries an answer to the question they are asking. It must make them feel more secure but it also must be in our own interest and it must not be provocative to the Soviets. We need to give them this answer very soon."[13]

In 1991, the Central and Eastern European countries were in a challenging situation. In addition to complete economic transformation from plan to market with Western assistance, their leaders were eager to establish the broadest possible ties. In March 1991, in a conversation with President Bush, Lech Wałęsa emphasized that "we resolutely desire to join Western Europe and the United States in political, economic and military terms." Wałęsa reiterated Poland's need for international security. He argued that "we are ready for cooperation in every respect, even military. This doesn't mean that we are anti-Soviet or anti-German, but rather that we are pro-peace and security." Meanwhile, the Warsaw Pact was effectively dissolved on March 30, 1991.

Bush did not feel in the position to give any sort of security guarantees. He emphasized the need to take a gradual approach. Bush understood Wałęsa's "sense of urgency." At the same time, he thought it impossible to provide immediate military assistance. Instead, he argued that "we still feel that the best assistance that we could possibly provide is to encourage our private sector."

Bush sensed Wałęsa's concern over the situation in the Soviet Union. Wałęsa watched Bush's diplomacy with Gorbachev very closely. Bush argued that "we support Gorbachev because he has been right before. [...] We must reward whatever he does that is cooperative. I know you are worried about gradualism on the part of the West and its response to Poland's needs, and I know you are also worried about military security."[14]

The West certainly rewarded Mikhail Gorbachev's cooperative security policy. In 1990, Kohl's financial help for the Soviet Union had been essential to buy his consent to Germany's unification, basically offering cash credits and covering the cost of removing Soviet forces from East Germany.[15] In 1991, the West Germans were unilaterally funneling massive amounts of assistance to Moscow to shore up the Soviet economy. Time and again, Helmut Kohl justified his actions stating "it certainly was not in the West's interest for instability to reign in the Soviet Union. That country had to be integrated into the world economy."[16]

To that end, Mikhail Gorbachev was invited to participate in the G-7 Summit in London in 1991. However, the USSR failed to stabilize. With the coup of August 1991, Gorbachev lost power and the USSR was on the path towards its dissolution.[17]

A Euro-Atlantic Security Initiative: The Establishment of the North Atlantic Cooperation Council

The August 1991 coup had affected the thinking in Central and Eastern Europe in profound ways. Ronald Asmus wrote that "the initial announcement of the coup had sent shivers down the spines of many in the region and reminded them how vulnerable their newly won freedom and independence might be."[18]

Central and Eastern European leaders immediately requested clear signal of support both from Washington and NATO headquarters in Brussels. Both Havel and Wałęsa worried about the lack of meaningful security guarantees. NATO's hand of friendship and the establishment of NATO liaisons offices meant little in the fall of 1991. József Antall of Hungary felt that the coup in Moscow had been proof that it had been right to have acted in haste to get the Soviet troops out of Hungary. He emphasized that "it would have been horrible if this had taken place under the former situation."[19]

The August 1991 coup highlighted the urgency to build a basis for a new peace order in Europe based on cooperative security as long as Mikhail Gorbachev was still in power. It underlined the need to construct a "new Euro-Atlantic community" of nations in an effort to provide the Central and Eastern European countries a perspective for closer ties with the West going beyond NATO's hand of friendship.[20]

President Bush advanced two initiatives to address both challenges.

First, following the aborted coup in Moscow, he proposed a unilateral move on nuclear weapons. Bush was eager to make progress while he still had Gorbachev as a partner.[21] His proposals entailed the idea of getting rid of all tactical nuclear weapons except those launched from the air. Other elements of the Bush initiative took bombers and missiles off alert, pressed de-MIRVing of missiles and canceled some nuclear modernization programs. The purpose of the Bush initiative was to signal to the leaders and the peoples in the Soviet Union that NATO's policy would enhance their security and build stability.[22]

Bush's second initiative was aimed at the transformation of Europe's security architecture; Secretary of State James Baker and Hans-Dietrich Genscher issued a common declaration highlighting their ambition to create a "Euro-Atlantic Community that extends East from Vancouver to Vladivostok." This vague rhetoric pointed to moving on with something more tangible from London in 1990. They emphasized that "the Atlantic link, European integration and cooperation with our Eastern neighbors are the linchpins of this community." And their premise was that promoting democratic institutions in Central and Eastern Europe "complements the maintenance of a common defense in ensuring security".[23]

The Baker-Genscher declaration was the birth hour for the establishment of the North Atlantic Cooperation Council (NACC). The aim was to institutionalize NATO's new relationship with the new democracies of Central and Eastern Europe and the Soviet Union and to formalize "the liaison relationship by establishing a more routine set of meetings among the sixteen and the liaison countries, perhaps as a "North Atlantic Cooperation Council."[24]

Genscher told Bush and Baker that it was imperative "to give the Soviets some kind of a framework for continuing to participate in Europe and also to prevent Balkanization of the Soviet Union or Eastern Europe." Moreover, he stressed that Germany wanted full associate and then full membership in the European Community (EC) for the Central and Eastern European countries. His verdict was clear: "We now have to decide how to help the Central and Eastern Europe countries and the Soviet Union: We cannot let them fail."[25]

Genscher was for EC membership for the Central and Eastern European countries, and also for loose but formalized NATO ties with them and the USSR. The establishment of the NACC was a means to find a way to expand relations and dialogue between NATO and the Central and Eastern European countries. It was intended to provide assurance of U.S. participation and to place NATO in the forefront of European security.[26]

The timing was as important as the content of the NACC initiative. There was as yet no blueprint for the transformation of Europe's security system. In December 1991, Poland, Czechoslovakia and Hungary were granted associate EC status. However, their future relationship towards NATO remained unclear.

In October 1991, President Bush's National Security Advisor, Brent Scowcroft, told Václav Havel that Czechoslovakia's relations to NATO "is in the nature of the growing European community as it relates to NATO. […] We are interested in close relations, but there is a debate over how to expand and how fast. This is caught up in the question of Europe and its relation to NATO and the European defense system."[27]

NATO's Rome Summit in November 1991 was the birth hour for the NACC. NATO's Heads of State adopted a declaration on peace and cooperation in order to define a new security architecture in Europe. Moreover, they welcomed the prospect of a strengthening of the role of Western European Union (WEU), both as the defense component of the process of European unification and as a means of consolidating the European pillar of the Atlantic Alliance.

A month earlier, NATO Secretary General Manfred Wörner had stressed that, in a broader sense, the purpose of NATO's Rome Summit was to "describe NATO's role with the context of the Euro-Atlantic framework and the transatlantic axis which is fundamental both to European order and to the new world order." Wörner made the point that "we need a new picture of NATO, not as a military alliance confronting the Soviet Union, but as a military alliance confronting instability and uncertainty, and as a political alliance gaining in importance for establishing and carrying out this new European and world order."[28]

The rapid collapse of the Soviet Union, however, quickly outpaced NATO's adaption.

Central and Eastern European leaders were not content with closer institutional cooperation short of membership. Polish Prime Minister Krzysztof Bielecki highlighted his country's need to join the institutions of the West: "When we are members of the family of the democratic community, we will feel secure." Bielecki favored a dissolution of the Soviet Union and its conversion to a collection of sovereign states. Only thus would the promotion of democracy be feasible, he argued. In fact, as he told Bush, "for me the Soviet Union doesn't exist."[29]

Helmut Kohl held a different view. He favored cohesion, stability and a continued role for Mikhail Gorbachev in a new Russian or post-Soviet federation. Kohl believed that "a catastrophe awaits us if the USSR disintegrates completely."[30]

In the autumn of 1991, Bush held a middle position: He continued to support Gorbachev while he established contacts with the republics and its leaders such as Yeltsin, Kravchuk, Nazarbayev and others.

In, 1992, Russia's need for economic assistance and the emergence of the Western relationship with Boris Yeltsin's government overshadowed Central and Eastern European pleas for NATO membership. In February 1992, Russia's domestic situation and its economic reforms were clearly the most pressing item on the agenda of President Bush's first summit meeting with Boris Yeltsin.[31]

Western policymakers did not address the issue of NATO's opening in public. George Bush thought that a public debate over NATO's opening might upset the emergence of the Euro-Atlantic security order. In June 1992, he told Antall that "we do have a responsibility to be a stabilizing force in Europe, also with Russia. In that respect we have unique responsibilities."[32]

Nonetheless, behind the scenes a strategy debate was under way over NATO's opening. In March 1992, Britain's NATO Ambassador John Weston argued in favor of an early declaration by NATO "of its readiness to accept in due course enlargement by any new member state of the European Union that is willing to assume the full obligations of NATO membership." Weston reiterated that there was an urgent need to address NATO's enlargement question at a time when the future enlargement of the European Union was taken for granted. His idea to meet potential Russian concerns was "to persuade them that they are sui generis because of Russia's seize and importance and that these require a special relationship with major world players."[33] Rodric Braithwaite, one of John Major's key foreign policy advisers, pointed out that "the trick would be to persuade the Russians that, as a Eurasian power, their future remained global, not narrowly European."[34]

The public debate over NATO's opening became more urgent with the outbreak of war in the former Yugoslavia, in particular Bosnia-Herzegovina, in April 1992. In May 1992, Havel, Wałęsa and Antall met in Prague to declare that their goal was full-fledged NATO membership.

NATO's opening, however, was not yet on the Western agenda. The Bush Administration did not take a position. When Braithwaite visited Washington in July 1992, his impression was that the Americans agreed with the premise that only NATO could provide the kind of security that potential new members of the European Community sought. But the Bush Administration was reluctant to take the lead. Braithwaite pointed out that "the British could not make the running alone. The Americans needed to be active now, without seeming to dictate."[35]

In 1992, against the background of the Balkan wars and Russia's economic free-fall, NATO mostly avoided the delicate enlargement question. At its Spring Ministerial Meeting in 1992, the Alliance mainly discussed its new responsibilities in crisis management: NATO committed itself to support peacekeeping missions under the roof of the CSCE.[36] The December 1992 NATO Ministerial produced an empty statement on "enhanced security from Vancouver to Vladivostok."[37] The debate on NATO's opening was postponed until 1993—with a new American President.

Notes

1. See Mary E. Sarotte, "A Broken Promise? What the West really told Moscow about NATO Expansion," *Foreign Affairs*, Vol. 93, No. 5 (September/October 2014), p. 96; Mary Elise Sarotte, "Not One Inch Eastward? Bush, Baker, Kohl, Genscher, Gorbachev, and the Origin of Russian Resentment toward NATO Enlargement in February 1990," *Diplomatic History*, Vol. 34, No. 1 (January 2010), pp. 119–140; Svetlana Savranskaya and Tom Blanton, "NATO Expansion. What Gorbachev Heard," National Security Archive Briefing Book #613, December 12, 2017, https://nsarchive.gwu.edu/briefing-book/russia-programs/2017-12-12/nato-expansion-what-gorbachev-heard-western-leaders-early, accessed February 23, 2019; Kirk Bennett, "Russia and the West. What Gorbachev Did Not Hear," *The American Interest*, March 12, 2018, https://www.the-american-interest.com/2018/03/12/gorbachev-not-hear/, accessed February 23, 2019.

2. See Mark Kramer, "The Myth of a No-NATO-Enlargement Pledge to Russia," *The Washington Quarterly* 32:2 (Spring 2009), pp. 39–61; Philip Zelikow, "NATO Expansion Wasn't Ruled Out," *International Herald Tribune*, August 10, 1995, p. 5, http://www.iht.com/articles/1995/08/10/edzel.t.php, accessed February 23, 2019.

3. See Joshua Itzkowitz Shifrinson, "Deal or No Deal? The End of the Cold War and the U.S. Offer to Limit NATO Expansion," *International Security*, Vol. 40, No. 4 (Spring 2016), pp. 7–44.

4. For the context, see Strobe Talbott, *The Russia Hand. A Memoir of Presidential Diplomacy* (New York: Random House, 2002); James M. Goldgeier and Michael McFaul, *Power and Purpose. U.S. Policy Toward Russia after the Cold War* (Washington DC: Brookings Institution Press, 2003).

5. Ronald Asmus, *Opening NATO's Door, How the Alliance remade itself for a new Era* (New York: Columbia University Press, 2002), p. 11.

6. See Mary Elise Sarotte, *1989. The Struggle to Create Post-Cold War Europe* (Princeton: Princeton University Press 2009); Jeffrey A. Engel, *When the World Seemed New. George H. W. Bush and the End of the Cold War* (New York: Houghton Mifflin Harcourt 2017); Kristina Spohr, *Post Wall, Post Square: Rebuilding the World after 1989* (London: Harper & Collins, 2019 (forthcoming)).

7. Verbatim Record of the North Atlantic Council Meeting with the Participation of the Heads of State and Government, 5 July 1990, in: NATO Archives, C-VR (90)36, Part I, available online under https://www.nato.int/nato_static_fl2014/assets/pdf/pdf_archives/20141218_C-VR-90-36-PART1.PDF, accessed February 12, 2019. See also Liviu Horovitz's contribution in this volume.

8. See James M. Goldgeier, *Not Whether But When. The U.S. Decision to Enlarge NATO* (Washington DC: Brookings Institution Press, 1999). See also Stephen J. Flanagan's contribution in this volume.

9. Memcon Bush and Mazowieki, 29 September 1990, see https://bush41library.tamu.edu/files/memcons-telcons/1990-09-29--Mazowiecki.pdf, accessed March 6, 2019.

10. Memcon Bush and Antall, 18 October 1990, see https://bush41library.tamu.edu/files/memcons-telcons/1990-10-18--Antall%20[1].pdf, accessed February 17, 2019.

11. Memcon Bush and Havel, 18 November 1990, see https://bush41library.tamu.edu/files/memcons-telcons/1990-11-18--Havel.pdf, accessed February 17, 2019. On Bush's account, see George Bush and Brent Scowcroft, *A World Transformed* (New York: Alfred A. Knopf, 1998), pp. 404–405.

12. See Jon Meacham, *Destiny and Power: The American Odyssey of George Herbert Walker Bush* (New York: Random House, 2016).

13. Memcon Bush and Genscher, 1 March 1991, see https://bush41library.tamu.edu/files/memcons-telcons/1991-03-01--Genscher.pdf, accessed February 17, 2019.

14. Memcon Bush and Walesa, 20 March 1991, see https://bush41library.tamu.edu/files/memcons-telcons/1991-03-20--Walesa.pdf, accessed February 17, 2019. For the background, see Lech Wałęsa, *The Struggle and the Triumph: An Autobiography* (New York: Arcade Publishers, 2016) (Reprint Edition).

15. See Hanns Jürgen Küsters, ed., *Dokumente zur Deutschlandpolitik (DzD), Sonderedition aus den Akten des Bundeskanzleramtes 1989/90* (Munich: Oldenbourg Verlag, 1998); Aleksandr Galkin and Anatolij Cernaev, eds., *Michail Gorbatschow und die deutsche Frage* (Munich: Oldenbourg Verlag 2012).

16. See Transcript, Heads of Government Talks, London Economic Summit, Lancaster House, 15–17 July 1991, in: The National Archives (TNA), Prime Minister's Office, PREM 19, Vol. 3284.

17. For the context, see Svetlana Savranskaya and Tom Blanton, eds., *The Last Superpower Summits. Gorbachev, Reagan, and Bush Conversations that Ended the Cold War* (Budapest: Central European University Press, 2016); William Taubman, *Gorbachev. His Life and Times* (New York: W.W. Norton, 2017); Vladislav M. Zubok, *A Failed Empire. The Soviet Union in the Cold War from Stalin to Gorbachev* (Chapel Hill: University of North Carolina Press, 2007).

18. Asmus, op. cit., p. 16.

19. Telcon Bush and Antall, 19 August 1991, https://bush41library.tamu.edu/files/memcons-telcons/1991-08-19--Antall.pdf, accessed February 24, 2019.

20. Joint Statement by Secretary of State James A. Baker III and Hans-Dietrich Genscher, Minister for Foreign Affairs of the Federal Republic of Germany, Washington DC, 3 October 1991. For the context, see Robert Hutchings, *American Diplomacy and the End of the Cold War. An Insider's Account of U.S. Policy in Europe, 1989–1992* (Washington DC, Baltimore, London: Woodrow Wilson Center Press and Johns Hopkins University Press, 1997).

21. Bush and Scowcroft, op. cit. pp. 539-547.

22. Telcon Bush and Gorbachev, 27 September 1991, see https://bush41library.tamu.edu/files/memcons-telcons/1991-09-27--Gorbachev.pdf   ,accessed February 17, 1991. For the background see Svetlana Savranskaya and Thomas Blanton, eds, "Unilateral U.S. nuclear pullback in 1991 matched by rapid Soviet cuts," Briefing Book #561, September 30, 2016, https://nsarchive.gwu.edu/briefing-book/nuclear-vault-russia-programs/2016-09-30/unilateral-us-nuclear-pullback-1991-matched, accessed February 17, 2019.

23. For the context, see Hans-Dietrich Genscher, *Erinnerungen* (Munich: Siedler Verlag, 1995); James A. Baker, *The Politics of Diplomacy. Revolution, War and Peace, 1989–1992* (New York: G.P. Putnam's Sons, 1995).

24. Joint Statement by Baker and Genscher, 3 October 1991, op. cit.

25. Memcon Bush and Genscher, 3 October 1991, see https://bush41library.tamu.edu/files/memcons-telcons/1991-10-03--Genscher.pdf, accessed February 17, 2019.

26. See Stephen J. Flanagan, "NATO and Eastern Europe. From Liaison to Security Partnership," *The Washington Quarterly*, Vol. 15, No. 2 (1992), pp. 141–151.

27. Memcon Bush, Scowcroft and Havel, 22 October 1991, see https://bush41library.tamu.edu/files/memcons-telcons/1991-10-22--Havel.pdf, accessed February 17, 2019.

28. Memcon Bush and Wörner, 11 October 1991, see https://bush41library.tamu.edu/files/memcons-telcons/1991-10-11--Woerner.pdf, accessed February 17, 2019.

29. Memcon Bush and Bielecki, 11 September 1991, see https://bush41library.tamu.edu/files/memcons-telcons/1991-09-11--Bielecki.pdf, accessed February 17, 2019.

30. Memcon Bush, Kohl and Genscher, 7 November 1991, see https://bush41library.tamu.edu/files/memcons-telcons/1991-11-07--Kohl.pdf, accessed February 24, 2019.

31. Memcon Bush and Yeltsin, 1 February 1992, in: George Bush Library (GBL), National Security Council Files, Nicholas R. Burns and Ed Hewett Files, CF01421-009.

32. Memcon Bush and Antall, 10 July 1992, see https://bush41library.tamu.edu/files/memcons-telcons/1992-07-10--Antall.pdf, accessed February 17, 2019.

33. Memorandum from Weston to Goulden, "The Future of NATO: The Question of Enlargement," 3 March 1992, in: TNA, PREM 19/4329.

34. Memorandum from Braithwaite to Major, "The Enlargement of NATO and the Community," 27 July 1992, in: TNA, PREM 19/4329.

35. Ibid.

36. See Telnon 205 from Oslo to FCO, "North Atlantic Council in Ministerial Session: Oslo: 4-5 June 1992," in: TNA, PREM 19/4329.

37. See Press Communique M-NACC-2(92)109, 18 December 1992, in: TNA, PREM 19/4329.

Chapter 3

The George H.W. Bush Administration's Policies vis-à-vis Central Europe: From Cautious Encouragement to Cracking Open NATO's Door

Liviu Horovitz

More than two decades after the 1997 Madrid NATO summit, scholars still debate why the U.S. government under President William J. Clinton favored inviting Poland, Hungary, and the Czech Republic to join the transatlantic Alliance. Given that American foreign policy is often marked as much by continuity as it is formed by change, this chapter seeks to leverage the greater current access to the documents of the George H.W. Bush Administration to sketch the situation that Clinton officials found when assuming office.

Overall, I seek to outline how the Bush Administration's priorities towards Central Europe were embedded in its broader approach vis-à-vis Europe. In a nutshell, I argue that U.S. views towards Central Europe evolved from cautious encouragement of politico-economic reform in 1989, to addressing regional concerns in order to achieve German reunification within NATO in 1990, and, by the time Bush left office, to a consensus around the necessity of opening the Alliance's door to Central European states.

To substantiate my arguments, I rely primarily upon internal Administration memoranda—documents mostly collected at the Bush Library; upon U.S. exchanges with British officials—recently declassified by the UK National Archives; and upon numerous interviews with former Bush Administration policymakers.

Struggling for European Stability and American Influence in 1989

As the Bush Administration assumed office in January 1989, its key players believed that they had to manage Soviet retrenchment, chaperone German ambition, and retain U.S. influence over European affairs.[1] With the Soviet economy crumbling, General Secretary Mikhail Gorbachev was trying to reform his country. To gain the necessary breathing space, he was pursuing détente with the West. Moscow's behavior could reduce tensions and, potentially, end the Cold War. Nevertheless, U.S. officials concluded it also endangered cohesion within the Western Alliance.[2] In addition, pressures were mounting in West Germany for the continent's dominant economic power to take advantage of Soviet weakness to bring the two German states closer to each other.[3] At the same time, the European Community was moving towards deeper economic integration, stoking fears of protectionism among Washington policymakers.[4] Against this background, White House planners concluded that, if the United States wanted to avoid long-lasting instability or objectionable consolidation in Europe, it had to work to mitigate the continent's existing explosive potential and to remain a European power over the long term.

The new foreign policy team held that a slowdown of European developments was necessary to secure these distinct American aims. This assessment had a major impact on the Administration's views on Central European affairs.[5] The Reagan Administration had embraced Soviet efforts at normalizing relations and reducing armaments.[6] In contrast, some Bush officials thought the Kremlin's reforms were not genuine, but just a ruse to rejuvenate the communist system.[7] A majority within the new administration, however, worried more about either *perestroika*'s failure or its success.[8] Were Gorbachev to move ahead too swiftly either at home and abroad, he might be toppled from within. Change in both the Soviet Union and Central Europe would have to wait.[9] Were the Soviet reformer to succeed in normalizing Soviet relations to the West, the threat from the Kremlin would diminish and communism would probably vanish. And yet, such success could also flush U.S. forces out of Europe, unravel the transatlantic Alliance, and lessen American influence over the continent. Such an outcome would complicate the U.S. management of global economic and political relations—priorities that mattered a lot to many within the Bush Administration.[10]

Confronted with these trade-offs, the most cautious American policymakers thought best a U.S.-Soviet arrangement over Central and Eastern Europe. The Administration's principal decisionmakers, however, believed Washington could achieve more.

Days before Bush's inauguration, former Secretary of State Henry Kissinger visited Moscow. He delivered a letter from the incoming President, one stating that the new Administration would need time to "reflect."[11] However, ostensibly in his personal capacity, Kissinger also hinted at the "idea" of a USSR-U.S. "condominium over Europe." Such an agreement would ensure that the Europeans "do not misbehave," Gorbachev told the Politburo, and noted that this was an opportunity not to be missed.[12] Kissinger was concerned that the Kremlin would lure the Western Europeans into a deal. The Soviets might remain engaged in the continent's affairs, while the United States—having won the ideological confrontation—would return home. As a solution, Kissinger's condominium arrangement could have had both powers retrench.

Bush officials saw few reasons for such extreme cautiousness.[13] Soviet weakness involved risks, but also offered opportunities.[14] Maybe it was possible to eradicate communism, have the Soviets out of Europe, and keep the Americans in—thereby retaining Washington's say in Western European affairs.[15]

To achieve these multiple aims, the Administration not only needed to address German aspirations, but also for the Soviet Union to both implement reforms and avoid breakdown—a needle that proved anything but easy to thread.[16]

On the one hand, U.S. policymakers understood that if the Soviet Union were to stagnate in a "frustrating, seemingly endless, struggle" to "reform its society from above while preserving central control," the states in Eastern and Central Europe would revert to a "historical pattern of fractious and unstable internal politics, persistent economic weakness, and bitter national rivalries," and cause great problems for European stability.[17]

On the other hand, American officials knew that moving ahead too fast might bring Gorbachev down.[18] There was "a big opportunity" in Central Europe, Bush told Canada's Prime Minister Brian Mulroney already in January 1989, "if we can get our act together." However, he argued, "there is also danger," as pushing too far might cause the situation to get out of control. At that point, the President believed, "the tanks might come in." His conversations with British Prime Minister Margaret Thatcher reveal that the West had neither the interest nor the willingness to intervene in such a situation.[19]

Working within these confines throughout 1989, the Administration concluded that promoting reforms in Central Europe aided overall U.S. goals but remained a risky business.[20] As the region was becoming more independent, the United States should "exploit" these openings, but had to do so in a "prudent way," a key official wrote.[21] Thus, in his April 1989 foreign policy statement on the region, Bush stated that he wanted Central Europe to be "free, prosperous, and at peace." However, to the dismay of many who sought a more resolute Washington push, the President added that his government was pursuing these goals "with prudence, realism, and patience."[22] In Eastern Europe, Bush's overall goal was not to "stir up trouble," but also not to pursue a "post-Yalta arrangement," one in which he would be "sitting with the Soviets to divide spheres of influence," he told the Italian leadership in May 1989. Instead, he wanted to promote democracy and capitalism without being so "flamboyant" that the Soviets would "feel the need" to take actions that would reverse "movement towards freedom."[23] Numerous American Allies shared Washington's concerns vis-à-vis the involved risks.[24] Thus, when Bush visited Poland and Hungary in July 1989, his message remained one of cautiousness and restraint.[25]

At the same time, other politico-economic constraints limited the Administration's efforts. On the one hand, significant domestic pressures from various supporters of Central European nations pushed for action, and U.S. officials were aware that economic assistance was their "best lever."[26] On the other hand, much stood in the way of employing such instruments. In contrast to Europe or Japan, the United States had few economic links to Central and Eastern Europe. In addition, separating dealings with the Soviet Union from those with its satellites proved a challenging feat. Also, if the United States was to offer Poland or Hungary "special treatment" on the "debt front," this would compromise Washington's overall policy towards debtor countries, undermining negotiations with other key middle-income creditors.[27] Further, the foreign policy bureaucracy faced stark domestic fiscal constraints. The NSC staff reported that meetings broke down whenever the question of spending American taxpayer dollars came up.[28] Last but not least, U.S. officials faced a chicken-or-the-egg-problem: they were not convinced that piecemeal economic and political reform would slowly lead to more reforms, stability, and prosperity; therefore, they were reluctant to invest too many resources before major reforms were implemented.[29]

Pursuing German Reunification within NATO in 1990

A year into the Bush Administration, it became clear that the Brezhnev Doctrine was defunct. Gorbachev would neither employ force nor condone its use, German reunification was impending, and Washington needed to act if it wanted to secure its influence in Europe.[30] To avoid West Germany becoming a disenfranchised giant at the continent's core, the White House had already supported the concept of eventual unification in spring 1989, and, by the beginning of 1990, decided to reinforce Bonn's efforts to achieve a rapid resolution.[31]

To assuage the concerns of Germany's neighbors and avoid European balancing against Bonn's new-found power, the U.S. government pledged to uphold NATO and retain armed forces in Europe for years to come.[32] Yet for Washington to be able and disposed to do so, a unified Germany had to remain in NATO, subordinating its military to the integrated NATO command, willing to host American troops, and ready to maintain U.S. nuclear weapons on its soil.[33] Obtaining both Germany's unification and sustaining its membership in NATO under such conditions was not going to be easy. Bush officials expected there would be opposition in both West and East.[34]

Against this background, the White House also understood that U.S. policy towards Western, Central, and Eastern Europe was tightly linked together.[35] "Our future as a European power will depend in large measure on how well we grasp these new opportunities," the NSC wrote to the President at the beginning of 1990. Germany was quickly filling the European power vacuum in Central Europe. Soon, the only powers with "real influence" in the region were going to be Germany and the Soviet Union, the NSC argued. On the one hand, this was "not the architecture of a stable European security order," American officials believed, as such a framework invited a return to the "cyclical pattern of Russo-German conflict and condominium that bedeviled Europe from 1870 to 1945." On the other hand, U.S. engagement would help shape German reunification, manage "an eastward drift" in Germany's policy, and strengthen the "future position" of the United States within European security and economic affairs. Thus, the NSC resolved that the United States had to remain engaged in Central Europe "between Germany and Russia."[36]

To both tie Germany to the West and stabilize Central Europe, the Administration had to beat back alternative approaches to European security in the region.[37] "The idea of a neutralized Germany would [...] fit into the fanciful visions among some in the new leadership [in Central Europe] of a demilitarized Europe of perpetual peace," Scowcroft wrote to Bush in January 1990.[38] On the one hand, leaders like Václav Havel of Czechoslovakia not only harbored "pro-American sentiments," but thought of future American engagement as a necessary "counterweight" to German economic and political power. Nevertheless, Bush officials believed these newcomers to power politics did not yet grasp the links between economic, political, and military affairs. Havel sought a bloc-free, demilitarized Europe. Scowcroft described him as "a man with a mission and in a hurry."[39]

Therefore, in a number of subsequent meetings at the White House, the President sought to impress upon Havel the interconnecting nature of the numerous elements underpinning an American involvement in Europe. "It is clear that the presence of American troops is a stabilizing factor," the Central European leader concluded, to the relief of his U.S. interlocutors.[40]

At the same time, the American government worked to dispel an emerging Polish-German border dispute. A solution was needed in order to both ease unification and to have Warsaw distance itself from Moscow, abstain from balancing against Bonn, and see the new German state in a positive light. During winter 1989, seemingly for domestic political reasons, German Chancellor Helmut Kohl refused to state publicly that Poland's Oder-Neisse Western border was a settled matter. To gain leverage with Bonn, Warsaw dragged its feet on having Soviet forces go home and kept talking about retaining Moscow involved in European security affairs.[41] Polish decisionmakers started considering a return to European ententes—balances in which France and Britain would ally with Poland and others to counter German power.[42] "In the past, peace was only guaranteed when a strong France was aligned with a strong Poland," a Warsaw official told a policymaker in Paris. Last but not least, to have their voices heard, the Poles were also trying at the beginning of 1990 to insert themselves into the German reunification process.[43]

The U.S. government understood that it had to deal with the issue. Not only were Polish concerns by themselves hindering reunification, but the unsettled border question offered European powers in both West and East a convenient tool to delay—and, potentially, to derail—reunification.[44]

The White House pushed the German leadership to find a solution.[45] By the end of March 1990, Kohl was telling Bush that he was "firmly determined" to accept the current border even if it was "a bitter burden of history."[46]

At the same time, Bush worked on the Poles to have them accept a compromise. Not only was Washington offering to put pressure on the German Chancellor, but the quickly emerging singular superpower was providing Polish decisionmakers with reassurances that a Germany in NATO and an American presence in Europe would limit Bonn's future ability to leverage Warsaw.[47] Maybe both Americans and Soviets "could remain in Germany," Polish Prime Minister Tadeusz Mazowiecki told Bush. "You may be right," the President answered, but gently pushed in the opposite direction, arguing that the window of opportunity for Soviet "pulling back" was unlikely to last for all too long.[48]

Having successfully dealt with these crises of the day, Bush officials realized already by the spring and summer of 1990 that Central European affairs were bound to remain in a state of flux. Soviet power would all but fade away—at least momentarily, while German influence would expand at a brisk pace. Thus, U.S. policymakers judged that all Central Europeans thought American "association" would be a "potential counterweight" to efforts by the French and Germans to establish political and economic "spheres of influence."

At the same time, some in the region were already realizing that security concerns would not remain dormant forever, and were asking for institutional reassurance arrangements.[49] "How would NATO respond if Czechoslovakia applied for membership?" Havel's security advisor asked an NSC official. With the Warsaw Pact gone but outside of NATO, where would these states find security in the "Europe of the future," White House analysts probed.[50] In the short term, non-binding security assurances might suffice. Over the long term, however, this was questionable.[51]

Nonetheless, U.S. officials were still very cautious. They argued that before Germany was unified and Soviet forces were gone, Washington should "avoid being seen" as rushing in to "fill the void" left by a Soviet Union in retreat.[52]

Shepherding Integration and Cracking Open NATO's Door in 1991–1992

The ink on Germany's unification not yet dry, the Administration started worrying about the sustainability of U.S. influence in Europe— the core concern vis-à-vis the continent during Bush's last two years in office.[53] With a unified Germany in NATO, the United States had made itself the renewed guarantor of European security.[54] As a consequence, European powers were quickly developing contradicting incentives.[55] On the one hand, they wanted to ensure that Washington did not gain too much leverage over them—with Paris at the forefront of such efforts.[56] On the other hand, Europeans wanted to obtain credible assurances that the United States was still willing and able to provide for the continent's security—a goal particularly important to smaller powers.[57]

U.S. officials worried that the Europeans might pursue alternative security arrangements. Some worried that European decisionmakers might be "seduced" by "pan-European collective security." Others were afraid that leaders on the continent might even be more inclined to pursue an independent Western European "defense pillar."[58] Bush policymakers feared that European security integration could potentially render NATO obsolete, thereby depriving the United States of its main lever of influence over the continent and severing the transatlantic bond.[59]

Managing European efforts at security integration proved a challenge.[60] Offsetting attempts at limiting American influence worked best when Washington's commitments were trusted. However, at home, political pressures for a "peace dividend" and the popular mood were pushing against America's obligations—both in Europe and all around the world.[61] Also, it quickly became clear (as had been the case during the Cold War and despite some Bush officials hoping the opposite) that America's security position in Europe could not be easily or quickly translated into leverage over economic or political affairs—a fact that diminished domestic support for engagement even further.[62]

Whereas the Iraq intervention gave Washington a credibility boost,[63] the Bush Administration's decision against going to war when the Yugoslav crisis erupted in 1991 reinforced doubts in Europe about U.S. willingness to spend blood and treasure to ensure the continent's security.[64] Within this context, and given that most threads of Europe's future ran through Paris, throughout both 1991 and 1992 Bonn remained reluctant to block a French push towards increased European security independence.[65]

Against this background of transatlantic relations, security questions in Central Europe were becoming more salient. With the Warsaw Pact now history, political leaders in East and West believed the region was sliding into a security vacuum. Washington tried reassurance. At their June 1991 meeting in Copenhagen, NATO foreign ministers concluded that security would be "safeguarded" through "interlocking institutions." Two months later, the August coup in Moscow was a stark reminder that there was little beyond words to ensure security. "It was quite a shock," a former Hungarian politician remembered.[66]

Expanding German influence and Western European ambivalence posed other problems. All Central Europeans were looking to Germany for trade and investment, but uncertain how Bonn would use its clout.[67] Washington's reticence to get involved and European inability to agree upon a common approach towards the breakup of Yugoslavia suggested that in the absence of institutional frameworks, Western powers would be primarily looking out for themselves. Last but not least, neither Paris nor London envisaged the Central European states joining the European Community for at least two decades.[68]

Accordingly, the French foreign minister told Bush already in spring 1991 that the former Warsaw Pact countries wanted to "join NA-TO"—a longing that only intensified over the next months and years. "They realize that the only firm ground in Europe is the Atlantic Alliance."[69]

Bush officials believed that U.S. steps in Central Europe had to take into account Washington's priorities relative to Moscow. The United States was facing a Russian "political landscape" that "few Americans understand," Scowcroft told the president. He advised walking a fine line between encouraging reform and avoiding entanglement.[70] U.S. Secretary of State James Baker sent a somewhat more ambitious message from Moscow in September 1991: "We have a tremendous stake in the success of the democrats here."[71] And yet Americans officials were aware that the Russian economy was broken, the pace of reform slow, and the outcome uncertain.[72] Becoming too involved bore certain risks and ambiguous benefits.[73] At the same time, U.S. officials believed that much spoke against organizing an "anti-Soviet coalition" whose frontier would be the Soviet border. Moscow would react negatively, potentially leading to a "reversal" of the "positive trends."[74]

As 1991 ended, U.S. officials argued it was strategically wiser to hold NATO's expansion as an ace up the Western sleeve. The NSC suggested that the key to "keeping the Russians out of Europe" was "the unspoken but credible threat to extend the Alliance eastward if Russian expansionism is ever rekindled."[75]

Over the subsequent months, Washington planners assessed that Central Europe's yearning for American involvement offered both challenges to and unique opportunities for cementing U.S. influence in Europe—influence that was deemed necessary for achieving broader U.S. political and economic goals. In terms of challenges, the Central Europeans' fears—rekindled by recent instability and American hesitancy—ranked high. U.S. analysts concluded if the U.S. government blocked NATO expansion, the "new democracies" would lose interest in a transatlantic bond and seek entrance into Western European security structures.[76] Nobody in the region believed seeking such shelter was "ideal." In America's absence, there was "little military teeth" in European frameworks.[77] And yet, within a decade, the Europeans, led by Paris, would merge security and economic institutions, with the

Community thus becoming the "de facto keeper of European peace."[78] As a consequence, NATO would be marginalized. Washington would retain "indirect and implied" security responsibilities due to the linkage between the Alliance and Western European security structures. Equally, the U.S. government would have "little to say" about European decision-making.[79]

Nonetheless, American officials thought there was also opportunity, if only Washington would take advantage of the current "period of flux."[80] On the one hand, Western Europe was becoming more assertive.[81] Its leaders believed Washington wanted "a say" in European affairs but was no longer willing to "invest the corresponding financial and security resources." Hence, they were building parallel institutions, thereby limiting American clout. On the other hand, Central Europeans were among the strongest proponents of Washington's "continued involvement" in Europe.

Against this background, the CIA argued that the U.S. position as "the only global power" still gave it "leverage with the Europeans." The United States had a clear comparative advantage: Europe's post-Cold War structure on the "political/military dimension of security" contained a "glaring gap," providing Washington with a "stronger hand." Therefore, the analysts concluded that a "reliable and predictable" U.S. commitment to assist in dealing with regional tensions "in the eastern half of the continent" would increase the U.S. government's sway in both West and East.[82]

During Bush's final year in office, a consensus appears to have slowly emerged: Washington should offer the Central Europeans the perspective of joining NATO. The French believed already at the end of 1991 that the Americans were tilting towards "seeking to offer" the countries in Central Europe "Alliance security guarantees."[83] During the same time period, analysts who would later serve in the Clinton Administration argued for elaborating criteria for admitting new members to the NATO club.[84] By the end of March 1992, the NSC was arguing that the United States should "signal" to the East Europeans that they "may become eligible" for NATO membership.[85] By June 1992, policy planners seemed to believe that a consensus was emerging within the Administration towards opening "up the Alliance to new members," although details had yet to be "worked out."[86]

Four months before Bush left office, a State Department memorandum stated that that "the benchmark will be high (and will take years to achieve)," but that the United States "will finally be giving" the states from this region "a yardstick by which they can measure their progress." American diplomats also admitted that "handling Russia will be critical." The U.S. government could not accept the British view "that Russia can never join NATO." Such a step would be interpreted by Russians as a "long-term strategy to isolate it from Europe."[87]

Conclusion

Throughout Bush's time in office, the dual goal of keeping Europe both stable and integrated within the quickly expanding American order required Washington to maintain its influence on the continent. To that end, the Administration's best bet was to carefully manage the demise of communism, help ease the Soviets out of Europe, and arrange for the United States to remain the continent's security guarantor.

During 1989, this meant cautious encouragement of reform. During 1990, it involved garnering support for German reunification in NATO. And during 1991-93, it meant pushing back against French-driven European security integration efforts and a slowly emerging consensus that Central European states should be admitted into the Alliance.

To the hard-nosed policymakers of the Bush Administration, keeping Central Europe away from NATO involved undeniable risks. Offering these states an accession perspective brought opportunities to advance both stability and influence. However, it also opened a "Russian Question" in European politics. As they left the corridors of power, Bush officials passed on these trade-offs to the incoming administration. It might be that President Clinton and his associates built their choices on a completely different set of concerns. And yet, if continuity is any guide, students of NATO enlargement could start by investigating whether Bush-era imperatives still applied in the mid-1990s.

Notes

1. Robert L. Hutchings, "Memo for Scowcroft: National Security Council Meeting on Western Europe and Eastern Europe," April 4, 1989, George H.W. Bush Presidential Library (BPL), NSC Collection, Robert D. Blackwill Chronological Files 30542-001, April 1989 [1].

2. CIA Directorate of Intelligence, "Moscow's 1989 Agenda for US-Soviet Relations," February 1989, BPL, NSC Collection, Condoleezza Rice Soviet Union/USSR Subject Files CF00719-017, US-USSR Soviet Relations [3]; and Peter W. Rodman, "Memo for Scowcroft: Eastern Europe: Why Is Gorbachev Permitting This?" July 28, 1989, BPL, Scowcroft Collection, 91124 Soviet Power Collapse in Eastern Europe (July 1989).

3. Brent Scowcroft, "Memo Bush: Dealing with the Germans," August 7, 1989, BPL, Scowcroft Collection, 91120 Soviet Power Collapse in Eastern Europe—SNF—May 1989 [1].

4. Charles Stuart Kennedy, "Interview with William Bodde," October 5, 1998, Diplomatic Studies and Training, Foreign Affairs Oral History Project (ADST) - available online; and CIA Directorate of Intelligence, "EC-1992: The Revitalization of Europe," January 25, 1989, BPL, Scowcroft Collection, 91148 Other (January-March 1989).

5. For a good review of the Bush Administration's policies towards Central Europe in 1989, albeit relying on a different logic than the one proposed here, see Gregory F. Domber, "Skepticism and Stability: Reevaluating U.S. Policy during Poland's Democratic Transformation in 1989," *Journal of Cold War Studies* 13, no. 3 (Summer 2011), pp. 52–82.

6. James G. Wilson, *The Triumph of Improvisation: Gorbachev's Adaptability, Reagan's Engagement, and the End of the Cold War* (Ithaca: Cornell University Press, 2014); see also Lou Cannon, "Interview with George Shultz," September 21, 2006, James A. Baker Oral History Project—available online at the Princeton Mudd Library.

7. Robert M. Gates, "Letter to Nixon," December 18, 1989, BPL, NSC Collection, Robert M. Gates Chronological Files CF00948-015, Chron File (Official): Classified 1989 (Part II) [1 of 3]; Charles Stuart Kennedy, "Interview with Raymond F. Smith," January 14, 2009, ADST; or Philip Zelikow et al., "Interview with Brent Scowcroft," November 12, 1999, University of Virginia, Miller Center, George H.W. Bush Oral History Project - available online.

8. George H. W. Bush, "Memo for Agencies: Comprehensive Review of US-Soviet Relations," February 15, 1989, BPL, NSC Collection, Robert D. Blackwill Chronological Files 30542-002, January February 1989 [2]. Also, telephone interview with Joint Chiefs of Staff (JCS) official, Zurich, April 2018.

9. Interviews with Department of State (DOS) and National Security Council (NSC) officials, Washington DC, March and December 2018.

10. James A. Baker, "Key Impressions from the Trip," March 1989, Princeton Mudd Library James A. Baker Papers (JAB), 108.3.1989 Mar; also, John E. Fretwell, "Telegram to FCO: Quadripartite Meeting of Political Directors," November 8, 1989, The National Archives of the United Kingdom (TNA), PREM 19/2682.

11. George H. W. Bush, "Letter to Gorbachev," January 13, 1989, JAB, 108.1.1989 January.

12. Anatoly C. Chernyaev, "Notes from the Politburo Session," January 21, 1989, Wilson Center Digital Archive - available online.

13. Interviews with NSC officials, New York and Washington, October and December 2018.

14. James A. Baker, "Talking Points Cabinet Meeting," January 23, 1989, JAB, 108.1.1989 January; and Dennis B. Ross, "Memo for Baker: Shaping Soviet Power," February 21, 1989, JAB, 174.2.Key Points Memos 1993.

15. George H. W. Bush, "Memo for Agencies: Comprehensive Review of US-East European Relations," February 15, 1989, BPL, NSC Collection, Robert D. Blackwill Chronological Files 30542-002, January February 1989 [2]; Peter W. Rodman, "Memo for Scowcroft: 'Kissinger Plan' for Central Europe," March 14, 1989, BPL, Scowcroft Collection, 91124 Soviet Power Collapse in Eastern Europe (March-April 1989); and Cabinet Office Staff, "Sir Robin Butler's Formal Meeting with General Brent Scowcroft," April 3, 1989, TNA, PREM 19/2891.

16. For an excellent overview of developments in the region and U.S. behavior, Jeffrey A. Engel, *When the World Seemed New: George H. W. Bush and the End of the Cold War* (Boston: Houghton Mifflin Harcourt, 2017), pp. 199–230.

17. Brent Scowcroft, "Memo for Bush: Your Meetings in Brussels with NATO Leaders," November 29, 1989, BPL, Scowcroft Collection, 91116 German Unification (November 1989); but also Hutchings, "Memo for Scowcroft: National Security Council Meeting on Western Europe and Eastern Europe."

18. Eric Melby, "Memo for Scowcroft: Your Revised Talking Points for White House Summit Group Meeting," July 5, 1989, BPL, Scowcroft Collection, 91124 Soviet Power Collapse in Eastern Europe (June-July 1989).

19. Unknown Author, "President's Meeting with Prime Minister Mulroney," February 10, 1989, BPL, Memcons and Telcons (M&T)—available online; also, Henry A. Kissinger, "Meeting with Gorbachev," January 17, 1989, JAB, 108.1.1989 January; for a clear statement that neither Washington nor London would have intervened, Charles D. Powell, "Letter to Wall: Prime Minister's Meeting with President Bush at Camp David," November 25, 1989, TNA, PREM 19/2892; and

Robert L. Hutchings, *American Diplomacy and the End of the Cold War: An Insider's Account of US Diplomacy in Europe, 1989-1992* (Washington, D.C. : Baltimore: Johns Hopkins University Press, 1997), pp. 8, 10.

20. Brent Scowcroft and Peter W. Rodman, "Memo for Bush: Repudiating the Brezhnev Doctrine," June 20, 1989, BPL, Scowcroft Collection, 91117 May-June 1989.

21. Brent Scowcroft, "Memo for Bush: Getting Ahead of Gorbachev," March 1, 1989, BPL, Scowcroft Collection, 91117 January-April 1989. The original memo was drafted by Condoleezza Rice.

22. George H. W. Bush, "Remarks to Citizens in Hamtramck, Michigan," April 17, 1989, BPL, Public Papers—available online.

23. Philip D. Zelikow, "Bush Meeting with Ciriaco De Mita, Prime Minister of Italy [2]," May 27, 1989, BPL, M&T; also, George H. W. Bush, "Remarks to the Citizens in Mainz, Federal Republic of Germany," May 31, 1989, BPL, Public Papers—available online.

24. Robert Blackwell, "National Intelligence Council: July Warning and Forecast Report," July 21, 1989, BPL, NSC Collection, Peter W. Rodman Files CF00206, Europe - Eastern, 1989; Ralph Singler, "Bush Telephone Conversation with Robert Hawke, Prime Minister of Australia," July 5, 1989, BPL, M&T; or Brent Scowcroft, "Bush Meeting with Francois Mitterrand, President of France," July 13, 1989, BPL, M&T.

25. For instance, Brent Scowcroft, "Bush Bilateral Meeting with Wojciech Jaruzelski, Chairman of Poland," July 10, 1989, BPL, M&T; or Condoleezza Rice, "Bush Meeting with Meiczyslaw Rakowski, Prime Minister of Poland," July 10, 1989, BPL, M&T.

26. Robert D. Blackwill, "Memo for Scowcroft: Strategy toward Poland and Hungary," September 19, 1989, BPL, NSC Collection, Peter W. Rodman Files CF00206, Europe - Eastern, 1989.

27. Condoleezza Rice, Adrian Basora, and Timothy Deal, "Memo for Scowcroft: Initiatives for the President's Trip to Poland and Hungary," June 14, 1989, BPL, Scowcroft Collection, 91124 Soviet Power Collapse in Eastern Europe (March-April 1989); Robert D. Hoffmann, "Memo for Scowcroft: Re-Capturing Western Leadership in Eastern Europe," September 8, 1989, BPL, Scowcroft Collection, 91124 Soviet Power Collapse in Eastern Europe (July-August 1989).

28. Robert D. Blackwill, "Memo for Scowcroft: Presidential Initiative for Poland and Hungary," July 3, 1989, BPL, Scowcroft Collection, 91124 Soviet Power Collapse in Eastern Europe (June-July 1989); and Adrian Basora, "Memo for Scowcroft: Presidential Decisions for His Trip to Poland and Hungary," July 3,

1989, BPL, Scowcroft Collection, 91124 Soviet Power Collapse in Eastern Europe (June-July 1989).

29. Peter W. Rodman, "Memo for Scowcroft: Eastern Europe: Why Is Gorbachev Permitting This?," August 8, 1989, BPL, Scowcroft Collection, 91124 Soviet Power Collapse in Eastern Europe (July 1989); Robert B. Zoellick, "Memo for Baker: Cabinet Meeting Presentation," September 5, 1989, JAB, 108.9.1989 Sept; also, Domber, "Skepticism and Stability," 56 and 61.

30. Robert D. Blackwill, "Memo for Scowcroft: The Beginning of The Big Game," February 7, 1990, BPL, NSC Collection, Robert D. Blackwill Subject Files CF00182-020, German Reunification 11/89-6/90 [1]; Brent Scowcroft, "Memo for Bush: Objectives for US-Soviet Relations in 1990," January 13, 1990, in Svetlana Savranskaya and Thomas Blanton, *The Last Superpower Summits: Reagan, Gorbachev and Bush at the End of the Cold War* (Budapest and New York: Central European University Press, 2016), document 88, pp. 587-589; and Harvey Sicherman, "Memo for Ross: Our European Strategy: Next Steps," March 12, 1990, JAB, 176.9.Malta Summit, 1989.

31. Robert Blackwill, "Bush Meeting with Helmut Kohl, Chancellor of the Federal Republic of Germany," May 30, 1989, BPL, M&T. The internal debates in November-December 1989 were confirmed in numerous interviews with former NSC and DOS officials, October-December 2018.

32. George H. W. Bush, "Outline of Remarks at the North Atlantic Treaty Organization Headquarters in Brussels," December 4, 1989, BPL, Public Papers—available online.

33. Brent Scowcroft, "Memo for Bush: Meetings with German Chancellor Helmut Kohl," February 24, 1990, BPL, Scowcroft Collection, 91116 German Unification (January-February 1990).

34. For an overview, Frédéric Bozo, Andreas Rödder, and Mary Elise Sarotte, *German Reunification: A Multinational History* (London: Routledge, 2017).

35. For White House thinking on the links between global questions, Germany, and Central Europe at the beginning of 1990, Robert L. Hutchings, "Memo for Scowcroft: Your Breakfast with Kissinger: Managing the German Question," January 26, 1990, BPL, NSC Collection, Robert L. Hutchings Files CF00683, 1989 [6].

36. Brent Scowcroft, "Memo for Bush: US Policy in Eastern Europe in 1990," January 1990, BPL, NSC Collection, Robert D. Blackwill Chronological Files 30547-010, January 1990; see also Unknown Author, "Meeting of the National Security Council," January 22, 1990, BPL, NSC Collection, NSC Meetings Files 90001-034 NSC0037a—January 22, 1990—Conventional Forces in Europe Initiative, Arms Control, Germany Federal Republic; and Robert L. Hutchings, "Memo for Scowcroft: US Policy Toward the New Eastern Europe," May 11, 1990, BPL,

Scowcroft Collection, 91125 Soviet Power Collapse in Eastern Europe (February-May 1990).

37. Robert B. Zoellick, "Proposed Agenda for Meeting with the President 16 February 1990," February 16, 1990, JAB, 115.7. White House Meeting Agendas 1990.

38. Brent Scowcroft, "Memo for Bush: Responding to a Soviet Call for a German Peace Conference," January 1990, BPL, NSC Collection, Robert L. Hutchings Files, CF00683, January 1990 [2].

39. Brent Scowcroft, "Memo for Bush: Meeting with President Vaclav Havel of Czechoslovakia," February 17, 1990, BPL, Scowcroft Collection, 91125 Soviet Power Collapse in Eastern Europe (February-May 1990).

40. Unknown Author, "Bush Meeting with President of Czechoslovakia Vaclav Havel," February 20, 1990, BPL, M&T.

41. CIA Directorate of Intelligence, "Update on European Views on German Unification and the Two-plus-Four Dynamic," April 4, 1990, BPL, NSC Collection, Robert D. Blackwill Subject Files CF00182-021, German Reunification 11/89-6/90 [2]; also, Vojtech Mastny, "Germany's Unification, its Eastern Neighbors, and European Security," in Frédéric Bozo, Andreas Rödder, and Mary E. Sarotte, eds., *German Reunification: A Multinational History* (London: Routledge, 2017), p. 208.

42. Adrian Basora, "Memo for Scowcroft: Impressions from Warsaw, Budapest, Vienna and Belgrade," March 2, 1990, BPL, Scowcroft Collection, 91125 Soviet Power Collapse in Eastern Europe (December 1989-January 1990).

43. Gregory F. Domber, "Pivots in Poland's Response to German Unification," in Bozo, et. al, op.cit., p. 190.

44. Charles D. Powell, "Letter for Wall: Prime Minister's Talk with President Bush," February 24, 1990, in Patrick Salmon et al, German Unification 1989-90: Documents on British Policy Overseas, Series III, Volume VII (London: Routledge, 2010), document 155, pp. 310-314.

45. Robert Blackwill, "Bush Meeting with Helmut Kohl, Chancellor of the Federal Republic of Germany," February 24, 1990, BPL, M&T.

46. Robert Hutchings, "Bush The President's Telephone Call to Chancellor Helmut Kohl of the Federal Republic of Germany," March 20, 1990, BPL, M&T.

47. Brent Scowcroft, "Memo for Bush: Meetings with Prime Minister Tadeusz Mazowiecki of Poland," March 20, 1990, BPL, Scowcroft Collection, 91116 German Unification (March-April 1990).

48. Unknown Author, "Bush Meeting with Prime Minister Tadeusz Mazowiecki of Poland," March 21, 1990, BPL, M&T; also, Unknown Author, "Bush Follow-up Meeting with Prime Minister Tadeusz Mazowiecki of Poland," March 22, 1990, BPL, M&T.

49. Lawrence S. Eagleburger, "Memo for Baker: Impressions from Hungary, Poland, Austria and Yugoslavia," March 1, 1990, BPL, Scowcroft Collection, 91125 Soviet Power Collapse in Eastern Europe (December 1989-January 1990); see also Stephen Barrett, "Telegram to FCO: Poland and German Reunification: Mr Baker's Meeting with Jaruzelski," March 11, 1990, TNA, PREM 19/3100_2 - available online.

50. Robert L. Hutchings, "Memo for Scowcroft: Military Exchanges with Eastern Europe," August 16, 1990, BPL, Scowcroft Collection, 91125 Soviet Power Collapse in Eastern Europe (August-October 1990).

51. Robert L. Hutchings, "Memo for Scowcroft: Your Meeting with Foreign Minister Jiri Dienstbier of Czechoslovakia," September 28, 1990, BPL, Scowcroft Collection, 91125 Soviet Power Collapse in Eastern Europe (August-October 1990).

52. Robert L. Hutchings and Michael Hayden, "Military-to-Military Contacts with Eastern Europe," August 16, 1990, BPL, Scowcroft Collection, 91125 Soviet Power Collapse in Eastern Europe (August-October 1990).

53. See, for instance, Unknown Author, "Summary of Conclusions: European Strategy Steering Group Meeting of November 29-30, 1990," December 1990, BPL, NSC Collection Barry Lowenkron Subject File CF01527-032, ESSG [European Strategy Steering Group]: ESSG Meeting of European Pillar—[March 27, 1991]; and Unknown Author, "The Rome Summit and NATO's Mission," February 1992, BPL, NSC Collection, Barry Lowenkron Subject File CF01527-019, ESSG [European Strategy Steering Group]: ESSG Meeting—February 21, 1992.

54. An excellent analysis of the evolving conundrum is CIA Directorate of Intelligence, "The Dynamics and Momentum in Europe for the Organization of a European Security Identity," March 6, 1991, BPL, NSC Collection, Barry Lowenkron Subject File CF01527-034, ESSG Papers for March 10 & 11 Meetings—[March 6, 1991].

55. The best overview I could find is David C. Gompert, "Memo for Agencies: Meetings of European Strategy Steering Group," March 6, 1991, BPL, NSC Collection, Barry Lowenkron Subject File CF01527-034, ESSG Papers for March 10 & 11 Meetings—[March 6, 1991].

56. David C. Gompert, "Memo for Scowcroft: European Views on NATO's Future," November 12, 1990, BPL, Scowcroft Collection, 91149 Other (November 1990) [1]; also Tony Wayne, "Memo for Scowcroft: Next Steps with France," June 19, 1991, BPL, NSC Collection, Nicholas Rostow Subject Files CF01329-006

NATO [2]; and "Memo for Scowcroft: Consultations with the French on the Alliance and a European Security Identity," September 11, 1991, BPL, NSC Collection, Nicholas Rostow Subject Files CF01329-006 NATO [2]; revealing are Percy Cradock, "Letter to Powell: Meeting with Admiral Lanxade," January 9, 1991, TNA, PREM 19/3344; and "Memo to Major: European Security and Defense," March 7, 1991, TNA, PREM 19/3326.

57. James F. Dobbins, "NATO's Future: Political Track of the Strategy Review: Questions to Ask Ourselves," October 22, 1990, National Security Archive, NATO Expansion: What Gorbachev Heard - available online.

58. David C. Gompert, "Memo for Scowcroft: Our Goals in CSCE," October 22, 1990, BPL, NSC Collection Condoleezza Rice 1989-1990 Subject Files CF00716-006, CSCE (Conventional Security & Cooperation in Europe); and, for the best overview, David C. Gompert, "Framework for Discussion of US Strategy Toward Organization of a European Defense Identity," March 26, 1991, BPL, NSC Collection, Barry Lowenkron Subject File CF01527-032, ESSG [European Strategy Steering Group]: ESSG Meeting of European Pillar—[March 27, 1991].

59. Heather Wilson, "Memo for Scowcroft: Office Call with SACEUR General Jack Galvin," January 5, 1991, BPL, Scowcroft Collection, 91150 Other (January-April 1991) [1]; also Anthony A. Acland, "Telegram to FCO: NATO and European Security," February 17, 1991, TNA, PREM 19/3326.

60. An overview is Brent Scowcroft, "Memo for Bush: NATO and European Integration," March 11, 1991, BPL, Scowcroft Collection, 91150 Other (January-April 1991) [1].

61. For instance, Brent Scowcroft, "Memo for Bates: The President's Meeting with the Cabinet," November 29, 1989, BPL, Scowcroft Collection, 91117 November 1989; or Unknown Author, "NATO and the East: Key Issues," January 1992, BPL, NSC Collection, David C. Gompert Subject Files CF01301-009 European Strategy [Steering] Group (ESSG).

62. A great example are the negotiations surrounding trade. See, for instance, Ewen A.J. Fergusson, "Telegram to FCO: Secretary of State's Meeting with Baker: US/EC Declaration," November 19, 1990, TNA, and "Telegram to FCO: Secretary of State's Meeting with Baker: GATT," November 19, 1990, both in TNA, PREM 19/3191—available online; revealing for the US attempt to link security and economic affairs is Charles D. Powell, "Letter to Wall: Prime Minister's Meeting with President Bush: Camp David, 21 December," December 22, 1990, TNA, PREM 19/3208.

63. Brent Scowcroft, "Bush Meeting and Dinner with Italian Prime Minister Andreotti," March 24, 1991, BPL, M&T.

64. Ivo H. Daalder and I.M. Destler, "The Bush Administration National Security Council: Oral History Roundtables: The Bush Administration National

Security Council," The National Security Council Project (Washington D.C.: Brookings Institution, April 29, 1999), 28–29; and David C. Gompert, "Memo for Scowcroft: Peacekeeping in Europe," April 29, 1992, BPL, NSC Collection, Barry Lowenkron Subject File CF01527-035, ESSG: Peacekeeping in Europe - April 29, 1992. Also, interview with DOS official, Washington DC, November 2018, and telephone interviews with DOS and NSC officials, Zurich and Washington DC, April and December 2018.

65. David C. Gompert, "Memo for Scowcroft: Cracks in the European Pillar," February 25, 1991, BPL, Scowcroft Collection, 91150 Other (January-April 1991) [1]; Charles D. Powell, "Letter to Gozney: Anglo-German Summit: Prime Minister's Meeting with Chancellor Kohl," March 11, 1991, TNA, PREM 19/3354; or David C. Gompert, "Bush Expanded Meeting with Helmut Kohl, Chancellor of Germany," September 16, 1991, BPL, M&T; revealing is Unknown Author, "Transcript Baker 1-on-1 Meeting with FRG FM Kinkel at the Department of State," June 30, 1992, JAB, 111.5.1992 June. Also, interview with DOS official, Washington DC, November 2018.

66. Johns Hopkins SAIS, Foreign Policy Institute, "Open Door: NATO Enlargement and Euro-Atlantic Security in the 1990s" Workshop, March 12, 2019.

67. Barry F. Lowenkron, "The President's Meeting with Secretary General of NATO Manfred Woerner," October 11, 1991, BPL, M&T.

68. Stephen J. Wall, "Letter to Gozney: Anglo/French Summit," June 24, 1991, TNA, PREM 19/3346.

69. David C. Gompert, "Bush Meeting with Francois Mitterrand, President of France," March 14, 1991, BPL, M&T. "The Poles and others were feeling like they had been orphaned and asking in which house they were going to live in," an NSC interviewee told me in Washington DC in December 2018.

70. Brent Scowcroft, "Memo for Bush: Coping with the Soviet Union's Internal Turmoil," April 1991, BPL, Scowcroft Collection, 91119 March-May 1991; for the background, Jack Matlock, "Memo to Scowcroft: Gorbachev's Current Concerns Regarding Our Relationship," May 7, 1991, BPL, Scowcroft Collection, 91129 Gorbachev-Sensitive January-June 1991 [3].

71. James Baker, "Memo for Bush: Wednesday's Meetings in Moscow," September 11, 1991, BPL, Scowcroft Collection, 91129 Gorbachev (Dobrynin) Sensitive January-June 1991 [1]; see also Lawrence S. Eagleburger, "Memo for Bush: Your Visit to the USSR," July 25, 1991, in Svetlana Savranskaya and Thomas Blanton, The Last Superpower Summits: Reagan, Gorbachev and Bush at the End of the Cold War (Budapest and New York: Central European University Press, 2016), document 134, pp. 864-867.

72. For instance, Ed A. Hewett, "Memo for Scowcroft and Gates: Highlights on the Current Soviet Situation," April 19, 1991, BPL, Scowcroft Collection, 91119

March-May 1991. Also, interview with DOS official, Washington DC, December 2018.

73. Brent Scowcroft, "Memo for Bush: Proposed Presidential Letter to Gorbachev Responding to His Request for Additional CCC Credits," April 30, 1991, BPL, Scowcroft Collection, 91129 Gorbachev (Dobrynin) Sensitive January-June 1991 [2]; CIA Directorate of Intelligence, "Gorbachev's Future," May 23, 1991, BPL, Scowcroft Collection, 91129 Gorbachev (Dobrynin) Sensitive January-June 1991 [1]. Dennis B. Ross, "Memo for Baker: Coordinating Conference Strategy," January 13, 1992, JAB, 178.2. Miscellaneous Book Materials, 1993-1995.

74. Dobbins, "NATO's Future: Political Track of the Strategy Review: Questions to Ask Ourselves."

75. Gompert, "Memo for Scowcroft: Our Goals in CSCE."

76. Brent Scowcroft, "Memo for Bush: The US, NATO, and Peace-Keeping in the Post Soviet Era," May 22, 1992, BPL, NSC Collection, Nicholas Rostow Subject Files CF01329-005 NATO [1].

77. David C. Gompert, "Implications for NATO of Expanded WEU Membership," March 26, 1992, BPL, NSC Collection, David C. Gompert Subject Files CF01301-009 European Strategy [Steering] Group (ESSG).

78. David C. Gompert, "US Security and Institutional Interests in Europe and Eurasia in the Post-Cold War Era," February 19, 1992, BPL, NSC Collection, David C. Gompert Subject Files CF01301-009 European Strategy [Steering] Group (ESSG); and "Peace-Keeping in the Post-Soviet Era," May 16, 1992, BPL, NSC Collection, David C. Gompert Subject Files CF01301-009 European Strategy [Steering] Group (ESSG).

79. David C. Gompert, "Managing NATO-WEU Expansion," July 20, 1992, BPL, NSC Collection, Nicholas Rostow Subject Files CF01329-005 NATO [1].

80. David C. Gompert, "Memo for Howe: ESSG Meeting, Monday, March 30, 1992," March 30, 1992, BPL, NSC Collection, David C. Gompert Subject Files CF01301-009 European Strategy [Steering] Group (ESSG).

81. Unknown Author, "US Recommendation for NATO Relations with the Franco-German Corps," September 17, 1992, BPL, NSC Collection, Nicholas Rostow Subject Files CF01329-005 NATO [1].

82. CIA Directorate of Intelligence, "The United States in the New Europe," January 22, 1992, BPL, NSC Collection, Barry Lowenkron Subject Files CF01527, ESSG [European Strategy Steering Group]: ESSG Meeting - February 3, 1992. Telephone interview with NSC official, Washington DC, December 2018.

83. Simon Webb, "Letter to Gozney: CDS Meeting with Admiral Lanxade," October 28, 1991, TNA, PREM 19/3345.

84. Hans Binnendijk, "NATO Can't Be Vague About Commitment to Eastern Europe," *The New York Times*, November 8, 1991.

85. Gompert, "Implications for NATO of Expanded WEU Membership."

86. Ed A. Hewett, "Memo for Scowcroft: Prime Minister Major and NATO Membership," June 5, 1992, BPL, NSC Collection, Nicholas Rostow Subject Files CF01329-005 NATO [1].

87. Unknown Author, "Expanding Membership in NATO," September 17, 1992, BPL, NSC Collection, Nicholas Rostow Subject Files CF01329-005 NATO [1]. "The Russians would not like it, but so be it," an NSC official told me. Telephone interview, Washington DC, December 2018. "A lot of us thought that way, but it never became policy," he added. "We believed in [NATO expansion] in concept, we believed in it as an outcome that had to be protected, but we did not pursue it."

Chapter 4

NATO From Liaison to Enlargement: A Perspective from the State Department and the National Security Council 1990–1999

Stephen J. Flanagan

Introduction

This chapter offers perspectives on the development of the internal U.S. government debate on NATO's transformation and enlargement and how these initiatives pursued by the George H.W. Bush and Clinton Administrations supported a common strategy to shape a new post-Cold War security order in Europe. It is written from my vantage point as a member and later Associate Director of the U.S. State Department's Policy Planning Staff 1989-1995, National Intelligence Officer for Europe 1995-97, and the Senior Director for Central and Eastern Europe at the National Security Council Staff 1997-99—during accession of the Czech Republic, Hungary, and Poland to the Alliance.

Throughout that period, I was deeply involved in the U.S. government and public debate and Alliance consultations on NATO's future missions and membership. This chapter draws on my recollections from that period, contemporaneous publications and speeches that I authored, and recently declassified government documents that I wrote, as well as the scholarly literature.

My analysis focuses heavily on the earliest debates on NATO's transformation and enlargement within the U.S. government during the George H.W. Bush Administration, which has received less scrutiny by scholars than the period after 1994, which is addressed in several other chapters in this volume.

The record illustrates that the framework for what became the Partnership for Peace (PfP), as well as considerable groundwork for NATO enlargement, was already well developed by the end of the 1992, as the Bush Administration was winding down. When the Clinton Administration entered office in 1993, the lines of debate that had unfolded quietly during Bush Administration were relitigated, and became more public after 1994. However, the critical questions of whether, why, when, and how NATO should invite any of the new democracies of Central and Eastern Europe to join the Alliance were examined by the Bush Administration during 1991-92. This debate was shaped by entreaties from Central and East European leaders as well as concerns in Washington and key West European governments about wider instability in the wake of the Soviet collapse and Yugoslav Civil War.

To be sure, many difficult questions required further, often contentious, internal deliberations, diplomatic engagement, and political-military assessments before NATO would open its door and the successful March 1999 round of enlargement could be completed. Nevertheless, the strategic rationale, political preconditions, and general military requirements of enlargement had been framed by the time the Clinton administration took office. This reflected the broad, bipartisan political support in the United States during the 1990s that welcoming the Central and Eastern European states into the Euro-Atlantic community after the collapse of the Warsaw Pact was the logical culmination of five decades of political support for their freedom, and that it would enhance both Alliance and overall European security.

Europe Whole and Free

Even as the revolutions in Poland, Hungary, and other Central and Eastern European countries were still unfolding, President Bush articulated, in his May 1989 speech in Mainz, Germany, the U.S. policy goal of working with other governments to realize a Europe "whole and free," which was far from a sure thing. Bush advanced four proposals to heal Europe's divisions: strengthen and broaden the Helsinki process to promote free elections and political pluralism; end the division of Berlin; pan-European action to address environmental problems; and accelerated negotiations to achieve dramatic reductions in NATO and Warsaw Pact conventional force levels and military capabilities, including a detailed set of specific proposals.[1]

As most of those revolutions were completed, the Bush Administration articulated its strategy for adapting proven Western institutions to lead and share responsibility in shaping the "architecture" for continued peaceful change. Secretary of State James A. Baker III first outlined the U.S. approach in a December 1989 speech in Berlin. Baker contended that no single institution would be capable on its own of addressing the complex political, economic, and security challenges required to realize a new European order.[2] He argued that NATO remained valuable and could serve "new collective purposes." He labeled NATO's first new mission Allied efforts in the ongoing Vienna talks on Conventional Forces in Europe (CFE) to realize deep reductions in military forces. He said that the Alliance could be a forum for coordination of other elements of engagement with the East. The European Community (EC) could play a vital role in the economic and political development and integration of the Central and Eastern European states. He noted that the United States was committed to building up the Conference on Security and Cooperation in Europe (CSCE), particularly in the areas of promoting democratic institutions, peaceful resolution of disputes, greater openness in military affairs, respect for human and political rights, and adherence to the rule of law.

During a period when some, including Václav Havel and West German Foreign Minister Hans-Dietrich Genscher, were calling for dissolution of both Cold War alliances and development of a new, all-European security structure (around the CSCE), the Bush Administration's planning was animated by the conviction that the new architecture should build on the strong foundations, core principles, and complementary capabilities of NATO, the EC, and CSCE.[3] Administration officials believed this approach was prudent and that trying to establish entirely new structures in a period of rapid change and political uncertainty—including about the scope of the EC's further integration—was fraught with risk. Moreover, NATO was seen as the most effective institution to guarantee European peace and security, including among its members, and as a hedge against instability or the reversal of political reforms in Central and Eastern Europe and Soviet revanchism. NATO was also central to retaining U.S. influence in Europe.

German Unity and NATO Enlargement

With the opening of travel between and East and West Germany and the fall of the Berlin Wall, German unity became the focus and a critical first step in the Bush Administration's strategy in advancing wider European integration. The administration moved quickly to support the manifest aspirations of the German people for rapid unification despite the strong reservations of other European governments, particularly those involved in the postwar occupation, about the security implications of a unified Germany. Before those three governments would relinquish their postwar rights, they wanted assurances that a reunited Germany with combined military forces would not pose a threat. To address these concerns, the February 1990 Ottawa Open Skies Conference—the first meeting of the 29 members of NATO and the Warsaw Pact since the revolutions of 1989—was repurposed as the United States worked nimbly to fashion the set negotiations that became known as the "2+4 Talks," involving the two Germanys plus the four occupying powers.

A central question in the talks was the status of a unified Germany in NATO. The United States made clear that it supported German integration in NATO, and that while the USSR had no *droit de regard* over this decision in accordance with principles of the Helsinki Final Act, Washington would accomplish this goal through an inclusive dialogue and support measures to assure Moscow this would be achieved in a way that did not threaten the security of the Soviet Union or any other European state.[4] German diplomacy served as an important lubricant in the negotiations with Moscow.[5] Another key factor was close coordination among leaders and senior officials in Washington and key European governments. This negotiation approach would later be cited as a model that could be emulated during the early debates on enlargement during the Clinton Administration.

In the September 1990 Treaty on The Final Settlement on German unity, the two German governments affirmed their commitment not to manufacture or possess nuclear, biological, or chemical weapons and endorsed the declaration of the Federal Republic of Germany in the context of the Conventional Armed Forces in Europe (CFE) negotiations to undertake deep reductions in the personnel strength of their combined German armed forces within three to four years. The two governments also agreed that only territorial units not integrated into NATO military structures would be stationed on the territory of the former German Democratic Republic (GDR), and that no forces of other states would be stationed or conduct military exercises there until the completion of the withdrawal of the Group of Soviet Forces in Germany. The Treaty established that after the Soviet troop withdrawals from the GDR and East Berlin were completed, German forces fully into integrated NATO military structures could be stationed in the territory of the former GDR—without nuclear weapons carriers—but foreign armed forces and nuclear weapons or their delivery systems could not. Finally, the Treaty codified the right of a united Germany to belong to alliances with full rights.[6]

Assertions by Soviet and Russian officials—and some U.S. diplomats—that U.S. and German leaders offered informal assurances during the 2+4 negotiations that NATO would eschew further enlargement remain contentious. These assertions have been roundly refuted by senior U.S. officials involved in the negotiations. Over the last decade scholars have been able to examine the U.S., German, and Soviet archives on this matter. A number of scholars have presented findings that support the statements of U.S. policymakers that NATO enlargement beyond the GDR was not discussed with the Soviets during this period. As Mark Kramer concluded: "Gorbachev did receive numerous assurances during the "2+4" process that helped to sweeten the deal for him, but none of these had anything to do with the enlargement of NATO beyond Germany." [7] Other analysts contend that U.S. and German officials did have discussions with the Soviets in early February 1990 that could have been interpreted as eschewing expansion beyond the GDR. In particular, Baker told Gorbachev, "there would be no extension of NATO's jurisdiction or NATO's forces one inch to the east."[8] However, this statement was not further elaborated or codified in an agreement, and even Gorbachev admitted it was made in the context of the early phases of negotiations on German unity.[9] Moreover, there was no discussion of NATO enlargement to Central and Eastern Europe in the Bush Administration at that time. The Soviets received financial assistance from Germany and the commitments on military deployments and force levels in the Treaty on the Final Settlement, in exchange for agreeing to a united Germany being a full-fledged member of NATO, but there was no promise to freeze NATO's borders.[10]

The Development of Liaison

During 1990, the Bush Administration's European strategy discussions focused on transformation of NATO and relations with the Soviet Union and the post-Communist Central and Eastern European governments with the goal of promoting stability and mutual understanding. While there was a recognition that the Alliance would eventually need to address the interest of many Central and Eastern European states to join NATO, taking a public stance on the issue was assessed to be premature and could risk trouble with Moscow, which still had several hundred thousand troops deployed in the region.

A small interagency planning group began drafting a NATO summit declaration that included several dramatic initiatives including: declaring nuclear weapons as truly "weapons of last resort," eliminating nuclear artillery, proposing a new military strategy, seeking further force reductions in a CFE II, inviting former Warsaw Pact countries to establish missions to NATO, and strengthening CSCE.[11]

At their July 1990 Summit in London, NATO Heads of State and Government endorsed these initiatives as a first step in NATO's post-Cold War transformation. NATO formally extended a "hand of friendship" to the former Warsaw Pact countries, inviting them to form a new relationship with the alliance. The declassified verbatim record of the London Summit reflects that Allied leaders discussed the need to transform NATO for new missions, while retaining its collective defense capabilities. President Bush argued that the most important step in engaging the Soviet Union and the new East European democracies was to invite them to establish permanent liaison missions to NATO. *Liaison* would facilitate an active dialogue and demonstrate that the Alliance had changed and was listening to Eastern security concerns. He noted that this would give the Central and Eastern European countries a channel to NATO and an alternative to a "reformed Warsaw Pact," without alarming the Soviets. He also suggested inviting Gorbachev to a future NATO Summit to help overcome the Soviet image of NATO as an enemy. The leaders also explored how to develop cooperative political and military activities.[12]

Initial Stirrings: Moving Beyond Liaison

The first detailed discussions of NATO enlargement in the U.S. government unfolded during spring and summer of 1991. It was stimulated by several factors. There was growing concern in Washington and Bonn that leaders and the wider public in Central and Eastern European countries were losing hope in the promise of integration in Euro-Atlantic political, economic, and security institutions and that this disappointment might lead to backsliding on implementation of difficult reforms or even the emergence of extreme nationalist political leaders, or the spread of the sectarian violence that was unfolding in Yugoslavia. In addition, the failed August 1991 Soviet coup raised fears of further instability and even revanchism in Moscow. While this abated somewhat in the wake of the collapse of the USSR, Central and Eastern European governments remained anxious to build closer ties with NATO and the EC. EC governments, however, were focused on development of the Union (Maastricht) treaty; Central and Eastern European leaders assessed the prospects of their integration were off in the distant future. The CSCE remained mainly a forum for dialogue on security, and other architectural constructs, such as President Mitterrand's Atlantic to the Urals European Confederation, failed to gain much traction.[13]

In February 1991, the Warsaw Pact's military structure was dissolved by defense and foreign ministers and the last meeting of its Political Consultative Committee was held in Prague the following July, ending any notion that a reformed, or more political pact could provide for Central and Eastern European security.[14]

In March 1991 Václav Havel, then President of the Czech and Slovak Federative Republic (CSFR), became the first East Central European leader to address the North Atlantic Council. However, some Allies were reluctant to issue a joint NATO/CSFR statement on basic principles of relations, which appears to have led other Central and Eastern European governments to decide not to push too hard on NATO's door at that time. Allied reluctance also raised concerns in Central and Eastern European capitals that NATO governments were more interested in allaying Soviet concerns than in helping them emerge from the legacy of Communist rule.

The following month Polish President Lech Wałęsa, after a disappointing meeting with the EC seeking economic assistance, lamented that "the Iron Curtain could be replaced by a silver curtain, separating a rich West from a poor East."[15] Still, some of the Central and Eastern European countries continued to ask the difficult question: if NATO is an alliance of democracies committed to promoting and protecting common values, how long would they have to be democracies before membership became an option?

Allies were pursuing liaison in ways that would avoid any delay of Soviet force withdrawals from the Central and Eastern European countries or undercut Eastern reformers who were arguing for more cooperative security relations with the West. A number of NATO governments were initially reluctant to develop the liaison program beyond information exchanges and increased contacts to practical cooperation and to have any differentiation among countries in the conduct of liaison activities. I argued that this hesitation existed in large measure because Allies had yet to fully consider, or convey to liaison governments, what the long-term objectives and parameters this function should be. In a May 1991 policy planning paper, I presented a range of possibilities from information exchange to limited partnership and even "candidate membership."[16]

By that time, leaders in Poland, Hungary, and the CSFR had already signaled NATO membership was a long-term goal.[17] At the June 1991 meeting of NATO foreign ministers in Copenhagen, Secretary Baker advanced several principles to clarify the objectives and guide the development of the NATO liaison relationships. Baker noted that NATO liaison complemented the activities of other forums and formed a web of relations that would further integrate the Central and Eastern European countries into with the West. Although liaison functions were not designed to extend a security guarantee, they did seek to foster greater security throughout Europe by building trust and reducing misunderstanding. Baker called for:

> new mechanisms for the Eastern countries to interact with members of the alliance so they would develop a better understanding of NATO's nature and operations and to foster the security concerns to all participating states; cooperation in areas where NATO had specialized technical expertise, such as civil emergency plan-

ning, for coping with common problems; and flexible relationships responsive to evolving needs of these countries in transition on a differentiated basis that reflected their progress toward of democratization and demilitarization.[18]

Ministers issued a separate statement pledging to build "constructive partnerships with the Soviet Union and the other countries of Central and Eastern Europe in order further to promote security and stability in a free and undivided Europe." The statement identified several concrete initiatives including: meetings of officials and experts on security policy, military strategy and doctrine, arms control and defense conversion; intensified contacts between senior NATO military authorities and their counterparts in the Central and Eastern European states, including visits to military training facilities; participation of Central and Eastern European experts in certain Alliance activities, such as scientific and environmental programs; exchange of views on subjects such as airspace management; expansion of NATO information programs in the region; and parliamentary exchanges.[19] These principles were endorsed and expanded by the Rome Summit later that year that year and were further developed through the Partnership for Peace.

The Rome Summit and the NACC

The Copenhagen Declaration was an important step in providing all Central and Eastern European states an initial roadmap for their integration into the Western security system. By the fall of 1991, however, the liaison program was at a critical juncture. There was a growing consensus in the Bush Administration that the Alliance had reached the limits of dealing with the Central and Eastern European states through diplomatic liaison and dialogue. There was agreement that these governments would need concrete Western advice and assistance if they were to succeed in their reforms and become members of the Euro-Atlantic community.

The senior interagency European Strategy Steering Group (ESSG) identified the upcoming Rome Summit as an opportunity to actualize the Copenhagen pledge of partnership and to advance practical programs of cooperation. The group decided not to pursue discussion of NATO membership that time. In September, I was asked to draft a memo for the ESSG that outlined a number of initiatives for Allied consultations, and was also authorized to "test market" these at a meeting of the NATO Atlantic Policy Advisory Group in early October.[20]

Washington's assessment was shared by the German government, which led to the joint statement by Secretary of State Baker and German Foreign Minister Hans-Dietrich Genscher on October 2, 1991. The two ministers proposed the establishment of a North Atlantic Cooperation Council to institutionalize dialogue with liaison countries and several specific proposals for developing practical cooperation for consideration at the Rome Summit.[21]

The Baker-Genscher initiative was generally welcomed by Allies and most provisions were adopted at the Rome Summit in November 1991, except for one to start planning with liaison countries for joint action on disaster relief and refugee problems,. In their Rome Declaration, NATO heads of state and government announced the adoption of a new Allied Strategic Concept for a time of diminished threat but continuing instability, based on three mutually reinforcing elements: dialogue; cooperation; and the maintenance of a collective defense capability. The leaders avowed that Allied security was "inseparably linked to that of all other states in Europe," and that "our common security can best be safeguarded through the further development of a network of interlocking institutions and relationships."[22] They agreed to expand the scope of the Alliance's liaison program with the Soviet Union and the five Central and Eastern European members of the former Warsaw Pact, and welcomed participation by Estonia, Latvia, and Lithuania, which had recently regained independence. The new program included both deepened dialogue and practical cooperation. To help oversee and guide this effort, NATO foreign ministers invited their nine liaison counterparts to form a North Atlantic Cooperation Council (NACC).

The first meeting of the NACC was held in Brussels at ministerial level on December 20, 1991. The foreign ministers of 24 countries (16 NATO, 8 Central/Eastern Europe)—and Soviet Ambassador Afanassievsky, who announced the formal end of the USSR and Yeltsin's statement of Russia's interest in NATO membership—agreed to develop "a more institutional relationship of consultation and cooperation on political and security issues," including:

Annual ministerial-level and bimonthly meetings at the ambassadorial level, as well as ad hoc gatherings, as circumstances warranted; Regular meetings of the NATO Political, Economic, and
Military Committees, the APAG, and the NATO military authorities with liaison states; Consultations on defense planning, arms
control, democratic concepts of civil-military relations, civil-military coordination of air traffic management, science and the environment, and the conversion of defense production to civilian
purposes; New efforts to distribute information about NATO in
Central and Eastern Europe through liaison channels and the
embassies of member states.[23]

In his intervention, Secretary Baker proposed that the NACC develop as the primary consultative body between NATO and liaison states
on security issues; assume oversight of the liaison program; and play a
role in helping to manage future crises in Europe.[24]

The second NACC ministerial in March 1992, which included all
the states of the former Soviet Union except Georgia (which joined
the following month), approved a NACC work plan, including intensified consultations and cooperative activities in the areas that had been
agreed to at the initial meeting. A December 1992 ministerial also adopted a work plan for 1993 with a provision for joint planning and
training for peace-keeping, and the NACC later established an Ad Hoc
Group on Cooperation in Peace-keeping, which included several non-
aligned countries with substantial experience in the field that were not
members of NACC—Finland, Sweden, and Austria (which joined PfP
after its formation in 1994 and the EU in 1995).[25]

The development of the NACC during this period did not abate the
manifest interest of a number of Central and Eastern European states
and former Soviet republics in even closer ties with NATO and eventual membership. Indeed, leaders in Warsaw, Prague, and Budapest continued to press for a path to eventual membership.

While the Bush Administration elected not to pursue a policy of
formal Allied consideration of enlargement during the election year of
1992, there was an internal debate over the rationale, modalities, and
timing of eventual NATO enlargement. During the summer and fall of
1992, I prepared several memos for senior State Department officials
on various aspects of NATO enlargement, including one reviewing key

considerations in preparing the groundwork with Allies for a debate, another setting out criteria for enlargement, and one on how to treat Russia, including keeping the door open to its eventual membership. The European Bureau of the State Department and officials in the European Directorate of the National Security Council (NSC) were also exploring the enlargement issue, which in my recollection was the subject of several ESSG meetings.

In early 1992, I was also granted permission by the State Department to publish a paper in *The Washington Quarterly* that outlined some of our deliberations within the Bush Administration on the further development of the NACC and enlargement, which I posed as a series of questions.[26] On future enlargement, I argued that the first step Allies needed to take was a careful consideration of how the core functions, particularly collective defense, could be applied to a broader group of states. I asked since NATO now emphasized that it was an alliance of democracies with historical ties and common values, what was the basis for excluding other such countries in Europe that might apply for membership? Could NATO develop a set of criteria for membership that would give transforming Central and Eastern European states the roadmap to fuller integration they were seeking? Beyond democratic and economic reforms, what other political, military, and geostrategic considerations should be articulated? I cited an op-ed that Hans Binnendijk, then Director of Georgetown University's Institute for the Study of Diplomacy, had written following a discussion we had about the issue in November 1991, in which he set out an illustrative set of criteria that any new members of the Alliance might be expected to meet.[27]

Finally, I floated a proposal to address concerns within the U.S. and other Allied governments about how to manage the addition of the still transitioning Central and Eastern European states to NATO membership in a way that would preserve the Alliance's political cohesion and military capabilities. Perhaps bilateral "association agreements" could be developed as codicils to the North Atlantic Treaty through which Central and Eastern European states that met certain criteria would be invited to adhere to articles 1 through 4, but not the collective defense obligations of articles 5 and 6 of the Treaty. Under this phased approach to enlargement, "associates" would thereby have the right to seek consultations with members states when threats to their security and territorial integrity arose, but decision-making authority on any action to be taken would remain vested in the full members of the North Atlantic Council.

A quiet debate and growing consensus on enlargement continued through the end of the Bush Administration, however, senior leaders were contending with a number of more pressing issues, including the aftermath of the first Gulf War, the Madrid Peace Process, and the escalating war in Bosnia-Hercegovina. Moreover, Secretary Baker and key members of his team had moved in late summer to the White House to work on the Bush reelection campaign.

I was authorized to present a paper outlining some of the afore-mentioned considerations concerning enlargement to counterpart policy planners and other officials at an October 1992 meeting of the NATO Atlantic Policy Advisory Group meeting in the Netherlands. It is noteworthy that in his final intervention at the North Atlantic Council Ministerial meeting in December 1992, Acting Secretary of State Larry Eagleburger stated that the Allies could not keep kicking the enlargement issue down the road, saying that the deepening partnership could "could contribute to transforming the composition of the Alliance itself."[28]

The Initial Clinton Debate

The debate on NATO enlargement resumed in early 1993 as the Clinton Administration undertook various policy reviews, including on overall European strategy and the crisis in the Balkans—which had greater urgency. This phase of the debate has been ably chronicled by former officials and scholars on both sides of the Atlantic and is subject to nuanced reassessments in several other chapters in this volume, particularly the two by Daniel S. Hamilton.[29] I therefore focus here on a few pivotal developments and highlight several threads of continuity in the debates from the Bush to Clinton administrations.

Under Clinton the initial focus on NATO's relations with the East was to build upon and improve the NACC and other elements of engagement with Russia. President Clinton called for a NATO summit in early 1994 to address these challenges. This set in motion intense and sometimes contentious interagency preparations of the agenda and deliverables.

There were three main elements of the Summit approach. First, give NATO, through the NACC or other outreach arrangements, new capabilities for joint action with NACC partners on common security concerns, with a focus on peacekeeping. Second, make adjustments in the military and political structures that recognized the EU's desire for more autonomy and U.S. interests in more equitable burden sharing. Third, adapt the Alliance's military structures to address new challenges within as well as outside of Europe.

Some in the Clinton Administration wanted to continue to avoid taking a position on NATO enlargement, mainly out of concerns of damaging still fragile relations with Russia. Others, including Under Secretary of State Lynn Davis and I, contended that this would be a mistake. We argued that NATO needed to play a role in both providing all European countries a means to cooperate on common security concerns and serving as a hedge against failure of the democratic transformation in the East.

In a paper prepared for Secretary of State Warren Christopher in September 1993, we argued for an incremental approach that would transform the NACC into an operational organization that could develop a partnership on peacekeeping and other security activities with the Central and Eastern European countries and former Soviet republics. The second element of this approach would be a clear commitment to open NATO to new members, along with the announcement of criteria or standards that aspirant countries would need to meet. These standards would be couched in a way that would not *a priori* be seen as excluding Russia, Ukraine, or other newly independent states in Eurasia. In addition, new arrangements with Russia and Ukraine could also be developed to counter perceptions that NATO's enlargement was directed at them. Rather than offering all the NACC governments the right to consultations with NATO akin to article 4 of the North Atlantic Treaty, as was the interagency proposal at the time, we suggested making that the first step in a phased approach to NATO membership that would proceed from an Article 4 to an Article 5 commitment based on the progress aspiring members had made on achieving the criteria and their readiness to contribute to collective defense. We postulated that this would result in the extension of full membership to several Central and Eastern European states by 1998 and others in later phases, including a peaceful, democratic Russia.[30] Our memo was also designed to allay concerns that the Clinton Administration might rush into a process of enlargement.

Our phased approach was set aside by principals, who felt extending Article 4 commitments could create ambiguity about collective security guarantees. However, principals did agree to support NATO's Open Door policy at the Summit. What many in the government didn't appreciate at the time was that President Clinton, National Security Advisor Lake, and others were already convinced, including through discussions with Havel, Wałęsa, and other Central and Eastern European leaders in April 1993 at the dedication of the Holocaust Museum in Washington, that enlargement was the right thing to do, and could be achieved in a way that did not isolate Russia.

The other key achievement of the Brussels Summit in January 1994 was the formal establishment of the Partnership for Peace (PfP). PfP was designed to strengthen practical cooperation between NATO and non-member countries of Europe and Eurasia through individual programs tailored to partners' capabilities and needs, with implementation linked to progress on reforms. The Summit also sought to cast PfP as playing a key role in the "evolutionary process of the expansion of NATO."

A number of Central and Eastern European governments and their supporters in the United States expressed great disappointment that NATO did not make a more explicit commitment to NATO enlargement in Brussels. Some derided PfP as a "second class waiting room" that did not address their long-term security concerns.

To counter this narrative, the Administration quickly dispatched U.S. Ambassador to the UN Madeleine Albright, Joint Chiefs of Staff Chairman General George Shalikashvili, and State Department Policy Planning Staff member Charles Gati to the Visegrád countries. Albright and other officials presented PfP as the "the best path'" to NATO membership, and that message, reinforcing the linkage to membership, engendered active Central and Eastern European engagement in PfP.

While the phased approach to enlargement was set aside, Paragraph 8 of the Partnership for Peace Framework Document issued at the Brussels Summit granted PfP members who perceived a threat to their territorial integrity, political independence, or security a right, analogous to Article 4 of the North Atlantic Treaty, to consultation with NATO.[31]

The Debate After 1994

The internal Clinton Administration debate on NATO enlargement in 1994-1995 featured vigorous exchanges between those who wanted to continue the development of PfP, to avoid loss of Russian cooperation on nuclear and conventional arms control, and those who contended that a failure to offer a more explicit roadmap to NATO membership risked the creation of an unstable security vacuum in Central and Eastern Europe and possible backsliding on democratic and military reforms. Some in Washington and Allied governments were also greatly concerned that as NATO developed this new relationship with the East, it was essential to maintain the political cohesion and military effectiveness of the Alliance, and that adding more members too quickly could erode these important aspects. This debate ultimately led to agreement to launch the 1995 NATO Study on Enlargement, which clarified the purpose and established a clear set of principles. These principles guided the process that led to the accession of the Czech Republic, Hungary, and Poland to the Alliance in 1999, and seven more Central and Eastern European countries in 2004.[32]

Key Lessons and Implications for the Future

NATO enlargement played a central role in healing the Cold War division of Europe and providing the security environment that facilitated a peaceful and successful democratic transition of much of Central and Eastern Europe. It was vital to realizing President Bush's vision of a Europe "whole and free." It was by no means a foregone conclusion that this transformation of the Alliance or the region could be achieved so effectively in less than a decade. It required careful planning, skillful diplomacy, and a firm commitment to principles.

The historical record reveals that the strategic rationale, political preconditions, and general military requirements of enlargement had been framed during the G.H.W. Bush Administration and brought to fruition during the Clinton Administration. This continuity reflected the broad, bipartisan political support in the United States and in most other NATO countries during the 1990s for welcoming the Central and Eastern European states into the Euro-Atlantic community and that it would enhance both Alliance and overall European security.

Enlargement of NATO to Central and Eastern Europe was not an objective or in the political calculus of senior U.S. policymakers when the negotiations for German unification began. However, the 2+4 process provided a diplomatic model that would could be emulated and adapted in the realization of the firsts post-Cold War round of NATO enlargement during the Clinton Administration. The United States and other Allies made clear that they supported the integration of a united Germany in the early 1990s and later the independent countries of Central and Eastern Europe into NATO. They cautioned Moscow that it had no veto over the sovereign decisions of these countries in accordance with principles of the Helsinki Final Act and later the Charter of Paris, but that the process would be undertaken through an inclusive dialogue and achieved in a way that did not threaten the security of the Soviet Union, Russia, or any other European state. This principled and transparent strategy, together with skillful diplomatic engagement, achieved the key goals of stabilization and reintegration of Central and Eastern Europe into the community of European democracies.

Another key factor was strong but inclusive U.S. leadership, which featured close coordination among heads of state and government and senior officials in Washington and key European governments, including Russia. While the Alliance has been unable to establish a durable and effective cooperation with Russia, this was not for lack of effort. As Alexander Vershbow outlines in his chapter in this volume, the United States and other Allies expended enormous effort to engage Russia as a partner, and to even hold out the prospect of NATO membership, and achieved real gains until the events of 2014.

Twenty years ago, leaders in Central and Eastern Europe asked the question: if NATO is an alliance of democracies committed to promoting and protecting common values, how long would they have to be democracies before membership became an option? Today with backsliding on reforms in Poland and Hungary and increasingly authoritarian, nationalist rule in Turkey, it is increasingly clear that NATO can no longer ignore this retreat from the principles without damage to the Alliance's cohesion and standing in the world.

With respect to hard security, the thirteen countries that have joined the Alliance since 1999 have for the most part demonstrated an enduring and lately an increasing commitment to providing for their own defense and to contributing within their means to collective defense, crisis management, and cooperative security. Through their continuing and varied contribution to the full range of NATO missions, these countries have more than met the relevant principles of the 1995 Study on Enlargement that their membership should contribute to Alliance and wider European and global security.

Notes

1. George H.W. Bush, "A Europe While and Free," Remarks to the Citizens in Mainz, Rheingoldhalle, Mainz, Federal Republic of Germany, May 31, 1989. As of March 3, 2019: https://usa.usembassy.de/etexts/ga6-890531.htm.

2. James A. Baker III, "A New Europe, a New Atlanticism: Architecture for a New Era," Address to the Berlin Press Club, December 12, 1989, U.S. Department of State, *Current Policy*, no. 1233 (December 1989). As of March 2, 2019: http://digitalcollections.library.cmu.edu/awweb/awarchive?type=file&item=690688.

3. By 1991 Havel and his advisors became convinced that "NATO was thus the only effective organization left that could offer a genuine guarantee of a country's security in a rapidly changing world." See Michael Žantovský, "In Search of Allies: Vaclav Havel and the Expansion of NATO, *World Affairs*, 177, No. 4 (Nov.-Dec. 2014), pp. 47-58.

4. See James A. Baker, III, *The Politics of Diplomacy: Revolution, War & Peace*, 1989-92 (New York: G.P. Putnam's Sons, 1995), pp. 209-16, 232-57,

5. See Kristinia Spohr, "Germany, America and the shaping of post-Cold War Europe: a story of German international emancipation through political unification," *Cold War History*, 2015, Vol. 15, No.2, pp. 221-43.

6. German Tribune, *Treaty on the final settlement with respect to Germany*, September 12, 1990, Articles 3,5,6.

7. See Mark W. Kramer, "The Myth of a No-NATO-Enlargement Pledge to Russia, *The Washington Quarterly*, Spring 2009. As of February 22, 2019: https://www.csis.org/analysis/twq-myth-no-nato-enlargement-pledge-russia-spring-2009.

8. Joshua R. Itzkowitz Shifrinson, "Deal or No Deal? The End of the Cold War and the U.S. Offer to Limit NATO Expansion," *International Security* 40, no. 4 (2016), pp 7-44.

9. "Promises Made, Promises Broken? What Yeltsin Was Told About Nato In 1993 And Why It Matters," *War on the Rocks*, 2016. As of March 3, 2019: https://warontherocks.com/2016/07/promises-made-promises-broken-what-yeltsin-was-told-about-nato-in-1993-and-why-it-matters/.

10. Mary Elise Sarotte, "A Broken Promise? What the West Really Told Moscow about NATO Expansion," *Foreign Affairs*, Vol. 93, No. 5 (September/October 2014), pp. 96-7. As March 2, 2019: https://www.foreignaffairs.com/articles/russia-fsu/2014-08-11/broken-promise.

11. Baker, *The Politics of Diplomacy*, op. cit., p. 257.

12. NATO Office of Public Affairs, "1990 Summit: a turning point in 'East-West' relations," As of March 3, 2019: https://www.nato.int/cps/ic/natohq/news_116133.htm?selectedLocale=en.

13. Mitterrand's European Confederation envisioned three concentric circles of integration: 1) a deeper, federal integration among the then 12 EC member states, (2) a wider Common Market including Central and Eastern Europe with the prospect of eventual membership in the EC, and (3) cooperation with the Soviet Union on security issues. See Frédéric Bozo, "The Failure of a Grand Design: Mitterrand's European Confederation, 1989-1991," *Contemporary European History*, Vol. 17, No. 3, (Aug. 2008), pp. 391-412.

14. Vojtech Mastny and Malcolm Byrne, *A Cardboard Castle? An Inside History of the Warsaw Pact* (Budapest and New York, Central European University Press, 2005), pp. 65-72.

15. Joel Haverman, "Walesa Asks Economic Support but Western Europeans Resist," *Los Angeles Times*, April 4, 1991. As of March 2, 2019: http://articles.latimes.com/1991-04-04/news/mn-2680_1_economic-support.

16. "NATO Liaison: General Principles for Development," SPEUR 2178, May 14, 1991. George H.W. Bush Presidential Records, National Security Council, Barry Lowenkron Files, NATO Files. FOIA Number 2000-0233-F. Thanks to Prof. Joshua Shifrinson of Boston University for sharing this document.

17. See M.E. Sarotte, "The Convincing Call From Central Europe: Let Us Into NATO, NATO Enlargement Turns 20," Snapshot, *Foreign Affairs*, March 19, 2019. As of March 26, 2019: https://www.foreignaffairs.com/articles/2019-03-12/convincing-call-central-europe-let-us-nato.

18. U.S. Department of State, Office of the Assistant Secretary/Spokesman, "Intervention by Secretary of State James A. Baker, III at the North Atlantic Council, June 6, 1991," Press Release, Copenhagen, June 7, 1991.

19. NATO, "Partnership with the Countries of Central and Eastern Europe," Statement issued by the North Atlantic Council Meeting in Ministerial Session in Copenhagen 6-7 June 1991. As of March 2, 2019: https://www.nato.int/docu/comm/49-95/c910607d.htm.

20. "New Directions for NATO Liaison: Building an Effective Partnership with the East," SPEUR 2583, September 27, 1991, George Bush Presidential Library, NATO Files; "NATO and the East Beyond Liaison," Paper for the NATO APAG Meeting in Elounde, Crete, October 9-11, 1991, SPEUR 2471, Unclassified.

21. U.S. Department of State, Office of the Assistant Secretary/Spokesman, "Joint Statement by Secretary of State James A. Baker, III and Hans-Dietrich Genscher, Minister for Foreign Affairs of the Federal Republic of Germany," Washington, D.C., October 2, 1991.

22. NATO Press Service, "Declaration on Peace and Cooperation," Press Release S-1(91) 86, Rome, November 8, 1991, paras 9 and 3. As of March 3, 2019: https://www.nato.int/cps/en/natohq/official_texts_23846.htm.

23. NATO "North Atlantic Cooperation Council Statement on Dialogue, Partnership and Cooperation," Press Release M-NACC-1(91) 111, Issued on 20 Dec. 1991. As of March 3, 2019: https://www.nato.int/cps/en/natohq/official_texts_23841.htm?selectedLocale=en.

24. U.S. Department of State, "Intervention by Secretary of State James A. Baker, III Before the North Atlantic Council, Brussels," December 20, 1991.

25. U.S. Department of State Archive, "Fact Sheet: The North Atlantic Cooperation Council," Bureau of European and Canadian Affairs, Department of State, May 9, 1997. As of March 3, 2019: https://1997-2001.state.gov/regions/eur/nato_fsnacc.html.

26. Stephen J. Flanagan, "NATO and the East: from Liaison to Security Partnership." *Washington Quarterly*, Spring 1992, pp. 141-151. As of March 3, 2019: https://www.tandfonline.com/doi/abs/10.1080/01636609209550097?journalCode=rwaq20. This was a revised version of a paper I presented at an October 1991 "Congressional-Executive Dialogue on the Future of NATO," organized by Stanley Sloan of the Congressional Research Service.

27. These criteria included: acceptance of the rule of law; renunciation of all territorial claims; support for self-determination of subnational groups; willingness and capability to offer mutual assistance to other member states; and acceptance of some limited decision-making authority (not a full veto) in NATO for a certain transition period. Hans Binnendijk, "NATO Can't Be Vague About Commitment to Eastern Europe," *International Herald Tribune* (Paris), November 8, 1991, p. 6.

28. James Goldgeier, *Not Whether but When: The U.S. Decision to Enlarge NATO* (Washington: Brookings Institution, 1999), p.18.

29. See especially Ibid.; and Ronald D. Asmus, *Opening NATO's Door: How the Alliance Remade Itself for a New Era* (New York: Columbia University Press, 2004).

30. "Memorandum to Secretary Christopher, "Strategy for NATO's Expansion and Transformation," September 7, 1993, Declassified, National Security Archive. As of March 9, 2019: https://assets.documentcloud.org/documents/4390816/Document-02-Strategy-for-NATO-s-Expansion-and.pdf.

31. NATO, On-Line Library, "Ministerial Meeting of the North Atlantic Council/North Atlantic Cooperation Council," NATO Headquarters, Brussels, 10-11 January 1994. Partnership for Peace: Framework Document. As of March 26, 2019: https://www.nato.int/docu/comm/49-95/c940110b.htm.

32. NATOe Library, Official Texts, "Study on Enlargement," 03 September 1995. As of March 5, 2019: https://www.nato.int/cps/en/natohq/official_texts_24733.htm.

Part II

Pushing to Join the West

Chapter 5

NATO Enlargement: Anchor in a Safe Harbor

Géza Jeszenszky

"It is not good for man to be alone," says the Holy Bible. While it is a phrase usually quoted in marriage ceremonies, it is also true in politics. On November 16, 1997, when a binding referendum was held in Hungary on accession to NATO, 85.33 per cent of those who cared to vote understood that it was in the interest of the security, welfare and brighter future of the nation to join the political and military alliance that united most of the world's economically and militarily strongest democracies.[1] NATO enlargement was of great historical and political significance not only for Hungary but for all Central Europe, indeed for the whole world.

Overcoming Misfortune and Misjudgments

The vast area between the two largest European nations, the Germans and the Russians, home to at least twenty national groups, was traditionally the object of fights for influence and control by the two neighboring great powers, occasionally joined by the Ottoman Empire and even Sweden. When the smaller countries (in what some have called *Zwischeneuropa)* were independent, they did their best to fight off invaders, but were often also involved in armed conflicts with neighbors over territorial and/or dynastic issues.

In the early modern age, at the 1878 Congress of Berlin, four empires—the Habsburg, Ottoman, Russian and Prussian-German—ruled over Central and Southeastern Europe. The First World War lead to the break-up of those empires and to the independence of most of their subdued nationalities. Border disputes and the treatment of thirty million people belonging to national minorities made the region easy prey for Hitler and Stalin. The United States and the West European democracies did very little to prevent World War II, which led to the horrors carried out by the Nazis and later by the Bolsheviks. The spread of

Soviet communism to the West was blocked seventy years ago by the creation of NATO.

The basic principle of NATO, common defense, is not new in the heart of Europe. The idea to stand up jointly to aggression and to defend the land and the people against invaders is very old there. It is enough to refer to the common struggles against the Ottoman onslaught from the 14th to the 18th century, to the mutual sympathy and support by volunteers in the various uprisings and wars for national independence in Poland, Hungary and Italy in the 18th and 19th centuries, and above all to the solidarity shown in all the Central European countries for the efforts to get rid of the inhuman and irrational dictatorship imposed upon them by the Soviet Union after the end of the Second World War. Hungary in 1956, Czechoslovakia in 1968, and Poland several times but particularly in 1980-81 underscored the strong attachment people in the eastern half of Europe felt towards freedom and democracy, the cornerstones of Euro-Atlantic values and principles.

Ever since the adoption of Christianity more than a thousand years ago, the three nations that signed the Washington Treaty in 1999 have followed a Western political, cultural and religious alignment. They adopted the Latin (rather than the Cyrillic) alphabet, had feudal Diets, and also a Reformation. In Hungary (including today's Slovakia) the final delivery from Turkish (Ottoman) rule in the late 17th century was the result of a huge international army liberating Buda and pushing on to Belgrade, then an Ottoman stronghold.

Later, educated Central Europeans were deeply impressed by the Enlightenment, the American Revolution, and by the material progress the West achieved in the early 19th century. In 1848 Hungary attempted to introduce the liberal political principles that were beginning to guide countries on the two sides of the Atlantic, only to be suppressed by the joint military forces of the Habsburg and the Russian Emperors. Hungary's leader, Lajos Kossuth (in exile) advocated the close association of the United States and the liberal States of Europe, becoming one of the first Atlanticists, and also proposed a confederation of the smaller Danubian countries.

As a historian I have always seen two tendencies or symptoms which were responsible for the many tragedies that had befallen upon the peoples of what the British historian Hugh Seton-Watson called "the sick heart of Europe." One was what I call the "invasion and partition" syndrome: neighboring great powers threatening, invading, subduing the smaller nations and imposing upon them foreign domination and usually also a backward social and political system. The Tsarist (later Soviet) and the Ottoman Empires were the most obvious examples. This misfortune was clearly a running theme in the history of Central and Eastern Europe. Another sad feature was what might be called the "ganging up against your neighbor" phenomenon: quarrels over borders and the treatment of national minorities (due to overlapping national territories), and the effort to enlist the support of the great powers in the internecine conflicts. That was more the result of misjudgment than misfortune, because in the long run all the Central Europeans were bound to pay a high price for being caught in the crossfire and becoming cannon-fodder in the wars of the giants.

However, one can also see misjudgment in the policy pursued by the Great Powers towards Central Europe as well. The peace treaties ending the First World War produced "an apple of Eris" for Central Europe, giving rise to discord and territorial disputes among the peoples of the region. Appeasement of Hitler and later of Stalin was a fatal and avoidable mistake. The lofty ideals expressed in the Atlantic Charter and the Yalta Declaration on Liberated Europe were perceived as a pledge that Central Europe would not be given up to the Soviet Union. Nevertheless, mainly for military reasons, the United States did not prevent the Soviet Union from turning every country under the control of the Soviet Army into a satellite of the Soviet Union by 1949.

All through the years of communism, the vast majority of Central Europeans looked at the West and NATO as the ultimate hope that one day freedom would be restored to them. It is a sad story to recall how the hopes of the Hungarians and others were dashed, how in 1956 Soviet leaders turned down U.S. President Dwight D. Eisenhower's promise not to seek new allies in Central Europe but in exchange to allow Hungary and its neighbors to become free. 1956, 1968 and 1971 were all misfortunes for Central Europe, helped by the mistakes committed by the West.

Potential Conflicts in the Post-Cold War Security Vacuum

It is evident (but seldom mentioned nowadays) that the existence and strength of NATO saved peace during the Cold War. The important role NATO played in the post-communist era in Central Europe, in the former Soviet satellites, is even less noticed. The aim to join NATO was a major incentive to consolidate democracy (as well as the market economy) and to overcome national antagonisms.

The collapse of communism was received with relief and joy in the West, but there was an understandable fear that old passions, prejudices and grievances would be released from the deep-freezer of Communism, and ethnic strife and national conflicts might re-emerge between peoples in the post-communist countries. Those premonitions proved right where it was least expected, in the former Yugoslavia, but such conflicts did not occur elsewhere in Central Europe, certainly not in a way threatening peace. Why? Because the foremost aim of all post-communist societies was prosperity (valued even more than independence and democracy), and Euro-Atlantic integration was seen as the best way to achieve that.

During the Cold War NATO was the official enemy of the Soviet Union and its satellites, who were rightly called "the captive nations." Yet Americans were never and nowhere as popular as in those countries who found themselves on the wrong side of the Iron Curtain. Several attempts by Central Europeans to regain their freedom and independence were foiled by the Soviet Union. Finally, in 1989 Central European countries were able to become free and independent, even though most were still members of that alliance of the unwilling, the Warsaw Pact, and Soviet forces were still stationed on their territories.

The main foreign policy objectives of the reborn, democratic Hungary were set forth in the government program, presented after the free elections held in Spring 1990: the development of a relationship of trust with the Western democracies, participation in European integration, good relations with all of its neighbors, and support for the rights of national minorities.

The first task was the termination of the Warsaw Pact and the withdrawal of the Soviet occupation forces, to reduce the danger of a return to Soviet Communism. The second was cordial relationships with

Hungary's neighbors. We anti-communist leaders hoped that on the basis of the common suffering under the dictatorships, and the common acceptance of Western, Atlantic values, a new solidarity would emerge between the "new democracies," and the former communist countries would follow the example of post-World War II Western Europe by putting aside all quarrels, and would concentrate on political, economic, environmental and cultural recovery. The third aim of Hungary's foreign policy was the protection of the Hungarian and other national minorities, who were victims of a kind of double oppression under communism. The Helsinki process, with its emphasis on human rights, was most promising in that respect.

The program was put into practice with a speed unexpected in over-cautious Western capitals. Hungary took the lead in dismantling the Warsaw Pact. In what turned out to be the last meeting of the leaders of that body in Moscow on June 7, 1990 Hungarian Prime Minister Antall declared:

> Here I would like to emphasize that Hungary welcomes the new Soviet stance acknowledging the importance of American military commitments in Europe. We believe the military presence of the United States to be a stabilizing factor that will continue to have a definitive positive influence even after German re-unification. During the process of forging European unity, it is expedient to rely on stable Atlantic co-operation, which proved in the course of two world wars that Europe and North America are inseparable. We do not wish to exclude the peoples of the Soviet Union from the unified Europe. We oppose merely shifting the line that divides Europe eastwards. The only credible alternative is the complete elimination of such divisions.[2]

He proposed the radical revision of the Pact, called for the immediate liquidation of its military organization, and proposed talks "to review the nature, the function and the activities of the Warsaw Treaty." President Gorbachev still hoped that both military-political alliances could be dissolved, but Antall contradicted him: "During the process of forging European unity, it is expedient to rely on stable Atlantic cooperation." He added that "the Soviet Union must be part of the process of European integration."[3]

Gradually Hungary enlisted the agreement to that program all the former satellites, and the Warsaw Pact was formally dissolved on July 1, 1991. By that date the last Soviet soldier had already left Hungary.

In my role as Hungary's Foreign Minister, I already visited NATO in Brussels on June 28-29, 1990. I found a sympathetic friend in Secretary-General Manfred Wörner, whom we invited to visit Hungary. Prime Minister Antall then had most cordial talks with Wörner at NATO Headquarters on July 17-18, 1990.

All the leaders of the new, non-communist governments wanted to guarantee that the great political and economic changes were irreversible. The failed coup in Moscow on August 19-20, 1991 was an ominous warning. Although on August 21 the North Atlantic Council came out with a statement in support of democracy, reform and independence in Central and Eastern Europe, and President Bush as well as Secretary-General Wörner placed encouraging phone calls to Antall and myself respectively, we knew that if the coup had succeeded and Moscow had sent back its troops, NATO would have found it difficult to do more than protest.

The Visegrád Cooperation, established among Hungary, Czechoslovakia, and Poland upon the initiative of Antall on February 15, 1991, greatly facilitated the dissolution of the Warsaw Pact. Having achieved that with Gorbachev's agreement, we were convinced that the fundamental political changes of 1989/90 could be guaranteed and made irreversible only by entering the European Community and membership in NATO. The latter aim was not publicized, however, until the Prague Summit of the Visegrád 3 in May 1992.

At that time NATO was still far from being ready to endorse the idea; instead it created the North Atlantic Cooperation Council (NACC), which brought together the members of NATO and of the dissolved Warsaw Pact.

What was needed was a strong campaign, primarily in the United States, to convince its leaders and the public that it was in the interest of NATO to expand eastward, and that post-Soviet Russia's likely opposition to the idea should not prevent its realization.

That aim was far from being shared by all in the West. John Matlock, U.S. Ambassador to the Soviet Union in 1987-91, wrote a retrospective opinion article in the *Washington Post* on March 16, 2014 deploring the fact that NATO had admitted members of the former Soviet bloc. By doing so, Matlock argued, NATO had violated "the understanding that the United States would not take advantage of the Soviet retreat from Eastern Europe."

Fortunately, eventually most American decision-makers, from President Clinton to Members the U.S. Senate, respected the desire and determination of the Central Europeans to join the foremost Western security organization. The late Ron Asmus (who left us painfully early), Steve Larrabee and others played a most important role in convincing leaders and public opinion in the United States about the wisdom of enlargement. The ongoing crisis in the Balkans acted as a catalyst for seeing enlargement as the best way to stabilize Central and Eastern Europe. (The present crisis in Ukraine has likewise reinforced the view of NATO as a force for stability.) According to Asmus, "the purpose of NATO enlargement was to help lock in a new peace order in Europe following communism's collapse and the end of the Cold War. We wanted to promote a process of pan-European integration and reconciliation that would make the prospect of armed conflict as inconceivable in the eastern half of the continent as it had become in the western half. ...it was also our hope that new allies from Central and Eastern Europe, having fought hard to regain their freedom and independence, would also bring fresh blood, ideas and enthusiasm to NATO and help us transform it for a new era."[4]

If a free Central Europe had been left in the no-man's land between NATO and the Russian Federation, tensions over national minorities between Poland and Lithuania, Romania and Serbia, Bulgaria and Macedonia (and probably Turkey, too), not to mention Hungary and three of its neighbors, might have engulfed the whole area.

Following the experts meeting of the CSCE in Geneva in July 1991, it became obvious that the recommendations of that body adopted in June 1990 in Copenhagen were not being carried out by the countries having large national minorities. Fortunately, the strict observation of human rights, including the rights of national minorities, was declared a prerequisite for NATO as well as for EU membership.

The prospect of joining the two Euro-Atlantic institutions proved a strong incentive for proper behavior in the applicant countries. It helped them reach important bilateral accords, like the treaties Poland, Hungary and Romania signed with their neighbors between 1991 and 1996. (I find it most regrettable that later on NATO, like the EU, paid little attention to the strict observation of the rights of minorities, or honoring CSCE and Council of Europe commitments.)

First Steps: Coming Out of the Cold

All the members of the erstwhile Soviet bloc welcomed the new strategic concept of NATO, adopted in November 1991 in Rome, which expressed a willingness to cooperate with them. But this was still a far cry from membership in the cozy club.

Prime Minister Antall addressed the Atlantic Council on October 28, 1991 and expressed his gratitude for NATO: "We knew that if Western Europe could not remain stable, if the North American presence would cease in Europe, then there wouldn't be any solid ground left for us to base our hopes upon." He also emphasized that Central Europe represented a strategically very important space, a link towards the southern arm of the Alliance and an essential hinterland. Antall called for an active role in solving the crisis in Yugoslavia—which was only emerging then.[5]

We were fortunate in having in Manfred Wörner a man as Secretary-General who not only sympathized with the nations emerging from Soviet captivity but had an intimate knowledge of their concerns. Formerly the Minister of Defense in the Federal Republic of Germany, Wörner made a great contribution to NATO rising to the challenges of the post-communist world. Central Europeans should preserve his memory most fondly.

Hungary became a very active member of the NACC, which was set up on December 20, 1991. In my contributions to the meeting of the Foreign Ministers I proposed several measures to deepen the ties between the two halves of Europe, e.g. bilateral consultations especially in conflict managements, devoting special attention to the democratization of the newly independent states (former Soviet republics), and the "human conversion" of the large officer corps of the former Warsaw Pact.[6] December 21, the last day of the NACC meeting was Stalin's birthday. It was also the day that the Soviet Union formally dissolved, as announced by the Soviet Ambassador during the NACC conference.

Together with its Visegrád partners Hungary decided to push for early membership in NATO – not as an alternative to the much hoped for membership in the European Community, but as a complement. This intention was announced publicly at the Prague summit of the Visegrád states on May 6, 1992. From that day until my last day in office, and after that as a member of the Opposition in Hungary's Parliament, also as President of the Hungarian Atlantic Council (1995-1998), I worked relentlessly for Hungary's accession. Prime Minister Antall used his considerable international reputation and influence for the same aim until his early death in December 1993.

During this time the two of us were careful not to appear as anti-Russian. We shared the view, held primarily by the United States and Germany, that it was highly desirable to help the Russian Federation become a strong and prosperous democracy, and to bring it as close to NATO as possible. Therefore, we did not bang on the door at Brussels for immediate admission.

In that spirit, at the second meeting of the NACC on March 10, 1992, I welcomed all the independent successor states of the former Soviet Union. "Apart from the CSCE this body has become the second institution to embrace the newly independent states and to offer them partnership, cooperation and a stabilizing fabric of international relations and interlocking institutions, they could hardly find elsewhere than in the Euro-Atlantic community of shared values and objectives."[7]

The brutal war first in Croatia and then in Bosnia, the frequent violations of Hungarian airspace by Yugoslav planes, and the danger of ethnic cleansing spreading to the Hungarian communities of Vojvodina, a formerly autonomous province of Yugoslavia (before 1919 an integral part of Hungary), compelled Hungary to be very active in urging the international community to stop the bloodshed and to prevent it from spreading further. With that purpose in mind, on October 31, 1992 Hungary opened its airspace for NATO's AWACS planes to monitor the military activities in the Balkans. It was followed by angry reactions from Belgrade. Milošević and his media continuously used threatening language towards Hungary and the large Hungarian minority in the Vojvodina, holding it as hostage.

We knew that even rump Yugoslavia was a formidable military power and was eager to draw Hungary into a military confrontation. NATO understood our predicament. In response to a letter by Prime Minister Antall, Wörner expressed what could be interpreted as a verbal guarantee: in carrying out international obligations under the U.N. sanctions and in making airspace available for AWACS planes monitoring the observance of U.N. resolutions, Hungary could count on the support of the Alliance.[8]

Germany was an early advocate of the recognition of Croatia's and Slovenia's independence. While Chancellor Kohl, grateful to Russia/ USSR for allowing and accepting German unification and membership in NATO, did not want to antagonize Russia in any way, his Minister of Defense, Volker Rühe, was eager to help the new democracies of the East by welcoming their inclusion in NATO.

The French were at best lukewarm about the idea, as they did not like the idea of NATO becoming larger and stronger. They proposed other European models (excluding the United States), such as a "European Confederation" or strengthening the West European Union. The United Kingdom, influenced mainly by military considerations, thought that the British were not ready to die for Warsaw.

The ultimate decision, however, clearly rested with the United States. There the expansion (the term was soon changed to the more innocent sounding enlargement) of NATO was a subject of heated discussions under the new Clinton Administration. The details, meticulously recounted by several authors, make exciting reading even today.[9]

Many Americans, some of them fellow authors in this volume, played a most important role in convincing the leaders and public opinion in the United States about the wisdom of enlargement. On the Republican side they were given strong support by Senator Richard Lugar, Republican from Indiana, while the Secretary of State, Warren Christopher (not exactly a sanguine person) was for long at best undecided. Other officials and experts (Steve Oxman, Strobe Talbott) appeared to be skeptical, fearing that Russia would be alienated by the Alliance approaching its borders.

On the other hand, we, Polish, Czech and Hungarian politicians were increasingly vociferous in the counter-arguments. Clinton, impressed by the heroes of Central Europe's anti-communist revolutions, was inclined to agree with us, but he did not want to go down in history as the President "who lost Russia," alienating Yeltsin, the man who was instrumental in the break-up of the Soviet Union.

Although we were aware of the misgivings most NATO members had about diluting the Alliance and admitting officers who had been trained in the Soviet Union into their ranks, we thought that even a campaign for membership would increase our security, and we should persist in our efforts to convince the skeptics that an enlarged NATO would guarantee the peace and stability of Europe.

A very emphatic expression of our wish was the first NATO "political-military workshop" held in a former Warsaw Pact country, in Budapest, on June 3, 1993. It was attended by many high-ranking NATO officers and officials, and offered an opportunity to articulate our arguments in favor of enlargement.

Prime Minister Antall opened the meeting in the impressive chamber of the Upper House of Parliament with a forceful address. He put cooperation between Hungary and NATO in an historical perspective, highlighting the deep roots Atlantic ideals had in Hungarian political thought, and recounting how Walter Lippmann and others had appeased Stalin. Hungary's prime minister also assured his audience that "we are supporters of the renewal of Russia, supporters of Russian reformist endeavors." With remarkable foresight Antall envisaged for NATO a new function in a volatile world, where "social and political fundamentalism may in the North-South conflict manifest itself and assail the world as the Bolshevism of the 21st century." Finally, the Prime Minister emphasized that in international politics, too, prevention should replace reactive behavior.[10]

In my own contribution I listed the many difficulties and dangers Central Europe was facing at the time, and pointed out that the present security institutions (NATO, CSCE, West European Union) were incapable of handling the existing and potential conflicts and crises. My conclusion was that "the Western democracies must play their part in establishing the security of this region, far more seriously than they have done so far. The reason for this is not simply a moral obligation, but their self-interest."[11]

The message was obvious: NATO must open its ranks. A week later I flew to Athens for the next NACC meeting, but it was preoccupied with Bosnia, and Christopher put enlargement on hold by preferring to plan a Combined Joint Task Force (CJTF) to deal with other unexpected crises.

The conference was followed by a morning cruise on June 12. With Hungary's Ambassador in Brussels, Granasztói, we managed to sit on the deck besides Wörner—to the exasperation of Romanian Foreign Minister Melescanu, who was keen only that Hungary should not become a member of NATO before Romania.

Despite his strong sympathy for Hungary, Wörner's main concern was the survival of NATO per se, when many people predicted its termination as an old instrument of the Cold War. He listened carefully to our reasoning that the stability and success of the new democracies required the West to include them formally in its institutions, and that a consolidated NATO could largely take over the role of the CSCE and the rather inefficient U.N. Security Council.

V3 Pressure, Washington's Pondering, and Yeltsin Acquiescing

In Washington the debate in 1993 narrowed down between the Pentagon (Les Aspin) accepting enlargement only in the distant future (provided Russia agreed), and the State Department, which gradually endorsed the view that the West must rise to the unique opportunity and accept Central and Eastern Europe as its partner.

On August 25, 1993 the world could hardly believe the news that on his visit to Warsaw, after a late evening discussion with President Wałęsa, President Yeltsin accepted that it was Poland's sovereign decision to join NATO, and that it did not hurt Russia's interests. "Yeltsin must have been drunk," was and still is the general explanation, but Asmus shows rather convincingly that the Russian leader accepted Wałęsa's arguments for a common Western orientation. In the coming months he increasingly came to like the prospect that Russia, too, might join the Western Alliance. Although his advisors and—even more—most Russian politicians were opposed to this turnaround, for

Yeltsin it was enough if the Visegrád countries were not given preference over Russia.

Antall, the foremost advocate of Central Europe's membership, was already seriously ill with non-Hodgkin's lymphoma. While under special treatment in Cologne he continued to advance our drive for NATO membership. On October 4, 1993, in the wake of the dramatic collision between Yeltsin and the anti-reformist, anti-Western Russian politicians in the Russian Duma, Antall reminded President Clinton in a letter of Hungary's standing in the Gulf War, throughout the Balkans and now the Russian crisis. That and the overall performance of Hungary warranted speeding up its integration into NATO.

On October 19 the Prime Minister turned again to the American President. Seven weeks before his death he pleaded in a letter for the upcoming NATO summit to make preparations for the Visegrád Group's accession to NATO. "I remain convinced that this would also assist the reform forces in Russia, as I mentioned in my letter of September 14 to President Yeltsin." The rest of the letter set forth why that was the time to act, arguments which have been proven true by subsequent events, including a reference that an enlarged NATO could help Turkey "as a counter-balance to pan-Islamic, fundamentalist (Shiite), and should occasion arise, Russian imperial endeavors."[12]

The answer was a long phone call placed by Secretary Christopher to Antall from the plane which took him on a visit to Budapest and Moscow. I gave a lunch in the Budapest Hilton in honor of the Secretary of State; it was followed by a walk by the two of us on Fishermen's Bastion. Having taken note of Hungary's specific reasons for NATO membership, Christopher assured me that the Partnership for Peace (PfP) would take all the new democracies much closer to NATO and would ensure their security. In a joint press conference, where PfP was formally announced, my guest told reporters: "I assure you we would never disregard or in any way underrate the significance of these countries." One of his top aides told reporters that the Administration wanted to "open the door" to the eventual expansion of NATO that could eventually include Russia and other countries of the former Soviet bloc.[13]

I decided not to show any disappointment: "We welcome the U.S. proposal for a partnership in peace. It accepts the idea of expanding

NATO and it *prepares* participating countries for military collaboration," I told the correspondent of the *Washington Post*. The paper later explained that "For Hungary in particular, the threat from the south is more than hypothetical. At the start of the Balkan war in mid-1991, Serbian warplanes violated Hungarian airspace repeatedly and even dropped a cluster bomb on the border town of Barcs. Hungary had no way to respond, because Moscow took away Hungary's air defense system when its troops departed in 1991." I was quoted that since membership in the European Community (by now the post-Maastricht European Union) proved to be still far away, "NATO came forward as an alternative [. . .] as a shortcut to anchoring us into the Western world." Asked whether a closer relationship with NATO did not involve substantial risks, I said Hungary's experience has been just the opposite: after we agreed to allow NATO AWACS surveillance planes to monitor the traffic over Serbian-dominated Bosnia from Hungarian airspace, Serbia became less aggressive.[14]

Unlike the Poles, who did not hide their disappointment, I really perceived PfP as an important step towards enlargement. On that basis the Hungarian government publicly welcomed the concept.

In the coming weeks and months, I used every possible opportunity, bilateral meetings, articles, interviews and speeches in NATO countries (France, Britain, five locations in Germany) to win over hesitant politicians and the public. The gist of my argument was that the West must "make hay while the sun is shining," should admit the Visegrád Three *before* Russian opposition to it would harden. My motto was the Latin wisdom *vincere scis, Hannibal, victoriam uti nescis*: "you know how to win, Hannibal, you do not know how to use victory." The West needed to use of its victory in the Cold War.

I also expressed confidence in Yeltsin. He (unlike Milošević) "never said that all Russians must be kept within Russia, and by this a most terrible war was averted." I argued that the expansion of the area of stability and security in what the Russians somewhat alarmingly liked to call the "near abroad" would not harm Russian interests; on the contrary, it would help to make the Western border zone of Russia safe. But Central Europe should not be required to wait for Russia to develop into a stable democracy – a very lengthy undertaking at best, a fraught, stillborn venture at worst.

I reiterated those arguments at a conference organized by the Hungarian-born financier George Soros in Budapest on November 12, adding that in my opinion his idea of a "Grand Alliance" between NATO and Russia was only a distant possibility, and it should never be created above the heads of the Central Europeans. My conclusion was that "Central Europe today is a no-man's-land and there is a tendency for any vacuum to be filled. If the West does not fill it there will be others to put in a claim."[15]

The Decisive Meeting in Prague

In preparation for the NATO summit to be held in Brussels in January 1994, I wrote a non-paper in October 1993 and sent it to all NATO foreign ministers. Its main message:

> We understand that the Alliance is now in the process of redefining its role and responsibilities so as to be able to meet the new challenges in Europe. This redefinition should take into consideration the security needs of the whole continent. It means that NATO should find practical ways to gradually extend its sphere of influence as well as sphere of activity to the Central and Eastern parts of the continent. Hungary believes that this task cannot be accomplished without embracing the idea of extending the Alliance to the democratically most mature states of these regions. We understand that such a decision could be realized only gradually, as a process, in which the first concrete steps should be already taken by the coming NATO Summit. We consider those principles very important, because in the process of the extension nobody should be allowed to feel to be left out, isolated or interpret it as a step directed against its security interest. Therefore, while extending the membership to the most advanced and stable countries of the region it is necessary to create cooperative mechanisms to satisfy the security needs of those countries which are not—yet—mature enough for more intensive cooperation. This means that the legitimate security interests of Russia, Ukraine and others must be taken into account and taken care of in the form of enhanced cooperation and coordination, in order to avoid that any—irrational—feeling of isolation should prevail. Extension of NATO should be carried out in a way which strengthens the security of present members of the Alliance as well as its internal cohesion.

> That is why we are in favor of gaining membership for the Viseg-
> rád countries, since we are convinced that the membership of these
> countries would significantly contribute to NATO's security by
> stabilizing & securing Central Europe. There is no danger of in-
> troducing internal disputes in the Alliance. These countries have
> made significant progress in the transformation of their societies
> and economies and have no problems relating to their borders.

In order to calm down the opponents of enlargement I raised the
possibility of a transitional status:

> We can envisage NATO to establish a new status, that of associa-
> tion, which in the interim period would provide us a possibility to
> participate in the political mechanism of the Alliance, while grad-
> ually preparing our military capabilities to obtain the necessary
> level of compatibility. During this period the ties of cooperation
> could grow constantly in every field, which would render mutual
> benefits, and the advantages of the extension could be seen more
> clearly for all sides. We strongly believe that NATO's decision on
> the extension of the Alliance would be a very important step pro-
> jecting stability in itself, stimulating countries in this part of our
> continent to strive even more decisively to stabilize the direction
> of their development based on the values of the present members
> of NATO.[16]

On November 18, 1993, I addressed the Strauss Symposium in Munich. I pointed out that now we had the opportunity to realize Franz
Josef Strauss' vision of a free and independent belt between Russia and
Western Europe by NATO accession. I was confident that "Once the
norms and attitudes that emerged in Western Europe after World War
II come to prevail in Central and Eastern Europe, if they permeate
the political elites, the young generations and the armed forces, existing tensions are likely to be significantly reduced."[17] Secretary General
Wörner privately told me at the Symposium that he would gladly accept Hungary immediately in NATO; the problem was that there were
eleven applicants, and obviously all of them could not be accepted at
once or possible at all.

At the NACC meeting in Brussels on December 3, in a partly im-
promptu speech, I gave a very positive interpretation of PfP. Having
made a reference to the famous Cold War novel *The Spy Who Came in
from the Cold*, I said that

We in Central and Eastern Europe have also come in from the cold, from the Cold War, from the wrong side. We were given a hero's welcome, but later, when the party was over, the air started to cool. Now, after the announcement of Partnership for Peace and the many contributions heard today, and having read and studied carefully the speech made yesterday by the Secretary of State, Mr. Warren Christopher, all this has had a warming effect on us. His words show that our thoughts have indeed been given careful consideration. These statements serve to reassure Hungary that the position which we already took when we were still in opposition at the end of 1989 has been a right one. We were calling for a continued strong American presence in Europe and for partnership for us in NATO. The Secretary of State's speech recognized the existence of a security vacuum and the need to fill it with the concerted action of free nations. That readiness to expand the Alliance is something which has long been advocated by the Central Europeans. Hungary's contribution in the military field will be both intellectual and in a modest way practical, consisting especially in providing support services for peacekeeping, as we are already doing through our help to the UNPROFOR mission in former Yugoslavia.

I assured my colleagues that

The extension of the area of stability and security to Central Europe cannot do harm to Russian interests, let alone pose a threat to that country or to any other. On the contrary, it will make the Western border zone of Russia safer. A stable and eventually prosperous Central Europe will improve the economic chances of Russia and Ukraine, and encourage their democratic forces, because Central Europe has long been seen by them as a testing ground, as a model within their reach. The democracies and the democrats of Central and Eastern Europe are the friends and supporters of democracy in Russia. They can best support the latter by their own rapid success. But for that we need rapid accession to the Western institutions.

[…] Partnership for Peace marks a good start. But its expansion, in my view, can only be gradual, and the countries that are more ready for membership should be given the green light first, for the time being by applying Article 4 of the Washington Treaty. I see no danger in this kind of differentiation, because it will encourage others to follow the democratic model of the Central Europeans and increase the incentive to conform to the standards of smoothly functioning democracies. [...]

In conclusion, I would state that democracy, prosperity and stability are interdependent, and like the European Union and NATO, they can only spread eastward gradually. It is like the old Western frontier in 19th century America. Once it started to move westward, democracy, the rule of law, stability and prosperity spread, and eventually reached the shores of the Pacific. One day the new Eastern frontier will pass by Moscow, reach Siberia and end up in Vladivostok and the Western coast of the Pacific. Once we will have won the Wild East we will be able to deal seriously with global problems, like how to bridge the North-South divide, or the threat of fundamentalist intolerance. So Partnership for Peace is not an end, it's only a means to prepare for the tasks of the coming years.[18]

After Brussels I flew to London, and had talks among others with Defense Secretary Malcom Rifkind. He listened politely to my words but I saw that he remained skeptical.

I expanded on the subject more fully in my talk on December 6, 1993 at the University of London's School of Slavonic and East European Studies, the institution where I spent much time in 1975 while doing research for my book on the British image of Hungary. I spoke about the lessons of appeasing Hitler in the 1930s and Stalin in the first half of the 1940s: Central Europe was then recognized by the Western democracies as of special interest first for Germany and then for the Soviet Union. By resolute and timely action both the Second World War and the Cold War could have been averted. At present I saw dangerous tendencies, not in Yeltsin's policies, but in those of his hardline opponents. My argument was that by admitting the Visegrád countries into NATO we could ensure that the no-man's-land between Germany and Russia would no longer be an attractive and obtainable prize for the Russian red-brown nationalists.[19]

Since Foreign Secretary Douglas Hurd was not in London during my visit, I sent him a memo on NATO enlargement. My emphasis was on Russia, warning that the larger the space its nationalists see available, "the more likely it is that Russian imperialism will re-emerge." I asked the British Government to "pay more attention to accommodating the legitimate concerns of the Central European countries," and to "send an encouraging signal" to them.[20]

I was aware that several NATO countries were less ready to offer security guarantees to former Soviet satellites than the United States, therefore I was eager to put forward my arguments in their media, too. In a long interview with Per Nyholm of *Jyllands-Posten*, the leading Danish newspaper, I explained why the Central Europeans were pressing for membership in NATO. We feared not Yeltsin's Russia but the possibility of a new, neo-imperialist Russian Great Power (if Yeltsin failed), to whom Central Europe may be abandoned just as had happened under Hitler, and later under Stalin. I argued that as NATO got closer to Russia, stability and prosperity was going to spread towards it.[21]

In my interview to a French newspaper I repeated the above argument, adding that Hungary was let down in 1956, too, but at least the best intellectuals of France then showed their solidarity. While NATO was not an institution for solving national and ethnic conflicts, it was an excellent school for collaboration between armies and politicians coming from different nations.[22]

Polish leaders did not hide their disappointment that despite Yeltsin's go-ahead the United States offered only PfP instead of membership in NATO. President Clinton sent the Czech-born U.N. Ambassador Albright, the Polish-born General Shalikashvili and Hungarian-born State Department adviser Charles Gati to pacify the Poles and to enlist Hungarian support.

On January 7, 1994 they had very hard talks in Warsaw. President Wałęsa told them that PfP only fed Russian imperialist designs, "in order to tame the bear it must be put in a cage and not allowed to roam in the woods." Foreign Minister Olechowski said a full presidential library could be filled by Western promises. What Poland needed was a timetable with fixed dates.[23]

The American team flew on to Budapest. My tactics differed from that of the Poles. I trusted in the force of our arguments and knew that in Washington a strong lobby of emigrants from Central Europe was also pressing the Administration. Albright and Gati assured me that the arguments of our late Prime Minister had reached their target. President Clinton endorsed the idea of eventual enlargement, the question was only "when and how."

Those words enabled me to say at the press conference at the Atrium Hyatt Hotel on January 8 that "since the very moment Secretary Christopher laid out the main principles of PfP to us in Budapest in October, the Hungarian Government has fully and articulately supported it. This program will, we trust, help prepare us for fulfilling the various responsibilities that arise from being a full member of NATO. [...] I am convinced that one day, I hope soon, we will become full members of the organization. It is not a matter of *if*, but a matter of *when*. [...] instead of regarding this [PfP] as *something* given instead of *everything*, we regard this as *something* given instead of *nothing*."[24]

The American guests welcomed Hungary's position and they were the first to make the soon famous statement that NATO enlargement was no longer in doubt, "the only question is when and how."

All of this allowed me to be cautiously optimistic in another long interview, this time on January 10 for the Polish weekly paper *Polytika*. I said that a year earlier most NATO countries did not accept the idea of admitting new members, since then we had made substantial progress. In Prague we would be able to argue how important Central Europe was and that the U.S. should not focus only on Russia. I rejected that the present situation could be regarded as our having been let down, let alone betrayed. We were simply being left too long in a waiting room. A stable Central Europe would set a good example for the other transition countries by showing them it is worth their while to carry out political and economic measures similar to ours.[25]

President Clinton was very forthcoming at the NATO Summit in Brussels on January 9-10. Speaking to the Allied leaders he referred to responsibility before history: he condemned U.S. isolationism; the time had come to incorporate the newcomers from the East. He promised that Partnership for Peace would start a process leading to the enlargement of NATO—but not in the immediate future. That would leave time for accommodating Russia.

The final communiqué sounded encouraging: "We expect and would welcome NATO expansion that would reach to democratic states to our East, as part of an evolutionary process, taking into account political and security developments in the whole of Europe.[26]

Upon receiving the news in Budapest I called a press conference. I pointed out that the last few weeks demonstrated the fallacy of the view that Central and Eastern Europe had been written off by the West. Prime Minster Antall's frequent warnings that the West was unprepared for the collapse of communism were at last beginning to be heeded; now, certainly from our perspective, the right answers were emerging. President Clinton declared that the security and the future of the area between NATO and Russia were regarded to fall within the interests of the United States. Sixteen NATO members accepted the principle of widening the Alliance. I was satisfied that the idea was not to push the Iron Curtain somewhat to the East, so that Hungary would become a frontier zone, perhaps a battlefield—but that Russia, too, was becoming a partner. That would be far more comforting than its *raison d'etre* as a revived rival superpower. Far from being a sell-out, PfP was a self-selecting process that rewarded those who took the lead, but it also encouraged those who lagged behind. The Brussels decisions were also good news for Ukraine, as they offered a perspective towards the West. We regarded PfP as a straight line leading towards NATO. Hungary was going to utilize all the possibilities for political, diplomatic, military and logistical consultation and collaboration, so that within a few years we would meet all the requirements for NATO membership. We were ready to bear all the costs for our security.[27]

I spoke in the same vein to the Hungarian program of the Voice of America. Answering the question about the difference between the Polish and the Hungarian reaction to PfP, I pointed out that Poland's past, having been partitioned four times in history, and the role played in them by Russia, made Polish worries fully understandable. In that interview I expressed my gratitude to the Hungarian-American Coalition and to those Hungarian-Americans who helped our case in Washington, coordinating with the Government of Hungary.[28]

The U.S. President and his entourage arrived in Prague on January 11, 1994 to meet the leaders of the by now four Visegrád countries, following Czechoslovakia's velvet divorce in 1993. Meeting President Havel in the afternoon, Clinton made it clear that PfP left time both for NATO and the applicants to prepare, while not alienating Russia and Ukraine. If a new threat from the East would emerge the answer would be immediate enlargement. Havel accepted the logic but asked for a public statement along it.

In the late afternoon Strobe Talbott invited me to a discussion. I knew his stance, his concerns about keeping Russia a cooperating partner. That was Hungary's position, too, I told him. I set forth my views on where the real threats for Russia were coming from and that NATO enlargement in fact served the interests of Russia. I did not expect an immediate endorsement of my arguments, but Talbott clearly appreciated that Hungary was keen not to push Russia in the direction of the hard-liner nationalists.

The next day, the U.S.–V4 meeting was friendly, albeit a bit formal. There was no heated discussion on a date for admission into NATO. Hungary's new prime minister, Boross, felt somewhat ill at ease among so many glamorous persons talking about issues which concerned him far less than Wałęsa and Havel – and myself. At the much-awaited press conference President Clinton reaffirmed that "while the Partnership is not NATO membership, neither is it a permanent holding room. [...] It changes the entire NATO dialogue so that now the question is no longer whether NATO will take on new members but when and how." Havel was satisfied as far as saying that he hoped Prague would go down in history as the opposite of Yalta, as the symbol of the re-unification of Europe. Wałęsa agreed to participate in PfP, adding "We welcome American generals in Europe: General Motors, General Electric..."[29]

Following upon the Prague meeting NATO's Assistant Secretary General Gebhardt von Moltke held consultations in Budapest on February 3-4, 1994 with Deputy State Secretaries Iván Bába and Zoltán Pecze on how to proceed with the Partnership. I signed the PfP Framework Document in Brussels on February 8, while my deputy, State Secretary János Martonyi, submitted the PfP Presentation Document to Deputy Secretary General Sergio Balanzino on June 6.

How to Win the East: Pushing the Frontier Eastward

By this point all six political parties represented in the Hungarian Parliament, including the three in opposition, supported the drive for membership in NATO. Although in the Spring 1994 Hungarian election campaign both the opposition Free Democrats and the Socialists called for a referendum on NATO membership (while my Hungarian Democratic Forum thought the decision fell within the competence of the Government, subject to parliamentary ratification), the new coalition government elected in May, led by Socialist Gyula Horn, continued close cooperation with NATO and was an active participant in the Partnership for Peace programs.

The whole matter now depended on the United States—how the State Department, the National Security Council, the Department of Defense, and the President, together with his advisers, sorted out their differences and dealt with the issue of membership in NATO. As a member of Parliament now in the opposition, I continued to work for that very end, attended many international conferences, spoke at several American universities and at other fora on the importance of membership for Hungary and its Visegrád partners. My arguments were partly historical, referring to the tragic consequences of appeasement (of Hitler and later of Stalin) and to the success story of the American western frontier in the 19th century. Let me present part of a typical talk of mine.

> Central Europe today is a no-man's land and there is a tendency for any vacuum to be filled. With the gradual enlargement of NATO, a strategically most important space would be incorporated into the stable zone of Europe. The admission of the states of Central Europe would establish an important link between the separate areas of NATO. The value of the air space and the territory of the applicants were evident during the Gulf War and even more today with the peace mission in Bosnia. Central European membership is more than enlarging the defense perimeters of NATO; it is the most important step in conflict prevention, in projecting security, in consolidating the newly won frontiers of democracy.
>
> NATO has proved to be an excellent educational institution in bringing together countries with a long tradition of mutual suspicions and even conflicts. A similar role is badly needed in Central and Eastern Europe. Left alone those states, without guidance and help, might again end up not simply in petty quarrels, but being reincorporated in a new sphere of influence, even in a restored military bloc. Plans for such have obviously not died yet, and that must be the real explanation for the growing opposition shown by

Russia to its former satellites acceding to the Washington Treaty. The former members of the Soviet bloc cannot help seeing that opposition as a most serious challenge to their sovereignty. It should not be answered by a policy which shows elements of appeasement.

The question is whether to provide unconditional support to Russia as long as there is at least a faint hope to see there a government basically friendly to the West, if necessary subordinating principles, the interests of the smaller nations that emerged from Soviet captivity, or to link help to more or less strict conditions, both in the field of economic and social policies, thus impressing upon Russia the advantages of continued cooperation with the West. Of course, everybody is aware of the importance of Russia, its nuclear arsenal, its pride and the danger of hurting it. It is difficult not to share the view that all efforts have to be made to avoid a new confrontation between Russia and the West. The question is how to support healthy forces and not offering a new chance for those who think that the best solution for the problems in Russia lies in the restoration of the Soviet Union, perhaps even the Soviet Empire. [...]

In my view in the case of Russia it is appeasement to accept anything that smacks of a veto over expanding NATO eastward. Russian arguments about expansion being a threat to Russia or at least seen by its people as such is a rather flimsy pretext for dictating policy to others, this time utilizing not the strength but the relative weakness of Russia. This argument must be reversed: the expansion of the area of stability and security to Central Europe does not harm Russian interests [...] it will make the Western border zone of Russia stable and safe. That would enable Russia to deal with the real threats to its security, which appear to exist rather in the South and the East. A stable and eventually prosperous Central Europe will be also very advantageous for the countries east of it as it will improve their chances for following suit quickly. It will encourage the democratic forces of Russia and Ukraine because Central Europe has long been seen by them as a testing ground, as a model within reach. Today—as a recent survey shows—the majority of Russians do not consider themselves and their country as part of Europe. If the real Europe, the institutionalized one, moves closer to them, they are more likely to discover the advantages of partnership than while their isolation continues. Today there is a de facto cordon sanitaire between Russia and the West. Is it in the interest of anyone that it would remain there?

Russia and Ukraine must indeed be offered special partnership by NATO, but not to the detriment of the Central Europeans, not as polite way of delaying their accession, slowing their integration. People in Central and Eastern Europe shudder if they hear any-thing that reminds them of a deal over their heads. They remem-ber when they were encouraged to seek 'an organic relationship' with the Soviet Union. It would be the biggest blunder of the still ongoing 20th century to repeat what failed miserably in the 1930's and in the 1940's. Reading some articles in the New York Times and quite a few British and American writers brings up memories of the London Times of the 1930's and the other appeasers. The voice of aloofness, expressed by pragmatic realists, should remind us that appeasement was pursued not by die-hard conservatives, or so-called right-wing people, but by moderate, intelligent Realpoli-tiker, by self-confident professional diplomats and by experienced journalists.

Once there was a westward-moving Frontier in America which greatly contributed to the consolidation and prosperity of a conti-nent. Today there is a kind of eastward moving frontier in Europe, and that can help solving many of the problems of the present and the future. That new frontier must be helped to move quickly, not restrained. The process of enlarging western institutions could have, should have started long ago. By postponing or denying the admission of new members into NATO we are not helping the cause of democracy in Russia but rather the forces of reaction. If the western institutions do not fill the security vacuum in Central Europe there will be others to put in a claim. As a famous, shrewd aggressor once put it: 'there is no space without a master', and even if that notion professed by Hitler no longer holds true, NATO and/or WEU, by expanding eastward and consolidating Central Europe, will exclude any chance for others to try to influence that 'grey zone' against the will of the inhabitants. The democracies and the democrats of Central and Eastern Europe are the friends and supporters of democracy in Russia. They can support the lat-ter best by their own rapid success, but that requires adequate pol-icies by the western world, a conscious break with attitudes which remind people of appeasement.

> My conclusion from this historical and political survey is that there is a very narrow edge between offering genuine friendship (if you like partnership) and inviting disaster by giving too much away without guarantees for proper behavior.
>
> To sum up the lessons of the recent past: we have to be careful. There are dangers which can be avoided, but if the lessons of history are not taken to heart then we may well see our hopes dashed again. Winston Churchill ended his monumental account of The Second World War on a pessimistic note: 'the Great Democracies triumphed and so were able to resume the follies which had so nearly cost them their life.' *Videant consules* ... The leaders should be watchful.[30]

I continued to believe that Russia's real concern should not be NATO enlargement. In the Foreign Affairs Committee of the Hungarian Parliament I told visiting Russian parliamentarians that enlargement would allow Russia to concentrate on the real threats to its security: Islamic fundamentalism in its South, potential rivalry in the Far East, particularly around Siberia and Central Asia, and internal dangers like lack of law and order, economic free fall, infrastructural backwardness, grey economy, corruption and poverty. They did not disagree.

With NATO's decision to intervene in the war in Bosnia in order to bring it to an end, and with the establishment of IFOR to implement the decisions of the Dayton Peace Accords, the strategic importance of Hungary became manifest. The Government, supported by the opposition parties, offered the territory and air space of Hungary for the Bosnia peace mission. Soon Americans learned the name of the small Transdanubian village Taszár and its air base, which became one of the centers of the operation. An engineering corps unit of the Hungarian Army joined the troops in the field in Croatia and Bosnia, and they soon proved their value by building and reconstructing bridges and roads. The Hungarians, especially those who lived near the NATO base, soon directly experienced the difference between the uninvited Soviet Army and the invited U.S. Army. Those Hungarians who had genuine fears about Hungary's involvement could also see the value and significance of Hungarian participation in that unselfish international venture and the advantages accruing for the Hungarian Army of close cooperation with NATO units in the field and in command. When the

Hungarian Parliament voted on participation in SFOR, the yes vote was unanimous.

Hungary's Treaties With Its Neighbors

In the American debates on NATO enlargement it was not self-evident that all the Visegrád countries would be invited to accede to the Washington Treaty. Poland was the strongest candidate due to its history (heroic resistance both to Nazism and communism) and size, also the large Polish-American community. The strongest argument for the Czechs was their geographical location. Slovakia's case was rather weak because of the authoritarian policies of the Mečiar Government. Hungary's strong points were the 1956 uprising, the role in 1989 in the fall of the communist dominoes, and the strong Atlanticism of the Antall Government.

There was one problem for Hungary, however: the fear of tensions and conflicts with its neighbors over Hungarian minorities. The existence of close to three million Hungarians (in speech and identity) in the region of the Carpathian Basin is a consequence of history. They are not immigrants or descendants of colonists; their ancestors lived in the Kingdom of Hungary for over a thousand years. They were cut off from the main body of the Hungarians by the Peace Treaty of Trianon, signed in 1920. Between 1938 and 1941 Hungary regained some of the territories lost in the peace treaty thanks to arbitration by Germany and Italy, only to lose them again in the 1947 Peace Treaty signed in Paris. Since 1945, reinforced by the democratically elected Hungarian governments after 1990, Hungary sought a solution for ensuring the future of the Hungarian communities, not by changing the present borders but by changing their nature, by making them transparent and by advocating measures and policies towards them recommended by the CSCE and the Council of Europe, in order to safeguard their future existence.

Since the early 1990s the Hungarian governments sought to strengthen various international documents on minority rights and to include guarantees for their observation into bilateral agreements with their neighbors.[31] By the end of 1992 Hungary concluded a whole network of bilateral treaties and conventions with a number of European countries: Italy, France, Germany, Poland, Russia, Ukraine, Croatia and Slovenia; all contained clauses on the rights of national minorities.

The Antall Government was also ready to sign treaties with Slovakia and Romania, which had the largest Hungarian minority population, only it insisted on clauses which would have improved their legal and actual status. Contrary to certain assumptions the obstacle was not the so-called territorial clause affirming recognition of the present borders. For fifty years Hungary had never questioned the validity of the peace treaty of 1947 and never voiced any territorial claim against any neighbor. A special article renouncing territorial claims even for the future was included in the treaty between Hungary and Ukraine, concluded on December 6, 1991, immediately after Ukraine became an independent state.

The obstacle in the negotiations with Slovakia and Romania was not the inclusion of such a territorial clause but the intolerant policies shown in those countries towards the Hungarian minorities and the lack of any will to change that. The Antall Government was of the opinion that unless those two countries were ready to change some of their laws, and even more so their practice, it was useless to conclude empty treaties.

The elections of 1994 changed the situation only in one respect: the new government of Gyula Horn was ready to accept considerably less in terms of improvements in the situation of the Hungarians in those two countries. While the international community paid very little attention to the bilateral treaties Hungary signed between 1991 and 1994, there was almost universal acclamation when the socialist-led coalition government signed a so-called "basic treaty" (the term borrowed from the German *Grundvertrag*) with Slovakia on March 19, 1995 and with Romania on September 16, 1996.

Without questioning the good intentions of the politicians and journalists who welcomed these treaties as clearing the last obstacles in the way of Hungary's joining NATO and the European Union, a more detailed analysis shows the flaws of these documents, notably that they do not go far enough in eliminating the real problems. Tensions exist not so much between Hungary and her two neighbors but rather between the majority nation and the Hungarian minority in Slovakia and Romania respectively. That is why all the controversy around these treaties centered on how the minority issue was being handled.

The two countries had little reason to worry about their borders, but in the new treaties they received a new promise: the Contracting Parties declared that they would respect the inviolability of their common state border and each other's territorial integrity. They confirmed that they had no territorial claims on each other and would not raise such claims in the future (Article 3.1. and Article 4 respectively). According to the Hungarian-Slovak treaty, "The Contracting Parties confirm that their interests and endeavors are identical in relation to integration into the European Union, the North Atlantic Treaty Organization and the West European Union and in relation to the Council of Europe and the Organization for Security and Co-operation in Europe, and they declare they resolve to extend each other support in this respect." The treaty between Hungary and Romania contained a similar clause.

The Hungarian-Slovak treaty confirms that the protection of the national minorities falls within the scope of international cooperation and, therefore, is not an exclusively domestic affair of the states concerned, but constitutes a legitimate concern of the international community (Article 15.1). The Romanian treaty contains no such phrase.

Both treaties confirm that cooperation in the field of national minorities constitutes an important contribution to their integration into the European Union, or (in the case of Romania) into Euro-Atlantic structures (Preamble).

Both treaties contain an Article according to which the Contracting Parties shall strengthen (in the Slovak-Hungarian treaty) or promote (in the Hungarian-Romanian treaty) the climate of tolerance and understanding among their citizens of different ethnic, religious, cultural and linguistic origin (Article 14).

The Hungarian-Romanian treaty condemns xenophobia and all kinds of manifestations based on racial, ethnic or religious hatred, discrimination and prejudice, and declares that the parties will take effective measures in order to prevent any such manifestation (Article 14) According to the Romanian treaty, the persons belonging to national minorities shall have, individually or in community with other members of their group, the right to freely express, preserve, and develop their ethnic, cultural, linguistic and religious identity (Article 15.2).

Both treaties contain an Article according to which the Contracting Parties refrain from policies or practices aimed the assimilation of persons belonging to national minorities against their will, shall protect these persons from any action aiming at such assimilation and shall refrain from measures that would alter the proportions of the population in areas inhabited by persons belonging to national minorities (Article 15.2d in the Hungarian-Slovak treaty, Article 15.9 in the Hungarian-Romanian treaty).

Each treaty was quickly ratified by the Hungarian Parliament. That should have dissipated any worry that the admission of Hungary into NATO would have imported tensions into the Alliance.

Nobel Peace Prize for NATO

My efforts and those of many other people came to fruition at the July 1997 NATO summit held in Madrid: the Czech Republic, Poland and Hungary were invited to accede to the Washington Treaty. The Socialist-Free Democrat coalition government of Hungary felt that membership should be endorsed by the people and called for a referendum on the issue. An information campaign on NATO was launched, and non-governmental organizations such as the Hungarian Atlantic Council did their utmost to show the public the importance and value of NATO membership. The result—85 percent voting yes—exceeded even my hopes.

That did not settle the issue, however. All NATO members had to agree, including the United States. The U.S. Senate had to confirm the decision with a two-thirds majority. In talks and by writing to newspapers in the United States, I did my best to help convince the U.S. public and the decision-makers of the advantages of enlargement and Hungary's inclusion. I argued that historically and culturally as well as geographically the three Central European countries were the closest to Western Europe. They were the pioneers of the changes in 1989/90; it would be most unfair to continue keeping them out in the cold. Economically they were doing well; they were on their way to membership in the European Union.

I thought it had also become obvious that the Visegrád Three did not have "a long history of border, ethnic, nationalist, and religious disputes" among them, as was raised by a number of U.S. Senators in a letter they sent to President Clinton on June 25, 1997. But was there really a serious danger that in the future U.S. soldiers would be expected to give their lives for the protection of Warsaw, Prague or Budapest? During the Cold War no Americans died for those three countries, but many cried for them in 1956, 1968 and 1981, and indeed during all those terrible decades when they were subjected to Communist misrule.

I argued that after Central European countries joined NATO, Americans were as unlikely to have to die for them as they had to die for London and other NATO capitals. NATO had proved to be a credible deterrent and would remain so. It would be stronger, not weaker, when the Central Europeans, who had already proved their value among others in the Gulf War and even more in the Bosnia peace mission, would become members as a result of the vote in the U.S. Senate .

It was far from easy to gather the necessary votes, but after thorough discussion the proposal was passed. On March 12, 1999 the Foreign Ministers of the Czech Republic, Hungary and Poland formally acceded to the Washington Treaty at Independence, Missouri, the State of President Harry S. Truman, who initiated NATO. I had the privilege to attend the ceremony as Hungary's Ambassador to the United States. Hungary's then and present Prime Minister, Viktor Orbán, wrote in his Preface to a volume published on that occasion: "We are proud of our NATO membership. We see it as a recognition of all the achievements that the Hungarians have made in the decade we are leaving behind. [...] We know that participation in one of the most successful alliances of modern history is our best guarantee against known and also yet unknown security threats."[32]

NATO has indeed brought peace and stability to the eastern half of Europe, including the proverbial Balkan powder keg. That is why I am quite serious in suggesting that NATO deserves the Nobel Peace Prize for having prevented a third World War after 1949, having prevented local tensions and conflicts in Europe after the Cold War, and in general for its contribution to a stable new Europe.

Notes

1. The first account of Hungary's exciting and rewarding journey to NATO is Lajos Pietsch, *Hungary and NATO* (Budapest: Hungarian Atlantic Council, 1998). Accession was celebrated by a bilingual collection of essays edited by Rudolf Joó: *Hungary: a Member of NATO* (Budapest: Ministry of Foreign Affairs, 1999).

2. For Antall's intervention in Moscow see József Antall, *Selected Speeches and Interviews*. Edited by Géza Jeszenszky (Budapest: József Antall Foundation, 2008). (Hereafter Antall Speeches) pp. 249-56, quote on 252-53.

3. Ibid. Cf. Bennett Kovrig, *Of Walls and Bridges. The United States and Eastern Europe* (New York: New York University Press, 1991) p. 326; Robert L. Hutchings, *American Diplomacy and the End of the Cold War, 1989-1992* (Baltimore and London: The Johns Hopkins University Press, 1997), p. 240.

4. *NATO Review*, Summer 2003.

5. Antall Speeches, p. 275.

6. See my speech in *Magyar Külpolitikai* Évkönyv *1991* [Hungarian Yearbook on Foreign Policy], Budapest, 1991, pp. 398-99. My proposals were not taken up. It was called "an opportunity missed" that could have saved lives. See Rob de Wijk, *NATO on the Brink of the New Millennium* (London and Washington: Brassey's, 1997), p. 65.

7. From my own records.

8. J. Antall to M. Wörner, March 8, 1993, and Wörner's answer, March 24, 1993. Copies in my possession.

9. Ronald D. Asmus, *Opening NATO's Door* (New York: Columbia University Press, 2002) is an authentic and detailed account by one of the major movers. It was published in a Hungarian translation, *A NATO kapunyitása* (Budapest: Zrínyi Kiadó, 2003). My references are to the Hungarian edition. Cf. Gerald B. Solomon, The *NATO Enlargement Debate, 1990-1997* (Westport, CT: Praeger, 1998), which does not say much about Hungary, while George W. Grayson, *Strange Bedfellows. NATO Marches East* (New York: University Press of America, 1999) offers a good short version of the story.

10. *Antall Speeches*, p. 332-34.

11. G. Jeszenszky's statement, "Security Issues in Independent Central Europe," June 3, 1993. From my own records.

12. Antall to President Clinton, October 19, 1993. Draft letter in my possession.

13. "Reassuring Eastern Europe, Christopher Praises Hungary's Reforms," *The New York Times*, October 22, 1993.

14. *The Washington Post*, November 17, 1993.

15. Text from my own records. I expressed those ideas, among others, in the Czech *Hospodárské Noviny* (November 11, 1993), and in the *Frankfurter Allgemeine Zeitung* (November 18, 1993).

16. Paper in my own records, written in October 1993.

17. The text of my address is among my own records.

18. From my own copy of my intervention delivered on December 3, 1993, also published by the Hungarian Foreign Ministry as *Current Policy* 1993/36. In my talks and articles in the coming years I often used paragraphs of that text.

19. "The Lessons of Appeasement," *The Hungarian Observer* [Budapest], January 1994. A version of that appeared in *BIGIS Papers* 3. 1995, pp. 27-35.

20. Memo by Foreign Minister Géza Jeszenszky for Foreign Secretary Douglas Hurd, December 16, 1993. In my own records.

21. "Ungarn vil ind i NATOs sikkerhed," *Jyllands-Posten*, January 8, 1994. p.2, Section 2.

22. January 8, 1994, the Hungarian text is among my papers.

23. Asmus, op.cit., pp. 107-110.

24. My opening statement on January 8, 1994, kept in my own records. I am indebted to [present Professor] Enikő Bollobás, then Head of the Atlantic Department at the MFA, who was an invaluable help and adviser in our drive for membership in 1993-94.

25. Based on the report issued by the Polish News Agency PAP, January 10, 1994. The interview appeared on January 15, following the Prague meeting, and it is among my records.

26. Grayson, op.cit., p. 86, Asmus, op.cit., p. 112.

27. My own notes for the press conference.

28. Rádiófigyelő [Radio Observer], January 11, 1994, in my own records.

29. Grayson, op.cit., pp. 86-87. Cf. Asmus, op.cit., p. 113.

30. Géza Jeszenszky, "The New European Frontier," *Society and Economy in Central and Eastern Europe*, 20 (1998/1): 45-57. Cf. my essay "Central Europe and Appeasement," *Uncaptive Minds*, 9 (1996-97). Nos. 1-2, pp. 5-10.

31. Those efforts are summarized in my essay, "Hungary's Bilateral Treaties with the Neighbours," *Ethnos-Nation*, (Köln) 1996. [1997] Nr. 1-2. pp. 123-128.

32. *Hungary: a Member of NATO*, op. cit., pp. 11-12.

Chapter 6

Hungary's Motivations and Steps on its Path to Enter the Euro-Atlantic Community

László Kovács

Hungary has been part of Christian Europe for over one thousand years. Hungarian tribes, led by Árpád, arrived from Asia in 896 and settled down along the Danube and the Tisza, the two rivers that continue to dominate Hungary today. Saint Stephen, who would be the first king of the country, appealed to Rome for the crown, and his requested was granted. The Bavarian princess he chose as his wife was escorted to Hungary by Bavarian knights.

For centuries, Hungarians proved successful in halting and driving out various forces attacking Europe from the east, including the Mongolian Tartars and, ultimately, the conquering Ottoman Turks, who ruled the country for 150 years. Subsequently, Hungary became and for a long time remained part of the Habsburg Empire, mounting a series of wars of independence against its masters over the centuries. The so-called Compromise of 1867 led to the formation of the Austro-Hungarian Monarchy as part of the Habsburg Monarchy. This dual kingdom, with the two countries sharing the same monarch, continued to rule other peoples in the region until World War I, which Hungary was instrumental in triggering on the side of Germany and Austria, and eventually lost. In the aftermath of the war, Hungary had to relinquish two-thirds of its territory and population, but remained part of Europe.

Later, Hungary once again made a major contribution to the outbreak of World War II as a supporter of Nazi Germany and its ally, fascist Italy. Once again, the country emerged from the war as one of the losers, sustaining enormous damage in terms of material assets and human lives. After the German occupation in 1944, Soviet Russia moved in beginning in April 1945, effectively tearing Hungary from the western half of Europe and engulfing it in the Warsaw Pact and Comecon. It was along the Austro-Hungarian border that the infamous Iron Curtain was erected and fortified, laying a mine barrage between what became two different political, social and economic systems, and thus two different cultures and ways of life.

The revolution and war of independence that broke out on October 23, 1956, proved that the people of Hungary had not resigned themselves to their fate and refused to accept Soviet rule or the political, social, and economic arrangement imposed by the Soviet Union, including the single-party scheme and the eradication of democracy, liberty, and the market economy.

The revolution was crushed by the Red Army. Mátyás Rákosi, the dethroned dictator, was granted asylum in the Soviet Union and replaced at the helm by János Kádár, the protégé of Moscow, who had served time in prison under the Rákosi régime. Kádár proceeded to rebadge the Communist Party and meted out death sentences and harsh prison terms to the revolutionaries in a wave of vengeance he called "consolidation." Imre Nagy, the Prime Minister of the revolutionary government who had returned to Hungary after spending decades in the Soviet Union, was executed along with several of his "accomplices." With the work of retribution complete, and having learned the lessons of the revolution, in the second half of the 1960s Kádár began to introduce cautious economic reforms. From the early 1970s, he played an active role in assisting the détente between East and West, and participated in the wording and promulgation of the Helsinki Accords in 1975.

After 1975, János Kádár instructed the Foreign Department of the party headquarters to start building bridges between the Hungarian Socialist Workers' Party (formed in 1957) and the Social Democratic parties of Western European countries. This marked a major turning point in East-West relations, given that the Soviet bloc had been ruled by communist hegemony, whereas many countries in Western Europe had been governed by Social Democrats, solo or in coalition with other parties.

Starting in the early 1980s, a handful of senior officials of the Hungarian Socialist Workers' Party, particularly of the Central Committee and the Departments of Foreign Affairs and Economic Policy, received the permission of János Kádár and assistance from Chancellor Helmut Schmidt to enter into a dialogue with the German member of the European Commission (EC), Wilhelm Haferkamp, and his staff. The objective of the discussions was to phase out the quotas imposed on

Hungarian exports to Community member states, followed by paving the way toward industrial cooperation between Hungary and the EC.

The phasing out of quotas clearly improved Hungary's market opportunities, while the initiative of industrial cooperation aided our ability to benefit from the relations forged with the most advanced European countries in other ways as well.

On the Hungarian side a select small group of six senior party and government officials, including First Secretary János Kádár and Prime Minister György Lázár (and me), were dealing with EC matters, as well as, obviously, the six senior staff members who actually conducted the negotiations with Brussels.

To this day I do not know whether the highest echelons of the Soviet leadership were ever briefed on these meetings. The matter was certainly never brought up by Soviet officials to their counterparts in Hungary. I find it highly likely, however, that the KGB was informed about the meetings taking place, although they probably never found out what had transpired at those meetings. Having first-hand experience with the inner workings of a single-party system, I can even imagine that nobody wanted to "burden" the political leaders in the Kremlin with such "unsavory" information. It is important to remember in this regard that, by the fall of 1982, Brezhnev had been struggling with a terminal disease, and died at the end of the year. He was followed as party head and chief executive of the country by an equally ill Andropov, who had served as Moscow's ambassador to Budapest during the 1956 Revolution, and later as KGB chief. He died a year and a half later himself. Chernenko, his successor as General Secretary, died in 1985. In all likelihood, the KGB simply refrained from "inconveniencing" the ailing leaders with such intelligence.

In the spring of 1985, Mikhail Gorbachev was elected to lead the Soviet Union as Secretary General of the Communist Party. His arrival and moves towards economic reforms encouraged the Hungarian leadership to disclose the fact and the purpose of the talks that had been taking place with the EC since the early 1980s, and to delegate the task of their continuation to competent government members instead of central party officials. In the fall of 1988, Deputy Prime Minister József Marjai, who also represented Hungary in the Comecon, and I (by then serving as Deputy Minister of Foreign Affairs) signed an agreement that provided not only for industrial cooperation and the phasing out of export quotas but also for the establishment of embassy-level diplomatic relations between Hungary and the EC. In those days, the Comecon, of which Hungary was a member, did not even recognize the existence of the Common Market.

An important, if delicate, moment in the process of opening up to the West had come in November 1982, shortly before Brezhnev died, when Hungary—subsequent to the decision of the party's Central Committee—submitted its application to join the IMF and the World Bank. This move had previously been considered and rejected point-blank by Brezhnev in various meetings with Kádár over the years. It was a vital step because gaining membership in both institutions in the summer 1982 enabled Hungary to access loans from international financial markets on much more favorable terms.

Even more spectacular was the step Hungary took toward opening foreign relations to the West when Soviet-American arms control negotiations over intermediate-range nuclear missiles (INF) ground to a halt in late 1983. NATO's double-track decision of 1979 had entailed that, in the event that the Soviet Union failed to withdraw beyond the Ural Mountains (or even reduce) its SS-20 missile arsenal, then stationed in the western parts of the country (from where Great Britain and West Germany easily fell within range), then NATO would proceed to deploy Pershing 2 and cruise missiles in the United Kingdom, the Federal Republic of Germany, Italy, Belgium, and the Netherlands, to ensure striking capability on the European territory of the Soviet Union. Since the SS-20s were still in place at the end of 1982, NATO began preparations for its reciprocal deployments.

Soviet Foreign Minister Andrei Gromyko responded by announcing the cessation of the Geneva INF arms control talks, blaming NATO for making it impossible for the Soviet Union to remain at the negotiating table. A few days later, premiers Margaret Thatcher (UK), Bettino Craxi (Italy), Wilfred Martens (Belgium) and Helmut Kohl (Germany) unveiled plans to make a trip to Hungary – as a sign that they wanted to keep relations with Eastern Europe going, irrespective of a potential re-freeze of superpower relations. The tacitly obvious purpose was to ease tensions related to the INF issue, which threatened to reignite the Cold War. Citing Gromyko's statement, Hungary's

Ministry of Foreign Affairs proposed that the visit be declined, while the foreign department of the party headquarters argued in favor of receiving the delegation.

Finally, on the recommendation of Kádár himself, the party's Political Committee decided to accept the visit, which duly took place with the participation of Thatcher, Craxi, Kohl, and Martens. The Soviet leadership essentially glossed over the Budapest meeting in silence. In subsequent years, senior NATO officials and the leaders of the aforementioned countries repeatedly spoke in words of praise about Hungary's openness to receive the four premiers, contrasting Hungary's positive attitude with the aloofness of other countries in the Soviet bloc, which seemed to hark back to the days of the Cold War.

This opening up of foreign relations—or rather Hungary's new *Westpolitik*—on the eve of its domestic democratic turn, which ushered in a favorable change in the international perception of Hungary, was supplemented by visits Prime Minister Károly Grósz paid to various countries, including Austria, Greece, West Germany, the United States, and Canada, as well as from concurrent visits to Budapest by several dignitaries from NATO member states, such as the Presidents of West Germany and France, the Queen of the Netherlands, the Queen of Denmark, and the King of Spain.

This series of visits culminated in the summer of 1989, when U.S. President George H.W. Bush came to Budapest. No other country in the Soviet bloc had ever managed to stage such a sequence of mutual visits, alone or together. The more positive opinion being formed in the West of Hungarian foreign policy further benefited from the restoration of diplomatic ties with the Vatican and Israel, which Hungary had formerly severed under Soviet orders, and from newly established diplomatic relations with South Korea and South Africa.

A further highly symbolic and momentous episode, as part of the overall campaign to open the country to the world beyond the Iron Curtain, took place on September 10, 1989, when Hungary decided to open its western border with Austria, effectively allowing East German refugees who had been staying for months in Hungary to leave for the Federal Republic of Germany. Just over a year later, Germany was unified. German Chancellor Helmut Kohl proclaimed that "Hungary knocked the first brick out of the Berlin Wall."

Without the democratic turn, the establishment of a multi-party system and the rule of law, the reinstatement of safeguards for basic liberties, and the first free elections, Hungary would not have been able to join Euro-Atlantic organizations. By the same token, it also must be said that had it not been for the decisions, measures, and initiatives taken in Budapest that I have outlined above, Hungary would never have received the amount of attention, recognition, and support the Euro-Atlantic Community provided to facilitate the country's accession and smooth integration.

During the brief days of the 1956 revolution and war of independence, most Hungarians preferred a neutral future for Hungary. Later, too, arguments for neutrality resurfaced in the wake of the democratic transition. Proponents cited Austria as the model to emulate. I and others of the new Hungarian Socialist Party, founded by the reformists, pointed out that in the case of Austria, neutrality had never been a problem because it had never been questioned by Austrian public opinion or the international community since the adoption of that country's State Treaty in 1955. By contrast, Hungary had been a member of the Warsaw Pact, and therefore envisioning a neutral state in our case would have cast doubt over the seriousness of our efforts to join the Euro-Atlantic Community. On a more practical level, as we insisted on pointing out, the cost efficiency of national defense would be much greater if we became a member of NATO. We cited the examples of Sweden and Finland, two neutral countries spending far more on their own defense than Norway, a country of comparable size and conditions but within the fold of NATO. The vast majority of the Hungarian public—in part persuaded by the Hungarian Atlantic Council, with its solid backing by intellectuals—concurred with this logic, and the issue of neutrality was taken off the agenda. Furthermore, neutrality seemed ill-advised in view of aggressive moves by Russia, including its former involvement in Afghanistan, its "near abroad" rhetoric and wrangling with the Baltics over border treaties.

Hungary's early decision to push for NATO membership now seems all the more justified in hindsight, given Russia's 2008 military action against Georgia and its 2014 attack on Ukraine, particularly its annexation of Crimea and its military backing of secession efforts mounted by Russians living in that country.

Hungary's first democratic elections in 1990 produced a three-party coalition government led by József Antall and his Hungarian Democratic Forum (MDF). From the start the new government and the three parties in opposition agreed that Hungarian foreign policy had to strive to achieve three interrelated goals. First, we had to join the Euro-Atlantic Community and its institutions, including NATO and the European Union. Second, we needed to finally establish good relations with neighboring countries, in part by putting behind us centuries of mutual wrongs and grievances. Third, we had to recognize the duty to protect the interests of Hungarian minorities living across the border and support them in their rightful pursuits and ambitions.

NATO and the European Union provided the additional incentive for Hungary and our neighbors to normalize relations by expressly and unambiguously stipulating this as a cardinal condition for the accession of former Soviet bloc countries.

I became Minister of Foreign Affairs of Hungary's second government after the régime change. That government was a coalition between the Hungarian Socialist Party and the liberal Alliance of Free Democrats. In the spring of 1996, I received an unmistakable hint from a senior national security official in the United States that we stood a good chance of becoming one of three countries to participate in the first round of NATO enlargement, provided that we signed a Basic Treaty with Romania (akin to the one already signed between Hungary and Slovakia) prior to the NATO Council session scheduled for the summer of 1997. Since we managed to fulfill this condition, we were able to join in the first round.

I remain convinced that we stayed on the right course thereafter when we chose to endorse, rather than to thwart, Romania's own ambitions of acceding to NATO. This had a beneficial influence on our ties with our neighbor.

I believe that the reigning government of Hungary, led by Viktor Orbán, would be well-advised to follow a similar path. Gestures in the service of improving bilateral relations would accomplish more on behalf of the Hungarian minority in Ukraine than obstructing Ukrainian advances to NATO. The Hungarian Socialist Party, now in the opposition, continues to urge the Orbán government to meet its obligations that come with NATO membership, including an annual 0.1 percent increase of its defense budget and participation in NATO's peace-building and peacekeeping missions. Finally, we affirm that NATO's involvement in the fight against international terrorism is essential.

The failure and ultimate fall of the Soviet model, foisted upon Hungary with its communist ideology, single-party rule, and insistence on a planned economy, did not come entirely as a surprise. The writing had been on the wall in Hungary for decades, perhaps from the start, or certainly since 1956. It was just a matter of time, especially after Hungary started to introduce the "goulash economy" in the late 1960s and to open up to the West. The democratic overhaul in the late 1980s—aided by the prevailing state of international relations—was accomplished by inside reformers who gradually turned against what had been a dead-end street from the start, in unison with the popular will, which point-blank rejected the single-party system – and by default the decade-long Soviet imposition of Communist ideology on the socio-economic and political order and the Red Army presence on Hungarian soil.

Subsequently, two referenda supporting Hungarian membership in NATO and the European Union demonstrated, without the shadow of a doubt, that the overwhelming majority of Hungarian citizens preferred to become part of the Euro-Atlantic Community. Indeed, the process of our integration within both organizations was a seamless one.

The 2010 domestic elections, however, brought an unfavorable shift in Hungary's relations with its Western Allies: the relations between the new Orbán government—now in power for nearly a decade—and the central institutions of the two organizations, as well as the majority of the member states, have deteriorated. The verbal back-and-forth with the European Union has been escalating, and in recent months even Hungary's ties with NATO have come under strain due to Orbán's edging closer to a Russia bogged down in conflict with the Ukraine, even as the latter is eyeing NATO membership.

I personally and firmly believe that creating or maintaining tensions with the two organizations of the Euro-Atlantic Community, of which Hungary is a member, is blatantly antagonistic to our very real interests. This is an untenable situation, which Orbán's government must remedy at the earliest opportunity.

Chapter 7

NATO Enlargement: Like Free Solo Climbing

András Simonyi

For my generation, joining the NATO Alliance was a historic opportunity and potentially a dream come true. But at times it seemed like free solo climbing Yosemite's "El Capitan" rockface: there were no ropes. One mistake and we could have plunged to our death. We were performing an acrobatic political act without a safety net. We did indeed break some bones. But then, looking back, that was part of the excitement, the thrill of doing something really great. Those of us who witnessed the process and the raising of the Hungarian flag at NATO Headquarters twenty years ago achieved something that cannot be repeated. We were among the first former members of the Warsaw Pact, the former adversaries, to join NATO.

It was never a given that NATO would open its door to Hungary, Poland and the Czech Republic. After the fall of communism in Central Europe in 1989 and following the collapse of the Soviet Union in 1991, "revolution" fatigue soon became apparent in many parts of the West. This was a clear case of complacency: the belief that the threats and challenges of the East-West conflict as we knew them were a thing of the past. The ghost haunting the captive nations of Eastern Europe for almost half a century was now thought to be gone. "What's the rush?" Western leaders would ask. "What's the urgency?" "Take it easy," they would suggest, as we in turn pressed forward our desire to join.

No doubt there was a constant element of wanting to appease the Russians, a silly feeling of guilt in some NATO circles for the demise of the Soviet empire, a quasi-apology for upsetting the "cozy" East-West relationship of detente. Apologizing for what? For keeping half of Europe hostage for fifty years? For causing lasting damage to the minds of generations? For suppressing democracy, freedom of thought and freedom of speech? I am forever grateful for the few supporters who initially backed our quest, who believed in us.

Still, the most compelling reason for our drive, the sense of urgency to anchor ourselves in the community of democracies, was more than just the possibility of an external threat to our new-born democracies by a resurgent Russia. Our institutions of democracy were new. The democratic instincts of our elites were weak or idealistic or both. The damage caused by forty years of "socialist experimentation turned bad" was huge, and the forces of restoration were present, strong and lurking in the shadows. No one had imagined the enormity of the tasks ahead of us as we embarked on the process to overhaul the command economy and to establish the rule of law. There was no prior experience in turning around a complete society: simultaneously converting to a market economy *and* moving from dictatorship to democracy. Back-sliding was the real worry.

I will not attempt a full exploration of Hungary's road to NATO membership. I only want to give an account of a few important moments, perhaps my favorite ones in the process. Some of them were "historic and defining," others simply funny. All of it was part of a process of making history. And history is made of the actions of people.

AWACS? What the H... is That?

It was October 1992. I had only been Deputy Chief of Mission (DCM) for NATO at the Hungarian Embassy for a few weeks when the phone rang in my make-shift office on Rue Mignot Delstanche in Brussels. It was an unforgettable call from my colleague at the U.S. NATO Mission, DCM Minister Counsellor Alexander "Sandy" Vershbow. I barely knew my way around town and had only been to NATO Headquarters once. Still I was very aware that this was a U.S.-led institution, and a call from the second-in-command at the U.S. representation was not going to be a conversation about rock and roll music (*As it turned out, it soon was about that as well!*). This was going to be important.

We discussed the increasingly tense situation in Bosnia, the issue of enforcing the U.N. decision of a no-fly zone on Serbian president Milosevic' forces, and NATO's possible role in such an operation. Sandy's question was simple and straight forward: Would Budapest allow NATO AWACS planes to cross into Hungarian airspace to execute their mission? Would Hungary permit these Allied planes to land in

Hungary in case of an emergency? He explained that he had just come out of a meeting of the North Atlantic Council: this was an ask by all 16 nations.

It was unexpected. My immediate problem was that I didn't understand the question at all. What in God's name is he talking about? What's this "avaks"? However, I understood the wider importance immediately, and considered it a real opportunity for Hungary. Already during my very short first few weeks in Brussels, I knew that the process of edging towards NATO would be hard. Only Central Europeans saw NATO membership as a far-away, beyond-the-horizon prospect. We would have to look for "accelerators," as I called our actions. We should seize every opportunity to prove our usefulness to NATO partners, to underscore that we would be net contributors to the Alliance, not just free riders.

Sandy Vershbow's call was one of those opportunities. But there were serious security considerations as well. A war raging just some hundred miles from the Hungarian border in former Yugoslavia posed a threat to our security.

I called a couple of friends in Budapest. By now well-educated and armed with the necessary expertise on "AWACS," I called on Ambassador György Granasztói, who passed Vershbow's request on to Budapest. A day later, I —not the Ambassador — received a call: it was Foreign Minister Jeszenszky.

"Prime Minister Antall wants to talk to you."

"Mister Minister, are you sure he wants to talk to me?" I asked.

"Yes, you. You talked to the Americans, right? So it's you he wants." He handed the phone to Antall.

I had met our Prime Minister a few times in the past, but would never have thought he would want to talk to me, the second secretary. Antall was straight-forward: "Tell me how this will impact our efforts to become members? Would the U.N. resolutions give us cover?" Even if I was uncertain, I gave him very confident, positive answers to both questions.

"Yes, Mr. Prime Minister. I can confirm both!" I knew this was the answer he wanted to hear.

"That's all I need to know!" he responded. "Tell the Americans that we will need a decision by Parliament, but that I support their request."

One small step for Hungary, one giant leap for NATO. This was our very first step on the long road to accession, which would be fraught with difficulties and sabotaged by opponents, inside and outside the country. But in the end, Hungary would be included in the first round of enlargement. Those who believed in Hungary's rise and that the success of our transition lay in our full integration into the West had a great ally in Prime Minister József Antall. He was very clear about his ambition to bring the country into both NATO and the European Communities, as the EU was called at that time. He insisted we push as hard as we could, and move as fast as possible. He did not care in which of the two institutions we first crossed the finish line.

Sandy Vershbow was pleasantly surprised at the quick and positive Hungarian response. This was history in the making in two ways. It would be NATO's first out-of-area operation, and it would be conducted with the help of a former member of the Warsaw Pact. It required the proper level military cooperation and coordination. It was no doubt a major decision on both sides. It would also be the beginning of a lifelong friendship between me and Sandy Vershbow, who is not just a great diplomat but, as I soon found out, a great drummer as well. Soon we would be comparing notes about our common love for rock and roll and form the first garage band in the history of NATO. We called it the Combined Joint Task Force.

It would be hard to exaggerate the impact the opportunity to support the NATO operation had on us Hungarians, even if it was short of any guarantee that NATO would assist us if Milošević retaliated by attacking Hungary or the Hungarian minority in Yugoslavia. But Antall weighed the risks and the benefits, and took a bold decision. I thought, "We are now on our way into NATO."

Unfortunately, many in the NATO orbit saw it differently. This was made very clear to me by NATO's Political Director at the time, the American John Krindler. At our first meeting, a courtesy call in early October 1992, we had a nice chat about the wonderful revolutions that had swept through Eastern Europe just three years before. Then I explained to him that I was the new diplomat at the Hungarian Embassy and my job was to get Hungary into NATO. He got agitated and visibly angry he said: "Sir, you are going too far...!"

Dead End Street

Yes, at that time we did go too far. But that was the idea. Over the next few years, at every juncture, we Hungarians went too far. We did this on purpose. We were, in a way, driving the process. We felt a sense of urgency, even a fear, that this window of opportunity to enhance our security and stabilize our weak democracy (which in the ensuing decades has proven to be a lot weaker than I thought) would not last forever. It was also a crash course in understanding the inner workings of the Alliance, including the importance of formal and informal relationships. Nevertheless, as much as we tried, it was still very difficult to navigate the corridors of NATO.

The first steps to involve us under the NATO framework came quickly in the form of the North Atlantic Cooperation Council (NACC), which first met in December 1991, and included all Central and Eastern European countries and the USSR, though ironically the first gathering took place on the very day the USSR was dissolved. This was followed in January 1994 by announcement of the Partnership for Peace (PfP) program. At the time PfP was a stark disappointment for those of us who were aiming for full membership. Elevated at first through participation in the AWACS mission and in our bilateral discussions, we soon became depressed; there was no sign that NATO was now ready to truly open its doors to new members. Instead, all of us in the post-Soviet sphere, including Russia, were offered "close cooperation." We felt betrayed. This was clearly not what we had hoped for.

In NATO sometimes small things make a difference. Personal relationships for sure. Immediately after the PfP announcement, one of my most difficult and toughest conversations took place with Robert "Bob" Beecroft, Head of the Political Section of the U.S. mission to NATO (and later U.S. Ambassador to Bosnia 2001-2004). It was at the annual Knokke-Heist meeting of NATO—a kind of retreat, where issues of the day were discussed: obviously the Bosnia humanitarian crisis, which was getting to the top of the agenda, and of course, this new Partnership for Peace. Bob wanted to know my views, "how I felt about this great new program."

As always, the conversation was agreeable, Bob Beecroft being one of the friendliest and most emphatic persons I have met, an exceptionally smart and shrewd U.S. diplomat. The discussion was between two devoted diplomats who understood what was at stake. I bluntly told him that if this exercise was meant to "appease" the eager Central Europeans, it was the wrong idea. I am sure my message surprised him.

"This is a disappointment." I said. "Not at all what we had expected. It's a dead end street and we see this as a way to sidetrack our ambitions to become members." And, I stressed, "I'd like you to convey home to Washington that some of America's best friends in Central Europe feel let down." Bob could have easily ended the conversation.

But he did not discard my criticism. On the contrary. He was generous in his response. He promised to convey my message, a promise he kept. He also told me that we, the ambitious Central Europeans - the Czechs, Poles, Hungarians—can and should turn this around (I wasn't sure about that!). He also advised me to think of ways Hungary could be useful to the Alliance. Hungary should prove every step along the way that it would be an asset, not a burden.

At the first session of the Partnership for Peace, Foreign Minister Géza Jeszenszky, with a flat face, endorsed the program.

Bumps on the Road

Unfortunately, by then, the clearly pro-Western Prime Minister Antall had passed away and our support for the AWACS operation was suddenly cast into doubt in Budapest. The new interim Prime Minster, an inexperienced former restaurant manager, Péter Boross, from the conservative MDF party, was clearly against Hungary's NATO membership and thrust hurdles on the already slow track upon which we were moving. Our support for NATO's AWACS campaign regarding Bosnia also nearly fell apart. This operation was so important to NATO that Secretary General Manfred Wörner summoned me to his office one day (again in the absence of Ambassador Ganasztói) and sent a very clear message to Budapest about "how this would be viewed by allies."

We kept the line, but barely. I received unexpected help, support and guidance from Sergio Balanzino, NATO's great Deputy Secretary General. And I would never find out why Gianni Jannuzzi, the Italian Permanent Representative, defied all rules and obligations to keep me informed about the debates and proceedings in the Council. He kept us in line and gave us tremendous encouragement. I became his adopted diplomatic son, and his Chief of Staff Stefano Pontecorvo (today Italy's ambassador in Pakistan) my new Best Friend Forever.

In the spring of 1994, there were elections in Budapest, and the political left, led by Gyula Horn, won a landslide victory. I knew Horn from the past. He was a decent man with an honest Western inclination. He was a communist turned social democrat who had been foreign minister before the Berlin Wall fell. He knew the Russians better than any other on the political stage and for that reason he supported our NATO membership. Even before the changes in 1989, he had alluded to the possibility that Hungary one day should be a member of NATO. So I was now no longer worried about any volte face at Hungary's highest levels on the NATO question. Foreign Minister László Kovács was another stalwart. Both he and Horn had been architects of the historic day when Hungary gave refuge to East Germans, ultimately allowing them to leave via Austria to West Germany in late summer and early fall of 1989, triggering a series of events that culminated in the fall of the Berlin Wall.

NATO, however, was worried. Would the rise of the left mean restoration of communism? Would it mean that the steps taken towards a market economy and democracy would now be halted? Would this mean that suddenly Hungarians would echo Russian "worries" about the dangers of NATO enlargement?

Horn and Hungary as a whole had to prove themselves. The first thing the government did, as a sign of its commitment, was to elevate the independent representative to the rank of Ambassador. I remember the Belgian colleagues freaking out: you have no status, you can't be an ambassador. But, as I had understood by now: if the United States accepts me as an ambassador, then I will be the ambassador to NATO. And Robert Hunter, the U.S. Ambassador to NATO, liked the idea.

I thus became the very first non-member Ambassador to be "accredited" to NATO. We also pushed hard for a presence at NATO Headquarters. I soon moved into the compound. I still have a piece from the ribbon-cutting ceremony, signed by Minister Kovács and Secretary General Javier Solana.

In 1995, an informal defense ministerial was held where a Study on NATO Enlargement was discussed. It stated that nations aspiring to join the Alliance were expected to respect the values of the North Atlantic Treaty, and to meet certain political, economic and military criteria. It was as if the study had been tailor-made for Hungary (criteria mostly abandoned since!). These criteria included: a functioning democratic political system based on a market economy and checks and balances; fair treatment of minority populations; a commitment to resolve conflicts peacefully; an ability and willingness to make a military contribution to NATO operations; and a commitment to democratic civil-military relations and institutions. I was ecstatic. This was the signal I had been waiting for. Our moment had arrived. I met my friend Hans Hækkerup, the Danish Defense Minister, in Copenhagen. He told me of the discussions around the first "batch" of possible new members. Then came the cold shower: Hungary is not in the first group, he said, only Poland and the Czechs.

That was devastating news. I immediately discussed this with Foreign Minister Kovács. We agreed on the need to do whatever it took to be in the first round. Horn was totally behind us. Whatever we could come up with. He called me in person to discuss, and pressed hard for a plan. But for the moment there was no plan.

The Opportunity

This is not the place to describe the horrors of the Bosnian genocide, and in no way would I want to suggest that we were cynical about that terrible war and all its victims, and that our position was driven by sheer interest in getting to NATO membership. But we now knew, however, that there was considerable skepticism about Hungary in Washington and in most allied capitals. Nevertheless, I also knew that, given the opportunity, we would be able to prove ourselves. One way or another we would catch up with the Poles and the Czechs. It would just be a matter of time when that opportunity would present itself.

And such an opportunity came after the signing of the Dayton accords on November 21, 1995.

I had become friends with General Jeremy McKenzie, the Deputy SACEUR, a fine British soldier. We had been talking a lot and also discussed the role for NATO in implementing the Dayton accords. He had this idea, very early on, that Hungary could play a significant role once the peace agreement was signed, given its geographical location and the AWACS experience. He made it clear to me that if "we were ever asked to provide support" we should say yes. He said this would give Hungary that long-awaited special opportunity.

Jeremy was right. When U.S. Ambassador Robert Hunter invited me to his office to ask if Hungary would be ready and able to host U.S. troops as part of the Implementation Force (IFOR) for Bosnia-Herzegovina, I did not blink. I asked him if a response the next day would be soon enough. I also told him that I would do my best to secure a positive response from Budapest. I was confident we would do so, since I had already discussed this possibility with Kovács, and he too was enthusiastic (I knew very little about the fight he had on the issue with our arch-conservative defense minister). I knew for sure this was going to be a game changer: U.S. troops stationed on Hungarian soil, American soldiers on the ground in the former Warsaw Pact.

"Tell us how we can help, Mr. Ambassador," I told Hunter a day later. He smiled and said "I knew Hungary would not disappoint!"

The next thing I knew I was on a plane to Hungary with Jeremy McKenzie. The Hungarian military, conservative by definition, was not ready. At the talks where the Chief of Staff politely explained at length the details of Hungary's military reforms, McKenzie suddenly asked if there was a map of Hungary "somewhere" at the Ministry. The hosts were curious. Why would the DSACEUR want a map? They brought out the map. Jeremy pointed at the one base which would eventually become the site of the IFOR base: Taszár.

"This is the base I want to visit," he exclaimed.

The Hungarian generals were furious. They did not want NATO to take over Taszár. They thought it was a set-up, orchestrated by me. Which was of course true. But they did not like civilians like me to interfere. At that time they still did not understand the concept of political leadership and civilian control. But Jeremy's insistence bore fruit. The next day we flew to Taszár.

Thus started one of the truly great military operations, a breakthrough in the cooperation between NATO and aspiring non-member nations. It was a huge political, military and logistical challenge. It would be a success. We made history. The whole episode changed the chemistry between Hungary and NATO. Taszár turned out to be much more than just another element in our quest for membership. It was also a statement about the relationship between Americans and Hungarians. It was something of which we could be proud. NATO fulfilled its historic mission to stabilize Bosnia, and my country performed well with NATO. The people of Taszár proved to be fantastic hosts to U.S. troops.

Years later, as ambassador to the United States, I was on my way from Cleveland to speak at the Rock & Roll Hall of Fame. My driver exceeded the speed limit and a morose trooper flagged him down. The trooper was angry. The driver explained that his passenger was the Hungarian ambassador. The officer walked over to my side of the car, asked me to pull down the window, saluted and said the following, smiling: "Sir, a few years ago I served in the Army and I was posted to the town of Taszár. I want to thank you and your countrymen for your kind hospitality. Would you please ask your driver to drive safely!?" And he escorted us all the way to the Pennsylvania border. What are the odds?!

We made it to the first round of those to walk through NATO's door. At the 1997 Madrid summit, the Poles, the Czechs and the Hungarians were invited to start accession talks. By that time, we had another great ally in the U.S. administration: Madeleine Albright, who of all the allied foreign ministers best understood our difficulties and the importance—for us—of NATO enlargement. Sandy Vershbow was now Ambassador and Permanent Representative to the North Atlantic Council. It was an uplifting moment when President Clinton in a private conversation thanked Hungary for its support to the U.S. troops in Bosnia.

Rather than detailing the agenda items, and the nitty-gritty, of the two-year accession process, I want to recall a few more memorable moments. When we were asked to provide details of our armed forces and military spending and about the contributions we would make to the alliance, I was approached by the ambassador of one of the smaller founding members. He told me that we needn't worry too much about the numbers: he would show us how to "make them look bigger than they actually are." What he really meant was that they did not carry their fair share of the burden, but that they knew how to cook the books. I would remember this conversation in the future whenever the debate about burden-sharing heated up again and again over the next twenty years.

I also recall conversations about the importance of democratic credentials of member states. It was assumed that the new members would be firmly-rooted liberal democracies, with a guarantee for the rule of law, a clear separation of powers and a multiparty system. I was less optimistic. At a certain point I recall some talk about the introduction of safeguards in case there would ever be any backsliding in the democratic credentials in new member states. Even the idea of an "expulsion clause" was discussed, to have a mechanism in place should a new member backslide on its commitments. Only a few of us took the position that perhaps that wasn't such a bad idea. Unfortunately, the expulsion clause was deemed unnecessary. I was no prophet, but we knew our history.

Strawberry Fields Forever

In 1998 there were elections in Hungary. The leader of the Young Liberals, Viktor Orbán, won and became prime minister. We would soon celebrate our membership in NATO. We would also prepare for war. The situation south of the border was getting increasingly tense, and Europe once again was looking on helplessly as Serbian leader Slobodan Milosevic was creating yet again a humanitarian crisis, this time in Kosovo. So even as we were rejoicing over the historic moment of membership, we had to prepare for the possibility of a hot war, now as members of NATO.

On March 19 1999, I stood by Prime Minister Viktor Orbán as the red, white and green Hungarian flag was raised at NATO Headquarters. I have no reason to doubt his honesty when he spoke about the Alliance being the key to Hungary's future. His eventual political volte-face, his turning away from the principles and values enshrined in the Treaty, his appeasing approach towards Russia, was nowhere to be seen, even in traces. For Horn and Kovács, who had done so much to get there, 1999 was a bittersweet moment: they were not invited to the ceremony. I felt bad about that. I believe in broad bipartisan cooperation across party lines on basic issues pertaining to the security and progress of our country. The achievement of membership simply fell into Orbán's lap. He had done very little to get us there.

On March 24, 1999, the bombardment of Yugoslavia began. I remember a short conversation on the secure NATO line with Orbán. I told him something that perhaps was a bit brash: "We will start bombing tomorrow. I hope your hand will not shake when you press the button" (meaning ordering the high alert of the Hungarian Armed Forces).

He responded firmly: "It won't." Our baptism by fire began.

No one could have imagined that we would join an Alliance, created to avoid war, and that then essentially on day one we'd find ourselves as NATO members actually going to war. But that's what it was. War. In a neighboring country. No other member state had to endure the risks that Hungary had in those days. To his credit Orbán stood firm, even in the face of Russian threats. The population, too, was remarkably solid in its support of the government. Even as novices, we did not take decisions lightly, at times fighting hard to push back unreasonable U.S. military demands. But we understood our obligation as new members to make sure we would not get in the way of a successful operation. We were not immune to the dangers to our citizens and in particular the Hungarian minority in Serbia. They could have become targets not of a NATO attack but of Serbian retaliation. We had to step into the role of a responsible member overnight. But we were ready—also to take a strong stance against Russian efforts to undermine NATO.

My favorite anecdote from those days is one I kept to myself for twenty years. As the operation was underway, I received a call from Foreign Minster János Martonyi.

"We've got a problem" he said.

"What is that János?" I inquired.

"It's strawberry season. The Hungarians in Vojvodina are out picking strawberries. They cannot be hit. Tell NATO that we'll send them the coordinates where the strawberry fields are."

I called DSACEUR General Dieter Stöckmann and presented the request.

"No big deal, Hungary has done enough. Send me the coordinates, András. Tell the Minister that his Hungarians will be fine. Send me some nice strawberries."

Strawberry Fields Forever.

Warning Signs on the Road Ahead

When in 2000 Vladimir Putin emerged as the "compromise" successor to Boris Yeltsin, we Hungarians, the Poles, and the Czechs were among the few who saw this as a writing on the wall that the cozy, even if somewhat chaotic, decade of transition in Eastern Europe was now over. I recall a conversation with NATO Secretary General George Robertson about my worries. I told him that Putin's arrival meant "the old guard" was back. He told me that like all Hungarians I worried too much, and that I should not judge Putin on the basis of our experience with Russia in the past. I have enormous respect for George Robertson, he was a great Secretary General, but I did not agree with him.

I proved to be right. Yeltsin's successors, heirs to the Russian tradition of disruption, embodied an almost genetically-coded aversion to the West, and an anger (wrapped in a sense of humiliation) for losing the Cold War. Those feelings were all there. They were far from gone. We had felt the Russians breathing down our neck throughout the accession process. And we had also seen that some allies would go weak in their knees at the opposition expressed by the Kremlin to our membership. It was only a matter of time when Russia would flex its muscles again. Twenty years ago, Vladimir Putin might have seemed to some like a "nobody," a weak outsider. But having a deep understanding of Russia, we were uncomfortable already then.

When I left NATO in 2001, the Alliance was in great shape. I had no doubt that our accession was the best thing that ever happened to us, maybe in a thousand years. Regrettably, the developments some ten years later were less encouraging. But that story is for someone else to tell.

Chapter 8

Václav Havel and NATO:
Lessons of Leadership for the Atlantic Alliance

Jan Havránek & Jan Jireš

In 2019 the North Atlantic Treaty Organization (NATO) celebrates its seventieth anniversary and twenty years since its first post-Cold War enlargement. As both sides of the Atlantic commemorate these historical achievements, NATO faces challenges to its security, cohesion and credibility.

Since 2014, NATO has been confronted with a significantly deteriorated security environment, marked by Russia's aggression in Ukraine and continued instability in Europe's southern neighborhood. In response, the Alliance has implemented the biggest reinforcement of its collective defense posture since 1989 and has recommitted to the fight against terrorism.

This adaptation has made NATO safer, but the world remains a dangerous place. Russia continues to disregard international law and treaties. It is testing NATO's unity and resolve, employing hybrid techniques against its neighbors and the Alliance itself. It is engaging in cyber-attacks against allies and interfering in their democratic processes. Moscow has continued its military build-up and has explicitly called NATO an "enemy."

In Europe's southern neighborhood there is little prospect for stability despite NATO's efforts at counter-terrorism, capacity building and regional partnerships. China is emerging as a strategic competitor to the United States and Europe. Diplomacy, commerce, and innovation, but also conflict, are happening in cyber-space.

Internally, NATO's credibility is under stress. Traditional gaps in threat perception persist among NATO allies. The transatlantic link, NATO's bedrock, is pressured by (not so) latent anti-Europeanism and anti-Americanism and occasional heated rhetoric by political leaders. A growing capability and technology gap between the United States and Europe, and a lack of sufficient defense spending on the part of most European allies (well below NATO's agreed benchmark of 2% of GDP) are sources of friction and frustration. The renaissance of EU's defense dimension brings a powerful element of misunderstanding and potential rifts to NATO. Meanwhile, the Alliance is struggling to clearly articulate its role in the Middle East and North Africa and its approach to the partner countries in general. NATO continues to expand (with North Macedonia in line to become its 30th member soon) but there are no clear accession timelines for any other aspirant countries (Bosnia and Herzegovina, Georgia and Ukraine).

These trends raise fundamental questions pertaining to NATO's very existence: is NATO fit for purpose to address the challenges of today? Is it still the relevant venue for America and Europe to work together? What can be done to rectify these problems and ensure that NATO remains the glue of the West?

We believe the answer can be found in the analysis of NATO's reinvention after 1989. Since 2014, the new cycle of NATO adaptation has happened "on the go" without much historical reflection. It might, therefore, be useful to analyze the previous major transformative period, which took place mainly in the 1990s.

Specifically, we will examine the relevance of former Czech President Václav Havel's policies and philosophy. Democratization and enlargement were central pieces of NATO's transformation process, and Havel was their key proponent. He was not alone in this quest, of course. but he was one of the most eloquent, widely respected and convincing protagonists. Through his persistence, Havel managed to give NATO enlargement almost spiritual meaning. His endeavors culminated in 2002 at NATO's summit in Prague, where he facilitated the largest wave of enlargement in NATO's history.

We acknowledge the visions put forward by other Western and Central European policy makers, including George H. W. Bush, Bill Clinton, Madeleine Albright, Volker Rühe, Lech Wałęsa and József Antall. The emergence of President Havel's leadership in this debate is a particularly fascinating phenomenon, and one that has not been fully appreciated. After exploring Havel's views on the transatlantic Alliance and the West, we shall present some ideas as to which lessons NATO can draw from these views today.

*   *   *

With the end of the Cold War, NATO searched for a new purpose and identity within a changing European security order. This search for legitimacy emerged from the fog of geopolitical uncertainty between 1989 and 1992 and against the backdrop of two major geopolitical changes: the re-establishment of German unity and the break-up of the Soviet Union. The debate on NATO's future revolved around a number of scenarios, ranging from the dissolution of the Alliance (alongside the Warsaw Pact) to the conversion of the Alliance into a pan-European security organization, as Havel initially suggested, that could include Russia.[1]

Over the course of the year 1990, the countries of Central Europe joined their Western counterparts in their quest for maintaining NATO beyond the Cold War. In June 1990, NATO invited leaders of the post-Communist countries to visit and establish liaison offices at its headquarters, confirming the end of an era of confrontation. Václav Havel was the first head of state from Central and Eastern Europe to take up the call, visiting NATO HQ in March 1991 and voicing his support for Alliance's preservation.[2]

For many leaders, including Havel, the Spring of Europe was at its height. Germany was now reunited and the Warsaw Pact had just agreed to dissolve itself. Soviet troops were withdrawing from the territories of the former Soviet satellite states. The Helsinki Process had been revived through the Charter of Paris.

By the summer of 1991, however, high hopes had been replaced by anxieties. Separatist and nationalistic tendencies around the former Eastern Bloc, the violent breakup of Yugoslavia, and the looming collapse of the Soviet Union demonstrated that there would be no "end of history."

The August 1991 coup attempt in Moscow was the final drop in Václav Havel's contemplation on NATO's relevance. It was utterly clear that Europe needed NATO as a stabilizing factor, and Havel was from then on determined to seek his country's membership in the Alliance.[3]

Initially, it seemed like an impossible mission. The scepticism of opening NATO to new members carried over from the Bush to the

Clinton administration. As late as spring of 1993, nobody in the United States was seriously considering enlargement.[4]

Havel's frequent public praise for the Alliance as a body contributing to the security of both its members and non-members, however, added a layer of legitimacy to the debate on NATO's continued existence and its potential expansion. His international reputation, combined with his insistence that the Alliance was fundamentally beneficial to European security and, therefore, in the interest of everyone, even the countries outside of it, helped to buttress the case for adapting and reinventing it.[5]

In April 1993, when Václav Havel, Lech Wałęsa and Árpád Göncz persuaded President Bill Clinton at the opening of the Holocaust Memorial Museum to start considering NATO expansion to Central Europe, the Alliance's survival as a physical institution was no longer in question. However, there was a considerable and growing risk that, without an updated purpose responding to the new realities of and challenges to Euro-Atlantic security, it would gradually lapse into irrelevance and, as a consequence, lose support of both the American public and its elected representatives. A NATO that continued to exist formally but had been hollowed out would then be increasingly unable to provide the vital institutional framework for the West as a political community.[6]

This gloomy scenario was something that both President Clinton and his Central European counterparts wanted to prevent. For Havel in particular, seeking NATO membership was not primarily about the narrow national interest of his "rather insignificant country" but about contributing to the security, stability and general well-being of Europe and the West as a whole.[7] In line with his lifelong devotion to the principle of individual responsibility for the broader world, he believed it was his and the Czech Republic's obligation to facilitate the establishment of a new security order benefiting the entire continent and beyond. Everyone was to be a responsible stakeholder in the future of Europe, the West and the humanity: "As I have said many times, if the West does not stabilize the East, the East will destabilize the West."[8]

Clinton's solution for saving NATO's relevance was to go "out of area"—both in the sense of enlarging the Alliance and moving to engage in peace-enforcement and stabilization operations beyond its territory. This formed the basis of the "new transatlantic bargain."[9] President Havel embraced this approach as he believed in the necessity of both elements. His April 1993 conversations with Clinton in Washington were not just about pitching NATO membership but, in equal measure, about convincing the U.S. president to intervene in Bosnia to stop the ethnic violence.[10]

The inception of the Partnership for Peace (PfP) and the "anatomy of the decision" to enlarge are well documented in literature and in this volume.[11] Václav Havel's leadership on NATO continued after March 1999. The same month that the Czech Republic, Hungary and Poland joined the Alliance, NATO launched a military operation without U.N. authorization against Slobodan Milošević's rump Yugoslavia to prevent further violence in Kosovo.

For new members like the Czech Republic and its leadership, the Kosovo campaign was "baptism by fire."[12] Václav Havel was one of very few Czech politicians who supported the operation; others, including in the cabinet, were reluctant if not openly against. To Havel, however, the air campaign made sense. In addition to the principle of allied solidarity, Havel emphasized the humanitarian aspect of the intervention:

> If it is possible to say about a war that it is ethical (...) it is true of this war. [The Alliance] is fighting in the name of human interest for the fate of other human beings. It is fighting because decent people cannot sit back and watch systematic, state directed massacres of other people. (...) This war gives human rights precedence over the rights of states. (...) The Alliance has not acted out of licence, aggressiveness or disrespect for international law. On the contrary, it has acted out of respect for the law, for the law that ranks higher than the protection of the sovereignty of states. It has acted out of respect for the rights of humanity, as they are articulated by our conscience as well as by other instruments of international law.[13]

His view of the Kosovo campaign was by no means utilitarian. Rather, it was an expression of his principled opposition to appeasing evil.

Havel's stellar moment came in 2002, when Prague hosted the first NATO summit behind the former Iron Curtain. The summit, short before the end of his tenure as president, was the culmination of his NATO efforts. Havel did not stop advocating for further NATO enlargement once his own country joined. Already in April 1999, when addressing the U.S. Congress, he named Slovakia, Slovenia, Romania, Bulgaria and the three Baltic countries as potential new members.[14] In Prague in 2002, NATO invited these seven countries to become members in the largest wave of enlargement in its history. It was this decision that solidified NATO's Open Door policy as we know it today.

But merely one year after the September 11 terrorist attacks, Prague was equally adamant about the need for NATO to transform to face new threats. Earlier that year, NATO and Russia had established the NATO-Russia Council, marking a new era of cooperation in Europe. For Václav Havel, the mission he set out in the early 1990s was accomplished.

*   *   *

Václav Havel was among the leaders who saw the historic opportunity to "do for Europe's East what NATO had helped achieve for Europe's West" after the Second World War, namely consolidate democracy, economic and political integration, de-nationalize defense, and make war unthinkable.[15] Their aim was to safeguard NATO's continued existence through transforming its mission, ultimately through extension of its membership.

Havel spent much time and effort thinking about NATO, its purpose and its mission, as demonstrated in a number of his essays, speeches, interviews and newspaper articles. He never approached NATO as a utilitarian military alliance but always as something much bigger, broader and more important.

He identified several important roles of NATO that stay relevant today. First, NATO as an institutional embodiment of the West, and a political, and even spiritual, community based on shared values. Second, NATO representing a distinct "civilization" that must be aware of the geographical limits of its expansion. Third, the Alliance as an indispensable vehicle for continued transatlantic cooperation and for American engagement in European affairs. Fourth, the West and NATO as promoters of international norms, particularly in the area of human rights. And finally, NATO as a community of friends based on mutual trust and a strong sense of responsible leadership.

The West as a spiritual community based on shared values

Havel regarded NATO as something more than just a practical military instrument to protect a piece of territory. For him, NATO was a tangible embodiment of the Western community of values.[16] He and his Central European colleagues were not ashamed of praising the virtues of Western values defined, in a rather conservative fashion, as an amalgamation of classical philosophy and law, Christian spiritual heritage and Enlightenment rationality. NATO membership was to be, among other things, a badge of honor confirming Central Europe's "return" to Western values after a long period of forced separation.[17]

In Havel's mind, the primary reason for Central Europe's membership in NATO was, therefore, not pragmatic geostrategy but the fact that the region now shared the allied countries' values and aspired to establish democratic political systems. Not admitting them as members would not only be unjust and unfair, it would also be self-defeating: rejecting newly democratic countries eager to join would undermine NATO's legitimacy as representative and protector of the Euro-Atlantic community of democratic nations. As he remarked to Allied foreign ministers at the NATO Headquarters in March 1991:

> We feel that an alliance of countries united by a commitment to the ideal of freedom and democracy should not remain permanently closed to neighboring countries which are pursuing the same goals. History has taught us that certain values are indivisible; if they are threatened in one place, they are directly or indirectly threatened everywhere.[18]

Havel believed the West was morally responsible for the fate of post-communist countries precisely because it had waged (and won) the Cold War: "From [Western support for democrats in the Soviet Bloc] arises a great responsibility for the West. It cannot be indifferent to what is happening in the countries which, constantly encouraged by the Western democracies, have finally shaken off the totalitarian system."[19]

Three years later, at the time when Central Europeans were anxious about what they believed to be the sluggish progress of the NATO enlargement process, and when the Bosnian war was still raging, Havel wrote, rather angrily, that Western failure to create a new stable and durable order in Europe would "demonstrate that the democratic West has lost its ability realistically to foster and cultivate the values it has always proclaimed and undertaken to safeguard and to which end it has built its arsenal of weapons. Such as state of affairs would be far more than just a crisis of the East; it would also be a crisis of the West, a crisis of democracy, a crisis of Euro-American civilization itself."[20]

Havel was not ignorant of NATO's and the West's fair share of internal problems and challenges. After all, his lifelong oeuvre as playwright and essayist focused on the universal issues of the corruption of power, the dehumanizing impact of modern technology, the alienating nature of bureaucratic structures, and the resulting loss of human identity. His response to this modern human condition was an everyday quest for authenticity, responsibility and "living in truth."[21]

A number of lessons for today's NATO can be derived from these simple rules. First, reducing relationships among allies to mere transactionalism is an anathema to how Havel saw the Alliance. Transactionalism does not provide sufficient basis for NATO's long-term viability and relevance. What is needed is a clear sense of purpose, rooted in a set of values and principles that extend beyond today—and beyond bookkeeping.[22]

Second, NATO being a community of nations based on common Western values meant that it could play an important role in consolidating Central Europe's newly established democratic political systems. Havel regarded the conditionality required to achieve membership as one of key benefits of the enlargement process, to the point of actually wishing for a stricter enforcement of membership criteria.[23]

In the same vein, Havel expected that NATO and other multilateral Western institutions would keep playing an active role in further cultivating new members' democratic systems as well as their sense of responsibility. He would thus expect a stronger effort by both NATO and the EU to mitigate democratic backsliding in their member countries.

Unlike the EU, NATO does not have formal instruments to exert pressure on its members to change their policies. This stems from the fact that the Alliance is a strictly intergovernmental organization based on the principle of consensus, with each ally holding a veto power over every decision. Thus, the disciplinary power that works well before accession diminishes once membership is gained.

On the other hand, NATO possesses informal mechanisms to discipline its members. First, there is peer pressure, exercised first and foremost by the United States as the chief contributor of military assets needed for Alliance's deterrence and defense. Second, the very nature of NATO's collective defense "guarantees" requires that allies behave themselves and demonstrate adherence to NATO's core values. The language of Article 5 of the North Atlantic Treaty is deliberately vague and, for all intents and purposes, the execution of a collective defense operation depends on the political will of Allied governments at the given moment. This means that all NATO members must systematically work to maximize other allies' motivation and goodwill to come to their assistance when subjected to an attack. Thus, it can be argued that allies grossly disrespecting Alliance values in times of peace invite a breach of allied solidarity in times of crisis and war.

From Havel's perspective, there is just one way to make these corrective mechanisms work: responsible leadership on the part of all Allied countries that puts collective good over narrow political interests and stems from the urge to live an "authentic" life based on the identity of one's moral impulses, words and deeds.

NATO as a distinct "civilization"

The polarization of Western societies that has become a norm over the past decade flattens Western political discourse to the point of meaninglessness and reduces policy options to an artificial binary choice between progressivist transnationalism and protectionist nativism. Our discursive landscape used to be much richer. Debates were less about two extremes and more about fifty shades of grey. Václav Havel's thinking represented one such shade of nuance.

On the one hand, Havel's persistent criticism of ethnic nationalism, his principled internationalism and his advocacy of humanitarian intervention turned him into a hate figure for nativists in his own country and abroad. On the other hand, his philosophy included a number of rather conservative elements that would make some of his progressivist admirers blush.[24]

These two approaches mix nicely in Havel's concept of "home" (*domov*). He regarded the sense of belonging to be indispensable for the true expression of one's identity and authenticity. This applied to him personally, too. He never considered himself a cosmopolitan in the conventional sense and his identity as a Czech, shaped by his country's history and intellectual traditions, was a crucial factor in developing his worldview and his policies. In other words, Havel was far from rejecting the notion of national identity or denying its importance.[25]

His idea of belonging to a "home," however, was much more complex and inclusive than that of conventional ethnic nationalists. For him, the individual was at the center of a structure consisting of concentric layers, each adding an element to one's overall identity. Ultimately, all these layers were important to one's fullness of being. They included family, profession, an immediate social circle, national community and language, Europe, Western civilization, and, eventually, humankind.[26]

National identity is thus important but not exclusive, since it always is, or should be, complemented by all those other layers, and should not be exerted in a hypertrophied way that suppresses them. At the same time, this approach means that Havel saw culturally and historically defined civilizations, broadly in the Huntingtonian sense, as important frameworks for respective national identities, providing them with coherent value systems.[27]

This is how he perceived the West and NATO. He gradually came to see the Alliance as an institutional expression of Western civilization. This meant that Russia could not become a member, due to obvious geostrategic reasons and, equally importantly, because of the fundamental incompatibility of Western and Russian values. This conviction of his only grew stronger as Russia's democratization faltered and ultimately stalled, and as the country reverted to some of the traditional patterns of behavior inherited from its imperial and Soviet past.[28]

This does not mean that Havel regarded Western civilization to be perfect. Rather the opposite was the case. From the very beginning of his intellectual endeavor, he had critically reflected upon Western modernity and the unintended (and sometimes intended) negative consequences of some of its key features for both individuals and the environment, leading to the loss of authenticity in life and damage to the cherished idea of "home."[29] After all, he regarded the communist regimes of Eastern Europe to be just more extreme, brutal and primitive versions of Western modernity, or simply its uglier siblings.[30] In this,

Havel followed in the footsteps of such complex thinkers as Reinhold Niebuhr (whom he most probably never read) and, for that matter, George Orwell.

From the notion of civilization as an element of one's "home" stemmed Havel's clear idea of NATO as a political community of nations bound by shared values and framed by a shared cultural outlook. This means NATO should not be regarded as an all-inclusive, universal organization. It was to remain a fundamentally Western body with a clear sense of where its borders should be. As he argued,

> Historical experience shows that vague, indistinct or disputed frontiers are one of the most frequent causes of wars. Every political entity must know where its territory begins and where it ends. (...) Where is [NATO's] frontier then? In my personal opinion, its starts with the border between Russia and the Baltic States and follows the Russo-Belarusian and Russo-Ukrainian border down to the Black Sea. This is absolutely obvious from the map, and it has more or less historical and cultural basis too.[31]

For Havel, civilization was a precious component of one's identity, and NATO was to be an institutional framework of the Western civilization, providing it with clear borders.[32] At the same time, Havel's view of civilization was clearly not as culturally deterministic as that of Huntington. It was Russia's political tradition hampering democratization and its imperial idea that were incompatible with NATO membership, not its orthodox religious affiliation per se.

Moreover, at no point in his life was Havel a Russophobe. As his biographer observes, he actually never developed a "concept of the enemy." Not even Communist Czechoslovakia's authorities who jailed him unjustly were "enemies" in his view. Rather, he tried to analyze their motivations and understand them.[33] Likewise, he did not hate Russians and often pleaded for a cooperative relationship between the West and Russia.[34]

Indispensability of transatlantic cooperation

For Havel, the fact that NATO was a transatlantic institution (or rather *the* transatlantic institution) was by far its most appealing feature. He wholeheartedly subscribed to the notion that the Alliance's chief purpose was to "keep the Americans in." The crucial challenge of the 1990s was how to secure this goal in the long run.

A part of the answer was to be, of course, the enlargement and the new sense of purpose it would generate for NATO. This was precisely the area where Central Europeans could contribute to the future relevance if not survival of the Alliance: not primarily through their limited defence capacities but by playing a role of responsible stakeholders in Western security architecture and by providing the U.S. administration with the opportunity to transform the Alliance to make it relevant for the new era.[35]

Havel's strong Atlanticism was obviously driven by a mix of motivations, both practical and philosophical. As for the practical side, he understood perfectly well that the United States was the only relevant actor capable of and willing to invest in the stability and security of Europe through its continued leadership in NATO. As he put it, "In the 20th century, it was not just Europe that paid the price for American isolationism: America itself paid a price. The less it committed itself at the beginning of European conflagrations, the greater the sacrifices it had to make at the end of such conflicts."[36] After all, as Ron Asmus and Alexandr Vondra noted, if there was one largely positive historical experience that Central Europe has in common, it has been with the United States.[37]

When it came to his philosophical motivations, the starting point is the fact that he was born and raised in a deeply Atlanticist cultural and political milieu, whose underlying tenets he retained throughout his life. The Havels were among the most prominent families in interwar Czechoslovakia, which, for all intents and purposes, was a creation of American Wilsonianism. Its democratic public philosophy, including some of its constitutional principles, was inspired by American Jeffersonianism. This came about, of course, mainly thanks to President Tomáš Garrigue Masaryk, who adopted his American wife's Unitarian faith and made an unashamedly Jeffersonian case for Czechoslovak independence during the First World War.[38]

The Havel family was devoted to Masaryk and shared his public philosophy, including his admiration for the United States and the American values of republican virtues and civic responsibility. In a sense,

Masaryk and the Havels were Atlanticists long before this concept was invented as a practical political doctrine in the 1940s.

Havel, though aware of great-power interests, identified a powerful streak of selflessness and idealism in American foreign policy, generally conducive to the well-being of smaller European nations. As in earlier periods, in the 1990s the United States could and would, through its deep political and military engagement in European affairs, contribute to the taming of European powers' darker impulses, or so Havel believed. While Havel and other Central European Atlanticists fully trusted the United States, they were at least occasionally wary of their fellow Europeans.[39]

Havel's approach to the transatlantic link was again heavily civilizational, informed by his understanding of Western culture and history. As he put it in 1991,

> Europe is deeply bound, through shared civilization, with North America, its younger brother. Three times throughout the twentieth century, America saved Europe from tyranny; three times it helped liberty and democracy prevail in Europe. It cannot keep saving Europe forever (…), however, it is so essentially linked to it— through its culture, values and interests—that not even Europe's integration and certain emancipation should break this natural bond. To the contrary, the peaceful linkage of these two continents could be of the principal stabilizing factors in the global context.[40]

For all these reasons, the transatlantic bond was supremely precious to Havel. He regarded it as a value in itself and worth preserving at considerable cost, as exemplified by his support for the 2003 invasion of Iraq, which tainted his reputation in the eyes of the war's opponents in both the United States and Europe. He was aware, however, that a value-based and durable transatlantic bond was conditioned upon practically demonstrated responsibility of all allies and the unity of their words and their deeds.

The West as a promoter of international human rights norms

When it came to NATO's preservation and transformation in the 1990s, Havel never focused solely on the issue of enlargement. Above all, he strongly believed that a crucial purpose of the Alliance was to be an international norm entrepreneur, particularly in the area of human rights. That is why he invested as much effort in convincing President Clinton to intervene in Bosnia as he did to put NATO enlargement on his policy agenda.

Havel's motivation to embrace humanitarian interventionism was deeply rooted in both Czechoslovakia's history and its intellectual traditions. "Munich" in particular provided a lesson in the sense of both moral unacceptability and practical foolishness of trying to appease evil. As he declared in March 1993, "We must accept our own share of responsibility for peace and justice in Europe. As people who once became the victims of a shameful concession to a bully in Munich, we must know even better than others that there must not be concessions made to evil."[41]

Michael Žantovský argues that this is the core belief of the "Havel Doctrine" of humanitarian intervention understood as "shared responsibility of people to stand up to evil (...) and the unacceptability of appeasement, inaction or indifference in the face of evil."[42]

At the same time, Havel was acutely aware of humanitarian intervention's moral and practical difficulties. Contrary to his contemporary reputation in some circles as either naïve do-gooder or cynical facilitator of American imperialism, he frequently spoke of the pitfalls of humanitarian intervention: "One must constantly and carefully scrutinize such humanistic arguments to determine that it is not a pretty façade concealing far less respectable interests."[43] He did not shy away from juxtaposing the Czechoslovak experiences of 1938 and 1968. While "Munich" led him to the conclusion that evil must be resisted at the very beginning, the suppression of the "Prague Spring" alerted him to the need to consider thoroughly the declared motives for an intervention and to "ask ourselves (...) whether it is not some version of the fraternal assistance."[44]

Havel's emphasis on NATO's role (and, indeed, its indispensability) in preventing or ending gross violation of human rights again illustrates his ambitious view of the Alliance's mission. He did not want the Czech Republic and other Central European countries to join a mere collective defence pact. Just as he expected responsibility for the world from individuals and from countries, he expected it from NATO as well.

"Alliance" as a community based on trust and responsibility

As we have established, "responsibility" was a key element of Havel's lifelong moral outlook, closely linked to the concepts of "identity" and "authenticity," and a prerequisite for "living in truth" in the sense of unity of conscience, words and deeds.[45]

In his own case, this was exemplified not only by his principled opposition to Czechoslovak communist authorities in the 1970s and 1980s to the point of sacrificing his health and even risking his life. In his presidential career he also showed remarkable courage and leadership by becoming an early advocate of causes not entirely uncontroversial.[46] Dissolving the Warsaw Pact and pressing NATO to open up to the East are obvious examples but there are many more: his early support for German reunification, meeting the Dalai Lama, pushing for U.S. military interventions in the Balkans, and promoting Russia's democratization.

His emphasis on assuming responsibility led him to advocate for an active role of Czechoslovakia and the Czech Republic in international security. To gain membership in the Alliance, his country was to be a shining example of mature, responsible behavior. In other words, Central Europe was to be security provider and not just security consumer.[47] An early example of this approach was Czechoslovakia's military contribution to Operation Desert Storm and, later, the Czech Republic's significant military deployments in peacekeeping missions in Croatia and Bosnia.

In 1991, Havel explained this attitude explicitly:

> This is why we have a heightened sense of obligation to Europe. Our wish to become a NATO member, therefore, concerns more than international security guarantees, it grows out of a desire to shoulder some responsibility for the general state of affairs on our continent. We don't want to take without giving. (...) Too often, we have had direct experience of where indifference to the fate of others can lead, and we are determined not to succumb to that kind of indifference ourselves.[48]

Needless to say, such a principled stance also bore practical fruits in helping the Clinton Administration make a more credible case for

NATO enlargement. By making practical contributions to international security and demonstrating their sense of responsibility, the Central Europeans could counter accusations that by seeking NATO membership "all they wanted was a security umbrella for a rainy day with the Russians."[49]

This emphasis on the need of his own country being responsible and mature stemmed from Havel's firm belief that even the smallest countries have agency in international affairs, precisely because if they are courageous and authentic they can exert moral and thus also political influence. Again, this notion stemmed from Havel's understanding of Czechoslovakia's history and his refusal to see it as a mere victim of foreign powers but as an actor at least partially responsible for the bad things that happened to it.[50]

Havel's thinking on the concept of responsibility, however, went further. His ultimate ambition, at least in the early 1990s, was to turn his own country into a sort of "spiritual state" and a model to follow not only by fellow post-communist countries in Central and Eastern Europe but other parts of the worlds as well. Very much in the Masarykian tradition, he regarded Czechoslovakia/Czech Republic as a "project" rather than a mere piece of territory.[51]

Of course, such a view bears a close resemblance to the American self-image going back to the Pilgrim Fathers. This thinking was adopted and reshaped by Masaryk and his disciples as early as in the 1880s and later turned into an official doctrine of Czechoslovakia. In other words, the ultimate goal of the dominant tradition of Czech political thought stretching from Masaryk to Havel was finding "meaning" and "purpose," defined in moral terms, of the very existence of Czechs and their country.

Their answer was that unless Czechs assume their share of responsibility for the well-being of Europe and, even more ambitiously, unless they contribute to the cause of humanity as a whole, there is not much of a point in their existence as a distinct national community. This peculiar intellectual tradition explains the strong emphasis Havel put on responsible behavior of individuals as well as countries.

Moreover, he stressed that executing responsibility requires ability to make sacrifices: "We came to understand (…) that the only genuine values are those for which one is capable, if necessary, of sacrificing something." Faced with what he perceived as Western wavering in its determination to expand NATO, he asked "Why has the West lost its ability to sacrifice?" He accused Western leaders of lacking imagination and courage and being overly fond of the status quo.[52]

Implications for today's NATO are obvious. NATO's future is in peril unless all allies start behaving responsibly, which means, among other things, demonstrating solidarity with and providing assistance to every member feeling threatened, delivering on their solemn commitments (including investing in defense and capability development), contributing their fair share to NATO's operations, and refraining from rhetoric that may undermine the credibility of Alliance's deterrence.

Conclusions

Václav Havel's contribution to the transformation of NATO in the 1990s was fundamental. Through his leadership and talent, Havel was able to project his values and convictions into the largest effort to bring peace and stability in Europe after the Cold War: NATO enlargement. He managed to do so in a fluid period of history when old systems ceased to exist and new ones were being born. In such times of uncertainty, Havel's example demonstrates that value-based leadership has a stabilizing effect.

As we stressed, Václav Havel was not the sole contributor to NATO's transformation and there is certainly not one single ideal type of leadership for NATO. But he represented a type of leadership that would benefit the Alliance today. Here are five reasons why.

First, Václav Havel was the embodiment of political and moral courage, stemming from his lifelong effort to "live in truth." These personal qualities gained him respect long before he became the president of Czechoslovakia. Havel also stuck to principles of morality while in office, regardless of consequences to his political standing and popularity. For example, his staunch support for NATO's intervention in Yugoslavia was contrary to the widespread popular beliefs at the time of the operation (and also to date). In the era of rising populism, virtues such as morality and courage are counter-intuitive and antagonistic to the mainstream, post-truth politics.

Second, Havel skillfully blended morality and ideas into practical politics and decision-making. He believed that it was his "responsibility to emphasize, again and again, the moral origin of all genuine politics, to stress the significance of moral values and standards in all spheres of social life."[53] His campaign to support the enlargement of NATO, a very practical project, had a strong moral component from the very beginning, but so too did his domestic endeavors. This connection between morality and practical politics is mostly absent today. International politics is polarized: on the one hand, we see realpolitik downgraded to transactionalism or zero-sum games; on the other hand, fundamentalism and radicalism leave no space for practicality.

Third, Havel's sense of strong responsibility for community shaped his attitude towards NATO and the West. Havel believed in a direct link between morality in politics and the mission to serve. Genuine politics, Havel wrote in 1992, is "simply a matter to serve those around us: serving the community."[54] In this spirit, he served throughout his life: in the theater, as a dissident, during the Velvet Revolution, as the President of the Czech Republic, and as the head of state of a NATO ally.

Fourth, Havel saw in NATO a tool for Europe's transformation, integration and democratization, an institution allowing Europe to help itself and to contribute to international security beyond its borders. He saw NATO not just as an alliance of collective defense but also as an organization of collective security focused on stabilizing what is within its territory. This is in line with NATO's current mission, including its effort to build a credible defense in Europe.

Fifth, Václav Havel sought a larger goal for NATO. Enlargement was a core element of his NATO policy, but only in the sense of being a vehicle to achieve a redefinition and transformation of the Alliance. In May 2002, prior to the Prague Summit, he outlined two objectives of NATO's redefinition: first, identifying the Alliance's approach not only to Russia but also to China, India, Africa, and other parts of the world; and second, opening NATO's door, "while at the same time setting a definite limit on its possible future enlargement. Otherwise, no future enlargement will make sense."[55]

All of this was to be undertaken in the context of an accelerated internal transformation. On the eve of the Prague Summit, Havel added:

If the Alliance is to be meaningful today it must be an organization equipped with a large quantity of information processed promptly and professionally; an organization capable of taking split-second decisions and, wherever this becomes necessary, of immediately engaging either its permanent rapid deployment forces, perfectly trained and constantly ready, or specialized forces of various armies that will be capable of confronting modern dangers.[56]

Almost two decades later, these principles of NATO transformation still apply.

Notes

1. Ronald D. Asmus, *Opening NATO's Door. How the Alliance Remade Itself for a New Era* (New York: Columbia University Press, 2002), pp. 7-17. See also Václav Havel, Speech to the Assembly of the Council of Europe, May 10, 1990.

2. Václav Havel, Speech at NATO Headquarters, March 21, 1991.

3. Alexandr Vondra, "Václav Havel: Remembering the Big Little Man," *NATO Review*, 2012.

4. James M. Goldgeier, "NATO Expansion: The Anatomy of a Decision," *The Washington Quarterly*, Winter 1998, pp. 86-92; Asmus, op. cit., pp. 18-25.

5. For an early example of Havel's public praise for NATO as a useful building block of the European security order and how this was appreciated by the U.S. government, see the declassified memoranda of conversation between Havel, Czechoslovak Minister of Defense Luboš Dobrovský and U.S. Undersecretary of Defense Paul Wolfowitz in Prague on April 27, 1991. This particular "transitional" phase in Havel's evolving view of NATO, of course, succeeded his early-1990 idea to dissolve both the Warsaw Pact and NATO as relics of the Cold War and preceded his later policy of openly seeking Czechoslovakia/Czech Republic's membership in the Alliance.

6. Asmus, op. cit., pp. 25-26.

7. "*If we appeal to the West not to close itself off to us, and if we demand a radical reevaluation of the new situation, then this is not because we are concerned about our own security and stability, and not only because we feel that the security of the West itself is at stake. The reason is far deeper than that. We are concerned about the destiny of the values and principles that communism denied, and in whose name we resisted communism and ultimately brought it down.*" Václav Havel, "A Call for Sacrifice: The Co-Responsibility of the West," *Foreign Affairs*, March/April 1994, p. 4.

8. Václav Havel, "NATO's Quality of Life," *New York Times*, May 13, 1997.

9. This principle was first articulated in Senator Richard G. Lugar's speech delivered in June 1993. See Richard Lugar, "Out of Area or Out of Business: A Call for U.S. Leadership to Revive and Redefine the Alliance." Speech to the Overseas Writers' Club, Washington D.C., June 24, 1993. Lugar's ideas, including the notion of the new transatlantic bargain, were expanded in Ronald D. Asmus, Richard L. Kugler, and Stephen F. Larrabee, "Building a New NATO," *Foreign Affairs*, September/October 1993, p. 28-40.

10. See Michael Žantovský, *Havel: A Life* (New York: Grove Press, 2014), pp. 435-436. For other accounts of the April 1993 meetings between Clinton, Havel, Wałęsa and Göncz in Washington and their impact on Clinton's thinking, see

James M. Goldgeier, *NATO Expansion: The Anatomy of a Decision*, op. cit., pp. 87-88; Ronald D. Asmus, op. cit., *Opening NATO's Door*, pp. 23-25.

11. Ibid.

12. Vondra, op. cit.

13. Václav Havel, Address to Members of the Senate and the House of Commons, Ottawa, April 29, 1999.

14. Václav Havel, Speech to the Congress of the United States, Washington, DC, April 23, 1999.

15. Madeleine K. Albright, NATO Expansion: Beginning the Process of Advice and Consent, Statement before the Senate Foreign Relations Committee, Washington, DC, October 7, 1997.

16. This notion appeared in a number of Havel's speeches and articles on NATO, European security and Czech foreign policy. And early example is his speech to NATO foreign ministers at the Alliance's headquarters in Brussels on March 21, 1991. A later example is his op-ed published in the *New York Times* in 1993 (Václav Havel, "New Democracies for Old Europe," *New York Times*, October 17, 1993). A mature version can be found in Václav Havel, *NATO's Quality of Life*, op. cit.

17. Again, this is a recurring theme in Havel's writing. See, for example, Václav Havel, "New Democracies for Old Europe," op. cit., *"We have always belonged to the western sphere of European civilization, and share the values upon which NATO was founded and which it exists to defend. We are not just endorsing such values from the outside: over the centuries, we have made our own contribution to their creation and cultivation. Why then should we not take part in defending them?"*

18. Václav Havel, Speech at NATO Headquarters, op. cit.

19. Ibid.

20. Václav Havel, "A Call for Sacrifice: The Co-Responsibility of the West," *Foreign Affairs*, March/April 1994, p. 3.

21. Žantovský, *Havel: A Life*, op. cit., p. 99; Václav Havel, *Power of the Powerless: Citizens Against the State in Central-Eastern Europe*, 1978 (Routledge 2009).

22. Throughout his life, Havel portrayed *"political (and economic) matters as phenomena secondary to cultural and moral questions. The latter define the frame against which the former acquire their concrete form and meaning."* David S. Danaher, *Reading Václav Havel* (Toronto 2015), p. 40.

23. *"Be strict with us before our entry into NATO! We are a nation of talkers!"* Havel's letter to Madeleine Albright, December 7, 1998, quoted in Michael Žantovský, *Havel: A Life*, op. cit., pp. 483-84.

24. James De Candole, "Václav Havel as a Conservative Thinker," *The Salisbury Review*, December 1988.

25. Václav Havel, *Letní přemítání (Summer Meditations)*, Prague 1991, pp. 19-20. See also Martin C. Putna, *Václav Havel: Duchovní portrét v rámu české kultury 20. století* (Václav Havel: A Spiritual Portrait in the Context of Twentieth-Century Czech Culture), Praha 2011, *in toto*.

26. See Kieran Williams, "Václav Havel," in Jonathan Wright and Steven Casey, eds., *Mental Maps in the Era of Détente and the End of the Cold War 1968-91*, p. 157. *"Even if the imagery might imply an order of receding intensity, each layer of domov was considered essential to a robust identity."* For Havel's definition of "home" and the concentric circles forming one's identity, see Václav Havel, *Letní přemítání*, op. cit., pp. 18-20. See also Martin C. Putna, *Václav Havel: Duchovní portrét v rámu české kultury 20. století*, op. cit., pp. 283-84.

27. Havel, *Letní přemítání*, op. cit., pp. 19-20.

28. See Havel's increasingly critical opinions on Russia after 2000, such as in Václav Havel, "Five Points on the Issue of NATO," *The New Presence*, Summer 2008, p. 27. (*"A dictatorship of a fairly new type is coming into existence to the east of the area under NATO protection. All basic human and civic freedoms are gradually and quietly being suppressed under the banner of aggrieved ideology that everybody is doing Russia wrong."*)

29. See Kieran Williams, op. cit., pp. 156-57. *"Havel (…) diagnosed a crisis of all forms of industrial society, a crisis outwardly manifested in impersonal, oversized bureaucratic states, soulless consumerism, ecological ruin and the nuclear arms race, but at root a crisis of modern man's ability to vouch for a truth and be consistent in an identity in his relations with others."*

30. Putna, *Václav Havel*, op. cit., pp. 151-153. For a complex account of Havel's critical view of the West and the East as two versions of humanity's existential crisis, see David S. Danaher, op. cit., pp. 138-49. As put by Danaher, Havel considered the (post)totalitarian regimes of Eastern Europe to be *"grotesquely exaggerated forms of the late twentieth-century consumer industrial society that has been perfected in the West."*

31. Havel, "Five Points on the Issue of NATO," op. cit., pp. 25-26.

32. Havel, "NATO's Quality of Life," op. cit., *"The alliance should urgently remind itself that it is first and foremost an instrument of democracy intended to defend mutually held and created political and spiritual values. It must see itself not as a pact of nations against a more or less obvious enemy, but as a guarantor of Euro-American civilization and thus a pillar of global security."*

33. Žantovský, *Havel: A Life*, op. cit., pp. 108-109.

34. Ibid. *"An enlarged NATO should consider Russia not an enemy, but a partner."*

35. Asmus, *Opening NATO's Door*, pp. xxv, 18.

36. Havel, "New Democracies for Old Europe," op. cit.

37. Ronald D. Asmus and Alexandr Vondra, "The Origins of Atlanticism in Central and Eastern Europe," *Cambridge Review of International Affairs*, Volume 18, Number 2, July 2005, p. 204

38. Putna, *Václav Havel*, op. cit., pp. 55-63. For Jeffersonian influences on Czechoslovakia's founding, see the "Declaration of Independence of the Czechoslovak Nation by its Provisional Government," also known as the Washington Declaration, which was drafted in Washington, D.C. and published in Paris on October 18, 1918.

39. Asmus, *Opening NATO's Door*, op. cit., pp. 12, 23.

40. Havel, *Letni premitani*, op. cit., p. 64.

41. Havel's address on the occasion of the unveiling of a monument to T.G. Masaryk, Olomouc, March 7, 1993, quoted in Žantovský, *Havel: A Life*, op. cit., p. 434.

42. Ibid.

43. Václav Havel, To the Castle and Back, quoted in in Žantovský, *Havel: A Life*, op. cit., p. 435.

44. Havel's opening speech at the conference "The Transformation of NATO," Prague, November 20, 2002, quoted in in Žantovský, *Havel: A Life*, op. cit., p. 492. "Fraternal assistance" was the euphemistic expression used by Soviet propaganda to whitewash the motives behind the 1968 invasion of Czechoslovakia.

45. See, for example, in Žantovský, *Havel: A Life*, op. cit., pp. 99, 191, 450; Danaher, op. cit., pp. 145, 171, 193. The themes of living in truth and the sense of responsibility for things higher than one's own personal survival are key messages of Havel's most famous essay, "The Power of the Powerless," written in 1978.

46. Williams, op. cit., p. 160. *"What made the words of Socrates, Jesus, Giordano Bruno or Jan Hus convincing (...) as expression of truth was not so much their content as the willingness of the speakers to provide their personal guarantee (...) by dying rather than recanting. This language of avouching by one's words and actions, including self-sacrifice, as a guarantee of truth (...) recurred throughout Havel's writing."*

47. Žantovský, *Havel: A Life*, op. cit., p. 444.

48. Havel, "New Democracies for Old Europe," op. cit.

49. Ibid, p. 443.

50. Williams, op. cit., p. 168. *"Havel refused to see Czechoslovakia's history and location as grounds for either fatalistic submission to foreign armies or passive pining for foreign rescue."* This attitude of his can be traced back to 1969, when Havel engaged in a

fiery dispute with Milan Kundera on the interpretation of the Prague Spring and the Warsaw Pact invasion of 1968. While Kundera romanticized Czechoslovakia as a noble and hapless victim of its unfortunate geography and aggressive neighbors, Havel provided a sober analysis of events and argued that *"Our destiny depends on us. The world does not consist (…) of dumb superpowers that can do anything and clever small nations that can do nothing."* Quoted in Žantovský, *Havel: A Life*, op. cit., p. 120.

51. Putna, *Václav Havel*, op. cit., pp. 283-84, 329-35. Havel, of course, failed. As Putna puts it, *"Havel's attempt from the early 1990s to turn his homeland into something more than just a "regular" small country, to make it a spiritual, intellectual and moral center of European and global significance, in effect failed. The Czech Republic remained to be precisely just one of the "regular" small states."*

52. Václav Havel, "A Call for Sacrifice," op. cit., pp. 4-5.

53. Havel, *Letní přemítání*, op. cit., p. 94.

54. Ibid, p. 98.

55. Václav Havel, "Quo Vadis, NATO?" *The Washington Post*, May 19, 2002.

56. Václav Havel, Opening speech at the conference "The Transformation of NATO," Prague, November 20, 2002.

Chapter 9

The 20th Anniversary of Poland's Accession to NATO

Ryszard Zięba

Geostrategic Location and a Sense of Threat from Russia as the Background for Poland's Bonds with the West

Poland is a middle-rank country located in the heart of Europe. The end of the Cold War and German reunification saw Poland revert to its old worries of being stuck between "two enemies," Germany and Russia—the feeling of being caught in a grey security zone, or a so-called *Zwischeneuropa*, which might again become the focal point of power political rivalry between these two big neighbors.

Since Poland had been part of the Eastern bloc, Polish political elites feared that Russia, the Soviet successor state, would seek to keep Poland in its sphere of influence. As early as September 1989, Poland decided to pursue the policy of a "return to Europe." The shortest path would lead through Germany and continuing the reconciliation processes would be at the core of engagement. Consequently, after the Soviet collapse Poland began to see Russia as its main threat.

The process of settling historical differences with Russia only exacerbated these fears and brought further misunderstandings. The most important of these turned out to be the two countries' distinct visions of European security. Having favored pan-European solutions based on the Conference on Security and Cooperation in Europe (CSCE) for many years, Poland quickly opted for seeking accession to NATO. After all, the CSCE could only provide soft security, just like the EU—whose Eastern enlargement appeared soon even more remote than NATO's potential opening to the East.

Meanwhile, Russia—though going on a charm offensive to NATO itself with Yeltsin speaking of partnership—reinforced its own efforts to build a pan-European security system based on an ever more institutionalized CSCE. Poland thus opted for group security with the West and collective defense provided by NATO, and Russia chose collective security—following the traditions of the USSR.

Changing Priorities: From Accession to the EU to Membership in NATO

Out of concern for its national security, post-communist Poland opted for hard security guarantees, i.e., obtaining the collective defense guarantees offered by the North Atlantic Alliance. There were several reasons, however, why Poland could not obtain those guarantees straight away.

First, in 1989-1991 NATO underwent an identity crisis as a military alliance being gradually deprived of its opponent in the form of the USSR and the Eastern Bloc.

Second, transitional arrangements remained in force due to the fact that forces of the former USSR temporarily remained on the territory of the eastern *Länder* of the united Germany and on the territory of Poland and elsewhere in former Warsaw Pact (and Baltic) states.

Third, the United States and its Allies tried not to irritate Russia with an excessively rapid eastward expansion of their multilateral structures.

Fourth, the ethnic conflicts that broke out in the former Yugoslavia and the former Soviet Union destabilized the international situation and called for cooperation between the West and Russia.

Fifth, Western elites were reluctant to perpetuate military blocs, as they believed in the concept of an era of democracy and peace, as put forward by liberal American political scientist Francis Fukuyama.

In this situation, Poland's political elites focused in the first instance on the other fundamental aims of their policy—the country's development. They introduced radical economic reforms (the Balcerowicz Plan) and established close ties with the European Community and the emerging European Union through an Association Agreement in 1991. The policy of "returning to the West," pursued since 1989, also entailed joining the Council of Europe (1991) and establishing contacts with the Western European Union (WEU). Collaboration with Germany and France within the framework of the Weimar Triangle (since 1991) was another important aspect of this course. Poland bound itself to the "institutional West" in order to ensure a continued progression on its development and civilizational advancement free from the Soviet yoke, and to get closer to the West's security structures, specifically NATO and WEU.

For the political class that emerged out of the democratic opposition from the communist period, focusing on an increasingly institutionalized CSCE was a temporary pan-European solution pending Poland's accession to NATO. This was the viewpoint of Foreign Minister Krzysztof Skubiszewski, and it was supported by Democratic Union politicians. The strong post-communist Left supported this security policy and saw Poland's accession to the European Union as its most important international policy aim. This was met with understanding in the West, and American politicians and experts stated outright that Poland should first join the EU and establish itself as a democratic state capable of collaboration; this in turn could pave the way to one day gaining NATO membership.

In such circumstances, during the first years of the democratic transformations, Polish foreign policy prioritized the aim of accession to the European Union. This viewpoint was not that of Jan Olszewski's nationalist-right government, which was in power briefly (Dec. 1991-June 1992) and took unsuccessful steps, especially in the United States, to obtain at least "partial" security guarantees from NATO. As we know, the North Atlantic Treaty does not provide for any form of association or partial membership. Moreover, the government proved unable to resolve any of the serious problems affecting Poland's relations with Russia. If anything, it complicated them further by raising contentious historical issues such the Katyń Massacres (1940). In addition, Polish President Lech Wałęsa was impatient with the West's cautious stance with regard to the efforts of Central European countries to join NATO, and attempted to blackmail the West in the spring of 1992 with his idea of setting up a "NATO-bis" alliance.

Initially, there was no coherent position on Poland's integration with Western structures among the Polish political class. Although the post-communist Left tended to favor Poland's accession to the European Union during the first years of transformation, some voices on the Left made allowance for Poland's accession to NATO. One such example was President Wojciech Jaruzelski's advisor, Colonel Wiesław Górnicki, who spoke of the need for Poland's accession to NATO as early as 1990 in the daily *Życie Warszawy*. It was an isolated opinion, however, especially as at the time Poland was still a member of the Warsaw Pact. It should also be borne in mind that there were many outstanding security policy experts at the Ministry of Foreign Affairs under Krzysztof Skubiszewski, such as Andrzej Towpik, for whom Poland's membership in NATO was a foreign policy aim. Along with the new officials—mostly from the Democratic Union—appointed by the post-Solidarity forces, they formed a competent team preparing Poland conceptually for the steps leading to NATO membership.

The first important and successful initiative of the Polish Ministry of Foreign Affairs and the Chancellery of President Lech Wałęsa was the preparation, along with Czechoslovak and Hungarian diplomats, of a joint declaration by the three countries' leaders. It was issued in Prague on May 6, 1992. The leaders of the Visegrád Triangle countries appealed for further qualitative development of relations between the three countries and the North Atlantic Alliance and stated that their "long-term objective remains their full-fledged membership in NATO."[1]

Two days later, on May 8, 1992, while announcing closer ties with NATO in the Polish parliament, Minister Skubiszewski for the first time explicitly declared that Warsaw's aim was to gradually and effectively integrate Poland with the Alliance's security system, with NATO membership in due course.[2] In his subsequent statements for the press in June 1992, Skubiszewski reiterated Poland's intention to join NATO "step by step,"[3] and from that moment on, this was the principal objective of Poland's foreign and security policy.

In July of that year, Prime Minister Hanna Suchocka said in her Sejm *exposé* that her government would strive to accelerate the process leading to Poland's membership in the North Atlantic Alliance. In October 1992, during an interview with the Secretary General of the Alliance and the North Atlantic Council in Brussels, Suchocka stated clearly, and in the presence of Defense Minister Janusz Onyszkiewicz, that Poland's aim was to become a NATO member. She did not receive a positive reply, but was told that the Alliance would focus on cooperation within the North Atlantic Cooperation Council (NACC).

NATO Secretary General Manfred Wörner, who was very friendly towards Poland, mentioned during talks in a narrower circle that certain Allies were resisting the idea of enlargement, but noted that NATO was open to such an option in the future and gave assurances that Poland was part of the small number of candidates for membership.[4]

On 2 November 1992, President Wałęsa signed two program documents adopted by the National Defense Committee: "The Premises of Polish Foreign Policy" and "The Security Policy and Defense Strategy of the Republic of Poland," in which Poland officially announced that its goal was to join NATO.[5]

Not long afterwards, one of the experts connected with the Democratic Left Alliance (SLD) voted in favor of a gradual rapprochement with NATO and indicated how this should be achieved. In early 1993, he wrote that "Poland intended to achieve membership in NATO gradually. The way to do this was to establish the closest possible bilateral military cooperation with the members of the North Atlantic Alliance and multilateral cooperation within NATO, which also included involvement in the NACC. The task during this initial period of rapprochement with NATO was for the Polish Armed Forces to gradually attain technical and functional compatibility with Western armies."[6]

Soon Poland's efforts to join NATO were made easier, largely due to political changes at home and on the international stage. In October 1993 the center-left coalition government of the Democratic Left Alliance (SLD) and the Polish Peasants' Party (PSL) was formed; one month earlier the withdrawal of Russian troops from Poland had been completed (and from former East German territory in mid-1994). The Democratic Left Alliance, which initially saw security in terms of pan-European regulations (CSCE), remained fixated on Polish accession to the EU. As they governed the country, Democratic Left Alliance politicians came to appreciate the difficulty of adapting Poland to EU standards, and as they shared government with President Wałęsa, they came to prefer Poland's accession to NATO, not least because this was easier to attain. The center-liberal political circles of the opposition Freedom Union (former Democratic Union) had pronounced themselves much earlier in favor of NATO membership. But they only presented their position fully in the *Poland-NATO Report*, which was published in October 1995. Its main authors, Przemysław Grudziński and Henryk Szlajfer, joined by Janusz Onyszkiewicz, Andrzej Olechowski, Andrzej Ananicz and Krzysztof Skubiszewski, publicly called for Poland to first opt for NATO membership, as this was easier than meeting EU membership criteria.[7]

It can therefore be said that the years 1993-1995 saw the emergence of a consensus between Poland's principal political forces, from right to left, about the country's foreign policy priorities. The idea of joining NATO *prior* to gaining membership in the European Union carried the day. This led to a systematic and ongoing deterioration of Poland's relations with Russia, which had been against NATO expansion to the East since the fall of 1993. Indeed, it produced a deepening impasse in Polish-Russian relations that no political force in Poland was able to overcome. Russia was not interested in overcoming this impasse either, and rejected the Partnership for Transformation concept put forward by Polish Prime Minister Waldemar Pawlak and Foreign Minister Andrzej Olechowski in 1994.

Polish Cooperation with NATO Prior to Accession

An issue of key importance in convincing Poland's future allies, and especially the United States, to accept it as a NATO member, was the Polish-American cooperation established at a very early stage in the sphere of intelligence. The first significant Polish intelligence operation of this type took place in 1990, during the unfolding of the Persian Gulf crisis. It ended with the spectacular spiriting of CIA agents out of Iraq. This operation has always served to legitimize Poland in the eyes of its NATO allies. A similar motive guided the center-left SLD/PSL government's dispatch of a 51-person contingent of commandos from the GROM unit to Haiti in October 1994, as support for the Multinational Forces, to manage the situation following the overthrow of that country's military junta. Another unequivocally positive role was played by Polish military intelligence services during the wars in former Yugoslavia. The Americans didn't mind that professionally active Polish special services had a communist pedigree and had even conducted successful operations against the United States.[8] Unfortunately, the effectiveness of these services was hampered by some Polish governments (above all by those of Jan Olszewski and Law and Justice—PiS), guided by the obsession of vetting and eliminating proven, often outstanding, aces of the Polish intelligence services from communist times.[9]

Ever since Poland was interested in membership in the North Atlantic Alliance, it feared that newly emerging institutions like the North Atlantic Cooperation Council (NACC) or the Partnership for Peace (PfP) would be substitutes. The pronouncements of President Lech Wałęsa—who warned President Bill Clinton's envoys Madeleine Albright, General John Shalikashvili and Charles Gati in January 1994, prior to the Brussels NATO summit, that Poland would not even join PfP—were especially critical.[10] However, during an official dinner of the heads of the Visegrád Group states with the U.S. president held in Prague on January 12, Wałęsa said of the PfP that it was "a step in the right direction, however too small. I hope that today's talks will define the time horizon and that our progress on the way to NATO will be faster."[11]

Poland nevertheless joined the PfP in February 1994, and the following September the first NATO military maneuvers took place in Biedrusko near Poznań. Military cooperation within the PfP framework served to adapt Poland to NATO standards and contributed to bringing Poland closer to membership in the Alliance. The Partnership for Peace Planning and Review Process (PARP), thanks to which partner countries were able to cooperate more closely with NATO forces in order to achieve interoperability objectives, was especially important. In practical terms, Polish military collaboration with NATO took the form of Poland's participation in IFOR, which was implemented in Bosnia and Herzegovina following the Dayton peace agreements and which put an end to civil war in that country. In February 1996, a 670-person strong Polish contingent joined IFOR and served as part of the Nordic-Polish Brigade. From December of that year, the Polish unit (which had been reduced to about 500 soldiers) was included in the next NATO mission—SFOR.

In the fall of 1994, Poland, along with the Czech Republic, Hungary and Slovakia, was included in the American military aid program (the so-called Brown amendment), and on December 1, 1994, the North Atlantic Council adopted the breakthrough decision to initiate internal debate within the Alliance about the manner and principles of its en-largement and the impact that this would have on European security. The option of NATO opening itself to new members was accepted by the Alliance's 16 members.

Poland was impatient and sought, mainly in Washington, to accel-erate NATO's enlargement eastward. President Lech Wałęsa's efforts were successfully continued by his successor from SLD, Aleksand-er Kwaśniewski. However, the United States tried to secure Russia's acquiescence to NATO's historical admission of the former East Bloc countries. This was not made any easier by the pronouncements made in the fall of 1995 by President Wałęsa or Defense Minister Zbigniew Okoński (appointed by Wałęsa), who feared that Poland might become a second-class NATO member and who demanded that Washington deploy nuclear weapons on Polish territory. This led to nervous reac-tions in Moscow.

A very positive role in the efforts leading to Poland's admission to NATO was that of Jerzy Koźmiński, Poland's ambassador in the Unit-ed States in 1994-2000. I personally had the opportunity (as a fellow at George Washington University during the 1994-95 academic year), to see how persistent he was in his efforts to persuade political circles in Washington and the U.S. public to expand NATO. I remember that instead of complaining about Poland's abysmal geopolitical situation and the threat from the East, he sought to convince the Americans of how good a deal they would be making by accepting Poland as a NATO member.

Jan Nowak-Jeziorański, National Director of the Polish-American Congress at the time, also played an important role. This is evidenced by his extensive publicity work, published in Poland years later, upon which he embarked during this period.[12] In general, the Polish-Amer-ican community played a major role in the difficult process of persuad-ing U.S. decision-making circles to expand the North Atlantic Alliance so as to include Poland. The very positive advisory role of Professor Zbigniew Brzezinski, associated with the Democratic Party, cannot be overestimated.

One issue hindering Poland's diplomatic efforts to become a NATO member was the worryingly insufficient civilian control over the Polish armed forces. The problem was symbolized by the political activity of

General Tadeusz Wilecki, who was appointed Chief of General Staff of the Polish Army by President Lech Wałęsa in August 1992. This general openly criticized the Sejm and the government, and in autumn 1994, with the support of other generals and President Wałęsa, forced the civilian minister of national defense (Admiral Piotr Kołodziejczyk, retired) to resign. General Wilecki was also a serious problem for the next president, Aleksander Kwaśniewski who, acting in response to Washington's expectations, decided to dismiss this general in March 1997.

Polish authorities faced another very sensitive problem on the way to NATO membership, and this was the issue of the investigation—renewed by Polish prosecutors—of Colonel Ryszard Kukliński. He was a former spy who had worked for the Americans, had informed them in 1981 of General Jaruzelski's preparations for martial law, had fled Poland and had been sentenced in absentia to death for treason. The matter was not taken up by the governments with a Solidarity pedigree or by President Wałęsa, but by the SLD/PSL government, and the main politician who brought about the positive closure of this difficult matter in September 1997 was the SLD leader, Minister of the Interior Leszek Miller, one of the former secretaries of the communist party in Poland. This example shows how Poles, including those from the old system, wanted Poland to join NATO. The Polish authorities, in keeping with regulations, carried out a controversial operation and resolved the last obstacle, which was the fact that Kukliński had until then been officially seen as a traitor in Poland and as a hero in the United States. Before the matter was formally closed, President Bill Clinton thanked the Polish government during his visit to Warsaw in July 1997.

The American political class found it difficult to come to terms with the fact that since 1993 the government in Poland had been formed by two parties who had originated in the communist system, the Democratic Left Alliance (SLD) and the Polish Peasants' Party (PSL), while in December 1995, the SLD's chairman, Aleksander Kwaśniewski, was elected president of the country. However, they quickly came to terms with this by observing the concrete actions of the post-communists. Although deep divisions persisted in internal politics, the political class at that time was guided by a *raison d'état*, which demanded that it continue its efforts to secure Poland's accession to NATO and the EU. Even Lech Wałęsa—who had rendered great services for the country and was bitterly disillusioned by his defeat in the 1995 presidential elections—during his visit to the White House in March 2016, spoke telling and wise words to President Clinton:

> Mr. President, you need not fear for Poland. Poland is in good hands. Those that govern it, have nothing in common with Russian communists. I do not like them of course, this is natural and you most certainly understand this. But they are intelligent and educated—often in your country and at your cost—who know capitalism and understand it. They have even come to like democracy, they are Westerners and pro-American. More than this, in a sense they have to be better than us, because everyone is now looking over their shoulder. We will win next time, but they won this time.[13]

Meanwhile, Poland was dissatisfied with the cooperation being established at many levels between NATO and the Russian Federation. This so-called Yalta Syndrome (fear of the West coming to an understanding with Russia at Poland's expense) appeared on many occasions, for example NATO's proposal to include Russia to the PfP program, the signing of the Founding Act on Mutual Relations, Cooperation, and Security between NATO and the Russian Federation of May 27, 1997 in Paris, the Rome Agreement of May 28, 2002, and the Lisbon Summit's 2010 offer that Russia collaborate in building an anti-missile shield.

This made the development of Poland's relations with Russia difficult and appeared to confirm Poland's alleged Russophobia in the eyes of some European allies. It has to be said that under the nationalist-right governments of the Law and Justice party (2005-2007 and since the fall of 2015), such allegations were not entirely groundless, even if Moscow was and remains uninterested in the normalization of relations with Warsaw. Russia treated Poland through the prism of its relations with the United States, and saw Poland as a U.S. client-state. In recent years Russian political science too has been criticizing Poland and Russia's other Western neighbors increasingly often, and referring to them as "limotrophs" implementing America's anti-Russian strategy.[14]

One of the most serious issues connected with Russia's opposition to NATO enlargement was Poland's fear of becoming a second-class member of the Alliance. As a concession to weaken Russia's opposition, the United States and NATO had pledged in 1990 that, just as with the eastern *Länder* following German reunification, NATO would not expand its infrastructure to the territory of new member states and that no substantial NATO combat troops would be permanently stationed there.[15] This was formalized in May 1997 during the signing of the Founding Act in Paris.

Before the decision to invite new members to the Alliance was formally announced at the NATO summit in Madrid on July 7, 1997, the Polish delegation was asked by Secretary General Javier Solana to sign the so-called "3 x NO declaration": NO to substantial NATO armed forces on the territory of states joining the Alliance; NO to military installations and bases; and NO to nuclear warheads. A member of the Polish delegation described it years later:

> Silence fell. President Aleksander Kwaśniewski was quickest to re-
> act: 'Gentlemen, we wish to join NATO, but at the outset you wish
> to treat us as second-rank members.' The NATO side expected
> this and replied 'This will not be the case. Should anything bad
> take place in the East, we will change these provisions immediate-
> ly.' It was clear that precedence had been given to Russia and it is
> with its authorities that NATO had first negotiated. We quickly
> signed the document, and only then could negotiations begin.[16]

Poland first ignored this forced political obligation, and went on to question it in the second decade of the 21st century as it advocated the building of the NATO anti-missile shield in Poland and to reinforce NATO's eastern flank.

Polish Disputes with Russia about NATO Policy

Upon joining NATO in March 1999, Poland became an import-ant member of the Alliance from a geostrategic point of view. It obtained Allied guarantees in the event of aggression by a third country, an expression widely seen in Poland as synonymous with Russia. To the north, Poland borders on Russia's Kaliningrad District, and to the east it shares a border with Belarus (bound to Russia by a military alliance since 1994), and with Ukraine—a state that was formally neutral and which was balancing between Russia and the West. Nearly half of Poland's southern border is with Slovakia, a country which was outside the Alliance until the spring of 2004. The fundamental concern of the Polish authorities was to secure the country militarily from any possible Russian aggression. For this reason, from the moment Poland joined the Alliance, it pushed for obtaining the same military status as that enjoyed by the "old" members, despite the above-mentioned NATO understandings with Russia. Polish politicians didn't treat these pledges to Moscow, or the provisions of the Founding Act, as treaty obligations. It has to be said that this latter document was not a legally binding treaty, but its binding force is de facto almost equally valid, similarly to the CSCE Final Act of 1975. The Western Allies have respected the original political understanding with Russia as regards the additional permanent stationing of substantial combat forces, and for as long as they saw no need to reinforce the Alliance's eastern flank, there was no problem. Such a need arose toward the end of the first decade of the 21st century.

It was under the vigorous leadership of Vladimir Putin that Russia eventually embarked on a policy of balancing the influence of the West. This was foreshadowed by Putin's famous speech at the Munich Conference on Security Policy of February 2007. The following year Russia reacted with disproportionate force to Georgia's attack on its troops, stationed as CIS peacekeepers in South Ossetia. Poland and other countries in the region felt an increased sense of threat, and feared the possibility of Russian armed aggression. In this situation, on August 20, 2008 Poland signed an agreement with the United States to build elements of a U.S. anti-missile shield on Polish territory.

Poland then began to demand that NATO strengthen its collective defense function enshrined in Article 5 of the North Atlantic Treaty and that it bring its contingency plans from 2001 up to date. This was Poland's position prior to the Lisbon Summit of November 2010 and in subsequent years. After Russia's annexation of Crimea in 2014, Poland further demanded a military reinforcement of the Alliance's eastern flank. All these steps and demands led to protests from Russia, which invoked, among other things, the stipulations of the Founding Act.

Another problem in NATO-Russian relations turned out to be NATO's "Open Door" policy, which Poland strongly supported and which presupposed further expansion of the Alliance, especially to former Soviet republics, that is, initially Lithuania, Latvia and Estonia, and, from 2008, also Ukraine and Georgia.

Polish-Russian relations also deteriorated as a result of the two countries' rivalry in the post-Soviet area. Poland took an active part in supporting U.S., NATO and EU policy which sought to promote democracy in Eastern Europe, included support of "color revolutions", and the EU's Eastern Partnership program. These Western initiatives were aimed at supporting democratization as well as a pro-Western orientation in the foreign policy of the former Soviet republics. Russia, on the other hand, saw this as interference in the internal affairs of the countries which lay in what it believed to be its sphere of influence, or what it called its "near abroad."

From the perspective of the theory of political realism, it has to be said that the motives officially put forward by Warsaw, Washington and Brussels, namely "supporting democracy," were just a cover for tensions already unfolding between the West and Russia over the future of the non-Russian post-Soviet states and their geopolitical orientation at stake. Side-by-side with the United States, Poland played a leading role in this contest.[17] Such a policy was due to the concept Warsaw had adopted on the threshold of the post-Cold War period and which called for strengthening the independence of Poland's immediate eastern neighbors as well as Georgia, in order to preclude Russia's reversion to an imperial policy.[18]

This was compounded by the strong anti-Russian sentiments, verging at times on outright Russophobia, of most Polish politicians, especially right-wingers. Poland showed its greatest commitment to supporting an anti-Russian political course with regard to Ukraine during the Orange Revolution at the turn of 2004/2005, and the so-called Dignity Revolution which began in November 2013. In the latter case, Poland's eagerness clearly overtook that of NATO and EU partners when it initiated economic sanctions against Russia, proposed that NATO sell weapons to Ukraine and, above all, when it sought to reinforce NATO's eastern flank and have all NATO allies increase military spending. Poland's determined course not only threatened the cohesion of the Alliance when it was accepted with some reservations by a number of European Allies but, above all, it eliminated Poland as one of the mediators in the Ukrainian crisis, a role that it could have played following the initially successful initiative of the Weimar Triangle in February 2014.

The Consequences of Poland's Accession to NATO and of its Pro-American Attitude

Poland's accession to NATO in 1999 had consequences not only for Poland's security, but also for NATO as a whole. The following are accession's most important consequences for the North Atlantic Alliance.

First, it strengthened Poland's security and U.S. involvement in European security issues by extending NATO security guarantees to two other Central European countries in the first instance and seven more in 2004.

Second, it enlarged the Atlanticist (and pro-American) wing within the Alliance. Proponents of an autonomous EU defense policy, France above all, began to refer Poland as an American "Trojan horse" in an integrating Europe, and following Poland's intervention in Iraq, in the German press Poland was referred to as the "Trojan ass" in connection nature of this operation, which had not been legitimized by the United Nations.

Third, it launched the process of an asymmetrical shaping of European security, it strengthened the security of Central Europe but not that of Eastern Europe, as involving Russia on a large scale in this process proved unsuccessful.

Fourth, Poland seeks to set the example in terms of contributing to NATO's defense capabilities. In 2002, it undertook to spend no less than 1.95% of GDP on defense as compared to the previous year. In 2018, it raised this figure to 2.0% of GDP, and on August 15, 2018 President Andrzej Duda announced that he would increase it to 2.5% of GDP in 2024, that is to about $31 billion annually.[19] This is an enormous effort, and doubts were voiced loudly in Poland about whether the government in Warsaw could really afford it. U.S. President Donald Trump praised Poland for this and singled it out as an example to follow by other allies, 23 of which did not attain the 2.0% of GDP figure recommended at the Newport NATO summit in September 2014. It is a pity that Poland's steadily increasing military budget does not lead to increased security to a degree making it certain that Poland's territory will be defended in the event of a possible war with Russia. On the other hand, the militarization of Polish and NATO security policy is not helping to strengthen international security, it weakens it by spurring an arms race, as Russia is responding with its own increasingly modern armaments.

Fifth, the reinforcement of NATO's eastern flank during the second decade of the 21st century has only ostensibly increased the security of the Allies, especially that of the Central European members. But it has strengthened Russia's determination to counterbalance NATO expansion. As a result, the militarization of security has begun, and the opportunities for multilateral pan-European negotiations (at the OSCE forum) and bilateral dialogue with Russia are not being used.

Sixth, continuing the process of NATO enlargement so as to include post-Soviet countries, especially when raised in 2008 regarding Ukraine and Georgia, entailed crossing a "red line" with regard to Russia.[20] This triggered sharp Russian countermeasures in the form of the Georgian War in 2008 and the Ukraine crisis in 2014. By annexing Crimea and militarily supporting the secession of the Eastern Ukraine's Donbas area, Russia signaled emphatically that it would not hesitate to use force and violate international law in order to protect its great-power interests. All in all, this means that the states making up the Euro-Atlantic security system are potentially heading for a great war in which there would be no winners. Poland was one of the main supporters of politics from a position of force which led to a situation reminiscent of the Cold War during the Ukraine crisis.[21]

A few years after joining NATO, Poland moved toward a clear policy of "bandwagoning" with regard to the United States. The most important signs where Poland's participation in America's invasion of Iraq in March 2003, its subsequent administration of one of the stabilization zones in that country, followed by new arms purchases from the United States once in April 2003 an agreement was signed for the purchase of F-16 multi-purpose planes. In September 2004, U.S. Deputy Secretary of State Richard Armitage and Polish Deputy Minister of Foreign Affairs Adam Daniel Rotfeld inaugurated a strategic dialogue between Poland and the United States. It was a low-level dialogue, although bilateral visits took place at the highest level. The bandwagoning policy in the following years, especially during the Law and Justice government, reduced Poland to the role of a U.S. client state and satellite.

The militarization of security policy as pursued by the United States and Poland neither strengthens the North Atlantic Alliance's security, nor increases Poland's national security. What's more, it hinders NA-TO's internal cohesion, since the leading Western European allies, Germany and France, are in favor of a cautious Eastern NATO policy and pragmatic cooperation with Russia, not least in security matters. On the other hand, Poland considers its security interests as identical with those of the United States and, therefore, unquestionably supports unilateral U.S. actions (such as the suspension of the INF treaty) and even encourages them, like the proposal to build "Fort Trump" on its territory. The danger is that this course may lead to Poland's strategic isolation, because Trump's America is no longer fully predictable.

Notes

1. Summit of the Visegrád Triangle: Declaration of the Highest Representatives of the Triangle Countries—Prague, May 6, 1992, *Zbiór Dokumentów-Recueil de Documents*, 1992, No. 3, p. 175.

2. The right-wing Konfederacja Polski Niepodległej (KPN) party, which was not a member of the government coalition, criticized the idea as it preferred to base Poland's security on the concept of Międzymorze (Intermarium), which Poland had championed unsuccessfully in the 1920s.

3. *Polska Zbrojna*, June 19–21, 1992.

4. R. Zięba, *Polityka zagraniczna w strefie euroatlantyckiej*, Warsaw: Wydawnictwo Uniwersytetu Warszawskiego, p. 46.

5. *Przegląd Rządowy*, No. 12 (18), December 1992, pp. 73-81.

6. A. Karkoszka, "Polityka bezpieczeństwa Polski," *Sprawy Międzynarodowe*, Vol. XLVI, 1993, No. 1, p. 98.

7. A. Ananicz et al., *Poland-NATO Report*, Warsaw: Institute of Public Affairs, Euro-Atlantic Association 1995. It was later published in *European Security*, Vol. 5, No. 1, Spring 1996, pp. 141-166.

8. E. Żemła, Gen. Radosław Kujawa: Tajemnice zdradza się tylko raz. Polskie służby tego nie zrobiły, Onet.pl, 12 March 2019, https://wiadomosci.onet.pl/tylko--w-onecie/20-lat-polski-w-nato-gen-radoslaw-kujawa-o-procesie-akcesyjnym-do--nato/q4s2s5v, accessed March 26, 2019.

9. It is worthwhile to mention that the few living Polish heroes of the Iraq operation were stripped of their retirement pensions in 2017 under the new "de-ubicizing" law (from UB—the Security Agency).

10. T. Lis, *Wielki finał. Kulisy wstępowania Polski do NATO*, Kraków: Wydawnictwo Znak 1999, pp. 91-95.

11. See *Materials and Documents*, Vol. 3, No. 1-2/1994, p. 319.

12. J. Nowak-Jeziorański, *Polska droga do NATO: Listy, dokumenty, publikacje / Poland's Road to NATO: Letters, Documents, Publications*, Wrocław: Towarzystwo Przyjaciół Ossolineum 2006.

13. T. Lis, op. cit., pp. 232-233.

14. S. N. Bukharin, N. M. Rakityanskiy, *Rossiya i Polsha: opyt politico-psikhologicheskogo issledovaniya fenomena limitrofizatsii. Posobiye dlya pravyashchikh elit limitrofnykh gosudarstv*, Mosow: Institut Russkoy Tsivilizatsii 2011.

15. J.R. Itzkowitz Shifrinson, "Deal or no deal? The end of cold war and the US offer to limit NATO expansion," *International Security*, Vol. 40, No. 4, Spring 2016, p. 16 *et seq.*; Former U.S. Ambassador to the Soviet Union: The U.S. and NATO Are Provoking the Ukrainian Crisis, Centre for Research on Globalization, September 05, 2014. https://www.globalresearch.ca/former-u-s-ambassador-to-the-soviet-union-the-u-s-and-nato-are-provoking-the-ukrainian-crisis/5399602 Accessed April 2, 2019.

16. K. Turecki, Jerzy Maria Nowak: Usłyszeliśmy—"macie to podpisać". Bez tego nie bylibyśmy w NATO, March 13, 2019. https://wiadomosci.onet.pl/tylko-w-onecie/polska-w-nato-jerzy-maria-nowak-o-kulisach-negocjacji/wsdpxzp, accessed March 26, 2019.

17. For more see R. Zięba, *The Euro-Atlantic Security System in the 21st Century: From Cooperation to Crisis*, Cham (Switzerland): Springer International Publishing 2018, pp. 159-165.

18. Z. Brzezinski, "Premature of Partnership," *Foreign Affairs*, Vol. 73, No. 2, March–April 1994, p. 80.

19. Prezydent: Polska mogłaby wydawać na wojsko 2,5 proc. PKB już w 2024 roku, PAP, August 15, 2018. https://businessinsider.com.pl/finanse/prezydent-andrzej-duda-25-proc-pkb-na-obronnosc-w-2024-r/2n9ztq4, accessed March 25, 2019.

20. *Były ambasador USA w ZSRR Jack Matlock: Ukrainie lepiej będzie bez Krymu*, An Interview of Jack Matlock to Polish Press Agency, PAP, March 21, 2014.

21. S. Cohen, *War with Russia: From Putin & Ukraine to Trump & Russiagate* (New York: Hot Books, 2018).

Part III

Opening NATO's Door

Chapter 10

Opening NATO's Door

Volker Rühe

Making the Case

On March 26, 1993 I was the first ministerial-level official to argue that NATO should open its door to aspiring candidates in Central and Eastern Europe.

In my Alastair Buchan Memorial Lecture at the International Institute for Strategic Studies (IISS) in London, I placed the issue of NATO's opening in the broader context of the changes that had unfolded since the end of the Cold War.[1] It was time to create a new architecture for Europe that transcended the old divides of Versailles, Yalta, and the Cold War.

For the first time in European history we had the opportunity to build cooperation across all of Europe on the basis of democracy and market economies. Institutions designed for half of Europe had to be prepared to open their doors to new democratic members. This was as true for the European Union as it was for NATO.

The deepening and the widening of the European Union had to proceed in tandem. Without opening to the East, EU member states would never be able to advance their own cooperation. "Without our neighbors in Central and Eastern Europe," I argued, "strategic unity in Europe would remain an illusion."

This applied also to NATO. "We must not exclude our neighbors in the East from Euro-Atlantic security structures," I insisted. "Eastern Europe must not become a conceptual no-man's-land…and the Atlantic Alliance must not become a 'closed shop'." Opening Western institutions was not only important, I argued, it was urgent.

At the time, in my lecture and in other writings, I argued that "the success of the reforms in Central, Eastern and Southeastern Europe

217

is the greatest strategic challenge of the Euro-Atlantic community…if the West does not stabilize the East, then the East will destabilize the West." I warned that if Central Europe were to be left in a strategic vacuum, a turbulent and insecure in-between Europe (*Zwischeneuropa*) would emerge, and "sooner or later Russia and the European Union, or even Russia and Germany would come into conflict regarding their respective influence" in the region.[2] Such a situation could be in the interest of no country, including Russia.

What we needed was the right balance between cooperation and integration. It was important to sustain the momentum for cooperation with Russia and translate that into practical steps so that Russia would be recognized as a strategic partner for NATO, and would itself feel to be such a partner, while simultaneously ensuring that the special nature of such a partnership did not hinder or suppress the process of integration of other partner countries into Western institutions.[3]

Managing the German Debate

I didn't consult my Chancellor, Helmut Kohl, on the content of my speech. If I had, I could not have given the lecture.

As Chancellor of a coalition government, Helmut Kohl could not be as forward-leaning as I was. That was clear. But if governing is just about compromising, you don't succeed. I was neither shy nor insecure on that point. Internally, I pressed Kohl quite hard on NATO's opening. He was still reticent for various political and tactical reasons. He never threatened to fire me if I went public with my views, but he and my colleague Hans-Dietrich Genscher, Germany's Foreign Minister and a member of our coalition partner, the Free Democratic Party (FDP), tried to slow me down. Genscher was against opening NATO to new members. Genscher never said we could not achieve such a goal, he simply didn't want to do it.

I disagreed and decided to go public. I was concerned that Alliance discussions on the issue had become desultory. Some weeks earlier, ambassadors to the North Atlantic Council had discussed informally in off-the-record session the possibility of NATO membership for Central and East European countries. The debate was inconclusive. I was convinced that this was an inadequate response to the desire of these countries to join the Alliance. There was a danger of drift. It was time to put the topic on the international agenda.

I deliberately chose the IISS because it is a special place to give an important speech, and because of my close friendship with Helmut Schmidt. I did not consult Schmidt beforehand, but I wanted my speech to have a historic background. I recalled Schmidt's own ground-breaking speech at the IISS in 1977, when he warned that the Soviet Union was deploying a new generation of mobile intermediate-range missiles with multiple warheads that could decouple European from U.S. security unless NATO matched the new Soviet threat. Schmidt's speech led to NATO's dual-track decision to deploy intermediate-range missiles and also to negotiate with the Soviet Union the removal of this entire class of weapons from Europe, a strategy that ultimately proved to be successful.

When I gave the speech, my views were in opposition to my own government's official position. But I had had a history of not asking Helmut Kohl before making important speeches.

In 1985 I gave a speech in the Bundestag on German-Polish relations and on the Warsaw Treaty, which had been signed by West German Chancellor Willy Brandt and Polish Prime Minister Józef Cyrankiewicz in December 1970.

In the treaty, both parties accepted the existing border, the Oder-Neisse line, which the Allied powers imposed on Germany at the 1945 Potsdam Conference. The German Bundestag ratified the Warsaw Treaty in May 1972. Nevertheless, the Treaty's Article IV stated that it did not supersede earlier treaties such as the Potsdam Agreement, so the provisions of Warsaw Treaty could be changed by a final peace treaty between Germany and the wartime Allies, as provided for in the Potsdam Agreement. Some conservatives interpreted this to mean that the German-Polish border had not been ultimately settled. This was of great concern to the Poles.

In my 1985 speech I said clearly that if Germany would again be united, its eastern border would be the Oder-Neisse line. I considered the Warsaw Treaty as politically binding for a united Germany. Poland and Germany had common strategic interests. Poland wanted a democratic neighbor in the West. The only precondition was that the border question had to be resolved. It was incumbent upon Germany to reassure the Poles on this point.

Kohl understood my rationale, but the speech made him angry because once again he had other political and tactical considerations in mind. For Kohl, my speech was another political headache. Franz Josef Strauß, the Bavarian leader of the Christian Social Union (CSU), the sister party of the Christian Democratic Union (CDU) to which Helmut Kohl and I belonged, demanded that Kohl throw me out of the party. Kohl refused. But he was not happy.

Formative Experiences

My Polish experiences were formative when it came to shaping my views of opening NATO's door. In the 1980s I was Deputy Leader of the Parliamentary Group of the CDU/CSU responsible for Foreign Policy, Defense and German-German relations. In the early part of that decade I was already in Poland meeting *Solidarnosc* people living in the underground, for instance Janusz Onyszkiewicz, at the time *Solidarnosc*'s press spokesman and later my close friend as Defense Minister. After the declaration of martial law in December 1981, Onyszkiewicz had been arrested. He was later released, but he was still banned, living in illegality. In 1984 I met him nonetheless. I'm sure many spies were surveilling us, but I knew that the Polish authorities couldn't do anything. In fact, I invited him to a reception at the German embassy in Warsaw with all the official Polish authorities. I didn't ask the German Ambassador. He would have said no. I just brought him. I wanted Janusz Onyszkiewicz to be my guest. The Poles were just stunned by this.

My intensive political contacts with Polish interlocutors during that time made me realize that the Polish opposition was more in favor of German unity than most in Germany and in my own party. Those fighting their own regime in Poland believed they had a vital interest in having a democratic, unified Germany as a neighbor. After unification in 1990 I felt politically and morally obliged to stand up for the unity of Europe, to ensure that those countries that had enabled us all to overcome the division of Europe and the division of Germany enjoyed the same sense of security that we did, and to help prepare the path for them to be integrated into Western structures.

My second main motivation for opening NATO's door emerged in the context of German unification. During that process, I was Secretary General of the CDU. As the unification unfolded, it became clear to me that as Germany and Europe emerged from the Cold War, it would be wrong and dangerous for the eastern border of NATO and the European Union to coincide with Germany's eastern border, because then the border between stability and instability would be identical with Germany's eastern border. It was incumbent upon us to extend the Western space of stability eastward.[4]

After I became Germany's Defense Minister in 1992, my contacts with Central and East European policymakers were renewed. It was very clear that with the breakdown of the division of Europe, the Poles, the Czechs, the Hungarians and the Baltic states wanted to be members of the European Union and of NATO.

My Polish friends approached me and they said: We want the same security as Germany. And we can only get that in NATO. I shared their opinion that they deserved the same security as Germany.

Full Steam Ahead

I never liked the expression NATO expansion. I prefer the term opening of NATO. At a very early stage, I decided to develop a concept for the opening of NATO, very much with the help of Admiral Ulrich Weisser, who led my policy planning staff. Without Weisser, I could not have done it.

Weisser and I alone produced the IISS speech; he wrote the final draft. We had not informed anyone of the content.

After the speech, the German generals with us on the flight back to Germany were both surprised and depressed. They said that this was a blow to NATO that we would feel for many years. The domestic reaction was also skeptical.

I didn't care about domestic criticism; my approach was strategic. The Central and East European countries did more for Germany's unification than anybody else. How can you have a European Union where some countries feel safe and others do not? I was undeterred and determined to press ahead. But I had to win over my government, the Americans, other NATO allies, and to thread the needle with the Russians.

In Germany, I had a good relationship with Chancellor Kohl. He never threatened to fire me. But I remember at least one instance—and I think there were more—when Kohl took me aside after a Cabinet meeting telling me that he and Yeltsin were in the sauna and Yeltsin had complained about me, arguing that he had to get his Defense Minister under control. And then Kohl told me to stay out of debates over NATO's opening. I didn't, of course. I knew that he was not going to fire me.

People in the Chancellery, for instance Kohl's National Security Adviser Joachim Bitterlich, said, "Don't listen to Rühe." They argued that I did not represent the German position and the Chancellor's view. They were very much against our approach. In some instances, the Chancellery did not inform me about its talks with U.S. interlocutors. But the Americans informed me about their talks with the Chancellery, which is very unusual.

In my own ministry, the German generals were also against NATO's opening. One general stated in an interview that Polish tanks were not good enough for NATO. I told him: "If you say this again, I will fire you. We will give the Polish our tanks for one Deutschmark," which we later did. It shows you: the military were not thinking in geostrategic terms. Many of them were totally against it.

Klaus Kinkel, my colleague as Germany's Foreign Minister, was not a strategic thinker. He was totally undecided on this issue. I really took the leading role, but made sure that the German Foreign Office was not totally pushed to the side. Wolfgang Ischinger, the director of Kinkel's policy planning staff and later the Political Director of the Foreign Office, was more open, and he and Admiral Weisser cooperated closely.

It was easier to open NATO without Genscher. Kinkel was not as strong. But Genscher was kind of a one-man *ancien régime*. He still had a lot of influence with Kinkel. We often had difficulties with the Foreign Office. Weisser approached me regularly asking for permission to go to the Foreign Office to talk things over with Ischinger to keep him informed. Weisser also always informed the Chancellery. At some point, we needed the whole government behind us.

I did not have many discussions with Social Democrats about NATO's opening. Karsten Voigt, the foreign policy spokesman for the SPD, was quite open to it. But I had enough challenges in my own government and in the U.S. Administration. The Social Democrats and the other parties could not help me with that.

Moving the Americans—and the Alliance

When I first talked to the Americans in 1993 about opening NATO's door, they were against it. Their position only changed after the mid-term elections in 1994. Bill Clinton and Strobe Talbott had both been Rhodes Scholars in Oxford, and they were both so-called "Russia-firsters." You can also see this when you look at the documents and the talks between Clinton and Yeltsin. That was also true for my American counterparts Les Aspin and Bill Perry.

After Strobe Talbott became Deputy Secretary of State, I had a conversation with him on opening NATO. I said, "Strobe, listen to me. The Poles want to be a member of the European Union. And they deserve the same security as Germany and France, don't you think so?" I added that "If we don't give them the same security, this will be the end of NATO. Why? Because they will then form something in between Russia and NATO, some security organization." I asked him, "do you think that this is in the interest of America?" I think he understood that if we didn't open NATO to them, there was a danger that NATO would break up. There was a beginning of a change of mind in 1994.

Meanwhile, I had to move things forward within the Alliance. The NATO bureaucracy did not want to expand. In one ludicrous memo they expressed concerns that a bigger NATO would mean there would not be enough parking spots at NATO Headquarters.

NATO Secretary General Manfred Wörner, in contrast, supported my efforts. In a speech on September 10, 1993, he said that NATO was not a closed shop, that the option of membership remained open, and that it was time to give a concrete perspective to those countries of Central Europe that sought membership and that the Alliance considered to be viable candidates for membership.

Wörner and I worked together to organize the NATO Defense Ministers' Meeting in Travemünde, Germany on October 20-21, 1993. This was my first big NATO conference as Defense Minister. I had been in office just for a year and a half.

While preparing for the conference, I learned from my people that the United States intended to float a proposal for something called a Partnership for Peace. We were concerned that it was a means to avoid NATO's opening. I sent Weisser to Washington on October 12 and 13, 1993 to find out where the U.S. Administration stood on the issue. Weisser returned believing that our position could be aligned with that of the Clinton Administration. He reported that the German and U.S. sides agreed that NATO had to undergo an internal adaptation that equipped it to deal with new missions, and that Western security structures had to be opened to new members. He added, however, that the U.S. interagency discussions were still not uniformly aligned. These differences were encapsulated in the idea of the Partnership for Peace.[5]

It was imperative for us to use the Travemünde meeting to build a consensus on NATO's opening. In remarks to the press before the event began, I made it clear that the Central and East Europeans had to be offered a clear membership perspective. The question was no longer "whether," but rather "when" and "how."[6]

As expected, discussions at the meeting centered on the nature of the Partnership for Peace (PfP), which U.S. Defense Secretary Les Aspin proposed and which had been developed by U.S. General John Shalikashvili, who intended PfP to be an alternative to NATO membership. I disagreed.

The Americans knew I was their friend even when I was fighting with them. I was not and am not anti-American. I was and remain very pro-American and always approach things with a transatlantic perspective. I visited the United States for the first time in 1963 and since entering the Bundestag in 1976 I had cultivated close relations with many American colleagues in the Congress, in the government, and in the think tank world. The Americans knew me and took my position very seriously. They listened to my argument that we would destroy NATO if we did not open it.

Manfred Wörner played an important role in Travemünde. He very much agreed with me. He had cancer, but he had lots of fighting spirit to support me. Without him, I would not have been able to turn around the Travemünde meeting. In his role as NATO's Secretary General, he could not confront the Americans as sharply as I could. But he played his role consummately as Secretary General by summarizing that there appeared to be consensus on two points. First, there was support for NATO enlargement, and that a process to this effect should be initiated at the January 1994 Brussels Summit. Second, there was support for the U.S. concept of a "Partnership for Peace" as a useful step in this process, but not as an alternative.[7]

In the end, Wörner and I crafted the language reporting on the conclusions of the meeting so that PfP could also be understood as offering a path to eventual NATO membership. The nuanced language was underestimated at the time. It was finalized despite U.S. concerns. My good friend Hans Haekkerup, the Danish Defense Minister, as well as the Dutch and the Canadians, were instrumental in securing the final language that opened NATO's door.

Hans Haekkerup was my closest ally in Europe. He was totally in favor of opening NATO's door. He was from a small country, but he was a strategic thinker. Together, we conceived the idea to establish a joint Danish-Polish-German corps, consisting of three divisions, in Szczecin. We started this process in 1994, three years before the 1997 Madrid Summit, where the first invitations were extended. This initiative could not have been done by Germany and Poland alone. Denmark played a very big role. In the old NATO, before 1990, there was a joint Danish-German command in Rendsburg. So, Hans suggested that we had to do something new to foster the process of opening NATO up. I suggested Szczecin. It has developed very well. In the meantime U.S. forces are also now there.

The effort to change U.S. and Allied opinion took time. If one looks back, it is astonishing: people did not understand the kind of problems that we would have had if we had not opened up NATO. I think that without NATO's opening, the European Union would not have survived as an institution.

The Clinton Administration did not fully turn in our direction until after the U.S. mid-term elections in November 1994. Even in September 1994, at a meeting of NATO Defense Ministers in Seville, Spain, my U.S. counterpart Bill Perry warned me about moving too fast. Perry is a friend of mine and I hold him in high esteem. At the time he told me that President Clinton did not like what I was doing. His advice was "Don't push too much. You will run into big problems."

Richard Holbrooke played an important role in this process. In 1993, he came to Germany as the U.S. Ambassador. Weisser and I managed to convince him that NATO's opening was a good thing. When he went back to Washington in 1994, he changed the attitude of the Clinton Administration.

The RAND Story

I had the political strategy in mind to open NATO. But I needed help to implement it. That's why I hired RAND. I needed them to put some flesh on my ideas and to outline the next steps. There were so many things to do.

Weisser and I had long been familiar with RAND. They were open, and they were in favor of our approach. RAND helped us to develop a step-by-step effort. Every three to six months RAND analyst Ronald Asmus would come over to report on what they had been working on. We then decided on the next studies. Asmus and I knew each other very well. Weisser was the go-between.

Essentially I paid RAND to help me do something that was against the foreign policy position of the United States. RAND was very courageous to work with me. U.S. government representatives warned them against it. But I was very unconventional.

No German think tank supported me. They were all against it. The *Stiftung Wissenschaft und Politik* (SWP) would have been the only think tank in Germany that could have really helped me to develop the steps toward NATO membership for the Central and East European countries. I asked them. Michael Stürmer, the head of SWP, was totally against it.

There are multiple ironies to the RAND story. At one point I shared the RAND studies with the Clinton Administration and with my Polish colleagues. I told them the studies were free. I had already paid for them. I said, "If it will influence you, that's enough for me." The studies were indeed influential. In 1997, in fact, Asmus even joined the Clinton Administration to implement the strategy.

Bosnia and German Responsibility

Between 1994 and 1997 we continued to work through the details of opening NATO's door. The conflict in Bosnia weighed heavily on our efforts. Without an end to the Bosnia crisis it seemed unlikely that there would be a consensus behind opening NATO to new members. Here again Richard Holbrooke played a major role by securing the Dayton Peace Accords.

When it came to implementing the Dayton agreement, Germany's role as an Alliance member was scrutinized. Through the Cold War Germany security and defense policy was focused on challenges in central Europe. There was little domestic support for German participation in foreign military missions. But in the post-Cold War period it was clear that Germany would be called on to join such efforts.

From the outset of my tenure as Defense Minister I argued that Germany had to take on the same responsibilities as its Alliance partners with regard to the use of military power.[8] In the summer of 1992 one of my first calls as German Defense Minister was to U.S. Defense Secretary Richard Cheney. He was clear that Washington expected greater German contributions to foreign military missions. I decided I would not come back to Washington until I had changed the German position. A major theme in my March 1993 IISS speech was Germany's responsibility to be a more proactive member and leader of the international community.

It was unbelievable to me that Germany did not contribute to U.N. military operations. One of my first acts as German Defense Minister, in May 1992, was to send German non-combat troops to participate in the U.N. mission in Kampuchea. Later in 1992 we send an navy air patrol as part of a NATO mission in the Adriatic. In 1993, we sent German non-combat forces to participate in the blue-helmet U.N. mission in Somalia. The deployments were controversial at home. Only in July 1994 did the Federal Constitutional Court rule that Germany's 1949 Constitution did not prohibit participation in multilateral peacekeeping or combat operations, and that German troops were permitted to join military missions abroad if the parliament approved.

Nonetheless, German participation in implementing the Bosnian peace posed a real challenge. Helmut Kohl was quite reluctant to deploy German forces for historical reasons. He referred to the role of the Wehrmacht and the Croatian Ustaše during World War II. I thought that our participation in the mission would be worth it if we could save many lives. I was determined that something like Srebrenica should never happen again. I was encouraged by the attitude of the Americans, who expected a united Germany to be part of these new roles of NATO. Manfred Wörner was also supportive. He believed that either we "go out of area" or "we go out of mission." Others didn't. It was quite a fight in Germany. Our coalition partner, the FDP, was against the deployment of German forces to Bosnia. Some Social Democrats, such as Karsten Voigt and Norbert Gansel, supported me. The Greens were totally opposed (later on, they agreed with my approach when we participated in the mission in Kosovo in 1999). In the end we managed to get a majority, and we joined the Bosnian implementation force.

Holbrooke gave us a call one morning to say that while watching television he had seen the Iron Cross on the surface of a Tornado jet in the sky over Sarajevo. He emphasized that this was a signal that Germany was a full member of the new missions of NATO.

If we were to succeed in adapting NATO to new missions and new members, Germany had to show that it was a reliable ally. Bosnia was a watershed for these efforts. Shortly after the end of the war, I met with Croatian President Franjo Tudjman. He believed that Europe ended right after the town of Banja Luka. For him, Bosnia was Turkish and a part of the former Ottoman-occupied territory, whereas my intention was not just to fulfill Germany's role in NATO but also to work for the integration of what I call secular European Muslims. I am still convinced that if we had not intervened, al-Qaeda's headquarters would not be in Afghanistan, but in Sarajevo. There was already money coming in from Saudi Arabia. We had to show that we were willing to fight for the human rights of Muslims in Europe. That was our mission: to play a full role in NATO's new missions. And the other part of our mission was to fight for the rights of European Muslims, also later in Kosovo.

Deciding the "Who"

With the Bosnian peace being implemented and Alliance efforts at adaptation underway, and following the U.S. and Russian elections in 1996, the stage was set for the debate on who would be the first countries to walk through NATO's door. That decision was to be taken at the 1997 Madrid NATO Summit.

From the beginning I agreed with the American approach, which Strobe Talbott summarized as "small is beautiful." If we brought in too many countries in the first round, it would appear as if this would be the end, and others would not be able to join later. But we envisaged NATO's opening as a process, not an event. If we wanted to bring in the Baltic states and others in later, it was just the right thing to bring three in first.

I was the first German political leader to name publicly the Czech Republic, Hungary and Poland as Germany's preferred candidates to walk through NATO's door.[9] As usual, I was ahead of my government—and the Alliance.

Kinkel again was undecided. The French, the Italians, the British, who had initially been against NATO's opening, were unclear about their preferences. The French position was rather ironic. When they first saw that they could no longer stop NATO's opening, they argued that it should proceed along the lines of the French version of NATO membership, i.e. without military integration. I told the Poles this, to which they replied, "They are fools."

Initially, the French rejected NATO's expansion. The French then reversed course and favored bringing in five countries in the first round, including Romania. Chirac's argument was that they had much better tanks than the Poles. That was a very superficial view. My response was: I am not interested in the quality of their tanks. I am interested in their mindset.

Kohl was very slow to change his mind on opening NATO. He argued that it was very important to influence Yeltsin. The idea was not just to open NATO, but to develop a strategic relationship with Russia. While he had voiced support for enlargement earlier, he only decided on three new members a few months before Madrid. He was still angry with me for pushing too hard. He didn't invite me to join the Summit. I didn't care. I was just happy. NATO was about to open its doors.

Shortly before Madrid, a German-French meeting was held between Kohl and Chirac. Chirac asked our delegation whether we were in favor of three, four or five new member states. Kinkel first said we are for three, four and five. That was typical for him. Then I said we are for three. Kohl did not say anything. But Kohl supported the American position.

A related challenge was what to tell aspirant countries who would not be among those asked to join NATO in Madrid. By 1995 it was apparent that we would not take in a large group of aspiring members. I visited the Baltic states August 21-23, 1995 to break the news.[10] Estonian Prime Minister Lennart Meri attacked me in private when I told him we would likely start with three new NATO members. He was concerned that the process would end with three. He said: This is another Munich 1938.

I said you don't talk to us like this. This is not another Munich, this is Brussels. I am the one who started the process to open NATO at all. And now you criticize me because we don't bring in the Baltic states in the first phase. I was very outspoken. Later on, he understood that this was the right process: small is beautiful. His views had historic roots. Back in 1941, Meri's family was deported to Siberia. In the 1990s, he feared that Estonia and the Baltic states might be left out again. That was never my intention. But I understood his anxiety.

Managing Relations with Russia

As the process of integration proceeded, it was important to establish new patterns of cooperation with Russia. Only a few short weeks after my IISS speech, I conducted talks with the Russian leadership in Moscow on April 13-17, 1993. As I reported to the Chancellor upon my return, I came away with a number of observations. Russian Foreign Minister Andrey Kozyrev made it clear that Russia was guided by the geopolitical and geostrategic national interests of a normal country, and that a threat from the West no longer played any role in such considerations. My counterpart, Defense Minister Pavel Gratchev, added that Russia now considered the real threats to emanate primarily from the south. Russian leaders emphasized that they sought a closer bilateral relationship with Germany, also in military-security issues; during my visit we signed a agreement on military cooperation. It struck me that NATO-Russia cooperation was opening a perspective for Central and Eastern European countries to draw closer to NATO and EU structures, and simultaneously for a new more intensive partnership between Russia and NATO to develop.

I continued to have regular meetings with the Russians, both in Germany and in Russia. In 1994, I went to St. Petersburg. I met Mayor Anatoli Sobchak and spent two days there. His deputy sat to his left: it was Vladimir Putin.

I met very often with Boris Nemtsov, Yevgeny Primakov, and Dmitry Rogosin, a member of the Duma who later became Russia's Ambassador to NATO. I met with Vyacheslav Trubnikov, who ran Russia's Foreign Intelligence Service, and Anatoly Chubais, who was Deputy Prime Minister and then chief of the Russian Presidential Administration. I also had many contacts with the community of strategic thinkers in Moscow. One of my most important contacts was Sergey Karaganov, who is still there and who had already been there during Soviet times. Another important contact was Deputy Defense Minister Kokoshin.

In our conversations, my Russian interlocutors did not try to change my strategic position. But we did try to work out things and to develop a strategic relationship. I explained my position that NATO was opening, not expanding. I told them that it was my conviction that Russia also deserved the same security and that one day we also might be open for Russia.[11]

The relationship between NATO and Russia had always been difficult. The Allies only met as a group with the Russians after we had found a 100 per cent consensus in NATO. We missed some opportunities. In some instances, it would have been possible to discuss some issues with the Russians beforehand, for instance topics relating to the Middle East. I was also ready to have some Russian thinkers relegated to NATO's international staff. It goes without saying that you have to discuss crucial things only among the NATO member states. But there were many other issues which we could have invited the Russians to discuss, to give them the feeling and the reality that they could join the debate when it was still open.

My discussions with the Russians were not always pleasant. We had particularly difficult interactions related to the war in Chechnya. On New Year's Eve in 1995, the Russian army sent in 500 young, recently-drafted and half-drunk soldiers into Grozny. Most of them were killed. What I learned later on and what really angered me was that their only training with hand grenades had been throwing snowballs in St. Petersburg. I promptly disinvited Grachev from the Munich Security Conference. Kohl said: What are you doing? Yeltsin complained as well.

Nonetheless, I tried to develop a strategic relationship with Russia. One example was my proposal, which I developed in 1997 and 1998, to develop a military transport plane as a joint venture between Airbus and the Russian aircraft company Antonov. We talked to the Ukrainians about it. Their President was very much in favor, and the Russians also. Even the French President sent me a letter saying that France agreed that this could be studied. Politically and strategically, it would have been a clear signal that we were engaged in common projects, and that we lived in a new world, not just with treaties and words, but in a very practical way. We would have been able to show that it was not the old NATO expanding, but a new NATO opening together with a new relationship towards Russia. Unfortunately, the Schröder government did not follow up on this initiative. They gave in to the interests of Airbus and to West European industry.

I was strongly in favor of modernizing Russia. In the 1990s I did not fear a Russian backlash. Yeltsin was trying to reform Russia. It was chaos. Putin tried to bring back order and hierarchy. Unfortunately, we did not find the appropriate response to Putin's pleas for a common zone of trade and economic interdependence.

Notes

1. An edited version of the speech may be found at Volker Rühe, "Shaping Euro-Atlantic Policies: A Grand Strategy for a New Era," *Survival*, 35:2, pp. 129-137, DOI: 10.1080/00396339308442689.

2. Volker Rühe, *Deutschlands Verantwortung: Perspektiven für das neue Europa* (Berlin: Ullstein, 1994), pp. 21, 59.

3. Ibid., p. 120.

4. For further exploration, see Ulrich Weisser, *Sicherheit für ganz Europa: Die Atlantische Allianz in der Bewährung* (Stuttgart: Deutsche Verlags-Anstalt, 1999), pp. 23-59.

5. Weisser, op. cit., pp. 45-47.

6. Ibid, p 49.

7. Ibid, p. 51.

8. Volker Rühe, "Sinn und Auftrag der Bundeswehr im vereinten Deutschland," speech of April 2, 1992, *Bulletin*, No 37, April 7, 1992, p. 346.

9. See "Bewertung der künftigen Rolle Moskaus," *Frankfurter Allgemeine Zeitung*, May 12, 1995.

10. See "Rühe fordert von Lettland und Litauen Geduld bei der Annäherung an EU und NATO," *Süddeutsche Zeitung*, August 23, 1995; "Letten wollen die Zusicherung der NATO: Rühe brenst Hoffnungen auf einen schnellen Beitritt," *Handelsblatt*, August 23, 1995; Kristina Spohr Readman, *Germany and the Baltic Problem After the Cold War: The Development of a New Ostpolitik 1989-2000* (London: Routledge, 2004), pp. 182-184.

11. In 2010 I published a piece in *Der Spiegel* with Admiral Weisser, Frank Elbe and General Naumann arguing in favor of Russian membership in NATO. We explained that it was not our intention to expand the old NATO. Our article was much welcomed by President Medvedev and also by his advisers and the think tank people in Moscow. See Volker Rühe, Klaus Naumann, Frank Elbe and Ulrich Weisser, "Open Letter: It's Time to Invite Russia to Join NATO," *Der Spiegel*, March 8, 2010, http://www.spiegel.de/international/world/open-letter-it-s-time-to-invite-russia-to-join-nato-a-682287.html.

Chapter 11

NATO Enlargement:
Perspective of a German Politician

Karsten D. Voigt

In April 1994, at the height of the debate about an eastward en-largement of NATO, the Trilateral Commission met in Vancouver. I was asked to open the debate. Former U.S. Secretary of State Henry Kissinger and former U.S. National Security Adviser Zbigniew Brzez-inski were asked to comment. Kissinger remarked that this was a his-toric day. Not only did he agree with me—which happened seldom enough—he also agreed with Brzezinski: all three of us were advocat-ing for an eastward enlargement of NATO. Our motives, however, were different.

My motives reflected predominantly political goals that could not have been achieved in the course of the reunification of Germany, or the need to address challenges that had became clearer in subsequent years.

First, the goal of the reunification of Germany was achieved in Oc-tober 1990, but the goal of overcoming the division of Europe and re-alizing a lasting European peace order had not yet been accomplished.

On November 21, 1990, the member states of the former Confer-ence on Security and Cooperation in Europe (CSCE) had agreed, with the Charter of Paris, on the basic normative principles of a future, fair, democratic, and constitutional peace. The reality, however, was that those standards were not upheld consistently across the vast space from Vancouver to Vladivostok. This was especially true in the area of secu-rity policy.

Until the fall of the Berlin Wall, for most German politicians the CSCE process and arms control policy agreements between East and West, in particular the INF Treaty and the SALT I and SALT II trea-ties, were the most important instruments for overcoming tensions and divisions in Europe. In the first few months after the fall of the Berlin

Wall, I would not have thought it realistic to strive for membership of a united Germany in NATO. Only after my talks in January 1990 in Washington and then in Moscow did I change my opinion and advocate first internally within my Social Democratic Party (SPD) and then publicly for NATO membership of a unified Germany.

On January 27, 1990, Robert Blackwill and Steve Hadley on the U.S. National Security Council informed me confidentially about the concept of the "Two Plus Four" talks to facilitate the unification of Germany.[1] I agreed with Blackwill that the Soviet Union could agree to NATO membership of unified Germany—if we were careful to ensure that the Soviet side understood the talks were truly "Two Plus Four" and not "Five Against One," the "One" being the Soviet Union. Only a few days later, on February 2, 1990, German Foreign Minister Hans-Dietrich Genscher held talks in Washington about the concept of "Two Plus Four" talks. Subsequently, on February 8, 1990, Secretary of State Baker also spoke in Moscow about this concept.

On February 6, 1990, I spoke for the first time in a session with SPD foreign policymakers about the possibility of membership of unified Germany in NATO. At that time, the majority of SPD members were still advocating for overcoming the security-political division of Germany within the framework of a reformed and strengthened pan-European CSCE. Thus, this was still in the draft for my speech for the "Wehrkunde" Munich Security Conference of February 2–4, 1990.

On February 12, 1990, there was another session of the foreign affairs working group of the SPD. Here, Egon Bahr, supported by the leading representatives of the newly-established party of the GDR, including Markus Meckel, Hans Misselwitz, and Walter Romberg, argued that a unified Germany should belong neither to NATO nor the Warsaw Pact, but rather to a pan-European security system. I objected and argued that the SPD must at least support an effort to sound out the possibility of membership of a unified Germany in NATO.

On February 27 and 28, 1990, Bahr and I flew to Moscow.[2] When the SPD party caucus (*Fraktion*) asked me to accompany Bahr, I was well aware that he and I represented different opinions. We spoke in Moscow with Foreign Minister Shevardnadze, Politburo Member Yakovlev, and Marshall Akhromeyev. Valentin Falin also participated in the talks with Yakovlev. Bahr explained his concept of a reformed and strengthened OSCE. At this point I interrupted him and explained that it was necessary to at least consider the possibility of NATO membership. Our Soviet interlocutors did not contradict Bahr. His ideas did not seem unsympathetic to them. But only Falin actively supported Bahr. Otherwise, our Soviet partners seemed to be much more interested in economic questions and good relations with the United States.

After our return from Moscow, I was convinced that there was an opportunity to maintain the NATO membership of a unified Germany. After that, I advocated first within the party and then also publicly for this.

Even though such an outcome would be favorable for Germany and Germany's neighbors, it was important that such a decision not deepen the division of Europe. The CSCE Charter of Paris was one response. But it alone would have been an unsatisfactory solution to the German (security) question. It would have guaranteed no effective multilateral integration of the German military, even though all of Germany's neighbors wanted this. In addition, due to the veto possibility of each individual CSCE member state, it would not have been in a position to protect CSCE members against the threat of military force in times of crisis.

The SPD was a very early advocate for the inclusion of Eastern European democracies in the Council of Europe and in the European Communities/European Union. Eastward enlargement was of great significance for the consolidation of the rule of law and respect for human rights. Yet neither the Council of Europe nor the larger, post-Maastricht EU carried any significance for military security policy.

The enlargement of the Council of Europe was completed relatively quickly in the mid-1990s. The enlargement of the EU, in contrast, was conditioned on significant economic and social transformations by the former Soviet satellite states. Therefore, contrary to our original conceptions, EU enlargement was realized only much later than the enlargement of the Council of Europe and NATO. In 1995, only Finland, Sweden, and Austria (all firm democracies and successful economies) became EU members and thus stepped out of the shadow of the Cold War.

At the beginning of 1990, individuals active in peace research and on the left of the SPD discussed the possibility of contractual agreements between NATO and a reformed Warsaw Pact and between the EU and a reformed COMECON. In my opinion, however, the dictatorial internationalism in the Warsaw Pact and in COMECON could not be transformed into a voluntary internationalism -- and in fact, both organizations soon fell apart. Added to this was that Poland, Czechoslovakia and Hungary were pushing for a withdrawal of Soviet and Russian troops from their countries and as close a connection to the EU and NATO as possible.

The membership of post-Soviet Russia in NATO received some support both in Germany and in the United States in the first half of 1990. I never approved of this. In my opinion, a NATO of which Russia was a member would be transformed from a system for collective defense into a system of collective security. In case of larger conflicts in Europe, such a transformed NATO would probably frequently not be able to act, because, due to the principle of consensus, it would always require the agreement of all members, that is, also of Russia.

Even after the dissolution of the Soviet Union at the end of 1991, Russia regarded itself as a world power and large European power. This self-image made it unlikely that it would come to terms with the dominant role of the United States in NATO. Russia's membership in NATO would diminish some problems, but create many new ones. Furthermore, from the very beginning, countries such as Poland saw the United States and NATO as an instrument of protection against Russia. For these reasons, I contradicted Deputy U.S. Secretary of State Strobe Talbott when, during a discussion at the American Academy in Berlin on March 20, 1998, he pleaded for the inclusion of Russia in NATO. It was important, I said, to bind Russia closer to Europe, but not to bring it into NATO.[3]

At the end of 1991 and in early 1992, I began to advocate for the eastward enlargement of NATO. Two ideas were decisive for me here. First was the multilateral embedding of Germany in the East according to the example of relations with our Western European neighbors in NATO and the EU. Second, at the same time, the enlargement of NATO needed to reinforce the trajectory then underway toward greater security cooperation throughout all of Europe. Therefore, in my opinion, the step of integration into NATO should be tied to the step of closer cooperation/collaboration with those countries, especially Russia, who were not able or willing to join NATO. In addition, I was convinced that the political and military strategy of NATO and its defense-political deployment would have to be changed so that it would be clear that Russia could be perceived as a partner rather than an opponent of NATO.

Today, NATO regards itself reinforced again as a system of collective defense, especially against risks that originate in Russia. This shift of accent had been required by the Baltic states and Poland since the beginning of their membership. In Germany, this shift of accent was first shared by the vast majority of members of the Bundestag as a consequence of Russian behavior in the 2008 Georgian conflict, and the 2014 annexation of Crimea and Russian aggression in eastern Ukraine.

A second complex of problems arose in connection with the unification of Germany. European politicians such as British Prime Minister Margaret Thatcher, French President François Mitterrand and others sought to reanimate concepts of the "balance of power" and the "concert of powers." For centuries, these concepts were the cause of conflicts and wars in Europe. German policy regarded it as a European interest to replace these concepts with multilateral systems of cooperation and integration, as had been practiced successfully in the preceding decades in Western Europe, also now in Eastern Europe.

At the 2+4 talks, the four former victorious powers, that is, the large powers at the end of World War II, were in agreement that the defense policy of a unified Germany had to be integrated multilaterally. Because the Soviet Union presented no viable alternatives to this, in the end, the Western concept of the integration of unified Germany into NATO prevailed. Thus, with the agreement of the Soviet Union, the first eastward enlargement of NATO was agreed upon, namely the enlargement of NATO territory to include the territory of the former German Democratic Republic (GDR). At that time, this was not called the first post-Cold War enlargement of NATO, but in fact it was the first, and a precursor to the subsequent enlargements.

In order to make this first NATO eastward enlargement (I did not yet speak of an initial enlargement in 1990, but only later in the context of the enlargement of NATO to include Poland, Czechoslovakia, and Hungary) acceptable to the Soviet Union, some special arrangements were agreed: no permanent stationing of foreign troops would be allowed on the territory of the former GDR. Because Germany was forbidden to possess atomic weapons, this meant factually a nuclear weapon-free status for the territory of the former GDR. These agreements about the military status of the former GDR territory later also became the example for similar agreements for the further eastward enlargements of NATO.

The former victorious powers were not the only countries worried about the future foreign and defense policy behavior of a unified Germany. Other neighbors of Germany, e.g. Poland and Denmark, shared these concerns. From their point of view, the integration of a unified Germany into NATO and the stationing of U.S. troops in Germany guaranteed that unified Germany could also not pursue any aggressive or revisionist policies in the future. Because Germany did not have such policies in mind, these arrangements in the interest of "enlightened self-containment" were also in Germany's own interest. In this manner it was guaranteed that Germany could not do what Germany also did not intend to do. Locking Germany into multilateral structures was a good basis for good relations with all of its neighbors, including those in the East.

A third set of issues arose because at the same time the Eastern Bloc was disintegrating, national conflicts within and between countries increased in Southeastern Europe and Yugoslavia. These conflicts were frequently conducted with force. The 1994 Partnership for Peace (PfP) was an instrument for moderating the effects of these conflicts. In that the settlement of such conflicts became a precondition for acceptance in NATO or in the EU, it was possible to solve or at least contain such conflicts. The SPD supported the Partnership for Peace.

On the basis of the treaties concluded in 1990, over the next few years Germany and many of its European partners concluded numerous bilateral agreements. It became the declared goal of German policy to strive for just as good a relationship with its eastern neighbors as with its western neighbors. With an eye on this goal, those advocating for closer cooperation between the EU and the Eastern European states grew in number and influence. Full integration into the EU, however, assumed such extensive economic and social changes that even with the best intentions it could only be achieved after quite a few years.

In this context, Russia only came into question as a cooperation partner for the EU and not as a full member. Its self-image as a sovereign nuclear global power and large European power could not be reconciled with the restrictions on sovereignty associated with full membership in the EU.

When I began to advocate for the concept of an eastward enlargement of NATO at the end of 1991/beginning of 1992, I assumed that Russia would be against former members of the Warsaw Pact joining NATO. There was almost no chance to change Moscow's mind. However, Russia also had very limited possibilities to prevent it.

As Chair first of the German-Soviet and later the German-Russian parliamentary group in the Bundestag, I was always in favor of close partnerships and relationships with this country, which is so important for Europe. Particularly after the disintegration of the Soviet Union, I believed it was important in the interest of lasting stability in Europe to design the eastward enlargement of NATO politically and militarily so that it would at least be palatable to Russia. Despite all differences of opinion, conflicts, and conflicting interests, today I am still in favor of continuing to attempt to find cooperative solutions with Russia.

The idea of an eastward enlargement of NATO did not emerge on one day in 1990, but rather as the result of a lengthy process. Today, Volker Rühe and I each believe that we were the first to advocate for this concept. I no longer remember when we discussed this goal for the first time. However, when we spoke about it initially, we were both aware that we were a minority within our respective parties. It was clear to us that in the beginning there was also no majority in the United States for an eastward enlargement of NATO. Without active U.S. support for an eastward enlargement of NATO, a German commitment would have been futile. And so, both of us, each according to his abilities, sought support in Washington. Leading U.S. foreign affairs policymakers such as Strobe Talbott and Richard Holbrooke, who were reluctant in the early 1990s, later became engaged proponents.

Richard Holbrooke became a proponent during his time as Ambassador in Germany in the year 1993. In talks with him at this time, I emphasized especially that without an eastward enlargement of NATO and later of the EU that it would also be more difficult for Germany to incorporate our legitimate striving for good relations to Russia into multilateral frameworks. As a matter of course, that would only exacerbate the anxieties with which our Eastern neighbors approached a unified Germany. Locking Germany into multilateral structures would serve German and European interests equally. It would also solve many geostrategic problems from past centuries.

While others saw the Partnership for Peace as an alternative to NATO enlargement, Volker Rühe and I regarded it as a precursor. In these years, I spoke about this several times with Admiral Ulrich Weisser, the head of the planning staff at the Ministry of Defense. As leader of the study group for security of the German Council on Foreign Relations, I regularly invited him to sessions of the study group. I remember that we both explained the concept of an eastward enlargement of NATO in the study group. Over the next years we continued our discussions. In Volker Rühe's chapter in this volume, he emphasizes the important role Admiral Weisser played.

Volker Rühe advocated among the Christian Democrats and as Defense Minister for the eastward enlargement of NATO. I did this as foreign policy speaker for the SPD in the Bundestag, through my intensive contacts with diplomats in other European countries and in the United States, through discussions in think tanks and calculated publicity work.

Throughout this period, I actively sought to shape public and parliamentary opinion to win support for enlargement of the Alliance within a broader frame of cooperative security across the European continent. In the following, based on my notes and my shuttle diplomacy of that time, I offer impressions of this process, which in the end contributed to gaining strong majorities for the eastward enlargement of NATO in the German Bundestag, in other European states, and in the United States.

From January 15-20, 1992, I flew to Jamaica to attend a seminar of the Congressional Program of the Aspen Institute. The topic was relations with the post-Soviet region. Eleven U.S. Senators and five members of the U.S. House of Representatives attended, as did several U.S. specialists, such as Robert Legvold and Robert Blackwill. I was invited in order to familiarize the U.S. representatives with a German point of view. The presence of Janusz Onyszkiewicz from Poland and Andrey Kortunov and Vladimir Lukin from Russia served the same purpose. Russians, e.g. Vyacheslav Nikonov and Alexei Arbatov, also participated in later seminars in Vienna, Istanbul, St. Petersburg, Warsaw, and Berlin. Onyskiewicz and I took the opportunity to present our arguments for a NATO eastward enlargement; the Russian participants confronted the representatives with their counter-arguments. In this respect, the seminar fulfilled its purpose.

In all of the following years, up to ratification of the NATO enlargement, I continued to participate in these Aspen seminars in different places. The American participants changed. But over the years, prominent Senators and Congressmen such as Lindsey Graham, William Roth, Mitch McConnell, Joe Liebermann, Nancy Pelosi, Jon Kyle, Sam Nunn, and Richard Lugar participated. Professor Michael Mandelbaum was responsible for preparing the content of these seminars. It spoke in favor of his democratic discussion culture that he kept inviting me even though he himself was against an eastward enlargement of NATO.

When it came to working with Members of the U.S. Congress, both through the Aspen sessions and in my work within the North Atlantic Assembly, my cooperation was especially close with the Republican Senator William Roth and his advisor Ian Brzezinski.

In February 1992 I called for a "security partnership agreement" that would include Eastern European democracies in a reformed NATO if they would heed the rights of national minorities and abandon any mutual territorial claims against one another. I believed that there was an opportunity to connect transatlantic ties and pan-European tasks with one another conceptually and practically better than ever before. Since the creation of new security structures in Europe was exceedingly urgent, I argued that it was realistic to utilize existing structures as the basis for the new architecture. Even former opponents of NATO, I argued, now considered the Alliance as a factor for stability in Europe. This was a qualitatively new moment, especially since NATO itself had offered the Eastern Europeans and the former USSR its partnership and friendship. However, I added, NATO would have to transform itself from an alliance based on military deterrence into a comprehensive security alliance.

I called for an amendment to the North Atlantic Treaty in which NATO would state that it was an institution in the service of the CSCE and the North Atlantic Cooperation Council. NATO should deploy its capabilities in the interest of the CSCE to mitigate crises, prevent conflict, and avoid the re-nationalization of defense. A changed NATO, I said, should be open to all CSCE states and members of the Cooperation Council. I realized that the inclusion of new members and an amendment to the North Atlantic Treaty with the goal of stabilizing pan-European security would require unanimity and the formulation of an overall concept by NATO. But this should not stop NATO from already declaring its readiness to include stable Eastern European democracies as full members in the future. The prerequisite would be that the countries in question could not make any mutual territorial claims and they would have to guarantee the rights of national minorities. At the same time, I rejected the idea of security guarantees provided by the alliance of member states of the CIS (Community of Independent States). The Social Democratic Press Service commented on my proposal with the words: "It honors the SPD that its foreign policy speaker Voigt is the first to present a comprehensive concept for the creation of a security partnership between the Western states and those of Eastern Europe."[4]

Before going public with my views, I had discussed this concept with the foreign policy and security policy representatives of the SPD. Some embraced it; others opposed it.[5]

Soon thereafter, József Czukor, the Hungarian envoy and later Hungarian Ambassador to Germany, visited me to discuss my approach. I explained my concept of NATO enlargement and requested that Hungary make an application for admission to NATO. As he told me years later, he then wrote a report to his government. They were very astonished and would have liked him to ask whether I really meant what I said, and how I imagined such a request could be realized.

I continued my efforts in March 1992 by contributing an article to the "*Entscheidung*," the newspaper of the Christian Democratic youth organization, about the "Westernization of Eastern Europe as a Mission." Each country in Eastern Europe had its own traditions, I wrote.

But it would be foolish to believe that these traditions would lead to better democracies, better adherence to the rule of law or better economic reforms than had already been realized in the West. Therefore, the "Westernization of the East" was a progressive concept.

For me, part of this concept of the "Westernization of Eastern Europe" also involved, where possible, leading previously communist parties to the political culture of Western European social democracy. In these years, I was the representative of the SPD to the "Socialist International" and what was called at the time the "Alliance of Social Democratic Parties" in the European Community (today called the "Party of European Socialists"). Here, I advocated for the cooperation with and later membership of these parties. In coming years, many of these former communist parties voted in their respective parliaments for their countries to join NATO.

On March 3-4, 1992, I participated in the first seminar organized by the North Atlantic Assembly (today the NATO Parliamentary Assembly) in Kyiv. In my speech to the seminar participants, I advocated for close cooperation of Ukraine with NATO, however consciously did not speak about membership of Ukraine in NATO. A Russian-speaking German whom I was paying was working at the time—with his cooperation—for a Ukrainian representative in the Verkhovna Rada, the Ukrainian parliament. She organized appointments for me with the foreign minister and the most important party groups in the parliament. At these meetings, we discussed the future relationship of Ukraine to NATO and the EU.

In early April 1992, Polish President Lech Wałęsa visited Bonn. In the course of his visit, he held talks with members of the foreign affairs committee of the Bundestag. In the process, he advocated for the membership of Poland in NATO, at the same time, however, set forth confused ideas about NATO and Poland's future security-political role.

On May 22, 1992, I flew to Copenhagen at the invitation of the supreme commander of the Danish forces. In my lecture to the Danish Academy for Defense, I explained not just my ideas about an enlargement of NATO. I also advocated for having NATO be available in the future for peacekeeping deployments of the UN and the OSCE. I also made this request because it would make it easier to gain support for the eastward enlargement of NATO in countries such as Denmark and within the SPD.

On October 1, 1992, I flew to Bucharest as Chair of the Defense Committee of the North Atlantic Assembly. There I held talks with President Iliescu, Foreign Minister Nastase, Defense Minister Spirou, and the chairs of the most important committees. I also visited Romanian military units. In Romania, agreement on the eastward enlargement of NATO was unanimous. However, my partners in the talks absolutely wanted to be present at the first enlargement round. They feared that there would not be additional rounds.

A letter from Berndt von Staden, our former Ambassador in Washington, had already presented me with similar worries. He came from the Baltic region, and he too that there would not be additional enlargement rounds. If that would be the case, then the political and security position of the Baltic states could be more exposed than without any enlargement. I tried to dispel these worries with a note about additional enlargement rounds. But naturally I was not certain about this either.

At the SPD's national party convention in November 1992, I advocated for the eastern opening of institutions previously limited to the West. I said that NATO would remain a system of collective defense and would not be transformed into a system of collective security. But in future, NATO could increasingly perform functions of collective security and thus perform pan-European functions. I did not mention the goal of an eastward enlargement of NATO in this speech.

In the following months and years, I continued this exceptionally large number of talks with German, European, and American politicians, diplomats, and specialists. In the process, I used my function in the Bundestag, in German and international social democracy, to think tanks and transatlantic networks, in order to promote the concept of the eastward enlargement. Because there were countless appointments, in the following I will mention only a few talks and meetings.

From June 8-10, 1993, I flew to Slovenia. There, among other things, I met President Kucan. In my talks, there was also discussion of the eastward enlargement of NATO. However, the primary concern was the violent conflicts in Yugoslavia and the possible escalation of these conflicts. Only after Slovenia was recognized internationally as an independent state did the question of NATO membership become an important goal for this country.

Shortly after my visit to Slovenia, I met RAND analyst Ron Asmus on June 14, 1993. to discuss the eastward enlargement of NATO. We and other American proponents met repeatedly in the following months and years to compare notes and our impressions.

As the Brussels NATO Summit slated for January 10, 1994 approached, it became apparent that NATO governments were ready to adopt the U.S.-inspired Partnership for Peace, but were not yet prepared to offer aspiring countries any real perspective for membership. I felt this was wrong. On December 21, 1993, I issued a statement on behalf of the SPD Bundestag parliamentary group about the upcoming summit:

> The proposals for a Partnership for Peace previously discussed at NATO fall short in two ways. On the one hand, they are lacking sufficiently concrete and binding proposals that could truly help Russia on its imperiled path to democratic and economic reforms. On the other hand, the perspective of membership in NATO and the European Union is missing, for which the Central European reform states are rightly urging.

> As close a partner-like cooperation with a hopefully further democratizing Russia and the integration of those Central European democracies that want this and that are already capable of this should create a stable network of NATO and the European Union with our Eastern neighbors.

> At the same time, NATO and the European Union should urge all Central European states to seek good neighborly relations with Russia and one another. However, at the same time, there may be no doubt that none of our Eastern neighbors has a veto right with respect to the membership of another state in the European Union or NATO.[6]

I reinforced the message the next day in an article for the *Frankfurter Allgemeine Sonntagszeitung,* in which I criticized NATO and EU governments for failing to offer Eastern European states any membership perspective.[7] Partnership for Peace was not enough.

On January 17, 1994, a representative of the German Federal Foreign Office, Wilfried Gruber, reported to the "International Relations" study group of the German Council on Foreign Relations on the NATO Summit conclusions with regard to the enlargement issue. In advance of this summit, the Alliance had been confronted with a dilemma. On the one side were the Poles and other Visegrád states, who pushed hard. On the other were the Russians, who rejected a geographic enlargement of NATO. The Summit result was a double-track decision. On the one hand, Allies affirmed the principle that NATO's door was open to new members. On the other hand, this would be an evolutionary process—hence the Partnership for Peace.[8]

Not only was I disappointed with the Brussels Summit outcome on membership, I felt it did not go far enough in demonstrating that NATO, too, had to change, and that a new relationship with Russia had to be forged. On February 6, 1994, I wrote another article in the *Frankfurter Allgemeine Sonntagszeitung*. I reiterated my support for NATO enlargement, but underscored that it had to be proceed together with a change in NATO strategy and deeper cooperation with Russia.[9]

I increasingly used my function as Chair of the German-Russian parliamentary group in the Bundestag to speak with Russian politicians, specialists, and diplomats about the concept of NATO and EU enlargement. For instance I was in Moscow from February 9-14, 1994 and spoke there with the chairs of all party groups of all parties except for communist party leader Zyuganov and the right-radical Zhirinovsky.

In many talks with Eastern European politicians, the mixture of domestic policy, party political, and foreign policy arguments was striking. The President of the Romanian parliament visited me on April 28, 1994. He requested a private meeting. There, he asked me about the chances for his Social Democratic Party to be included in the "Socialist International." More important to him, however, was inclusion in the "Party of European Socialists," because he hoped, not without good reason, that this could facilitate his country's prospects to join the European Union. In particular, he urged that Romania be included the next round of NATO enlargement.

From July 16-20, 1994, I flew to RAND in Santa Monica. There, I discussed with Ron Asmus, Robert Blackwill, and Steve Larrabee and others conceptual details of a NATO enlargement and the respective debates about this, especially in the United States and in Germany, but also in other countries. I also explained my ideas about the role of the North Atlantic Assembly (today's NATO Parliamentary Assembly) in the further process.

In Washington in November 1994, I was elected President of the North Atlantic Assembly. In my inaugural address, I emphasized that while the Assembly had no power, it could exert influence. I made the case that it should use this influence to build support for an eastward enlargement of NATO and incorporation of Eastern European parliamentarians into the customs and culture of transatlantic relations. This way, the Assembly could also contribute to overcoming the division of Europe.[10]

In the Assembly there was still no consensus about the eastward enlargement of NATO. However, over two years the Assembly working group on this topic had made a significant contribution by clarifying questions to be considered. Shortly before the Washington meeting, the working group's "Report on NATO Enlargement" was published. Co-Chairs of this working group were Republican U.S. Senator William Roth from Delaware and Democratic U.S. Congressman Charlie Rose from North Carolina.

As Rapporteur, it was my task to prepare this report. As part of this process, I had sent a letter to all leaders of the associate delegations of Bulgaria, the Czech Republic, Hungary, and Slovakia. In this letter, I asked them to write to the working group whether they were—beyond the Partnership for Peace concept—interested in NATO membership. If so, I asked them in which type of membership they were interested:

- participation in integrated command structure (not France; special Spanish status);

- deployment of non-indigenous ground and air forces in peacetime (e.g. Germany, UK, Netherlands);

- only deployment of non-indigenous air forces in peacetime (e.g. Turkey);

- no deployment of non-indigenous forces in peacetime (e.g. Norway);

- total integration of all indigenous forces in NATO command structure already in peacetime (Germany only);

- no nuclear weapons deployment in peacetime (e.g. Norway/ Denmark).

Each delegation was clear: they wanted to be fully integrated members of the Alliance. In the 10-page report (plus appendix), the working group described and analyzed practically all arguments for and against enlargement and all relevant questions in the context of this debate.[11] I later sent these same questions to those from Belarus and Russia who represented their parliaments at the Assembly. They answered me in February 1995.

The Belarus delegation emphasized the significance of the decision to join the Partnership for Peace. Belarus wanted to be a territory free of nuclear weapons. For the foreseeable future, however, Belarus did not want to join NATO. Many people in the population, they said, would be concerned if NATO came closer to the borders of Belarus. This would be especially true if troops or, in particular, nuclear weapons were stationed in the vicinity of Belarus.[12]

The Russian delegation emphasized in its 5-page letter of February 2, 1995, "We regard NATO today not as an enemy or as a threat of any nature against the new, democratic Russia. We have the right to rely on a similar approach of the North Atlantic block with regard to Russia... Russia is attempting to set up a broad-based and deep cooperation with NATO based on the principles of mutual respect, mutual benefit, and friendship." The Russian parliamentarians went on to call for a comprehensive pan-European security model. "A transformation of NATO in the interest of European unity is of vital importance," they continued. "NATO's December agreements form a stark contrast against this backdrop...there are numerous other, international organizations such as the European Union, the Council of Europe, and the West European Union, in which membership would be a much more persuasive confirmation of belonging to Europe than would participation in NATO, which represents a transatlantic organization...it's time to reject the chronic complex with respect to the role of Russia in Europe."[13]

On January 24, 1995, I invited all members of the SPD Bundestag parliamentary group to a discussion of the topic "NATO enlargement." Over previous months it had become clear that a clear majority of foreign affairs policymakers of the SPD *Fraktion* supported this concept. Our task now was to gain stable majority support in the entire party group.

Meanwhile, I continued discussions on NATO enlargement with members of the "International Security" study group of the German Council on Foreign Relations that I was leading. On February 13, 1995, I invited its members to a discussion on the topic "New perspectives on NATO enlargement." The discussion was introduced by one representative from the Foreign Office, the Defense Ministry, and the German Institute for International and Security Affairs (SWP). Uwe Nerlich of the SWP pleaded for a careful rather than overly hasty NATO enlargement. The representative of the Foreign Office was not specific with respect to the endorsement of an enlargement, however he pleaded against haste—also with regard to Russia. The representative of the Defense Ministry expressed himself somewhat more positively about NATO enlargement, however then concentrated more on the individual questions that would have to be considered in the context of a possible enlargement.

In the discussion, the vast majority of the participants assumed that there would be an enlargement of NATO. In their remarks, they concentrated on the different positions of the individual Central European states, on the interests of the Baltic States, on specific German points of view and interests, and the relationship to Russia.[14]

Soon after that, from March 15-17, 1995, I flew to Moscow as President of the North Atlantic Assembly. I met with Russian Foreign Minister Kosyrev, Deputy Minister of Defense Kokoshin, various parliamentarians, including the Vice-President of the Duma and counsel of the Federation, members of the commission of foreign affairs and defense, and many political analysts. All of my interlocutors, without exception, declared themselves opposed to an enlargement of NATO, with Kozyrev being the most inflexible among them.

The meeting with Kozyrev was more a monologue than an exchange of views. Immediately after Kozyrev entered into the room he began to object, even before he sat down. The 20-page protocol of the secretary's office of the Assembly notes that "The Minister of Affairs described his position using a very simple formula: no to enlargement, yes to partnership." He argued that an enlargement of the Alliance would undermine cooperation between NATO and Russia and be incompatible with partnership. NATO enlargement would reduce the NATO-Russia partnership to nothingness. It would put an end to the democratic experience in Russia, and Russian public opinion could not comprehend the expansion of this military alliance. The NATO Enlargement Study underway at that time would in itself undermine cooperation with Russia; the publication of criteria would mark a new stage. Russian opinion would interpret this as an overture to negotiations, like the trigger of an irreversible process (which he qualified as an "avalanche of enlargement").

I responded by saying that I was personally in favor of enlargement, but did not think that NATO would reach a firm decision about the 'who' and the 'how' before the Russian elections. I reviewed with Kozyrev the main conclusions of the Assembly's deliberations, which encouraged the integration of new members into the Alliance in parallel with pursuit of cooperation with Russia.[15]

On May 24, 1995, the spring meeting of the North Atlantic Assembly began in Budapest. It was the first time that such a meeting was held in a former member state of the Warsaw Pact (a meeting was later held in Bucharest from October 9-12, 1997). Public interest was accordingly great. As main speakers, I had invited Volker Rühe and Richard Holbrooke, two committed proponents of enlargement. Both fulfilled my expectations. The speech was very important to Holbrooke, as Daniel Hamilton recounts in Chapter 1 of this volume. He used it not only to argue for enlargement, but to send the East Europeans a "tough love" message that NATO was unlikely to open its door to new members unless and until they resolved their own historical disputes and made real progress on political, economic and security reforms.

Among the Assembly parliamentarians, in addition to the Germans, the Scandinavians professed themselves very early as supporters of an enlargement. The British and French delayed for a long time—if for different reasons.

On June 13-14, 1995, I flew to Sofia as Assembly President. In Bulgaria, the discussion about a possible NATO enlargement had developed completely differently than in Romania. The parliament was deeply divided with respect to this question. A minority of the parliamentarians—the so-called "Euro left" and the conservative opposition—wanted to be in the first enlargement round if possible. The socialists who then reigned—a party that arose from the former communist party—was at that point still largely skeptical to dismissive. The proponents of membership in the EU were more numerous. The socialists advocated for close relations with Russia, but due to a possible EU membership wanted at the same time to become members of the "Confederation of Socialist Parties," the later "Party of European Socialists."

I had meetings with the President of the National Assembly, Sendov, with Deputy Foreign Minister Alexandrov, Defense Minister Pavlov, with Prime Minister Videnov, with the President of the Republic, Zhelev, and representatives of all political parties.[16] In my talks, I constantly emphasized that Germany as member of NATO would simultaneously maintain good, close relations with Russia and that our NATO membership would not harm our relations with Russia. No pressure would be exerted on Bulgaria to join NATO. Bulgaria would first have to decide whether it wanted to become a NATO member. Important also would be that Bulgaria seek good relations with its neighbors, and especially not let familiar border problems from Bulgaria's earlier history erupt again. But even then, there would be no automatic acceptance of Bulgarian membership to NATO. It was easy to join the Warsaw Pact, but difficult to leave it again. In NATO, the situation was reversed.

The Bulgarians made me the honorable offer of addressing their parliament. In this speech, I once again summarized the arguments from the foregoing talks into an overall concept.

I had been in Romania as Chair of the Defense Committee of the North Atlantic Assembly in October 1992. Now I flew to Bucharest from September 12-15, 1995 as Assembly President.[17] I had meetings with President Iliescu, Prime Minister Văcăroiu, the foreign and defense ministers, the leader of the Romanian delegation to the Assembly, the President of the House of Deputies, and all political parties. The Romanian interest in joining NATO as early as possible was even more perceptible than during my visit in 1992. All interlocutors wanted Romania to be considered in the next round of enlargement. They emphasized that they were striving for a similarly long-term reconciliation with Hungary as the one between Germany and France. They would make efforts to maintain good relations with all neighbors and would also respect the rights of national minorities.

From October 17-19, 1995, I flew to Warsaw as Assembly President.[18] Part of the program was a wreath-laying at the Tomb of the Unknown Soldier. This event was a very special and emotional element for a German politician. My interlocutors were President Wałęsa, the Prime Minister, the Defense Minister, the Marshall of the Sejm, the Chairman of the Foreign Affairs Committee, the Marshall of the Senate, the Undersecretary of State for Foreign Affairs, the Chair of the Defense Committee, the First Deputy Chief of the General Staff, and representatives of all political parties.

All my interlocutors wanted to become members of NATO as early as possible. They were concerned about the slowing down of this process. I remarked that this was "regrettable, but to be expected." There were four different sources for this caution: those worried about guarantees—the "Article Fivers;" those concerned about Alliance cohesion—the "NATO protectionists;" those worried about Russia—the "Russia-firsters"; and those who saw the strengthening of OSCE as a solution—the "pan-Europeans." I raised the issue of civilian control of the armed forces several times. This problem was not always taken as seriously as one would have wanted.

History played a direct or indirect role in all discussions. In my meeting with the Marshall of the Senate, my Polish interlocutor mentioned the Russian desire for a sphere of influence. I answered "that if NATO enlargement was seen in terms of spheres of influence, it became a zero-sum game; it should be seen as stabilizing by providing reassurances and confidence. If the Poles and Czechs were alone, they would become nervous if the United States or Germany were to cooperate with Russia. Membership in NATO would give these countries the confidence to cooperate with Russia. Remaining ´outside´ meant that each offer of cooperation would be seen as a competing influence; the old game in this region would start again."

My meeting with Wałęsa was dramatic. He was obviously very frustrated with what he considered to be the slow pace of enlargement. He told me he had already obtained a written agreement from Russian President Boris Yeltsin that Russia had no objections to Polish aspirations to join NATO and the EU. When I responded that Yeltsin appeared to have changed his mind, Wałęsa agreed this appeared to be so, but retorted that NATO should have taken a "man's decision." NATO was a military alliance; he had done his military service and knew what it was to take decisive decisions. What he had realized two years earlier would now take three years to materialize.

It was a question of whether or not the West would take a courageous decision, he said. It was essential not to talk of confrontation or of individual countries but of Europe. There was one continent and one civilization, not individual categories. The later enlargement was implemented the higher would be the price. Now was the opportunity to overcome the division of Europe.

In concluding the meeting, Wałęsa appealed for an acceleration of the process. Time would not wait, he said. Life would be safer and collective capabilities greater. "We join you to defend you," he told me, as we said goodbye.

I continued my campaign to win majority support in my party for NATO enlargement. On November 6, 1995 I sent to all members of the SPD Bundestag parliamentary group "10 theses about the eastward enlargement of NATO. I later used the 10 theses as the basis for a February 1996 article in the *NATO Review*.[19]

10 theses about the eastward enlargement of NATO

1. So that the principles of Europe—human and minority rights, democratic pluralism, rule of law, and freedom from violence—become the reality of a unifying Europe, beyond the strengthening of the OSCE, the European Union, the WEU, and NATO must exercise pan-European functions in that they open themselves up to the East for cooperation and integration.

2. The eastward enlargement of NATO relies, like that of the European Union, on the principle of the parallelism of integration and cooperation. The integration of new members and the deepening of cooperation with those who are not or not yet in a position or not willing to join.

3. The eastward enlargement of NATO should contribute to stability through integration. It is not provoked by an acute military threat. Therefore, in the new member states, there do not need to be any nuclear weapons or any foreign troops stationed there.

4. The eastward enlargement of NATO and the European Union should complete the already completed multilateral integration of Germany into the West. This obligates Germany in the interest of stability in Europe to consider the interests of its neighbors when pursuing its own values and interests. The eastward expansion shall prevent a bilateralism in German politics toward the East that is problematic for Germany's neighbors in the East and West.

5. NATO is interested in good, close partner-like relations with Russia and Ukraine. The process for accepting new members into NATO must accompany parallels mechanisms of cooperation. A security partnership to be secured contractually between Russia and NATO should allow for Russia's singular status as nuclear power and as permanent member of the Security Council. Russia should be informed immediately about decisions within NATO and be consulted on questions of collective security in Europe. In addition, the OSCE should be strengthened. Parallel to agreements with Russia, a security partnership with Ukraine should be striven for.

6. Above all, the eastward expansion of NATO is a political decision about whether states that want to join can support the values and principles of the alliance. The minimum conditions that must be fulfilled: democracy and a free-market economy must be anchored; the new member state must be in a position to promote the principles of the Washington Treaty and contribute to the security of the North Atlantic territory; its membership must bring a security gain for both sides, which means unresolved conflicts such as territorial and minority problems may not be brought into the alliance, it must be in a position to bear appropriately the costs of membership, each new member must have the agreement of all 16 NATO members in the ratification process, and its inclusion may not prevent the inclusion of other candidates.

7. Adherence to these minimum conditions is required in order to maintain democratic credibility and NATO's ability to act. This also means that not all states that want to join will join at one time. Accession negotiations should begin in the second half of 1996. This also means that Russia's fear that NATO will rush into an eastward enlargement is unfounded.

8. It is anticipated that some of the young European democracies will be able to join NATO earlier than the European Union. No conscious obstacles should be placed in the way of their integration efforts. Therefore, there is a conceptual relationship between the

enlargement of NATO and the European Union, but no necessary temporal parallel.

9. The dynamic of the enlargement process should be maintained despite current objections. The enlargement study passed by the NATO council at the start of October [1995] represents an important step even if the study does not make any clear statements about some important questions, for example, with respect to the beginning of the accession negotiations and about partnership relations with Russia and Ukraine.

10. The decision about the enlargement of NATO will be made solely by the 16 member states and the candidate countries; there is no veto right from a third party. The eastward enlargement is not directed at anyone. It prevents the re-nationalization of the security policy of the Eastern European states and thus serves stability and security in Europe overall. A nationally organized security policy of the Eastern European states can become a motive for the arming of these states. Furthermore, an integration of these states into NATO can be used for increased disarmament efforts. For this, first and foremost, additions to the Conventional Forces in Europe Treaty (CFE) should result in lower upper limits.

On December 4, 1995 at the Friedrich Ebert Stiftung, I used the 10 theses to discuss NATO enlargement with German peace researchers, who still harbored great reservations about the issue. I placed the debate in the context of German domestic politics. "With the end of the power and system-political bipolarity between East and West," I argued, "the basis has been removed for the previous bipolarity between CDU and SPD in the discussion of foreign affairs and security policy in Germany." I also framed the debate on NATO in the context of broader changes to the architecture of European security. "The OSCE should not just be maintained, but also strengthened," I said. "However, anyone who proclaims the strengthening of the OSCE not as an additional measure but rather as a substitute for the eastward enlargement of NATO and WEU is really talking about the sacrifice of a deeper integration with and between states that are ready and in a position for a deeper multilateral integration of their foreign and security policy.... An enlarged NATO bound to Russia and Ukraine by a treaty is still not a system of collective security. It is still a system of collective defense, but it fulfills functions of collective security."[20]

That same day I led another session of the "International Security" study group at the German Council of Foreign Relations on "How do we continue with the NATO eastward enlargement?" I asked NATO Assistant Secretary General for Political Questions, Ambassador Gebhardt von Moltke and Russian Ambassador Terechov to provide opening statements. Based on the explanation of the official position of NATO and the Russian Federation, subsequently all aspects of the NATO enlargement were discussed.[21]

From May 25–June 2, 1996, I visited Poland again as President of the Assembly. In addition to talks with most of the leading politicians and in the relevant ministries, I was given the honor of addressing the Sejm, the Polish parliament. In the process, I emphasized that I would speak not just as President of the NATO Parliamentary Assembly, but also as a German politician. From my point of view, the enlargement of NATO was a historical setting in which centuries-old dilemmas in relations between Russia and Poland could be overcome. We Germans could work closely with Russia without having Poland feel threatened on account of this. And Poland, as a member of a multilateral transatlantic alliance, could develop close, constructive relations with unified Germany and in the end also with Russia without requiring reinsurance through bilateral treaties with Western partners. This bilateral reinsurance of Poland in the West would never have proven reliable in the past.

From June 15-17, 1996, I flew to Bratislava, Slovakia as President of the Assembly. The talks with the President, the Foreign Minister, the Defense Minister, and the various parties and committees in the parliament were very constructive. My interlocutors urged that Slovakia be considered for the next round of the NATO enlargement. My indication that this also depended on the development of democracy and the rule of law in Slovakia met with resistance. Some partners in the talks even asserted that there was a secret agreement with the Russian leadership to the detriment of Slovakian membership. My talk with Prime Minister Vladimír Mečiar were contentious. He did not accept my argument that the decision about inclusion in NATO would not be made based on geostrategic considerations, but also assumed as a prerequisite Slovakia's adherence to democratic principles and the rule of law.[22]

From September 14-17, 1996, I flew to Kyiv as President of the NATO PA. I held talks with President Kuchma, Prime Minister Lazarenko, the Defense Minister, the President of the Parliament, and the relevant committees and party groups of the parliament. In my talks, I remained true to my earlier position. I favored cooperation between Ukraine and NATO, but not membership. With the Foreign Minister, I went through point by point a list I had made of European treaties and organizations of which Ukraine could be a member without being a member of the EU. I did not talk about the question of future membership of Ukraine in the EU. However, this topic was addressed by several Ukrainian interlocutors. Several participants in the talks advocated for a NATO membership of Ukraine. Some of those who desired this believed it was unrealistic. Others advocated for non-alignment, linked to a close cooperation with NATO. Regardless of which position the Ukrainian politicians represented, each discussion was overshadowed by the question about the relationship of Ukraine to Russia.[23]

From October 21-23, 1996, I visited Estonia, where I met with the President, the Prime Minister, the Defense Minister, the President of the Parliament, and the most important committees and party groups in the parliament. In Tallinn, all of my interlocutors wanted Estonia to join NATO. The dominant reason for this was the fear of Russian revisionism. I could understand this fear, but I did not share it at that point. I supported the Baltic states' desire to join NATO, but only in a second enlargement round. Before that point it would be possible to reinforce cooperation with NATO and naturally also with the EU on many levels. President Meri expressed the fear that if Poland entered NATO and the Baltic states did not, this could cause problems with respect to Kaliningrad. In an address to the Estonian parliament, I had the opportunity to give reasons for the overall concept of the policy of NATO enlargement.[24]

I completed the series of my visits to future NATO member states with a visit in Prague from October 29-31, 1996. There, I met all the politicians important for the question of joining NATO. Czech President Havel especially impressed me.

From January 23-26, 1997, I flew to Moscow for a conference of the Friedrich Ebert Stiftung. After the talks there, I stated again that the members of NATO should not wait for the agreement of Russia for NATO enlargement. At best, Russia would tolerate such an enlargement, but would not explicitly agree to it. I represented the same conviction in speeches to the Bundestag on February 28 and June 26, 1997. By the time I delivered these speeches, a clear majority of the leadership of the SPD now advocated for NATO enlargement. At that time, the SPD would also have been in favor of including a larger number of states, e.g. also Romania and Slovenia, in the first enlargement round.

On March 21, 1997, I flew to Tokyo for the meeting of the Trilateral Commission. In connection with this meeting, the Tokyo office of the Friedrich Ebert Stiftung organized appointments for me with parliamentarians and at the foreign and defense ministries. One of the topics was the possible consequences of an eastward enlargement of NATO on the security situation in East Asia. In September 1998, I flew to Asia again, this time to Beijing and Tokyo. At the talks in both capitals, there was concern about the possible consequences of the eastward enlargement of NATO for East Asia. The greater concern, however, was the future foreign policy of Germany in case of a government coalition between the SPD and the Greens.

To round out the picture: On May 12, 1997, Joschka Fischer and I went to our old favorite pub from the times of the 1968 student movement, the "Club Voltaire" in Frankfurt. There, with moderate success, I defended the concept of an eastward enlargement of NATO. The vast majority of the Greens were still against it at that time. But it became clear: after the end of the Cold War, the foreign policy front lines between the parties in Germany had begun to change.

On July 8-9, 1997 at the Madrid NATO Summit, Alliance leaders invited the Czech Republic, Hungary and Poland to join the Alliance. On March 26, 1998, 554 of the 621 members in the Bundestag—including almost all members of the CDU, FDP and SPD as well as a minority of the Greens—agreed to the entry of the three countries into NATO. Only 37 members voted against, and 30 abstained. By the time the three new members took their seats at NATO's 50th anniversary summit in 1999, Germany's new Chancellor, Social Democrat Gerhard Schröder, and Germany's Green Foreign Minister, Joschka Fischer, welcomed them into the Alliance.

Notes

1. During the subsequent 2+4 Talks the foreign policy spokespersons of the parties represented in the Bundestag, which included me, were regularly informed of progress by the State Secretary in the Foreign Office Dieter Kastrup. We were informed that the German position was that except for the question of Poland's western border the negotiations were not to discuss 3rd state issues of any kind. Such an extension of the negotiating framework would be counter to German interests.

2. For details about the talks in Moscow and their context, see my article "Anfang 1990: Die SPD, Moskau und die NATO-Frage," in *Das Blättchen*, Vol. 19, No. 5, February 2016.

3. See the summary of the discussion in the *Süddeutsche Zeitung*, March 21, 1998.

4. Parallel to the democracy movements, nationalistic ideologies and national conflicts were increasing in Eastern Europe and the Soviet Union, also in Caucasus, in Yugoslavia, and also in the Baltic states. This thawing of mentalities and conflicts suppressed during the Cold War was of great concern to me at that time. This analysis was also a reason for me to work against these tendencies with effective multilateral structures. For a summary of my remarks, see *Parlamentarisch-Politischer Pressedienst*, PPP, February 25, 1992. In: Archiv der Sozialen Demokratie, Depositum Voigt.

5. According to the protocol of the conclave of the speakers of the SPD Bundestag parliamentary group on February 21, 1992. it was said quite rightly: "Brigitte Schulte sees significant differences in the question of the enlargement of the NATO alliance and future role of the CSCE, the Council of Europe, and NATO overall." Availabile in: Archiv der Sozialen Demokratie, Depositum Voigt,

6. Press release from December 21, 1993. Archiv der Sozialen Demokratie, Depositum Voigt.

7. Karsten D. Voigt, "Die NATO, Osteuropa und Russland," *Frankfurter Allgemeine Sonntagszeitung*, December 22, 1993.

8. Protocol of the session of the "International Relations" study group of the DGAP, January 17, 1994. In: Archiv der Sozialen Demokratie, Depositum Voigt.

9. Karsten D. Voigt, "Osterweiterung der NATO ja, aber nicht Hals über Kopf," *Frankfurter Allgemeine Sonntagszeitung*, February 6, 1994.

10. Speech at the meeting of the NATO-PA on November 18, 1994. In: Archiv der Sozialen Demokratie. Depositum Voigt.

11. Defense and security committee—Working Group On NATO Enlargement, November 1994. Archiv der Sozialen Demokratie. Depositum Voigt.

12. Letter to Karsten Voigt from Ivan Tsyareshko, Leader of the Belarus Delegation to the North Atlantic Assembly, February 7, 1995. In: Archiv der Sozialen Demokratie. Depositum Voigt.

13. Letter from the Deputy Chair of the Federation Council, Viktorov, from 2/2/1995. In: Archiv der Sozialen Demokratie. Depositum Voigt.

14. Protocol of the session of the "International Security" study group of the DGAP, February 13, 1995. Archiv der Sozialen Demokratie. Depositum Voigt.

15. Resume et bref compte rendu de la visite du president Karsten Voigt a Moscou, 15 au 17 Marc 1995. In: Archiv der Sozialen Demokratie. Depositum Voigt.

16. Summary and brief account of the visit to Sofia by president Voigt, June 13-14, 1995. In: Archiv der Sozialen Demokratie. Depositum Voigt.

17. Summary and brief account of the visit to Bucharest by President Karsten Voigt. September 12-15, 1995. In: Archiv der Sozialen Demokratie. Depositum Voigt.

18. Summary and brief account of the visit to Poland by President Karsten Voigt. October 17-19, 1995, 28 pages long. In: Archiv der Sozialen Demokratie. Depositum Voigt.

19. In: Archiv der sozialen Demokratie. Depositum Voigt.

20. Manuscript of the lecture in: Archiv der sozialen Demokratie. Depositum Voigt.

21. Protocol of the session in: Archiv der Sozialen Demokratie. Depositum Voigt.

22. Summary and brief account of the visit of President Karsten Voigt, June 15-17, 1996, In: Archiv der Sozialen Demokratie, Depositum Voigt.

23. Summary and account of the visit to the Ukraine by President Karsten Voigt, September 15-17, 1996. In. Archiv der Sozialen Demokratie. Depositum Voigt.

24. Summary and brief account, President Karsten Voigt´s visit to Estonia October 21-23, 1996. In: Archiv der Sozialen Demokratie. Depositum Voigt.

Chapter 12

Enlarging NATO: The Initial Clinton Years

Jenonne Walker

The end of the Cold War presented the West with obvious opportunities but also with a tangle of challenges and trade-offs that policy makers knew they could only imperfectly understand. Trying to deal sensibly with the dizzying pace of change sometimes seemed like painting a moving train. Top American diplomat Larry Eagleburger captured the times when he answered a question about whether he was guilty of nostalgia for the Cold War: "Hell, I'm nostalgic for last week."

Western governments wanted to do all they could to help stabilize the independence of Central and East European states—former Soviet satellites and republics alike—and aid their transition to democracy and market economy. At the same time, they wanted to support democratic forces within Russia and build a constructive relationship between it and the West. Most Washington career officials, civilian and military, saw a possible conflict between these goals, but President Clinton never seemed to waver from his belief that he could do both. Western leaders also had to deal with question of NATO's own role and relevance once the military threat to its members was believed to have disappeared, especially in light of its unwillingness to resist Serbian aggression in Bosnia. These issues, in turn, were related to the political and security role of the European Union, now presumably less in need of American military protection and apparently eager to take more responsibility for its own security—and what its evolution might mean for NATO, for good or ill.

All the former Soviet satellites, and several of its former republics, felt an urgent need to be firmly linked in some Western structure. Most looked first to the European Union, with its tight political links and the economic benefits of membership. As realization grew that EU membership would face tough conditions and take a long time, attention turned to NATO.

Like good bureaucrats almost always almost everywhere when faced with hard issues, the first instinct in the West was delay. There were various reasons, some better than others. Much as we wished the countries of Central and Eastern Europe well, the old system had been comfortable for the West. Decades of planning and training and playing together had formed close bonds among civilian and military security officials across the Atlantic which were unlikely to be replicated, and could well be diluted, by the addition of those whose backgrounds and perspectives inevitably would be different. One senior American diplomat bemoaned, "nothing will ever be the same" if NATO enlarged. As former Secretary of Defense James Schlesinger told a Washington conference, "governments tend to go on doing what they know how to do well; that's how they get into trouble." But it also was clear that none of the Central or Eastern European states was yet ready for NATO or EU membership and that continuing changes in all of them made it hard to know which would be ready to become members, or when.

In addition to skillfully managing the unification of Germany within NATO (a united Germany, untethered from multilateral structures, would have alarmed its neighbors to the west as well as east), the George H.W. Bush administration focused almost exclusively on supporting the transition to market economies—a key issue given the importance to democracy of economic health and a strong middle class. The Clinton administration continued those efforts and added more direct support to the underpinnings of democracy—non-governmental organizations, journalists, judicial and police reform, local governments.

On NATO membership, senior working level officials in the Clinton administration at first adopted the mantra of the Bush administration: it was "a question for the future, not now." From the beginning, however, any paper sent to the President with those words would be returned with his left-handed scrawl in the margins: "why not now?" American support for Central and Eastern European integration into NATO and other Western structures, as broadly as possible and as soon as possible, was consistently driven from the top.

The question was what "as possible" reasonably could mean. As Washington saw the NATO issue, it was not only which countries might join and when, but also how to help them prepare for membership and how to strengthen Western ties with those who could only join later, or maybe never.

The Defense Department was most wary, understandably so about taking on new commitments to defend countries in the midst of rapid change and unable at that time to contribute much or anything to their own defense or even to support NATO forces if necessary. However unlikely a military threat then seemed, military planners are paid to prepare for worst cases. Money also mattered. The cost of assimilating new NATO members could be substantial; whatever new funds Congress might provide, some diversion of Defense Department resources was likely. Opinions within both the State Department and the NSC staff varied, and those of individuals changed along the way.

At the June 1993 NATO Foreign Ministers' meeting in Greece, Allies agreed to a Washington proposal for a Summit in December 1993 (later slipped to January 1994). I was then Senior Director for Europe on the U.S. National Security Council (NSC) staff and thus chaired senior Interagency Groups for crises (Bosnia) and issues of equal concern to two or more Departments (NATO). As soon as we returned home from Greece, I convened an Interagency Group to prepare for the Summit. Other key members were the State Department's Principal Deputy Assistant Secretary for European Affairs Alexander Vershbow (later U.S. Ambassador at NATO and then to Russia); Deputy Under Secretary of Defense for Policy (soon to be Under Secretary) Walter Slocombe; and Chief of Strategic Plans and Policy for the Joint Chiefs of Staff General Barry McCaffrey. Each of these was backed by an impressive group of experts who contributed significantly. All participants also were deeply engaged in Bosnia, which in fact absorbed most of our time and attention. The same was true for the Principals Committee to which we reported: National Security Advisor Tony Lake; his Deputy Sandy Berger; Secretary of State Warren Christopher; Secretary of Defense Les Aspin; Chairman of the Joint Chiefs of Staff Colin Powell; Ambassador to the UN Madeleine Albright; and Director of Central Intelligence James Woolsey.

All members of the Interagency Group agreed from the outset that the Summit Communique should take concrete new steps, not just affirm Allies' devotion to NATO—and that Washington should have proposals to that end when European allies returned in September from summer holiday.

NATO's relations with its neighbors to the east topped the agenda. There already was a North Atlantic Cooperation Council (NACC), established in 1991 during the George H. W. Bush Presidency, to which all European states—including Russia—sent representatives for consultations with NATO's North Atlantic Council on a range of issues. The State Department had a list of ideas for upgrading NACC, ranging from the mildly substantive to assigning its non-NATO members free parking places at Alliance headquarters. The NSC staff felt strongly that something more was needed—a recognizably significant departure rather than a grab-bag of small improvements to existing arrangements.

At the Group's initial meeting I laid out the bones of what became the Partnership for Peace (PfP), an idea that was elaborated by all. Indeed it became apparent that American officials at NATO had been thinking along similar lines and their ideas were fed into the Washington process. NATO would invite all European states, again including Russia, to join the PfP and send permanent staffs not only to NATO headquarters outside Brussels but also to its military command at Mons, Belgium. Non-NATO PfP members would plan and exercise with NATO members for possible operations. There were to be no criteria for joining the PfP, but non-NATO members would share with NATO their plans for military and political reforms. (When I asked Sweden's Deputy Foreign Minister how they would feel about the requirement to share Sweden's plans to become a democracy, he smilingly said they understood its purpose and would be happy to comply.)

Washington knew that NATO had an "out of area" problem: to remain relevant after the Cold War it had to do more than continue preparing to repel a highly unlikely Russian attack on Western Europe. "Out of area or out of business," the saying went. To address this problem John Shalikashvili, the American General who was then Supreme Commander of NATO's military forces and soon to become Chairman of the U.S. Joint Chiefs of Staff, proposed creation of Combined Joint Task Forces (CJTF): multinational, multi-service headquarters units which would plan and train to direct military operations beyond NATO's geographic area. Non-NATO members of the PfP could participate.

Shalikashvili also proposed that the European Union—then acting as the Western European Union or however it chose to organize its security and defense cooperation—could use a CJTF or other NATO assets for operations in which NATO chose not to participate. NATO, including the United States, would have to approve the use of NATO assets, but after that the operation would be under EU/WEU control. (NATO of course does not "own" combat forces, which are under national control until and unless assigned to a specific NATO mission. NATO's own assets at that time included, for example, an Airborne Warning and Control Systems (AWACS) and some logistics capabilities such as a pipeline.)

This was an American proposal for the Summit, not a concession to the French or others as some have suggested. It was a dramatic departure for Washington, which for years had seen NATO as the key instrument of its influence in Europe and viewed any other form of security cooperation as potentially a mortal rival. It was understandably controversial. One senior American diplomat then posted in Europe sent a fax to his Washington peers saying all that remained was to "rename the Alliance OTAN" (the French acronym for NATO).

I suspected that some in Washington hoped that making European-only military operations dependent on NATO assets, and thus subject to U.S. veto, would curb European efforts to build truly separate arrangements; capabilities would be "separable but not separate." But Bosnia had made Clinton Administration leaders, very much including Shalikashvili at NATO and Colin Powell speaking for the Joint Chiefs of Staff, keenly aware that there could be situations calling for Western military engagement in which the United States would not want to participate—and that NATO would not act without significant U.S. involvement. Also, at that time of enthusiasm for European integration among West European governments and people, it was believed that acting to "build Europe" might gain more popular support for defense efforts than contributing to an American-led enterprise, thus strengthening NATO's own "European pillar."

All this—creating the PfP and CJTFs, making NATO assets available for European Union missions—was agreed relatively easily at the senior working level. Two things slowed formal approval. One was the name. The working title had been Peacekeeping Partnership, until the killing of 18 American soldiers in Somalia in October 1993 made "peacekeeping" a dirty word in Washington. There was a longish pause until a Pentagon official came up with "Partnership for Peace." The other was more substantive. A newly-arrived senior political appointee in the Defense Department wanted to upend things and require each non-NATO country to apply for Partnership membership and its fitness be judged by NATO. His bosses didn't support him but thought he should be given a hearing by the Principals Committee. Both these issues should have been resolved quickly, but the Principals were meeting almost daily on the Bosnian morass and it took time to get their attention. The delay added to suspicions, in Central Europe and elsewhere, that Washington was stalling.

We saw the PfP and CJTFs as related to the question of NATO enlargement. Participating in them would help Central and Eastern European states learn to operate with NATO and could prepare at least some of them for membership. They could be in at the beginning of the CJTFs, rather than just signing on to longstanding NATO activity.

Decision

With regard to NATO enlargement itself, all understood the strong commitment of the President, his National Security Advisor, and the Secretary of State. Some key political-level officials, notably Secretary of State Christopher and U.N. Ambassador Albright, initially wanted the NATO Summit at least to designate some Central and East European states associate members, or candidate members, or set a timetable for admitting new members—something more than just promising pie in a distant sky. All members of the Interagency Group were more cautious. While few if any voiced outright opposition to NATO enlargement, some clearly wanted to delay it as long as possible. And even those more supportive (or at least resigned) believed that part of their job was ensuring that their political masters understood the possible pitfalls both of enlargement and of its careless handling.

The arguments for enlargement were understood by everyone. Whether or not Central and East European states faced a military threat, the confidence and therefore stability provided by NATO membership could underpin economic and political reforms, much as had been done for West European countries in the Alliance's early days. Membership could ingrain patterns of cooperation among peoples and governments previously wary of each other. It could promote key elements of democracy like civilian control of the military and transparency of military budgets. Finally, it would have been very hard for Western leaders to say that Luxembourg might need NATO's military protection, but Poland never would.

A less admirable reason for some to push NATO enlargement was to distract attention from Washington's unwillingness to oppose Serbian aggression in Bosnia. Enlargement was to make NATO seem vigorous, on the move, despite its absence from Europe's worst conflict in the Alliance's history. The shadow of that war loomed over everything. One senior political-level official in the State Department even drafted a speech arguing explicitly the need to "enlarge NATO to save it," but was dissuaded from being so blunt in public.

At the same time the Clinton Administration, from the President on down, was doing all it could, in big ways and small, to build a constructive relationship with a Russia which at that time seemed open to one. No one expected Moscow to like the idea that its former enemy would move closer to its borders and absorb some of its former satellites and possibly even, in time, republics. No one could be sure how much NATO enlargement might damage Russia's relations with the West or democratic forces within Russia. But all on the Interagency Group took the problem seriously.

Some East Europeans also urged caution. The Ukrainian Foreign Minister told us that he knew his country would not be among the first new NATO members, but urged that it be given five years or so to entrench its independence before NATO took in other former communist states.

We also had concerns about whether early NATO membership would necessarily be an unmitigated good for potential new members. Would it lead them to divert resources from building strong economies to unnecessary defense spending? While defense contractors did urge aspiring countries to do just that, NATO's military leaders, including top American generals like Shalikashvili, toured the region telling them that big ticket items like supersonic fighter jets were not necessary and that less expensive things like NATO-compatible communications gear were far more important. As one member of the U.S. delegation to NATO put it: "we care less whether they have their own supersonic jets than whether their airfields can refuel ours." Another concern was whether, given the importance of democracy in NATO's criteria for new members (see below), countries doing well, and so less in need of the stabilizing benefits of membership, would be admitted while those still struggling might be seen by their publics as having been rebuffed. (To their credit, countries not in the first batch of new members redoubled their efforts, with public understanding and support.)

If NATO were to designate associate or candidate members, how could it be sure which they should be? At the time of NATO's January 1994 Summit, Slovakia probably would have been included, but under Prime Minister Mečiar it soon experienced a period of political backsliding that kept it from being among the first new members.

These and other considerations, such as the cost of assimilating new members, formed the bulk of a Pros/Cons paper the Interagency Group submitted to the Principals. The paper did not turn any of them against NATO enlargement. But it did persuade all that the January 1994 Summit should be only the beginning of a slower process than some, in Washington as well as in the Central and Eastern European countries themselves, had hoped. President Clinton's Deputy National Security Advisor Berger remarked on the paper, "this shows that it (NATO enlargement) is a lot more complicated than we thought." Another member of the Principals Committee noted, after reading the paper, that "it looks like this (a general commitment to NATO enlargement, without further details) is all we can do for now" (at the January 1994 Summit).

With one exception, there was no disagreement among members of the Interagency Committee on what the pros and cons were and how to describe them, even though some struck different balances and so reached different conclusions. It was a remarkably congenial and cooperative effort. The exception was a newly appointed political appointee in the Pentagon who pressed me forcibly on the telephone to eliminate key "pros" for NATO enlargement. I refused and he dropped the matter.

On the issue of criteria for membership, there was easy agreement that democracy, market economies, respect for human rights and the sovereignty of others should come first and military factors put farther down the list. Among the latter, civilian control and defense budget transparency were listed ahead of military capability and interoperability with NATO. The Clinton Administration understood that the chief incentive for political and economic reform in the former communist east would be the lure of European Union membership, but wanted NATO to contribute what it could. Its Summit proposals were designed to that end.

Washington bungled the rollout of its package. Final details of the PfP (its name, whether there would be conditionality) were decided just before a previously scheduled NATO Defense Ministers meeting in December 1993. Secretary of State Christopher first briefed his opposite numbers by telephone, and then Secretary of Defense Aspin elaborated the proposal to his fellow Defense Ministers. Press accounts of the latter meeting gave the impression that PfP was a substitute for NATO membership rather a step toward it at least for some.

That suited most West European Allies just fine. While none objected publicly to NATO enlargement in principle, few wanted to move as rapidly as President Clinton. Many in the public thought Germany was an exception, especially when its Defense Minister Rühe published an op-ed in a major American newspaper supporting rapid enlargement. But at the same time Chancellor Kohl was urging President Clinton to slow down lest he damage relations with Russia.

In the end, the January 1994 NATO Summit communique declared that the Alliance "expects and would welcome" expansion to "democratic states of the east" in an "evolutionary manner." Allied briefings stressed that this could include Russia. While we were still in Brussels, I shared a television interview with Kenneth Adelman, a prominent Republican security expert. When asked if I really believed Russia might ever join NATO, Adelman, luckily for me, jumped in with the perfect answer: "I don't ever expect to see Russia in NATO, but I didn't expect to see the Berlin Wall come down or the Soviet Union to disintegrate."

The Summit language meant different things to different people. To many it seemed a reiteration of the old "question for the future but not now" attitude. West Europeans allies went home comfortable that the issue had been settled for the foreseeable future. Russian security officials may have had a similar reaction; they voiced no objections to the Summit outcome when I joined Under Secretary of Defense Frank

Wisner in briefing them on the margins of President Clinton's subsequent meetings with President Yeltsin in Moscow. Strobe Talbott's chapter in this book relates the far more important Clinton-Yeltsin discussions then taking place. Central and Eastern European states were understandably disappointed. But Madeleine Albright and General Shalikashvili had previewed our positions in pre-Summit visits, which helped soften the blow. More important was President Clinton's affirmation, when he met Central European leaders in Prague immediately after the Summit, that enlargement was a question of when, not if.

To dispel impressions that the NATO Summit language on enlargement had been just a place-holding temporizer, National Security Advisor Lake directed that a study be launched on the when and how of enlargement. He wanted to keep the issue out of America's 1994 mid-term elections, but in the meantime to use the study to show commitment and momentum. Some West European allies felt they'd been misled.

The View From Prague

I was still on the NSC staff when Lake asked for the study, but I left in the summer of 1994 to prepare for a new post as U.S. Ambassador to the Czech Republic. From that vantage point I saw how one candidate country was preparing for NATO membership, and the role of the U.S. Embassy there.

On the whole the Czech course was quite smooth. NATO and EU membership were each enthusiastically supported by Czech leaders across the political spectrum and by the populace. The beginning of serious NATO air action in Bosnia on August 31, 1995 strengthened this feeling; the Czech Foreign Minister and other key figures told me excitedly "this shows that NATO still is relevant." One exception was Prime Minister Klaus, who told me privately that NATO membership would be a waste of money, but acknowledged that he could not say so publicly or try to make opposition the position of his party or the Czech government.

The U.S. Embassy's Defense Attaché arranged for Czech military and civilian defense officials to participate in a wide array of training programs on how to work with NATO, while both it and the Political Section discussed parliamentary oversight with Czech legislators.

Washington wanted its ambassadors in Central Europe to promote NATO membership, but that was scarcely necessary in Prague. A small minority did see NATO as only a war-fighting body and claimed Washington should focus instead on conflict prevention. I spent quite a lot of time trying to ensure that Czechs understood what NATO was and was not, including the conflict-prevention importance of deterrence, and explaining the Clinton Administration's support for the security roles of the Organization for Security and Cooperation in Europe, the Council of Europe, and especially the European Union. I also tried, with very limited success, to remind Czechs that they needed to pay attention to the West European parliaments that would have to ratify their NATO membership.

There were bumps in the road. A senior American general based in Europe came to town and told the press that the Czechs were failing in membership preparations, specifically because their defense budget was half that of Hungary and growing at half the pace. The opposite was true; he had his countries confused. I worried that his factual mistakes would have enabled Prime Minister Klaus to say we didn't know what we were talking about when we urged the improvements the Czechs did need to make. At the other extreme, the other NATO ambassadors in Prague and I were concerned when General Shalikashvili visited and said publicly that the Czechs were "ready now" to join, or when Madeleine Albright, by now Secretary of State, came to town and told them "welcome home."

None of these incidents, however, seemed to affect Czech preparations. They had decided early to concentrate first on building one Rapid Response Brigade and on English language training. The head of the Czech Army told me proudly that he would be the last in his job who was not fluent in English. In late 1995 they eagerly joined enforcement of the Dayton accords in Bosnia, welcoming the chance to show that their military could operate with NATO.

More troublesome for the Embassy was the competition between two major American defense contractors, each trying to persuade the Czechs that U.S. Senate ratification of their NATO membership depended on their buying its supersonic fighter airplane. Individuals in each company were eager to find evidence that the Embassy was favoring the other. This became so extreme that when former U.S. Senator

Bob Dole came to town, I felt I could not join his meetings because one of his law partners represented one of the companies, and the other likely would have accused me of helping him sell its rival's plane. Dole did not mention airplanes to the Czechs. Already a strong supporter of enlargement, he told me that he was visiting the candidate states so he could tell his former Senate colleagues that he had seen their fitness with his own eyes. Savvy about Washington, he understood and was gracious about my predicament.

The Clinton Administration's efforts to secure Senate ratification of NATO enlargement is covered in Jeremy Rosner's chapter of this book. U.S. Embassy Prague's participation was minimal. We arranged meetings for the steady stream (sometimes flood) of U.S. executive and legislative branch visitors to Prague (then the flavor of the month for Westerners). Czechs were less good at selling themselves (whether their military abilities, export goods, or cultural attractions) than Poles or Hungarians, but had solid progress to show and did so effectively to official American visitors. In February 1998, U.S. Ambassadors in the three candidate countries accompanied "our" Foreign Ministers when they traveled to Washington to make their case on Capitol Hill. In April of that year, the U.S. Senate ratified accession of the three to NATO.

Concluding Reflections

Other chapters in this book and talks with some of the authors show how the NATO enlargement story illustrates two recurring aspects of U.S.—and probably other—foreign policy making.

The first is that even those who participate in the same discussions can come away with different understandings of the decisions, depending at least in part on what outcome they wanted. While those of us working in the White House understood that deciding the "how and when" of enlargement might be tough going, we believed the basic decision to enlarge had been taken with the Summit language expecting and welcoming it. We saw that as the Summit's prime accomplishment. In sharp contrast, senior American diplomats who had been key participants in pre-Summit deliberations thought the Summit decided on PfP as a substitute for enlargement.

The second point is how little presidential decisions sometimes settle. The U.S. Defense Department's continued opposition to enlargement is well known, but it was not alone. It took a long time even to get the Enlargement Study underway. Implementation of other policies also was rocky. The ink was scarcely dry on the Summit decision that the EU could borrow and command a CJTF before NATO's top military commander (a U.S. general) began trying to ensure any operation using one would be under his ultimate command. Later, a new Assistant Secretary of State for Europe began cautioning European diplomats that EU security cooperation risked damaging transatlantic ties, although President Clinton had made no decision to change American support for it.

There is nothing new in this. Except on long-running, major crises requiring continued presidential/prime ministerial involvement in the details, heads of government in most countries, their foreign ministers and national security advisors, do their best thinking on an issue, make a decision, then necessarily move on to the next problem, unable to monitor implementation of what they think they have mandated. Harry Truman was exaggerating but had a point when he said, as Eisenhower was about to assume the presidency: "Poor Ike. He'll sit at this desk and say "do this, do that" and nothing will happen."

Chapter 13

Redrawing the Maps:
Rethinking Atlantic Security in the 1990s

John C. Kornblum

How best to focus Western security institutions has been a never-ending task for Alliance nations since 1949. The Atlantic community in its present form emerged from widespread concern about the Soviet threat. Its reach expanded during the 1950s when NATO provided a foundation for the first steps towards European integration. With this new task added, NATO emerged as the most important transatlantic link, whose importance surpassed the original focus on the Soviet Union. These mutually supporting goals defined the Atlantic community for forty years. This evolution was much on the mind of many European and American officials as the post-Cold War era began to unfold.

Ironically, NATO was originally a European project to keep the Americans engaged on the continent, while European unity was originally an American effort to disengage itself from a permanent presence on the continent. After the project for a European Defense Force failed in 1954, however, NATO assumed a more central role and the American umbrella became more permanent.

NATO's guarantee of European stability and democracy played a central role in support of the first steps towards European unity. Failing a common European defense structure, NATO was needed as a means of reassuring Europeans that Germany would not reassert its power against them. Embedding a rearmed Federal Republic within NATO was the best solution. Germany entered the Alliance in 1955.

Throughout this era, NATO also served increasingly as a bulwark against the reemergence of isolationist tendencies in the United States, such as the efforts by Montana Senator Mike Mansfield to pull American troops from Europe in the 1960s and 1970s. Continued Congressional recommitment to NATO in the face of Donald Trump's isolationism is an important demonstration of how central the Alliance remains to maintaining Atlantic unity

The Core of the Post-Cold War Debate

In short, the security debate in the 1990s was about much more than strategies for dealing with post-Soviet Russia. As a result of the dramatic changes of the past thirty years, NATO's post-Cold War role has in fact become even more complex. Defense against Russia has evolved into efforts to maintain both dialogue and deterrence in Russia and in the countries it borders, especially those in Central Europe who ultimately have joined NATO. Germany is now a central member of the Atlantic community, but its firm anchor within NATO ensures that it will not be unsettled by instability emanating from Russia or elsewhere. And, as the current U.S. Administration demonstrates, isolationist tendencies remain strong in America. Without NATO and the military security link, it is unlikely that the American commitment to an Atlantic partnership would continue.

Add to this NATO's key role in "out of area" crisis such as the Balkans and Afghanistan, and the fundamental strategic importance of NATO to both sides of the Atlantic becomes clear.

U.S. Assistant Secretary of State Richard Holbrooke focused the American position on these basics in a much-commented article in *Foreign Affairs* in the Spring of 1995, in which he declared that as a consequence of its Cold War engagement, American had become a European power. But even today, neither Americans nor Europeans have fully comprehended NATO's role as a geopolitical fulcrum for the Atlantic world.

Since 1990 Europeans seem to have forgotten the fact that NATO is essential to progress in European integration. Especially after the debacle in the Balkans, EU leaders seriously misread their strategic situation. Rather than understanding the importance of maintaining the strategic link with Washington, they were convinced that European defense should be sought primarily through stronger European institutions outside the Alliance. In so doing, they effectively removed NATO from their vision for a European future.

The low point occurred at the Berlin NATO Ministerial meeting in June, 1996, when French President Jacques Chirac, mostly for domestic political reasons, torpedoed a plan to join the conventional capabilities of Europe and the United States into an integrated structure within NATO. From that point on, Europe and America travelled in opposite strategic directions. One result is that the American public, whether Democrat or Republican, is returning to more traditional American nativism and is becoming restive over what is seen as an inadequate European contribution to the common defense.

This growing transatlantic gap represents the most important threat to NATO's future and thus to the security of the Atlantic Community. American demands for higher defense contributions, or more economic access or political support in third countries, were once tempered by the sense of mutual support embodied in Atlantic ties. No longer. Younger elites from both parties no longer have a sense of the strategic dilemmas for American interests presented by the complexities of Europe. Now America decides on whatever goals seem to be attractive at the moment. This tendency towards "transactional diplomacy" was as active during the Obama administration as it is now under Trump.

The Road to NATO Enlargement

The roots of the negative American reaction to European strategic reluctance could already been seen in the debate over NATO enlargement after 1990. In the United States, differences arose between those who might be called the geostrategic lobby, who argued that Europeans could take care of themselves, and that eliminating the danger of nuclear war, if necessary over the heads of the European allies, was America's main goal in a post-Cold War world.

This group focused more on military-security considerations than on NATO's importance to solidifying civil society in Europe and the Atlantic world. They believed urgent defense needs required the West to focus primarily on building new sorts of security cooperation with our former foe, Russia, and above all not "threatening" Russia with an expansion of Western security structures. This group believed America's sole task in Europe had been to hold back or defeat Russia—nothing more.

Such thinking in fact harkened back to President Truman, who put it most directly as he signed the NATO treaty in 1949. The United States had no intention to remain a protecting power for Europe. We expected rapid moves towards unity and to the formation of a European Defense Force which would be an equal partner of the United States.

Numerous well-known security experts, analysts of Russian behavior and those who wished to limit American foreign commitments argued strongly against any changes, including NATO enlargement, which could stoke new sorts of conflict with Russia.

Those who focused on civil society, on the other hand, argued that to flourish, the West should expand its vision beyond traditional military security strategies and focus also on building a unified, democratic community of those who wished to be part of it, including of course Russia. They did not reject efforts at a new security dialogue with Russia, but argued that failure to build civil society in the newly liberated countries of the Warsaw Pact could undermine any progress made on military-security issues.

Countries just emerging from Communism needed protection that only membership in NATO (and the EU) could afford them. History would reassert itself and the road to unity would be difficult. The Atlantic community had evolved into a partnership of democratic countries. An equally important Western goal should be to steady this partnership and help the countries of Eastern and Central Europe join the family of democratic nations.

This group argued that a strategy focused primarily building a new security arrangement with Russia, even if it had newly become non-Communist, would have been a bet against history. Democracy was our strongest suit. Modernizing and expanding our own institutions was the only logical way of supporting democracy in Russia as well.

Practical political arguments also played a role. Large numbers of Americans traced their origins to Eastern and Central Europe. The West had not always stood up for the freedom of these countries during the Cold War. Both Presidents Clinton and George W. Bush felt a moral responsibility for these interests as well.

Thirty years later, these debates have been reignited by the many new challenges presented by aggressive Russian behavior. The debates have evolved into an even more fundamental rethinking of the goals and identity which should be defined for the West in a new age of global digital integration.

Focus on building stability for the newly democratic nations has proven to be correct. But many new challenges such as technology, refugees, and above all national identity have overwhelmed many existing assumptions. New forms of conflict, such as cyber warfare, outside challenges such as terrorism and refuges and a general drop in awareness of the importance of the Atlantic community require new impulses, in particular where Russia is concerned.

The complexities are endless and right now we haven't yet even developed a vocabulary to help us define what needs to be done. But we can be sure of one thing—modern civil society has been strengthened by extension of Western institutions into Central and Eastern Europe. This democratic foundation will remain the West's most important advantage in dealing with competitive visions for the digital future from Russia and elsewhere.

How Enlargement Came About

Many persons and institutions played a role in defining a new strategy in the 1990s. This is an account from the viewpoint of one whose professional role during the 1990s, as described below, touched on all of the issues involved. My task at the State Department, beginning in 1994, was to implement what the President and others had decided—which was the enlargement of NATO.

The critical phase which led to the decision to enlarge NATO in 1997 was guided primarily from the Bureau of European Affairs in the State Department, where I was senior deputy and then Assistant Secretary of State. The key State Department personality was Assistant Secretary Richard Holbrooke, who had a mandate from the President to make enlargement a reality. He often worked independently of other agencies, including the National Security Council.

Defining a Strategy

The foundation of the Holbrooke strategy was to fit NATO into a longer-term vision of the Atlantic, which included a permanent American presence, and in fact defined the United States as a European power. This was the philosophy which Holbrooke and we on his team had

grown up with, but as the following years would show, it was counter-
intuitive for much of the American political establishment.

We were aware, however, that regardless of the fundamental changes
already imposed on the strategic map of Europe, much more was to
come. Our goal was not to draw up a perfect strategy for the 1990s.
Rather, we hoped that by strengthening and modifying existing institutions, we could provide a firm foundation for protecting Western interests during the many upheavals ahead of us.

Nothing has turned out perfectly. Russia remains a disruptive force
in Europe and the world. Western Europeans have essentially abandoned military security as a central task of their governments. But
when we see the way in which Europe has unified into a democratic community, when we note the progress toward freedom in several
former Soviet dependent states, we can be proud to register that the
West's ability to reorient and expand its goals and institutions nearly
three decades ago represents one of the most successful diplomatic and
political achievements of our era.

Background for the Debate

As the Soviet Union entered its final days, Western leaders were
faced with several fundamental questions:

- How should we maintain military and political security? What
  changes were necessary and how far should they go? How should
  the role of institutions, especially NATO, be defined? I took part
  in many discussions of this issue at NATO headquarters after 1989
  and helped formulate the program set forth in the London Communique in 1990, parts of which are quoted below.

- What was the role of post-Soviet Russia? Which tools would best
  suit our needs in dealing with it? How could we best integrate this
  new Russia into the modern post-Cold War world?

- And above all: How could our community of democratic Atlantic
  nations ensure that former Warsaw Pact countries, which had suffered for decades under authoritarian rule, would not again threat-
  en Western security by drifting into dictatorship and decay? This

point was stressed repeatedly by European Allies and by the nations of Central Europe themselves.

The Question of Russia

Since much of postwar Atlantic and European cooperation was aimed at reducing a perceived threat from the Soviet Union Russia, decisions of how to deal with the post-Soviet Russian rump state were central to the process. Many of them remain controversial, and the current situation is in no way satisfactory. After an initial period of co-operation in the very early 1990s, Russia has soon began to revert to a self-centered, hostile approach to its immediate neighbors and to the West. In response, the West has responded by reducing the level of cooperation and moved to sanctioning Russian behavior.

In particular, most recently Russia has even invaded neighboring countries and threatened to expand both conventional and nuclear capacity. Hence, much of the framework for future cooperation worked out with Russia in parallel with NATO enlargement has stopped functioning, although many of the institutions are still intact.

Some blame Western behavior in the 1990s for today's situation in Russia—some twenty years on. To me, that contention is ludicrous. Not building a security foundation for democracy in Europe would have been a concession which probably would have emboldened Russia to mix in the affairs of its weak neighbors.

Not to have built this democratic community would have risked our security much more than any event in Russia could have done. Choosing Russia over Europe would have been an historic blunder of epic proportions.

We need only imagine a situation in which Poland or Hungary were struggling to maintain a democratic system—something we are witnessing in fact right now in 2019—while Russia taunted them from the sidelines. We need only ask if Estonia, Latvia and Lithuania would have remained attack-free and independent without joining NATO and the EU. We need only to observe remind ourselves of Russia's earliest pressures on Georgia and Armenia, which much predated NATO enlargement, or its invasion of Ukraine virtually without pretext.

And to be totally honest, we need only to recall the strong words of then German Defense Minister Volker Rühe in 1993 warning of the consequences of allowing Germany to sit alone on NATO's eastern border.

Over the past fifteen years, new threats from Russia, such as cyber warfare and aggressive use of natural resources, have complicated the debate. None of them are related to NATO. Other new elements are is the growing strength and ambition of China (including its dealings with Russia as regards the Arctic Sea route and raw materials mining/ exploration) and its consequences for the global balance of power, major instability in South Asia and the Middle East, and the security challenges created by massive movements of refugees into both Europe and the United States.

As a result, the original security equation for Russia and the independent nations of the former Soviet Union has expanded significantly beyond its 1990s definition. Thirty years later, we are again at a major point of redefinition. Russia is now only one of many complex new challenges—albeit a significant factor of course.

As in the past, Russia's power to disrupt is greater than its ability (or desire) to cooperate. As a participant in the 1990s exercise, I believe that we can be grateful that our institutions successfully met the challenge to change. But it is also clear that both the United States and Europe are now in the midst of a new era of fundamental upheavals which go far beyond question of military security in Europe.

New technologies are likely to change both the practice of diplomacy and the definition of security in fundamental ways. As in the past, the West is the leader of this new era, but success is far from certain. The transatlantic format of NATO, the EU and the OSCE, which we established in the 1990s, is more important than ever.

Western democracy continues to offer the best operating system for the new digital world. Initial arguments about expansion of Western institutions have in many ways been overtaken by events. Our focus on Russia must now be built into a much broader strategy which includes China, India and several other important/ pivotal regions of the world.

Back to the Roots

My judgments on these issues were based to considerable extent on my good fortune of having taken part in the structural reordering from five vantage points:

- As U.S. Minister and Deputy Commandant of Forces in divided Berlin in the 1980s, I was able to watch the steady decline of East Germany and absorb the political consequences of what was happening. When German Defense Minister Volker Rühe warned that Germany could not be left on NATO's eastern border, I recalled that President Reagan's famous Brandenburg Gate speech had been aimed not at Gorbachev, but at Bonn. The goal was to stifle growing tendencies in the Federal Republic to favor a deal with Gorbachev, which would have cemented the division of Europe.

- I was Deputy U.S. Representative to NATO from 1987–1991. As such I directed the American role in negotiation of several important NATO positions, including the Conventional Forces in Europe negotiations, the CSCE Charter of Paris and the two declarations issued at meetings of NATO Foreign Ministers and at the Summit in 1990.

- I was Ambassador and head of the American delegation to the CSCE from 1991–1994. In this role, I chaired the American delegation to the Helsinki review conference in 1992 and opened the first U.S. Mission to the CSCE in Vienna in that same year. I also played a major role in redefining the CSCE in Helsinki and in transforming it into the OSCE at the Budapest summit in 1994. My experience with what became the OSCE in 1994 went back to the drafting of the Helsinki Final Act in the mid-1970s. Over the years, I became a strong believer that more active use of the tools of civil society could play an important role in building security in Europe.

The Helsinki preparatory conference in 1992 was fascinating for another reason. This gathering of senior officials (from all over Europe, America, Canada, including Russia and the other post-Soviet republics as well as Yugoslavia's successor states) was the only existing relevant forum for discussion of the Balkan wars as they unfolded in 1992.We spent many dozens of hours discussing events and recommending policy options for the international community. We notably welcomed Slovenia, Croatia, Bosnia, Macedonia and Albania as new CSCE participating states. In July of 1992, we suspended Serbia's seat in reaction to its aggression in Bosnia.

- From 1994–1997 I was Principal Deputy and then Assistant Secretary for European Affairs in the Department of State. In this role, my task was to implement strategies defined by the President and others. This included American strategy on important aspects of NATO enlargement and other institutional changes taking place during the 1990s. I personally negotiated several of the arrangements, including the NATO-Russian Founding Act. In addition, I was deputy head of delegation to the Dayton Balkan negotiations and later American special envoy to the Balkans. I also authored much of NATO's Berlin decision in 1996 which created a framework for closer NATO-EU military cooperation.

- Finally, from 1997–2001 I was American Ambassador to Germany, in both Bonn and Berlin. In this function, I worked closely with the German government on Balkan issues, including refugees from Kosovo and NATO's bombing of Serbia in 1999, and conducted a continuing dialogue with the new SPD/Green government (from 1998).

Having the advantage of viewing the world from these much differing perspectives led me to become a strong supporter of an integrated approach to security. This was the approach I adopted when I arrived in Washington in 1994.

Eventful Years

NATO's first official reaction to demise of the Warsaw Pact came at the Summit meeting held in London, July 5-6, 1990. Secretary General Manfred Wörner set the tone in his opening remarks: "The Cold War belongs to history. Our Alliance is moving from confrontation to cooperation. [...] Never before has Europe had such a tangible opportunity to overcome the cycle of war and peace that has so bedeviled its past."

The Summit Communique continued in the same spirit:

> Our Alliance must be even more an agent of change. It can help build the structures of a more united continent, supporting security and stability with the strength of our shared faith in democracy, the rights of the individual, and the peaceful resolution of disputes.

Significantly, the London Communique did not foresee enlargement of the Alliance. It went only as far to extend a "hand of friendship" across the old East-West divide and proposed a new cooperative relationship with all the countries of Central and Eastern Europe. But the London Declaration and other statements of that era left no doubt that most Allies believed that NATO should evolve beyond its defensive role and put more stress on building a more far-reaching structure of peace. Despite the ensuing debate among various experts in Washington, by 1990 the die had already been cast. Article 2, the passage of the NATO Treaty which provided for consultation and support of freedom along all allies, was to many, the future of the Alliance.

NATO sought to give substance to this concept with establishment of the North Atlantic Cooperation Council (NACC) on December 20, 1991. The NACC was explicitly created as a forum for dialogue and cooperation with NATO's former Warsaw Pact adversaries—not as a stepping stone for enlargement.

It was an irony of history that as the final communiqué of the inaugural NACC meeting was being agreed, the Soviet ambassador announced that the Soviet Union had dissolved during the meeting and that he now only represented the Russian Federation. Multilateral political consultation and cooperation helped build confidence and paved the way for the launch of the Partnership for Peace (PfP) in 1994, which established concrete programs of cooperation with non-NATO members, primarily in the East.

Interesting was the fact that at that January 1994 PfP summit, U.S. President Bill Clinton characterized the Partnership for Peace as a "track that will lead to NATO membership" and that "does not draw another line dividing Europe a few hundred miles to the east."

While the issue of enlargement had not yet been addressed, these first reactions and NATO's 1991 revised strategic concept began a restatement of NATO's goals from that of a defense Alliance to an institution for dialogue and change.

The 1991 document gave prominence to economic, social and environmental issues as a means of promoting stability and security in the Euro-Atlantic area as a whole. Dialogue and cooperation would be essential to managing the diversity of challenges facing the Alliance.

Parallel to the NATO transformation was a joint East-West effort to add new commitments to the Helsinki Process and to transform the Conference for Security and Cooperation in Europe into a more formal organization.

The Charter of Paris, signed at a Summit of CSCE participating States in November, 1990 followed NATO's example by reaffirming and deepening the original principles of the CSCE, establishing new mechanisms for consultation and cooperation and agreeing to work further in conjunction with a CSCE Summit scheduled to be held in Helsinki in 1992.

I should stress that this was a thorough reordering of broader European security cooperation. As head of the American delegation to this meeting, I spent six months in Helsinki preparing the program approved at the summit.

Our goal was to establish the CSCE as a functioning pan-European framework for day-to-day work on areas of possible tension. Both military confrontations and human rights violations were areas the CSCE should tackle and were thereby included in our final report.

During the preparatory phase, we agreed a comprehensive reorganization of the CSCE process and added substance to commitments made in Paris. The Document compiled in Helsinki remains the operating manual for the OSCE. While recent confrontations, especially with Russia, have hindered some OSCE operations, it remains a key institution for human rights, civil society and conflict prevention in Europe. By 1992 it had evolved into a pan-Eurasian format that would ultimately include over fifty members.

Equally important was the debate surrounding the extension of European Union membership to the countries of the former Warsaw Pact (especially after the Cold War neutrals Finland, Sweden and Austria had joined in 1995; and the GDR, as a special case, had effectively been absorbed into the West German state structures through unification in 1990 and thereby automatically become part of the EC/EU).

A consensus grew in support of using EU membership as a tool to push democratic development in these countries. With a current membership of 28, there is a wide feeling in the EU, that the promise of membership is still one of Europe's most important foreign policy tools. EU enlargement was also an important element of our (American) comprehensive security strategy. NATO could provide the protection but not the political and economic foundation for a wider community of democratic states.

Parallel to these events, the United States, both in official and private capacities, worked hard to promote establishment of the free market economies in the former Comecon countries, including Russia. Former U.S. Deputy Secretary of State Richard Armitage played an important role during the George H.W. Bush Administration in supplying humanitarian aid (and financial assistance, mostly via the IMF) to Russia.

But EU membership would be long-term goal, as the criteria of the *acquis communautaire* post-Maastricht posed significant hurdles for the transforming states that were undergoing serious electoral revolutions and economic shock therapy. Seeking stability and security Eastern Europeans increasingly looked to NATO and the United States.

Movement Towards Enlargement

By early 1994 arguments in favor of NATO enlargement were growing in both Europe and the United States. Central European countries were especially vocal in their call for NATO membership. German Defense Minister Volker Rühe was an early supporter of an "open door policy," noting that in a reunified Europe, Germany should not be left alone on NATO's eastern border. But the United States government was far from unified on the strategy to be followed.

The arrival of Richard Holbrooke as Assistant Secretary for European Affairs in 1994 and the establishment of a separate Bureau for Russia and CIS affairs under Strobe Talbott in 1993 were important events. While the existence of two Bureaus did not survive beyond the Clinton Administration, it was useful at this critical point to have an independent focus on Russia. I arrived in the European Bureau as principal deputy in early June of 1994, coming directly from the CSCE Mission in Vienna.

By this time, the outlines of a broader, integrated approach to European security were becoming more evident. The fact was that events following the fall of the Soviet Union were so complicated and unmanageable, that any policy had to be one both of planning and of improvisation.

As a first step, we quickly adopted this three-pronged approach based on the key institutions of NATO, the EU, and the CSCE/OSCE as our basic framework for defining a sense of direction for Atlantic and European security cooperation.

Hopes for a democratic belt around Russia and the idea that the West would work first on that were unrealistic. But working closely with Russia to help define and meet its needs was an important part of our strategy. President Clinton's decisions to build close ties to Yeltsin have been criticized in various quarters. I strongly doubt, however, that without Clinton's strong bond with Yeltsin that Russian acceptance of enlargement would have been possible at all.

Also important were the views of the Federal Republic of Germany. Rühe's argument that Germany should not be left isolated in the East was of considerable influence, as were the strong desires of the Visegrád countries to find a home in the West. Germany was also crucial in sweetening the pill for Russia and for Yeltsin by financial means—and just like Bill cultivated his bond with Boris, Helmut Kohl worked his sauna friendship with the Russian also.

We should also not forget that the Balkan war was a major focus during all of this period. Our success in maintaining cooperation with Russia during the Balkan war and in using NATO as the foundation for the IFOR peacekeeping force added considerable credibility to a broader future role for NATO.

A final, important consideration was an assumption about the future, on which Richard Holbrooke and I agreed. Developments in Europe and with Russia would be unpredictable. A strong American role would be essential. But as events since 2000 have also demonstrated, isolationism was a deeply held emotion in the United States and we could not be certain that a continued strong American engagement in Europe could take taken for granted.

To us this meant that while the three existing security arrangements—NATO, EU and the newly upgraded OSCE—should be strengthened, the real bastion would in American eyes be NATO. It has a deeply rooted credibility in the United States, not possessed by anyone or anything else. Observing the many U.S. Senators and Congress members who demonstrably supported NATO at the 2019 Munich Security Conference more than proves the point.

We could at that time not foresee NATO's important role in Afghanistan or its stabilizing role in Central Europe, but generally these were the types of considerations we had in mind. If a new strategy were based on NATO, it would have a better chance of surviving, for example, than one built on cooperating with Russia. Again, recent events, including a more isolationist American administration, have demonstrated how important it will always be to keep American NATO membership functioning and up to date.

The *Foreign Affairs* Article

By the fall of 1994, Holbrooke had been given the task getting American preparations for enlargement going and to jump start the process in NATO. He turned in his usual superb performance. As a first step, the European Bureau prepared for Holbrooke's signature an article later published in the Spring 1995 edition of *Foreign Affairs*, which set forth the overall concept for the first time in a public document. In the article, Holbrooke argued that forty years of postwar engagement had cemented America's role as a European power. Neither the Europeans nor the United States could prosper if this American link were broken. The article set forth a building block approach to post-Cold War security, based on NATO, the EU and the OSCE.

Holbrooke welcomed an expanded role for NATO, including new members, but suggested that "NATO, the European Union (EU), and the other major institutions of the West are not clubs that one joins simply by filling out membership applications. Over time, each has evolved values and obligations that must be accepted by each new member."

This sentence was carefully chosen. It was meant to pave the wave for organizing the American and NATO bureaucracies into a step-by-step NATO enlargement process, which could be managed and defended with each forward step. First there would be consultations on the requirements of membership, then a judgment as to whether one or the other country was eligible and only then membership. And this is exactly the process which was followed. One country, Slovakia, actually did not meet the requirements and therefore did not join in the first group.

Getting the process started within the U.S. government was a different story. As noted above, entrenched communities such as arms control, Soviet specialists etc. continued to be vocal in their rejection of any enlargement of NATO. They either argued that any lasting peace in Europe must include a Russian role, or that adding new members would stretch Alliance resource too thin. Much of the Pentagon, and especially the Joint Chiefs of Staff, were also known to be against enlargement. Letters with many signatures were being sent to the newspapers and the Administration rejecting enlargement.

Despite this opposition, President Clinton himself was already making positive noises, including an important statement in Warsaw in July 1994. NSC chief Tony Lake was strongly in favor. But the all-important inter-agency consensus among all relevant players in the U.S. government had not yet been constructed. That was our job.

Gore Speech in Berlin

As a first step, we came up with a high level, direct means of getting the process moving. On September 9, 1994 Allied and Russian troops were completing their departure from Berlin. Vice President Gore was scheduled to deliver a speech on the occasion. A torn knee prevented him from going to Berlin, but he delivered the speech by satellite.

The text, which I had drafted, contained many positive sentiments and also announced the founding of an American Academy in Berlin, which would substitute cultural exchange for American military presence.

Gore was a strong advocate of enlargement and reacted with humor when I suggested that the Defense Department might come beating at his door if he included the language on NATO. In the speech, the Vice

President talked about the need for NATO and other organizations to adapt adjust to the new situation in Europe or they would stagnate. He added: "Everyone knows that the economic and political organizations tailored for a divided continent must now adapt to new circumstances—including acceptance of new members—or be exposed as mere bastions of privilege…Beyond Partnership for Peace, and the NACC, several countries have already expressed a desire to become members of the Alliance. We shall begin our discussion on this important question this fall."

This simple sentence, "We shall begin our discussion on this important question this fall," masked considerable debate in Washington and in the Administration. The Pentagon, including Secretary of Defense Bill Perry, was especially skeptical. Armed with a Vice Presidential statement signifying that a decision had been taken, Holbrooke skillfully pushed the Joint Chiefs of Staff to take the lead in the "process of examination." There was some pushback from the Defense Department, but the White House backed up Holbrooke's procedure. He was able to move the process forward. By December NATO Allies were also ready to move ahead. The Ministerial communique recorded the following agreement:

> We expect and would welcome NATO enlargement that would reach to democratic states to our East, as part of an evolutionary process, taking into account political and security developments in the whole of Europe. Enlargement, when it comes, would be part of a broad European security architecture based on true cooperation throughout the whole of Europe….
>
> Accordingly, we have decided to initiate a process of examination inside the Alliance to determine how NATO will enlarge, the principles to guide this process and the implications of membership. To that end, we have directed the Council in Permanent Session, with the advice of the Military Authorities, to begin an extensive study. This will include an examination of how the Partnership for Peace can contribute concretely to this process.

This examination was a serious one. Candidate countries were presented with catalogues of requirements and a list of individual implementing agreements (STANAGs) they would be expected to fulfill. Inside the U.S. Government, the State Department guided a complicated process which consumed months of meetings. It would be more than two years before enlargement was settled. But after the Ministerial in December, 1994, there was little doubt that it would occur.

The other key was Russia. While perhaps not set down formally, it was generally accepted that the Alliance could not enlarge if Russia was opposed. President Clinton had been working on Yeltsin assiduously, but the Russians kept turning hot and cold. A very cold moment came in December 1994 at the OSCE Summit in Budapest when Yeltsin warned that NATO enlargement could lead to a "cold peace." But Clinton agreed to attend Yeltsin's celebration of the end of World War II in 1995 and held several other discussions which moved him forward.

Jim Collins, Strobe Talbott's senior deputy, and I were given the task of designing agreements that would convince the Russians we were taking them seriously. The result was the NATO-Russia Founding Act and the NATO—Russia Partnership Council. We also agreed similar arrangements with Ukraine.

I took part in the closing negotiations in May, 1997 led by Secretary of State Madeline Albright. The details focused mostly on Russia's desire to ensure that NATO did not expand militarily up to its border. After several near break downs of the discussions, language was found and Russia agreed.

I had great hopes for these agreements, but they turned out to be less successful than expected. One reason in my view was that NATO Headquarters itself did not implement them, especially the Partnership Council, sufficiently. Many Russian complaints about Western behavior after NATO enlargement are in my view not accurate, but this one is: Both the NATO staff and the member nations dropped the ball.

Our original idea had been that Russia would be treated as an honored partner. As has been reported elsewhere, both President Clinton and others offered the Russians the prospect of future membership in NATO. Yeltsin never took us up on the offer, and the Europeans rejected it anyway. But the spirit was a positive one.

Unfortunately, the Russians were soon complaining, rightly in my view, that they sat almost as if they were in Court, being grilled by the allies. I myself took the opportunity a few years later to complain to then NATO Secretary General de Hoop Scheffer about the lack of respect offered the Russians in Brussels. After scowling at me for a few minutes, Scheffer said I was right.

Of course, other major events intervened. A year after NATO enlargement was agreed, Russia suffered a near economic meltdown. Yeltsin was on the ropes, both politically and health wise and a new era was waiting in the wings. He chose Putin to make sure that his personal legacy would be honored.

Whatever the intervening events, few would argue that the basic goal of the 1990s had been achieved: to strengthen and update existing institutions as a means of maintaining security and democracy in Europe.

Since then, the nations of Europe have evolved beyond all expectations. Democracy is beginning to take hold in important parts of the former Soviet Union such as Georgia and Ukraine. The NATO of 2019 is a much different animal than the Alliance I knew in the late 1980s. So are the European Union and the Organization on Security and Cooperation in Europe. Many are knocking on our door, asking for entry. No one is crying to join Russia.

We can now be proud of a democratic community of nations, numbering nearly 1 billion inhabitants, which stretches from the Finnish and Estonian borders in the Northeast to the tip of Alaska in the far West. This complex community is not totally unified and not perfect. But all of its members are guided by the democratic principles of modern civic society.

This to me in the most important result of our efforts nearly thirty years ago. In my mind, there is no doubt that without enlargement of NATO and the EU, this community would today not exist, and several states in proximity to Russia would be hanging tenuously to their independence.

Chapter 14

Toward NATO Enlargement: The Role of USNATO

Robert E. Hunter

The story of how NATO took in new members from Central Europe following the end of the Cold War has been told from many perspectives. This chapter looks at what happened from the perspective of the United States Mission to NATO (USNATO), which played a crucial role both in creating the architecture of the "new NATO" and in negotiating many of its elements, at times not only for the United States but also for NATO as a whole. This chapter is in part a personal account, relating to my own service at NATO as the U.S. Permanent Representative from July 11, 1993, to January 1, 1998—the most significant period of NATO's transformation in the post-Cold War era, building on what had already been done in the George H. W. Bush administration.

This chapter will focus on those developments most relevant to NATO enlargement. That of necessity brings in many more factors. These include NATO's role in ending the war in Bosnia, but this chapter will only deal with Bosnia as it impacted on the Alliance's overall transformation and the enlargement issue.

By the time the first NATO enlargement was formally decided in July 1997, the work of transforming the Alliance to deal effectively with post-Cold War security challenges in Europe was essentially completed. The basic design of that era continues to be preeminent in today's functioning of NATO. Since then, NATO has continued to adapt and to meet new demands, especially those which followed Russia's seizure of Crimea in February 2014. Unfortunately, in my judgment, some decisions taken since 1997 affecting NATO have had adverse effects, not so much on NATO as an institution but on its ability effectively to meet European and transatlantic security requirements. Most important were ill-thought-out excessive further enlargements of NATO until it now numbers 30 Allies and, related to that, miscues in Western, especially U.S., policies and actions toward the Russian Federation. Complemented by Russian actions, these essentially ruined the chances for creating a European security structure that might have avoided repetition of some of the historic errors that plagued Europe and international society in the past.

Creating a Grand Strategy for Europe

As a nation, Americans have almost never articulated a grand strategy for the United States in the outside world and then taken steps to implement it—except occasionally at time of war. Usually grand strategy comes into being the other way around: as a summary of individual goals, strategies, and actions which are seen in retrospect as coherent and comprehensive.

One major exception to this general rule was the peacetime effort to restructure European security following the end of the Cold War. The effort began not as a summary of individual elements but as a central proposition for the United States that was contained in a few short words: "to create a Europe whole and free"—to which a few more words, "and at peace," were later added. They were contained in a speech by President George H. W. Bush in Mainz, Germany,[1] five months before the Berlin Wall opened; but they provided the framework for what followed, certainly in U.S. policy toward Europe and also for most European countries (plus Canada), at least west of Russia and Belarus.

Thus, none of the steps to implement the Bush grand strategy, both during his administration and during much of Bill Clinton's administraion, took place in a vacuum or reflected just experimentation. While the character of each individual policy and action was not predetermined, each did evolve within the broader context of the Bush grand strategy and was judged, at least in the West, in terms of how it contributed to pursuit of that grand strategy, undertaken primarily by NATO and the European Union.[2]

The Core Elements of the Grand Strategy

As efforts to implement the Bush grand strategy moved forward, the key elements, in virtually all of which US mission at NATO played a central role, were as follows:

- Ratifying the United States' engagement as a European power;

- Preserving key elements of NATO, including the integrated military command structure;

- Confirming the end of the "German problem," which had begun even before formation of the German Reich in 1871;

- Taking the Central European countries "off the geopolitical chessboard,"[3] and including them in Western and NATO institutions, as independent, democratic nations (NATO efforts were conducted in parallel with those of the European Union);

- Reaching out to Russia, seeking to involve it in wider European security and other institutions and practices without posing threats to its neighbors;

- Ensuring a special place for Ukraine as an independent country;

- Breaking down barriers between NATO and the European Union (including the Western European Union [WEU]);

- Acting, both on its own and with other institutions, to end conflict in Europe (Bosnia and later Kosovo) and to help keep the peace afterwards; and

- Undertaking ancillary efforts (in addition to ongoing NATO cooperative practices), including shifting the primary orientation of post-reduction NATO militaries in Europe (especially those of the United States) from an easterly to a south-easterly direction and moving most USAF assets from north to south of the Alps; creating the Combined Joint Task Force (CJTF) concept as a key element of NATO peacekeeping; expanding NATO cooperation with the Conference on (later Organization for) Security and Cooperation in Europe (CSCE/OSCE); and beginning the process of reintegrating France fully into NATO defense and military structures.

Taken together, these steps were designed to follow the theory and practice of the creation of European security, writ large, in the late 1940s, plus development of transatlantic relations: a combination of political, economic, strategic, and military relations, which also included important roles for the private sector and what came to be known as non-governmental organizations (NGOs). In effect, these are organic, mutually supportive institutions and practices, within a core set of political commitments. They were designed precisely to play these roles.

Before President Bill Clinton came to office, there had been preliminary steps, including a U.S. decision to remain deeply committed to NATO, plus collective allied decisions to continue honoring the Treaty of Washington of April 4, 1949, as well as to preserve the Alliance's institutions, notably the North Atlantic Council—where Allied decisions are taken—and the integrated military command structure. The latter remains historically unique and is a basic element in the Alliance's being and, if need be, its ability to implement the Treaty's Article 5: the "Three Musketeers" provision of an all-for-one and one-for-all response to external aggression. The Alliance had also taken other preliminary steps toward preserving, reforming, and restructuring the Alliance, for example creation of a North Atlantic Cooperation Council (NACC) in December 1991 (the first meeting of which coincided with the dissolution of the Soviet Union), "as a forum for dialogue and cooperation with NATO's former Warsaw Pact adversaries."[4]

NATO 1993: Still a Backwater

In general, however, the NATO Alliance was essentially marking time in a new world without a major enemy (the Soviet Union) and thus without a central organizing principle. While the Alliance and its subordinate institutions were still ticking over, it was essentially in a holding pattern; there were even voices on both sides of the Atlantic (some of which still persist) calling for NATO to be abolished as out of date and no longer necessary or, at least, having no serious purpose to justify keeping it in being, except perhaps as a passive insurance policy in the event that Russia, in particular, would at some point in the future pose an active threat to the alliance or any of its members.

That NATO as an institution was seen at senior levels in Washington as essentially a backwater was marked by the decision of the U.S. Permanent Representative (ambassador), Reginald Bartholomew, to leave that position in March 1993, after only 10 months, to become the lead U.S. negotiator on the Bosnia war, which, as the worst conflict in Europe since the Second World War, was on the radar.[5] This led to my being offered NATO, as opposed to being U.S. ambassador to the European Communities, an appointment that was already in the works. NATO ambassador was certainly not seen as the plum job it later became.[6]

My first step was to phone NATO Secretary-General Manfred Wörner, a friend from my days on the NSC staff in the Carter administration. "What can I do for you?" I asked. "Get me a summit," he replied. So I worked to get that done. My second step was to ask to see the draft intervention to be given by Secretary of State Warren Christopher at the forthcoming June NATO foreign ministers meeting in Athens, although I was not yet in the government. I believed this was particularly important because of Christopher's first trip around Europe in February, when he asked the Allies what should be done about Bosnia rather than presenting Clinton Administration ideas. There was no sense of American leadership. This reminded me of Vice President Walter Mondale's first trip to Europe soon after the 1977 inauguration: the same lack of U.S. leadership; the same failure of advisers to provide substance; the same failure with the Allies and thus their wondering about the strength of a new U.S. administration's commitment to NATO and European security—as well as its competence.[7]

The Athens ministerial draft, prepared by the State Department Office of European Affairs, in my judgment showed virtually no awareness of the massive changes taking place and the challenges that lay ahead. I wrote a totally new draft, laying out key themes, outlining some specific proposals, and demonstrating U.S. leadership. I took it directly to Stephen Oxman, the newly-installed Assistant Secretary for European and Canadian Affairs, who accepted it as the basis of what Christopher would say at Athens. Most of it survived the State Department bureaucracy. It helped to restore Christopher's reputation with his colleagues. It laid out, within the overall grand strategy of a "Europe whole and free," much of the basic framework for detailed U.S. initiatives during that crucial year in creating a new architecture for NATO and European security overall. It also began the process of demonstrating American leadership, a *sine qua non* throughout NATO's history for Alliance success. Notably, however, it did not occur to me to include one idea that became important: that NATO should take in new members! But Christopher did raise the subject: in his intervention at the foreign ministers' meeting, he said that "...at an appropriate time we may choose to enlarge NATO membership. But that is not now on the agenda."[8]

Starting Out in Brussels

This was background to my arrival in Brussels on Sunday, July 11, 1993 and a meeting of the North Atlantic Council the following day to begin planning for the summit, "penciled in" for the following January in Brussels, for which I had gained agreement in Washington. I met with my able mission team that afternoon to game out our approach for Monday's meeting of the North Atlantic Council, the "NAC," to start summit planning and for which I had written most of my formal Washington instructions.

What follows is an account of what was done to meet the needs of European security, writ large, and of transatlantic relations, from the perspective of efforts at NATO and with a special focus on USNATO. To begin with, it will focus in detail on the period through the January 1994 Brussels summit, by which time most of the elements of the new architecture for European security—as I called it from that time forward—had been formulated, though many details and implementation took considerable time and efforts in Washington, other allied capitals, and at NATO to get done. As I noted later, the fact that it took nearly six years from the start of the NATO restructuring process until the first three Central European countries were welcomed as alliance members testified to all the other things that had to be done to increase the chances that enlargement would strengthen rather than weaken NATO and keep open possibilities for accommodation with Russia on European security matters.

As these efforts and roles developed, I believe it represented a virtually-unique engagement by U.S. officials based abroad in the Washington interagency process. Beyond doubt is that, while direct contacts between Washington and foreign capitals were important, as well as ministerial and summit meetings, most of the practical negotiations regarding NATO's future were conducted in Brussels. Simple math will indicate that this would be difficult to carry out on an iterative basis from Washington—how to get each of the United States' 14 European allies plus Canada to reach agreement on a round robin basis.

Many times, of course, only a handful of Allies would count—most often the United States, the United Kingdom, France, and Germany—with the others trusting their decisions, but at the extreme when all had to be involved, as often happens around the negotiating table at either the ambassadorial (NAC) or subordinate level, the number of iterations from a distance would be staggering. Great complexity was involved even when ambassadors came instructed, if they were to have to compromise to get agreement (consensus) in the NAC.[9] With the necessary give and take, often a compromise would be reached that then got sent back to capitals *ad referendum*, on a take-it-or-leave-it basis. Most often each capital, including Washington, would "take it." With the leadership of USNATO at Alliance headquarters on most issues and being, as the United States, the "800-pound gorilla," U.S. positions regularly (but not always!) prevailed.[10]

For my fifteen colleagues on the Council, plus the Secretary General and other NATO officials, the important thing was not that "Hunter" had arrived, but that the United States would again be represented by an ambassador after a gap of four months (despite the abilities of the *chargé*, Alexander Vershbow, who later succeeded me as ambassador in January 1998). Having the United States represented at the level of ambassador was a touchstone for the allies of U.S. commitment and purpose. It was also useful for this individual to be a political appointee, as had prevailed with only a few exceptions until Foreign Service Officer Reginald Bartholomew, as opposed to being a member of the Foreign Service. The notion was that a political appointee would more readily have access if need be to the U.S. president than someone whose onward career would be determined within the State Department. It also didn't hurt that I had been working on NATO issues for 30 years. Further, I had in the past worked closely with the new Secretary of Defense, Les Aspin, a matter of consequence at NATO, given the nature of the work and the fact that NATO is the only post where the U.S. ambassador has unfettered access to the Secretary of Defense (who also has his own representative in Europe, under the ambassador's authority) as well as the Secretary of State.[11] That relationship, which ensures that the NATO ambassador will in effect be part of the interagency process back in Washington, proved invaluable, as did my working relationship with the Supreme Allied Commander Europe (SACEUR), Gen. John Shalikashvili, who soon became chairman of the Joint Chiefs of Staff.[12] Indeed, in this early period, many of the ideas for NATO's future were worked out primarily between my mission and the Defense Department, then accepted within the interagency process.[13]

Throughout my first two years at NATO, Bosnia was a major issue for NATO, although it tended to be dealt with only episodically, generally when the Bosnian Serbs had attacked one of the cities that had been designated as "safe areas," from which heavy weapons were excluded and which were supposed to be places where civilians could be safe from the conflict. But since Bosnia did not figure prominently in the restructuring of NATO until mid-1995, this account will not delve deeply into that subject.

Partnership for Peace

While the persistent challenge of the Bosnia war was always in the background at NATO-Brussels, far greater attention was paid to preparations for the forthcoming NATO summit and the accompanying demonstration of renewed U.S. leadership, which had fallen from its high-water mark of the remarkable diplomacy that had been so critical in the soft landing of the Cold War, the opening of possibilities with Russia in the wake of the Soviet Union's dissolution, and the unification of Germany. These Bush administration achievements (many by the president himself) made possible what we in the Clinton Administration were then able to do. Indeed, the continuity involved highlights one of the most critical aspects of U.S. engagement in NATO since the early days after its creation: U.S. domestic political and public support has always been bipartisan. There have often been disagreements on the details, but never on the basic U.S. commitment to NATO. For U.S. ambassadors to NATO, this has always been a godsend; I found that particularly so during my tenure when the U.S. Senate was controlled for the first year-and-a-half by the Democrats and the last three years by the Republicans.

A key moment came in early September, when the International Institute for Strategic Studies (IISS) held its annual conference in Brussels. Secretary of Defense Les Aspin was invited to speak and he planned to arrive with a full Defense Department team. Key was the Deputy Assistant Secretary for European and NATO Policy, Joe Kruzel, a remarkable public servant who tragically died on Mt. Igman in Bosnia in August 1995. He and I planned the visit by Aspin to Brussels and I offered to convene a seminar at my ambassadorial residence, Truman Hall. Joe and I organized it around a morning session that would include a number of the leading strategic thinkers from the ranks of the IISS conference attendees, following by a lunch with Secretary General Wörner, and then an afternoon just with U.S. government officials, who, in addition to key members of my staff, were primarily from the civilian and military sides of the Defense Department, plus key U.S. commanders in Europe.

As we planned the agenda, Kruzel and I, working closely with Gen. Shalikashvili and also with the State Department and NSC staff,[14] focused on what became a central factor both in architecture for post-Cold War European security and for the forthcoming NATO summit. We devised an approach that would embrace within NATO's purview those Central European and other countries that had emerged from the wreckage of the Warsaw Pact, the Soviet Union, and then also the Former Yugoslavia. But at the same time this would be without NATO inviting any of them to join the Alliance, with the critical Article 5 guarantees and membership in allied military commands and command structure. We sought to thread several needles: in particular to give these countries, which had just emerged from communist governments and Soviet control, a sense of engagement in the West and especially with NATO, but at the same time without weakening NATO's military capabilities (notably Allied Command Europe) and sense of common commitment (Article 5 of the Washington Treaty). Indeed, the Pentagon's Joint Staff and SHAPE were strongly opposed to the enlargement of NATO. Concern about weakening NATO militarily was in addition to the added burdens of having potentially to defend more countries, especially when they would not have the requisite national military capacities and infrastructure to make such defense feasible.

Around the table that afternoon on September 11th came agreement among the key U.S. government security officials to finalize a concept based mostly on the Kruzel-Shalikashvili-Hunter initiative, which came to be called Partnership for Peace (PfP).[15] It would not include roles for non-NATO countries in the "high end" of military activities, with full integration in NATO commands and military activities, but rather at the "low end" of peacekeeping. The most important tool in implementing this concept would be for military personnel from NATO allies to work with the militaries of what came to be known as "partner" countries. These could include all countries that were members of CSCE, then 52 in number, stretching all the way through to Central Asia.[16]

As we at USNATO then took the lead (with SHAPE) in elaborating PfP, it developed several principal aspects. Working with Kruzel and his colleagues at the Defense Department, along with the State Department and the NSC staff, PfP was embedded in the NACC and then, at the 1997 Madrid summit, in a successor organization which came to be called the Euro-Atlantic Cooperation Council (EAPC): essential differences being that the latter also permitted the inclusion of the European neutral and non-aligned countries, plus enhanced involvement for all members in NATO activities. As I told key officials of the Swedish and Finnish governments when they joined PfP, with their capabilities they would be on the "teaching rather than the student staff" for other partner countries.[17]

PfP focused on the military institutions of the countries that joined, with the understanding that, with their existing structures, they could in most cases play a significant role in the democratization of these countries, while at the same time being reformed, trained, and equipped to play roles in peacekeeping, in league with NATO allied peacekeeping elements, as well as for potential use by the United Nations.[18] While the United States played the leading role in sending uniformed personnel to work with national militaries, many of the other allies also took part.[19]

As Kruzel, General Shalikashvili's people, and my team and I developed the PfP concept, along with SHAPE/EUCOM[20] and some input from State and the NSC, we decided on three functions for it to perform, in addition to being a lead element in democratization and confidence-building to underpin economic development:[21]

- It helped to prepare partner militaries to undertake peacekeeping missions, while also giving them access to NATO standards and command practices (plus use of English, the NATO military language) that are essential for the militaries of different countries to work together;

- It helped prepare partner countries to become ready for NATO membership; and

- For those countries that would not join NATO—either by their own choice or because NATO would not invite them to join—it would give them an enduring form of security just by having this engagement with NATO. I termed this kind of arrangement their being within the penumbra of NATO security, even without the Article 5 commitment. My reasoning was simple: that if a non-member of NATO were subjected to external aggression, the alliance might anyway decide to respond militarily (or in other ways) even without Article 5, as happened with U.S. responses against North Korean aggression (1950) and Iraqi aggression (1990). This then might have a quasi-deterrent effect or at least would reduce the chances of miscalculation by a potential aggressor.[22]

In retrospect, PfP has proved to be one of NATO's most successful ventures and an essential precursor to enlargement.

NATO, the European Union, and France

Long before being appointed U.S. ambassador to NATO, I had been concerned about virtually non-existent relations between NATO and what became the European Union. Indeed, I regularly said that these were "two institutions living in the same city (Brussels) on different planets!" That practice of institutional pride and division—which also, of course, represented the differences in membership and of structure and purpose—seemed to me to violate the principle that security had to be a combination of political, economic, strategic, and military activities. This was especially so following the end of the Cold War, when it was necessary to create new bases for European security and the political and economic development of countries that had emerged from communism and, in fact, in some cases had become truly independent for the first time in decades.

From the U.S. perspective, however, shared in particular by Britain, with its sense of special relationship with Washington and ambivalence toward "Europe," there was also worry that the Western European Union could compete with NATO and lead to a weakening of alliance capabilities, political as well as military. The State Department in the Bush administration had been assiduous in trying to limit the writ and activities of WEU.

I judged otherwise even before I went to Brussels. During the Cold War, the United States did not want WEU (or any other institution or arrangement) to get in the way of NATO and of U.S. strategic leadership because of the need for central direction of confrontation with the Soviet Union. With the end of the Cold War, that argument fell to the ground. I saw virtue in the EU having both a more effective foreign policy and defense component. I argued that if an effective WEU would lead European members to spend more on defense and to build more useful capabilities than they would do just for NATO, that was a net plus. In any event, as I argued and has proved true, if there is ever a disagreement between NATO and WEU as to which would have primacy, NATO, the "big kid on the block," would always prevail; further, if European security were at risk from external aggression—i.e., a resurgent Russia—only the United States could be effective: that means NATO. My reasoning did not convince some State Department people who continued to fret, wrongly, that WEU (and its successors) would steal NATO's thunder and U.S. primacy in the transatlantic relationship.

I had also long been interested to see whether France could be reintegrated in NATO's military command structure. Again, with the Cold War over and thus any incentive in Paris to gain flexibility in dealing with Moscow,[23] that incentive had gone away. Further, during Operation Desert Storm (Kuwait/Iraq) in 1991, the French military realized that being outside of NATO military institutions for so long had led it to miss much military modernization. Thus, it had to put its forces under U.S. command. I saw an opportunity for NATO here.

When the French ambassador to NATO, Jacques Blot, invited me to lunch early in my tenure, I suggested that he and I explore a possible deal: that I would work to get the U.S. government to back off on its opposition to a strong WEU if Blot would work to move France in the direction of rejoining NATO's integrated command structure. We agreed and sold the basic concept to our respective governments. This led in 1995-96 to complex negotiations between NATO and the WEU[24] that created a useful and viable relationship between the two institutions.[25] Fortunately, I was able to prevail with Washington that U.S. relations with the WEU would be run out of USNATO rather than out of the U.S. mission to the European Union. On my initiative and with Washington's approval, I also organized France's return to the NATO Military Committee and International Military Staff, necessary first steps toward its full reintegration in NATO's military structures in 2009.

Resolving this issue also helped with enlargement, as it increased the chances of cooperation/coordination between NATO and the European Union, both as they extended informal mechanisms into Central Europe (PfP and its EU analogues), and parallel processes of taking in new members.[26]

Travemünde

As the Alliance was preparing for the January 1994 Brussels summit, key was a set of U.S. proposals in October, part deriving from initiatives at the USNATO mission and part originating in Washington, more at the Defense Department and the NSC than at the State Department. Following interagency agreement, they were deployed with Allies by both Christopher and Aspin. The former presented the ideas in a cable to U.S. ambassadors for Allied leaders; much more attention-getting was a unique event at NATO to that point, an informal meeting of defense ministers, without all the ceremony and circumstance that tended to circumscribe the semi-annual regular meetings. German Defense Minister Volker Rühe offered to host, and the meeting was held in Travemünde, not coincidentally in Rühe's part of the country.[27] With all the allies to be gathered in one room at ministerial level, attention naturally focused on Travemünde and Secretary Aspin, rather than on Secretary Christopher's cable.[28]

This was clearly foreseen as the moment when the United States would need to show that it would be both able and willing to lead at NATO, especially for the transformation that the alliance would have to undergo in order to remain relevant. Already, there were widespread calls for its dissolution, including on Capitol Hill, and questioning whether it could have relevance in the absence of a central organizing principle, as the Soviet Union had been. I argued that NATO's principal objective was to *create confidence in stability*—a relatively low-cost but certainly high-value insurance policy. If a major measure of this stability could be achieved—with its heavy dose of psychology—that would enable people to get on with their lives, which I have long argued should be the end of international politics.

Because of the importance of the forthcoming meeting, Manfred Wörner agreed to visit Washington and discuss the key issues with President Clinton. This would also help to lock in the political significance of other developments for NATO and gain U.S. blessing at the highest level.[29] Clinton's main message was that despite talk about the possibility of NATO soon taking in new members, the United States could not at this time support that course. He deployed some of the arguments advanced by the Pentagon, such as had led to the compromise in creating Partnership for Peace. Notably, however, it had been decided in the interagency process that at some point enlargement would happen.[30]

On the day of the Travemünde meeting, I sat with Aspin on the helicopter from Hamburg Airport and went through his final briefing book.[31] The talking points included an announcement that the United States was abandoning its commitment to use airpower in Bosnia, thus also no longer supporting a NATO role in stopping the war. I told Aspin that, if he made that statement, he might as well forget the other U.S. proposals: any hope for U.S. leadership and a positive response by Allies would be dead. Aspin read the talking points, then said: "You're right. I won't do that."

At the start of the defense ministers' meeting there was a forest of glum faces, until Aspin laid out the U.S. proposals, from the small (Combined Joint Task Forces—CJTF, as a means for making NATO peacekeeping effective) to the large (NATO peacekeeping itself, Partnership for Peace, and support for the WEU in the form of a European Security and Defense Identity).[32] The mood shifted instantly: here was proof positive that the United States was taking NATO seriously and was reasserting its traditional and indispensable role as leader. There was rapid agreement on the entire U.S. agenda for the Brussels summit. Enthusiasm was so great that one additional idea that Aspin had only laid down in passing—that NATO should at some point involve itself in limiting proliferation of weapons of mass destruction and ballistic missiles—was seized upon by his colleagues and added to the summit agenda. All these proposals and the sense that the United States "was back" offset concerns that the defense ministers had little to say about the war in Bosnia. Indeed, Travemünde was probably the most important moment for NATO, at least in the Clinton Administration, except for 1) decisions that led directly to the NATO airstrike campaign in Bosnia in August-September 1995 that ended the war; and 2) decisions taken in 1997 regarding NATO enlargement and relations with Russia and Ukraine.

The 1994 Brussels Summit

Still, the Brussels summit on January 10-11, 1994, was not an anticlimax. But the fact that Travemünde (and Secretary Christopher's parallel presentation of the U.S. proposals to his European and Canadian colleagues) had done so much to show American leadership and set forth a coherent approach to the future of European security meant that the summit itself did not require as much heavy lifting at the level of heads of state and government that is often true at NATO.

In his remarks at the summit meeting, Clinton moved the ball forward on the possibility of NATO enlargement, in line with a public speech he had made the day before in Brussels,[33] when he said about Partnership for Peace: "…[it] will advance a process of evolution for NATO's formal enlargement. It looks to the day when NATO will take on new members who assume the Alliance's full responsibilities." Also, the summit declaration did "reaffirm that the Alliance remains open to the membership of other European countries"—though at that point that did not connote any decision or haste to arrive at one. However, Clinton advanced U.S. thinking in almost-decisive fashion in Prague immediately afterwards. In a press conference with Visegrád leaders,[34] he said: "While the Partnership is not NATO membership, neither is it a permanent holding room. It changes the entire NATO dialog so that now the question is no longer whether NATO will take on new members but when and how."[35] Notably, however, many subsequent statements by different officials of the US government, some recently declassified, indicate that the U.S. position on enlargement was not always consistent and was often open to different interpretations.[36] This was to cause considerable difficulties down the road and, in some ways it still does.[37]

After Brussels: The Role of USNATO—Major Themes

Following the Brussels summit, work began in earnest to build on basic architecture for the future of European security. USNATO, which had played a major role in creating that architecture, was in the thick of things. We focused not just on dealing with other parties in Brussels, SHAPE, and the other NATO commands,[38] which collectively make up the NATO organism and are a major source of its strength. We also had to play a role with Washington, which included reporting what was going on in Brussels, making recommendations, and receiving instructions on what to do; we also often played an informal role in the Washington interagency process, even though 3800 miles and six time-zones distant.[39]

The last-named was possible in part because represented at the mission were elements from the Departments of State and Defense (civilian and military), acting on a fully-integrated basis, and because of the many differences of view and priorities within the Washington bureaucracy. I realized we had to balance a series of differing U.S. perspectives, or trade-offs, and if we didn't do it at USNATO, often nobody else could. In addition to NATO-WEU relations, the most significant of these issues were:

- Preserving the effectiveness of NATO military operations (and decision-making) versus deeper involvement of partner countries;

- Keeping NATO small or expanding it, with the attendant issues of decision-making (consensus principle) and taking on added burdens, including potentially under Article 5; and

- Giving priority to aspirations of Central European countries (membership) or trying to avoid excluding Russia and, by so doing, potentially leading to a new Cold War.[40]

I saw my special responsibility to keep the strength of the Alliance, Central Europe, and Russia all in view and, regarding Washington bureaucratic struggles, to help prevent overemphasis on any one perspective to the detriment of the others, thus to damage U.S. and Western interests.[41]

In the process, I always shared with all the key people at USNATO everything that I knew, especially when I returned from trips to Washington—something of a rarity in the "knowledge-is-power" part of the U.S. government,[42] at least on the civilian side. Two benefits resulted: first, after thoroughly discussing issues with senior members of my team, State and Defense, civilian and military, and my making a decision, people in the Washington bureaucracy who had lost the battle of our recommendations would phone their counterparts at the mission, only to be told that they had had a fair shot and would honor my decision. Second, we never had a leak from the mission. That comes from showing trust and confidence in one's colleagues.

Partners' Adaptation

The first of the three central problems—preserving NATO's military effectiveness—was easiest to deal with, at least in helping the militaries of non-NATO PfP members adapt to NATO methodology and create military capabilities able to function with NATO. But how could they play a role in taking decisions on peacekeeping operations, given that they would be putting their troops at risk? The solution was to invite non-ally troop-contributing nations to join in decision-making meetings, but not to give them a veto on decisions (they could always elect not to take part). The Pentagon and Allied militaries were particularly sensitive on this point, especially in cases where a NATO ally wanted to include in a peacekeeping operation a neighbor from Central Europe that was not up to speed.

It was also widely recognized that NATO could only do part of the job: the European Union also had a major role to play in the adaptation and modernization of Central European countries, with as much integration with NATO's efforts as possible; and at USNATO we supported the relevant EU political and economic programs. In my judgment and that of some of my team, what the Central Europeans really needed, in addition to PfP, was not NATO membership (at the time there was no palpable threat) but close association with the EU and other programs for economic development. Universally, the Central European governments did not see it that way, and they had a major point. With their histories in the Second World War and the Cold War, strategic guarantees were uppermost. Indeed, given a choice between having a U.S. security guarantee without NATO and membership in a NATO where the United States did not give a guarantee, they would all choose the former. This was understandable because of the psychological value of a security guarantee for getting on with economic and other developments; whereas the opposite, membership in the EU, might not produce a serious security guarantee and uncertainties would continue.[43]

Enlargement

The second problem, relating to NATO enlargement, was far more difficult. Soon after the Brussels summit, when the full import of decisions had become evident—that is, PfP now, membership later and perhaps not at all—almost all Central European states expressed deep reservations about PfP, especially fearing that "later" would indeed mean "never." There were also people in the Washington bureaucracy who were more anxious to take in new members than to see them be effective allies, militarily or otherwise. For some, that included a belief that, the Soviet Union/Russia not posing a threat, NATO could be converted into a form of CSCE, indeed "NATO-lite." That view was stoutly resisted by U.S. and Allied militaries and by us at USNATO.

Even for Central European states which understood they had to be able to pull their weight before becoming NATO allies, there was reluctance to put great effort into PfP without a guarantee that membership would follow. I set myself the task of working closely with representatives of these states at NATO and impressing on them the need to develop capabilities that would make them ready to be allies. I held regular meetings with them at Truman Hall, the ambassador's residence. On the first such occasion, I made the following statement: "Pay close attention. Anyone here representing a country that would like at some point to join NATO, *you need to take PfP very seriously: repeat, very seriously.*" The message was not particularly welcome but it was understood. The same was true of a more graphic way I put it:

"NATO will only take in new members who are producers and not just consumers of security." The message began to get across. Thus, a year later the Latvian foreign minister told me that his country would not want to join NATO if thereby the Alliance would become weaker.[44] Several countries did indeed work hard at PfP, including in NATO peacekeeping exercises, the first of which, with partner militaries, was held at Poznan, Poland.[45]

I also delivered another clear message: that NATO membership would be closed to any country that chose to pursue ambitions or historical grievances against another state or ethnic group in Europe. The dead past had to bury its dead.[46] Given the number of grievances that had festered for so many years and in some cases decades or even centuries, this was a critical injunction. It was in general swallowed as the price of getting into NATO.

At the same time, Central European aspirants were worried that NATO and in particular the United States might give Russia a chance to block their entry, given the desire not to drive it away from the West. Thus, we made clear that no outside power—meaning Russia without naming it—would have any influence on NATO enlargement. I summarized that as NATO's allowing Russia (or any other outside country) "a voice but not a veto" on developments within the alliance.

I further advanced the ideas, though in retrospect this might have been a vain hope (this may be debated forever), that the overall architecture of European security and efforts to implement it—with a respected role for Russia—might be able to move European security beyond centuries' old concepts: the balance of power and spheres of influence. This ambition was consistent with George H. W. Bush's concept of a Europe whole and free. Obviously, it didn't work; but I remain unconvinced that it was given "the old college try"—by either side!

As the various processes developed, NATO also created Membership Acton Plans[47] for each aspirant country, to underscore the need for preparation to undertake full allied responsibilities. At the end of 1994, NATO also decided to conduct an Enlargement Study, related to preparing countries to join. As I wrote in *NATO Review*:

> Allied agreement to take in new members is a fact; debate now
> centres solely on the means. This year, the 16 Allies are delving

into questions of the how and the why of formal NATO expansion. They know they must answer these critical questions before they can either logically or beneficially proceed to the next level of decision: the who and the when of taking in new members.

The NATO enlargement study has two major, declared purposes. One is for the Allies to gain a clear knowledge of how NATO will function once it expands its membership—put simply, what they must do to ensure that a larger NATO will be the same strong defensive military alliance it is today. The other major purpose is to show prospective members precisely what they can expect as Allies—both their rights and their duties within the Alliance.

The study also has an unspoken purpose—to build confidence among the 16 Allies that, when they do decide on the who and the when of expanded membership, each of their several parliaments will give a strong and positive assent—and will mean it.[48]

However, despite the efforts underway to get aspirants ready to be allies in terms of military and other capabilities, and despite all the talk about criteria for membership, none of that really mattered, even though a country that was progressing in terms of capabilities would be easier to defend and would be demonstrating seriousness of purpose. In fact, there was and is only one criterion for NATO membership: that all of the existing NATO Allies are prepared to honor Article 5 of the Washington Treaty if the new entrant suffers external aggression. If so, membership is possible; if not, membership would be folly. Full stop.[49]

Russia

The third major problem of perspective and trade-offs led to the most intense disagreements in Washington: how to balance extension of NATO's formal writ into Central Europe with the desire not to drive Russia away or give it cause to believe that it was being taken advantage in its weak condition or was being "disrespected." There were two camps in Washington, each with strong views. The camp that was more concerned with bringing Central European countries into NATO had the advantage of President Clinton's support which I judged, rightly or wrongly, had a lot to do with domestic politics. Indeed, it always appeared to me that he was more concerned with domestic than foreign policy issues—a choice that a number of presidents make. For instance, on a visit to the Oval Office with Secretary General Willy Claes, Clinton did an excellent job in discussing NATO issues. After 15 minutes, the White House Chief of Staff, Leon Panetta, tapped on his clipboard to bring the meeting to an end. I signaled to Claes, who started to get up but then asked Clinton: "How is the economy, Mr. President?" Clinton promptly sat back down. It was as though he had received a huge injection of adrenalin. For the next half hour, he expatiated vigorously on the U.S. economy: at that moment, I understood where his heart really lay.

Notably, the only foreign policy speech Clinton gave in his 1996 reelection campaign was in Detroit on October 22, following a campaign stop in Hamtramck, a town surrounded by Detroit and heavily populated by people of Central European nativity or ancestry. Clinton said that "By 1999, NATO's 50th anniversary and 10 years after the fall of the Berlin Wall, the first group of countries we invite to join should be full fledged members of NATO."[50]

He also tried to thread a needle by reaching out to Russia: "NATO will promote greater stability in Europe and Russia will be among the beneficiaries. Indeed, Russia has the best chance in history to help to build that peaceful and undivided Europe, and to be an equal and respected and successful partner in that sort of future." It was an important effort and, even today, it is not possible to judge whether it might have worked or was doomed to fail: whether reemergence of great-power politics, based on competition if not also confrontation, was inevitable or not.

Even as the United States and key Allies were attempting to turn an historical page with Russia and the conduct of international relations, Russian leaders remained skeptical. This included Boris Yeltsin, who was president throughout the key period.

It was obvious to us at USNATO that the two camps in Washington—Central Europe-heavy and Russia-heavy—would have a difficult time in pursuing both objectives; indeed, discussions, even in the White House Situation Room, sometimes became acrimonious.[51]

In Brussels, meanwhile, my team and I detected early-on that the Russian leadership was skeptical even of PfP: they could read as well as anyone else that one theme for PfP was as a precursor for NATO enlargement. But who would be included and how fast it would happen was obviously as opaque in Moscow as it was in Washington and elsewhere in the Alliance. There was also some skepticism about PfP in the U.S. government, including the U.S. ambassador in Moscow. As a result, I got the NAC to propose a mission to Moscow at the beginning of March 1994 to explain what PfP was and what it wasn't, both to try convincing the Russians that it was in their interest to join (thus, of course, giving them a hearing and respect by NATO), and to get the U.S. ambassador on board![52] The sheer fact of the visit was a plus: while we were not paying court to Russia, we were showing that it was not just being shunted aside in what (PfP) was to that point the leading edge of NATO reform.

After a good deal of nurturing, Russia did indeed join PfP in June 1994, when Foreign Minister Andrei Kozyrev visited NATO. Moscow also sent officers to take part in a military Partnership Coordination Cell (PCC) at SHAPE.[53] The alternative, of course, was that it would be self-isolating and, among other things, would have no influence at all on the NATO enlargement process.

I worked in particular with Vitaly Churkin,[54] in 1994 Russia's new ambassador to Belgium, who, after PfP accession, also represented it at NATO, to explore possibilities for NATO cooperation with Russia. When he arrived, he was "full of beans," but soon realized that he would have to mind his manners to be taken seriously: the days of the Soviet Union were over, and he had to be civil even to representatives at NATO from the three Baltic states, carefully-chosen individuals who knew how to take care of themselves and their nations' interests. As part of my relationship with Churkin, designed to show that Russia could have a productive role with NATO, I was able to get a positive response from Washington to Churkin's request that Russia be allowed to bid on equipment contracts for Soviet-era aircraft (e. g., MiG-29s) that still dominated air forces of former Warsaw Pact states.

The person in the U.S. government who led the "Russia-firsters" and worked hardest to forge a productive relationship with Russia was Strobe Talbott, senior State Department person on Russian matters and from 1994 onward Deputy Secretary of State. Despite his seniority in the government, however, plus a close personal relationship with

Clinton, he faced intense opposition from the "Central Europe-first-ers." One of my jobs, even though on the other side of the Atlantic, was to try to find common ground, as well as to help reconcile the military side of the Pentagon to NATO expansion, through emphasis on aspirants' undertaking needed reforms.

The NATO-Russian relationship even progressed to the point that Moscow was prepared to conclude an Individual Partnership Programme (within PfP), as well as a paper on "NATO-Russia Relations Beyond PfP." This was to be done at the Alliance's foreign ministerial meetings on December 1, 1994. But in the interim, the enlargement camp in Washington had been reinforced by a new Assistant Secretary of State for European and Eurasian Affairs, Richard Holbrooke, who was deeply committed to bringing in new members as fast as possible, come what may and without concern for other matters then in play. His efforts on enlargement at times were well out in front of the tolerance of a number of Allies, as I heard from them in Brussels; they also went beyond what the Pentagon and some allied military leaders believed was the time needed to develop the partners' capabilities to the point of adding to allied security rather than detracting from it, i.e. becoming producers and not just consumers of security. The bureaucratic balance in Washington among different NATO goals was thus upset. Further, in mid-November Holbrooke was quoted publicly as saying that NATO would soon take in new members. Allies were disconcerted. His comments also struck a nerve with Yeltsin, who had already developed concerns about what he thought he saw developing with enlargement and that, I later learned, he had expressed directly to President Clinton.[55]

Thus, when Foreign Minister Kozyrev arrived at the NATO ministerial, he was—he told us—pulled back by an angry Yeltsin and instructed to deliver in closed ministerial session a strongly-worded rejection of the Individual Partnership Programme, plus blistering comments about enlargement. Afterwards, German Foreign Minister Klaus Kinkel publicly rebuked Holbrooke. "Satisfied, Dick?" he asked.

The Russian reaction happened despite NATO's carefully nuanced ministerial statement on enlargement, which could hardly have been less specific or forward-leaning, out of deference not directly to Russia but to some skittish allies:

> We expect and would welcome NATO enlargement that would
> reach to democratic states to our East, as part of an evolutionary
> process, taking into account political and security developments in
> the whole of Europe. Enlargement, when it comes, would be part
> of a broad European security architecture based on true cooper-
> ation throughout the whole of Europe. It would threaten no one
> and would enhance stability and security for all of Europe. The
> enlargement of NATO will complement the enlargement of the
> European Union, a parallel process which also, for its part, con-
> tributes significantly to extending security and stability to the new
> democracies in the East.[56]

In the NATO drafting sessions, every word had been haggled over
and every one counted. The first sentence of 34 words, buttressed by
the next two, was the most carefully-crafted and heavily-compromised
NATO statement of any during my four-and-a-half years as ambassador. Given the U.S. desire to get the alliance fully on record for enlargement and to create a basis for launching the Enlargement Study,
while also not going beyond the tolerances of several NATO allies
(wary either of new security responsibilities or of driving Russia away),
my team and I earned our keep in this drafting exercise. Nevertheless,
President Yeltsin was not mollified.[57]

There was even worse to come in striking a balance between Russia
and Central Europe: a week later at a Budapest summit meeting of the
Conference on Security and Cooperation in Europe (at that meeting it
was renamed as an Organization rather than a Conference, i.e. OSCE),
Yeltsin laid into President Clinton:[58] "Why are you sowing the seeds of
mistrust?...Europe is in danger of plunging into a cold peace...History
demonstrates that it is a dangerous illusion to suppose that the destinies
of continents and of the world community in general can somehow be
managed from one single capital."[59]

It took considerable time and effort, with Talbott in the lead in dealing directly with the Russians, aided by individual NATO allies, to put
this particular genie as much as possible back in the bottle. That never
totally succeeded.

A big moment to test possibilities in NATO-Russian relations came
at the time of NATO's air campaign in August-September 1995, when
the Alliance finally received approval to conduct a sustained air cam-

paign, which ended the war in 18 days. This was pursuant to a U.N. Security Council resolution which, for reasons of its own, Russia did not veto (neither did China), despite historic Russian ties to Serbia and their common Orthodox Christianity.[60]

Following the Dayton Accords, when NATO created an Implementation Force (IFOR) for Bosnia, the Russian military indicated a desire to be part of it: not to be left out of this most important venture in the center of Europe. To the Pentagon and us at USNATO, that seemed an ideal opportunity to work directly with the Russians within the framework of a NATO-led peacekeeping operation. But how to achieve it? Secretary of Defense Bill Perry invited the Russian defense minister, General Pavel Grachev, to meet in Brussels. In a session in my office at USNATO, the deal was struck, but there was a problem: Russia was not willing to put its troops under the command of NATO, the former enemy, while, from NATO's perspective, there could be no troops in IFOR that were not under a common command.

SACEUR, Gen. George Joulwan, came to the rescue. He recalled that U.S. and Soviet forces had met on the Elbe River at the end of World War II, and that this was the first time since then that Russian and American forces had had a chance to work together. He accepted that the Russians could not be under NATO command, but how about U.S. command? That would show that Russia was being treated more-or-less on the same plane as the United States. Grachev immediately accepted the idea, even though representatives of the Russian foreign ministry in the room tried to stop him.[61]

Arrows on charts Joulwan displayed thus showed the proposed chain of command. Russian troops would report to the U.S. European Command (EUCOM) rather than to NATO. The key element: SACEUR, the NATO commander, was the same person—General Joulwan—as the commander of U.S. Forces in Europe! Respect would be shown by the superpower, the Russians would have a major role, and they would not be under NATO. The Russians then sent highly-qualified troops to Bosnia, and Russians and Americans worked closely together, on different occasions rescuing one another from misbehaving Bosnian Serb soldiers. This was a high-water mark in Russia-NATO relations, even though achieved through a transparent sleight-of-hand.

Bosnia

Throughout the months in which NATO was being reorganized to deal with the key issues of European security—implementing the architecture, as I had dubbed it—Bosnia came in and out of prominence at NATO Headquarters, almost never "in" except when the Bosnia Serbs committed a military outrage, especially against one of the safe areas. But each time (a total of 8 decisions in the NAC), the alliance advanced its commitments, but to no overall effect until the very last set of decisions, following the horrific Bosnian Serb slaughter of more than 7,000 Muslim civilians at Srebrenica in July 1995.

However, much more than Srebrenica was involved in the change of views by some key Allies[62] on the use of NATO airpower. Since Travemünde in October 1993, NATO had been significantly transformed to meet post-Cold War challenges. By the summer of 1995, almost all the pieces were moving into place, including the prospect of enlargement. Only one key element—Russia—was still not clearly on track. There was widespread satisfaction at NATO Headquarters about its major achievements as a job well done. I also discovered that, when other ambassadors at NATO talked about its new architecture and practical steps, all said more-or-less the same thing as was in my script. I had made sure that all of them could claim a share in bringing about the new NATO: it was a corporate achievement.

Bosnia, however, stood in the way of unalloyed celebration. The challenge was clear. As RAND's Steve Larrabee put it, "How can you be so proud of what you have done when you can't even stop the war in Bosnia?"[63] This crystallized the issue: along with the triggering event at Srebrenica, there was realization that little of what NATO was doing for European security with its transformation could have political validation unless NATO (finally) acted in Bosnia.

Foreign ministers of key Allies met in London on July 21 and issued an ultimatum to the Bosnian Serbs.[64] The baton then passed to us at USNATO to codify with the NAC what became the last of the air strike decisions. The special NAC on July 25 that authorized bombing if triggered by impermissible Bosnian Serb military actions was one of the longest on record and stretched far into the night. It was successful in issuing a warning to the Bosnia Serbs, who ignored it and conducted further military actions against safe areas.[65]

The NATO bombing campaign, *Operation Deliberate Force*, started on August 30.[66] At NATO headquarters, there was a major shift of mood: finally, the Alliance was acting. There was an almost universal sense of accomplishment, even on the part of people from countries that had been most reluctant for NATO to act.

The mood was short-lived, however. Late that night, I was phoned by the Undersecretary of State for Political Affairs. Ambassador Holbrooke, by then chief Bosnia negotiator, was demanding a bombing pause so he could go to Belgrade and get Slobodan Milošević to end Bosnian Serb military action. I couldn't believe it; the chances of its working so soon after the bombing had started were absurd. And, once stopped, could we get the bombing started again?[67]

I woke up Secretary General Claes and relayed the request from Washington. He, too, was furious. Further, Holbrooke had asked that the call for a pause come not from him but from Claes! A good soldier, Claes agreed to do so.

In the morning, the Allies soberly absorbed the news but had to comply. Thus, Holbrooke went to Belgrade and, as we had predicted, came away empty-handed. Then there was a problem: how to get the bombing restarted. I proposed a method to Claes that, as Secretary General, he would declare that the original NATO decision was still in force and that the technical pause could be automatically ended. In other words, a new NAC decision would have to be taken to turn off the renewed bombing, and that would be subject to a veto (mine!). The NAC met and there was no objection.

Sixteen more days of air attacks and the war was over. Left was the wrapping-up in the Dayton Accords, which many of us at NATO saw as having the virtue of bringing the conflict to a formal conclusion, but also allowing Milošević to gain at the bargaining table much of what he and his Bosnia Serb proxies had lost in battle.

1997: On to the End Game

The rebuilding of NATO in all dimensions then continued apace into 1997, to be crowned by a summit. To accommodate the Secretary General, Javier Solana,[68] it was agreed to hold it in Madrid. Only one key element was missing: a way to include Russia in some way and not exclude it, keeping the door open to cooperation but not letting Moscow affect NATO decisions, especially enlargement. This led to proposals for a NATO agreement with Russia, setting out principles and specific areas for cooperation, while also steering clear of any hint that this would give Moscow a way to side-track other NATO efforts.

Unique among the steps toward remaking NATO, diplomacy with Russia was developed and orchestrated from Washington, led by Strobe Talbott, with little input from NATO-Brussels, other than formally. The fiction of full Allied involvement was preserved but the reality was Washington-Russia, although with a role for Solana as front man and me as the Alliance conduit with Washington. Thus, when the NAC had considered all the issues in the proposed NATO-Russia agreement, Solana said he would take all the ideas, ponder them over the weekend, and propose his own draft for the NAC on Monday. Over the weekend, the State Department produced its own consolidated draft for negotiations with Russia and cabled it to me. What Solana then tabled with the NAC was therefore, in fact, "made in Washington" and, with his imprimatur, was approved unchanged by the Council.[69]

Solana then took the lead in formal negotiations with the Russians on behalf of NATO. But, to be sure he kept on track, the United States quietly held his hand.[70] The result was agreement on a NATO-Russia Founding Act, a remarkable document in terms of possibilities for cooperation.[71] In addition to general principles to govern the relationship, the Founding Act listed 19 areas for practical cooperation. It also sought to resolve some difficulties the Russians had with NATO's potential military involvement in Central Europe. It was clearly unacceptable, both to the United States and to allies, for Russia to have a role in determining NATO policies. Yet the need was recognized to relieve some legitimate Russian security concerns about NATO's moving eastward.

As a result, at U.S. prompting, the NAC unilaterally agreed on two self-abnegating provisions, which were then imported into the Founding Act, untouched by Russian hands. In brief, these were:

- The member States of NATO reiterate that they have no intention, no plan and no reason to deploy nuclear weapons on the territory of new members, nor any need to change any aspect of NATO's nuclear posture or nuclear policy—and do not foresee any future need to do so....[72]

- NATO reiterates that in the current and foreseeable security environment, the Alliance will carry out its collective defence and other missions by ensuring the necessary interoperability, integration, and capability for reinforcement rather than by additional permanent stationing of substantial combat forces.[73]

As ever, there was some caviling in the NAC over the final agreement. Most came from the French. I suggested a work-around: that NATO propose that the summit-level signing of the Founding Act take place in Paris (at the Élysée Palace). All French objections instantly disappeared, and President Jacques Chirac hosted this prestigious event.

We still had a problem regarding architecture. Ukraine was in an anomalous position. It was clear to everyone (including the Ukrainians at that time) that it could not aspire to join NATO, certainly under prevailing conditions and perhaps never. Also, opinion in Ukraine was deeply divided. It was also necessary to reassure Russia that NATO membership would not extend that far but without at the same time leaving Ukraine in limbo.

The answer was to negotiate a special arrangement for Ukraine with NATO. The Secretary General delegated the task to us at USNATO and, working with Washington, my team negotiated with the Ukrainians. Final provisions were worked out between me and the Ukrainian representative to NATO, Ambassador Borys Tarasyuk, who later became Ukraine's foreign minister. The result, signed on July 9 at the Madrid NATO Summit, was a Charter on a Distinctive Partnership between NATO and Ukraine.[74] Like the NATO-Russia Founding Act, it included general principles designed to reassure Ukraine and a list of areas for practical cooperation. It also provided for "NATO-Ukraine meetings at the level of the North Atlantic Council at intervals to be mutually agreed..." a Ukrainian military mission at NATO, and NAC meetings "with Ukraine as the NATO-Ukraine Commission, as a rule not less than twice a year."[75] The Commission was thus created at the Madrid summit.[76]

Whom to Invite to Join NATO

The final significant matter was which countries to invite to join NATO. This was done at a foreign ministers' conference in Sintra, Portugal, on May 29-30, 1997.[77] At USNATO, we provided Washington with our best assessment of the thinking of key allies, notably Germany, the UK, and France. From the beginning of the process, Germany had been concerned to surround itself with NATO, as well as with the European Union. That meant Poland and the Czech Republic as the minimum and could also include Hungary and Slovakia, the other two from the so-called Visegrad Group, named for the Hungarian city where leaders of Poland, Czechoslovakia, and Hungry came together in February 1991.[78] Slovakia, however, had been scratched from the list because its prime minister, Vladimír Mečiar, was judged to be less than committed to democracy.

Britain's objective, we at USNATO determined, was to have as little enlargement as possible, in order primarily to keep from weakening NATO, both militarily and in its ability to take decisions. Its list, therefore, included all four Visegrad countries plus Slovenia, but then with a "hard stop:" an end to further NATO enlargement. For its part, we learned, France wanted Poland and the Czech Republic (the "surround Germany" factor), plus Romania.[79]

Thus, only five Central European aspirants were in play: the Visegrad three, Slovenia, and Romania. Obviously, the decision whether to admit a country was the United States to make, since its strategic commitment to new allies was most critical. Secretary of State Albright's comment was simple: "We believe in a small number; that number is three; so, we support Poland, the Czech Republic, and Hungary."[80] So that was it. Part of the U.S. reasoning had to do with gaining U.S. Senate ratification: it would be easier to gain approval—the strategic commitment of the United States to more allies—if there were only a few.

All this was ratified at the Madrid NATO summit, July 8-9, 1997, which also included the first meetings of the simultaneously-created NATO-Ukraine Commission and of the Euro-Atlantic Partnership Council (the latter having been created at the Sintra ministerial).[81] President Yeltsin declined to attend, however: enlargement was on the agenda. Nevertheless, I believed that, especially with the NATO-Russia Founding Act, Moscow had become reconciled to the first round of three countries to join NATO. That its complaints were muted had a lot to do, I concluded, with the basic policy that Russia had adopted toward Germany, beginning with its unification at the end of the Cold War and the entry of united Germany into NATO. This was consistent with a judgment I made about Germany's surrounding itself with NATO and the EU. In my words: "This generation of Germans wants to make it impossible for its children and grandchildren to do what its parents and grandparents did."

I also arranged for Senator Bill Roth (R-Del) of Delaware, the head of the U.S. Senate NATO Observer Group, which I had helped to create, to speak at the summit, and I also gained NAC approval for defense ministers of Allied states to attend, in order to increase the chances of integrating the different aspects of security and to increase support for NATO with the U.S. Congress and European parliaments. I also arranged for some other members of Congress to be present and encouraged Allies to do likewise.

The only major business done at the summit that had not already been completed or at least decided (e.g., Ukraine and the EAPC), related to the future of enlargement beyond the first three countries.[82] Most important was a debate that took place just among foreign ministers, about the eligibility of the three Baltic states at some point to join NATO. In order to avoid provoking Russia regarding states that had been part of the Soviet Union (and with two of them contiguous to Russia), Deputy Secretary Talbott opposed any mention of these states in the summit communiqué, but the Danish foreign minister said that there would be no NATO communiqué and no NATO enlargement if they were not mentioned. His views were thus included, as innocuous as they sound:

> We will review the process [of enlargement] at our next meeting in 1999...The Alliance recognises the need to build greater stability, security and regional cooperation in the countries of southeast Europe, and in promoting their increasing integration into the Euro-Atlantic community. *At the same time, we recognise the progress achieved towards greater stability and cooperation by the states in the Baltic region which are also aspiring members* [emphasis added]. As we look to the future of the Alliance, progress towards these ob-

jectives will be important for our overall goal of a free, prosperous and undivided Europe at peace.[83]

Responsibility for implementing the decisions of the Madrid summit was given to the North Atlantic Council in Permanent Session, which included us at USNATO. In the period ahead, many more decisions were taken that deeply affected the future of NATO and of European security overall. Most consequential for the near term were more decisions on further enlargement with their impact on NATO's relations with Russia. European security is still being affected by the consequences. Also, during the ratification process in the U.S. Senate, Senator Kay Bailey Hutchison (R-Tx) proposed to me (I was then out of government) the creation of a mechanism at NATO to deal with any new Allies that might backslide in terms of their responsibilities, including falling short on democracy. The person heading enlargement on Capitol Hill for the State Department instantly rejected this suggestion when I proposed it to him. In view of recent developments in Hungary and to a lesser extent in Poland, this was a most short-sighted view.

Notes

1. See A Europe Whole and Free: Remarks to the Citizens in Mainz. President George Bush. Rheingoldhalle. Mainz, Federal Republic of Germany, May 31, 1989, at https://usa.usembassy.de/etexts/ga6-890531.htm.

2. The Treaty on European Union was signed in Maastricht on February 7, 1992, and the European Union formally superseded the European Communities on November 1, 1993. For treaty text, see https://europa.eu/european-union/sites/europaeu/files/docs/body/treaty_on_european_union_en.pdf.

3. A phrase I invented.

4. See North Atlantic Cooperation Council (NACC) (Archived), at: HTTPS://WWW.NATO.INT/CPS/EN/NATOLIVE/TOPICS_69344.HTM?

5. Like some other observers, I had publicly taken a strong public position on the need for the United States to be actively engaged in trying to end the Bosnia War.

6. Nevertheless, the appointment process went rapidly, and I arrived at post on July 11, only the second Clinton Administration ambassador to do so, after Pamela Harriman to Paris, who proved to be an outstanding representative of our country.

7. This is a constant concern of European Allies with a new U.S. administration, even today so many years after the end of the Cold War. It betokens the critical role of the United States in European security. Beginning with my time on the NSC staff in 1977, I noted that the Allies always complained if the United States did too little; and they often complained if we did too much. I prefer that we be criticized for doing too much.

8. Quoted in Mart Laar, *The Power of Freedom—Central and Eastern Europe after 1945* (Tallinn: Unitas Foundation, 2010), p. 217.

9. No votes are ever taken in the North Atlantic Council or its subordinate bodies. Any ally can object to any proposal and it then fails. This is an important provision for building political cohesion and ensuring that, after a decision is taken, allies will not fail to carry out assigned military tasks. No ally ever has.

10. I was, of course, careful that we never made a formal proposal at the NAC or in subordinate committees for which we did not have written instructions by cable from Washington, other than in the midst of hot and heavy negotiations—e.g., on Bosnia air-strike decisions—where oral instructions from the State Department had to suffice. It was the State Department's task to get interagency clearance for the oral instructions.

11. This was established by DOD Directive 5105.20 of 1952, which is periodically updated. See https://www.esd.whs.mil/Portals/54/Documents/DD/issuances/dodd/510520p.pdf.

12. Even at SHAPE, adaptation to new circumstances was slow. Soon after arriving in Belgium, I visited General Shalikashvili at his headquarters at Supreme Headquarters Allied Powers Europe (SHAPE) and received a command briefing. It included the projection that Russia could field at least 99 army divisions by the year 2000. I was uncomplimentary (!) and Shalikashvili was embarrassed for this idiocy by his staff briefer. Following that, we forged a good relationship that paid dividends throughout our mutual terms of service.

13. USNATO is also the only fully-integrated U.S. foreign mission/embassy. It includes State and Defense personnel (military and civilian) plus some other smaller elements (in those days the later-abolished United States Information Service). It was a single team, under the ambassador's authority, without the stove piping that so often occurs in embassies with representatives of a multitude of Washington agencies. The United States, like the other allies, was also represented by a military delegation that reported to the chairman of the Joint Chiefs of Staff (in common NATO parlance the Chief of Defense or "CHOD") and formed the NATO Military Committee. See Structure of NATO, at: https://en.wikipedia.org/wiki/Structure_of_NATO.

14. Key NSC staff were Alexander (Sandy) Vershbow and Jennone Walker.

15. There were different names at different times. One was Peacekeeping Partnership; a second, based on Partnership for Peace, was P4P. The finally agreed acronym was PfP.

16. The CSCE standard was later used to denote those countries that the United States, at least, would see as potentially eligible to join NATO.

17. I was even able to stimulate Irish interest in joining PfP. After lengthy consideration, it finally did so in 1999, after I had left Brussels. This was a remarkable departure for Irish foreign policy, where in 1949 it had rejected a U.S. offer of membership in NATO, unless Britain were excluded (!). The Truman administration opted for the UK.

18. An essential objective was also the massive reduction of Cold War-era military formations and equipment, as both irrelevant to peacekeeping tasks and as burdens on national economies, an essential element both of democratization and development of these societies: functions of security, writ large.

19. In 1995, the commander of U.S. Air Forces in Europe (USAFE) told me that the "pers-tempo" of all the people in his command—that is, how were they spending their time—was more than 50% at any time engaged in PfP activities with partner militaries.

20. EUCOM is the U.S. European Command in Stuttgart, also commanded by SACEUR in his solely U.S. "hat." In parallel with PfP, SACEUR (U.S. General George Joulwan) developed what he called the U.S. European Command State Partnership Program, which fostered cooperation between the National Guards

of individual American states and the militaries of PfP countries. Thus, the Illinois National Guard partnered with Poland, the Maryland National Guard with Estonia, etc. These efforts were an effective supplement to PfP and are continuing.

21. This was not, however, a matter of creating civilian control of the partner militaries but rather the democratization of the broader societies. Indeed, in the Cold War, all of the Warsaw Pact militaries were under civilian control with the political commissar system.

22. This obviously did not work with regard to Ukraine and Crimea in deterring Russian aggression in 2014. That begs the question, however, whether what the United States was doing in Kyiv contributed to the Russian decision to invade. The crisis also took place against the background of the unthought-out 2008 Bucharest NATO summit's declaration that Ukraine and Georgia "will become members of NATO," thus clearly crossing a red line for Moscow.

23. I had always believed this to have been a central motive for President DeGaulle's expelling Allied Command Europe and NATO troops from French soil in 1966-67.

24. The key Washington official on this issue was Frank Kramer, Assistant Secretary of Defense for International Security Affairs.

25. I was also invited to lunch by the British ambassador, Sir John Weston, whom I had known well when he had been posted to the British Embassy in Washington. His single message: stifle WEU. Ironically, British opposition to significant elements of European integration was still alive and well in the 2016-19 British folly over Brexit!

26. Unfortunately, after I left NATO in 1998, opponents of a strong EU (and its successors) at the Departments of State and Defense undercut some of the key NATO-WEU provisions. The debate, which was settled in the mid-1990s, has also been (uselessly) revived during the Trump administration. See Robert E. Hunter, *The European Security and Defense Policy: NATO's Companion — or Competitor?*, RAND Corporation, 2001, free download at https://www.rand.org/pubs/monograph_reports/MR1463.html.

27. See Press Statement Meeting of NATO Defence Ministers Travemünde 20th-21st October 1993, at: https://www.nato.int/cps/en/sid-f8a07a2a-aff13dba/natolive/news_24026.htm.

28. See Elaine Sciolino, "U.S. to Offer Plan on a Role in NATO for Ex-Soviet Bloc," *The New York Times*, October 21, 1993, at https://www.nytimes.com/1993/10/21/world/us-to-offer-plan-on-a-role-in-nato-for-ex-soviet-bloc.html.

29. Ahead of Wörner's visit, I went to Washington and learned the White House was not prepared to provide a scheduled time for Wörner to meet with Clinton or

even to guarantee that one would take place. He could meet with National Security Advisor Tony Lake, and the president might "drop by." Wörner threatened to cancel his trip. I talked him out of it, made clear to Lake the political damage at NATO if there weren't an Oval Office meeting, and it did take place.

30. Sciolino, op. cit.: "The United States has decided to support an expansion of NATO that could eventually include Russia, the countries of Eastern Europe and other former members of the Warsaw Pact, a senior aide to Secretary of State Warren Christopher said today."

31. Usually, the secretaries of state and defense got their first look at the staff-prepared briefing books for ministerial meetings on the plane on the way to the conference site.

32. See Press Statement Meeting of NATO Defence Ministers Travemünde 20th-21st October 1993, at https://www.nato.int/cps/en/SID-F8A07A2A-AFF13DBA/natolive/news_24026.htm.

33. Remarks to Multinational Audience of Future Leaders of Europe, President Bill Clinton, Brussels, Belgium, January 9, 1994, at: https://usa.usembassy.de/etexts/ga6-940109.htm.

34. Czech Republic, Hungary, Poland, and Slovakia.

35. See The President's News Conference With Visegrad Leaders in Prague January 12, 1994, at: https://www.govinfo.gov/content/pkg/WCPD-1994-01-17/pdf/WCPD-1994-01-17-Pg41.pdf.

36. In a press conference with Russian President Boris Yeltsin in Moscow on January 14, Clinton emphasized Partnership for Peace, which Yeltsin looked at somewhat favorably, though he hedged his position: "…the idea may prove just one of the scenarios for building a new Europe." Clinton apparently misheard that as "Russia's intention to be a full and active participant in the Partnership for Peace." Clinton did add that PfP included that "NATO plainly contemplated an expansion." The President's News Conference With President Boris Yeltsin of Russia in Moscow, January 14, 1994, at https://www.govinfo.gov/content/pkg/WCPD-1994-01-24/pdf/WCPD-1994-01-24.pdf.

37. See "NATO Expansion: What Yeltsin Heard," National Security Archive, March 16, 2018, at: https://nsarchive.gwu.edu/briefing-book/russia-programs/2018-03-16/nato-expansion-what-yeltsin-heard. This account contains some documents that were not shared with USNATO at the time and thus did not directly affect our dealings with the issue.

38. These include at NATO Headquarters the U.S. Delegation to the Military Committee, which worked for the chairman of the Joint Chiefs of Staff, the other 15 national delegations, delegations from PfP countries, the Secretary General and his Private Office, the Deputy and Assistant Secretaries General, and the seemingly

myriad other NATO bodies (notably the civilian International Staff and the military International Military Staff).

39. At NATO Headquarters, we also received on average 7,000 official government visitors each year for meetings of the alliance's various bodies.

40. In 1994, less than three years had passed since the USSR dissolved; its forces had not that long before departed from Central Europe; and it could not be said for sure that military confrontation, which had ended, would stay ended.

41. I worked particularly closely with Joe Kruzel, until his death on Mt. Igman, and Secretary of Defense Bill Perry, one of the most effective holders of that office and a strong supporter of NATO and of what we were trying to achieve at NATO Headquarters. Both had clear-sighted perspectives on what needed to be done.

42. I found this to be mostly on the civilian than the military side (with some notable exceptions) of the U.S. foreign policy/national security bureaucracy. Regarding the latter, I was struck with how open U.S. officers were with one another and with their Allied counterparts, until I realized that, if there is not a full exchange of information, in combat people may die.

43. Many Central European states have argued that joining NATO would help them gain foreign investment. This has been a factor in what I believe to have been excessive NATO enlargement, but there is no evidence to support the proposition.

44. I asked him if he had ever heard of Groucho Marx.

45. Notably, at that exercise, which I attended to show the American flag, peacekeeping troops from Ukraine performed particularly well.

46. One notable example was Hungarian claims on Transylvania, which had been incorporated into Romania in 1918. Hungary was told it had to give up this claim in order to join NATO and it did so.

47. See Membership Action Plan (Map), NATO, at https://www.nato.int/cps/en/natohq/topics_37356.htm.

48. Robert E. Hunter, "Enlargement: Part of A Strategy for Projecting Stability into Central Europe," *NATO Review*, May 1995, at: https://www.nato.int/docu/review/1995/9503-1.htm.

49. This was a major reason why the NATO summit at Bucharest in 2008 was grossly irresponsible in declaring that "Ukraine and Georgia will join NATO." It was clear that not a single ally was prepared to fight for Georgia—and, when the short conflict began with Russia, none did; and that judgment also likely applies to Ukraine, as well. The upshot of that decision was to give credence to Vladimir Putin's domestic propaganda claim that NATO was seeking to "surround" Russia, but with no security benefit for Georgia, Ukraine, or the alliance. See Bucharest Summit Declaration Issued by the Heads of State and Government participating

in the meeting of the North Atlantic Council in Bucharest on 3 April 2008, at: https://www.nato.int/cps/en/natolive/official_texts_8443.htm.

50. Transcript of the Remarks by President W. J. Clinton To People Of Detroit, USIA, 22 Oct. 1996, at https://www.nato.int/docu/speech/1996/s961022a.htm.

51. I saw this first hand during a trip to Washington that included a meeting of senior officials in the White House Situation Room, when members of the two camps personally insulted one another.

52. Although I had proposed the mission, it was properly led by the dean of the NAC, Spain's Ambassador Carlos Miranda. This was actually an advantage since it showed that PfP was not just a U.S. venture.

53. Ironically, the PCC occupied a small building that had been used for Operation Live Oak, Cold War-era coordination by the three Western occupying powers in Germany—the U.S., UK, and France—plus the Federal Republic of Germany, regarding possible Soviet/East German threats or military action against West Berlin. When we took officers from the PCC nations to tour the building and to choose offices, the Russian delegation took the best for themselves.

54. See Robert E. Hunter, "Vitaly Churkin: The Consummate Professional," *Lobelog*, February 21, 2107, at https://lobelog.com/vitaly-churkin-the-consummate-professional/.

55. There is also still debate, including U.S. diplomats who were present, about whether the United States had promised Yeltsin at the time of German unification that NATO would not expand into Central Europe. When we were first considering NATO enlargement, I formally asked the State Department whether any such pledges had ever been made. I was assured that that had not happened.

56. Final Communique Issued at the Ministerial Meeting of the North Atlantic Council, 1 December 1994, at: https://www.nato.int/docu/comm/49-95/c941201a.htm.

57. See Leonid Velekhov, "Russia-NATO Betrothal Didn't Happen," *Sevodnya*, December 3, 1994, translated in CDPSP 46(48). In a late December letter to Clinton, Yeltsin explained the Russian reaction: "I proceeded from the assumption that we had agreed in Washington [in September 1994] not to act hastily, but rather to achieve, in the first place, agreement between us on Russia's full-scale partnership with NATO, and only after that to start tackling the issues of enlargement." Kozyrev later wrote that "[p]rior to the meeting, as a result of arduous and protracted negotiations, representatives of the 16 NATO member-states worked out a compromise communiqué. The Russian delegation had the text of the paper only a few hours before the official inauguration of the cooperation program between Russia and NATO. We did not even have time to translate the document into Russian, much less to analyze it in order to report to the president of Russia. How-

ever, the communiqué recorded positions on issues of direct concern to Russia. It described the future evolution of the alliance, including its eventual expansion eastward, with the emphasis on the expansion rather than on partnership with Russia. This created a new situation for Russia, which we needed at least to examine. Thus, it was decided to postpone signing the partnership instrument."

58. See "NATO Expansion: What Yeltsin Heard," op. cit.

59. See Sciolino, op. cit.

60. At least one reason Russia opposed he 1999 air campaign over Kosovo was that there was no U.N. resolution. Whether it would have vetoed such a resolution if the Western powers had proposed one is not clear.

61. Russian diplomat Yuli Vorontsov said in Russian that this must not be done. Grachev told him, in Russian, to shut up.

62. Britain worked hardest to prevent any use of NATO airpower to protect safe areas, to begin with at NATO and, if it was cornered there, at the U.N. through the Secretary-General or, if even that failed, on at least one occasion by instructing its military commander in the field not to act.

63. At a conference attended by senior NATO leaders organized by the German Institute for International and Security Affairs in Ebenhausen, Bavaria.

64. See John Darnton, "Conflict In The Balkans: The Strategy; Ambiguous Ultimatum: Allies Show Differences," *The New York Times*, July 24, 1995, at https://www.nytimes.com/1995/07/24/world/conflict-in-the-balkans-the-strategy-ambiguous-ultimatum-allies-show-differences.html.

65. See Press Statement by the Secretary General Following North Atlantic Council Meeting on 25 July 1995, at https://www.nato.int/docu/speech/1995/s950725a.htm.

66. See Operation Deliberate Force, at https://en.wikipedia.org/wiki/Operation_Deliberate_Force.

67. As is any ambassador's right, I asked for formal instructions by cable, which arrived a few hours later.

68. See Javier Solana, at: https://en.wikipedia.org/wiki/Javier_Solana. Having been Spanish foreign minister and with ambitions for the future in Spanish politics—never realized—this was a logical proposal.

69. The British ambassador, Sir John Goulden, took me aside after the NAC meeting and said: "Robert, when your people in Washington produce a draft and pass it off as Solana's, you could at least change American spellings to the British spellings we use here at NATO!"

70. Talbott sent Sandy Vershbow to Moscow to make sure that Solana got things right.

71. Founding Act on Mutual Relations, Cooperation and Security between NATO and the Russian Federation signed in Paris, France, May 27, 1997, at: https://www.nato.int/cps/en/natohq/official_texts_25468.htm. The Founding Act was revised somewhat at a 2002 NATO-Russia Council meeting in Rome, at: https://www.nato.int/docu/comm/2002/0205-rome/rome-eng.pdf.

72. Key elements of the wording of this paragraph were literally written on the back of a napkin at the NATO Headquarters restaurant at a U.S.-officials-only lunch, including me and key members of my team, plus Sandy Vershbow of the NSC staff. Vershbow was the chief draftsman.

73. The qualifiers "current and foreseeable security environment" became an escape clause for NATO following the Russian seizure of Crimea and military activities elsewhere in Ukraine, beginning in 2014. They permitted NATO to do military things in Central Europe while arguing that it has not violated the Founding Act.

74. See Charter on a Distinctive Partnership between the North Atlantic Treaty Organization and Ukraine, at: https://www.nato.int/cps/en/natohq/official_texts_25457.htm.

75. Regarding a name for the agreement, I told Tarasyuk we had proposed calling the NATO-Russia agreement a "charter," but Moscow had rejected it. "We'll take it," he said.

76. There was nearly a snag. I was back in Washington to go over final details for Madrid and mentioned to Strobe Talbott that NATO would meet with Ukraine at the summit in the context of the new Commission. Worried about the impact on the Russians, he disagreed vigorously. But he was overruled by Secretary of State Albright.

77. See Final Communiqué of the Ministerial Meeting of the North Atlantic Council in Sintra, Portugal, at: https://www.nato.int/docu/comm/1997/970529/home.htm. Notably, he communique also said: We also recommend to our Heads of State and Government to make explicit our commitment that the Alliance remains open to the accession of any other European state able and willing to further the principles of the Washington Treaty and to contribute to our common security.

78. See History of the Visegrád Group, at http://www.visegradgroup.eu/history/history-of-the-visegrad. Slovakia acceded to the group as an independent country, as did the Czech Republic, following the velvet divorce of December 31, 1992.

79. At USNATO, we believed French inclusion of Romania was calculated more to "get the U.S. goat" as anything else, since the Romance language connection was not serious.

80. Hungary's inclusion by the United States in the first enlargement was affected by its contribution to U.S. military efforts to keep the peace in Bosnia with the post-Dayton Implementation Force (IFOR). I was tasked to ask the Hungarian ambassador to Belgium, who represented his country to PfP, whether the U.S. First Armored Division could use the Hungarian military base at Taszár for transit to Bosnia. When I approached him with this request, the Hungarian ambassador, András Simonyi, asked: "Would tomorrow morning be too late for us to agree?" From that moment, Hungary was on the U.S. short-list to join NATO. President Bill Clinton visited the base in December 1995.

81. For documents, see NATO Summit, Madrid, Spain, 8-9 July 1997, at: https://www.nato.int/docu/comm/1997/970708/home.htm.

82. At the end of the summit, President Bill Clinton had a private meeting with leaders all of the Central European aspirant countries. It concluded with a "family photo" of all of them. Just before that, Madeleine Albright deliberately button-holed Prime Minister Mečiar of Slovakia, the "anti-Democrat," and proceeded to lecture him at length in Czech. As a result, he missed the family photo and saved Clinton the embarrassment.

83. Madrid Declaration on Euro-Atlantic Security and Cooperation Issued by the Heads of State and Government, at: https://www.nato.int/docu/pr/1997/p97-081e.htm.

Chapter 15

New Members, New Missions: NATO and Euro-Atlantic Architecture in the Second Clinton Administration

Daniel S. Hamilton

With the advent of President Clinton's second term, the evolving security architecture entered a new phase. The essential premise of U.S. strategy—that the United States, as a "European power," needed to help engineer a new interlocking architecture that could anchor a Europe that was whole, free and at peace—had become foundational to operational policies as well as public statements by the President and senior officials.

Progress had been made on each element of the emerging architecture during the Administration's first term. The prospect of walking through the doors of European and Euro-Atlantic institutions had accelerated aspirants' efforts to strengthen democratic institutions; make sure soldiers served civilians, not the other way around; and resolve lingering ethnic and border disputes.[1] With little fanfare, some small steps toward integration had been taken; 17 European countries had joined the Council of Europe, and the Czech Republic, Hungary and Poland had acceded to the OECD.

Nonetheless, there was no room for complacency. From Bosnia to Chechnya, more Europeans had died violently in the past five years than in the previous forty-five. Russia's trajectory remained uncertain. The EU enlargement process seemed stalled. There was very real prospect of renewed bloodshed in the Western Balkans.

President Clinton's new Secretary of State, Madeleine Albright, immediately underscored the urgency of the task. Europe's democratic revolution was not complete, she said. Much still needed to be done. Right after assuming office she asked me and Tom Malinowski to help her with an *Economist* piece in her name to set the stage for her inaugural visits to European Allies as Secretary of State, and for decisions the Alliance would have to make over the next six months.[2]

In the first term, the "how" and "why" of NATO enlargement had been determined. Now the "who" and "when" had to be answered, after which the ratification struggle had to begin. At the same time, the Administration's promise of a "new NATO" required the Alliance to complete its own internal transformation by streamlining commands, promoting European capabilities and welcoming Spain and potentially France into the integrated military command. The proposal for an Atlantic Partnership Council had to be implemented. Initiatives to integrate Russia, through a more robust NATO-Russia partnership and full participation in the G-8, had to move forward. A special relationship with Ukraine was still necessary.

It was also clear that NATO could open its door to some, but not yet to all, of the many aspirants seeking to join the Alliance. Already in the Clinton Administration's first term U.S. officials had been clear that enlargement must naturally begin with the strongest candidates, but that NATO's next new members would not be its last.[3] My long-time friend and colleague Ron Asmus, who had been working informally with Administration officials while outside the Administration at the RAND Corporation, now joined the State Department as Deputy Assistant Secretary for European Affairs, with responsibility for NATO and European regional political-military affairs. He argued successfully that the Administration's strategy should be "small is beautiful plus robust Open Door." This meant that only the strongest candidates should be invited for membership to ensure the principle of continued enlargement would be successfully established. That would pave the way for accession by others after that. This required a proactive strategy to reassure those not in the first wave that the door did indeed remain open to them, and to work together to create the conditions that would let them walk through that door.

President Clinton and his foreign policy team were now ready to advance the strategy. Significant decisions were made in a remarkable 44-day period between the May 27,1997 meeting of NATO heads of state and government at the Élysée Palace with Russian President Boris Yeltsin and the July 9,1997 NATO summit in Madrid, when leaders formally invited the Czech Republic, Hungary and Poland to join the Alliance. As U.S. Ambassador to NATO Robert Hunter noted, the decisions all reinforced each other: "each was indispensable to the success of the others and to the overall creation of a transatlantic security architecture that can succeed."[4]

First, the Alliance chose the first new members because they were judged to be the most likely to gain the support of the legislatures in the 16 NATO member states. Administration officials echoed Richard Holbrooke's mantra: NATO was not a club, it was a military alliance with high standards. Madeleine Albright drove home the point: "the enlargement of NATO must begin with the strongest candidates; otherwise it would not begin at all. But when we say that the first new members will not be the last, we mean it. And we expect the new members to export stability eastward, rather than viewing enlargement as a race to escape westward at the expense of their neighbors."[5]

Second, the Alliance affirmed that its door remained open to additional European countries ready and willing to shoulder the responsibilities of NATO membership. President Clinton stressed that NATO's next invitations would not be the last. Secretary Perry's fall 1996 comment set the tone: the answer to those not among the first three was not "no," it was "not yet." The Alliance engaged in a new phase of individual dialogues to help aspirants understand the implications of Article 5 responsibilities, work through obstacles to eventual membership, and maintain positive momentum.

Third, the Alliance decided to strengthen the Partnership for Peace (PfP), which then embraced 27 countries, including countries that weren't even part of the Warsaw Pact, including Austria, Finland, Sweden and Switzerland. Allies agreed to the U.S. proposal for an Atlantic Partnership Council, which they renamed the Euro-Atlantic Partnership Council (EAPC), to replace the defunct NACC and become the political voice of the Partnership for Peace: a forum for intensified political and security consultations and decision-making among Allies and partners on common activities.

Fourth, the Allies negotiated a NATO-Ukraine Charter and its operating arm, the NATO-Ukraine Commission, recognizing tacitly that the future of Ukraine could well be the key to many other Alliance strategic plans and objectives.

Fifth, NATO and Russia signed their Founding Act creating a Permanent Joint Council as the mechanism for Russia-NATO cooperation on a range of issues, from peacekeeping and theatre missile defense to nuclear safety, terrorism and disaster relief, all as part of a comprehensive and cooperative security architecture.[6] NATO reiterated that it had "no intention, no plan, and no reason" in the foreseeable future to station nuclear weapons on new members' soil, but that it may do so should the need arise. NATO further stated that military infrastructure "adequate" to assure new members' security under Article 5 of the North Atlantic Treaty would be maintained on their territory. The Alliance pledged not to place "substantial combat forces" in the "current and foreseeable security environment" on new members' territory, but underscored an intention to increase interoperability, integration, and reinforcement capabilities with the new states. In Paris, President Clinton declared that the quest for security in Europe "is not a zero sum game, where NATO's gain is Russia's loss and Russia's strength is an Alliance weakness. That is old thinking, these are new times."[7]

Sixth, NATO continued its internal adaptation by creating the means to build the European Security and Defense Identity (ESDI) within the Alliance, rather than separate from it, slimming down NATO's military command structure, reducing the number of headquarters from 65 to 20, preparing forces for operations under the command and control of Combined Joint Task Forces (CJTF) headquarters and comparable arrangements—one of which was represented by SFOR in Bosnia—and to improve its ability to conduct operations with nonmembers.[8] These and related reforms enabled the full integration of Spain into NATO's military command. France inched closer, although Chirac in the end was not prepared to agree to full reintegration.[9]

Five months after the Madrid Summit, NATO foreign ministers joined their counterparts from Poland, the Czech Republic and Hungary and signed the protocols of accession. In that same week, the European Council agreed to begin accession negotiations with the same three countries, as well as Slovenia, Estonia and Cyprus.

The "Litmus Test"

Major pieces of the architecture were now in place, but Secretary Albright pushed on the Baltic issue, which she called a "litmus test" of our overall strategy of integration. She said that there was perhaps no part of Europe which suffered more from the old politics of the Cold War and the zero-sum philosophy of the Cold War than did the Baltic republics. That was why there could be no better example of our success and the benefits of win-win cooperation than this region—if we got it right. She looked at Ron Asmus at the time and said, "Where is the strategy?" A team of us were put together to develop one. The result was essentially the Baltic Action Plan on steroids. It consisted of two elements: a Northern European Initiative and a U.S-Baltic Charter, anchored by a joint Commission.

During this time John Kornblum had moved on to become U.S. Ambassador to Germany. His successor as Assistant Secretary was Marc Grossman, who had been U.S. Ambassador to Turkey. As one of his first acts Grossman flew to the region in September 1997 to present the Northern European Initiative (NEI). The key goal of the NEI was to encourage stronger cooperation with and among the countries of the region, creating the conditions in which the question of integration, while controversial at the time, could be posed more positively in the future. The NEI was an effort to build closer ties to Nordic countries while embedding our engagement with the Baltic states in a broader framework that sought to create stronger regional cooperation (including the northwestern region of Russia) and cross-border relations in terms of business promotion, law enforcement, civil society, environment, energy, and public health. In each of these areas we established a number of concrete projects and activities. We knew that the United States wouldn't be the major player in these areas, but we thought we could play a modest and, in some niche areas, a crucial role. We were prepared to be a junior partner or a bigger partner depending upon the issue and depending upon what we could bring to the table.

Like the Baltic Action Plan, the NEI consisted of three tracks. The first was to help Estonia, Latvia, and Lithuania help themselves to become the strongest possible candidates for Western integration. Political goals included managing expectations regarding NATO, establishing Partnership commissions, facilitating border treaties, supporting recommendations of the OSCE's High Commissioner on National Minorities regarding inter-ethnic issues, starting EAPC regional discussions on security issues, and promoting inter-Baltic cooperation. Economic initiatives included facilitating Baltic entry into the WTO, promoting an open investment climate, and prodding Baltic-Russian commercial cooperation. Military goals included support for NATO activities, exploring eventual CFE accession, supporting the decommissioning of the Skrunda radar facility in Latvia in 1999, and increasing Baltic receptivity to Russian participation in regional PfP activities. We also sought to expand regional capabilities to fight transnational organized crime and establish effective export control and non-proliferation regimes.

The second track we called "Nordics Plus," which meant coordinating approaches with the Nordic countries, as well as Germany, Poland and the European Union on Russia/Baltic relations, a U.S. observer role in the Council of Baltic Sea States (CBSS), energizing commercial activities in the region, promoting regional energy strategies, and urging Nordic/German mentor roles in NATO activities, including the creation and strengthening of the Baltic Security Assistance (BALTS-EA) Forum of 14 Western nations, which was intended to help Estonia, Latvia and Lithuania develop their defense and eventually join NATO. We believed our Northern Europe Initiative and the European Union's Northern Dimension could complement and reinforce one another. [10]

The third track was to implement the kind of inclusive policy toward Russia envisioned in the Baltic Action Plan. This included enhanced cooperation among embassies in the Nordic and Baltic states and Russia, engaging regional public/private policy makers, including Kaliningrad in regional cooperation, linking SEED/Freedom Support Act activities, promoting military-military cooperation with regard to the Kola Peninsula, responding to Russian proposals on confidence- and security-building measures, urging joint planning for Baltic ports and other infrastructure projects, regional environmental objectives through the CBSS, coordinating nuclear waste management programs, and promoting the U.S. role in the CBSS task force on organized crime.

As Strobe Talbott put it, our goal was to encourage Russia, over time, "to view this region not as a fortified frontier but as a gateway; not as a buffer against invaders who no longer exist, but as a trading route and a common ground for commerce and economic development—in a word, that Russia will come to view the Baltics Hanseatically."[11] President Clinton and Secretary Albright believed that Russia would have to make that psychological and political adjustment itself, by its own lights, for its own reasons, in keeping with its own evolving concept of its national interest. But we and our European partners could help by applying the general principle of inclusiveness. That meant involving Russia to the greatest extent possible in the commercial, political, environmental and other forms of collaboration we were developing among the states along the littoral of the Baltic Sea. The Barents Euro-Arctic Council, the Council of Baltic Sea States, and the Arctic Council were models of what was required, and the United States would participate as appropriate.[12]

The second initiative was to give our activities through the Baltic Action Plan a higher political profile via a U.S.-Baltic "Charter of Partnership," to be signed by President Clinton and the three Baltic presidents, affirming our common goal of fostering the deeper integration of the Baltic states into the European and Euro-Atlantic mainstream. Ron led the negotiating team, which I joined. Initially, each of the Baltic states wanted its own bilateral charter; we had to convince them that a single document signed by four presidents conveyed a stronger message of support than three separate documents.

On January 16, 1998 the four presidents signed the Charter of Partnership, otherwise known as the Baltic Charter—a political statement of common principles intended to guide the deepening of mutual cooperation and advance common objectives, including, explicitly, "Baltic integration into the European and transatlantic institutions, such as the European Union, OSCE, the World Trade Organization and NATO." While the Baltic Charter did not specifically provide a U.S. guarantee of Baltic security or NATO membership, it did confirm the Baltic republics' inherent right to choose their own security arrangements. At the signing ceremony, President Clinton left little doubt of his commitment: "America is determined to create the conditions under which Estonia, Lithuania, and Latvia can one day walk through [NATO's] door."[13]

The goal of the Charter and accompanying measures was to help the leaders of these countries shift from a preoccupation that they might be left in some kind of a gray zone and instead focus on what they needed to do to make themselves the strongest possible candidates for future integration to European and Euro-Atlantic institutions. As Marc Grossman said,

> This administration's Baltic policy can be summed up in three
> words: Champion of integration. We want the United States to be
> the champion of integration of Estonia, Latvia, and Lithuania into
> European and transatlantic institutions. That is what the Baltic
> Charter is all about...This is a race that the Baltic states have to
> run themselves. But they understand that this race is a marathon,
> not a sprint. The point is to stay in the race and finish. We can
> help coach them--and make it clear that one day we want them to
> successfully cross the finish line.[14]

The Charter created a Baltic Partnership Commission to advance
the integration of the Baltic nations into transatlantic and European
structures. The Commission continued efforts as set forth under the
Baltic Action Plan. It sought to enhance regional cooperation by promoting Baltic, Russian, and Nordic participation in regional and international organizations. It quickly moved forward with a number of
initiatives, for instance the Baltic-American Partnership Fund (BAPF),
which was established by the United States Agency for International
Development and the Open Society Foundations. Each organization
initially provided $7.5 million to be spent over a ten-year period on
the continued development of civil society in the Baltic countries of
Estonia, Latvia, and Lithuania.[15] The three Baltic presidents jointly
announced that they would establish national commissions to study the
period of the Holocaust and of the totalitarian rule in each of their
countries. The Pentagon worked with each Baltic state to establish
long-term defense modernization plans that would help them develop small but modern and capable militaries. The Administration and
Congress also agreed to significantly increase security assistance for the
Baltic states under the Warsaw Initiative program.

Triple Crown

As the NATO ratification debate proceeded, the Clinton Administration's thinking was already shifting to what a larger NATO's purposes could be, and how NATO should relate to other instruments of
U.S. engagement. Secretary Albright wanted forward thinking. In fall
1997 I wrote a memo to her arguing that while the enlargement debate
was likely won, size was not purpose. In future the Alliance would not
only take in new members, it was likely to take on new missions. The

Alliance would need to maintain the Open Door and help to create conditions by which new members could add their strength to ours, while simultaneously aligning our NATO strategy with our overall architectural effort to position the transatlantic partnership as a geostrategic base from where we and our European partners, acting through and with our various institutions—including the EU—could address new threats to our common values and interests, many of which would come from outside of Europe. Albright liked the idea and asked me to follow up with Marc Grossman and Ron Asmus, with whom I had already been working closely.

Albright then pushed these themes at the NATO foreign ministers meeting in December 1997. Even as the Allies signed the agreements with Poland, Hungary and the Czech Republic to bring them into the alliance, Secretary Albright urged a wider NATO strategy to deal with other looming challenges, including the threat from nuclear, chemical and biological weapons in the hands of terrorists or countries like Libya, Iraq and Iran.

My boss Greg Craig asked me to prepare talking points for a new transatlantic bargain and to join him at the Secretary's annual retreat with her senior advisors on January 9, 1998. There, together with Marc Grossman, we pitched our ideas. She was receptive and asked us to send her a more detailed outline.

I worked with Ron and Marc to formulate a memo sent to Secretary Albright on January 15 proposing that the Administration use 1999 to define a new transatlantic bargain for the 21st century premised on the need for the United States and Europe to work together in an expanded transatlantic framework to solve problems both inside and outside of Europe. The premise of the strategy was two-fold: the United States remained a European power, and the transatlantic partnership remained America's geostrategic base when it came to global issues.

We prepared a speech for Secretary Albright before the New Atlantic Initiative on February 9 placing NATO enlargement in the context of our broader goals for our relations with Europe. There, she said that

> It is my great hope that Poland, Hungary and the Czech Republic will be part of a transatlantic partnership that is not only broader, but deeper as well; a partnership that is a force for peace from the

Middle East to Central Africa; a partnership that has overcome barriers to trade across the Atlantic; a partnership strong enough to protect the environment and defeat international crime; a partnership that is united in its effort to stop the spread of weapons of mass destruction, the overriding security interest of our time.

However old or new the challenges we face, there is still one relationship that more than any other will determine whether we meet them successfully, and that is our relationship with Europe. The transatlantic partnership is our strategic base—the drivewheel of progress on every world-scale issue when we agree, and the brake when we do not.[16]

The goal was to foster an inclusive, more self-confident and outward-looking Europe as a strategic partner for the United States in all these areas. As we opened our institutions to new members, we needed to expand the scope of our partnership to new areas.

Grossman billed this strategy as advancing the "Triple Crown" of mutual security, prosperity and democratic values. We identified three challenges that the United States and Europe had to address in coming decades.

The first challenge was within Europe: to support the continuing integration of the continent and build a broader Euro-Atlantic community, including new partnerships with Russia and Ukraine. The second challenge was between Europe and America: to deepen the bonds between our societies—the foundation of our relationship—as a positive force for change in the world. That meant building down commercial barriers to foster a closer, more open economic relationship, continuing to foster people-to-people exchanges, and generating closer political ties bilaterally and with the European Union. The third challenge extended beyond Europe and America: to improve our ability to deal jointly with challenges in the wider world—whether political, military, economic, criminal or environmental—that neither of us would be able to confront effectively alone.

We viewed these goals as mutually reinforcing. A safer, freer, more prosperous Europe was more likely to be America's global partner. And a more cohesive, outward-looking Europe that could act was more likely to be able to manage broad forces of change that could challenge stability, prosperity and democracy on the European continent.

At its core, the Triple Crown was our effort to make more explicit and operational what was, for the first time in European history, broad and implicit agreement across most of the continent that our underlying task—and opportunity—was to create a secure and increasingly prosperous community of democracies. Defining security in this broad sense had enabled us to project a new vision for the United States and Europe building together a "cooperative security space." This "common space" rested on a foundation of shared values, common norms of behavior and mutually-reinforcing institutions, and reached beyond the outdated frontiers of the Cold War.

Under the Triple Crown strategy, each of the three major pillars of the architecture—NATO, U.S.-EU relations, and the OSCE—would need to undergo further adaptation to reposition the U.S-European relationship so it could stabilize the European continent while advancing U.S. and European values and interests beyond Europe. The strategy required a new NATO with expanded missions, the reorientation of U.S.-EU relations to global challenges, and a retooled OSCE to promote democracy throughout the Euro-Atlantic region. Major summits were scheduled for each of these architectural pillars in 1999; the strategy foresaw using the three summits—Grossman called it the 'trifecta'—to advance this new bargain.[17]

First, however, the U.S. Senate had to agree to let the Czech Republic, Hungary and Poland walk through NATO's open door. As Jeremy Rosner recounts in this volume, the Administration mounted a major effort to secure a successful outcome. On April 29, 1998, by a vote of 80-19, the U.S. Senate ratified the accession of the three countries to the North Atlantic Treaty.

New Missions

Senate ratification was a new high in the Administration's campaign to reposition the transatlantic partnership for a new era. The ratification debates on each side of the Atlantic, however, revealed some potentially dangerous faultlines when it came to perceptions of NATO's purpose and its relevance to future security challenges. In essence, differences centered over the degree to which the Alliance should take on out-of-area challenges.

President Clinton framed the issue in a speech commemorating the 50th anniversary of the Berlin airlift on May 13, 1997: "Yesterday's NATO guarded our borders against direct military invasion. Tomorrow's NATO must continue to defend enlarged borders and defend against threats to our security from beyond them—the spread of weapons of mass destruction, ethnic violence and regional conflict."[18]

A new debate had emerged. Clinton's ambitious vision for the Alliance was overwhelming to those who believed that NATO's singular mission was to stabilize the European continent and to provide a hedge against a possibly resurgent or instable Russia. Proponents of this view argued that NATO, at its core, was essentially an insurance policy. Securing the territorial integrity of Europe and North America was an historic achievement. Alliances were inherently fragile, however, and doing more threatened strategic overload. Europeans who subscribed to this view were unenthusiastic about reorienting their militaries away from the traditional, less urgent and now relatively cheap mission of protecting European territory toward a more controversial, distant and expensive—if arguably more urgent—mission of addressing out-of-area challenges.

Having just become accustomed to the notion of a larger Alliance, many viewed this new debate as an attempt to shift the strategic goalposts. They argued that an effort to move NATO towards defending common interests underestimated current transatlantic problems, overlooked continuing dangers in Europe, risked the achievements of the past decade, and was yet another example of inconsistent U.S. priorities. Americans who shared this perspective added that the more successful the United States was in maintaining peace on the European continent at relatively low cost, the freer the United States would be to deal with security challenges elsewhere. Collective defense, together with enlargement, they said, was sufficient glue to hold the Alliance together. Their basic argument, to coin an old American homily, was "if it ain't broke, why fix it?"

Others, primarily in the United States, argued that while NATO was not yet "broke," it soon would be if Allies did not wake up to new dangers. The old glue was not enough; to survive, NATO needed to be capable of addressing new sources of conflict, most of which were beyond Europe's borders. They contended that in the new century the transatlantic community was more likely to face threats emanating from outside of Europe than from within it, whether posed by weapons of mass destruction, threats of disrupted energy flows, or instability in the former Soviet space or the Greater Middle East. A ballistic missile attack using an agent of mass destruction from a rogue state (concerns were growing about Libyan, Iranian and Iraqi capabilities) would be every bit as much an Article 5 threat as a Warsaw Pact tank had been two decades earlier.[19] Similarly, non-Article 5 threats, if not addressed early and effectively, could grow into Article 5 threats. Bosnia and Kosovo were examples. NATO, they asserted, should be our instrument of choice when Europeans and Americans decided to address military security challenges together. That meant it would need to be further adapted to be capable of addressing a spectrum of Article 5 and non-Article 5 challenges.

A third line of argument began to appear that essentially called for a division of labor: Europeans should worry about security in Europe and Americans should worry about security beyond Europe. Republican U.S. Senator Kay Bailey Hutchison of Texas (who, by 2017, ironically, had become U.S. Ambassador to NATO) became a prominent proponent of this view as part of the ratification debate.

The Clinton Administration believed the division of labor argument to be a false choice. It would leave the United States with the much more demanding and dangerous assignment. It would deprive Europeans of a voice on out-of-area challenges and relieve them of any broader sense of responsibility for common security dangers, even though Europe was just as wealthy and had similar global interests. It would also end America's still fundamental role as a European power. It would reinforce European inwardness and resentment, exacerbate American tendencies to pull away from European concerns, and ultimately corrode the Alliance.

For Washington, the real choice was not division of labor but a shared sense of risk and responsibility to respond to the challenges that faced the Atlantic community. The Clinton Administration wanted Europeans to step up and assume greater responsibility for security in Europe—but they also realized that the United States remained an essential element of stability on the continent. Administration officials understood that by virtue of its global posture, Washington would need to assume much of the burden defending common interests else-where—but they also realized that Europe was similarly challenged by such threats, and had resources and capabilities to contribute. Article 5 was and should remain the heart of the Washington Treaty. But Allies had to recognize that Article 5 threats could come from sources beyond NATO's immediate borders.

"If you ask where U.S. and European forces could face conflict in the decades ahead," Under Secretary of State Thomas Pickering said, "the answer must include scenarios beyond NATO's borders. During the Cold War, it made sense for Europeans to concentrate on the threat to their own territory and for the U.S. to assume the primary responsibil-ity for defending common transatlantic interests elsewhere. But such an arrangement makes less sense at a time when the direct territorial threat to Europe has diminished, and when new threats to our common interests may come from beyond NATO's immediate borders."[20]

In short, ratification of NATO enlargement was an important step, but only a step, toward a new transatlantic bargain. The Policy Plan-ning memo crystallized the debate and argued that on this fundamental question, NATO needed to continue to stabilize the European conti-nent, but increasingly had to be prepared to address challenges ema-nating from beyond Europe. The Secretary's January 9 retreat clarified our need to move ahead with this adapted approach. Senate ratifica-tion on April 29 enabled the administration to move forward with its broader vision for the transatlantic partnership, in which the two sides of the North Atlantic would continue to build a Europe whole and free while simultaneously developing the capacity to address challenges and threats from beyond Europe.[21] The "trifecta" of major upcoming summits afforded an opportunity to further develop the mutually re-inforcing nature of the institutional construct in ways that would not only address Europe's security challenges, but also position the United States and Europe to deal with challenges of a broader nature.

Administration officials now began to articulate the Triple Crown message. Meeting with her NATO counterparts in Luxembourg in May 1998, Secretary Albright talked about the President's desire to start a conversation on how we could best build a new and all-encompassing Euro-Atlantic partnership for the 21st century—and the role NATO should play as a key pillar in that partnership. The essence of that vision was a deeper form of cooperation with a Europe that could act as a partner—on the continent, across the Atlantic, and in the wider world. NATO would be the institution of choice when the United States and Europe had to act together militarily. The goal should be to create a larger, more flexible NATO committed to collective defense and capable of defending against a wide range of threats to our common interests, both on and beyond the European continent.[22] NATO would need to develop the defense capabilities to provide the forces for Article 5 collective defense and non-Article 5 crisis response missions.

Essentially, Albright was laying out the U.S. vision statement for NATO in advance of the Alliance's 50th anniversary summit in Washington in April 1999. In our view it was essential to break through the perception that NATO was only about keeping Europe stable, and to get Allies to embrace the idea of a common transatlantic community defending common values and interests.

Secretary of Defense William Cohen forcefully elaborated on this approach at a NATO defense ministers meeting in Villamoura, Portugal on September 24, 1998. The United States wanted to adapt NATO's defense capabilities to provide forces for Article 5 collective defense and non-Article 5 crisis response missions. EAPC Partners should be involved as much as possible in Alliance activities, particularly non-Article 5 missions. "Risks will remain unpredictable and multidirectional," Cohen said. "We must…commit ourselves to develop the defense capabilities required to carry out the full spectrum of existing and future missions." That included addressing the threat posed by the proliferation of weapons of mass destruction and their means of delivery by both state and non-state actors, which, Cohen contended, "is arguably our most significant potential Article 5 threat."

Cohen argued that NATO's new Strategic Concept, slated to be unveiled at the Washington NATO Summit, had to reflect the evolving strategic environment, building upon language from 1991 that stated "Alliance security must take account of the global context" and that "NATO must be capable of responding to multifaceted and multi-directional risks" if stability in Europe was to be preserved. "The crises will no longer come to us," he said. "We must go to the crises….We may operate as an Alliance, an Alliance with Partners, or NATO could provide forces to WEU for operations outside Alliance territory."[23] Cohen was quick to say that "this does not involve a global peacekeeping role for NATO," but he underscored that "our history as an Alliance is clear proof that we have interests in common that go beyond Article 5 defense of territory."[24]

Following these ministerial presentations, on October 28, 1998 I joined Grossman to present the Triple Crown concept to a "chiefs of mission" conference of U.S. Ambassadors posted throughout Europe. The upcoming summits (NATO, U.S.-EU and OSCE) presented a unique opportunity for the United States to articulate and build support for a new Euro-Atlantic partnership that would shape our political, economic and security interaction in coming decades. A Triple Crown task force was organized within the State Department to develop and integrate the substantive policy and outreach activities in the U.S. and Europe. I was asked to work with Grossman's Principal Deputy Tony Wayne, and Ron Asmus as co-leader of the Task Force, also in my brief capacity as Acting Director of the Policy Planning Staff.[25]

Each of the three major pillars of the architecture—NATO, the U.S.-EU partnership, and the OSCE—now needed to evolve.

The United States presented a package of proposals for the spring 1999 NATO Washington summit. They were designed to highlight its view of a new NATO for the new century, as set forth by Albright and Cohen. The core of the package was to be a new Strategic Concept that emphasized a larger NATO assuming new missions to project stability beyond its immediate borders as one central pillar of a new Euro-Atlantic community.[26] Reinforcing NATO as the institution of choice when North America and Europe decide to act together to address military security challenges would keep the United States engaged as a European power, while giving Washington credible and reliable partners to address security contingencies outside of Europe, and giving European countries a greater voice in U.S. regional diplomacy, for instance in the Middle East. NATO would have real and meaningful military missions securely tied to serious threats to Western vital interests, thereby renewing the Alliance's sense of purpose. And transatlantic preventive diplomacy and deterrence strategy would be deeply connected to NATO's potential use of force and thereby strengthened.[27] To meet these goals, force structures and doctrine would need to be realigned. European capabilities would also have to be improved, either as part of a NATO mission or in "separable but not separate" efforts to address security challenges should the United States, or NATO, choose not to be involved.

The other parts of the architecture also needed tending.

The United States, the EU, and the Struggle to be Strategic

U.S.-EU summits were now held twice a year as part of the New Transatlantic Agenda agreed in 1995, and a vast range of operational dialogues now took place among U.S. and EU interlocutors from across many different government agencies. The EU was not only America's major economic partner, it brought real resources to the foreign policy table, making some of Washington's most important initiatives possible. U.S.-EU common or complementary efforts were beginning to show some effect, from promoting nuclear safety in Ukraine and Russia to responding to hurricane disaster in Central America and defending human rights in many parts of the globe. The EU's $1.9 billion aid package for the Palestinians was fundamental to the Middle East peace process, and its aid to Eastern Europe—including Bosnia—was as large in real dollar terms as the amount America gave to Western Europe under the Marshall Plan. Together the United States and the European Union accounted for 90 percent of humanitarian aid around the world.[28]

Nonetheless, despite best efforts, the U.S.-EU relationship had still not overcome its image as a technocratic exercise with an overabundance of process disproportionate to actual output, a repository of issues dealt with in rather ad hoc fashion by a range of disparate agencies, with little sense of urgency or overall direction. Priorities were often mismatched; the United States looked for efficiency and concrete outcomes, while the EU sought legitimacy and symbolic U.S. validation of the ongoing process of European integration. Relations were beset by competitive impulses, underlying questions of trust, and mutual doubts about relative commitment and capacity.

The U.S.-EU relationship was close, but it was not strategic, in the sense that partners would share assessments about issues vital to both on a continuous and interactive basis; be able to deal with the daily grind of immediate policy demands while identifying longer-term challenges to their security, prosperity and values; and be able to prioritize those challenges and harness the full range of resources at their disposal to advance common or complementary responses. The U.S.-EU partnership simply punched below its weight.

In other regions of the world, the Clinton Administration was advancing an ambitious economic agenda; it was implementing NAFTA, seeking to open trade throughout the Americas, and advancing APEC's goal to achieve free and open trade and investment in the Asia-Pacific region by 2020. The U.S.-EU New Transatlantic Agenda, in contrast, set forth a relatively modest objective of building down transatlantic commercial barriers and addressing trade and investment obstacles case-by-case. Moreover, even this incremental approach had been completely overshadowed by EU fury with such U.S. laws as the Helms-Burton Act and the Iran-Libya Sanctions Act, U.S. challenges to the EU's "banana and beef" regimes, and other disputes.

Two U.S. Undersecretaries, Stuart Eizenstat and Thomas Pickering, the lead State Department officials driving the NTA process, sought to move the ball forward. I was involved in an internal working group that sought to give more substantive weight to our efforts to render the U.S.-EU partnership more effective. The premise of our work was that U.S. goals with respect to Europe—our most important trade and investment partner—should be no less ambitious than those in Asia and Latin America.

One challenge was to make the global dimension of the U.S.-EU partnership more operational so that we could act more effectively and quickly together in fast-breaking crises; identify and manage our differences before they impair our ability to work together; and, better anticipate and prevent emerging threats.[29] We started work to advance this dimension of the relationship at the spring 1999 U.S.-EU summit in Bonn.

We were also ready to consider again a more ambitious economic partnership, perhaps even revive the idea of a Transatlantic Free Trade Agreement (TAFTA). We found an ally in Leon Brittan, the European Commission Vice President and Commissioner for Trade, who by spring 1998 was ready to advance plans for a "New Transatlantic Marketplace" (NTM). The NTM proposal envisaged a political commitment to eliminate all industrial tariffs by 2010, create a free trade area in services, relax restrictions on intellectual property, remove technical barriers to trade through mutual product recognition and harmonization of standards, and conclude a bilateral agreement on investment.

The NTM proposal was adopted by the Commission on March 11, 1998. If implemented, it would have represented a huge leap forward in EU-U.S. relations. In the end, however, Brittan was unable to find sufficient support among EU member states. France was vociferous in its opposition, and Europeans were furious at U.S. sanctions legislation in the form of the Helms-Burton and D'Amato laws directed at Cuba and Iran/Libya, respectively, which had also affected European companies.

The proposals also found only lukewarm support from the Washington trade establishment. Other trade disputes were weighing down the relationship, and Brittan's plan ruled out audiovisual services and the possibility of negotiating agricultural subsidies, which would have been key incentives for U.S. support.

In the end, the most we could muster was the Transatlantic Economic Partnership (TEP), an initiative launched at the London U.S.-EU Summit on May 18, 1998. Elements of Brittan's proposals were salvaged, but the TEP was a watered-down version of the far more ambitious NTM. Work began to flesh out an action plan, which was launched at the U.S.-EU Summit in December 1998. The action plan initiated what were still relatively ambitious efforts to reduce barriers and improve regulatory cooperation in a dozen areas ranging from biotechnology, services and food safety to trade-related labor and environmental issues. [30]

Defining the OSCE's Niche

The OSCE was the third pillar of the architecture. Since the 1994 Budapest Summit it had been engaged in three major ways. The first was via conceptual discussion of the European security model; the second was through the growth and changing nature of its field missions; and the third was as a framework to accommodate Russian concerns and adapt the CFE Treaty to reflect post-Cold War realities.[31]

Partially in response to Russian disappointment at not having the OSCE formally designated at Budapest as the leading European security organization, the OSCE states launched an ongoing dialogue on a comprehensive security model for Europe in the 21st century. By 1996 a rough consensus had formed around a model of common and cooperative security, in which interlocking institutions in the OSCE area would collaborate in a nonhierarchical fashion on the basis of comparative advantage. This approach reflected a general assumption that the major security problems Europe would face at the end of the Cold War would come from conflicts not between but within states. Ethnic and national minority issues and the disintegration of states were major challenges. The principle of cooperation among mutually reinforcing institutions became the central theme of the OSCE's approach to the new security model for Europe.[32]

As these discussions continued, the OSCE's niche in the evolving security architecture was being defined on the ground through the growth and character of its operations in the field, which significantly increased and deepened its conflict prevention and management role and capabilities. Field missions in Estonia and Latvia had helped ensure Russia's continued fulfillment of its commitment to withdraw its military forces from the Baltic states, a process that was essentially complete by late 1994. The OSCE Minsk Group on Nagorno-Karabakh and field missions in Georgia, Moldova and the Former Yugoslav Republic of Macedonia remained busy. A field mission was established in Kyiv on constitutional law and economics. And as the war in Chechnya developed, Moscow surprised almost everyone by agreeing to accept an OSCE field presence in Chechnya in 1995. In January 1998 Belarus accepted the presence of an OSCE Monitoring and Advisory Group.[33]

Most significantly, after the Dayton Accords were agreed, the OSCE was entrusted—in tandem with the EU—with some of the most important aspects of post-conflict reconciliation and reconstruction in the Balkans. The United States gave wholehearted support to the OSCE's post-Dayton role in Bosnia and Herzegovina, overseeing elections and implementing the Dayton Agreement's disarmament and confidence-building provisions.[34] An OSCE field mission was also established in Croatia in July 1996.

The United States also used the OSCE as a platform to address some of Russia's most pressing security concerns. For instance, Russia complained that the CFE flank agreement limits were outdated and hampered its response to the security problems presented by the conflict in Chechnya. In November 1995 the thirty states parties, led by the United States, agreed to consider revising the flank provisions, and in May 1996 adopted changes to the areas included as part of the flank and agreed upon what amounted to more generous allotments for Russia for permanent and temporary deployments of troops and treaty-limited equipment in the region. The revisions were ratified by the U.S. Senate in a 100-0 vote, and went into force in mid-1997. Similarly, various CFE review conferences had led to agreement to adapt the CFE Treaty from its now-outdated bloc-to-bloc structure to a system of national and territorial limits. Negotiations began in 1997.

The next stage in the OSCE's evolution would come at its Istanbul Summit, which was scheduled for fall of 1999. We began to lay the groundwork for the Summit. Our major goal was to solidify the OSCE as the institution of choice for conflict resolution, expansion and protection of democracy and democratic institutions, defense of human rights, and identifying and addressing economic issues that could lead to conflict and threats to security. We sought to promote new tools such as police monitoring to allow greater proactive use of OSCE institutions in situations that seemed headed for instability or conflict. We were also keen to encourage the continued use of OSCE field missions. Such missions could serve as useful platforms offering synergies among various institutions and NGOs active on the ground in conflict or post-conflict situations. All of this underscored our approach to build mutually-reinforcing, non-hierarchical relations among complementary organizations.

"Hallelujah!"

On March 12, 1999, I joined Ron Asmus, Dan Fried, a number of members of Congress, and Czech Foreign Minister Jan Kavan, Hungarian Foreign Minister János Martonyi, and Polish Foreign Minister Bronisław Geremek on Secretary Albright's plane to the Harry S. Truman Library & Museum in Independence, Missouri. There she would sign a paper formally acknowledging receipt of the documents of accession by the three countries to the North Atlantic Treaty. Albright, a Czech-born refugee to the United States, chose the accession ceremony site to honor Truman, whom she often called "my first President," and to affirm to the American public the importance of the transatlantic Alliance.

As each foreign minister spoke at the ceremony about the significance of the moment, a palpable hush enveloped the room—but the underlying emotions were electric. Using different turns of phrase, each European spoke of returning home to a democratic community of shared values, and of their conviction that their tragic histories of oppression were finally at an end. Geremek, who as a leading Polish dissident in the 1980s had helped engineer the rise of the *Solidarnosc* trade union, declared that Poland was "no longer alone. Today it returns where it belongs--to the free world." Martonyi said the ceremony signified Hungary's "manifest destiny to return to its natural habitat." Kavan said "the Czech traumas of this century have now been relegated forever to history."[35]

Then Albright strode to the table on which, in May 1947, President Truman signed legislation providing $400 million of aid to Greece and Turkey, thereby giving reality to the Truman Doctrine announced that spring, and on which, on August 2, 1952, he signed a NATO protocol which would have brought the Federal Republic of Germany into NATO as part of the European defense community. While that protocol never came into effect, its objective was realized when Germany entered NATO in May 1955.[36]

Albright quickly signed the *process verbal*, attesting to the fact she had received the instruments of accession document. The Czech Republic, Hungary and Poland were now members of NATO. She captured the emotion of the moment by quoting what she called an "old Central European expression": "Hallelujah."

The ceremony marked the culmination of years of intensive effort. Yet Albright was intent on making her audience understand that enlargement was "only one element" of a larger goal. "NATO enlargement is not an event; it is a process," she declared. She framed that process within our overall efforts to create a new structure of security in which NATO's door would remain open, in which Russia and Ukraine and Europe's other democracies could find a place, and in which the interlocking institutions of Euro-Atlantic architecture would work to-gether in mutually reinforcing ways. "Although NATO stands tall, it does not stand alone," she said. "The EU, OSCE and NATO and its partners form the core of a broader system for protecting vital interests and promoting shared values."

Such a structure would not only be essential to ensure European stability, it offered a foundation from which Europe and North Amer-ica could address future challenges, such as terrorism and weapons of mass destruction, that could emanate far from European shores. The Truman Library event marked "the end of one era and the beginning of another," she told reporters. She used the occasion to turn attention to NATO's upcoming 50th anniversary summit in Washington, at which the Alliance was slated to present a new Strategic Concept—a blueprint for NATO in the 21st Century.[37]

That blueprint would design an Alliance that was "not only bigger, but also more flexible; an Alliance committed to collective defense, and capable of meeting a wide range of threats to its common interests; an Alliance working in partnership with other nations and organizations to advance security, prosperity and democracy in and for the entire Eu-ro-Atlantic region." She reiterated that collective defense was the "core mission" of the Alliance. But she was quick to add that

> NATO's founders understood that what our alliance commits us to do under Article V is not all we may be called upon to do, or should reserve the right to do. Consider, for example, that when French Foreign Minister Robert Schuman signed the North At-lantic Treaty, he characterized it as "insurance against all risks—a system of common defense against any attack, whatever its nature."

> During the Cold War, we had no trouble identifying the risks to our security and territory. But the threats we face today and may face tomorrow are less predictable. They could come from an ag-gressive regime, a rampaging faction, or a terrorist group. And we know that, if past is prologue, we face a future in which weapons will be more destructive at longer distances than ever before.[38]

In April at the Washington Summit, Allies approved the blueprint for a new NATO engaged in new missions, with new members, and with stronger partnerships. The Strategic Concept described a larger, more flexible Alliance, still committed to collective defense, but capable of meeting a wider range of threats to common Alliance interests. These included the proliferation of weapons of mass destruction and their means of delivery, regional conflicts beyond NATO territory, and transnational threats like terrorism. The Strategic Concept recognized non-Article 5 crisis response operations as a "fundamental task" of the Alliance and made clear the expectation that such operations would be conducted with Partners.

Aspirants had made a strong effort to push the Alliance to extend additional membership invitations at the Summit. There was no consensus to do so, however. Instead, Allies adopted a U.S. proposal to develop with individual aspirants a Membership Action Plan (MAP) that could provide a clear roadmap for a strong membership candidacy. The Alliance would commit to setting out clearly the major military interoperability requirements for aspiring members, expect aspirants to step up to challenging defense planning targets, and provide candid feedback on progress.[39] NATO leaders pledged to revisit the enlargement process at their next summit, which they said would be "no later" than 2002.

Integrating Southeastern Europe

By the time the Czechs, Hungarians and Poles joined NATO in March 1999, we had made considerable progress in our efforts to revitalize Euro-Atlantic security architecture and position it to address future challenges. The Washington Summit unveiled a new NATO as part of that effort.

Once again, however, Slobodan Milošević threatened to destroy what had been accomplished when he sent in troops and police to crush the mostly ethnic Albanian, mostly Muslim minority living in Kosovo, a province of Serbia. The OSCE, EU and NATO worked in concert to head off full-scale war in Kosovo: the OSCE mounted its largest field mission ever, the EU applied diplomatic pressure, and NATO threatened to employ military force against Serbia unless it stopped violence against the civilian ethnic Albanian population in Kosovo. Milošević responded by stationing 40,000 troops in and around Kosovo. They began to move from village to village, shelling and shooting civilians and torching their homes. Efforts by Allies and Russia to secure a peace agreement in Rambouillet, France collapsed a week after the accession ceremony in Independence, Missouri. One week later, NATO was at war.[40]

Throughout most of the Administration I had been only tangentially engaged on Balkan issues. Holbrooke told me to work on NATO and the architectural elements of Euro-Atlantic security while he focused on Bosnia. He asked me to scout out possible sites for what turned out to be the Dayton Proximity Talks at Wright-Patterson Air Force Base, and occasionally asked me what I thought as his team grappled with the "problem from hell." Otherwise my focus was elsewhere. As Kosovo descended into violence, however, I was concerned that our overall efforts would be sabotaged by continued Balkan turmoil.

My concerns were shared by counterparts from Germany, who had assumed the rotating Presidency of the European Union in the first half of 1999 as well as the annual Presidency of the G8. In a series of calls with Markus Ederer, at the time head of the Western Balkans office in the German Foreign Office, we agreed that Western efforts to quell violence in this region of Europe had to be better aligned with our overall efforts to project stability across the continent. We had been approaching the region tactically; a more strategic approach was needed.

The day NATO began its bombing campaign, in consultation with my colleagues in the European Bureau I wrote Secretary Albright a memo arguing that despite our best efforts we were destined to keep sliding from one conflict to another in the Western Balkans until we embraced a different approach to the region as a whole. We would win the war, I wrote, but victory would be hollow unless we and our European allies were prepared to offer Southeastern Europeans the same bargain we had offered those in Central and Northern Europe—to stand with them on reforms and to keep the doors to our institutions open, if they created the conditions to make it possible someday to walk through those doors.

At the time, this was a radical notion. Much of "mainstream" Europe still debated whether this region was truly part of Europe. The chronic violence plaguing the region was tragic, but was not viewed as directly relevant to European construction and integration. The dominant talk

364 OPEN DOOR: NATO AND EURO-ATLANTIC SECURITY AFTER THE COLD WAR

in Western Europe and the United States was of "exit strategies" rather than sustained efforts at stabilization.

We had to break this mentality. The Western Balkans were in fact part of Europe, and had to be offered the same perspective of integration as other parts of Europe—the alternative being more violence, conflict, and disintegration. Europe would not be secure, and would be unable to become the global partner we sought, until we transformed this region from a primary source of instability to a fully integrated part of the European and transatlantic mainstream. The only true exit strategy from the Balkans, I argued, was an integration strategy.

This would require us to use our full diplomatic, economic and military toolbox and draw on the interlocking institutional architecture we had created. NATO was important but insufficient. The OSCE would need to play an enhanced role. Most significantly, the European Union would need to agree that its own door was potentially open to Western Balkan countries. This might prove to be our biggest challenge, but it had to be done. Such an effort was not unlike the Marshall Plan, except this time the United States would not need to bear the financial burden alone or primarily. The European Union, our other partners in Europe and elsewhere, the international financial institutions, other international organizations, and the private sector could and should carry the largest share of this effort. Our job would be to mobilize such efforts.

I sent the memo to the Secretary under the heading "The Albright Plan." She responded that she liked everything but the name. She asked to recast the memo—without the name—as a "night note" from her to President Clinton. The President immediately agreed to the effort. I was double-hatted, representing both her Policy Planning Staff and the European Bureau, to coordinate an overall U.S. effort at regional stabilization. I worked closely with Tony Wayne and Ambassador Richard Shifter, who had been instrumental in promoting a regional law enforcement initiative called the Southeast European Cooperative Initiative (SECI).

Tony and I asked Markus Ederer and Wilfried Gruber, who had just completed his term as German ambassador in Belgrade, to fly to Washington to review our next steps. In those conversations we agreed to use the German-American channel to build consensus, both among countries of the area and by major partners, including the Russians, to a broad-based effort to stabilize the region, deepen cooperative ties among countries in the area, and to hold out the prospect of integration into the European and Euro-Atlantic mainstream. Germany would take the public lead in this effort, partly because senior U.S. officials were focused on the military campaign and partly because Germany's EU Presidency would be essential to build support in the European Commission and among EU member states, and its G-8 Presidency could be used to draw in support from Russia, Japan, and the international financial institutions.

President Clinton fully embraced the concept and made it his own. In an April 15 speech in San Francisco to the American Society of Newspaper Editors, the President framed the Kosovo campaign in the context of a U.S. South East Europe Initiative to strengthen overall Euro-Atlantic architecture, saying "we should try to do for Southeastern Europe what we helped to do for Western Europe after World War II and for Central Europe after the Cold War; to help its people build a region of multiethnic democracies, a community that upholds common standards of human rights, a community in which borders are open to people and trade, where nations cooperate to make war unthinkable."

We then used the presence of so many leaders at the Washington NATO Summit April 23-25 to secure support for an urgent, broad-based effort to stabilize Southeastern Europe and to give the people of that region a real perspective for integration into the European and Euro-Atlantic mainstream. By the time the military campaign in Kosovo would be over, we argued, a broader political/economic framework had to be in place that offered a means to set the entire region on a new course. We could not afford to keep sliding from one disaster to another in the Balkans. We proposed immediate negotiations to secure a political commitment to a "Stability Pact" for the region along these lines.

The response was overwhelmingly positive. Shortly thereafter, Tony Wayne and I led the U.S. team to negotiate the Pact with more than 40 countries and international organizations—including NATO, Russia, the EU, the OSCE, the Council of Europe, the United Nations, the World Bank, the IMF, the European Investment Bank (EIB) and the European Bank for Reconstruction and Development (EBRD)— at the Petersburg mountain retreat across the Rhine river from Bonn. Gruber, representing the EU Presidency, hosted the negotiations, with

Ederer energetically moving things forward, and German Foreign Minister Joschka Fischer lending needed political support to close the final deal. The document was agreed and finalized in early June, and then announced on June 10, the day NATO suspended air operations against Serbia.

During the same period Yeltsin's envoy Victor Chernomyrdin and Finnish President Martti Ahtisaari joined with Strobe Talbott to successfully prod Milošević to stop his aggression. Talbott recounts that "Chernomyrdin would be the hammer and pound away on Milošević, and President Ahtisaari would be the anvil against who the pounding would take place, so that Milošević would know what he had to do to get the bombing stopped."[41]

At its core, the Stability Pact was a bargain between integration and reform: the international community agreed to work to stabilize, transform and integrate the countries of the region into the European and Euro-Atlantic mainstream; they, in turn, agreed to work individually and together to create the political, economic and security conditions by which this could be possible. It was a political initiative to encourage and strengthen cooperation among the countries of the region, an effort to promote stronger democracies, civil societies, market economies and respect for human rights, and a commitment to facilitate, for those who sought it, full integration into Euro-Atlantic institutions.[42] Notably, Russia was one of the signatories. While our Russian colleagues evinced some heartburn when it came to the Pact's language about "Euro-Atlantic integration," in the end they agreed to it.

On July 30 President Clinton flew to Sarajevo to join the other leaders of the participating and facilitating countries and organizations of the Stability Pact to

> reaffirm our shared responsibility to build a Europe that is at long last undivided, democratic and at peace. We will work together to promote the integration of South Eastern Europe into a continent where borders remain inviolable but no longer denote division and offer the opportunity of contact and cooperation...We also reaffirm the inherent right of each and every state participating in the Pact to be free to choose or change its security and association arrangements, including treaties of alliance as they evolve.[43]

Following the Sarajevo Summit, German Chancellor Gerhard Schröder asked the head of his Chancellery, Bodo Hombach, to head overall efforts to implement the Stability Pact. Markus Ederer was his chief of staff and the key to the whole effort. I was asked to lead the U.S. government's engagement, working with Miriam Sapiro, my Policy Planning colleague who had moved to the National Security Council staff with James Steinberg. A wonderfully talented Foreign Service officer, Rosemary DiCarlo, joined the team and later succeeded me in the position.

The Kosovo campaign and the accompanying Stability Pact underscored the importance of the U.S-EU relationship as part of the evolving architecture. Through the Stability Pact the United States had pressed the European Commission and EU member states to accept, and also act, on the logic of their own approach to integration, by offering those aspiring to membership concrete perspectives that they could draw ever closer, and eventually join, the Union if they created the conditions necessary to walk through the EU door. Both in the Stability Pact agreement and in the Sarajevo Summit Declaration the EU committed to "making every effort" to assist those seeking integration into EU structures "to make speedy and measurable progress" toward that end.[44]

Despite the best efforts of our German counterparts and also European Commissioner for External Relations Chris Patten and his indefatigable aide Edward Llewellyn, however, getting the European Commission on board was a slog. I found myself flying as often to Brussels as to the Balkans to harangue EU colleagues to act on their commitment.

What seemed like an eternity from a U.S. perspective, however, was lightning-fast for the Commission. By the time we arrived at the OSCE's Istanbul Summit in November, European Commission President Romano Prodi was able to announce that the Commission would devote close to 12 billion euros to Southeastern Europe over the next six years. For non-accession candidates in the Western Balkans the EU developed a new type of contractual relationship, termed "Stabilization and Association Agreements," which provided for a closer association with the Union and a perspective of eventual integration.[45]

The European Union was beginning to define itself more expansively and inclusively: in December it invited Romania and Bulgaria to join Hungary and Slovenia, among others, in accession negotiations; it offered to include Turkey as a membership candidate; and it announced that as of 2003 it would be able to take in further new members.

Within a year the Stability Pact had initiated a series of regional initiatives and secured substantial pledges of financial support from a range of countries and international financial institutions.[46] By the end of the Administration's term European allies and partners were contributing more than 80 percent of the ground forces conducting peace-keeping operations in the region. They were providing humanitarian and reconstruction assistance to the region in the form of "quick-start" projects worth more than $2.2 billion dollars that were earmarked to rebuild infrastructure, reopen borders, and disarm local militias. EU members were contributing 60% of the funds for Kosovo. The U.S. and the EU were also able to harness their combined influence to leverage additional financial support from international financial institutions; the World Bank, the IMF, the EBRD, the EIB were all involved. These were all signs of a more balanced partnership in which the United States could exercise leadership but did not need to carry the biggest burden.[47]

Some observers and critics lost the forest for the trees, complaining about the Stability Pact's plethora of "working tables" and initiatives. In many ways, it was our "Euro-Chart" in miniature. The essential point of the Stability Pact, however, was not to get lost in the process but to keep focus squarely on the basic bargain. From the U.S. perspective, the prime purpose of the Stability Pact was to apply the same logic of integration to Southeastern Europe as we had applied to Central and Northern Europe. We had gained broad recognition that the people of the Western Balkans were not only part of Europe, they had to be offered the same perspective of integration as those in other parts of Europe. They would need to make the hard choices for reform that could make that possible; we would stand by them as they did. The alternative was more violence, more conflict, and further disintegration.

The New OSCE

Post-conflict efforts following the Kosovo war, together with the Stability Pact mechanisms for Southeastern Europe, which were subsequently placed under the auspices of the OSCE, underscored once again the importance of that organization, and the opportunity to advance our Triple Crown effort at its summit in Istanbul in November 1999.

At Istanbul we sought to promote our concept of mutually-reinforcing, non-hierarchical relations among the key institutions of Euro-Atlantic architecture, and in this context to solidify the OSCE as the institution of choice when it came to conflict resolution, expansion and protection of democracy and democratic institutions, defense of human rights, fundamental freedoms, and the rule of law, and identifying and addressing economic issues that could lead to conflict and threats to security throughout the Euro-Atlantic community. Negotiations on a new security model for Europe culminated in the elaboration and adoption of the comprehensive Charter for European Security at the Summit.[48] As William Hill recounts, the push for an all-inclusive agreement and document on European security was a logical outgrowth of and heir to the aspirations for an undivided Europe and comprehensive definition of security embodied in the Charter of Paris and other immediate post-Cold War documents and proposals. In Istanbul, Clinton called the OSCE "a unique institution grounded in the principle that the root of human insecurity is the denial of human rights...the charter we've negotiated recognizes that the greatest threats to our security today are as likely to come from conflicts that begin within states as between them."[49]

Building confidence and security within societies was what the OSCE had always done best. Election monitoring, peacekeeping, efforts to address trafficking, corruption, national minorities, and arms control/verification were all important aspects. Perhaps the OSCE's most vital work was being done through its field missions, including a high-profile presence in Chechnya and the largest field mission of its history in Kosovo. We wanted to empower the OSCE to become more operational in the areas of early warning, conflict prevention, management and resolution, and post-conflict reconstruction and reconciliation. In this regard, we sought to promote new tools such as police monitoring to allow greater proactive use of OSCE institutions in situations that seemed headed for instability or conflict. We continued to encourage OSCE field missions as "platforms" to synthesize the activities of international organizations and NGOs.

Kosovo demonstrated that the OSCE needed to organize and deploy its resources faster to areas of need. We proposed the formation of Rapid Expert Assistance and Co-operation Teams (REACT), a reserve capability within participating states that would enable the OSCE to deploy experts in elections, law, media, administration and policing rapidly for more effective conflict prevention, crisis management, and post-conflict rehabilitation.[50]

While the OSCE's responsibilities extended from Vancouver to Vladivostok, in practice it had become increasingly focused in its operational work in the Balkans. We wanted the OSCE to apply its tools throughout the broader Euro-Atlantic region, a point we underscored in our support for stepped-up OSCE engagement in the Caucasus and Central Asia.

We also sought to establish the OSCE as a comprehensive framework in which arms control and confidence-building could be important elements of our strategy. This was important for the adaptation of the CFE Treaty, in which a system of national and territorial ceilings replaced outmoded bloc-to-bloc calculations. The Adapted CFE Treaty was agreed at Istanbul, although NATO allies linked their ratification to Russia's commitment to withdraw its forces from Georgia and Moldova. A related advance came with agreement on the "Vienna Document," a real expansion and deepening of the commitments of all OSCE states with regard to information exchanges, visits and inspections, and other transparency measures.[51]

These initiatives and others adopted in Istanbul laid the groundwork for a more action-oriented OSCE whose value added was that it could potentially deal better with conflicts within societies than others, and that was better equipped with relevant tools to do so. By the end of the Administration in 2000, the 25th anniversary year of the Helsinki Final Act, the OSCE had twenty missions and about 3,000 personnel in the field, and continued to break new ground with a broad and flexible array of tools for conflict prevention, crisis management and post-conflict rehabilitation. By the end of the Clinton Administration, William Hill could write that "the OSCE truly flowered...perhaps reaching the zenith of its activity and influence."[52]

"Two Institutions in the Same City Living on Different Planets"

About this time Marc Grossman became Director General of the U.S. Foreign Service and Ron Asmus left the State Department. Secretary Albright asked me to succeed Ron, to work now with James Dobbins in the European Bureau's front office, with a portfolio that combined our continued work on regional political-military affairs and Nordic-Baltic issues while still overseeing U.S. efforts at Southeastern European stabilization and integration. When I found myself flying rather exotic routes from Tallinn to Thessaloniki or from Iceland to Istanbul, I couldn't help thinking we truly were experiencing a new Europe.

As the Clinton Administration drew to an end, most building blocks of a new Euro-Atlantic architecture had been put into place, with one curious exception: the strange non-relationship between the primary institutions of the West, the European Union and NATO, which Robert Hunter often described as "two institutions in the same city living on different planets."

Bosnia, Kosovo and a host of other crises underscored the need for improved European capabilities and better coordination mechanisms to deepen EU-NATO cooperation so that civilian and military efforts at crisis management worked more effectively together.[53] We believed that American popular support for a continuing U.S. role in Europe was increasingly related to the perception that America's European partners were willing and able to assume more responsibility not only for their own security but also for defending common interests of the transatlantic community in the wider world. A European defense initiative that bolstered European capabilities, if developed with care, could be a possible expression of that commitment and be mutually reinforcing with NATO initiatives. Common foreign and security policy was a logical next step in the European integration process and could help to avoid renationalization of European defense. U.S. support was also consistent with the premise of the Triple Crown strategy that the United States needed a strong and coherent European Union as a partner on the European continent and beyond.[54] A more coherent and capable European profile could equip the EU to assume the lead in the Balkans or to engage, if necessary, in areas such as Africa, where the United States was unlikely to play a prominent role. The United States needed to welcome enhanced European crisis management capabilities in situations where NATO—meaning, in practice, the United States—would decide not to become engaged.

Even those who supported such efforts, however, were concerned that European force commitments and capability pledges too often tended to be little more than empty exercises in European self-assertion. Americans across the board were both wary and weary of repeated European pledges that seemed to melt away with the next spring thaw. In American eyes, the EU effort not just to build a European Security and Defense Identity (ESDI), but to move to what would be called European Security and Defense Policy (ESDP), was not just a narrow technical topic for policy wonks. It was emblematic of a far larger strategic debate about how—and even whether—Europe and the United States could tackle in more equal and balanced fashion the security challenges posed by the post-Cold War world. If ESDP and the Union's Common Foreign and Security Policy were developed in ways that truly created greater European capabilities, not just more European process, they could be vehicles for a stronger, outward-looking Europe and a more balanced, global partnership with the United States.

The key was to shape and condition European initiatives so they would complement, rather than compete, with those of the Alliance.

Meanwhile, French and British experiences in the Balkans and elsewhere had laid bare key military deficiencies. Paris and London each realized they had to do something. Paris had long argued that the EU needed more muscular defense forces. The real change came from London.

UK Prime Minister Tony Blair had come to believe that Bosnia, Rwanda, and Kosovo were harbingers of a post-Cold War world in which the international community would be increasingly challenged to confront unprincipled actors who were engaging in wonton acts of ethnic cleansing and even genocide, and who believed they could use the principle of non-interference in a country's domestic affairs to shield themselves from international intervention. Blair, appalled by the failure of the international community to stop the Rwandan genocide, and having seen how the Bosnian tragedy had only been turned around by international intervention, was now frustrated by the threatened continued use of the veto by Russia and China blocking a U.N. Security Council Resolution on intervention in Kosovo.

Blair was convinced that the United Kingdom had to be equipped to act. Britain's Strategic Defense Review committed the UK to a real defense spending increase for the first time in 15 years. Britain was unlikely to engage unilaterally, however; it would need to work with others. Yet Blair believed that international mechanisms had to be facilitative; they could not be allowed to block what he deeply believed to be the moral imperative of humanitarian intervention. The UK and its European partners clearly needed to bolster their military capabilities, and when they chose to deploy them, they needed to be able to do so via whatever mechanism might prove appropriate given the specific case at hand—through the U.N., through NATO, through European efforts drawing on NATO assets when NATO chose not to be involved, or, if need be, through the EU alone.

Traditionally, the UK had been hesitant to provide the EU with "autonomous" defense structures. On December 4, 1998, however, London and Paris took a decisive step at their St. Malo summit. They concluded in a Joint Declaration that the EU "must have the capacity for autonomous action, backed up by credible military forces, the means to decide to use them and a readiness to do so, in order to respond to international crises." It was agreed that the EU should be able to act, whether using NATO assets or on its own "outside the NATO framework." The declaration also noted both that military action would take place "when the Alliance as a whole is not engaged," and that these European capacities should be developed "without unnecessary duplication." [55]

The White House wanted a clear U.S. response to the St. Malo Declaration. It was important to support this new emphasis on bolstering greater capabilities while ensuring that EU efforts could complement, rather than compete, with those of the Alliance. I was asked to draft an opinion piece; working with Deputy National Security Adviser James Steinberg and with Secretary Albright, the draft was massaged and appeared in the *Financial Times* on December 7 under the title "The right balance will secure NATO's future." The message: Clinton Administration support for greater European efforts would be conditioned by what Secretary Albright termed the "three D's:" no *discrim-*

ination against non-EU NATO members, no *decoupling* of European and North American security, and no *duplication* of NATO's operational planning system or its command structure.[56]

At the same time, the administration pushed hard for NATO to launch its own Defense Capabilities Initiative (DCI) at the Washington summit four months later. The DCI was designed to improve Allied forces' deployability, mobility, sustainability, survivability and effectiveness. It identified some 58 areas in which Allies were asked to make concrete improvements in their forces to fill specific capability gaps.

The collapse of the Rambouillet peace effort and the start of NATO's bombing campaign against Milošević reinforced Blair's views. To press his case, Blair took the unusual step of flying to Chicago on the eve of the NATO Summit to set forth his doctrine of humanitarian intervention. "The most pressing foreign policy problem we face," Blair said before the Economic Club of Chicago on April 24, 1999, "is to identify the circumstances in which we should get actively involved in other people's conflicts."[57] While framing the issue as a challenge for the U.N., Blair knew that Europe and the United States would have to be the motor behind new multilateral approaches to such issues.

The Kosovo war was the third out-of-area conflict North America and Europe had faced in the 1990s; such challenges indeed seemed far more likely in future than traditional threats to the territorial security of the Alliance. Being equipped to address out-of-area challenges, however, was going to be much easier for the United States, whose forces had been built around power projection rather than territorial security, than for the Europeans, whose Cold War forces had been oriented the other way around. By and large Europeans were unenthusiastic about reorienting their military postures from protecting European territory—familiar but less necessary—to projecting force beyond their borders—controversial but more necessary.

The Clinton Administration used these concerns to frame and guide its support for a more cohesive and responsive European foreign policy and above all, for more capable European defense. The Kosovo war affirmed to U.S. leaders and the U.S. military that not enough European armed forces were ready for the diverse, rapidly-evolving challenges of the post-Cold War world. In American eyes, Europe had been sluggish in its efforts to manage the shift away from the massed, terrain-based forces necessary for the Cold War toward more mobile, deployable and sustainable forces and improved lift, logistics and intelligence capabilities. Kosovo underscored European dependence on the United States for precision-strike capability, surveillance and intelligence assets, refueling, lift, logistics, and high-end command and control systems. European forces would need to become more mobile, deployable and sustainable. "A central lesson" of the Kosovo campaign, Secretary Albright and UK Foreign Secretary Robin Cook warned, was that "not enough European armed forces are ready for the diverse, rapidly evolving challenges of the post-Cold War world. Too many are trained and equipped to defend against a threat that no longer exists."[58]

The widening capabilities gap threatened Alliance unity by widening the faultlines we had sought to repair as we crafted NATO's new Strategic Concept. The U.S. military had been irritated that it had to provide 80 percent of the useful capability in the Kosovo air campaign, while needing to negotiate a consensus with 18 other countries on operational methods. Unless the Europeans could bolster their capabilities to fight alongside Americans, there was a danger that each side of the North Atlantic would address such challenges separately—the U.S. unilaterally, unconstrained by "war by committee," the Europeans via the EU or perhaps not at all.

The dangers were apparent. The United States was carrying virtually all the risk of defending common vital interests where they were now most threatened—beyond Europe's periphery. To take just one example, U.S. military plans included defense of Persian Gulf oil supplies without reliance on NATO Allies, even though the Allies depended more on Gulf oil than the United States.

It was time to jettison traditional U.S. concerns about a stronger European profile. The danger was European weakness, not European strength. It was time to end the counterproductive competition that had long existed between the EU and NATO; Secretary Albright wanted a "true strategic partnership." In a joint article, Secretary Albright and UK Foreign Secretary Robin Cook affirmed that "NATO remains the foundation of the collective defense of its members," but added it was important to craft "new arrangements to link the EU and NATO in unprecedented ways, laying the foundation for a true strategic partnership between the two key institutions of the West."[59]

Those new arrangements would mean that European contributions to NATO operations, in the Balkans and perhaps elsewhere, could be stronger and more effective. It meant that where NATO as a whole chose not to become engaged, the EU would be able to act in response to humanitarian crises, to provide disaster relief and also undertake peacekeeping tasks. It meant that European nations, inside and outside the EU, would be ready and able to offer forces for EU-led operations and be afforded the opportunity to participate, just as they had in NATO-led operations in Bosnia and Kosovo.

In such a context, Albright's 3D's could be addressed. To minimize duplication of effort, NATO had offered the EU assured access to NATO planning, which the EU welcomed. To address the danger of discrimination, the EU proposed new arrangements for close and continuous involvement of non-EU European allies. With such arrangements in place, there was less risk that North American and European security would be decoupled. Europe's contributions to NATO would be strengthened, relations between the European Union and non-EU European allies enhanced and Europe's ability to support the activities of the OSCE and the U.N. improved.[60]

The turnaround in British policy facilitated the transformation of the ESDI into the European Security and Defense Policy (ESDP) at the Helsinki European Council meeting in December 1999. At Helsinki leaders also announced a Headline Goal of bolstering European military capabilities with the aim of developing a future European Rapid Reaction Force by 2003 of 60,000 troops deployable in 60 days and sustainable for a year. It was intended to be a force capable of undertaking the full range of so-called "Petersburg Tasks," that is tasks ranging from rescue and humanitarian missions, through peacekeeping to that of combat troops in peacekeeping. By December 2000 forces to meet the Headline Goal were offered by EU countries, non-EU European allies and EU candidate countries. EU nations committed themselves to the capability improvements necessary to achieve the goal in full by 2003. NATO and the EU would work together to ensure that shortfalls were met and that the planning to meet capability goals of both organizations was coordinated.

To highlight the changing nature of relations I had pressed hard for a joint session of NATO and EU foreign ministers while NATO foreign ministers were in Brussels for their semiannual meeting in December 2000. It was a bridge too far; EU qualms prevented a formal meeting. As one of our last acts in office, however, we managed a work-around: Canadian and European foreign ministers would host an informal farewell event for Secretary Albright. Her counterparts from both NATO and EU member states agreed. After five decades, the two institutions had finally come together, if only over dinner.

Conclusion

The Clinton Administration's effort to recast Euro-Atlantic architecture for the post-Wall world went through three phases. The first was a period of distraction, division and indecision during the President's first year in office. A decisive second phase, punctuated by war and then imposition of peace in Bosnia, began with the NATO Brussels Summit in January 1994 and culminated in a flurry of summits in 1997 that resulted in special NATO partnerships with both Russia and Ukraine, internal and external adaption of the Alliance, including membership invitations to the Czech Republic, Hungary and Poland, and enhanced political and military cooperation with NATO's growing list of partners. The third phase, which lasted until the end of the Administration, was again punctuated by war, this time in Kosovo, even as the Administration sought to equip NATO for new missions, further energize the OSCE, and build a more effective and outward-looking U.S.-EU partnership.

As the 21st century dawned, the United States and its European Allies and partners had developed a Euro-Atlantic architecture of cooperative overlapping, and interlocking institutions that enabled new members to walk through the doors of NATO and the EU in ways that were not at the expense of other states or institutions.[61] A democratic peace had taken hold across much of the continent; Europe was more secure than at any time in the previous century. Yet Europeans were approaching with uncertainty and apprehension challenges of a generation. America's European Allies were more prosperous than ever, but the benefits of that prosperity were not yet shared fully among all Europeans. The Baltic republics remained anxious about their future. Slobodan Milošević, whose toxic brand of nationalism had inflamed the Balkans, was out of power, yet tensions still afflicted the region. Europe would not be secure until its northeastern and southeastern corners was transformed from sources of insecurity and instability into fully integrated parts of the European and transatlantic mainstream. And the transatlantic community's efforts to develop a new and sustainable partnership with Russia—itself in the midst of a generational transformation—remained a formidable work in progress.

The United States had a major stake in the outcome of these generational choices. During the 20th century American leaders learned the hard way that America's interests are deeply intertwined with the security and prosperity of Europe. Whenever we failed to make the investment required to protect those interests, we always ended up paying a higher price later. As the Clinton Administration left office, however, it was unclear whether the United States would sustain that investment.

America, a European power? Today, the question mark has returned.

Notes

1. Secretary of State Madeleine K. Albright, Remarks before the New Atlantic Initiative Conference, The Mayflower Hotel, Washington, D.C., February 9, 1998 https://1997-2001.state.gov/statements/1998/980209.html.

2. Madeleine K. Albright, "Why bigger is better," *The Economist*, February 15, 1997.

3. U.S. Deputy Secretary of State Strobe Talbott, "The Transatlantic Partnership in the Post-Cold War Era," October 5, 1995, U.S. Department of State Dispatch, October 23, 1995, Vol. 6, No. 43, pp. 762-764; U.S. Secretary of State Warren Christopher, Statement to the North Atlantic Council, December 4, 1996.

4. Robert E. Hunter, "NATO in the 21st Century: A Strategic Vision," *Parameters*, Summer 1998, pp. 15-29.

5. Albright, "Why bigger is better," op. cit.

6. William Hill, *No Place for Russia: European Security Institutions since 1989* (New York: Columbia University Press, 2019), pp 136-137.

7. Remarks by President Clinton at the Signing Ceremony of the NATO-Russia Founding Act," Paris, May 27, 1997, http://www.nato.int/usa/president/s970527.a.htm.

8. State Department Fact Sheet on the Enlargement of NATO, "Why enlarging NATO strengthens U.S. security," USIS Washington File, February 11, 1998, http://www.bu.edu/globalbeat/nato/sdfacts021198.html.

9. U.S. Ambassador to NATO Robert Hunter declared French reintegration into NATO at that time "about 95 percent done." Robert E. Hunter, "NATO in the 21st Century: A Strategic Vision," *Parameters*, Summer 1998, pp. 15-29.

10. Under Secretary of State for Political Affairs Thomas R. Pickering, "Shores of Peace: Advancing Security and Cooperation in the Baltic Sea Region," Keynote address at the Conference on Baltic Sea Security and Cooperation, Stockholm, Sweden, October 19, 2000, https://1997-2001.state.gov/policy_remarks/2000/001019_pickering_bssc.html; U.S.-Baltic Partnership Commission Communique, June 7th, 2000, http://www.bits.de/NRANEU/Enlargement/documents/BPC-communique.pdf; Remarks by U.S. Deputy Secretary of State Strobe Talbott, U.S.-Baltic Partnership Commission Press Conference, June 7, 2000, http://www.bits.de/NRANEU/Enlargement/documents/Talbott.pdf; Statement by James Rubin on the First Anniversary of the U.S. Baltic Charter of Partnership, Department of State, January 14, 1999, http://www.bits.de/NRANEU/Enlargement/documents/charter140199.pdf.

11. Strobe Talbott, "A Baltic Home-Coming: Robert C. Frasure Memorial Lecture," Tallinn, Estonia, January 24, 2000.

12. https://1997-2001.state.gov/policy_remarks/1998/980121_talbott_eursecurity.html; Conrad Tribble, U.S. NEI Coordinator Address at the conference, "The Northern Dimension: An Assessment and Future Development," Riga, Latvia, December 6, 1999 https://1997-2001.state.gov/policy_remarks/1999/991206_tribble_nei.html; "Estonia, Latvia, and Lithuania and United States Baltic Policy," Hearing before the Subcommittee on European Affairs of the Committee on Foreign Relations, U.S. Senate, July 15, 1998, https://www.govinfo.gov/content/pkg/CHRG-105shrg50539/html/CHRG-105shrg50539.htm.

13. The White House, "A Charter of Partnership Among the United States of America and the Republic of Estonia, Republic of Latvia, and Republic of Lithuania," January 16, 1997.

14. "Estonia, Latvia, and Lithuania…," op. cit.

15. "The Baltic-American Partnership Fund: Ten Years of Grantmaking to Strengthen Civil Society in Estonia, Latvia and Lithuania," November 2008, https://www.opensocietyfoundations.org/reports/baltic-american-partnership-fund-ten-years-grantmaking-strengthen-civil-society-estonia.

16. Albright, Remarks before the New Atlantic Initiative Conference, op.cit.

17. For Asmus' view of these discussions, see Ronald D. Asmus, *Opening NATO's Door* (New York: Columbia University Press, 2002), p. 279.

18. Cited in Thomas R. Pickering, "A Transatlantic Partnership for the 21st Century," Columbia University, December 8, 1998.

19. Iran was buying and developing long-range missiles. It had flight-tested a 1,300-km Shahab-3 missile and, within a decade, would be in a position to test a missile capable of reaching all NATO territory and much of the United States. Tehran had chemical weapons and was seeking nuclear and biological capabilities. Before the Gulf War, Iraq had loaded chemical and biological weapons into missile warheads, and was close to achieving a nuclear capability. U.S. analysts believed that UN sanctions slowed, but probably had not stopped, Iraq's efforts to produce weapons of mass destruction and develop or buy long-range missiles to deliver them. Libya also had chemical weapons capabilities and was trying to acquire missile capabilities. North Korea was building and selling long-range missiles and had assembled an arsenal with chemical, biological, and probably nuclear capabilities. It had developed and was on the verge of testing the Taepo Dong 2 missile that could reach U.S. territory. The United States projected that all of these states would have missile forces in the next 5 to 15 years that could be used to threaten the homelands of all NATO members. See White House, *A U.S. Strategy for the 21st Century*, Washington, DC., 2000.

20. Thomas R. Pickering, "A Transatlantic Partnership for the 21st Century," op. cit.

21. See Asmus, op. cit., p. 304.

22. Ibid., p. 290.

23. "Taking Stock of the Alliance's Defense Capabilities," Remarks by Secretary of Defense William Cohen at the Informal Defense Ministerial Meeting, Vilamoura, Portugal, 24 September 1998. Copy in author's possession.

24. Ibid.

25. Assistant Secretary of State Marc Grossman, "The Future of the US-Europe Relationship," Houston World Affairs Council, October 1, 1998. Under Secretary of State for Economic Affairs Stuart Eizenstat was also actively involved.

26. Asmus, op. cit., p. 304

27. Ronald D. Asmus, Robert D. Blackwill, F. Stephen Larrabee, "Can NATO Survive?" *The Washington Quarterly*, 19:2 (1996), pp. 79-101.

28. Thomas R. Pickering and Stuart E. Eizenstat, "Now Europe Should Look Outward," *Wall Street Journal Europe*, January 8-9, 1999.

29. The White House, "Fact Sheet: 1999 U.S.-EU Summit: Strengthening the Transatlantic Economic Partnership," June 21, 1999, https://clintonwhitehouse4.archives.gov/WH/New/Europe-9906/html/Factsheets/990621a.html.

30. See Ellen L. Frost, "The Transatlantic Economic Partnership," Policy Brief 98-6, September 1998, Institute for International Economics, https://piie.com/publications/policy-briefs/transatlantic-economic-partnership.

31. Hill, op. cit., p. 125.

32. Ibid., pp. 122-123.

33. Ibid., pp 126-127.

34. Ibid., p. 125.

35. All cited in Tyler Marshall, "U.S. Gives NATO's 3 Newest Members Official Welcome," *Los Angeles Times*, March 13, 1999, http://articles.latimes.com/1999/mar/13/news/mn-16828.

36. Secretary of State Madeleine K. Albright And Foreign Ministers of the Czech Republic, Hungary and Poland, "Remarks on Accession to the North Atlantic Treaty Organization," Truman Presidential Library , Independence, Missouri, March 12, 1999, https://1997-2001.state.gov/www/statements/1999/990312.html.

37. Marshall, op. cit.

38. "Remarks on Accession…," op. cit.

39. See the speech by U.S. Ambassador to NATO Alexander Vershbow before the PfP 5-Year Conference in Bucharest, Romania, February 28-March 2, 1998.

40. Hill, op. cit., p. 161.

41. In: PBS Frontline Interviews, https://www.pbs.org/wgbh/pages/frontline/shows/kosovo/interviews/talbott.html.

42. President Bill Clinton, "A Commitment to Stability for Southeastern Europe," June 21, 1999, https://clintonwhitehouse4.archives.gov/WH/New/Europe-9906/html/Factsheets/990621c.html.

43. Sarajevo Summit Declaration of the Heads of State and Government of the participating and facilitating countries of the Stability Pact and the Principals of participating and facilitating International Organisations and Agencies and regional initiatives, http://www.bosnia.org.uk/bosrep/augnov99/Sarajevo_summit.cfm. On the margins of the Summit the United States offered an economic aid package worth nearly $700 million for post-war reconstruction in the Balkans.

44. Ibid.

45. Statement of Daniel S. Hamilton, Special Coordinator for Implementation of the Stability Pact for Southeastern Europe and Associate Director, Policy Planning Staff, U.S. Department of State before the House Committee on International Relations, March 8, 2000, https://fas.org/asmp/resources/govern/000309_hamilton.htm.

46. Through the Southeast European Cooperative Initiative (SECI) the countries of the region worked with the United States and other European partners on a long-term plan to upgrade customs facilities, improve border access and fight cross-border crime and corruption. SECI's efforts laid the practical foundation for broader Stability Pact cooperation in these and other areas. The SECI-initiated regional Anti-Crime Center in Bucharest served as a locus for active cooperation among regional law enforcement officials against organized crime and corruption.

47. Under Secretary of State for Political Affairs Thomas R. Pickering, "America's Stake in Europe's Future," French American Chamber of Commerce, Washington, DC, November 3, 2000, https://1997-2001.state.gov/policy_remarks/2000/001103_pickering_transatl.html.

48. OSCE, Charter for European Security, Istanbul, 1999, https://www.osce.org/mc/17502?download=true.

49. Hill, op. cit., pp. 122-123.

50. Remarks by the President at Opening of OSCE Summit, Ciragan Palace, Istanbul, Turkey, November 18, 1999.

51. Hill, op. cit., p. 153-157.

52. Hill, op. cit., p. 153.

53. See Ronald D. Asmus and Richard C. Holbrooke, "Re-Reinventing NATO," Riga Papers, German Marshall Fund of the United States, 2006.

54. See, for instance, Robert Hunter, *The European Security and Defense Policy: NATO's Companion—or Competitor?* (RAND, 2002); Michael J. Brenner, *Europe's New Security Vocation* (National Defense University, January 2002).

55. Joint Declaration on European Defence Issues at the British-French Summit (Saint-Malo, 4 December 1998), https://www.cvce.eu/obj/franco_british_st_malo_declaration_4_december_1998-en-f3cd16fb-fc37-4d52-936f-c8e9bc80f24f.html. See also Gerard Errera, "Time to be serious about European defense," *Financial Times*, October 31, 2003. The term "autonomous"—appearing in such a declaration for the first time—and not clearly defined—has continued to bedevil discussion across the Atlantic.

56. See Madeleine K. Albright, "The right balance will secure NATO's future," *Financial Times*, December 7, 1998. "No duplication" was neither defined nor intended to mean that the EU should not develop certain capabilities that already existed in the Alliance; indeed much of the Clinton Administration's efforts, such as the NATO Defense Capability Initiative, sought to prod the Europeans into developing precisely such capabilities. This distinction has been lost on many analysts. The three D's were subsequently amended by NATO Secretary General Lord Robertson into the three "I's;" indivisibility of the transatlantic link; improvement of capabilities; and inclusiveness of all Allies. See Daniel S. Hamilton, "American perspectives on the European Security and Defence Policy," in Jess Pilegaard, ed., *The Politics of European Security* (Copenhagen: Danish Institute for International Studies, 2004), pp. 143-158, https://www.files.ethz.ch/isn/16947/politics_European_security.pdf, which updates an earlier chapter by the author in Esther Brimmer ed., *The EU's Search For A Strategic Role: ESDP and Its Implications for Transatlantic Relations* (Washington, D.C.: Center for Transatlantic Relations, 2002).

57. "The Doctrine of the International Community," Remarks by British Prime Minister Tony Blair to the Economic Club of Chicago, April 24, 1999, http://webarchive.nationalarchives.gov.uk/20061004085342/http://number10.gov.uk/page1297.

58. Madeleine Albright and Robin Cook, "Euro force will beef up Nato," *The Guardian*, November 25, 2000, https://www.theguardian.com/world/2000/nov/26/eu.foreignpolicy.

59. Albright and Cook, op. cit.

60. Ibid.

61. Hill, op. cit., pp. 129-131.

Chapter 16

Winning Congressional and Public Support for NATO Enlargement, and the Political Psychology of Collective Defense

Jeremy D. Rosner

The debate in the United States over ratification of the first post–Cold War enlargement of NATO demonstrated the potential for the country to act in a bipartisan way to refresh support for the Alliance in a new security period. That decision in the late 1990s, endorsed by a broad range of groups and experts from both parties, seems far from today's polarized partisan environment, but suggests some paths toward political progress on current national security challenges.

The Pivot from Policy Development to Ratification

By late 1996, NATO governments were moving toward consensus after a years-long transatlantic policy debate about NATO's evolution after the Cold War. In the United States, after over three years of policy development, President Bill Clinton declared in October of that year that he and his administration were ready to formally invite Central European states to the Alliance, to ensure "the Iron Curtain [is not] replaced by a veil of indifference."[1] He argued that enlargement would add capable allies to NATO, tamp down dangerous strategic insecurity in Europe's center, and help define a new and workable relationship between NATO and Russia.

But if there was support from policy makers, it was not clear there was equal support from NATO's publics and legislatures. This was a particular question in the United States, given the U.S. Congress's substantial, independent powers over foreign policy.

To be sure, there were many signs U.S. ratification could succeed. NATO remained popular with the public, with 63% favoring a sustained or increased commitment to NATO, according to an October 1997 Pew Research Center poll.[2] Presidents had rarely lost congressional votes on major treaties and foreign agreements since World War II. NATO enlargement had been part of the "Contract with America" that GOP House candidates touted in 1994, and President Clinton's Republican opponent during the 1996 election, U.S. Senator Bob Dole, had also pushed for the idea. A "NATO Enlargement Facilitation Act," endorsing the policy, cleared Congress with strong bipartisan support in mid-1996 and was signed by the Clinton Administration. In earlier times, the Senate had regularly given overwhelming approval to each previous request to add new members to the Alliance—Greece and Turkey in 1952; West Germany in 1955; and Spain in 1982.

Yet major uncertainties loomed:

- Although majorities of the American public after the end of the Cold War continued to say the United States should play an active role in world affairs, there had been a strong surge in the share who wanted more focus on domestic rather than global challenges. Reflecting this, Clinton had been elected promising a laser-like focus on problems at home.[3]

- Similarly, although the public held generally favorable views about NATO, there was little public understanding of what it would mean to extend NATO's robust security assurances to Poland, Hungary, and the Czech Republic—the first three states proposed for membership.

- The Cold War's end had emboldened Congress to challenge the executive branch more forcefully across a range of foreign policy issues, reflecting the historical norm that relative peace in the world means relatively less peace between Congress and the White House on national security.[4] President Clinton had only with great effort won a November 1993 House vote on the North America Free Trade Act. By 1999, the Senate would fall 19 votes short on approving the Comprehensive Test Ban Treaty, with a 51-48 vote against ratification.

- This would be the first (and, even now, the only) time a Democratic president sought approval for NATO's enlargement from a Republican-controlled Senate. That was the same partisan combination that led to defeat of the Treaty of Versailles after World War I.

- Republicans in Congress harbored particular animus toward this Democratic President. As during the Wilson Administration, animus toward the president was particular sharp from the Chairman of the Senate Foreign Relations Committee—Henry Cabot Lodge in 1919, Jesse Helms in 1997—the committee of jurisdiction on a NATO enlargement vote.

- Congressional Republicans had supported the NATO Enlargement Facilitation Act during the summer of 1996 partly to help Dole claim the issue as his own; but by early 1997 Dole had lost and it was Democrat Clinton pushing the idea as a signal initiative.

- Although support for NATO's enlargement was broad, it was comprised of what political scientist George Grayson later called a "strange bedfellows" coalition, including Republicans and Democrats, defense hawks and human rights idealists, unionists focused on the brave actions of Poland's Solidarity, and business leaders focused on the lure of new markets in Central Europe. Keeping this diverse coalition united was by no means assured.

For all these reasons, some foreign policy experts at the time doubted whether it would be possible to gain ratification. One said it would take a "feat of magic" given "skin deep" support for NATO, and a public that had been reluctant to send troops to Bosnia or money to Mexico to relieve the peso crisis.[5]

Facing such danger signs, President Clinton and Secretary of State Madeleine Albright decided to take special steps to ensure they would have the necessary public and congressional backing. They created a special office with the sole purpose of obtaining that support. It would be housed at the State Department, but "double hatted," reporting directly to both the Secretary and National Security Adviser Samuel "Sandy" Berger. Berger and Albright's Deputy Secretary, Strobe Talbott, asked me to lead the NATO Enlargement Ratification Office (S/NERO)—and, along with a gifted Foreign Service Officer (later U.S. Ambassador to Serbia and Pakistan) Cameron Munter, we began our work in early March 1997. A few weeks later, Albright and Talbott recruited Ronald Asmus, a RAND analyst who was one of the intellectual fathers of NATO enlargement, to be Deputy Assistant Secretary of

State for European Affairs, to lead the policy work on this effort, and Asmus became our close partner in achieving ratification.

Defining Success: "A Good Win"

On one level, S/NERO's goal was simple: getting the constitutionally-required "two-thirds of the Senators present" to approve an amendment to the North Atlantic Treaty. We knew that falling short of that goal would be a disaster. Woodrow Wilson's failure to achieve ratification of the Treaty of Versailles was not only a huge political setback for his administration and party; it also helped signal an American retreat from global affairs that would contribute to the worst moments of the rest of that century. We were determined not to permit a Senate defeat that would send a similar signal after the close of the Cold War.

But from the outset, the Clinton Administration approached the ratification effort not simply as a quest for 67 votes and a legal hurdle for adding three countries to the Alliance. Rather, the ratification campaign represented a broader opportunity to sharpen the American public's understanding of, and support for, the Alliance, and to ensure the public was ready to support the treaty's security commitments, particularly toward new members, in a new era.

Public support had always been the critical variable at the core of the Treaty's security guarantees. When Dean Acheson first explained the new Atlantic Alliance to the American public in 1949, he observed that the operation of Article 5—the Treaty's central promise of collective defense—was "not a legalistic question." He said it was rather "a question of faith and principle," linked to the "exercise of will."[6] It would ultimately be futile and dangerous to extend NATO membership to Central European states without ensuring the American public and Congress were truly prepared to treat an attack against one of them as an attack against all. A narrow victory in the Senate, or Senate consent without real public backing, would not suffice.

These factors framed S/NERO's work from the start. On February 26, 1997, just days before joining the administration, I sent a personal note to Albright, Talbott, Berger, and Deputy National Security Adviser James Steinberg, laying out what I felt should be the goals of the ratification effort. I argued our goal should not only be a win, but "a good win."

A "good win" meant obtaining not just the constitutional require-ment of two-thirds of the Senate, but a lopsided, larger-than-expected, and fully bipartisan margin. I argued we needed to show "broad, enthu-siastic U.S. support, both to make the ... security guarantees [to new allies] more meaningful, and to strengthen the U.S. as it pursues other foreign policy goals."

A good win also meant that the victory could not come at the expense of other U.S. interests, including constructive relations with Russia. Clinton had staked a good deal on building closer ties to Russia and President Boris Yeltsin. A win on NATO enlargement would be under-mined if pursued in a way that needlessly poisoned that relationship.

A good win also had to provide affirmation and political momen-tum for the Open Door concept—NATO's pledge that membership would remain open to qualified candidate states that were not in this first round of enlargement. I was confident that if we made the Open Door policy an explicit part of the debate and won strong Senate en-dorsement, then votes on future rounds would be less controversial. This proved to be true.[7]

Finally, a good win had to involve the broad public, to the greatest extent possible. As a student of public opinion on national security, I knew that the public pays relatively little attention to most foreign pol-icy issues, and that we would never make NATO's enlargement a topic of conversation at most American dinner tables. But I argued we need-ed to do all we could to take this issue to the public, and draw as many sectors of society as possible into the discussion. I felt the strength and legitimacy of NATO's security guarantees partly depended on this.

The February 26 memo suggested several things were necessary to achieve a good win. As noted, the effort needed to be bipartisan; but I argued that the harder half of achieving bipartisan support lay with winning Republican votes: "While most of the votes we need to pick up...are from Democrats on the left, the most serious prospect for de-feat entails a broad defection by Republicans on the right." My reading of Stull Holt's 1933 study *Treaties Defeated in the Senate* and other his-torical analyses underscored that treaties in the 20th century had nearly always been threatened by Republicans, not Democrats.[8] Despite scattered internal resistance to the idea of focusing the ratification campaign more on wooing Republicans than Democrats, the President's team ultimately sided with my recommendation.

Achieving a good win would also require deeply involving the Senate in the ratification process. Holt concluded that a key factor in the Senate's rejection of the Treaty of Versailles was Wilson's refusal to involve Senator Lodge and his colleagues more in the negotiations. My memo therefore urged the administration to invite the Senate to create a group that would have a real seat in the diplomacy, and it urged involving the House as well, since the House could play a major role in shaping this kind of national debate, even if it lacked a vote on the Treaty.

My memo argued that another key to success was creating a tangible sense of momentum and inevitability. If the outcome of the vote never seemed in doubt, it would depress the energy of opponents, make enlargement's critics seem more fringe, reduce the leverage of Senators seeking amendments, and contribute to a broader public and international sense that, at least in the United States, the wisdom of enlarging NATO was more a matter of consensus than dispute.

The Ratification Campaign

There is neither space nor need to describe here in detail the specific steps the Clinton Administration took to achieve ratification of the first round of NATO's enlargement. Several excellent books chronicle those actions, especially those by Asmus, Grayson, and James Goldgeier.[9] Yet it is worth noting a few points about the effort, especially those aimed at "a good win."

The importance of early diplomacy and signaling to Congress

Much of the work needed to ensure ratification preceded S/NERO's creation. President Clinton had already signaled unequivocally to Congress that NATO's enlargement was a personal priority; he had stressed it during his re-election campaign and in his 1997 State of the Union address.[10] In speeches and meetings with Congress, he and Secretary

Albright had clearly laid out enlargement's strategic rationale. Albright and Talbott had succeeded in driving the Alliance to create the "NATO-Russia Founding Act," and they, along with others, managed to walk a fine line important for ratification politics. The Founding Act was positive enough toward Moscow that it reduced anxieties (mostly among Democrats) that NATO enlargement would antagonize Moscow. But it also had enough red lines between Russia and NATO's own decision-making that it minimized concerns (mostly among Republicans) that NATO was giving Russia any kind of vote or veto. The State Department's former Europe chief, Richard Holbrooke, had helped solidify the inter-agency consensus behind enlargement. All this laid a strong foundation for later success in Congress.

The Senate NATO Observer Group

The President's top advisers quickly agreed with the idea of inviting the Senate to create an "observer group" to take part in the diplomacy that would precede ratification. Yet before they could act on this idea, Senate Majority Leader Trent Lott on March 21, 1997 proposed the idea himself, in a *Washington Post* op-ed.[11] This was a stroke of good fortune, since it put the Senate's own stamp on the idea, and linked it to one of the Republicans most needed for success. Lott's initiative meant that he would decide which Senators to involve, freeing us from that knotty question, given that multiple committees and individual Senators arguably had a stake in the issue. The Observer Group ultimately included 28 Senators, with an even partisan split, including key enlargement supporters and opponents.

There were some bitter early fights between the Observer Group and the administration over the Senate's role in diplomacy, especially the degree to which it could access classified diplomatic cables. But over some months, the two branches built a satisfactory process of cooperation, and the Group contributed significantly to the Senate's work. There were ultimately 17 meetings between the Observer Group and the President, members of his administration, or relevant foreign leaders. The administration also brought members of the Senate Observer Group, along with House members, to NATO's Madrid Summit in July 1997.

U.S. Committee on the Enlargement of NATO

In a saga filled with surprising turns, few were as unexpected or helpful as the appearance of Bruce Jackson. A central casting country-club Republican and Dole fundraiser, in October 1996 he reached out to NSC official (later U.S. Ambassador to Poland) Daniel Fried to offer the creation of an outside bipartisan committee to support the enlargement effort. Fried connected Jackson to me, and by the time S/NERO opened shop, the U.S. Committee on the Enlargement of NATO had become a vital part of the ratification effort. Jackson and his Republican co-leader, Julie Finley, hosted dozens of gatherings where members of Congress, staff, and journalists could meet visiting Central European leaders, and hear their case for enlargement first-hand. Jackson's and Finley's strong ties with Hill Republicans proved a key bridge across the aisle. The Committee ultimately ran ads in Capitol Hill newspapers (including one with an iconic photo of Albright and Helms, on the same stage, beaming at each other and holding hands) in support of NATO's enlargement.

Endorsements

An early and constant priority for S/NERO was getting endorsements from a wide range of organizations and luminaries. That not only showed broad public support—and dispelled the canard that this was only an issue of concern to ethnic Central European voters—but it also made it easy for senators who were just learning about the issue to be comfortable with it. We wanted to "close the off-ramps" for skeptical Senators by showing there was almost no segment of society that opposed the issue. Air Force Brigadier General Robert "Tip" Osterthaler spent weeks with S/NERO staff visiting leaders of veterans' organizations to make the case for NATO's enlargement. Munter flew uninvited to a meeting of the U.S. Conference of Mayors and came away with their endorsement. We ultimately obtained endorsements from over three dozen organizations—including the Veterans of Foreign Wars, the American Legion, the AFL-CIO, the National Governors Association, the American Jewish Committee, a range of state legislatures, three former presidents (including President Carter, after a direct pitch to him by Secretary Albright), and a wide range of national security experts and former officials from both parties.

Editorial boards

The ratification strategy aimed to generate as much nationwide media discussion as possible. To that end, we mounted a broad outreach to editorial boards at both the major national newspapers and local papers. Administration officials fanned out across the country to make the case. It was an uphill effort: according to Grayson, of the 68 North American newspapers that ultimately took positions on the first round of enlargement, 34 opposed the initiative, another 13 called for delaying the vote, and only 21 favored it.[12] The negative balance underscores that ratification was hardly a forgone conclusion. Yet there were some notable successes: the *Chicago Tribune* reversed its position to favoring enlargement after administration officials reached out to members of the editorial board and helped them meet with key Central European leaders.

The opposition

A final variable in the ratification effort was the nature of our opposition—not something of our making, but important to the successful outcome. The opposition benefited from some highly influential Senators, including some leading Republican voices on military matters, such as John Warner (Virginia), as well as respected voices on the Democratic left, including the liberal lion Senator Daniel Patrick Moynihan (New York). Opponents also had strength among prominent foreign policy writers, including the legendary diplomat George Kennan, Johns Hopkins academic Michael Mandelbaum, and Thomas Friedman of the *New York Times*, whose paper was among the many opposing enlargement. The Cato Institute added a libertarian voice against enlargement, while Ben & Jerry's co-founder Ben Cohen injected passion and funding.

This was a powerful mix, and the opponents attacked NATO's enlargement with some challenging arguments. Moynihan and others on the left argued that enlargement would alienate Russia and could trigger World War III. Former Secretary of State Henry Kissinger initially argued the administration had given too much away to Moscow in the NATO-Russia Founding Act. Senator Warner and former Senate Armed Services Chair Sam Nunn warned enlargement could degrade the Alliance by admitting weak militaries and indefensible geographies.

Peace groups and others on the left argued enlargement was a scheme to enrich U.S. arms makers. And a mix of left, right, and libertarian voices expressed concern over enlargement's cost to the United States, which remained a muddled issue until the end (figures ranged from Cato's estimate of $70 billion over a decade, to the administration's estimate of $1.5–2 billion over the same period). Ben Cohen helped finance full-page ads in the *New York Times* and other papers across the country.

Yet the opponents never seemed to have any centrally organized lobbying effort, and ultimately never did much to grow their ranks. They did not create the kind of education effort for elites provided by the U.S. Committee to Expand NATO. They did not work to get resolutions of disapproval from a broad range of civic organizations. All this meant that the ratification faced an opposition that was often articulate and quoted, but rarely organized or expanding.

In the end, the Senate voted April 30, 1998, to endorse NATO's enlargement, by a vote of 80-19 (Senator Jon Kyl of Arizona would have voted in favor, but had left to catch a flight). The lopsided margin obscures the clashes that endangered Senate approval until late in the game. The final days were spent combatting a series of hostile amendments (it was hostile Senate amendments and "reservations" that sank the Treaty of Versailles in the United States). One by Senator John Ashcroft (Republican from Missouri) proposed to limit NATO's missions to only defense of members' territories, ruling out NATO's involvement in conflicts like Bosnia; Ashcroft's provision was tabled by the Senate on an 82-18 vote. Another amendment, from Senator Warner, would have barred the admission of any other new members for at least three years; it failed, 59-41. Defeat of the Warner amendment was key example of the difference between a win and a good win. We could have accepted his proposed pause and still won admission for the first three states. But a good win, including robust endorsement of the Open Door policy, required defeating it.

Implications for the Future

Twenty years later, the first post-Cold War enlargement of NATO still seems an enduring success. It added new forces and capabilities to

NATO, strengthening the Alliance and the security of its members, including the United States. It created a process that continues to generate a magnetic appeal to those states still aspiring to membership, such as Georgia and Ukraine. It helped transform Central Europe from its historic role as a spawning ground for great power conflicts into a thriving area firmly anchored in the West, enabling roughly 100 million people to enjoy more freedom, security and progress. Few if any of the dire predictions of enlargement's proponents came true. There has been no evidence of NATO losing its military edge as the new states joined. There has been no explosion of America's NATO-related costs. Contrary to the dire warnings of NATO enlargement's fiercest critics, the 1998 vote did not trigger World War III.

As part of that overall effort, the U.S. ratification process in 1997-1998 ultimately met our standard of "a good win." The final margin was overwhelming. Support was solidly bipartisan. There was a real national debate, with a wide range of experts, interest groups, and media outlets taking an active part. The debate included an explicit rejection of efforts to shut NATO's "Open Door" policy. That in turn helped make all three of the subsequent rounds of enlargement virtually uncontroversial within the Senate and the public. Public support for NATO has remained undimmed, even as America's current president has tried to cast doubts on the Alliance's utility.

Yet some key questions about NATO's enlargement linger. This is particularly true regarding the debate over whether enlargement pushed Russia away from the West. While Vladimir Putin and other Russian leaders often criticize NATO's enlargement as threatening, there has been a surprising lack of high-quality, dispassionate research about whether this is just a talking point for them, or a genuine driving force behind Russia's drift toward increased confrontation and authoritarianism. Other authors in this volume contribute important new insights on this question, and hopefully their work will spur additional scholarship as well.

It also is worth examining how it came to be that the first three post-communist countries admitted to NATO are now among the Central European states veering furthest from liberal democratic norms. Hungary is ruled by a strongman-leader who has villainized immigrants (despite their paucity in Hungary), fanned anti-Semitism, suppressed media freedom, politicized the courts, and boasted about his illiberal model of governance. Poland is ruled by a party that has stacked the courts, politicized the public broadcaster, and imposed a government-sanctioned view of history. The Czech Republic has elected a prime minister who is a populistic oligarch.

It was not supposed to be this way. During the ratification process, we argued enlargement would bolster democratic norms by requiring applicant states to address a range of issues regarding their democratic bona fides. We also argued NATO membership would more firmly embed these countries within the liberal democratic culture of the trans-Atlantic community.

The strong turn toward populism in the Central Europe's first three NATO members may be a coincidence, and it is implausible that their political conditions would have been better had they remained outside the Alliance. But one experience a few years ago led me to wonder if the security that NATO has brought to Central Europe may have played a small role.

In early 2014, 16 years after S/NERO concluded its work, and long after the Baltics and additional Central European states had also joined both NATO and the EU, I was advising an Estonian party on their campaign for the European Parliament. The party was settling on a campaign message that focused on domestic issues, although some in the Western-oriented party argued for more of a focus on national security. Then, in late February and early March, Russia forcibly seized Ukraine's Crimean peninsula. Many in the party said, in effect, "Well, now we *must* focus on national security; all our voters will demand it." I replied that this was an empirical question, and set up focus groups to assess reactions among the party's rank-and-file.

We started our focus groups the way we begin virtually every group anywhere, with a broad question: how are things going in this country? Participants talked at length about bread-and-butter issues: employment, salaries, pensions, corruption, and the like. Not one person mentioned Russia or Crimea. Our moderator probed this striking omission: "What about Russia's actions in Crimea? Does this concern you?" "Oh no," responded a Tallinn man. The moderator asked why not. He responded, "Well, now we are in NATO."

I was fairly stunned, and wondered whether Estonia was really as safe from aggression by its huge eastern neighbor as this Tallinn voter assumed. On one hand, I was glad that Central European citizens in these new NATO states felt safe, with a confidence that the Alliance's Article 5 guarantees were meaningful. On the other hand, I worried that their perception of NATO's protections might lead them to pay too little attention to security issues in their own countries' politics, and wondered if this would leave more room for populist appeals on other issues.

Obviously, there are bigger forces creating openings for populism, which has upended politics in the United States as well as in Central Europe, which faced these populist headwinds with less well-established democracies than many other countries. But it is worth exploring the potential linkages between NATO's security guarantees and political dynamics within these states. And we should focus on how NATO (as well as other institutions, particularly the European Union) can continue to push to preserve liberal democratic norms among its members.

Closer to home, it is worth asking whether the successful 1998 ratification effort provides a broader model for bipartisan cooperation in the United States on national security issues. The short answer is: partly. It would be a mistake to suggest there is any magic wand that can wave away the toxic air of division and recrimination that hangs over Washington. As many studies reveal, partisan polarization in the United States reflects myriad long-term trends, from a more politicized mainstream and social media environment; to geographic sorting that has left more pockets of America either deep blue or deep red; to gerrymandering of congressional districts; to shifts in cultural beliefs. It is inevitable that these forces have made it harder to forge bipartisan support on national security issues, just as they have on most domestic issues. It also may be that the tactics that brought success in 1998 would not fare as well in this age of social media.

Yet there were a few elements of the success on NATO's enlargement that may hold some hope for progress, including:

- **Build on successful institutions.** Americans trust NATO. They did during the Cold War. They do now. This is a huge asset. During the ratification effort, we capitalized on that trust and the transatlantic values that helped build it. Even as Donald Trump reportedly has considered withdrawing the United States from NATO, public support for the Alliance has shown no signs of weakening, and bipartisan majorities in Congress have voted for resolutions reaffirming American support for NATO, and opposition to withdrawing from it. It may be that the enlargement debates helped to reinforce public and congressional support for NATO. At a minimum, the strength of that support means that internationalists may do well to use NATO as a substantive and rhetorical starting point, where applicable, in building their case for other initiatives.

- **Take opponents seriously.** During the enlargement effort I spent more time with Republican activists and members of Congress than at any other time in my life. We were determined to win them over. We knew that required hard listening, bringing them into the diplomatic process, having real respect for their concerns, and taking serious steps to address their worries. The bipartisan success of recent congressional efforts on issues such as Russian sanctions and disapproval of Saudi Arabia's war in Yemen suggest there may inherently be more room for non-ideological discussion and compromise on national security issues than on many domestic challenges like health care financing and reproductive rights.

- **Do not be overly cowed by public opinion—or Congress.** Decades of studying and working the seams between public opinion and national security policy have left me impressed with the malleable nature of that ground. As some scholars have noted, public opinion only rarely imposes binding constraints on the ability of a president to take action abroad. In the wake of events like the violent conflicts in the former Yugoslavia and Somalia, there were some good reasons that President Clinton and his administration could have spooked themselves into believing the public was unwilling to take on new security commitments abroad. It is good they did not. The public and Congress tend to judge national security pragmatically, more by results than ideology. Strong-willed presidents, with a clear plan, can usually get their way on national security if they act with confidence, clarity, and candor.

- **Reach out to the public—and at least civil society.** Although it may seem to contradict the previous point, there was great value in the effort the Clinton Administration made to take its case for NATO enlargement out beyond Washington. It is doubtful our efforts radically energized or changed mass public opinion. But the endorsements from a wide range of civic groups and meetings with editorial boards were quite important. In addition to "closing the off-ramps" for wavering senators, those efforts helped educate a key stratum of opinion leaders about NATO, its history, and its continuing relevance. It is a type of effort that can help bridge partisan divides across a range of national security initiatives today.

There was much that was unique about the politics surrounding the 1997-1999 ratification of NATO's enlargement. The historical moment; the bipartisan genesis; the strange-bedfellows coalition of supporters—these were all unusual and yet crucial to the outcome. The gusts of nationalism and protectionism blowing through American and global politics today make internationalist initiatives more challenging now in many ways. Yet the success of the ratification effort two decades ago helped establish an enduring point of relative consensus in the politics of American foreign policy and provides some guidance for how to sustain other internationalist initiatives in the years ahead.

Notes

1. Remarks of President W. J. Clinton to the People of Detroit; October 22, 1996; https://www.nato.int/docu/speech/1996/s961022a.htm.

2. The Pew Research Center for the People and the Press, "Public and Opinion Leaders Favor NATO Enlargement," News Release, October 7, 1997.

3. Polling by the Chicago Council on Global Affairs found the share of the public wanting the United States to "play an active part in world affairs" stayed nearly steady during this period, moving from 64% in 1986 to 62% in 1990 and 65% in 1994. Dina Smeltz, Ivo Daalder, Karl Friedhoff, Craig Kafura, and Lily Wojtowicz, "America Engaged: American Public Opinion and US Foreign Policy (Chicago Council on Global Affairs: Chicago, 2018), p. 2. At the same time, however, there was an 18-point spike after the Cold War in the share of the public that agreed with idea that, "we should not think so much in international terms but concentrate more on our national problems and building up our strength and prosperity here at home." The share agreeing rose from 60% in 1985 to 78% in 1991. "America's Place in the World: An Investigation of the Attitudes of American Opinion Leaders and the American Public About International Affairs" (Times Mirror Center for the People and the Press: Los Angeles, November 1993), p. 31.

4. Jeremy D. Rosner, *The New Tug-of-War: Congress, the Executive Branch, and National Security* (Brookings Institution: Washington, 1995).

5. Quoting Charles Kupchan, in Jeremy D. Rosner, "NATO Enlargement's American Hurdle: The Danger of Misjudging Our Political Will," *Foreign Affairs*, July/August 1996.

6. Dean Acheson, Speech on the proposed North Atlantic Treaty, March 18, 1949, p. 14. Truman Library website: https://www.trumanlibrary.org/nato/doc5.htm.

7. During mid-1997, as the administration was preparing for NATO's Madrid Summit and the decision about which states would first be added to NATO, the Romanian ambassador told me worriedly that if Romania were not made part of the first group of new Central European members then it would never gain membership. I responded that, to the contrary, if we did the first round right, Romania's addition in the next round would be largely uncontroversial. On May 8, 2003, four years after we gained strong Senate approval for the first round of enlargement, the Senate voted to support the admission of Romania and six other states by a vote of 96-0. It is true that the intervening events of September 11, 2001 had strengthened the hand of the U.S. executive branch on national security issues; but the content of the

debate on the second round of enlargement makes clear that the Senate felt many core questions on this issue had been settled in the 1998 debate.

8. Stull Holt, *Treaties Defeated by the Senate* (Baltimore: Johns Hopkins University Press, 1933).

9. Ronald D. Asmus, *Opening NATO's Door: How the Alliance Remade Itself for a New Era*, (Columbia University Press: New York, 2002); George W. Grayson, *Strange Bedfellow: NATO Marches East* (University Press of America: Lanham MD, 1999); James M. Goldgeier, *Not Whether But When: The U.S. Decision to Enlarge NATO* (Brookings Institution Press: Washington, 1999).

10. Transcript of Clinton's State of the Union, http://www.cnn.com/2005/ALLPOLITICS/01/31/sotu.clinton1997/index.html. James Lindsay and others have stressed the importance of clear signaling to Congress by presidents and their administrations about their national security priorities. See, for example, *Congress and the Politics of U.S. Foreign Policy* (The Johns Hopkins University Press: Baltimore, 1994).

11. Trent Lott, "The Senate's Role in NATO Enlargement," *Washington Post*, March 21, 1997, p. A-27.

12. Grayson, *op. cit.*, 137.

Part IV

A Place for Russia?

Chapter 17

Bill, Boris, and NATO

Strobe Talbott

Three consecutive American presidents—Ronald Reagan, George H. W. Bush, and Bill Clinton—were a virtual tag team in dealing with the end of the Cold War and its aftermath. Reagan cultivated a productive relationship with Mikhail Gorbachev, the last leader of the USSR. He was also the first to proclaim and forge a "partnership" between the superpowers.[1] It was on Bush's watch that the Berlin Wall collapsed, followed by the Iron Curtain, and the Warsaw Pact. That created the prospect, as he put it in 1989, of "a Europe whole and free."

The euphoria in Western capitals was not shared in Moscow. The unification of West and East Germany, in October 1990, meant that the North Atlantic Treaty Organization (NATO) would encroach onto what had been part of the Soviet zone of domination. The Western Alliance was expanding while the Warsaw Pact was evaporating, and Lieutenant Colonel Putin was back in St. Petersburg having burned secret documents in the K.G.B. outpost in Dresden.

The Bush Administration tried to soothe Soviet anxieties by assuring Gorbachev and his team that there were no plans for NATO beyond the new eastern German border.

As for Gorbachev and his aides, they were not concentrating on the future of the USSR's erstwhile allies; instead, they were increasingly worried about the fate of the Soviet Union itself. So was Bush. He was worried about chaos all across Eurasia.

After Bush flew to Moscow and Kyiv in the summer of 1991, he sensed that Gorbachev and the USSR might not be salvageable. The coup de grâce was a real coup against Gorbachev weeks after Bush's trip. When Boris Yeltsin moved into the Kremlin in December 1991, Bush assured him that America would maintain the substance and spirit of "partnership" with the new Russian state and its first leader.

The Bond

When Clinton moved into the Oval Office, he picked up where Bush left off. He was prepared to do all he could to help Yeltsin's economic and political reforms. Clinton had been a student of what used to be the Soviet Union. He made his first visit there in his early twenties, in Brezhnev's "era of stagnation." He recalled that young, liberal Soviet citizens he met on that trip pined for the motherland to become "a normal, modern country." He saw Yeltsin—and Gorbachev before him—as catalysts for the evolution.

Clinton devoted more of his time, energy, and political capital to Russia and Yeltsin than any other foreign nation or leader. They met during their overlapping terms in office eighteen times, nearly as many as all their predecessors going back to Harry Truman and Joseph Stalin combined.

Even during Clinton's transition, he was fixated on the upheaval in Russia and its neighborhood. He was getting intelligence briefings in Little Rock on mounting opposition from the diehard parliamentarians. "I don't want to appear to be letting Yeltsin hang out there," he said to me late in 1992, "naked before his enemies."[2]

Yeltsin was so desperate to get the transition between Bush and Clinton off to a good start that he sent a letter urging the president-elect to attend a meeting in a third country before Inauguration Day. That was out of the question, but Clinton took Yeltsin's impatience seriously: "His letter reads like a cry of pain. You can just feel the guy reaching out to us, and asking us to reach out to him. I'd really, *really* like to help him. I get the feeling he's up to his ass in alligators. He especially needs friends abroad because he's got so many enemies at home. We've got to try to keep Yeltsin going."

Once Clinton was in office, he focused on Yeltsin's economic reforms. If they failed, so would his political ones. He enlisted leaders in other capitalist democracies to join him in boosting the fledgling government in Moscow.

After all, Clinton's campaign-winning slogan had been "It's the economy, stupid!" He was also the first U.S. president who would use his whole term to treat his counterpart in the Kremlin as a partner, rather than an antagonist.[3] In much of 1993, NATO as such was not high on either the U.S. or Russian president's agenda, to say nothing about its expansion.

But others, in the United States and abroad, were already seized of the matter. The Poles, Czechs, Hungarians, and other Central Europeans protested vehemently, as did their diasporas in the United States. By far the most persistent and passionate among them was Jan Nowak-Jeziorański, a Polish exile whom I knew when I was a reporter in Eastern Europe and he was at Radio Free Europe in Munich. His broadcasts made him a celebrity in his native land.

The three Baltic states were a special case. They had been illegally annexed by Stalin as part of his pact with Hitler in 1939, and the United States and other Western countries regarded them as occupied territories and never accepted them as a part of the USSR.

Clinton used his first summit with Yeltsin in April 1993 to finance repatriation of Soviet-era officers who had settled down into retirement in what were now three new independent states. A month later, I met with Lennart Meri, the president of Estonia. His tone was one-third grateful, one-third skeptical, and one-third downright sarcastic. It was, he said, welcome news that elderly pensioners were returning to Russia. Even so, he was looking down the road to when Russian troops might re-occupy his country since Yeltsin was sure to give way to a more traditional Russian leader. The only way to protect Estonia was with membership in NATO under the American nuclear umbrella. Russia, he said, was a malignancy in remission; the Yeltsin era was, at best, a fleeting opportunity to be seized before Russia relapsed into tyranny at home and conquest abroad.

That same month, Presidents Lech Wałęsa of Poland, Václav Havel of the Czech Republic, and Árpád Göncz of Hungary came to Washington and made a vigorous case to Clinton for their countries' admission to NATO. There wasn't much response from the press nor the Russian government. However, when I flew to Moscow for consultations with Yuri Mamedov—my counterpart for all eight years in government—he remarked that it would be "discriminatory to Russia's interests" if NATO included former Soviet allies, to say nothing of former Soviet republics.

Throughout Clinton's first year, he was weighing the decision that only he could make on NATO enlargement. One caveat that he insisted on was that the post-Cold War NATO needed to be part of a number of new organizations that included the former Warsaw Pact members and the former Soviet republics, notably Russia. The hope was that, over time, Russia's mistrust of NATO and the Central Europeans' mistrust of Russia would fade. The Bush administration had already laid the ground for that strategy by initiating a NATO-sponsored body called the North Atlantic Cooperation Council (NACC) in 1991.

In June 1993, I joined Secretary of State Warren Christopher for the annual meeting of the NACC in Athens. For the purpose of a photo op, it was impressive: foreign ministers of thirty-eight countries whose governments—and militaries—had spent decades glowering at each other over the Iron Curtain were now gathered around a giant U-shaped table. They were thrashing out ways to cooperate on mutual interests with limited success. There was more squabbling than brainstorming.

Christopher spent much of the two days being accosted by Central Europeans wanting to know when they could join NATO, and Andrei Kozyrev, Yeltsin's foreign minister (and contributor to this project), pleading for assurances that the U.S. was not contemplating enlargement. In all those "pull-asides," sipping strong bitter coffee, Chris could say nothing more than that the matter was under study. What he didn't say—and shouldn't have—was that Clinton was leaning toward expansion not just of NATO but also a wider security and political architecture that included Russia and the other former republics.

The Decision

The process that brought Clinton to a final decision required numerous, diverse, and some disputatious discussions. Some in the Oval Office, some in the Situation Room, some in the East Wing, some on Air Force One, some over private meals, and—my least favorite—post-midnight telephone calls that began with an operator saying, "Please hold for the President." When that happened, I prayed that Clinton was on another call so I could get myself fully awake.

The overriding rationale was that while the Cold War was over, there were—and would continue to be—threats to peace and democracy in the Atlantic Community. Since that Community was expanding as former Eastern bloc states metamorphosed into capitalist democracies, so should the institutions that have undergirded it since the end of the World War II. The critical ones were the various early incarnations of the European Union, and the other was NATO. Had there not been an American-led Alliance, there would have been no integration—and, all too possibly, another catastrophic war.

There was a German-specific factor here. Helmut Kohl, the German Chancellor, along with Defense Minister Volker Rühe, was bound and determined, now that there was no Iron Curtain, to move the boundary of the "political West" eastward. Both were worried about instability on their borders and wanted reinsurance against a volatile Russia.

Clinton told me about Kohl's view, and I had a chance to hear it from the Chancellor himself in Bonn. In addition to its internal demons, Germany had been cursed in the 20th century by political geography. Immediately to the east were Slavic lands, historically regarded more as Eurasian than truly or entirely European. As long as Germany's border with Poland marked the dividing line between East and West, Germany would be vulnerable to the pathologies of racism and the temptations of militarism that can come with living on an embattled frontier. That frontier could disappear, he said, only if Poland entered the European Union. His country's future depended not just on deepening its ties within the EU but on expanding the EU eastward so that Germany would be in the middle of a safe, prosperous, integrated, and democratic Europe rather than on its edge.

"That is why Germany is the strongest proponent of enlargement of the EU," Kohl said to me, and the EU would not accept new members unless they were in NATO: "That's why European integration is of existential importance to us. This is not just a moral issue, it's in our self-interest to have this development now and not in the future."

Morality, however, is important as well, as leaders in Central Europe kept pounding into our heads. Their countries had suffered a brutal 20th century: chaos during the First World War, Nazi occupation during the Second World War, the post-World War II "liberation" by the Red Army who turned them into vassal states for the Soviet Union—with the collusion of the United States and Britain at Yalta. Were they going to suffer triple jeopardy in the 21st century?

There was another, more realpolitik concern in Washington and in Europe, including among the liberal presidents of the aspiring new NATO members. If the Alliance shut them out, there would be a danger that those countries would feel left to their own devices, including in dealing with tensions with their neighbors over ethnic and territorial issues. At a minimum, they were likely to beef up their military to the detriment of their economy. Worse, if the Central Europeans were relegated to what they feared would be a "security vacuum," they would turn inward for their salvation and resort to homegrown ethnic violence across borders of the sort that was happening in the Balkans.

And then, of course, Russians started using the phrase, not just "near abroad," but "*our* near abroad," which sounded like dog-whistling for revanchism.

Those were the pros in the ongoing debates in and out of government. There were, of course, cons, but the only one that Clinton really cared about was exacerbating Yeltsin's already fierce political opposition. In a meeting in London with Yuri Mamedov in late August 1993, I gave him a heads-up that the issue of NATO expansion would be on the table in early 1994 when President Clinton made his first trip to Moscow.

Mamedov grimaced. "Only our worst enemies would wish that topic on us," he said. "NATO is a four-letter word in Russian. Let's concentrate merely on the difficult jobs—like Bosnia and Ukraine—and not assign ourselves Mission Impossible."

An hour later a news bulletin announced that Boris Yeltsin had told a press conference in Warsaw that Russia had no objection to Poland's joining NATO. "In the new Russian-Polish relationship," Yeltsin proclaimed, "there is no place for hegemony and one state dictating to another, nor for the psychology of the 'big brother' and the 'little brother.'"

He and Wałęsa signed a joint declaration affirming that Poland had the sovereign right to provide for its own security and that if Poland chose to join NATO, it would not conflict with Russia's interests.

Mamedov was thunderstruck. Some of his colleagues claimed that their president had been expressing his "private opinion," not government policy. Others suspected that the Poles plied Yeltsin with his favorite beverage. They denied it—their president used logic. If Poland was snubbed by NATO, it would have no choice but to enter a bilateral alliance with Ukraine. He would much prefer to join NATO and the European Union. Both were committed to cooperating with Russia. Why not make a deal before the issue blows up and politicians are screaming?

Apparently, Yeltsin bought it: Poland was indeed a free country now—it had broken out of the Soviet empire, just as Russia itself had done. Yes, NATO was anti-Soviet in its origin, but Yeltsin was anti-Soviet himself. They shook hands and announced their agreement to the world.

Poor Kozyrev and Defense Minister Grachev. They had to double-team their boss and convince him that he was committing political suicide unless he rescinded the agreement with Wałęsa.[4] They succeeded in getting him to sign a letter, drafted by the foreign ministry and sent to the leaders of NATO member states, suggesting that the Alliance and Russia would jointly guarantee the security of the Central Europeans. It had a strong whiff of Yalta to the Poles and their neighbors. However, Yeltsin did not reverse the essence of what he had agreed with Wałęsa; in fact, his letter reaffirmed the right of any state to choose its own methods and associations.[5]

Within weeks, Kozyrev's and Grachev's concerns were all too accurate about the fury and strength of Yeltsin's opponents. All hell broke loose in Moscow. Unreconstructed Communists, holed up in their offices, sent armed thugs into the streets who killed several militiamen and later attacked the main television center, firing rocket-propelled grenades into the lobby, setting it ablaze. Rioters attacked government buildings, chanting "All power to the Soviets!" and carrying hammer-and-sickle flags and portraits of Stalin.

Yeltsin ordered the ministry of defense to crush the uprising with tanks in the streets, shelling the parliament itself, and jailing the ringleaders. When Yeltsin addressed his nation, it was more of a dirge and regret: "Nobody has won, nobody has scored a victory. We have all been scorched by the lethal breath of fratricidal war."

When I saw Clinton in the White House as the crisis abated, he gave me a rueful look and a remark that snapped my head back: "Boy, do I ever miss the cold war."

He didn't, but he was all the more concerned about "Ol' Boris" and his unpopular policies and his treacherous politics. Now that the anti-Yeltsin forces had failed with civil war, they did much better for their revanchist cause at the polls. In parliamentary elections in December, the perversely misnamed Liberal-Democratic Party—headed by the virulent ultranationalist, Vladimir Zhirinovsky—triumphed in a parliamentary election. The resurrected Communist Party, led by Gennady Zyuganov, also had a strong showing.

These two setbacks for Yeltsin—and for Russia—highlighted another reason for expanding NATO: the danger that Russia might break bad.

William Perry, the secretary of defense, along with General John Shalikashvili, the chairman of the Joint Chiefs of Staff, were uneasy about expansion unless Russia regressed to its predatory ways. They hoped that a new and expansive organization, Partnership for Peace (PfP), created in 1994, would be a way of slowing down extending NATO itself. But when their Commander-in-Chief made clear in October 1993 that he wanted to open the Alliance to the Central Europeans in his term, they saluted. Even though they were concerned about expansion, they could imagine the failure of Russian reforms. The Pentagon, somewhat reluctantly, adjusted its policy and talking points to include a "hedge" against Russian regression. That didn't help with our diplomacy with the Russians.

Yet Chancellor Kohl made the same point—in private—with incisiveness and foreboding: "New waves of nationalism are mounting in Russia. Seventy years of dictatorship have left the Russians in total ignorance of the world around them. Two generations couldn't get out into the world. Russia has a surprisingly free press, but the people have no experience in forming independent judgments. Pressures are building. The Russians are frightened. This is key to Yeltsin's psychology, and it reflects his people's psychology. You can make bad politics with a people's psychology—just look at 20th century Germany."

In conclusion, Kohl said Yeltsin might not be around too long, and we need to be wary about who might come after him.

The Hard Sell

Clinton used a tour in January 1994 to European capitals—Brussels, Prague, Kyiv, and Moscow—to go public on his decision. All he said was that NATO was creating the PfP for countries to the east all the way through Central Asia, and the Alliance would bring in new members in due course. He made those announcements in Brussels (NATO's headquarters) and Prague (an eager aspirant). That way, he had already delivered the bad news when he arrived in Moscow for a high-profile, good-news event that Yeltsin was hosting: the U.S. and Russian presidents had invited their Ukrainian colleague, Leonid Kravchuk, for the signing of the "Trilateral Statement" that removed all nuclear weapons from Ukraine in exchange for assurance of Ukrainian security and sovereignty.

Once the signing was over, Clinton had a private meeting with Yeltsin in which he went into his Boris-whispering mode: the two of them were going to work together on a new-age, capacious architecture, revolutionizing European security, emphasizing cooperation, peacekeeping, and structures that would take account of Russia's legitimate interests and aspirations. Yeltsin listened intently but saved his response for the press afterward. As we headed for the crowds, Clinton whispered to me, "Uh-oh."

Yeltsin's news for the world started out upbeat and on script: the integration of former communist countries into the structures of the West was a fine objective, and Russia looked forward to being part of that process. But then he pulled a fast one: that process, of course, would culminate with a big-bang, all-together-now "integrated together, in just one package ... That's why I support the president's initiative for Partnership for Peace."

Clinton demurred gently: the Brussels summit he had attended on this trip had made clear that NATO "plainly contemplated an expansion." That, he quickly added, was for the future, while PfP was "the real thing now."

When Yeltsin came to Washington in September of 1994, Clinton had updated his step-by-step persuasion of Yeltsin: "Boris, on NATO, I want to make sure you've noted that I've never said we shouldn't consider Russia for membership or a special relationship with NATO. So, when we talk about NATO expanding, we're emphasizing *inclusion*, not exclusion. My objective is to work with you and others to maximize the chances of a truly united, undivided, integrated Europe. There will be an expansion of NATO, but there's no timetable yet. If we started tomorrow to include the countries that want to come in, it would still take several years until they qualified and others said 'yes.'

"The issue is about psychological security and a sense of importance to these countries. They're afraid of being left in a gray area or a purgatory. So, we're going to move forward on this. But I'd never spring it on you. I want to work closely with you so we get through it together. This relates to everything else. When you withdrew your troops from the Baltics, it strengthened your credibility. As I see it, NATO expansion is not anti-Russian; it's not intended to be exclusive of Russia, and there is no imminent timetable. And we'll work together. I don't want you to believe that I wake up every morning thinking only about how to make the Warsaw Pact countries a part of NATO — that's not the way I look at it. What I do think about is how to use NATO expansion to advance the broader, higher goal of European security, unity and integration—a goal I know you share."

Yeltsin was listening intently. "I understand," he said when Clinton was done. "I thank you for what you've said. If you're asked about this at the press conference, I'd suggest you say while the U.S. is for the expansion of NATO, the process will be gradual and lengthy. If you're asked if you'd exclude Russia from NATO, your answer should be 'no.' That's all."

Just to be sure that Yeltsin understood, Clinton promised him that U.S. policy would be guided by the motto, "the three no's": no surprises, no rush and no exclusion."

That evening, during a reception and dinner at the Russian embassy, Yeltsin pronounced himself delighted with the working lunch and asked Clinton, as a personal favor, to attend the annual summit of the Conference on Security and Cooperation in Europe (CSCE) in early December in Budapest. Especially given how the day had gone, Clinton said "if it matters to you, Boris," and "if there's important business to do."

Sometimes a good deed does get punished. As promised, Clinton flew all night to Budapest for an event where he had no real role other than keeping close to his friend. Yeltsin, however, used the opportunity to throw a temper tantrum, excoriating the United States for throwing its weight around. What seemed to have sent Yeltsin into a tirade was the conflict in Bosnia. NATO's use of force in Bosnia was its first time going into combat in its existence. The Alliance that had been created to defend Western Europe from the Soviet Union and the Warsaw Pact was, with the Cold War over, stopping the first genocide in Europe since the Holocaust. For many Russians, however, Western forces were killing their fellow Orthodox Slavs. The headline out of the busted summit was Yeltsin's warning that the world was "in danger of plunging into a cold peace."

On Air Force One heading home, bleary-eyed and after letting off some steam, Clinton turned forgiving and philosophical. "I can't stay mad at Boris for too long," he said. "He's got a tough row to hoe." Clinton mused a bit about Yeltsin's quote of the day: "You know," he said, "I've been thinking about that 'cold peace' line of his. If that's what we end up with, it ain't great, but it sure beats the alternative."

Those of us on the Russia beat read into Yeltsin's outburst an omen: his heroic efforts to maintain Russia's partnership with the United States and its Allies might get increasingly difficult as long as NATO was at war in the Balkans.

Fortunately, that didn't happen in 1995. U.S. and Russian diplomats were collaborating in the Dayton Talks on peace in Bosnia that would produce an agreement at the end of the year.

Clinton, in Moscow for V-E Day in May, persuaded Yeltsin to begin a NATO-Russia dialogue and join the Partnership for Peace. That was an important step for developing a NATO-Russia relationship in parallel with NATO enlargement. In the fall, the two presidents met at Hyde Park, New York, and agreed on the terms of Russia's participation alongside NATO for keeping the peace in Bosnia. Secretary Perry and Minister Grachev worked out an agreement that a Russian unit would operate under U.S. command, not the four-letter word.

The Endgame

A partial hiatus settled in 1996 so that Yeltsin could get himself re-elected without too much ruction and criticism over the four-letter word. (It was also the year that Yeltsin underwent quintuple bypass heart surgery while Clinton was winning his own second term.) With that stressful year behind them, they returned in 1997 to important, delicate, and—for Yeltsin, painful— issues.

The knottiest was the eligibility of the Baltic states for NATO membership. Lennart Meri was unmerciful and passionate on that issue. When it was clear that Estonia, along with Latvia and Lithuania, were not going to be in the first tranche of inductees, he went after me with vengeance. When dealing with him—which meant reiterating our commitment to the Baltics and being pelted with skepticism—he made me think of an Old Testament prophet who, unlike Moses, was determined to not just see the Promised Land in the distance but settle there for the rest of his life. He showed up in numerous cities where the negotiations were going on, stalking me just so I knew that there would be hell to pay if, as he put it, "my country is Yalta-ed."

Exactly the opposite happened. Rather than being sacrificed to Moscow and Stalin like Central Europeans were at Yalta, the Baltics were Helsinki-ed by Clinton and Yeltsin. The venue of one of their most suspenseful and consequential meetings was in the Finnish capital, hosted by President Martti Ahtisaari in March 1997. (By appropriate chance, the Finns and Estonians are relatives, with similar languages.)

Clinton was in a cast and on crutches from a knee injury several days before. "Still," he said, "I'm going into this meeting with a lot more mobility than ol' Boris. We've got to use this thing to get him comfortable with what he's got to do on NATO."

Clinton was armed with good news about a target date for Russian accession to the World Trade Organization and using the Denver summit in June to "look and feel more like a G-8 than a G-7." He told the team in a huddle on the plane, "It's real simple. As we push ol' Boris to do the right but hard thing on NATO, I want him to feel the warm, beckoning glow of doors that are opening other institutions where he's welcome. Got it, people?"

The welcome dinner was ominous. Yeltsin was distracted, and polished off four glasses of wine and a glass of champagne. Afterward, Clinton said "It's no good." "Every time I see him I get the feeling that it's part of my job to remind him that the world really is counting on him and he can't go into the tank on us."

During a strategy session with Clinton, Madeleine Albright, who became Secretary of State in 1997, and Sandy Berger, the national security advisor, I started to suggest some talking points about the Baltic states, but Clinton didn't need either a script or a rehearsal.

The next morning, in a private meeting, Yeltsin seized the initiative: "The Helsinki Summit has got strategic significance not only for our two countries but for Europe and the world. It's important so that in the future we won't look back and say we returned to the cold war. Sliding backward is simply not acceptable...We were both voted into office for second terms, until the year 2000; neither of us will have a third term. We want to move into the 21st century with stability and tranquility... Our position has not changed. It remains a mistake for NATO to move eastward. But I need to take steps to alleviate the negative consequences of this for Russia. I am prepared to enter into an agreement with NATO, not because I want to but because it's a step I'm compelled to take. There is no other solution for today."

He had only one condition: Clinton had to promise that NATO would not "embrace" the Baltics. He proposed that they reach "an oral agreement—we won't write it down. This would be a gentlemen's agreement that won't be made public."

Clinton, looking relaxed, passed over the bizarre suggestion. Instead, he painted a rosy picture of a grand signing ceremony for the NATO-Russia charter: "You and I will be there to say to the world that there really is a new NATO and there really is a new Russia."

"I agree," said Yeltsin.

"Good," said Clinton. "But I want you to imagine something else. If we were to agree that no members of the former Soviet Union could enter NATO, that would be a bad thing for our attempt to build a new NATO. It would also be a bad thing for your attempt to build a new Russia. I am not naïve. I understand you have an interest in who gets into NATO and when. We need to make sure that all these are subjects that we can consult about as we move forward. 'Consult' means making sure that we're aware of your concerns, and that you understand our decisions and our positions and our thinking. But consider what a terrible message it would send if we were to make the kind of supposedly secret deal you're suggesting. First, there are no secrets in this world. Second, the message would be, 'We're still organized against Russia — but there's a line across which we won't go.' In other words, instead of creating a new NATO that helps move toward an integrated, undivided Europe, we'd have a larger NATO that's just sitting there waiting for Russia to do something bad."

"Here's why what you are proposing is bad for Russia. Russia would be saying, 'We've still got an empire, but it just can't reach as far West as it used to when we had the Warsaw Pact.' Second, it would create exactly the fear among the Baltics and others that you're trying to allay and that you're denying is justified."

"A third point: the deal you're suggesting would totally undermine the Partnership for Peace. It would terrify the smaller countries that are now working well with you and with us in Bosnia and elsewhere. Consider our hosts here in Finland. President Ahtisaari told me last night that we're doing the right thing in the attitude we're taking toward the future of enlargement. He said that Finland hasn't asked to be in NATO, and as long as no one tells Finland it can't join NATO, then Finland will be able to maintain the independence of its position and work with PfP and with the U.S. and with Russia."

"I've been repeating that I'd leave open the possibility of Russia in NATO and in any event of having a steadily improving partnership between NATO and Russia. I think we'll have to continue to work this issue, but we should concentrate on practical matters. However, under no circumstances should we send a signal out of this meeting that it's the same old European politics of the cold war and we're just moving the lines around a bit."

Clinton then explained that if Russia insisted on a legally binding treaty, opponents of the deal in the Senate would refuse to ratify it. Better, he said, was to settle for a political commitment of the kind the U.S. had been proposing as a charter.

"I agree," said Yeltsin.

Then Clinton circled back to Yeltsin's proposed gentlemen's agreement. He said it "would make us both look weaker, not stronger. If we made the agreement you're describing it would be a terrible mistake. It would cause big problems for me and big problems for you. It would accentuate the diminishment of your power from Warsaw Pact times. The charter will be a much more powerful and positive message. It's without precedent, it's comprehensive, and it's forward looking, and it's hopeful. It will move us toward a situation that's good for both of us."

"Bill," said Yeltsin, "I agree with what you've said. But look at it from my standpoint. Whatever you do on your side, we intend to submit this document to the Duma for ratification. But the Duma will take two decisions. First, it will ratify the document, then it will attach a condition that if NATO takes in even one of the former republics of the Soviet Union, Russia will pull out of the agreement and consider it null and void. That will happen unless you tell me today, one-on-one — without even our closest aides present — that you won't take new republics in the near future. I need to hear that. I understand that maybe in ten years or something, the situation might change, but not now. Maybe there will be a later evolution. But I need assurances from you that it won't happen in the nearest future."

"Come on, Boris," said Clinton, "if I went into a closet with you and told you what you wanted to hear, the Congress would find out and pass a resolution invalidating the NATO-Russia charter. Frankly, I'd rather that the Duma pass a resolution conditioning its adherence on this point. I'd hate for the Duma to do that, but it would be better than what you're suggesting. I just can't do it. A private commitment would be the same as a public one. I've told you — and you have talked to Helmut [Kohl] and Jacques [Chirac], you know their thinking — that no one is talking about a massive, all-out, accelerated expansion. We've already demonstrated our ability to move deliberately, openly. But I can't make commitments on behalf of NATO, and I'm not going to be in the position myself of vetoing any country's eligibility for NATO, much less letting you or anyone else do so. I'm prepared to work with you on the consultative mechanism to make sure that we take account of Russia's concerns as we move forward."

"Another reason why I feel so strongly: look at Bosnia. That's the worst conflict in Europe since World War II. The Europeans couldn't solve it. The U.S. was finally able to take an initiative there, and Russia came in and helped. It took me years to build support. What if, sometime in the future, another Bosnia arises? If the NATO-Russia understanding is done right, then Russia would be a key part of the solution, working with the U.S. and Europe. But if we create a smaller version of the larger standoff that existed during the cold war, there won't be the needed trust. This process of integrating Europe is going to take years. We need to build up the OSCE. It's not going to happen overnight. But if we make a statement now that narrows our options in the future, it will be harder to do the other good things we want to do."

"I know what a terrible problem this is for you, but I can't make the specific commitment you are asking for. It would violate the whole spirit of NATO. I've always tried to build you up and never undermine you. I'd feel I had dishonored my commitment to the alliance, to the states that want to join NATO, and to the vision that I think you and I share of an undivided Europe with Russia as a major part of it."

Yeltsin, looking glum, went to his second fallback: "Okay, but let's agree—one-on-one—that the former Soviet republics won't be in the first waves. Bill, please understand what I'm dealing with there: I'm flying back to Russia with a very heavy burden on my shoulders. It will be difficult for me to go home and not seem to have accepted NATO enlargement. Very difficult."

"Look, Boris, you're forcing an issue that doesn't need to drive a wedge between us here. NATO operates by consensus. If you decided to be in NATO, you'd probably want all the other countries to be eligible too. But that issue doesn't arise. We need to find a solution to a short-term problem that doesn't create a long-term problem by keeping alive old stereotypes about you and your intentions. If we do the wrong thing, it will erode our own position about the kind of Europe we want. I hear your message. But your suggestion is not the way to do it. I don't want to do anything that makes it seem like the old Russia and the old NATO."

"Well," Yelstin said, "I tried."

That afternoon, at Clinton's gentle insistence, he and Yeltsin reviewed how they would handle the press conference. Sandy Berger played a journalist throwing nasty questions at the two presidents. One was, "Have you made any secret deals here in Helsinki?" (That was the fear of Lennart Meri and the other Baltic presidents.)

With a rueful smile, Yeltsin said, "My answer will be: 'We wanted one, but we were rejected.'"

Yevgeny Primakov, Kozyrev's droll but canny successor as foreign minister, remarked, "Perhaps we should have one secret deal, and that's to make Madeleine the next secretary general of NATO."

As the two presidents got up to go face the press, Yeltsin grabbed Clinton by the hand, pumped it and said, "Bill, we have done powerful work."

The way was open for a ceremony to activate the NATO-Russia Founding Act in Paris in May. The atmosphere among the sixteen Allied leaders, the president of Russia, and Javier Solana, the NATO secretary-general, was, on the surface, upbeat. But there was a touch of forced solemnity, and Yeltsin seemed strained. When he signed the document, he first took a huge breath, wrote his name with a flourish, then gave Solana a bear hug and a big kiss on both cheeks.

Clinton had already done his heavy lifting in Helsinki—and so did Yeltsin—clearing the way for a Madrid summit that would begin the process of admitting the Czech Republic, Hungary, and Poland as NATO allies in 1999 and holding the door open for other Central European applicants, including the Baltic states, in the years to come.

Epilogue

The 50th anniversary of NATO, in late April 1999, was held under a cloud. NATO was bombing Serbia because Slobodan Milošević was committing genocide in Kosovo. Clinton had hoped that Yeltsin would come for the event, but Yeltsin could not possibly attend under the circumstances. The theory going around Moscow was that NATO was using the conflict between Serbia and Kosovo as a trial run for a future war when the Alliance would separate Chechnya from Russia.

On the last day of the NATO summit, Yeltsin had a telephone conversation with Clinton. There were forces in the Duma and the military, he said, that were agitating to send a flotilla into the Mediterranean in a show of support for Serbia, and to provide arms to Belgrade, including anti-aircraft systems that would endanger NATO pilots. Yeltsin told Clinton he had already fired one commander in the Far East who was trying to mount a battalion to go to Serbia.

Yeltsin had two suggestions, one of which sounded like a demand. The easy first was to make Victor Chernomyrdin the delegate in the diplomacy over Yugoslavia. Chernomyrdin was one of Yeltsin's several former prime ministers who had a productive relationship with Vice President Al Gore.

Then came Yeltsin's plea for a bombing pause. That was neither wise nor possible. The Allies at the meeting had just set firm conditions for a pause, and until Milošević met those, the bombing would continue.

Yeltsin exploded. "Don't push Russia into this war! You know what Russia is! You know what it has at its disposal! Don't push Russia into this!"

When Clinton heard the translation, he pursed his lips and furrowed his brow. He decided not to respond to what had come close to being a warning of the danger of nuclear war between the United States and Russia. Instead, Clinton chose to reiterate, in as positive a fashion as possible, the conditions for what Yeltsin wanted. The call, he said, had been helpful because it had "clarified" what would have to happen to bring about the pause. Clinton promised that Gore would call Chernomyrdin right away, and he would send me to Moscow to serve as a point of initial contact for the new U.S.-Russian initiative.

Suddenly soothed, Yeltsin pronounced himself satisfied: "I think our discussion was candid, constructive and balanced. We didn't let our emotions get in the way, even if I was a little more talkative than you."

"Goodbye, friend," said Clinton, relieved to be able to end the conversation on that note. "I'll see you."

Of all Clinton's conversations—face-to-face, or over the phone—this was the most dramatic of all. In a matter of minutes, the Russian president was warning the American president that they were at the brink of war, then agreeing to a U.S.-Russian diplomatic channel to deal with Milošević.

Chernomyrdin teamed up with President Martti Ahtisaari of Finland, representing the European Union, and myself, representing NATO. In the ensuing weeks, Chernomyrdin and Ahtisaari pounded Milošević into submission. Neither Ahtisaari nor Chernomyrdin were citizens of NATO countries, but both of them hewed the NATO line. Milošević hoped that Russia would protect him in the international community, but Chernomyrdin convinced him otherwise. The two envoys had brought a document of capitulation, and Milošević finally accepted it.

The bombing stopped. An international force, including NATO and Russian units, moved into Kosovo. Milošević, guilty of crimes again humanity, died in a prison cell in The Hague.

The bottom line: NATO had gone nearly 50 years never firing a shot or dropping a bomb in combat. Those munitions had been saved for the Soviet Army and its Warsaw Pact allies during the bad old days. NATO saw combat for the first time in the Balkans. Its presence there elided into a peacekeeping mission when and how it did because of the crucial and courageous role of Yeltsin.

There was irony in tragedy. His opponents used the episode to help advance their campaign to ruin his vision for Russia, and their champion would be Yeltsin's handpicked successor.

Notes

1. Gorbachev first used the word *partnerstvo* to an American official in a meeting with Reagan's Chairman of the Chiefs of Staff, Admiral William Crowe, on June 21, 1989. See Michael R. Beschloss's and my book *At the Highest Levels: The Inside of the End of the Cold War* (Boston: Little Brown, 1993), p. 83.

2. Most of the quotations from Clinton, Yeltsin, and others in this chapter are taken from my research and notes from my eight years at the State Department and from my book, *The Russia Hand: A Memoir of Presidential Diplomacy* (New York: Random House, 2002).

3. Ronald Reagan came into office with Leonid Brezhnev on the other side of the hot line. George H. W. Bush in his early months in the Oval Office was cautious about embracing Gorbachev. Bush ordered what came to be known as the "pause" to make sure Reagan hadn't leaned too far toward trust rather than verification. A factor was skepticism from Bush's secretary of defense, Dick Cheney. During that time, Gorbachev was in despair that he had lost a friend in the White House. Bush was known in Moscow for attending funerals for Gorbachev's predecessors—Brezhnev, Yuli Andropov, and Konstantin Chernenko. An intimate of Gorbachev told me on a visit to Moscow that Gorbachev mordantly suggested that Bush's *pauza* was a signal that he was waiting for yet another funeral, "either physical or political." Fortunately, Bush threw himself into efforts to help Gorbachev.

4. See Andrei Kozyrev's chapter for more on this episode.

5. The right of any country to choose its security arrangements was a principle to which Russia had already subscribed in several international covenants, such as the 1975 Helsinki Final Act of the CSCE charter, which allows each state "to define and conduct as it wishes its relations with other States in accordance with international law." Gorbachev had used the same formulation in May 1990 when he agreed that a unified Germany should be allowed to choose its own alliances, opening the door for its membership in NATO. See also Ronald Asmus, *Opening NATO's Door* (New York: Columbia University Press, 2002), pp. 37-40.

Chapter 18

Present at the Transformation: An Insider's Reflection on NATO Enlargement, NATO-Russia Relations, and Where We Go from Here

Alexander Vershbow

It's now twenty years since NATO's first post-Cold War enlargement when Poland, Hungary and the Czech Republic became the 17th, 18th and 19th members of the Alliance in March 1999. This began a process that has added a total of 13 new democracies from Central and Eastern Europe to NATO's ranks, with Northern Macedonia set to become the 30th member in 2019.

NATO enlargement was only one dimension of U.S. and NATO policy at the end of the Cold War aimed at consolidating peace and security across Europe, overcoming the division of the continent imposed by Stalin at the end of World War II and ratified at the 1945 Yalta Summit. The enlargement of NATO membership went hand in hand with the forging of a strategic partnership with Russia, formalized in the NATO-Russia Founding Act of 1997. A transformed NATO Alliance and an institutionalized NATO-Russia partnership were envisaged as the main pillars of a U.S.-led pan-European security system that sought to realize the vision of a Europe whole, free and at peace first articulated by President George H.W. Bush and reaffirmed by President Bill Clinton.

The ensuing twenty years have witnessed a lot of second-guessing about the wisdom of the decision to open NATO to the East, with more and more critics arguing that it was the "original sin" that led to the confrontational relationship with Moscow that we are dealing with today. As a participant in developing and implementing NATO's enlargement strategy, I remain convinced that it was the right thing to do in rectifying the injustices of Yalta and setting Europe's East firmly on the path of democracy and reform, rather than consigning these countries to a gray zone of instability and disintegration. At the same time, the United States and its Allies went the extra mile to demonstrate to Moscow that NATO enlargement posed no military threat to Russia and to establish a framework for NATO-Russia consultations and co-operation that is still functioning today.

In saying this, I don't deny that the West may have missed some opportunities over the years to cement a long-term partnership with Russia. We may have underestimated the psychological impact on the Russian people of the collapse of the Warsaw Pact in 1989 and the break-up of the USSR in 1991, the economic collapse during the 1990s, and the perception that the West no longer saw Russia as an important power.

But we shouldn't buy the false historical narrative the Russians have been peddling in recent years about how we deliberately took advantage of Russia after the end of the Cold War, how we sought to weaken or marginalize Moscow or allegedly encircled the country with NATO military bases poised for surprise attack. Nor should we dignify Putin's claims that we are trying to organize a people's revolution in Russia aimed at toppling his regime (as we supposedly did on Georgia and Ukraine).

The record shows that, in fact, the United States and its Allies made an extraordinary effort to reach out to Russia as a partner—and even as an ally—after the end of the Cold War and achieved a lot in the years until 2014. In the NATO-Russia Founding Act, NATO made unilateral commitments—still in effect today—to limit its deployment of nuclear weapons and combat forces on the territory of new members. These demonstrated that an enlarged NATO would not pose a military threat to Russia. Other factors played a larger role than NATO enlargement in the breakdown of the West's relations with Moscow that culminated in Russia's 2014 invasion of Ukraine.

The goal of an integrated European security system, with a prominent place for Russia, remains the right one, although it has never seemed as distant as it does today. Applying the lessons learned during the first round of NATO enlargement may help us in halting the further deterioration of the West's ties with Moscow and returning relations to the path of cooperation and partnership that both sides chose in the 1990s.

Hopes and Fears as the Cold War Ended

It is important to remember the historical context in which the NATO enlargement debate emerged. When the Berlin Wall fell in November 1989, I was serving as the Director of Soviet Union Affairs at the State Department. U.S.-Soviet relations had begun to change with the arrival of Mikhail Gorbachev and his turn to reformist policies epitomized by the policies of *glasnost* and *perestroika*. In those days, we only joked about the Soviet Union reconciling with its arch-enemy, the North Atlantic Treaty Organization. In December 1989, the invitation to the Soviet Desk's annual Christmas party had on its cover a cartoon depicting me on the phone with Soviet Ambassador Yuri Dubinin asking: "Let me get this straight, Mr. Ambassador. The Soviet Union doesn't want to destroy NATO, it wants to join it?!"

Merely two years later, however, as the new U.S. Deputy Permanent Representative to NATO, I attended the first Foreign Ministers' meeting of the new North Atlantic Cooperation Council (NACC) in Brussels in December 1991. The NACC was the first body established by NATO for consultations with its former Cold War adversaries. During the meeting's final moments, Soviet Ambassador Nikolay Afanasievsky announced that he couldn't sign the communique, because his country had ceased to exist. He had just learned that the Presidents of Russia, Ukraine and Belarus had signed the Belovezha Accords dissolving the USSR. Jaws dropped when, a few minutes later, the Chairman, NATO Secretary General Manfred Wörner, read out a telegram from President Boris Yeltsin declaring that the newly independent Russian Federation was interested in joining NATO.

This episode only confirmed that the glacial, predictable course of events that characterized the Cold War was a thing of the past. Indeed, history had gone into fast-forward mode—for better and for worse. The dissolution of the Warsaw Pact, the peaceful unification of Germany within NATO, the emergence of democracy and civil society in Central and Eastern Europe and the dissolution of the Soviet Union itself were mostly good news. But we were also confronted with the tumultuous and violent disintegration of the former Yugoslavia, the Armenian-Azerbaijani war over Nagorno-Karabakh, separatist movements in parts of Georgia and Moldova, and upheavals inside Russia itself, including the failed coup against Gorbachev in August 1991. That and subsequent dramatic events, such as the shelling of the Russian White House in 1993 and the first Chechen War beginning in 1994, showed that the turn toward reform and democracy was far from irreversible.

All these events made clear that we no longer had the luxury of standing on the sidelines and taking a passive, "wait and see" approach, simply reacting to events. Our shared interests with our traditional allies, and our shared values with the forces for change in Europe's East, demanded that we engage fully and seek to shape events in a pro-active way.

Some suggested that, with the disappearance of the threat of large-scale aggression, NATO had fulfilled its purpose and could go out of business like the Warsaw Pact. But U.S. and Allied leaders recognized that Europe was still a dangerous place. The consolidation of democracy in Central and Eastern Europe and in the former Soviet Union was far from assured. Instability in the Balkans and elsewhere along NATO's periphery suggested that the mission of the Alliance needed to evolve to meet changing circumstances. And the peoples of Central and Eastern Europe themselves were desperately keen to join Western institutions as they sought to consolidate their own transformations, escape the shadow of Soviet domination, and rejoin the European mainstream.

Rather than focusing solely on defense of NATO territory, the United States and its Allies agreed that NATO would need to go "out of area" in two ways: to reach out to its former adversaries to help them consolidate their reforms and avoid regional instability; and to use NATO's military power when necessary to deal with threats when prevention failed. Rather than just defending its borders, NATO would need to "project stability" beyond its borders—still a key part of NATO's mission today, even as collective defense has become job #1 once again in the face of Putin's aggression.

First Steps

The first steps in this direction were taken by the George H.W. Bush Administration, which spearheaded the review of NATO's Strategic Concept in 1991 and proposed the creation of the North Atlantic

Cooperation Council in 1991. President Bill Clinton, upon taking office in 1993, called for an early NATO Summit to build on these initial steps. It was in that year that the debate within the Administration, and within the Alliance heated up, as has been chronicled by James Goldgeier and the late Ron Asmus.[1]

The 1994 Brussels Summit launched the Partnership for Peace (PfP), the highly successful program that gave an operational dimension to NATO's interaction with Soviet bloc states and other interested parties, including neutral Sweden, Finland, Austria and Switzerland. It offered participation in NATO training, assistance with defense reforms and guidance on achieving interoperability and standardization with NATO, creating a set of partners that could operate with NATO in future peacekeeping missions. It was promoted by its authors at the Department of Defense as an alternative to NATO enlargement that would enable us to put off the admission of new members until the end of the decade. It was welcomed by Russia in that light, with President Yeltsin telling Secretary of State Christopher, when he first presented the PfP proposal, that it was a "work of genius."[2] As former Foreign Minister Andrei Kozyrev recounts elsewhere in this volume, Yeltsin deliberately ignored the other half of Christopher's message, that NATO was going to admit new members, if not immediately, then in the medium term.

In any event, it became clear immediately after the Brussels Summit that President Clinton had a much more rapid timetable in mind. He declared publicly on several occasions in 1994 that the "time has come" to consider the "when and how" of NATO enlargement. He had been deeply affected by his first encounters with Václav Havel, Lech Wałęsa and other Central and East European leaders at the time of the opening of the U.S. Holocaust Memorial Museum in 1993. They convinced him that he had to seize the opportunity to embed the new democracies in Western institutions, rather than risking that they would succumb to internal instability and militant nationalism as had happened in the 1930s. Of necessity, this process would need to start with NATO, since the more extensive requirements for accession to the European Union meant that EU enlargement would proceed at a much slower pace than NATO enlargement.

From Partnership to Membership ... and NATO-Russia Partnership

I joined the NSC Staff in June 1994 as Special Assistant to the President and Senior Director for Europe. I had been hired by National Security advisor Tony Lake, in part, because I was as forward-leaning as he and President Clinton on NATO enlargement. During the year before, when I was serving at the State Department as Principal Deputy Assistant Secretary for Europe, he also discovered I was a kindred spirit when it came to using NATO airpower in the service of diplomacy to end the war in Bosnia-Herzegovina.

With Lake's encouragement, and working as part of the self-styled NSC Troika with Daniel Fried, Senior Director for Central and Eastern Europe, and Nick Burns, Senior Director for Russia and Eurasia, we set to work on developing a strategy for achieving the President's vision. By the fall of 1994, the Troika had developed a roadmap entitled "Moving Toward NATO Expansion."[3] This short paper served as the vehicle for gaining interagency consensus. It became the blueprint for efforts led by the State Department to build a consensus within NATO, described by Daniel Hamilton in Chapter 1 of this volume.

The paper laid out the goals, rationale and timeline for a two-track strategy: on track 1, a process leading to an expanded NATO; and on track 2, a parallel process leading to an institutionalized partnership with Russia. The objectives were defined as follows:

- An integrated and inclusive security system for Europe, including but going beyond NATO expansion, while ensuring a prominent place for a democratic Russia.

- In the medium term, an expanded NATO, including the major Central and East European states who live up to our precepts, with the prospect of further expansion to others down the road.

- In parallel, an institutionalized relationship between NATO and Russia, which could take the form of a charter or treaty (an "alliance with the Alliance"). It should include a mechanism for consulting with Russia on NATO-led military operations and other subjects, but without giving Russians a veto over NATO decisions.

- The possibility of NATO membership for Ukraine and the Baltic States would be maintained; they should not be consigned to a gray zone or a Russian sphere of influence.

- New members would acquire all the rights and responsibilities of current members (full Article 5 guarantee) and would commit to eventual full integration in NATO's military structures. Full integration would not be required at the outset, however, and there would be flexibility on operational issues such as stationing of foreign forces.

- NATO enlargement would take place in coordination with the enlargement of the EU but would not be delayed to match the EU's likely slower timetable.

The rationale was set forth in these terms:

- To extend stability eastward and underpin the democratic reform process in Central and Eastern Europe, we needed to create a perspective that Partnership for Peace will lead to NATO membership for some PfP members.

- To make sure that enlargement was not seen as directed against any country, the process would need to be developed in parallel with a long-term strategy toward Russia that included intensified partnership with NATO and development of other institutions (CSCE/OSCE, G-8).

- The enlargement process would be evolutionary and merit-based. It would be linked to a continued, robust Partnership for Peace as the mechanism both for preparing new members and for deepening relations with countries not yet ready for, or interested in, NATO membership.

- We would downplay the "insurance policy" rationale for enlargement (i.e. as a strategic hedge against the return of a more aggressive Russia).

- Indeed, the possibility of membership in the long term for a democratic Russia should not be ruled out explicitly—although this position, while supported by President Clinton in his talks with President Yeltsin, was not accepted by many Allies or by some parts of the U.S. government.

The criteria for membership would not be overly specific, in contrast with the criteria for EU membership. There would not be an explicit checklist of military requirements; the focus would be on general precepts—democracy, market economy, responsible/good-neighborly security policies. On the military side, the general goal would be interoperability with NATO forces, with the precise standards to be refined as PfP evolved.

In terms of timing, the expectation was that the first explicit NATO decision to invite new members would be taken no sooner than the first half of Clinton's second term (1997 or 1998), which would allow time for building consensus inside NATO, improving the readiness of candidates via PfP, and, most importantly, working with the Russians on a NATO-Russia institutional relationship. In the meantime, we would avoid speculating on which countries were likely to be included or excluded from the first round.

Implementing the Roadmap

Over the next three years, the United States followed this roadmap almost to the letter, culminating in the signing of the NATO-Russia Founding Act in May 1997 and the decision to invite Poland, Hungary and the Czech Republic as the first new members at the Madrid Summit in July 1997. While some in Congress, as well as East European émigré groups, pushed for a quicker pace, the Clinton Administration's deliberate approach helped solidify Allied support and made it easier to gain Russia's acquiescence.

The process inside NATO went remarkably smoothly, thanks to the leadership of NATO Secretary General Javier Solana. During 1995, NATO conducted a Study on NATO Enlargement that forged Allied consensus on the precepts and criteria for considering new members.[4] The Study, completed in September 1995, declared that 1996 would be the year for "intensified dialogues" between aspiring members and NATO's political and military authorities. This was the process for assessing each candidate's progress on political, economic and defense reforms, improving relations with neighbors, and establishing democratic civilian control of its military.

The only drama within NATO came at the very end of the process, at the Madrid Summit itself, when France, supported by Italy, pressed unsuccessfully to add Romania to the first group of new members. They argued that this was necessary to achieve greater geographic balance—despite Romania's domestic instability. Although uncomfortable playing the "heavy," the United States rejected the French demand, but agreed to language noting Romania's progress as a face-saver for President Chirac.

Reaching agreement with Russia was far more difficult. The negotiations were complicated by the turbulence of Russian domestic politics, including Yeltsin's uphill struggle for reelection in 1996, when he faced a formidable challenge from Communist Party leader Gennadiy Zyuganov. Yeltsin was disappointed that the United States had moved quickly beyond Partnership for Peace, pressing ahead with its enlargement agenda rather than delaying the admission of new members until the end of the century. He appealed to President Clinton to slow the pace and defer any decisions until well after the 1996 Russian presidential elections.

Russian diplomats, while agreeing to the basic paradigm of a NATO-Russia charter and consultative mechanism to parallel enlargement, pressed the United States to renounce any deployment of nuclear weapons or conventional forces on the territory of new members. Yeltsin personally appealed to Clinton to rule out the possibility of membership for former Soviet republics, including the three Baltic states. These former Soviet republics were a special case, since their forcible incorporation into the Soviet Union as part of the Nazi-Soviet Pact of 1939 had never been legally recognized by the United States.

In order to get its way on these issues, Russia played hard to get when it came to joining PfP, which the United States and its Allies argued was an essential mechanism for forging NATO-Russia military-to-military cooperation. During President Clinton's visit to Moscow in May 1995, Yeltsin reluctantly agreed to sign the PfP Framework Document, more than a year after PfP's establishment. But negotiations proceeded at a glacial pace as Yeltsin fought for his political survival.

The potential for NATO-Russia cooperation got a boost from the conclusion of the Dayton Peace Agreement for Bosnia-Herzegovina in the fall of 1995. Russia, having been a participant at Dayton as a member of the Contact Group, agreed in principle at the Clinton-Yeltsin October Summit in Hyde Park, New York, to deploy peacekeepers to the NATO-led Implementation Force (IFOR). While the Russians insisted that their forces in Northern Bosnia be formally under U.S. rather than NATO tactical control, the operation showed that Russia and NATO could work together on the ground to meet post-Cold War security challenges.

The success in Bosnia gave impetus to the talks on what became the NATO-Russia Founding Act, which began in earnest after Yeltsin's 1996 reelection (a victory secured thanks to extensive U.S. and German support, both political and financial). While the official negotiations were headed by NATO Secretary General Javier Solana, it quickly became apparent that the Russians preferred to address the most sensitive issues bilaterally. With a NATO Summit scheduled for July 1997 to take the first decisions on enlargement, time was of the essence. Success was achieved thanks to the high-level engagement by newly appointed U.S. Secretary of State Madeleine Albright and U.S. Deputy Secretary Strobe Talbott with Foreign Minister Yevgeny Primakov, as well as direct engagement by President Clinton himself.[5]

Getting to Yes with Russia

Albright and Talbott formed a "flying squad" of senior U.S. officials and experts to tackle the issues one-by-one with Russian leaders, in close coordination with Solana and the NATO Allies. I was proud to be part of the team as NSC Senior Director. My experience as a former Deputy Ambassador to NATO helped me to come up with creative solutions to address Russian concerns without crossing any U.S. or NATO redlines.

We managed to address the first of Russia's concerns in December 1996, with the NATO Allies' decision that they had "no intention, no plan and no reason to deploy nuclear weapons on the territory of new members"—a unilateral commitment known as the "Three No's."[6] The Russians pressed for additional specificity that was ultimately reflected in the NATO-Russia Founding Act: "This subsumes the fact that NATO has decided that it has no intention, no plan, and no reason to establish nuclear weapon storage sites on the territory of those members, whether through the construction of new nuclear storage facilities or the adaptation of old nuclear storage facilities."

There were critics of the Three No's, both in the United States and in Central and Eastern Europe, who argued that the new Allies should have the same rights and responsibilities as older Allies and not be singularized. But given the dramatically reduced threat since the break-up of the Soviet Union, Allies considered this to be a cost-free gesture.

The United States and the other Allies did, however, reject Russia's demand for a similar ban on the stationing of conventional forces on the territory of new members. In this case, they agreed that a total ban would render new members "second-class allies" and reduce NATO's ability to defend them under Article 5. But considering the virtual disappearance of a credible Russian threat of aggression against Allies in Europe, NATO did not see the need for a large U.S. conventional deterrent presence as had been maintained along the inner-German border throughout the Cold War. Defense and deterrence could be carried out via reinforcement rather than permanent stationing. How to reflect this without limiting NATO's flexibility in the longer term was the challenge.

During one of the flying squad's consultations with Secretary General Solana in Brussels in early 1997, I scribbled a sentence aimed at articulating NATO policy along these lines. Known as the "sentence from hell," this proposal, with minor modifications, became the NATO policy on stationed forces that was announced on March 14, 1997: "In the current and foreseeable security environment, the Alliance will carry out its collective defense and other missions by ensuring the necessary interoperability, integration and capability for reinforcement rather than by additional permanent stationing of substantial combat forces."[7]

Although the security environment has changed dramatically since 1997 and Russia has violated many of its commitments under the Founding Act, the March 1997 statement continues to guide NATO decision-making, including on the scale of its enhanced Forward Presence battalions deployed in Poland and the Baltic states since 2017. If the Russian threat continues to grow, however, NATO may have no choice but to jettison this element of the NATO-Russia Founding Act and deploy much larger forces and strategic enablers along the Eastern flank.

Russia was generally satisfied with the "sentence from hell" when it was presented by the "flying squad." Although Allies refused to be more specific about the meaning of "substantial combat forces," they did agree to clarifications requested by Primakov in the Founding Act on the conditions in which reinforcement could take place: "In this context, reinforcement may take place, when necessary, in the event of defense against a threat of aggression and missions in support of peace consistent with the United Nations Charter and the OSCE governing principles, as well as for exercises consistent with the adapted CFE Treaty, the provisions of the Vienna Document 1994 and mutually agreed transparency measures." For their part, Allies underscored that there was a trade-off: by foregoing large stationed forces, NATO would need infrastructure to support reinforcement.[8] Russia conveniently forgets this point when complaining nowadays about NATO's (still modest) infrastructure on the territory of new members.

President Clinton personally rebuffed Yeltsin's persistent demands that NATO renounce the possibility of membership for former Soviet republics. At their Summit in Helsinki in March 1997, Clinton argued that the West did not recognize the Baltic states as having been legitimately part of the USSR, and that we could not in any case rule out any sovereign country's right to join an alliance; this was a basic principle of the 1975 Helsinki Final Act that Russia had long accepted, and it had been reaffirmed in the Paris Charter of 1990. Clinton also argued that ruling out the Baltic states or Ukraine would mean foreclosing the possibility of Russian membership in the long term—a point important to Yeltsin who, despite various zig-zags, still believed in Russia's Western trajectory. That settled it with Yeltsin, at least with respect to keeping NATO's door open to the Baltic states. But the issue would return with a vengeance eleven years later, when Ukraine's and Georgia's pro-Western leaders pushed to join NATO's Membership Action Plan.

With Russia's main concerns resolved, the Founding Act was signed on May 27, 1997, and the Madrid Summit convened on July 8 to decide on the first group of nations to be invited to join the Alliance. Both tracks of the 1994 Roadmap were now complete. A few weeks later, as I prepared for my onward assignment as U.S. Ambassador to NATO, National Security Advisor Sandy Berger sent the members of the Troika a copy of the Roadmap with the comment: "One for the textbooks—a policy well-conceived, well-executed, and well-present-ed. Congratulations!"

Kosovo: The First Test to the NATO-Russia Partnership

I took up my duties as U.S. Permanent Representative on the North Atlantic Council on January 2, 1998. The Ambassadors of NATO's three invitees, Karel Kovanda of the Czech Republic, András Simo-nyi of Hungary, and Andrzej Towpik of Poland, sat to my left in the North Atlantic Council as observers pending ratification by NATO's 16 parliaments of their accession. It was exciting to work so closely with the beneficiaries of my work in opening NATO to the East. I also welcomed the chance to develop the new NATO-Russia partnership with Russian Ambassador Sergey Kislyak, who had been one of my main interlocutors during the negotiations on the Founding Act. Little did we know that, within a year, NATO would be at war again in the former Yugoslavia—this time, over Kosovo—putting both the Alliance and the NATO-Russia partnership to the test.

As a member of the Contact Group, Russia was part of the diploma-cy that sought to press Serbian President Slobodan Milošević to grant autonomy to Kosovo. Moscow refused to push Milošević to compro-mise Serbia's sovereignty and agree to an international peacekeeping force, which the Allies judged essential to ending the violence and mak-ing an autonomy deal stick. With Milošević hiding behind the Russian position, the Rambouillet negotiations broke down in failure. NATO then delivered on its threat to use force against Serbia to compel it to accept the terms it had rejected at Rambouillet.

NATO—now including Poland, Hungary and the Czech Repub-lic—acted without explicit UN Security Council authorization since Russia had made clear it would veto any resolution authorizing force. Russia responded by suspending its participation in the NATO-Russia Permanent Joint Council (PJC).

NATO-Russia cooperation survived the test of Kosovo, although the crisis left permanent scars. Even with the PJC suspended, Russia (in the person of Prime Minister Viktor Chernomyrdin) played a crucial role in the diplomacy that persuaded Milošević to back down, sparing NATO the need for a ground invasion of Serbia. After the air campaign was over, Russia quickly returned to the PJC. And Yeltsin agreed to deploy Russian troops to the NATO-led Kosovo Force (KFOR), operating again under U.S. tactical control. Russian forces remained part of the mission until 2003.

Russia Reacts Calmly to the Second Round of Enlargement

Yeltsin's successor, Vladimir Putin, saw the 9/11 terrorist attacks in New York and Washington as an opportunity to build closer ties with the West as he consolidated power at home. At a special NATO-Russia Summit in Rome in May 2002, Putin and NATO leaders signed the Declaration on "NATO-Russia Relations: A New Quality" and established the NATO-Russia Council to replace the PJC.[9] Allies and Russia launched a series of joint counter-terrorism projects and continued to develop their dialogue and cooperation on a range of subjects, including the conflict in Afghanistan, arms control, non-proliferation, theater missile defense, and civil emergency planning.

While this upgrade in NATO-Russia relations was not explicitly conceived as a counterpart to further NATO enlargement, it helped Allies manage tensions over the second round. At the Prague Summit in November 2002, Allies invited seven Central and East European states to join the Alliance, including the three Baltic states together with Bulgaria, Romania, Slovakia and Slovenia. I was Ambassador in Moscow from 2001 to 2005, and I heard few complaints about NATO expansion to the Baltic states as having crossed Russian red lines, either at the time of the Prague Summit or when the seven new members formally joined the Alliance in 2004. Putin described the further enlargement of NATO as "counterproductive" but continued to take a pragmatic approach to relations with the Alliance.

New Challenges to West-Russia Relations under Putin

Relations between the West and Russia did begin to deteriorate after 2002, but the causes were not related to NATO or NATO enlargement. The 2003 Iraq War, while conducted via a U.S.-led coalition of the willing rather than through NATO, rekindled Russian objections to operations launched without a U.N. Security Council mandate.

While Moscow had been assured that Kosovo was a one-time exception to the rules, prompted by an impending humanitarian disaster, the U.S. decision to invade Iraq and topple Saddam Hussein suggested that the United States was making it a standard practice to bypass the U.N. Security Council, nullifying Russia's veto power.

A second factor contributing to Putin's suspicions was the Bush Administration's aggressive pursuit of ballistic missile defense (BMD) of the U.S. homeland, including a "third site" with installations in Poland and the Czech Republic. I recall accompanying Secretary of State Colin Powell to the Kremlin in December 2001 to inform Putin of President George W. Bush's decision to withdraw from the 1972 ABM Treaty. Putin reacted more with sorrow than anger at the time, and Russian experts accepted U.S. assurances that U.S. BMD plans were focused on defending against limited attacks by rogue states like Iran and North Korea and did not threaten Russia's assured retaliatory capability.

As U.S. plans advanced, however, Putin became increasingly convinced that the United States was seeking to negate that retaliatory capacity by deploying interceptors close to Russia's borders, which Moscow feared could embolden the United States to carry out a preemptive first strike. The fact that the third site would not, in reality, put the Soviet strategic deterrent at risk—because of its location and the small number (10) of interceptors—did not alter Putin's perception that the United States was undermining strategic stability.

The third factor that contributed to Russia's estrangement from the West was the Rose and Orange Revolutions in Georgia (2003) and Ukraine (2004). While the West viewed both as spontaneous popular rebellions against corrupt political leaders and, in the Ukrainian case, against Russian-backed efforts to steal the election on behalf of its preferred candidate, Putin saw things in a much darker light. These "color revolutions," in his view, were special operations planned and financed by the United States aimed at undermining Russia's interests in its "near abroad." The reformist leaders' pursuit of NATO and EU membership only confirmed Russian suspicions that the West, led by the United States, was determined to tear these countries from Russia's sphere of privileged interests. (This same perception influenced Putin's harsh reaction to the Revolution of Dignity in Ukraine in 2013 and the toppling of President Viktor Yanukovych.)

Another factor affecting Putin's mistrust of the West was the wave of terrorist attacks that spread across Russia in 2002-2004. Putin seemed to see the hand of the United States rather than Chechen separatists and home-grown Islamic extremists as behind the attacks. I remember watching Putin's chilling speech after the 2004 attack on the school in Beslan, North Ossetia. Clearly pointing his finger at the West, Putin said "Some want to tear off a big chunk of our country. Others help them to do it. They help because they think that Russia, as one of the greatest nuclear powers of the world, is still a threat, and this threat has to be eliminated. And terrorism is only an instrument to achieve these goals."[10]

U.S. criticism of the arrest of oil tycoon and political opponent Mikhail Khodorkovsky in November 2003 was also seen as confirming Western support for those seeking to weaken Russia and undermine the Putin system.

In sum, by the time of his blistering, anti-Western speech to the Munich Security Conference in 2007, Putin had concluded that the West had become increasingly dismissive of Russia's interests—circumventing its UN veto, undermining its status as a nuclear superpower with ballistic missile defense, fomenting pro-Western, anti-Russian movements in Ukraine and Georgia, and supporting forces seeking to destroy Russia from within. The fact that much of this perception was based on paranoia and worst-case assessments fed to him by Russian intelligence was beside the point.

Bust-Up At Bucharest

None of these factors were the consequence of NATO enlargement. But when the Bush Administration came to the April 2008 NATO Summit in Bucharest actively supporting the inclusion of Ukraine and Georgia in the Membership Action Plan (MAP), Putin's hostile reaction should have come as no surprise. He was not assuaged by explanations that MAP was not a guarantee of membership, since invitations to begin accession talks would require a separate, political decision by the North Atlantic Council. While Allies assured him that MAP was just the start of a more intensive phase of preparation, Putin couldn't abide the symbolism—the M in MAP was the issue.

Moreover, in contrast with the strategy Washington had adopted during the earlier rounds of NATO enlargement, the United States and other supporters of MAP for Ukraine and Georgia had not developed a "Russia track" of measures to mitigate Russian concerns. Lacking a Russia strategy, President Bush and his team were unable to convince key U.S. allies to support MAP in the face of Russian objections.

The resulting deadlock among the Allies at Bucharest led to the ill-conceived and hastily drafted compromise in which NATO leaders refused MAP but declared in the Summit communique that "these countries will become members of NATO."[11] This was a far more categorical commitment than would have been the case had NATO decided only to offer MAP to Ukraine and Georgia. Whatever Allies' intentions at Bucharest, the Summit outcome contributed to Putin's decision to launch the war in Georgia four months later. With Russia's invasion and occupation of Georgian territory, Putin had effectively drawn the red line on NATO enlargement to the former Soviet Union that Yeltsin had been persuaded not to draw in 1997.

One More Try under Medvedev

After the war in Georgia, Allies suspended the work of the NATO-Russia Council for a few months, but business resumed after the "reset" in U.S.- and NATO-Russia relations in 2009. With Dmitriy Medvedev occupying the Russian Presidency, another attempt was made by NATO and Russia to develop a "true strategic partnership" at the 2010 Lisbon Summit, the last Summit attended by a Russian President.

The flagship initiative was an effort to link NATO and Russian missile defense capabilities to create a cooperative system to defense against missile attacks by rogue states. This could have been a game-changer—joining NATO and Russian capabilities to counter a real and growing common threat, and demonstrating that NATO's missile defense capabilities were not aimed at undermining Russia's strategic deterrent. As Assistant Secretary of Defense for International Security Affairs, I was part of the U.S. negotiating team that pursued a bilateral missile defense agreement in 2011 and 2012, and I supported the NATO-Russia side of the negotiations in 2012 and 2013 as Deputy Secretary General of NATO.

Although Allies put a bold proposal on the table,[12] negotiations foundered by the end of 2013. With Putin back as President, it became clear that Russia's real goal was to convince the United States and NATO to cancel their planned missile defense deployments in Romania and Poland and rely instead on a Russian "sectoral" defense of NATO territory—a total non-starter.

The Arab Spring and NATO's 2011 intervention in Libya is where NATO-Russia relations really came a cropper. When Libyan dictator Muamar Qadhafi threatened to "kill like rats" tens of thousands of pro-democracy protesters in eastern Libya, Allies decided to intervene from the air to establish a no-fly zone and protect the Libyan people. U.N. Security Council Resolution 1973 authorizing "all necessary measures"[13] passed thanks to Russian President Medvedev's decision to abstain—presumably with the concurrence of then-Prime Minister Putin.

As NATO bombing of Libyan forces escalated and Qadhafi was overthrown, Putin and other Russian leaders became convinced that NATO had exceeded that mandate. It looked again that the United States and NATO were circumventing Russia's authority as a Security Council member as they had done in Kosovo and Iraq, with NATO becoming the instrument for regime change.

What Is To Be Done?

The breakdown in the West's relations with Russia was not caused by the NATO decision in 1997 to admit new democracies from Central and Eastern Europe. Indeed, the first and second rounds of enlargement went smoothly because the Alliance—guided by creative U.S. leadership—made a concerted effort to develop a real strategic partnership with Russia. This was not meant as compensation or a consolation prize but was an effort to ensure that a democratic Russia's voice was heard in European security.

Success was also achieved because NATO made a determined effort to allay Russian concerns about the military implications of enlargement. Even after the admission of the Baltic states to NATO in 2004,

Russia continued to reduce its forces along its Western flank.[14] This reflected an understanding that NATO enlargement was primarily a political project, and that NATO was living up to its commitments in the Founding Act on non-deployment of nuclear weapons on the territory of new members and on refraining from "additional permanent stationing of substantial combat forces."

Relations between Russia and the West faced multiple challenges during President Putin's first years in office, but these were not directly related to NATO. By 2007, Russia had become increasingly resentful at the West's alleged disregard for Russia's interests and increasingly paranoid about "color revolutions" as a catalyst for regime change in the "near abroad" and in Russia itself. Together with the lack of a "Russia track" to balance NATO's MAP for Ukraine and Georgia at the Bucharest Summit in 2008, this hardened Russia's animosity toward the Alliance. Today's Russia is now ready to use force to block any former Soviet republic's path to NATO, and it has sought (albeit less successfully) to block further NATO enlargement in the Western Balkans, including an attempted coup on the eve of Montenegro's accession in 2017.

The prospects for overcoming Russian objections to Ukrainian and Georgian membership are dim as long as Vladimir Putin remains in power. For Putin, the future of Ukraine and other former Soviet republics is as much about Russian domestic politics as it is about geopolitics. Putin fears the encroachment of Western ideas far more than the approach of NATO's borders. He worries that, if Ukraine succeeds as a prosperous, democratic, pro-Western state, it will fall out of Russia's orbit, foiling Putin's neo-imperial ambitions and setting a dangerous example for the Russian people, who could be inspired to start a "color revolution" in Russia itself. Thus, to protect the Putin system at home, Putin is determined to destabilize Ukraine, make it an unattractive candidate for NATO and the EU, and discredit Western democracy more generally through interference, influence operations and information warfare.

Given this ideological dimension, the standoff between NATO and Russia cannot be easily resolved. The West and Russia have conflicting visions of European security. The United States and its allies want to restore respect for the principles of the Helsinki Final Act—sovereignty, territorial integrity, no changing of borders by force, and respect for the freedom of all states to choose their security arrangements. Russia, on the other hand, rejects these principles and wants to pressure the West into accepting some sort of Yalta 2, a Europe divided into spheres of influence with limited sovereignty for everyone but Russia, and hegemony of big powers over small states.

Until Russia itself returns to the westward path its people and leaders chose at the end of the Cold War, our differences are likely to remain profound and the relationship largely competitive. The immediate priority for NATO should be to bolster its deterrence posture and strengthen Allies' resilience against cyber-attacks and information warfare. While Russia is unlikely to engage in direct military aggression against NATO, we cannot allow any possibility that Russia could attempt a limited land grab in the Baltic states using "little green men" as it did in Crimea.

NATO should not renounce its commitment to Ukrainian and Georgian membership as a long-term goal, but we and our Allies must be frank with Kyiv and Tbilisi that membership is effectively on hold for the foreseeable future. In the meantime, acting through NATO and bilaterally, we should use all available means to strengthen Ukraine's and Georgia's security and preserve their independence short of providing security guarantees, even as we hold their feet to the fire on reforms and the fight against corruption. A prosperous, democratic Ukraine and a prosperous, democratic Georgia may be the best counterweight to Russian aggression in the long run, but training and equipping these countries' armed forces with defensive weapons, and boosting their resilience against cyber-attacks and hybrid warfare, are also essential to help them defend themselves and prevent further Russian aggression.

As for the future of NATO-Russia relations, a return to partnership is out of the question as long as Russia is flouting the principles it pledged to uphold in the Helsinki Final Act and the NATO-Russia Founding Act. The litmus test for any return to normal business (and for any lifting of sanctions) must remain an end to Russian aggression in eastern Ukraine and withdrawal of its forces in accordance with the Minsk agreements. Until then, the United States and its Allies should focus their dialogue with Moscow on ways to reduce the risk of incidents between NATO and Russia from escalating to an unintended conflict and to increase transparency and predictability of our military activities.

Conclusion

Our vision of a Europe whole, free and at peace will remain incomplete as long as relations with Russia remain competitive and as long as Moscow seeks to deny its neighbors the right to choose their own future. But that should not diminish our pride in the progress we have made since the 1990s in enlarging the community of democratic nations committed to ensuring one another's security and united by the values of democracy, liberty and the rule of law. NATO's Open Door remains the right policy to encourage all of Europe's democracies to follow the path pioneered by Poland, Hungary and the Czech Republic when they joined NATO twenty years ago.

Notes

1. James M. Goldgeier, *Not Whether but When: The U.S. Decision to Enlarge NATO* (Washington, DC: Brookings Institution Press, 1999); Ronald D. Asmus, *Opening NATO's Door: How the Alliance Remade Itself for a New Era* (New York: Columbia University Press, 2004)

2. Strobe Talbott, *The Russia Hand: A Memoir of Presidential Diplomacy* (New York: Random House, 2002), p. 101

3. This summary is based on the author's personal notes and recollections.

4. North Atlantic Treaty Organization, *Study on NATO Enlargement*, https://www.nato.int/cps/en/natohq/official_texts_24733.htm.

5. See Talbott, op. cit.

6. The full decision, part of the December 10, 1996 NAC Ministerial communique, read as follows: "We reaffirm that the nuclear forces of the Allies continue to play a unique and essential role in the Alliance's strategy of war prevention. New members, who will be full members of the Alliance in all respects, will be expected to support the concept of deterrence and the essential role nuclear weapons play in the Alliances strategy. Enlarging the Alliance will not require a change in NATOs current nuclear posture and therefore, NATO countries have no intention, no plan, and no reason to deploy nuclear weapons on the territory of new members nor any need to change any aspect of NATOs nuclear posture or nuclear policy - and we do not foresee any future need to do so." https://www.nato.int/docu/pr/1996/p96-165e.htm.

7. Statement by the North Atlantic Council, March 14, 1997, https://www.nato.int/docu/pr/1997/p97-027e.htm.

8. "Accordingly, it will have to rely on adequate infrastructure commensurate with the above tasks." https://www.nato.int/cps/en/natohq/official_texts_25468.htm.

9. NATO-Russia Council Rome Summit 2002, https://www.nato.int/docu/comm/2002/0205-rome/rome-eng.pdf.

10. "Putin Tells the Russians 'We Shall Be Stronger,'" *New York Times*, September 5, 2004, https://www.nytimes.com/2004/09/05/world/europe/putin-tells-the-russians-we-shall-be-stronger.html.

11. Bucharest Summit Declaration Issued by the Heads of State and Government participating in the meeting of the North Atlantic Council in Bucharest on 3 April 2008, https://www.nato.int/cps/us/natohq/official_texts_8443.htm.

12. NATO proposed bringing NATO and Russian officers together in two centers, one to jointly monitor and provide early warning of ballistic missile attacks, the other to jointly plan and coordinate NATO and Russian missile defense operations to intercept ballistic missiles aimed at NATO or Russian territory. See author's January 2014 speech, "The Future of Missile Defense: A NATO perspective," https://www.nato.int/cps/en/natohq/opinions_106142.htm

13. United Nations, "Security Council Approves 'No-Fly Zone' over Libya, Authorizing 'All Necessary Measures' to Protect Civilians, by Vote of 10 in Favour with 5 Abstentions," March 17, 2011, https://www.un.org/press/en/2011/sc10200.doc.htm.

14. OSCE Vienna Document data for the Western Military District plus Southern Military District (formerly known as Leningrad, Moscow, and North Caucasus, Districts plus the Black Sea Fleet and Caspian Flotilla) show a steep drop in troops and equipment from 2000 to 2010, a continued but less precipitous drop from 2010 to 2014, and then an uptick 2014-present. If Russia thought NATO enlargement to be a threat, particularly the second round (2004), we would not expect to see numbers keep falling throughout the 2000s. The total reported troop numbers dropped from 236,525 in 2004 to 210,000 in 2008 to 200,000 in 2013 to 190,000 in 2014. Then shot back up to 220,000 in 2015. 216,787 were reported as of 1 January 2017). This is consistent with Battle Tanks (2004: 4000; 2009: 2720; 2013: 1063; 2017: 1264), APCs (2004: 13,000; 2009: 11,000; 2014 8,000; 2017: 8,400) and Artillery (2004: 4,278; 2010: 2,450; 2013: 1,986; 2017: 2,499). Combat aircraft and helicopter numbers were more variable. Source: NATO International Staff.

Chapter 19

Russia and NATO Enlargement:
An Insider's Account

Andrei Kozyrev

Russia versus NATO

When, led by the United States, European nations founded NATO on the principles of democracy, individual liberty and the rule of law, they made a major multinational political pivot in modern history. Parting from centuries-old efforts to gain territory and domination, they found their national interests in peaceful cooperation and prosperity. That's why emerging democracies want to join NATO. And that's why the totalitarian Soviet Union opposed it, and now authoritarian Russia along with undemocratic politicians elsewhere try to subvert it.

When in April 1992 the president of Czechoslovakia Vaclav Havel came to Moscow on an official visit, he had a brief chat with me away from the main action of the summit and explained the reason for joining NATO in his distinctive concise, simple, but insightful way: "I am not a fan of the military. We just want to join the Western democracies full-scale. Don't you?" That was the driving force behind the NATO enlargement, culminating in the first instance with the admission of Poland, Check Republic and Hungary in 1999: a process that has continued and is continuing ever since.

The Promise of the New Era

In December of 1991 the Russian Federation emerged not only as one of fifteen successor states to the collapsed USSR, but also as the continuation state that inherited membership in the U.N. Security Council and in all treaties, including Russian-American and multilateral treaties concerning nuclear weapons, most importantly in the Nonproliferation Treaty as one of the five nuclear states. America and other

Western powers helped us to achieve that outcome. But despite this Great Power status, the new Russia had to make a determined effort to overcome its isolation from the most prosperous democratic countries, which was not determined by any treaty and simply represented the bad legacy of the Soviet past. And the inherited Russian hostility towards NATO was a key political barrier on its way to join the club of great nations to which it belonged by dint of its size, economic potential, history and culture. That hostility could be removed only together with the entire Soviet heritage that reformers in the Yeltsin government tried to replace with political democracy and a socially conscious capitalism. My own credo was—and still is—that a democratic Russia would be as natural an ally of the United States and NATO as the tyrannical Soviet—or post-Soviet—system had been an enemy of the Western Alliance.

Already in December of 1991, the first popularly elected president of Russia, Boris Yeltsin, sent an open letter to the North Atlantic Coordination Council that reflected the Russian leadership's view that NATO could turn from being an aggressive military machine to an alliance of peaceful nations based on common values. "On this basis of deep reforms and common values," he wrote, Russia was eager to develop cooperation with NATO both in political and military fields. "Today we do not ask for Russian membership in NATO." But, Yeltsin's letter continued, he regarded it "as our long-term political objective."

There is a Russian saying that misfortune leads to fortune. Unfortunately, the text of the letter given to the press had a typo. The word "not" was absent. So, it read as "Today we ask for Russian membership in NATO, but regard it as our long-term objective." The next day we issued a correction. Fortunately, this drew additional attention to the meaning of the document that in essence was the same with or without "not." At that time no one except the bunch of discredited Communists challenged the concept directly. Some doubts were expressed only about the ability and good will of NATO to welcome Russia to the club.

Were we—the reformists around Yeltsin—delusional in our attempt to radically change the course of Russia? No. The mass movement representing our base was called "Democratic Russia" and we counted on a number of fundamental factors summarized below.

The Russian nation is based on European culture. Leo Tolstoy's *War and Peace* is partly written in French. The first attempt to establish a European style democracy had been undertaken in 1917 after the collapse of the tsarist rule, but it failed mostly because the provisional government inherited the backbreaking burden of World War I. When the second effort came, in 1992, the situation was radically different. No country was at war or even in conflict with Russia. Moreover, we counted on support from the West, particularly from the United States—politically, economically and strategically.

This bet was neither unprecedented nor unrealistic. Less than 50 years earlier Winston Churchill had called on the West to stand up to the challenge of the "Iron Curtain" of Stalin's domination, and America generously helped fragile democracies in Europe to survive and grow. Why couldn't similar efforts be undertaken as Russia tried to get rid of the "Iron Curtain" once and for all? It would have been not only in best interest of America and its Allies, but existentially important for them. Behind the Curtain sat a nuclear-missile force able to destroy America that also could have been demolished had democracy taken hold in Russia.

Apparently, George H.W. Bush realized that. Welcoming Yeltsin in Washington DC in June 1992, Bush said he was "totally convinced" of Russia's commitment to democracy and hoped to assist "in any way possible." He appeared to have bipartisan support. Democrat Richard A. Gephardt, the House majority leader, said that Mr. Yeltsin "delivered a loud, clear message that if there's going to be help, it needs to come now."

Yeltsin, too, was straightforward. "I didn't come here just to stretch out my hand and ask for help. No, we're calling for cooperation ... because if the reform in Russia goes under, that means there will be a cold war." Unfortunately that warning became an omen and today it's the reality.

To be sure, in 1992 tangible results were achieved in reducing the nuclear threat. The two presidents put Secretary of State Jim Baker and me in charge of that job. It was tough but rewarding, due to the professionalism, dedication and integrity of my counterpart. Not only were the numbers of nukes allowed for each party by the START II treaty 2-3 times lower than permitted by the previous START agreement, but also for first time ever Russia agreed to cut its superiority in intercontinental ballistic missiles, supposedly the most destabilizing first strike force, and the United States did the same in sea-launched ballistic missiles and strategic bombers. A political and legal international foundation was laid for preventing proliferation of Soviet nuclear weapons; over the ensuing years all were placed under control and gathered on the territory of the Russian Federation recognized as the only nuclear power among the post-Soviet states.

With regard to economic aid and assistance, however, America's contribution was much less impressive. While preparations for cooperation with Russia were in progress, President Bush was losing to Democrats in America. President Clinton was elected under the motto: "it's the economy, stupid"—by which he meant the U.S. economy. His administration promised and did help us, but mostly through programs of the International Monetary Fund. These were conditional on the reforms the government in Moscow swore to undertake. But what Russia really needed was immediate aid to set up the reforms in practical manner.

Simply put, the social cost and complexity of the reforms were too heavy a lift for the government in Moscow without commensurate Western assistance. Russian reformers were unable to provide sustained political leadership in the face of worsening pressure by reactionaries and nationalists. We failed for domestic reasons. We own historic responsibility for that. Yet, the West could have done more to prevent that failure. Soon a pattern was established of mutual financial and economic promises that were predictably unrealistic and thus politically damaging. Something of the kind followed also in the foreign policy field.

Troubled Partnership with NATO

In the early 1990s, the rapprochement of Russia with the West and integration of East European states into Western economic institutions were accepted even by hardliners in Moscow. Yet, the adversary image of NATO was—and is—the last line of their defense, as it guaranteed them a privileged position in the power structure of the "ceased fortress," whether it was called the Soviet Union or the Russian Federation.

To be sure, turning the two opposing military machines into allies was a monumental task. Yet it could be achieved. Step by step the military and security forces of democratic Russia should have become partners of their Western counterparts in fighting common enemies like rogue states, terrorists, drug-traffickers and so on. Advocating this perspective, in December 1993 I won 70% of the popular vote in a competitive election for the parliament membership in the region of Murmansk, which included the major naval base hosting the core of Russian nuclear-armed fleet.

It was clear that my solution required the radical and resolute reform of the military and security services inherited from the USSR. Yet President Yeltsin chose a KGB-associated veteran, Evgeny Primakov, to be chief of the foreign intelligence service. He also appointed other heads of military and security government bodies who were personally loyal to him but hardly zealous reformers. He argued that change was a tough process; it should be carefully controlled to maintain stability along the way. That was true, but in my view, stability should have been pursued hand-in-hand with resolute and robust action to transform the old structures.

Bearing in mind the complexity of the NATO issues, I had a confidential agreement to avoid radical public moves with Warren Christopher, U.S. Secretary of State in first term of the Clinton Administration. This was more or less similar to the kind of understandings I had with some Eastern European leaders who recognized that their desire to join NATO should be realized in stages and in consonance with Moscow. Slowly but surely, a discussion on finding a mutually acceptable solution between Russia and NATO gained steam.

Russia's Bad Surprise For America

Lech Wałęsa, the President of Poland, was not a patient person. When President Yeltsin arrived in Warsaw on a hot August day in 1993, Wałęsa invited him to a late private dinner. After midnight Yeltsin woke me up. He could hardly utter an apology for the late call and handed me a piece of paper with ragged handwriting and his signature. It was a last-minute insertion for the joint Russian-Polish declaration that had been prepared for a signature ceremony next morning. The paper endorsed Poland's aspiration to join NATO—right now.

In my heart I welcomed Yeltsin's addition. In my mind, though, I had no doubt that without any practical purpose the statement would wake up the sleeping dogs in Russia against NATO and those in Eastern Europe favoring NATO. Like all East European nations, Poland would not be ready to join NATO earlier than in a number of years. In the meantime, Russia would have to work out its cooperation with the Alliance.

Early at dawn the next morning, Defense Minister Grachev and I asked Yeltsin to have a more sober look at the matter. Then milder language was agreed with the Poles. The incident, including the "late night" formulation, leaked to the press, triggering a never-ending firework of political agitation across the spectrum of conflicting opinions and interests in Russia and elsewhere. I had to apologize to my American colleagues and other partners who were caught off guard and who had not yet given any green light to Central and Eastern European states about NATO membership.

Most importantly, as a result of this story and the leak, we all lost the ability to address the matter calmly, without politicized domestic and international pressures. Poland, the Czech Republic, and Hungary immediately demanded unambiguous responses from the United States and NATO on whether the Alliance was open to the new democracies. That amounted to an offer neither Washington nor Brussels could refuse in the long run. Jittery politicians in the West spoke of an imminent Russian threat, to the delight of NATO-fear-mongering hardliners in Russia.

Bridging the gap between Russia and NATO now became a burning task. Defense Minister Grachev visited Washington in 1993. He felt that the Pentagon was skeptical of NATO enlargement and preferred instead cooperation with Eastern Europeans and Russia through a mechanism called the Partnership for Peace (PfP). That was good news for Yeltsin, who now realized the hot nature of the problem and tried to push genie back into the bottle.

In October Secretary of State Warren Christopher came to Moscow as special envoy of the U.S. president to brief the Russian president on the new NATO policy and test his reaction. He was accompanied by Strobe Talbott, who played an important role in bridging U.S. and Russian positions. This is how Strobe describes the meeting in his book *The Russia Hand: A Memoir of Presidential Diplomacy*:

> Chris laid out our decision on NATO: we would not proceed immediately with enlargement but concentrate instead on developing the "Partnership for Peace"...Without letting Chris finish, Yeltsin spread his arms and intoned, drawing out the words, "Genialno! Zdorovo!" (Brilliant! Terrific!).

After "a brief review of other issues," the meeting was concluded. Christopher repeats this story in his memoirs. Declassified documents from U.S. and Russian archives also show that U.S. officials led Russian President Boris Yeltsin to believe in 1993 that the Partnership for Peace was the alternative to NATO expansion, rather than a precursor to it.

After leaving the meeting with Yeltsin, however, the U.S. visitors provided to me an "unabridged" message: the new policy was not *instead* of but rather a pathway *to* enlargement. Why at the meeting they switched to other issues without finishing their main presentation and clarifying the issue remained unclear to me. Allies were pleased by the news that Russia's president praised the PfP, and it was adopted as the NATO strategy. Primakov told Yeltsin that Clinton deceived him to get NATO approval and that the PfP was a trick to draw East Europeans into NATO, leaving Russia in the cold. The Russian press increasingly shared this suspicion.

Yeltsin preferred to stick to what he heard directly from Clinton's special representative and authorized me to sign up to the PfP on June 22, 1994.

America's Bad Surprise for Russia

Yeltsin then felt offended and betrayed when in December 1994 NATO approved a policy that could be summarized in a simple formula: the PfP "sets in motion a process that leads to the enlargement of NATO." He was also enraged by Clinton's recurring failures to consult—in fact a "courtesy call" would do—in advance of the U.S. bombings of Bosnian Serbs under NATO auspices. That was interpreted in

Russia as a sign that Moscow was seen by Washington and Brussels as a second-rate partner. In response, Yeltsin spoke of a new "Cold Peace" at the summit of the 53-nation Conference on Security and Cooperation in Europe.

To avoid the political firestorm igniting in Moscow, I worked strenuously to decouple the criticism of hasty enlargement from hostility toward NATO itself. "Hasty" was the key word meaning a tactical disagreement with a friendly alliance on when best to accommodate its potential new participants. Without this word, Russian opposition to enlargement implied strategic confrontation with an enemy trying to advance to our very borders.

By the end of 1994, the hard-liners were winning the day in Moscow, as an old-style security and governing bureaucracy, intermingled with crony oligarchs, was perverting democratic and market reforms.

Those forces restored state-controlled monopolies in key sectors of economy and wanted to keep out Western competition. They fostered 'seized fortress" propaganda for the Russian people while they and their families were enjoying lavish lifestyles in London, New York and French Riviera. Yeltsin was yielding to their pressure. Already in November 1993 Primakov published a report that NATO was still a threat to Russia. In this vein, he insisted on changing the policy formula on NATO from "No hasty enlargement—Yes partnership!" to the simple and bold proclamation: "No enlargement!" In early 1995 Yeltsin approved that change. Then he signed a program of modernization of Russian strategic nuclear forces.

The Bill–Boris Show

The historic opportunity for Russia to become a NATO ally might have still been saved had presidents Yeltsin and Clinton spoken more clearly and absolutely frankly to each other on the core of the matter and really worked at hammering out a solution. Yet, they were more fixated on representation, and were busy with the Bill—Boris amity show at their joint press conferences.

Apparently in an attempt to avoid the risk of adding the question "who lost Russia?" to his own domestic problems, Clinton preferred to downplay and paper over the growing rupture in the very foundation of the structure of partnership, i.e. common values. Yeltsin escaped into Soviet-style doublespeak (only too familiar to a former party apparatchik), one for domestic and another for foreign audiences. Both fudged and left issues open to interpretation or to being resolved in the future.

During 1995 Bill urged Boris to sign a PfP program of cooperation and to send a military detachment, even autonomous and symbolic, to Bosnia, making the NATO operation there look acceptable to Russia. In exchange Clinton promised to support Yeltsin's reelection campaign looming in 1996 with his less than 10% approval rating. Among other things, no visible steps would be taken towards NATO expansion during that year. This pathetic deal boiled down to mutual understanding that Boris would actually run under anti-NATO banners (and the West would look away). None of this addressed the NATO enlargement conundrum between the United States and Russia.

And then, at the beginning of 1996, Primakov succeeded me (later he became the prime minister) and Grachev was replaced by an even more traditionalist general. Russia was turning away from Western common values.

In 1997 the "Founding Act" between NATO and the Russia was added to the pile of goodwill declarations implemented as halfheartedly as they were signed. Yeltsin, in his radio address to the Russian people on May 30, described the Act as an effort "to minimize the negative consequences of NATO's expansion and prevent a new split in Europe." He then described the agreement—inaccurately, according to Western officials—as "enshrining NATO's pledge not to deploy nuclear weapons on the territories of its new member countries and not [to] build up its armed forces near our borders...nor carry out relevant infrastructure preparations." Russia continued to strongly oppose NATO also when the Alliance stopped Serbian cruelties in Kosovo in 1999 shortly after admitting Poland, Hungary and the Czech Republic as new members.

Conclusions and Outlook

The chance of alliance between Russia and NATO, which had opened in the early 1990s, was missed. Instead, the relationship degraded into hostility, veiled by diplomatic niceties that were thrown away at a later stage.

While the West failed to seize the opportunity and some diplomatic mistakes were made on both sides, the United States and NATO were on the right side of history by admitting new democracies to the Alliance and being willing to find an accommodation with Russia. It was Moscow that returned to its antagonism toward NATO, which has been intensifying ever since. Yeltsin's chosen successor president, Vladimir Putin, tried to hinder the West with a charm offensive in the early years of the 21 century and even hinted that Russia might join NATO. In the meantime, domestic anti-American and anti-NATO propaganda has continued to gain momentum. Today the Kremlin has left little doubt about its attitude toward the Alliance in words and in deeds.

NATO remains the main power to safeguard the liberal world order. It is under attack from autocratic, populist and extremist forces who claim that the organization is outdated. The Kremlin's champs and chumps in the West portray NATO as a bloc promoting American hegemony, expanding to the East and cornering Russia. It is reassuring however, that the U.S. Congress continues to display firm bipartisan support for NATO.

The prospects of a new opening in Russian–NATO relations will depend on the resilience and firmness of the Alliance and on deep changes in Moscow's domestic and foreign policy. I believe that sooner or later the Russian people will follow the suit of other European nations in finding their national interest in democratic reforms and cooperation with NATO and other Western institutions.

Chapter 20

Russia and NATO in the 1990s

Andrei Zagorski

Several clichés have become established in contemporary narratives explaining the evolution of relations between Russia and the West and particularly Russia and NATO in the 1990s.

Contemporary Russian mainstream discourse builds on the thesis that, following the end of the Cold War, it was particularly the United States that sought to extend its sphere of influence by conducting a policy of subjugation, or re-subjugation of former Communist countries, not least by integrating them into Euro-Atlantic institutions, especially NATO. In a nutshell:

> Starting with the negotiations on German unification, the West systematically took advantage of Russia's weakness. The West never acted in the spirit of the Charter of Paris, in which the indivisibility of security was a key concept. The West never tried to address security with Russia, only without it, or against it. The United States instead seized the opportunity to dominate international affairs especially in Europe. [...] The 'common European home' failed because the West was unwilling to build new, open security architecture—and to fulfil its promises.[1]

In pursuing this policy, the West allegedly broke an earlier promise to Soviet President Mikhail Gorbachev not to extend the Alliance any inch eastward.[2]

In the West and particularly in East Central Europe, Russian reactions to NATO enlargement in the 1990s tend to be presented as a linear policy pursued by Moscow since the collapse of the Soviet bloc. After the dismantlement of the Warsaw Pact the Kremlin allegedly followed the Soviet so-called 'Falin' and/or 'Kvitsinskii doctrine'—seeking to prevent East Central European countries from joining other military blocs (with NATO being the most prominent candidate), or from acceding to other sort of arrangements that could lead to the stationing of foreign troops and of military bases on their territory.[3]

The projection of this policy into the 1990s builds on an understanding (widely represented among my contemporary students) that, after the dissolution of the Soviet Union, the new Russia pursued the same policy and vehemently resisted NATO's enlargement.

There is a large body of evidence that seems to support this understanding. In his letter addressed to the leaders of major Western nations in September 1993, Russian President Boris Yeltsin strongly opposed NATO's eastward extension and instead offered to provide East Central European countries common security guarantees from Russia and the West. Minister of Defense Pavel Grachev admitted the sovereign right of East Central European countries to join alliances of their choice, but insisted that Russia had a sovereign right to retaliate. The Russian Foreign Intelligence Service was more specific in a public report released in November 1993, indicating that Moscow could reconsider its obligations under the 1990 Treaty on Conventional Armed Forces in Europe (CFE) should NATO extend eastward. Moscow also sought to persuade countries, such as Bulgaria, Romania or Slovakia, which early on appeared less determined to join the Alliance, to foster closer relations with Russia by offering them particular economic rewards.[4] These and many other manifestations of Moscow's anger with the emergence of NATO's debate to open its door to the East are often seen as confirming Russia's determination to resist the expansion of the political West into East Central Europe, which it, nevertheless, was unable to stop.

In this chapter I argue that none of those narratives, each implying a zero-sum game, correctly reflect policies pursued by either Russia or the West, or properly capture the highly dynamic and complex political processes that were involved with regard to managing NATO's eastward enlargement. By reconstructing the main moments highlighting the evolution of Russia–NATO relations in the 1990s, I argue that this was anything but a zero-sum exercise. On the contrary, it in fact remains a positive example of cooperative policies pursued by all parties leading to a successful joint decision-making by Russia and the West on an issue that was, admittedly, highly controversial.

This evolution should be understood against the broader background of both post-Communist Russian *Westpolitik* with the overall goal of integrating (or seeking some sort of association/affiliation) with the "political West," and the domestic political strife in a country where foreign policy issues played a significant role in the overall controversies. One must also take note of Moscow's strong interest to have a seat at relevant (institutional) tables to ensure that it would have a say as an equal partner in decision-making on major international issues, particularly on those relevant for Russia's national interests.

Policy choices made in Moscow during the 1990s changed as the European landscape continued changing. Between 1992 and 1995, Moscow pursued its 'first choice' of strengthening the Conference on Security and Cooperation in Europe (CSCE, contemporary OSCE) as the most inclusive, truly pan-European security organization. With the beginning of the EU/NATO enlargement debates in 1993–1994, Russia, too, adapted by seeking to institutionalize and develop mechanisms for political consultation, joint decision-making and joint action with both NATO and the EU—though, for many, this may have been only the second choice, or the 'plan B.' Moscow pursued this adaptation without abandoning the overall goal of seeking association with the "political West." This led to complex arrangements during the late 1990s—ones that allowed the Kremlin and the NATO Alliance to co-operatively manage the first wave of NATO enlargement, including the one in 2004, without jeopardizing Russia–West relations.

This chapter begins by addressing general issues relevant for the Russian policy toward the West, Europe and NATO in particular, before exploring Moscow's policy choices at different phases of the evolution of the European landscape in the 1990s. In doing so, it concentrates on Russian policy choices of the early and mid-1990s, and those made at the end of the decade as the Yeltsin government sought arrangements with NATO based on a positive-sum assumption.

Background

With due regard to the highly complex and dynamic landscape of European and domestic Russian politics, four considerations appear crucial for understanding the evolution of Russian policy and choices that affected its relations with NATO all through the 1990s:

- First, the overall vector of the Russian policy toward an integration into, or association with, the "political West."

- Second, the search for an appropriate institutionalization of Russia's relations with the West through different organizations giving Moscow a voice in joint decision-making on major international issues.

- Third, the highly dynamic and often dramatic political controversy in Russia challenging not only domestic but also major foreign policy choices made by the Russian Government.

- Fourth, the prioritization of the policy toward the post-Soviet space—the so-called "near abroad"—over many other directions of foreign policy.

Integration into or association with the West

The most important choice made by the Russian leadership with the end of the Cold War and the collapse of the Soviet Union was to favor a policy of integration into or association with the "political West" on the basis of shared values and interests which was expected to be framed as some sort of a 'strategic partnership.'[5] This choice anticipated a gradual formation of a wider community of democratic states, including Russia itself, that would fit into the definition of a pluralistic security community in the sense of Karl W. Deutsch and stretch from Vancouver to Vladivostok. Russian diplomat Vladimir Voronkov, being an eye witness of that period of the Russian policy, explains it simply: "Russia was not really weak; it was rather seeking—like any other state—its own place in the world. Such a search for identity took place under the influence of the dominant trend in the Euro-Atlantic zone at that time—the willingness of the majority of post-Communist nations to join NATO and the EU."[6]

Despite highly controversial foreign policy debates both within the Russian government and with the political opposition, seeking a close, or even an alliance-type relationship with the West was a deliberate choice of the country's leadership, which it pursued all through the 1990s (and a few years beyond).[7] While anticipating the post-Cold War world to become polycentric with the increasing number of new 'rising' or 'emerging' powers seeking to assert themselves on the international stage, the first Russian foreign policy doctrine adopted in April 1993 held that "Russia should firmly embark on the course of developing relations with those countries that could help to achieve the priority tasks of national revival, first of all with neighbors, economically strong and technologically advanced Western states and new industrial countries in various regions." Crucially, that choice was explained by the fact that Russia and the identified group of states were committed to "shared values of the world civilization as well as shared interests as regards core issues of global developments, in particular, as far as the maintenance of international peace and security, ensuring success of Russian reforms, strengthening stability in regions going through post-totalitarian trans-formation."[8] From this perspective, the West, including the United States and NATO, was not seen as an enemy or threat but rather as an eventual 'strategic partner' in assisting Russia's own post-Communist transition toward a democracy and market economy.

It was clear from the very beginning that any proper integration with the political West would require progressive and profound convergence of Russian domestic political and economic systems with those of the West. As long as the vector of post-Communist transition in Russia would remain compatible with that of East Central European coun-tries, the issue of a potential 'eastward extension of the West,' though important (not least in the context of domestic political strife), would not be central issue in Russia–West relations. That is because a trans-formed Russia, so it was hoped, would after all itself become part of the "political West."

Institutionalization of Russia–West relations

While seeking to develop relations of strategic partnership with the West, Moscow's main concern was to identify appropriate options for institutionalizing this relationship in order to ensure that Russia would have a voice in decision-making processes. Acceding to a number of "Western" organizations and institutions both global and regional (Eu-ropean), such as the World Bank and the International Monetary Fund, the World Trade Organization, the Organization for Economic Coop-eration and Development (OECD), the Council of Europe or the G7, was from the very beginning on the agenda of Russia's Western policy. This of course was a path on which the Soviet Union had already em-barked under Gorbachev.

The Yeltsin government pointed to an important 'institutional gap' that divided it from the leading Western nations. While post-Soviet

Russia as the USSR's successor state remained a permanent member on the U.N. Security Council with veto power, a participating state of the consensus-based CSCE/OSCE, and, since 1993, was a member of the Contact Group on former Yugoslavia, it was not a member of the G7, of NATO, or of the European Union.[9] The consequence was that Moscow was regularly confronted with a consolidated position of those groups of states after their joint decision-making process had been finalized, and was not itself part of that process. This is why Moscow sought to elaborate on inclusive institutional mechanisms that would give it a voice before final decisions would be taken in those groups.[10]

The objective of transforming the G7 into the G8 through the integration of Russia was formulated in the early 1990s, while the 1994 Partnership and Cooperation Agreement with the European Union provided for a mechanism for intensive political consultations and decision-making. The issue of establishing a mechanism for Russia–NATO political consultations grew in importance particularly against the background of the evolving enlargement debate.[11] While admitting the possibility of pursuing different options ranging from membership through different forms of association to a 'variable geometry' of institutional solutions,[12] the objective of Moscow was to form effective mechanisms for "joint decision-making by Russia and the West pertaining to the use of force, if necessary, and joint implementation of such decisions,"[13]

Domestic political controversies

The strategic foreign policy choice seeking closer association of Russia with the West was from the very beginning part and parcel of domestic political strife. The opposition to Boris Yeltsin and his foreign minister Andrei Kozyrev rallied not only in the Parliament but reached out into various branches of the government, political and economic establishments. This included over time the growing opposition to NATO enlargement that consolidated itself as the discussions in the West matured from 1993 onward. This opposition ultimately manifested itself in the establishment in 1997 of a parliamentary 'anti-NATO' group that included members of different factions in both chambers of the Federal Assembly and demanded that President Yeltsin take bold steps in order to arrest any extension of the Alliance into East Central Europe. In the few months from January through April 1997,

Figure 1. Responses to the question: "Should Russia beware of NATO member states?"

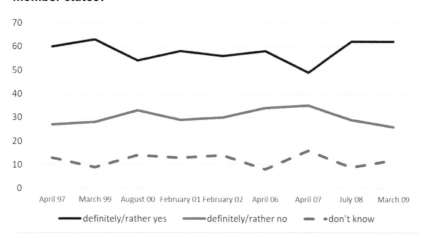

Source: Levada Center, March 31, 2009, http://www.levada.ru/2009/03/31/otnoshenie-rossiyan-k-nato/.

this group grew from 110 to 250 members and included four of six vice-speakers of the Duma and chairpersons of 17 of 28 parliamentary committees. It was definitely much larger, vocal and visible than the small parliamentary 'pro-NATO' group.

Russian public opinion was also divided on NATO, although popular anti-NATO mood was not as radical as the political opposition to Yeltsin. As shown in Figure 1, around 60 percent of respondents in surveys of the Levada Center tended to see NATO as a risk, if not a threat, to Russia in 1997–1999, while the number of those who did not remained under 30 percent. Figure 2 shows that the number of respondents ready to support NATO membership for Russia never exceeded 10 percent in 1996–1999 and continued declining thereafter. However, proponents of hard resistance remained a clear minority, too. The majority of respondents favored either simply staying away from any bloc policies, or developing a cooperative relationship with NATO.

Both the domestic political strife, in which the political opposition operationalized the NATO enlargement issue against the President, and inconclusive public opinion imposed significant constraints on

Figure 2. Responses to the question: "What policy better meets Russia's interest?"

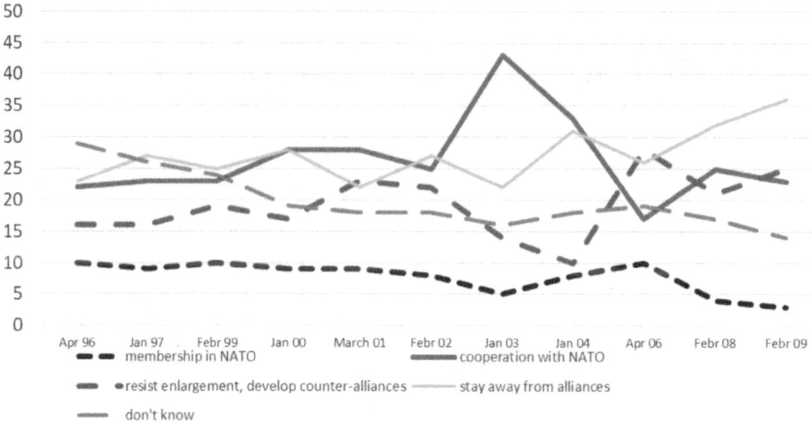

Source: Levada Center, March 31, 2009, http://www.levada.ru/2009/03/31/otnoshenie-rossiyan-k-nato/.

Yeltsin leading up to the 1996 Presidential elections, not least considering the advance of Vladimir Zhirinovsky's nationalistic Liberal Democratic Party and the Communists in the 1993 and 1995 parliamentary elections. It was clear that any conciliatory policy on NATO enlargement would boost the opposition. On the other hand, the possibility of a Communist or nationalistic backlash regarding NATO enlargement served as a plausible argument for Yeltsin to delay any formal decisions on NATO until after the Russian Presidential elections.

Prioritization of the 'near abroad'

Russian policy toward the post-Soviet space was one of the most controversial themes during domestic political debates of the early 1990s. The goal of consolidating New Independent States (NIS) around Russia (or consolidating 'Eurasia,' to put it in the language of the contemporary debate) was advanced particularly by the opposition as an alternative preferred path to the association of Russia with the political West.

Against the background of increasing differentiation among the NIS, Russia's 1993 foreign policy doctrine became a compromise growing out of the domestic debate. It formulated the goal of maintaining and strengthening the role of Russia in the post-Soviet space, developing the Commonwealth of Independent States (CIS) as a 'viable intergovernmental framework,' and the recognition by the West of Russia's 'special role' in that geographic area. While intended to help increasing Russia's political status in the world, it was also recognized that this policy could eventually become controversial with the West.[14]

This recognition led to the gradual development of the Russian understanding of what a new status quo in Europe should represent, while developing Russia's relations with the West. On the one hand, it implied a limit on Moscow's policy, which sought to draw a 'red line:' the eastward extension of the 'West' (at that time primarily NATO, but the EU would not be excluded) should not continue beyond the western borders of the former Soviet Union. On the other hand, the focus on the post-Soviet space effectively implied that the East Central region that the Soviet Union had vacated at the end of the Cold war was largely considered to have abandoned the Russian orbit, no matter whether the countries of the region would accede to Euro-Atlantic institutions or not.

The crux here was the fate of the Baltic states—being left in a sort of limbo. Although they were no formal part of the CIS, they were still considered by many to be part of the former Soviet space, and their integration into Euro-Atlantic institutions activated the same instincts particularly in the Russian domestic opposition as the discussion of eventual NATO membership for Ukraine in the late 1990s. Concerns raised by specific groups of the Russian establishment, and particularly by the defense community, added to the complexity of that debate.

This meant that, while not being seen as welcome, the integration of East Central countries into Western institutions would not be seen as an unsurmountable problem. The key concern related to the NIS, with the Baltic states representing a special and particularly sensitive case. The general expectation that could thus reconcile Moscow with NATO extension into the ECE region, including the second phase in 2004, was that either the Alliance would commit itself not to cross the 'red line' or, at least, that it would not cross it any time soon. As a senior

Russian diplomat put it in 2010, "NATO has already engaged all nations possible...Other states cannot expect membership or do not seek it...It means that many countries in the Euro-Atlantic in the near future, or even in the next few decades, will not be covered by the NATO and EU framework."[15] This was supposed to leave Moscow more time for the consolidation of its neighborhood by pursuing integration projects within the CIS.

Still, the objective of an association with the political West was not seen as being necessarily irreconcilable with post-Soviet integration, provided that the overall vector of post-Communist transformation of Russia and its neighbors would remain compatible with that of other post-Communist nations. In that case, the CIS, like the European Union, could represent another case of regional integration without challenging the concept of a wider Euro-Atlantic community from Vancouver to Vladivostok.[16]

It was also important that, during the 1990s, despite beginning debate over the 'near abroad' doctrine, the West and the international community in general refrained from actively engaging in conflict resolution in areas of the former Soviet Union. Although, at various moments, the possibility of dispatching U.N. or OSCE peace operations was considered (in particular, in Abkhazia, Tajikistan and Karabakh), both organizations reduced themselves to sending smaller teams of monitors and did not really challenge Russian operations conducted either on the basis of ad hoc arrangements, or under CIS auspices.[17] The most urgent issues of Russian troop withdrawal from and integration of Russian minorities in the Baltic states were addressed in a cooperative way with the assistance of the OSCE and the United States.[18]

Before the Door Begins Opening

In the early 1990s, when the prospect for any NATO enlargement remained still vague, the option of advancing the goal of integration with the West through further institutionalization of strengthening of pan-European institutions of the CSCE/OSCE on the basis of common values and goals enshrined in the 1990 Charter of Paris for a New Europe appeared plausible in Moscow. Russia was a full participating state of this consensus-based organization, and the CSCE did not trigger any anti-Western instincts in the post-Soviet Russian political establishment—at least not yet. Embarking on that path, Moscow did not simply set forth the footprint of Soviet policy during the late Gorbachev era, it also seems to have overestimated its own ability to persuade the West and particularly to overcome U.S. skepticism with respect to the CSCE.

The CSCE was seen in Russia as a main framework for shaping the evolving complex European community of states and the central institution that granted Russia full involvement in European affairs. It was also considered as an *inclusive* overarching framework for the formation of the 'Euro-Atlantic,' and after 1991 the 'Euro-Asian,' communities of states. The Russian foreign policy doctrine anticipated that a CSCE-based security architecture in Europe would provide a platform for cooperation with the European Union, NATO, the Western European Union and the CIS.[19] Having joined together with the former Warsaw Pact countries and NIS at the North Atlantic Cooperation Council (NACC) in December 1991, Moscow cautiously explored the possibility of a NATO membership.[20] However, before the enlargement debate began to take shape in 1993, the Alliance was really not seen as the top item on Russia's agenda.

Moscow welcomed the 1992 Helsinki decisions which took the CSCE institutions and structures to a new level and identified it as a regional arrangement under Chapter VIII of the U.N. Charter. It welcomed the progressive discussions of cooperative security within the organization and of the establishment of the CSCE Forum for Security Cooperation for this purpose and the strengthening of the CSCE Conflict Prevention Center.

In 1993 and 1994, Russia submitted proposals aiming at further strengthening the CSCE.[21] They were followed by the introduction, in 1994, of a comprehensive "Program for Enhancing CSCE Effectiveness."[22] In the Program, Moscow promoted the objective of giving the CSCE a central role in peacekeeping, strengthening of democracy and providing for security and stability in the Euro-Atlantic region. It anticipated to transform the CSCE into a fully-fledged, treaty-based regional organization partnering with the United Nations. The central element of the Program was the proposal to establish a CSCE 'Executive Committee' that would act in a similar way as the U.N. Security Council does. It would consist of no more than 10 permanent and non-permanent members and take binding decisions following the consensus rule. This vision was based on a hierarchical approach to European security architecture, implying that the CIS, NACC, the EU, the Council of Europe, NATO and the WEU should act as equal partners while the CSCE would be given an overall coordination role.

Following an earlier Russian proposal of late 1993 that suggested shifting the NACC from NATO to the umbrella of the OSCE and, for this purpose, to open its membership for neutral and non-aligned European countries,[23] the Russian Program proposal was met with much skepticism, for different reasons. While any sort of subordination of NATO would be unacceptable for the Alliance's members, small participating states in particular feared that the establishment of a CSCE "Security Council" would undermine the consensus rule and thus minimize their impact on decision-making. Other countries, such as Germany and the Netherlands, sought to offer alternative solutions that would strengthen the role of the organization.[24] Russian proposals did, however, inspire a decision by the OSCE to begin a structured discussion on a Common and Comprehensive European Security Model for the 21st Century. Yet, the debate on the 'Model,'[25] launched in 1995, resulting in the adoption of the 1999 OSCE European Security Charter, unfolded already in a different environment—one that was already defined by the beginnings of the NATO enlargement debate, which no longer was about 'whether' but had now turned to 'when and how.'

Anticipating Enlargement

It is often believed, that the Warsaw Declaration signed by Yeltsin during his visit to Poland in August 1993, in which he accepted Poland's intention to join NATO "in the long term," stating that it was "not in conflict with the interests of other states, including those of Russia,"[26] provided a boost to the discussion that had started months before. It served as the trigger for Moscow's mounting official rhetoric against enlargement that would follow in the fall of 1993. However, the main purpose of that rhetoric seems to have been not to begin a campaign to stop the enlargement but, rather, to buy time to sort out other important issues of Russia-NATO relations—not least which steps would be necessary for Moscow to adapt to this trend.

The most important question for Moscow was not "whether" NATO would enlarge, but "when" and "how". The question was also whether Russia would be part of the process in some way, or would it be left out. The above-mentioned 1993 Warsaw Declaration by Presidents Yeltsin and Walesa itself put the prospect in a long-term perspective and made the membership option (for Poland) conditional on the formation of a pan-European security architecture, thus not entirely abandoning the policy of strengthening the CSCE, which Russia continued to pursue. Foreign Minister Andrei Kozyrev emphasized at that time that the problem was not the enlargement *per se*, but a premature or hasty enlargement that would take place before other important issues had been dealt with. He did not exclude that, at some point in the future, either Russia would also join NATO, or both Russia and NATO would become part of a pan-European security system. What he explicitly ruled out was an expansion of NATO that would categorically exclude, or not involve Russia.[27]

Moscow had to respond to the challenge of the post-Cold War European order becoming increasingly NATO (and EU)–centric, for this would predictably lead to a progressive marginalization of the CSCE. At the same time Russia remained keen to ensure and appropriately institutionalize its own association with the "political West." As a result, Moscow adapted to the new trend by abandoning its previous policy of concentrating on the CSCE—largely at the expense of the organization—and by seeking to institutionalize direct political consultation and joint decision-making with NATO and the European Union. Recalling this period, Andrei Kelin admits that the interest in the OSCE gradually declined both in the West and in Russia. The agenda was dominated by concentrating on different platforms for the pursuit of Russian policy objectives in cooperation with NATO and the European Union.[28]

It remains open whether the changes in Russia's policy toward the ineffective CIS integration by launching, in 1995, a 'multi-speed' integration approach, was part of its response to the beginning NATO enlargement, or simply coincided with it. Russia's response to NATO was formulated in the context of the Partnership for Peace (PfP) proposal advanced by the United States and NATO beginning in the fall of 1993, and particularly after the program's launch in 1994.

In April 1994, President Yeltsin took the decision for Russia to join PfP. He did so with the support of the Ministry of Defense and the Security Council, against harsh criticism from the Russian Parliament. One month later, however, he appeared to make a U-turn, announcing during a visit to Germany that Russia would not sign the PfP Framework without a special protocol. As it turned out, his statement did not herald a reversal in Moscow's policy but, rather, a decision to institutionalize 'special' relations with the Alliance that would go beyond military-political cooperation provided for within the PfP program. Foreign Minister Andrei Kozyrev and Defense Minister Pavel Grachev clarified that Russia was prepared to sign the Framework Document together with an *additional* protocol or agreement to include detailed and reciprocal commitments of NATO and Russia in the political and military fields, and proposed to establish a mechanism for regular or ad hoc Russia–NATO consultations.[29]

In the event, on June 22, 1994, Kozyrev signed the PfP Framework Document on behalf of Russia. At the same time, at a press conference, a protocol on establishing a framework for enhanced political dialogue between Russia and NATO was presented.[30] This document anticipated an institutionalization of information exchange, political consultation, and the discussion of possibilities for cooperation in form of holding ambassadorial Russia-NATO "16+1" ad hoc meetings with the North-Atlantic Council or with the Political Committee. Following this, on July 2,1994, Russia submitted a very ambitious program for political and military cooperation with NATO.[31]

In the course of the negotiations, two documents were worked out with the Alliance: a Russia—NATO individual program for cooperation within the PfP and a document on broader cooperation including holding political consultations on a wide range of international security issues. Both documents were expected to be signed on December 1, 1994. But then Kozyrev declined from endorsing them at the last moment, referring to the decision taken by North Atlantic Council to commission a study that would spell out criteria for enlargement. That was seen as a principal decision to proceed with enlargement. Even if the decision not to sign the documents was initiated by Kozyrev, his proposal must have been approved by the President, who was concerned at that time that no formal decisions concerning enlargement would be taken by NATO before the 1996 Presidential elections in Russia.

No matter whether Kozyrev was instructed not to sign or whether he himself initiated that decision, it postponed the institutionalization of cooperation between Russia and the Alliance for two and a half years.

Negotiating Terms of Enlargement

As the first round of Eastern enlargement approached, Moscow considered available policy choices. Evgeniy Primakov, who in 1996 became Foreign Minister, listed them as follows:[32]

1. To reject NATO enlargement and exclude any relations with the Alliance. This option was considered a road to nowhere or a resumption of the Cold War.

2. Accept and not object NATO enlargement and, on this basis, seek an agreement that would govern Russia-NATO relations. This option was seen as a sort of capitulation that would not be accepted by the Russian public.

3. Without abandoning the negative appraisal of the enlargement, seek a negotiated "minimization of negative consequences," or reduce the damage for Russia's security and interests.

Option 3 was the favored one. It implied that (largely for tactical reasons and domestic consumption) Moscow would continue rhetoric policy opposing the enlargement but, at the same time, seek to negotiate a deal that would allow to establish 'special relations' with the Alliance.[33] Also, for tactical reasons, Moscow decided not to raise the possibility of membership for Russia during these negotiations based on the understanding that raising this question would weaken the rhetorical part of its policy and could provoke a big-bang enlargement. However, even at this time, Moscow did not yet abandon the membership option altogether.[34] It remained on the agenda until 2002.

This policy choice also anticipated that, prior to the enlargement, specific Russian concerns had to be addressed, particularly those raised by the defense establishment, and appropriate solutions identified and agreed upon. Like at the earlier stage, Moscow was also seeking establishing a mechanism for regular political consultations with NATO.

In particular, Moscow sought to:

- address specific military issues that served for concerns in the context of the enlargement, such as guarantees that neither nuclear weapons, nor foreign troops and respective military infrastructure would be permanently stationed on the territory of new members; agreement on the parameters for the adaptation of the CFE Treaty in order to exclude that the military power of NATO approaches Russian borders as a consequence of the enlargement;

- establish a consensus-based mechanism for consultations that would include Russia into joint decision-making on all issues that could affect its interest (effectively giving Russia a veto power on such issues);

- ensure continued transformation of NATO from being a collective defense alliance toward an organization addressing regional threats, first of all regional conflicts which were at the core of threats perceptions in the 1990s, and engaging in peace operations in cooperation with Russia;

- negotiate a legally binding document to be signed by heads of state or government.[35]

One of the key objectives of Moscow was to draw a 'red line' for NATO's eastward extension: the Baltic states and any other post-Soviet states should remain excluded from NATO.[36]

At the initial stage, the discussion of those issues was supposed to resolve, in a *sequential* (rather than parallel) way, three problems: further transformation of NATO, institutionalization of cooperation between Russia and the Alliance, and enlargement.[37]

Intensive and complex bilateral consultations held in 1996 and 1997 at the level of heads of state or government and especially of foreign ministers, particularly with the United States, France, Germany and the UK, as well as from January 1997 with NATO Secretary General Javier Solana, resulted in the adoption of several documents and decisions. Those included, inter alia, the signing on May 27, 1997 the Founding Act on Mutual Relations, Cooperation and Security between NATO and the Russian Federation, and the adaptation of the CFE treaty in 1999 that met Russian concerns. Although not included into the framework of negotiations, the transformation of the G7 into the G8 by including Russia was also facilitated by seeking a broader arrangement with the West against the background of the latter's extension to the east.

Most of concerns raised by Moscow at that time were addressed and resolved in a cooperative manner. The Permanent Joint Council, established by the Founding Act, was supposed to "provide a mechanism for consultations, coordination and, to the maximum extent possible, where appropriate, for joint decisions and joint action with respect to security issues of common concern." The document identified 19 initial areas for Russia–NATO cooperation. Members of the Alliance stated that they had "no intention, no plan and no reason to deploy nuclear weapons on the territory of new members, nor any need to change any aspect of NATO's nuclear posture or nuclear policy" and did "not foresee any future need to do so," and that they had "no intention, no plan, and no reason to establish nuclear weapon storage sites on the territory of those members, whether through the construction of new nuclear storage facilities or the adaptation of old nuclear storage facilities." They also stated that "in the current and foreseeable security environment, the Alliance will carry out its collective defence and other missions by ensuring the necessary interoperability, integration, and capability for reinforcement rather than by additional permanent stationing of substantial combat forces. Accordingly, it will have to rely on adequate infrastructure commensurate with the above tasks."[38]

The arrangement reached in 1997 paved the way to a swift adaptation of the CFE treaty in order to acknowledge the disappearance of the Warsaw Pact (or of the 'eastern group', to put in in the CFE language) and to give effect to and operationalize the Alliance's pledge that its enlargement would not result in a concentration of troops or stationing of nuclear weapons at the borders of Russia. Moscow's reciprocal commitment not to permanently station additional substantial combat forces in Pskov and Kaliningrad regions was formalized in December 1999 in the context of signing the Adapted CFE Treaty in Istanbul.

Comparing this outcome with Primakov's checklist of 1996 makes clear that only two of his objectives were not obtained at the end of 1990s.

First, the language of the Founding Act was explicit that its provisions "do not provide NATO or Russia, in any way, with a right of veto over the actions of the other nor do they infringe upon or restrict the rights of NATO or Russia to independent decision-making and action."

Second, no explicit or tacit agreement was reached on a red line which NATO should not cross by next rounds. Since it was already clear in 1997 that this process would not be limited to the Czech Republic, Hungary and Poland, this produced uncertainty particularly with respect to whether the Baltic states would be able to join the Alliance in the second round. However, the second round of enlargement in 2004 also did not generate a crisis in Russia–NATO relations, because both sides had a clear understanding of what they had agreed on and what they had not agreed on.

The signing of the Russia—NATO Founding Act and the establishment of the Joint Permanent Council operating at different levels and including political and military fields provided a significant boost to practical cooperation between Russia and the Alliance from 1998. Indeed, it is one of few instruments still relevant and operational which is observed by both Russia and NATO, despite the dramatically changed security environment in Europe.

Conclusions

Neither NATO's nor Russia's policies in the context of the enlargement debate in the 1990s were based on a zero-sum game assumption. Although the emergence of a 'NATO-centric' European security architecture was far from being Moscow's first choice, it did not adapt a policy of simply resisting enlargement. Instead, it sought to develop and institutionalize political consultations and cooperation with the Alliance, identify and raise specific security-related concerns and jointly seek for cooperative solutions. Public rhetoric accompanying this policy served the purpose of making the arrangement acceptable to the Russian public which would support developing a cooperative relationship with the Alliance.

Opening NATO doors for the enlargement in 1997/99 did not lead to a crisis in relations of the Alliance with Russia. Mechanism for cooperation established by the Founding Act began bringing fruits. The first meeting of the Joint Permanent Council was held at the ministerial level in New York on September 26, 1997, and agreed on the program for cooperation, including main themes for political consultation and directions for practical cooperation. In October 1997, first working groups were established. In March 1998, the Russian Permanent Mission at NATO was established. Russia and NATO agreed to exchange military liaison missions and agreed on the individual partnership program for 1998 including the participation of Russia in more than 70 events in 17 areas of cooperation, including 10 joint exercises.

In 1997–1998, political dialogue and cooperation between Russia and NATO expanded significantly helping to develop an atmosphere of growing openness and confidence between various agencies involved in projects. This experience also built upon positive cooperation between Russia and NATO in Bosnia (SFOR).

Russia–NATO relations only began deteriorating in 1999, not because of enlargement but because of NATO's airstrikes against Yugoslavia between March and June 1999. The immediate reaction of Moscow was to suspend its participation in the Joint Permanent Council, the implementation of all cooperative programs with NATO and any military-to-military communication at senior level. Although Russian 'sanctions' targeting NATO at that moment did not last long, and Moscow returned to cooperation, not least within KFOR in Kosovo, this was a moment when those opposing any rapprochement between Russia and NATO, Russia and the West, indeed those who failed to influence Moscow's Western policy during the early 1990s, began increasingly to have an impact on Russia's course after 1999. The cooperative moment of the 1990s was passing, just as did Yeltsin, who passed the baton to Vladimir Putin. Times as much as leaders were changing.

Notes

1. *Back to Diplomacy Final Report and Recommendations of the Panel of Eminent Persons on European Security as a Common Project* (Vienna: OSCE, 2015), p. 24.

2. For a recent overview of the recent historical research on the issue see, inter alia: Christian Nünlist, Juhana Aunesluoma, Benno Zogg, *The Road to the Charter of Paris: Historical Narratives and Lessons for the OSCE Today* (Vienna: OSCE Network of Think Tanks and Academic Institutions, 2017).

3. Marek Menkiszak, "Difficult Neighborhood: The Security Question in Polish Relations with the Soviet Union and Russia," in Roman Kuźniar, ed., *Poland's Security Policy 1989–2000* (Warsaw: Scholar Publishing House, 2001), p. 134.

4. References to this evidence are spread over several chapters in Andrei Zagorski, ed., *Russia and East Central Europe After the Cold War: A Fundamentally Transformed Relationship* (Prague: Human Rights Publishers, 2015).

5. Andrey Kozyrev, "Стратегия партнерства" ["Strategy of partnership"], in T.A. Shakleina (compiler), Внешняя политика и безопасность современной России. *1991–2002 [Foreign policy and security of contemporary Russia. 1991–2002].* Anthology in four volumes. Vol. I (Moscow: MGIMO et al., 2002) pp. 182–192.

6. Vladimir Voronkov, "The European Security Treaty after Corfu," in *Security Index*, 2010, No 1 (90), p. 61.

7. Igor Ivanov, "Внешняя политика России на рубеже XXI века: Проблемы формирования, эволюции и преемственности" ["Foreign Policy and Security of Contemporary Russia at the Brink of the 21st Century: Problems of Formulation, Evolution and continuity"], in T.A. Shakleina, ed., op. cit., pp. 207–208.

8. "Концепция внешней политики Российской Федерации (1993 г.)" ["Foreign Policy Conception of the Russian Federation, 1993"], in: T.A. Shakleina, ed., op. cit., pp. 21–23.

9. The EU was seen mainly as an economic bloc in the 1990s. The interest in developing and institutionalizing cooperation in the security field occurred in Russia with the beginning of the formation of the ESDP instruments after 2000. However, early in the 1990s Moscow was already in the process of negotiating a Partnership and Cooperation Agreement with the EU (signed in 1994) which established a flexible and intensive mechanism of regular political dialogue and joint decision-making at all levels. I elaborate later in the text.

10. Andrey Kozyrev, "Strategy of partnership," op. cit., p. 187.

11. Andrey Kozyrev, Преображение ["*The Transformation*"] (Moscow: Mezhdunarodnye otnosheniya, 1994], p. 202.

12. Ibid., p. 231.

13. Igor Ivanov, op. cit., p. 211.

14. "Foreign Policy Conception of the Russian Federation, 1993, op. cit., pp. 20, 23–27, 33.

15. Voronkov, op. cit., p. 61.

16. On this see Andrei Zagorski, Россия в системе европейской безопасности [*Russia in the European Security Order*] (Moscow: IMEMO, 2017], p. 10.

17. V.F. Zaemskiy, ООН и миротворчество [*UN and Peacekeeping*], 2nd Edition (Moscow: Mezhdunarodnye otnosheniya, 2012), p. 13.

18. On this see, *inter alia*, Ekaterina Furman, Nils Muižnieks, Gatis Pelnēns, "Latvia and the Russian Federation: Twenty Years of Relations", in Andrei Zagorski, ed., *Russia and East Central Europe After the Cold War*, op. cit., pp. 231–238; Sabine Machl, "The OSCE Missions to the Baltic States,", in IFSH, ed., *The OSCE Yearbook 2002* (Baden-Baden: Nomos, 2003), pp. 209–218; Nils Muižnieks, *Latvian—Russian Relations: Dynamics Since Latvia's Accession to the EU and NATO* (Riga: University of Latvia Press, 2011).

19. "Foreign Policy Conception of the Russian Federation, 1993, op. cit., pp. 37, 38.

20. Kimberly Marten, "Reconsidering NATO expansion: a counterfactual analysis of Russia and the West in the 1990s", in: *European Journal of International Security*, Vol. 3 (June 2018), No 2. (Published online first in November 2017), p. 7, https://www.cambridge.org/core/journals/european-journal-of-international-security/article/reconsidering-nato-expansion-a-counterfactual-analysis-of-russia-and-the-west-in-the-1990s/356448EA9D5C63C53BE1EC6B33FE470A.

21. *Diplomaticheskiy Vestnik* [*The Diplomatic Herold*], 1994, No 15-16, p. 23.

22. For the text of the Program, see: *Diplomaticheskiy Vestnik*, 1994, No 17-18, p. 13.

23. Andrei Zagorski, "Россия и Европа" ["Russia and Europe"], in A.Lopukhin, S. Rossi, A. Zagorski, eds., От реформы к стабилизации... Внешняя, военная и экономическая политика России (анализ и прогноз), 1993–1995 [*From Reform to Stability... Russian Foreign, Military and Economy Policy (Analysis and Forecast) 1993–1995*] (Moscow: MGIMO; Industrial Herald, 1995), p. 31.

24. For the debate of those years see, *inter alia*, Hans-Dietrich Genscher, "Strengthening the OSCE—An Indispensable Condition for a Just and Lasting Peaceful Order from Vancouver to Vladivostok," in IFSH, ed., *The OSCE Yearbook 1995/1996* (Baden-Baden: Nomos, 1997), p. 53; Kurt P. Tudyka, "The Attitude of Participating States Toward the OSCE," in *The OSCE Yearbook 1995/1996*, pp. 83–84.

25. For an overview of the discussion on the 'Model' see, inter alia, Heinrich Schneider, "The 'European Security Model for the 21st Century'—A Story without an Ending?" in IFSH, ed., *The OSCE Yearbook 1997* (Baden-Baden: Nomos, 1998) pp. 235–255.

26. For the text of the Declaration see: *Diplomaticheskiy Vestnik*, 1993, No 17—18, p. 16.

27. Andrei Kozyrev, *"The Transformation,"* op. cit., p.199.

28. "ОБСЕ наконец-то работает так, как должна была работать всегда" ["The OSCE Finally Operates in a Way it Was Always Supposed to"]. Interview with Andrei Kelin in PIR-Center, 2015, http://www.pircenter.org/articles/1957-obse-nakonecto-rabotaet-tak-kak-dolzhna-byla-rabotat-vsegda.

29. Andrei Zagorski, "Russia and Europe," op. cit., pp. 43–44.

30. *Areas for Pursuance of a Broad, Enhanced NATO/Russia Dialogue and Cooperation*, June 22, 1994, https://www.nato.int/DOCU/comm/49-95/c950531a.htm.

31. For details see Andrei Zagorski, "Russia and Europe," op. cit., pp. 44–46.

32. Evgeniy Primakov, Встречи на перекрестках [*Meetings at the Crossroads*] (Moscow: Centrpoligraph, 2015), pp. 220–221.

33. Ibid., pp. 222, 238.

34. Evgeniy Primakov, "Международные отношения накануне XXI века: Проблемы, перспективы" ["International Relations on the Eve of the 21st Century: Problems and Prospects"], in in: T.A. Shakleina, op. cit., ed., p 201.

35. Evgeniy Primakov, *Meetings at the Crossroads*, op. cit., pp. 225, 226, 227, 237.

36. Ibid., p. 226.

37. Primakov, "International Relations on the Eve of the 21st Century," op. cit., pp. 201-202.

38. Founding Act on Mutual Relations, Cooperation and Security between NATO and the Russian Federation, Paris, 27 May 1997 (https://www.nato.int/cps/en/natohq/official_texts_25468.htm).

Chapter 21

Explaining Russia's Opposition to NATO Enlargement: Strategic Imperatives, Ideas, or Domestic Politics?

Elias Götz

This chapter examines the sources of Moscow's opposition to NATO's opening eastward. The topic is timely and important, not only because of the twentieth anniversary of the first post-Cold War round of enlargement in 1999, but also because of its prominent role in the ongoing "who lost Russia" debate among Western scholars.[1] Previous studies have documented that from 1993 onwards large parts of the Russian political elite opposed NATO's eastward expansion.[2] But the sources of Russia's opposition remain a matter of controversy. At risk of oversimplification, one can distinguish between three different sets of explanations in the existing literature: one group of scholars emphasizes the role of strategic imperatives and national security considerations; a second group focuses on ideational factors such as Russia's status concerns and Cold War thinking; and a third group argues that Russian domestic political factors explain Moscow's position best.

Based on the work of area specialists and newly declassified U.S. transcripts of the conversations (over the phone or face-to-face) between Presidents Clinton and Yeltsin, I argue that Russia's opposition to the first round of NATO enlargement was driven by the interplay of strategic imperatives and status concerns. Cold War memories and domestic political factors played only a secondary role. Of course, my findings are somewhat tentative as most internal policy documents, diplomatic cables, and records of high-level meetings—especially on the Russian side—remain inaccessible.

I begin in the first part with an account of the evolution of Russia's stance towards the planned enlargement of the Alliance in the 1990s. The core of the chapter (sections 2-4) provides an assessment of the different explanations for Moscow's resentment against NATO expansion. The chapter concludes with a brief discussion of what the findings imply for the ongoing politico-historical debate about Russia's relations with the West.

Yeltsin's Russia and the NATO Enlargement Question

In late 1991 and early 1992, Moscow made it clear that it wanted to establish closer relations with the West. President Yeltsin and other high-ranking officials even aired the idea that Russia might someday join NATO. Meanwhile, voices in Central and Eastern Europe grew louder about seeking membership in the Alliance. The Kremlin, in response, adopted an increasingly critical stance towards the ambitions of those states and NATO's activism in Central Europe more generally.

This became clear in the summer of 1993. During an official visit to Warsaw in August, Yeltsin at first stated that he was principally not opposed to Poland's membership in NATO. But, as soon as the president had uttered his words, the Russian Foreign Ministry qualified these comments, arguing that this applied only if and when NATO established a special relationship with Moscow. A few weeks later, President Yeltsin sent a letter to the governments of the United States, France, Germany, and the United Kingdom in which he declared, "In general, we advocate that relations between our country and NATO be a few degrees warmer than those between the Alliance and Eastern Europe."[3] In the letter, Yeltsin also argued that "the spirit of the treaty on the final settlement with respect to Germany (...) precludes the option of expanding the NATO zone into the East."[4]

By June 1994, Moscow decided that it would join NATO's Partnership for Peace (PfP) program. The Russian leadership believed that the PfP framework was an alternative to NATO expansion—or at least a venue to exert some influence on the decision about enlargement.[5] Soon, however, it became clear that the Alliance was seriously thinking about admitting new members from among the former Soviet satellites. In July 1994, when President Clinton addressed the Polish parliament in Warsaw, he emphasized that "no country should have the right to veto (...) any other democracy's integration into Western institutions, including those ensuring security."[6] Clinton also reiterated the by now famous phrase that NATO enlargement was "no longer a question of whether, but *when* and *how*."[7]

Notwithstanding Western assurances that expansion would not be directed against Russia, many policymakers and military thinkers in Moscow objected vociferously. In July 1994, for instance, President Yeltsin stressed in his private conversations with Clinton, "I have to say candidly, Bill, that with respect to Poland, the position they take on this [NATO expansion] does not correspond very closely with ours."[8] In December 1994, at a Ministerial Meeting of the North Atlantic Council in Brussels, Foreign Minister Andrei Kozyrev unexpectedly announced that he would not sign the PfP accord out of protest against the initiation of a new NATO enlargement study.[9] A few days later, at the OSCE meeting in Budapest, President Yeltsin doubled down and warned that "Europe (…) is in the danger of plunging into a cold peace."[10]

By May 1995, Russia did approve the PfP Individual Partnership Program. But it remained opposed to NATO expansion plans. One month later, in June 1995, the Russian Council on Foreign and Defense Policy issued a report, entitled "Russia and NATO," capturing Moscow's attitude towards NATO expansion, which, so the report held, might lead to the "first serious crisis in relations between Russia and the West since the end of the Cold War." Furthermore, it argued that "especially in the United States, there is a desire to consolidate the geopolitical sphere achieved by 'winning' the Cold War." The report also stressed that although the "interest [of the Central and Eastern European countries] are understandable and legitimate (…) Russia does not consider [membership in the Alliance] an optimum and well-balanced response to their anxiety. If they join NATO, the security of the eastern and central European countries will be achieved at the cost of Russian security."[11]

Russian elites clearly resented the eastward expansion of NATO and made this public. Some of the more hardline figures threatened to take all kinds of countermeasures, including the stationing of nuclear weapons in western parts of Russia and Kaliningrad, withdrawal from arms control treaties, and even military actions in Eastern Europe. In private conversations with President Clinton, Yeltsin reiterated Russia's concerns about the prospect of a widened Alliance, but he did not issue any direct threats. Given Russia's economic and military weakness, there was also little Moscow could do to prevent enlargement. So Russian negotiators tried to secure formal reinsurances that NATO would not station nuclear weapons, military infrastructure, and combat troops on the territory of new NATO members. As Russia's new Foreign Minister Yevgeny Primakov declared in a 16+1 meeting with NATO in July 1996, "moving up NATO's infrastructure to our borders [is unacceptable]. On this basis, Russia is inviting NATO to conduct a dialogue, and now they have agreed to this."[12] Similarly, at the Helsinki Summit in March 1997, President Yeltsin made it clear that "[o]ur position has not changed. It remains a mistake for NATO to move eastward." But, seeing he could not stop the process anyway, he added: "I need to take steps to alleviate the negative consequences of this for Russia. I am prepared to enter into an agreement with NATO not because I want to but because it is a forced step."[13]

Seeking to allay Moscow's concerns, the Alliance proposed to set up an institutionalized form of cooperation, which was codified in the NATO-Russia Founding Act on Mutual Relations, Cooperation, and Security. The Founding Act entailed the creation of a forum for consultation, the Permanent Joint Council (PJC), and a non-binding declaration (Article 4) that "in the *current and foreseeable security environment*, the Alliance will carry out its collective defense and other missions by ensuring the necessary interoperability, integration, and capability for reinforcement rather than by additional permanent stationing of substantial combat forces."[14]

However, even after Moscow's signing of the Founding Act in May 1997, large parts of the Russian political establishment—including President Yeltsin and many of his associates—remained worried about NATO's eastern extension. This was reflected in Russia's revised National Security Concept, which was published in December 1997. The Concept stated, "The prospect of NATO expansion to the East is unacceptable to Russia since it represents a threat to its national security." The Concept also argued that "NATO's expansion to the East and its transformation into a dominant military-political force in Europe create the threat of a new split in the continent which would be extremely dangerous given the preservation in Europe of mobile strike groupings of troops and nuclear weapons."[15]

In essence, despite repeated reassurances by Western governments and Clinton himself that NATO expansion was not directed against Russia, and despite intensive U.S.-Russian dialogue, many politicians and strategists in Moscow saw it otherwise, opposing the enlargement outright. The question is, why? In what follows, I re-examine three prominent explanations in light of the evidence that has become available in recent years.

Russia's Strategic Imperatives

Some analysts have argued that Russia's opposition to the eastward extension of NATO was based on strategic imperatives and military security concerns. As Kenneth Waltz put it, "it is not so much new members that Russia fears as it is America's might moving ever closer to its borders."[16] Likewise, Charles Kupchan warned already in 1994 that "enlarging the alliance would alter the balance of power on the continent and make Russia feel less secure."[17] And Michael Brown cautioned, "Russian leaders will see any form of NATO expansion (...) as a change in the balance of power and an extension of Washington's and Bonn's sphere of influence."[18]

Indeed, as early as November 1993, Primakov, then head of the Russian Foreign Intelligence Service (SVR), warned that NATO expansion would "bring the biggest military grouping in the world, with its colossal offensive potential, directly to the borders of Russia. If this happens, the need would arise for a fundamental reappraisal of all defense concepts on our side, a redeployment of armed forces and changes in operational plans."[19] Likewise, analysts in the Russian defense ministry were concerned that "when Poland, Hungary, and the Czech Republic join NATO, the Alliance's territory will expand eastward by 650 to 750 kilometers. As a result, the 'buffer zone' between Russia and NATO would be substantially reduced."[20] And Defense Minister Pavel Grachev plainly stated, "if new members are admitted into NATO, Russia will have to take additional security measures."[21]

Indeed, virtually all Russian defense planners opposed NATO's eastward movement with reference to security concerns. One might say that this is unsurprising. After all, defense planners are paid to think in terms of worst-case scenarios. What is more, by playing up the potential threat posed by NATO expansion, Russian military officials might have hoped to advance the corporate interests of the armed forces, such as higher levels of defense spending and increased influence on foreign affairs. While there may be some truth to this argument—bureaucracies usually look after themselves—the significance of the Russian military's parochial agenda should not be exaggerated here, for two reasons.

First, existing research has shown that the military did not succeed in exerting significant influence on the Kremlin during the 1990s. As a RAND study concluded, "On critical resources issues such as the defense budget, pay, and military housing, the top brass has consistently been short-changed and failed to achieve its main goals."[22]

Second, and more importantly, concern about the prospective eastward enlargement of NATO was shared across the political spectrum. For instance, Russian privatization mastermind Anatoly Chubais, a known pro-Westerner, stated at the 1997 World Economic Forum in Davos that with regard to NATO expansion, "for the first time in the last five years, I personally am adopting the same position as Messrs, Zhirinovsky, and Zyuganov.[23] Similarly, the liberal opposition leader Grigory Yavlinsky declared in 1998, "Talk that this is a different NATO, a NATO that is no longer a military alliance, is ridiculous. It is like saying that the hulking thing advancing towards your garden is not a tank because it is painted pink, carries flowers, and plays cheerful music. It does not matter how you dress it up; a pink tank is still a tank."[24]

In other words, there was broad-based opposition to NATO expansion among Russian policymakers of different stripes, even as there were frequent disputes on economic, social, and domestic political matters. This suggests that Moscow's position regarding NATO expansion was shaped by structural or situational pressures rather than by the parochial interests of particular actors or institutions.

To be clear, few policymakers in Moscow believed that NATO expansion posed an immediate threat. Only the most extreme hardliners feared that the Alliance would initiate military strikes on Russia in the near future. Nevertheless, NATO remained a politico-military bloc and thus a potential danger. As the abovementioned quotes indicate, Russian policymakers focused on capabilities rather than intentions. Intentions, after all, can be misrepresented or change over time. As President Yeltsin put it in a one-to-one meeting with Clinton in May 1995, "It's a new form of encirclement if the one surviving Cold War bloc expands right up to the borders of Russia. Many Russians have a sense of fear. What do you want to achieve with this if Russia is your partner? they ask. I ask it too: Why do you want to do this?"[25] Likewise,

Russian Foreign Minister Primakov noted dryly, "For any reasonable politician, plans are a variable factor but potential is a constant factor. Having a powerful military bloc being formed on our borders or near our territory irrespective of whether it poses a threat today or not, is unpleasant. It is against our interests."[26]

Indeed, President Clinton himself reflected before the signing of the Founding Act, "they [the Russians] get our promise that we're not going to put our military stuff into their former allies who are now going to be our allies, unless we happen to wake up one morning and decide to change our mind."[27] Seen against this background, it is not difficult to understand why policymakers in Moscow remained concerned about the long-term strategic consequences of NATO expansion, despite repeated assurances of Western governments that the Alliance's move towards the East was not aimed at containing Russia.

Moscow's concerns were reinforced by the open-ended character of NATO enlargement. As the 1997 Madrid Declaration expressly stated (Article 8), "The considerations set forth in our 1995 Study on NATO Enlargement will continue to apply with regard to future aspirants, regardless of their geographic location. No European democratic country (...) will be excluded from consideration."[28]

Indeed, already by the mid-1990s, Western analysts and policymakers pondered publicly about the future inclusion of other Central and Eastern European countries, including some of the post-Soviet republics (in particular the Baltic states and Ukraine). This caused a shudder to run through the spines of Russian politicians. As Vladimir Lukin, the chairman of the Duma's Foreign Relations Committee, declared, "if NATO expansion were to aim at ultimate membership for the Baltic States and Ukraine, without Russia, that would be utterly unacceptable. No Russian could possibly accept the presence of a potentially hostile NATO within striking distance of Smolensk."[29] Likewise, Foreign Minister Primakov warned, "Russia cannot remain indifferent to the factor of distance—the Baltic countries' proximity to our vital centers. Should NATO advance to new staging grounds, the Russian Federation's major cities would be within striking range of not only strategic missiles, but also tactical aircraft."[30] And Yeltsin's foreign policy aide Dmitrii Ryurikov made it clear that if NATO included any "neighboring country" Russia would "revise its position towards the Western alliance."[31]

The list of such statements could go on, but the point is clear: government officials in Moscow were deeply worried about the possibility that NATO expansion's open-ended character would lead to the admission of countries from the former Soviet area, an area that Moscow considered to be its direct sphere of influence—its real "near abroad"—for historical, cultural, economic, and geopolitical reasons. Indeed, as the declassified memcons and telcons show, President Yeltsin repeatedly raised the issue with President Clinton. For example, at the Helsinki Summit in March 1997, he emphasized that "one thing is very important: enlargement should not embrace the former Soviet republics. I cannot sign any agreement without such language. Especially Ukraine."[32] President Yeltsin also noted, "We followed closely Solana's [the then-General Secretary of NATO] activities in Central Asia. They were not to our liking. He was pursuing an anti-Russian course."[33] And at the end of the Helsinki Summit, President Yeltsin even proposed to Clinton, "regarding the countries of the former Soviet Union, let us have a verbal, gentlemen's agreement — we would not write it down in the statement — that no former Soviet republics would enter NATO. This gentlemen's agreement would not be made public."[34] President Clinton rejected this politely but firmly.

Clearly then, strategic imperatives were central for Russia's resentment to the first round of NATO expansion. The leadership in Moscow was concerned especially about the possibility that NATO military infrastructure would be moved closer to the Russian border. Equally worrisome was the uncertainty about the long-term intentions of Western governments and their response to other aspirant countries given the open-ended character of enlargement.

Ideational Factors

How then did ideational factors play into Russian behavior? Some observers highlight how Russian policymakers suffered from a Cold War hangover, meaning that Moscow focused on the United States and NATO as potential threats because of deep-seated mistrust born of the Cold War. NATO, after all, had been established as a military alliance against the Soviet Union. It is therefore perhaps unsurprising that Russia, as the principal successor state to the USSR, was opposed to NATO's eastward extension. But the problem was also generational. As many decision makers had grown up and been trained during the East-West confrontation, vestiges of Cold War thinking were almost certainly present among parts of the Russian foreign policy establishment. As one observer put it, "present day Russian politicians and journalists are almost all themselves products of the USSR. A mistrust of Western, and especially American, motivations was inculcated in them during their childhood school days and in their early professional careers."[35]

That said, there are also obvious difficulties with viewing Russian opposition to NATO expansion as a straightforward extension of a Cold War mentality.

First, this line of reasoning cannot explain why resentment to NATO enlargement was shared across the political spectrum. As noted, even reformers such as Chubais and Yavlinsky—certainly no Cold Warriors—opposed the Alliance's enlargement.

Second, such an explanation ignores the fact that Russia cooperated with NATO on a wide range of issues, from the non-proliferation of nuclear weapons to counter-terrorism and military crisis management. Take the war in Yugoslavia. Although Moscow opposed air strikes, it supported key UN resolutions against Serbia and worked with NATO on the peacekeeping operation in Bosnia.[36] This would have been unthinkable during the Cold War; and it shows that the Russian leadership was willing to cooperate with the Alliance.

Third, in the transcripts of the calls and personal conversations between Presidents Yeltsin and Clinton, there are no discursive structures reminiscent of Cold War thinking. To the contrary, both presidents were well aware of the shadow of the past and wanted to overcome it. And yet, Yeltsin opposed the Alliance's enlargement. Thus, while the legacy of the Cold War most likely influenced Russian perceptions of NATO, it was certainly not the sole or even primary source of Moscow's resentment to eastward expansion.

A second variant of the ideational argument stresses the role of Russian status concerns. For example, Hilary Driscoll and Neil MacFarlane have pointed out that "[NATO] enlargement runs directly counter to commonly held Russian perceptions of themselves as a great power."[37] Taras Kuzio has similarly concluded that Russian resentment to NATO expansion can be attributed to "questions of coming to terms with loss of empire and Great Power status."[38] And Peter Shearman has argued that "[t]he majority of Russians, the elite and the wider population, has been consistently opposed to NATO expanding closer to Russia's borders, not out of any sense of direct military threat, but due to psychological factors linked to questions of prestige and identity."[39]

The leadership in Moscow, no doubt, was status-sensitive. This was visible in President Yeltsin's efforts to make Russia a member of the G7 group of advanced industrialized states. Likewise, Yeltsin often referred to status concerns when debating NATO expansion (and international affairs more generally) with President Clinton. Yeltsin complained, for instance, that "Russia is not consulted on some issues but Russia is a great power."[40] He also demanded "to get a clear understanding of your [Clinton's] idea of NATO expansion because now I see nothing but humiliation for Russia if you proceed."[41] Moreover, he stressed that "Russia is a great power to be reckoned with and that no problem can be addressed without Russia."[42] In particular, President Yeltsin was concerned that the post-Soviet Russian rump state would be relegated to a second-ranked power on the European periphery without a say in the formation of the continent's new post-Cold War order.

What is more, several scholars have argued that the Russian elite's conception of great-power status is bound up with a sense of entitlement to a regional sphere of influence along its periphery.[43] This helps to explain why Russian policymakers responded so strongly to NATO expansion's open-ended character and the possibility that former Soviet republics would join the Alliance in the future.

To acknowledge all this, though, is not to say that Russia's resentment to NATO expansion can be solely explained by reference to status concerns. As described above, there were also strategic imperatives at play. Indeed, in situations when strategic imperatives conflicted with status concerns, the former trumped the latter. For example, Russia was initially hesitant to become a member of the PfP program, for several reasons. One was that the program treated Russia on par with other post-communist countries and did not provide Moscow with a special role. This challenged Russia's view of itself as a great power. But, once Moscow came to regard PfP as a venue to influence and possibly hold up the process of NATO expansion (mistakenly, as it later turned out), status concerns were set aside and it decided to join the program.[44] In other words, status concerns are best understood not as the root cause of Moscow's opposition, but rather as a reinforcing factor that amplified Russia's strategically induced resentment to NATO's eastward expansion.

Domestic Politics

According to some scholars, domestic political developments in Russia were the key driver for Moscow's opposition to the planned enlargement of NATO. For example, Allen Lynch has argued that "the communist-nationalist political opposition to Yeltsin's government at home quickly realized that the prospect of NATO's extension eastward could be exploited so as to undermine the government's nationalist credentials. In response, Yeltsin just as rapidly moved to close the rhetorical gap with the communists, so that there is no longer a serious difference between government and opposition on the issue."[45] In this view, President Yeltsin started to oppose NATO enlargement—not because of strategic imperatives and status concerns—but because the issue served to placate communist-nationalist forces at home who challenged his presidency. This was especially important after the December 1993 parliamentary elections, in which Vladimir Zhirinovsky's right-wing party garnered 23 percent of the votes, not least due to his appeal among military servicemen.[46] Yeltsin therefore decided to adopt a more assertive stance towards the West in general and NATO in particular to boost his nationalist credentials.

While intuitively appealing, this explanation is problematic for several reasons.

First, there is a timing problem. As indicated above, members of the Yeltsin government began to oppose NATO enlargement by mid-1993, that is, prior to the strong showing of Zhirinovsky's party in December. Logically, therefore, the latter cannot have caused the former. Of course, Yeltsin had been under pressure from communist reactionaries and hardline nationalists since fall 1992. Thus, one might argue that he indeed had good reasons to placate nationalist voters in the run-up to the elections by adopting a tougher stance on NATO. If so, the gambit failed as right-wingers won almost a quarter of the votes.

Second, the underlying logic of the argument is built on shaky empirical ground. As public opinion research from the time shows, the majority of Russian citizens were not particularly interested in international affairs. Instead, they were preoccupied with plunging living standards, rising crime, and increased social insecurity. Accordingly, ordinary Russians were largely apathetic on the issue of NATO enlargement.[47] Seen against this background, it is not at all clear why the Yeltsin government would have wanted to adopt a tougher stance towards the West for electoral purposes.

Third, and related, although there existed nationalist forces in Russia that stridently opposed NATO expansion, the domestic politics argument overlooks that there also existed a powerful counter-lobby. Commercial and financial elites promoted close cooperation with the West. As James Goldgeier and Michael McFaul have demonstrated, "oil companies, mineral exporters, and bankers (...) emerged as the main societal forces pushing for greater Western integration [in the 1990s]."[48] This begs the question: why would the Yeltsin administration want to placate nationalists while incensing the equally (if not more) powerful pro-Western lobby? The logic of domestic politics provides no obvious answer to this question.

Fourth, the memoranda of conversation between Presidents Yeltsin and Clinton do not support the thesis that domestic political calculations were the primary driver behind Moscow's opposition to NATO expansion. Absence of evidence is not evidence of absence, as the saying goes. Still, one would expect that President Yeltsin had disclosed a domestic political rationale for opposing NATO expansion in private talks with Clinton, especially since the two had a close personal relationship. Indeed, Yeltsin's political survival and Russian elections figured prominently in their talks. But, apart from one passing comment, President Yeltsin did not link NATO expansion to his re-election campaign or domestic politics more generally.[49] This is surprising. Overall, then, while the domestic politics argument cannot be fully discarded, the available evidence casts considerable doubt on it.

Concluding Observations and Implications

The interplay of strategic imperatives and status concerns goes a long way to explain Moscow's resentment to the Alliance's eastward expansion. By contrast, there is limited evidence that domestic political calculations were the principal cause for Moscow's opposition. More specifically, my argument is that uncertainty about NATO's long-term intentions and the possibility that former Soviet countries might join the Alliance in the not-too-distant future were the central drivers behind Russia's negative view on enlargement. These strategic imperatives were reinforced by a latent fear that NATO expansion would demote Russia to a second-ranked power on the European periphery.

This conclusion implies that Russia would have objected to the eastward expansion of NATO no matter how the West would have packaged or presented it. The ambition of Central and Eastern European countries to join the Western Alliance was seen in Moscow both as a challenge to Russia's strategic interests and as a humiliation of its great-power status.

Some observers have argued that the West should have made a serious effort to integrate Russia into NATO during the early 1990s. Leaving aside the organizational and political challenges involved in embracing Russia as a full member, this would effectively have transformed the character of NATO. NATO would have become a collective security organization—that is, a UN-style body on the regional level—rather than a collective defense alliance. Given the well-known problems of collective security organizations and the different outlooks of the United States and Russia, it is doubtful that this would have contributed to establish a more stable and lasting security architecture in Europe.

Another option was to keep NATO in place but without expanding its membership. This, in Moscow's eyes, would have been a desirable outcome as Yeltsin kept telling Clinton, but it would have occurred at the expense, and over the heads, of the Central and Eastern European countries who were eager to join the Alliance. Moreover, large parts of the political establishments in the United States and Germany wanted to enlarge NATO towards the East, for a variety of economic, strategic, and ideological reasons. Why, one is left wondering, should these countries—and not Russia—set aside their interests?

Some observers have criticized that the West took advantage of Russia's weakness in the 1990s. That is correct, but misses the point. After all, the interests of states sometimes coincide and sometimes clash with each other; and in such situations the more powerful actor usually gets its way. This is a normal feature of international politics. It is likely, for example, that the Soviet Union would have acted in a similar way and extended the Warsaw Pact had it prevailed in the Cold War.

Instead, I would argue that lack of power political considerations—not their application—is one of the root causes of today's crisis. During the 1990s, Western governments grew accustomed to take a weaker Russia for granted. Policymakers in Washington, Brussels, and elsewhere forgot—so it seems—that the first round of NATO enlargement (as well as the second round) had been enabled by a highly asymmetric distribution of power. This changed, to some extent, as the increase in world energy prices and internal reforms under the Putin government led to the resurrection of Russian power in the mid-2000s. Accordingly, Russia adopted a more assertive stance and pushed back against Western advances into the post-Soviet space. In my view, therefore, only an approach that takes into account the configuration of interests *and* power will lead to a more stable European security order and a less adversarial relationship with Russia.

Notes

1. See, for example, Peter Conradi, *Who Lost Russia? How the World Entered a New Cold War* (London: Oneworld, 2017); William Hill, *No Place for Russia: European Security Institutions since 1989* (New York: Columbia University Press, 2018); Kimberly Marten, "Reconsidering NATO expansion: a counterfactual analysis of Russia and the West in the 1990s," *European Journal of International Security* 3, no. 2 (2017), pp. 135-161; Richard Sakwa, *Russia against the Rest: The Post-Cold War Crisis of World Order* (Cambridge: Cambridge University Press, 2017).

2. See, for example, J. L. Black, *Russia Faces NATO Expansion: Bearing Gifts or Bearing Arms?* (Lanham: Rowman & Littlefield, 2000); Roland Dannreuther, "Escaping the Enlargement Trap in NATO-Russian Relations," *Survival* 41, no. 4 (1999), pp. 145-164; Anatol Lieven, "Russian Opposition to NATO Expansion," *The World Today* 51, no. 10 (1995), pp. 196-199.

3. *Retranslation of Yeltsin Letter on NATO Expansion*, National Security Archive, George Washington University, https://nsarchive2.gwu.edu//dc.html?doc=4390818-Document-04-Retranslation-of-Yeltsin-letter-on.

4. Ibid. There is a longstanding debate among scholars as to whether a no-NATO expansion pledge was ever given to Russia. See, for example, Mark Kramer, "The myth of a no-NATO-enlargement pledge to Russia," *Washington Quarterly* 32, no. 2 (2009), pp. 39-61; Mary Elise Sarotte, "Not One Inch Eastward? Bush, Baker, Kohl, Genscher, Gorbachev, and the Origin of Russian Resentment toward NATO Enlargement in February 1990," *Diplomatic History* 34, no. 1 (2010), pp. 119-140; Joshua R. Shifrinson, "Deal or No Deal? The End of the Cold War and the US Offer to Limit NATO Expansion," *International Security* 40, no. 4 (2016), pp. 7-44; Kristina Spohr, "Precluded or Precedent-Setting: The 'NATO Enlargement Question' in the Triangular Bonn-Washington-Moscow Diplomacy of 1990-1991," *Journal of Cold War Studies* 14, no. 4 (2012), pp. 4-54.

5. Hilary D. Driscoll and S. Neil MacFarlane, "Russia and NATO after the Cold War," in *Almost NATO: Partners and Players in Central and Eastern European Security*, ed. Charles Krupnick (Lanham: Rowman & Littlefield, 2003), pp. 240-241.

6. Cited in Adrian Bridge, "Clinton pleases Poles with cash and NATO carrot," *Independent*, July 8, 1994.

7. Ibid. President Clinton had publicly uttered the phrase for the first time during his January 1994 trip to Prague. James M. Goldgeier, *Not Whether But When: The U.S. Decision to Enlarge NATO* (Washington DC: Brookings Institution Press, 1999), p. 57.

8. Telcon, 5 July 1994, https://clinton.presidentiallibraries.us/items/show/57568.

9. Martin Smith, "A Bumpy Road to an Unknown Destination? NATO-Russia Relations, 1991-2002," *European Security* 11, no. 4 (2002), p. 63.

10. Cited in Andrew Marshall, "Russia warns NATO of a 'Cold Peace'," *Independent*, December 6, 1994.

11. Cited in Roland Dannreuther, *Russian Perceptions of the Atlantic Alliance* (Final Report for NATO Fellowship, Edinburgh University, 1997), p. 18. The full text of the report is reproduced in Transition Online, *NATO Expansion: No Role for Russia*, December 15, 1995, http://www.tol.org/client/article/1708-nato-expansion-no-role-for-russia.html.

12. Cited in Dannreuther, *Russian Perceptions*, op. cit., p. 22.

13. Memcon, March 21, 1997, https://clinton.presidentiallibraries.us/items/show/57568.

14. *Founding Act on Mutual Relations, Cooperation and Security between NATO and the Russian Federation*, https://www.nato.int/cps/en/natohq/official_texts_25468.htm (emphasis added).

15. *Russian National Security Blueprint*, December 1997, https://fas.org/nuke/guide/russia/doctrine/blueprint.html.

16. Kenneth N. Waltz, "NATO Expansion: A Realist's View," *Contemporary Security Policy* 21, no. 2 (2000), p. 31.

17. Charles A. Kupchan, "Expand NATO—and Split Europe," *New York Times*, November 27, 1994.

18. Michael E. Brown, "The Flawed Logic of NATO Expansion," *Survival* 37, no. 1 (1995), p. 43.

19. Cited in Mike Bowker, "Russian Policy toward Central and Eastern Europe," in *Russian Foreign Policy Since 1990*, Peter Shearman, ed. (Boulder: Westview Press, 1995), p. 82.

20. Victor Israelyan, "Russia at the Crossroads: Don't Tease A Wounded Bear," *Washington Quarterly* 21, no. 1 (1998), p. 53.

21. Cited in Mark Kramer, "NATO, Russia, and East European Security," in *Russia: A Return to Imperialism?*, Uri Ra'anan and Kate Martin, eds. (New York: St. Martin's Press, 1995), p. 126.

22. F. Stephen Larrabee and Theodore W. Karasik, *Foreign and Security Policy Decisionmaking Under Yeltsin* (Santa Monica: RAND, 1997), p. 15.

23. Cited in Michael C. Williams and Iver B. Neumann, "From Alliance to Security Community: NATO, Russia, and the Power of Identity," *Millennium* 29, no. 2 (2000), p. 360.

24. Cited in Rick Fawn, "Realignments in Russian Foreign Policy: An Introduction," *European Security* 11, no. 4 (2002), p. 3.

25. Summary report on one-to-one meeting between Presidents Clinton and Yeltsin, The Kremlin, May 10, 1995, https://clinton.presidentiallibraries.us/items/show/57568.

26. Cited in Peter Shearman, "NATO Expansion and the Russian Question," in Robert G. Patman, ed., *Security in a Post-Cold War World*. (New York: St. Martin's Press, 1999), p. 168.

27. Cited in James M. Goldgeier and Michael McFaul, *Power and Purpose: U.S. Policy toward Russia after the Cold War* (Washington DC: Brookings Institution Press, 2003), pp. 204-205.

28. *Madrid Declaration on Euro-Atlantic Security and Cooperation*, https://www.nato.int/cps/en/natohq/official_texts_25460.htm?mode=pressrelease.

29. Cited in Anatol Lieven, "A New Iron Curtain," *The Atlantic Montly* (January 1996), p. 22.

30. Cited in Robert H. Donaldson and Joseph L. Nogee, *The Foreign Policy of Russia: Changing Systems, Enduring Interests* (Armonk: M.E. Sharpe, 2009), p. 216.

31. Cited in J. L. Black, "Russia and NATO expansion eastward," *International Journal* 54, no. 2 (1999), p. 252.

32. Memcon, March 21, 1997, https://clinton.presidentiallibraries.us/items/show/57569.

33. Ibid. Solana had toured the South Caucasus and parts of Central Asia in the spring of 1997, promoting closer ties between NATO and the countries in these regions.

34. Ibid.

35. Black, *Russia Faces NATO Expansion*, op. cit., p. 240. See also Driscoll and MacFarlane, "Russia and NATO," p. 235.

36. Bowker, "Russian Policy," pp. 87-88.

37. Driscoll and MacFarlane, "Russia and NATO," p. 253.

38. Taras Kuzio, "NATO Enlargement: The View from the East," *European Security* 6, no. 1 (1997), p. 52.

39. Peter Shearman, "The sources of Russian conduct: understanding Russian foreign policy," *Review of International Studies* 27, no. 2 (2001), p. 261.

40. Memcon, September 27, 1994, https://clinton.presidentiallibraries.us/items/show/57568.

41. Summary report on one-to-one meeting between Presidents Clinton and Yeltsin, The Kremlin, May 10, 1995, https://clinton.presidentiallibraries.us/items/show/57568.

42. Telcon, January 26, 1996, https://clinton.presidentiallibraries.us/items/show/57568.

43. Anne L. Clunan, "Historical aspirations and the domestic politics of Russia's pursuit of international status," *Communist and Post-Communist Studies* 47, no. 3-4 (2014), p. 284; Driscoll and MacFarlane, "Russia and NATO," p. 253.

44. On the international and domestic drivers of Russia's decision to join the PfP program, see Sten Rynning, "A Balancing Act: Russia and the Partnership for Peace," *Conflict and Cooperation* 31, no. 2 (1996), pp. 211-234.

45. Allen C. Lynch, "Russia and NATO: Expansion and Coexistence?" *The International Spectator* 32, no. 1 (1997), p. 85.

46. Jacob W. Kipp, "The Zhirinovsky Threat," *Foreign Affairs* 73, no. 3 (1994), pp. 84-85.

47. William Zimmerman, *The Russian People and Foreign Policy: Russian Elite and Mass Perspectives* (Princeton: Princeton University Press, 2002), pp. 187-215.

48. James M. Goldgeier and Michael McFaul, "The Liberal Core and the Realist Periphery in Europe," *Perspectives on European Politics and Society* 2, no. 1 (2001), p. 18.

49. Summary report on one-to-one meeting between Presidents Clinton and Yeltsin, The Kremlin, May 10, 1995, https://clinton.presidentiallibraries.us/items/show/57568.

Part V

The Russian Conundrum and the Balkan Backdrop

Chapter 22

NATO Enlargement 20 Years On

Malcolm Rifkind

Introduction

NATO enlargement did not begin in 1999 with the accession of Poland, the Czech Republic and Hungary. There have been, to date, seven enlargements beginning in 1952 with Greece and Turkey and ending (so far) with Montenegro in 2017. Accepting new member states has been the norm rather than the exception as regards the judgment and strategy of the United States and Western Europe.

But the admissions of Central European countries in 1999 and of the Baltic states in 2004 were different. Greek, Turkish, West German and Spanish accession were during the Cold War. Including these states enhanced the power and deterrent capability of NATO *vis-à-vis* the Soviet Union. The case for membership was overwhelming. Accession by Balkan countries in 2009 and 2017 had few military implications. They were contested by the Kremlin but, except with Montenegro, did not cause any significant controversy.

In comparison, the Central Europeans and the Baltic states were not just much closer to Russia. The Baltic states had been part of the Soviet Union. All these countries were also formerly part of the Warsaw Pact, and had been deeply integrated into Soviet military strategy. Neither Mikhail Gorbachev nor Boris Yeltsin supported enlargement. The Russian Duma and the military were increasingly hostile. Against that background it is worth noting, however, that only moderate damage was done to Western-Russian relations in the immediate aftermath of the 1999 and 2004 enlargements. The Kosovo War, NATO air strikes in Bosnia, NATO air attacks on Qadhafi's Libya in 2011 and ballistic missile defense programs caused much more serious controversy. Vladimir Putin's first public accusation of bad faith by the West in regard to NATO enlargement was not made until his speech to the Munich Security Conference in 2007 and then it was referred to in only a couple of paragraphs in a long speech with many other real or alleged grievances.

Background

The background to NATO enlargement in 1999 was, of course, the fall of the Berlin Wall and the end of the Cold War after 1989. It was a curious coincidence that these historic events occurred exactly 200 years after the fall of the Bastille and the French Revolution in 1789. But in reality, 3 separate, though interconnected, events occurred in these momentous years. The Cold War ended; Communism, as an alternative to Capitalism, collapsed throughout the Soviet bloc; and the Soviet Union, which was the Russian Empire, disintegrated being replaced by 15 independent states.

The United States and its European Allies had long sought, and worked towards, the peaceful end of the Cold War. Similarly, the West, obviously, hoped that, one day Communism would disappear but there was no expectation that that would happen in the foreseeable future. A Communist Party could, quite credibly, have remained in power in Russia after the end of the Cold War for many years.

Most extraordinary, and unpredicted, was the simultaneous disappearance, at the end of 1991, of the Soviet Union, otherwise known as the Russian Empire. Today's Russian Federation has, with the exception of the Kaliningrad enclave, European borders that are further from Western and Central Europe than they have been for centuries and are similar to those of Peter the Great's Russia in the 17th and 18th centuries.

That loss of territory, rather than the end of the Cold War or the disappearance of Communism, is what President Putin finds most distressing and unacceptable. In 2018, when asked what Russian historical event he would like to change, he replied "The collapse of the Soviet Union." In 2005 he had described that collapse as "a major geopolitical disaster of the century". He knows that modern Russia cannot be recreated with its previous boundaries but his annexation of Crimea, destabilization of eastern Ukraine and aggression towards Georgia are, in part, a consequence of his belief, and that of many Russians, that their nation's security and realization of its destiny has been imperiled.

It is worth reminding both ourselves and Putin that NATO was neither directly, nor indirectly, responsible for the disintegration of the Soviet Union. That had never been part of U.S. or NATO strategy. Indeed, when it became clear that this was likely to happen Western leaders were disconcerted and uncertain as to what should be their response.

I served as Defense Secretary of the United Kingdom from 1992-95 and as Foreign Secretary from 1995-97. I recall, and took part in, these debates both in London and at NATO meetings. While the British, and other Western governments, all recognized that the disappearance of the Soviet Union would dramatically weaken the risk of future aggression by any government in the Kremlin it was felt that it would also create major new risks and uncertainties.

Both Gorbachev and Yeltsin were moderate leaders who were determined to forge positive relations with the West and were anxious to modernize their countries and create open and more democratic societies. None of us knew who might end up as the leaders of an independent Ukraine, Kazakhstan, Belarus as well as other newly created states. Furthermore, these three countries, in particular, had large numbers of Soviet nuclear weapons stationed on their territory. Would they insist in holding on to them and becoming nuclear weapon states themselves?

These concerns even led to President George H.W. Bush visiting Kyiv, his address to the Ukrainian Parliament, and his unsuccessful attempt to persuade Ukrainian members of parliament to reconsider their demands for independence from Moscow. The Ukrainians, unimpressed, have, ever since, referred to his visit as the "Chicken Kiev" speech.

German Reunification

During the first year after the collapse of the Berlin Wall the predominant issue for both the United States and the Soviet Union was not the future of NATO *per se* or of the former Soviet satellite states in Central and Eastern Europe.

Rather it was whether the two divided parts of Germany should be allowed to reunite and, if so, on what terms. It is highly doubtful whether reunification could ever have been prevented given the enthu-siasm of the East German people and of Chancellor Helmut Kohl for the merger of the German Democratic Republic with the Federal Re-public. Margaret Thatcher tried to stop or delay it but found no allies.

It did not necessarily follow, however, that a reunited Germany would be able to be a member of NATO. That would extend NATO's borders, for the first time, to the Polish border. Soviet consent for such an enlarged NATO was not only required for diplomatic reasons. There were still very large numbers of Soviet troops and weaponry in the former GDR. Their withdrawal back to the Soviet Union, and the timing of that withdrawal, would require Soviet consent which could not be assumed.

It was during discussions on the relationship of a united Germany to NATO that the issue of future enlargement of NATO to include member states of the crumbling Warsaw Pact was first raised. The ini-tial exchanges were between the U.S. Secretary of State, James Baker and Mikhail Gorbachev in February 1990. It appears that Baker gave assurances that NATO would "not move an inch towards the east" and that NATO expansion would not be approved of by the United States.

It was also recorded that Gorbachev indicated that "a broadening of the NATO zone is not acceptable" and Baker responded "We agree with that." The German Foreign Minister, Hans-Dietrich Genscher, had indicated a similar view saying that "NATO should rule out an expansion of its territory towards the East."

The "Treaty on the Final Settlement with Respect to Germany" was signed in Moscow in September 1990. Its terms were consistent with a reunited Germany being part of NATO, including the territory of the former GDR. The United States, the Federal Republic and other Western signatories, for their part, accepted that, apart from German troops, no other NATO troops nor any nuclear weapons would be sta-tioned in the territory of the former GDR.

It is undeniable that both Baker and Genscher indicated to Gor-bachev that there was no interest in the expansion of NATO beyond the territory of the former GDR. It seems also to be the case that that was, at that time, the sincerely held view of the President of the United States and the Governments of other NATO members.

However, these were incidental, verbal statements. They do not appear to have been replicated in any formal written exchanges between Moscow and Washington. Nor is there any reference to them in the Treaty that led to German reunification. Furthermore, I am not aware that Gorbachev sought any written statements or legally binding assurances which were refused by the West.

It is interesting, in this context, to compare the Treaty on German reunification with the Austrian State Treaty of 1955 which led to the Soviet withdrawal of all its forces from Austria. The Austrian State Treaty was signed in May 1955 by the USSR, the United States, the United Kingdom, France and Austria. The issue of whether Austria would be free to join NATO or be neutral was not mentioned in the Treaty, though political union with Germany was forbidden. However, as soon as all Soviet troops had left Austria, the Austrian Parliament, in October 1955, declared permanent neutrality for the country which meant that it could not join NATO. It was well understood that the Soviet Union would not have withdrawn from Austria if that commitment had not been given in advance.

While it would have been inappropriate to include, in a Treaty providing for German reunification in 1990, commitments that NATO would not seek, nor permit, further enlargement of the Alliance, there was no procedural nor legal reason why there could not have been a separate written assurance to that effect, at that time, between the Soviet Union and the Western powers if both sides were in agreement. No such formal commitment was given. So far as I am aware, no such request was made by Gorbachev.

Polish, Czech and Hungarian Membership

The circumstances in which expansion of NATO was agreed in 1997 and occurred in 1999 were fundamentally different to those of 1990 and this should be borne in mind when allegations of bad faith are made. Not only had the Warsaw Pact dissolved itself in 1991 but the Soviet Union had ceased to exist at the end of that year and had disintegrated into 15 separate states of which Russia and Ukraine were the largest.

In May 1990 Gorbachev had suggested to James Baker that a new security structure should replace both NATO and the Warsaw Pact.

However, the subsequent collapse of both the Warsaw Pact and the Soviet Union created a security vacuum in Central and Eastern Europe which had a profound impact on thinking in Washington. The new Russian Federation would not have been able to replace the Soviet Union by filling that security vacuum as they could never have received the consent of the newly liberated East Europeans and Baltic states. It also followed, that NATO, with or without new members, could, no longer, be presented as an anti-Soviet coalition. What, as a consequence, became much more attractive was a NATO whose membership would transcend the old boundaries and reflect a new Europe with shared democratic values and security interests.

U.S. and European views as to whether NATO expansion would be acceptable were also influenced by Yeltsin, who had become President of the new Russian Federation after the disappearance of the USSR. In speeches in Warsaw and Prague in 1993 he indicated that, based on the Helsinki Final Act, every state could decide, for itself, whether to join an alliance.

The Poles and others used Yeltsin's remarks to put pressure on the West to allow them into NATO, alleging that it was now clear that Russia would be relaxed if they did. Yeltsin changed his position because of pressure from the Duma and Russian military, but by then the damage had been done.

Yeltsin, subsequently, argued for a new European security structure which would include Russia. He proposed that Russia should have a privileged relationship with NATO. This led, not to any offer to Russia of membership in NATO, but to the U.S. initiative of a Partnership for Peace (PfP) which would cover all European states including Russia and which could be a basis for possible long-term NATO membership. In January 1994 Clinton informed Yeltsin that he did not wish to speed up NATO expansion but that Russia could not expect to have a veto. The refusal to allow a Russian veto on enlargement was repeated on several occasions.

It needs to be borne in mind that while the Americans and European governments were changing their views on NATO expansion to the East the main pressure for enlargement was coming not from the existing members of NATO but from the Poles, Czechs and Hungarians. This was partly because they were nervous that Russia, one day, might again threaten their independence and freedom. But it was also their deep belief that their economic as well as their security interests required their full integration in both NATO and the European Community and that both of these objectives should be achieved as soon as possible.

They received strong support from Germany for these aspirations but other Western Europeans, including the UK, were more cautious. Most of the East and Central Europeans, apart from Poland, would bring little significant military capability to NATO, relations with Yeltsin might be damaged and London and other capitals were much more concerned about the collapse of Yugoslavia and the war in Bosnia than about NATO enlargement.

During my own years as British Defense Secretary and then Foreign Secretary, from 1992-1997 it was Bosnia and not NATO enlargement that dominated my time. There was not only concern that the war in Bosnia might spread throughout the Balkans but that Turkey and Greece might get drawn in. Géza Jeszenszky, the Hungarian Foreign Minister, visited me in London in December 1993 to lobby for NATO membership. In his chapter in this volume he has recorded that I "listened politely" to his words "but I saw that he remained skeptical."

It was also a consideration that during these years the Russian Foreign Minister, Andrei Kozyrev, was helpful rather than obstructive as Britain, France and the United States sought to resolve the Bosnian crisis. Russian support could not be taken for granted. Historically, they were very close to the Serbs and were strongly opposed to any use of NATO in air strikes against Milošević's Bosnian Serb allies. I chaired the Lancaster House conference in London, in 1995 shortly after the Srebrenica massacres. The Americans, British and French were determined to use air strikes against the Bosnian Serbs if there were further attacks on "safe areas." At Lancaster House Kozyrev could not support the use of NATO for this purpose but he was willing to abstain rather than wreck the unity of the conference. That co-operation was much appreciated.

However, it was the case that over these first few years after the end of the Cold War the interests and priorities of existing members of NATO and the new applicants were gradually coming into alignment in important respects.

Despite the end of the Cold War the United States saw a continuing need for NATO not only to guarantee European security but as part of Washington's wider determination to ensure the continuity of its own global leadership. That pointed not only towards maintaining the NATO alliance but also allowing new states, which now shared Western values, to join if they so wished.

European members of NATO shared this view. They were not only sensitive to the enthusiasm of Poles, Czechs and Hungarians to join their ranks. They also remained very nervous that the political instability and economic collapse that was continuing in Russia might lead to a power grab by extreme nationalist politicians who would have little interest in Yeltsin's reform agenda and desire to move closer to the West.

Furthermore, the collapse of Yugoslavia and the subsequent savage conflicts in Bosnia and Croatia as well as in the Caucasus was a reminder of how latent nationalist and ethnic rivalries in Hungary, Romania and elsewhere in Central Europe could lead to massive internal instability if the countries between NATO and Russia were left in a limbo outside both NATO and the European Community.

To those general considerations one other advantage of enlargement should be mentioned. Much has been made, over the years, of common membership of the EU being crucial to Franco-German reconciliation after centuries of mutual enmity. In a similar way Poland becoming a partner of Germany not just in the EU but also in NATO, was a historic change for the better.

The outcome of these developments was the invitation that was made at the 1997 NATO Summit in Madrid to Poland, the Czech Republic and Hungary to join the Alliance which they did in 1999.

To try and reassure the Russians that the enlargement of NATO did not imply indifference or hostility to them a NATO-Russia Permanent Joint Council had been agreed before the Madrid Summit. This was accepted by Yeltsin but it is doubtful if he was very impressed. It had already been emphasized by the United States and others that Russia could not expect any veto either on NATO membership nor on NATO's actions out of area.

Further Enlargement of NATO

In 2002, a further 7 countries, the Baltic states, Romania, Bulgaria, Slovenia and Slovakia were invited to join NATO. They did so in 2004. Croatia and Albania joined in 2009, Montenegro in 2017 and North Macedonia is expected to become a member in the near future.

The most contentious of these admissions were the Baltic states: Lithuania, Latvia and Estonia. Unlike the other new members, they had formerly been part of the Soviet Union. Their acceptance into NATO was seen as a particular provocation by many Russians especially as it would bring NATO's borders close to St. Petersburg. The Russians were reminded, however, that the forced annexation of the Baltic states into the Soviet Union by Stalin in 1940, during the Second World War, had never been recognized de jure by the United States, the United Kingdom and many others.

Quite apart from Russian hostility to their admission there was a serious debate within the Alliance as to whether NATO would be strengthened or weakened by Baltic membership. Joining NATO meant that the Baltic states would receive the same defense guarantee as any other member under Article 5 of the NATO Treaty. But they would be at the geographic extremity of NATO territory, sharing a border with the Russian Federation and with only a relatively narrow corridor of land linking them to Poland and the rest of the alliance. Being very small they would be unable to add, significantly, to NATO's military capability.

As the UK's Defense Secretary, I shared these concerns. I had visited the Baltic states in 1993. While in Riga I met the President of Latvia who wanted to know when his country would be admitted to NATO and why there seemed likely to be such a delay. I had advised him to be patient and had pointed out that if anyone ten years earlier had predicted that in 1993 the President of an independent Latvia would be discussing with a British Defense Secretary Latvia's admission to NATO they would have seemed to be living in a world of fantasy!

Over the subsequent years Western leaders accepted that to make an exception of the Baltic states would be unreasonable and unwise. They would have become a no man's land between Russia and NATO, like Belarus. They were non-Slav and, historically, part of Central Europe. While their defense against serious Soviet aggression would be extremely difficult, that had been even more true of West Berlin during the Cold War. As with West Berlin it has been essential, in recent years, that NATO as a whole make clear to Moscow, unambiguously, that it takes its obligations to the Baltic states as seriously as to any other member.

The Baltics, especially Estonia, have been the victims of Russian attempts at destabilization in recent years but, unlike Ukraine and Georgia they have not lost control of any of their national territory. Being members of NATO must be, at least part of, the explanation.

Should NATO have refused enlargement to the East?

It was always open to NATO to refuse to enlarge the Alliance after the end of the Cold War. No country was guaranteed membership even if it met the normal NATO criteria of being democratic, respecting the rule of law and observing Western values.

The Alliance had to decide not just whether an applicant state wished to join and shared NATO's values. A decision also had to be reached by NATO as to whether it was in the Alliance's own interest to accept all new applicants or any one of them. Two questions, on this aspect, needed to be answered.

First, would security in Europe, as a whole and for existing members of NATO, be enhanced or diminished by enlargement? The Alliance concluded that enlargement would enhance Europe's security. There is little evidence to suggest that that judgment was wrong. The new members have been well integrated into the Alliance; there have been significant increases in their defense spending; and both old and new NATO members have responded well to Russian destabilization by agreeing robust forward positioning of a NATO presence in the Baltic states and Poland.

The other question that needed to be considered before accepting a new member state was whether NATO members, especially the United States, would be prepared to deliver the Article 5 guarantee, both in letter and in spirit, if the applicant state was subject to aggression by a third party. Delivering the Article 5 guarantee did not, automatically, mean going to war if a member state was attacked but a military confrontation with an aggressor was implied if other measures did not stop aggression. The worst outcome for NATO would be to promise an Article 5 guarantee to a new member state but not deliver it despite aggression from a third party. There would not only be legitimate cries of betrayal from the country concerned. The whole credibility of NATO as a source of security for all of its existing members would also be gravely undermined.

It was for these reasons that despite being a strong champion of Ukrainian and Georgian independence I, and many other NATO ministers, have never supported their membership in NATO. It was never credible that, for example, Russian aggression towards Georgia over South Ossetia or against Ukraine in the Donbas would have led to war between Russia and NATO if Russia refused to desist. It is difficult to believe that these two countries could have been fully integrated into NATO or that the political will would have existed in the United States or Western Europe for an all-out war with Russia on their behalf.

In contrast, any attack on NATO territory in Central or Eastern Europe would be a quite different matter as it would have been if there had been aggression against any member state during the Cold War.

Some have argued that the benefit of NATO membership would have been that Russia would never have risked aggression towards Georgia or Ukraine if they had become members of NATO. One can never know what might have happened but one should not enter into solemn treaty obligations, involving a potential declaration of war, based simply on an assumption that one would never be called upon to honor such obligations.

Would Putin be much friendlier to the West today if there had been no enlargement?

The admission of former Warsaw Pact states must have been a factor in Putin's disillusion with the West, but the evidence points to enlargement being only one consideration and not the most serious.

The most virulent criticism by Moscow of NATO began with the Kosovo War when NATO planes bombed Serbia for over two months without any U.N. Security Council resolution and in the face of strong Russian protests. The bombing began 12 days after Poland, the Czech

Republic and Hungary joined NATO. There were riots outside the U.S. Embassy in Moscow and the Russians saw this as hard evidence that NATO, when the West so wished, would be an offensive not just a defensive alliance.

The Kosovo war occurred while Yeltsin was still President. The use of NATO air power to help destroy the Qadhafi regime in 2011 caused equal anger with Putin and convinced him that the United States was determined to use NATO as a prime arm of its foreign policy and in a manner that would often be in direct conflict with perceived Russian interests.

NATO has declined to accept Ukraine and Georgia as new members but the United States had sought to propose otherwise at the Bucharest Summit in 2008. Their views did not prevail with other NATO members but Putin has continued to believe that this might still happen. Putin also chose to believe that the Orange Revolution in Ukraine in 2004 and the overthrow of Yanukovych in the Maidan in 2014 were orchestrated by the United States with the support of other NATO powers. That, and not earlier NATO enlargement, was the excuse used by Putin to try to justify the annexation of Crimea.

Should Russia have been offered membership?

A more intriguing question is whether a historic mistake was made, at the time of the NATO enlargement agreed in 1997, by not inviting Russia, also, to become a member of NATO or, at least, to have a more formal relationship with the Alliance. Such a proposal might seem naïve and extraordinary today but it had some respectable advocates at the time.

Until the Madrid NATO Summit in 1997, which agreed to invite former Warsaw Pact states to join the Alliance, their remained powerful opposition to enlargement from within the U.S. foreign policy establishment. Shortly before the Summit a letter was delivered to President Clinton, arguing that NATO enlargement would be a historic mistake. It was signed by many luminaries including Robert McNamara, Gary Hart, Edward Luttwak, Paul Nitze, Sam Nunn and Richard Pipes.

The legendary George Kennan, who had drafted the Long Telegram in 1946, described enlargement as the most fateful error in the
entire post-Cold War era.

Henry Kissinger and Zbigniew Brzezinski took the opposite view.
Kissinger was characteristically eloquent and blunt in his evidence to
the U.S. Senate:

> Basing European and Atlantic security on a no man's land between
> Germany and Russia runs counter to all historical experience, es-
> pecially that of the interwar period. It would bring about two cate-
> gories of frontiers in Europe, those that are potentially threatened
> but not guaranteed, and those that are guaranteed but not threat-
> ened ... NATO expansion therefore represents a balancing of two
> conflicting considerations: The fear of alienating Russia against
> the danger of creating a vacuum between Germany and Russia
> in Central Europe.... I would strongly urge the Senate to ratify
> NATO enlargement.[1]

Those who opposed him argued that Russia was being humiliated.
They suggested that enlargement to the east would be like the Versailles Treaty which had led to Hitler and another world war, whereas
after 1945 Germany and Japan had, successfully, been brought back
into the family of nations as partners and as new democracies.

Some suggested that if enlargement was necessary it should include
Russia. Charles Kupchan of Georgetown University made that case.
But there was a crucial qualification made by Kupchan. He wrote that
"As long as Russia continues down the path of democracy"[2] its mem-
bership of NATO would be appropriate.

As British Defense Secretary, in January 1994, I sent a paper to the
Prime Minister, John Major, suggesting that, while it was unrealistic
for Russia to become a member of NATO, a new category of associate
member could be created to meet Russian interest in closer integration
with Western security. This did not seem unrealistic to me at the time.

George Kennan made a similar assumption to that of Kupchan about
Russia's new democratic credentials. He argued "Russia's democracy
is as far advanced, if not farther, as any of these countries we've just
signed to defend from Russia."[3] That might have been true in 1997.
It has, certainly, not been true since Putin's rise to power. Today, there

may still be more freedom in Russia than during Soviet times, but democracy and the rule of law are noted by their absence. Russia has reverted to an authoritarian dictatorship where the Russian people have little power to determine their ultimate destiny.

The reality is that, even in 1997, Russian membership of NATO would have been impossible unless the West could have accepted that NATO would cease to be a military alliance and become just another political organization like the OSCE. The Russians could never have accepted that their armed forces would become part of the Integrated Military Structure under overall American leadership. Even France had balked at that under de Gaulle.

Nor could NATO have accepted a Russian *de facto* veto on its operations which the Russians would have insisted on. If America was going to continue to guarantee the security of Europe it had to be through a NATO that could be used "out of area" as in Bosnia, Kosovo and Libya without the need for the Kremlin's consent.

If NATO had not enlarged, might Putin have permitted Russia to continue to move towards a more pluralist and democratic political system?

While Putin paid lip service to democratic values in his first years in power he soon lost interest. There is no evidence that supports any suggestion that NATO enlargement was relevant to his increasing authoritarianism and hostility to democracy.

Yeltsin, and Gorbachev to some degree, appear to have been genuine in their desire to transform Russia into a democratic and pluralist society. They were comfortable with Western values, which they felt could be adopted by post-Communist Russia.

Putin was different. It was not just his KGB background that explains his enthusiasm for centralizing power and eliminating organized opposition. The reality is that Gorbachev and Yeltsin, as reformers interested in pluralism, were more unusual in Russian history than is Putin. He, rather than either of them, is the natural successor to the Tsars and autocrats of Russian history.

Many in the West assumed that as Communism collapsed the Russian people, and their leaders, would not only adopt a capitalist economic model but would be attracted to liberal multi-party democracy and a vigorous and independent civic society.

That might have had a chance of happening if Yeltsin had nominated someone like Boris Nemtsov to succeed him. Fatefully, he chose Vladimir Putin instead. Putin's immediate priorities were not to expand democracy. They were to rescue Russia from a descent into internal anarchy and to crush the insurgency in Chechnya. The more he consolidated his personal power the less he was interested in sharing it with the Russian people.

It is clear that whatever might have happened with regard to NATO enlargement would not have influenced Putin in his exercise of power within Russia over the last two decades.

Without NATO enlargement might Ukraine and Georgia not have been subject to Russian aggression and deprived of their territorial integrity?

There was little doubt that, after the overthrow of Yanukovych, the new Ukrainian Government would be fiercely pro-Western and aspire not only to membership of the EU but also of NATO.

Although membership, at least in the short term, was never likely there had been some Western leaders advocating NATO membership for Ukraine and Georgia. Putin's fears were understandable even though his reaction was indefensible.

The timing of the annexation of Crimea and the aggression in the Donbas were influenced by the downfall of a pro-Russian President in Kyiv but they were part of a much wider strategy already developed by Putin. Putin realizes that Ukraine can never be reabsorbed into a new Russian Empire. But he has long believed that it could be fatally weakened by loss of control of much of its territory bordering the Black Sea. Georgia has been suffering similar loss of its territorial integrity for years, in Abkhazia and South Ossetia.

Putin had held those views for some time, but while Yanukovych was in power he felt he could rely on a compliant Ukraine without resorting to overt aggression. The Maidan in 2014 changed all that.

Conclusions

There are fundamental, geopolitical considerations that help explain why NATO enlargement to the East was right and why we are highly likely to have very difficult relations with Russia for the foreseeable future.

There was an assumption in the West that the collapse of Communism, the end of the Cold War and the disintegration of the Soviet Union would lead to a Russia that would recognize that it was no longer one of the world's two superpowers and might, therefore, become "another" European power like Germany, France or the United Kingdom.

But the Cold War after 1945 did not occur just because Moscow was ruled by Communists with a global, Marxist ideology. The Soviet Union was also the successor to the Russia of the Tsars which, for several hundred years, had extended its territory, absorbed much of historic Poland as well as what are now the Baltic states, and during the nineteenth century, after the Congress of Vienna, exercised unprecedented power in helping determine the destiny of much of Europe.

Soviet leaders, ruling from the same Kremlin as the Tsars, inherited many of these aspirations and expectations. That, as well as a desire to spread Communism, explains why they enforced their control of the countries of Eastern Europe that they had liberated from the Nazis. When the Soviet Union disintegrated and old Russia reappeared it is hardly surprising that a new generation of Russians, and Putin in particular, should, in the absence of an ideology, have returned to traditional Russian nationalism which has characterized Russian history since the days of Peter the Great.

Indeed, it is arguable that even if Putin had been willing to allow Russia to evolve towards a democratic and pluralist society that might have been combined with an expansionist foreign policy not that different to what we have experienced.

Russia, because of its massive size, its Orthodox Church, its Slav heritage and its Eurasian landmass can never be just another European country. It is quite possible that, whoever succeeds Putin in due course, will, like him, wish to see a Russia that has the power to limit the independence of its self-proclaimed "near abroad" and help direct the future of Europe as a whole. That will make Russia an uncomfortable neighbor for the rest of Europe.

This is the challenge we have faced not just from 1917 or 1945 but since the early nineteenth century. That should concern but need not depress us. It is worth recalling the remark of Lord Palmerston during the Crimean War:

> The policy and practice of the Russian Government has always been to push forward its encroachments as far and as fast as the apathy or want of firmness of other Governments would allow it to go, but always to stop and retire when it met with decided resistance.

The West will need, both by diplomatic means and through NATO, not only to protect the independence of its member states but also to impress on Moscow the unacceptability of Russia seeking to limit the freedom of Ukraine, Georgia and other post-Soviet states to determine their own destiny.

The British, French, Spanish and other former empires have gone forever. Russia, too, ceased to be an empire at the end of 1991 with the collapse of the Soviet Union. It is time for the Russian Federation to recognize not only the letter but the spirit of that historic change.

Notes

1. Testimony by Henry A. Kissinger to the Senate Foreign Relations Committee, October 30, 1997.

2. Charles A. Kupchan, "The origins and future of NATO enlargement," *Journal of Contemporary Security Policy*, Volume 21, 2000, pp. 127-148.

3. Thomas L. Friedman, "Foreign Affairs; And Now a Word From X," *New York Times*, May 2, 1998, https://www.nytimes.com/1998/05/02/opinion/foreign-affairs-now-a-word-from-x.html.

Chapter 23

Beyond NATO Enlargement to Poland, the Czech Republic, and Hungary: A French Reappraisal

Benoît d'Aboville

It is well known that victory has many fathers and defeat none. The process of NATO enlargement was no different. Bill Clinton, Helmut Kohl, Hans-Dietrich Genscher, François Mitterrand, Margaret Thatcher, Mikhail Gorbachev, Boris Yeltsin, Václav Havel, Lech Wałęsa, to name a few leading figures, without forgetting others who led democratic countries aspiring to join NATO, emerged as key players in a very personalized diplomatic process, involving a plethora of direct contacts and personal relationships.

In France, given the political stakes, the issue became the domain of President François Mitterrand and his closest Elysée aides, especially Hubert Védrine and Foreign Minister Roland Dumas, a personal friend of the President, who had a good personal relationship with German Foreign Minister Hans-Dietrich Genscher. Jacques Chirac, who succeeded Mitterrand in 1995 and who had previously been Prime Minister during the period of political "cohabitation" in 1986-1988, also focused on the issue. Both Mitterrand and Chirac were supported by a diplomatic establishment still wary of Moscow. Until the war in Bosnia, the military stayed largely on the margins.

Throughout the process France, as well as most of the other Allies, including the United States, sought to maintain the right balance between the candidate countries' understandable impatience and the fear of weakening the reformist Moscow leadership under both Gorbachev and Yeltsin, which was seen as shaky and divided on the issue.[1]

The risk of missing what was considered as an historic but perhaps fleeting window of opportunity was preeminent in the mind of Polish, Hungarian and Czech leaders, who were hammering the message in NATO capitals.

The situation in Moscow therefore became a constant preoccupation for Western leaders, and put them in a quandary. The aborted coup of August 1991 and the collapse of the USSR had served as a powerful reminder of the weakness of the Kremlin leadership. It was seen as a call for accelerating the opening of NATO up to the East. At the same time, Mitterrand and other Western leaders, at least until 1994, remained cautious so as not to endanger the political survival of their Moscow interlocutors, who constantly reminded them of the stiff opposition they were facing.

A Cautious Mitterrand

From the outset, Paris was convinced that once German reunification had been achieved on Western terms, Washington would do everything to convince Moscow of the need for NATO's enlargement, whatever the Allies might think or propose. Mitterrand himself shared this view and told Gorbachev so.

The inclusion of unified Germany within NATO—a remarkable achievement of President Bush and Secretary Baker and their teams in liaison with a determined Chancellor Kohl—led indeed to the Alliance's widening to Central and Eastern Europe, even if the two issues were separated at the start. The question was therefore not the end game, but the timing (the French were pleading for patience) and the framework. The Conference on Security and Cooperation in Europe (CSCE) was considered the obvious place to host such a process, as Moscow was already a member.

As those questions were obviously had great bearing with regard to the new organization of post-Cold War Europe and its implications for the future of NATO, it appeared quickly that Paris and Washington, while sharing the same views regarding the status of the reunified Germany,[2] did not have exactly the same priorities regarding a new political framework.

France opposed the Soviet idea of a "neutralized Germany with no NATO military structures in the territory of today GDR." In January 1990 in Paris, Mitterrand reminded U.S. Deputy Secretary of State Larry Eagleburger that "it has always been the wish of USSR and it was unacceptable."

Within the German SPD, however, the same concept had long been advanced as a way to facilitate reunification. It was somewhat reintroduced into the debate by German Foreign Minister Genscher in his Tutzing speech of January 31, 1990.[3] He was immediately opposed by President Bush, who convinced Chancellor Kohl to distance himself from his coalition partner.

Mitterrand agreed with Bush, using the reasoning U.S. Secretary of State James Baker presented early to Gorbachev: would it not be better for Moscow to have Germany within NATO and therefore anchored into the West, rather than to have a loose neutral Germany, unhinged and likely to raise the anxiety of its neighbors?

Mitterrand used the same line with Gorbachev when they met bilaterally in Moscow on May 25, 1990. Other schemes, denied of any practicality, were also proposed by Gorbachev during the same meeting, when he mentioned to a skeptical Mitterrand that Germany could belong either in both political camps or even adopt what the Soviet leader called "the French model," i.e. a non-military integrated member within the Alliance. Gorbachev even alluded to the possibility of the USSR being a member both of the still-existing Warsaw Pact and of NATO.

It puzzled many French observers that Moscow did not attempt to throw a spanner into the process at a time when it could have been still possible for the Russians to stop it. This view is shared by historian Mary E. Sarotte: "for a moment in February 1990 the Soviets could have made an agreement with Washington freezing NATO expansion to the East in not including East Germany within NATO. Gorbachev didn't do it and the opportunity vanished."[4]

Even so, it took four years more of intra-Alliance debates, the 2+4 negotiations, and many bilateral discussions with Moscow to arrive at the point when the Central and East Europeans could be told that the question was no longer "if" but "when," as President Clinton stated publicly after his January 1994 Prague lunch with the leaders of the "Visegrád" group—Czechoslovakia, Hungary and Poland.

Until 1997, the French were much less confident than the Americans that the Kremlin would accept NATO enlargement sincerely and for the long term. They were not persuaded that President Clinton and the "Bill-Boris" personal relationship was the key to explain the weak resistance of the Russian leaders. Paris indeed suspected that Moscow would sooner or later try every trick to derail the process, including, under various guises, by using the old theme of the "European Common House." Hence the repeated French insistence to embed German reunification and the enlargement of NATO into a new general architecture of Europe, which, without isolating Moscow and giving it veto power, would not appear to exclude Russia from the "new Europe."

The Paris CSCE Summit of November 1990 was considered as a successful first step in this direction. But it was only by 1996 and with the NATO-Russia Founding Act of May 1997 that it was reasonably possible to put aside the prospect that a last-ditch change of heart of the Kremlin would endanger the process.

Mitterrand knew, of course, that he did not possess any leverage with Moscow similar to that of the United States. The fact that Clinton had stated, right at the start of his first term, that his personal political priority was to build a new American-Russian relationship was reassuring for the men in the Kremlin. They thought that they could still count on Washington to consider Russia as the Great Power it had been until now, at the very moment they were discovering that they were losing their place and role in Europe (this is precisely what Putin would denounce later on in 2007 as Yeltsin's fatal misjudgment). At the same time, they were expecting, as a quid pro quo, a massive influx of financial and economic aid to redress their floundering economy. They believed that Washington was the key. In point of fact, however, Washington resisted Helmut Kohl's entreaties at G-7 meetings, considering that an unreformed Soviet system would not make good use of international aid.

Throughout this period, President Mitterrand remained convinced of the need of a cautious step-by-step approach to both NATO and EU enlargement. He spoke of a timeframe of "10 to 15 years." His stance was utterly disappointing for the candidate countries. The issue would come to a head with them at the time of his ill-fated "Confederation" proposal.

In addition to his personal tendency to put events in an historical perspective and thus, in his formulation, "give time to the time," Mitterrand had two additional political motivations.

The first was that while NATO and EU enlargements did not need to proceed in lockstep, as everyone understood from the start, Central Europeans needed both security guarantees and urgent economic aid. The Germans, for obvious reasons, were especially keen in stabilizing their immediate neighborhood with the support of the European Community (EC). As early as 1992 the EC was already working through the Commission of Jacques Delors to develop a program to that end.

For the French President, however, consolidating the EC in the wake of German reunification was a much higher priority than NATO enlargement. At the start, Mitterrand didn't hide his concern about Bonn's attitude: would reunification make Bonn less interested in the EC's drive towards political union and the building of a European monetary system? Kohl, who was keen about a deeper political union after the fall of the Berlin Wall, soon reassured Mitterrand, even accepting an acceleration of the preparations for the European monetary union, for which Paris had been pushing. The Maastricht EU summit at the end of 1992 put to rest Mitterrand's concerns.

He remained much more worried about the implications of EU enlargement rather than that of NATO, however. Premature accession of Eastern and Central European countries to the EU could, in his view, not only divert the political attention and diplomatic endeavors of other Europeans partners from this process, but also "dilute" the EU. Moreover, both Mitterrand and his successor, Jacques Chirac, suspected that London was using enlargement to slow down the European integration project and to continue to reduce it into a free market zone. For Paris, therefore, "deepening" of the EU had to precede its "widening." As a result, the political and diplomatic work undertaken to implement deeper EU integration at summits in Maastricht in 1992, Amsterdam in 1997 and, for Chirac, Nice in 2000 would overshadow by far in Paris the concerns about NATO preparations for its own enlargement.

As far as NATO was concerned, Paris also proposed "a renovation of the Alliance" as a prerequisite for its actual widening. Given France's special position as a non-integrated Ally, Paris had a weak card. Nevertheless, France, under Mitterrand, and later more actively under Chirac, tried to establish a link between its support for NATO enlargement and Allied agreement to recognize a "European pillar" within the Alliance. It was a way to reconcile the French view that NATO needed to renew and revamp its structures in view of broadening its membership with its aim of bolstering the European Defense and Security Identity (ESDI) within the transatlantic Alliance.

Mitterrand's second political motivation for moving slowly on NATO enlargement stemmed from his personal conviction that NATO, having lost its military *"raison d'être"* after the dissolution of the Warsaw Pact, would also slowly lose its political relevance. At that time, NATO's "existential problem" was indeed common talk in Europe, and not only in Paris. Most of the French political-military establishment was convinced that, even with a different political role, NATO would remain a necessary military organization. Yet, Mitterrand's personal views were more ambiguous. In 1999 he told a puzzled German President Richard von Weizsäcker that, in his view, "there is a reality: NATO is fading away, and there is a virtuality: European defense is reinforcing itself."

In retrospect, President Mitterrand underestimated Washington's willingness to act on what it perceived to be its strategic interest in giving a new role and saliency to NATO by enlarging it externally and renovating it internally.

Already in 1989 President Bush had set forth the vision of a "Europe whole and free." In 1994 President Clinton called for "a peaceful and undivided Europe." For Washington, a "Euro-Atlantic approach" was not only the right solution to fill the new security and political void in Central and Eastern Europe, it was also a way to maintain a strong American presence on the continent, at a time when numerous voices in the United States were calling for a reduction of the U.S. troop presence on the continent after the dissolution of the Warsaw Pact.

Much to the regret of Paris, the NATO London Summit in July 1990 did not signal that the "Europeanization" of NATO, as advocated by France, could be part of the actual "renovation" of NATO. Allies instead focused their attention eastward. At the NATO Summit in Rome in November 1991, the Allies offered institutional cooperation with the new Eastern Europe democracies through the creation of the North Atlantic Coordination Council (NACC), even if, at that stage, it was designed more as a framework for political dialogue than a program for preparation of a full-fledged adhesion. It would be later systematized with the institution of the Partnership for Peace (PfP).

In fairness, one should note that some "historic" members of the Alliance, such as the UK, Turkey, and parts of the German military establishment, as well as East Central European aspirant countries themselves, were concerned about the possible negative military implications of enlargement, the weakening of the Article 5 security guarantee and the prospect of more problematic diplomatic management of a larger and less homogenous Alliance. This line would be later used by the opponents to enlargement during the ratification debates in the U.S. Senate in 1999, including by Henry Kissinger, U.S. Senator John Warner, and George Kennan. Those concerns, however, were not expressed in Paris.

Paris and the "Kidnapped Europe"

Mitterrand's cautious approach toward the candidacy of Poland, Czech Republic and Hungary to join the EU and NATO was a paradox, given the President's own personal history and the steadily growing sympathy expressed by the French public toward the cause of freedom and democracy in Eastern Europe.

Especially since the 1970s, and even earlier, France had a tradition of hosting a very active community of intellectuals and dissidents from those countries, which Milan Kundera—himself a Czech émigré from the 1958 "Prague Spring" who had lived in Paris since 1975—described famously as the "kidnapped Europe."

Pavel Tigrid, an aide to Jan Masaryk, a former employee of Radio Free Europe, and a close friend of Václav Havel, was a Paris publisher of a review entitled *Svedectvi*, which became the rallying point for the post-1968 Czech dissidents. Earlier, with the remaining press funds of the Polish Brigade, which distinguished itself at the Monte Cassino battle in 1944, a group of Polish intellectuals, meeting in Maisons Laffite under the direction of Jerzy Giedroyc, had founded the magazine *Kultura* and began to send clandestinely to Poland the works of writers like Czesław Miłosz (who later emigrated to California), Leszek Kołakowski (living in Oxford), Gustaw Herling-Grudziński (living in Naples), and artist Józef Czapski. Bronisław Geremek had been obliged to leave Poland at the time of the anti-Semitic purge of the hard line Natolin faction fighting Gomulka within the Polish Communist Party.

He took refuge in France and was given a post to teach at the College de France. The Hungarians could count on François Fejtő.

Kot Jeleński and Georges Liébert linked the Paris émigrés with the Ford Foundation, the reviews *Contrepoint* and *Encounter*, Radio Free Europe and Radio Liberty, as well as international networks such as the Pen Club.[5] Most importantly, in Paris, they were supported by a cluster of well-connected and influential French intellectuals, including the poet Pierre Emmanuel, Raymond Aron, George Nivat, François Bondy and Pierre Hassner.

Following the Prague Spring and the first demonstrations by *Solidarnosc*, a growing fraction of French public opinion, beyond the Parisian intellectual circles, had started supporting actively the quest for freedom in the East European countries. The reason was not only popular support for human rights and cultural freedom but because it was also a way for leftist intellectuals and politicians to demonstrate that they were breaking from the political grip of communism.

For a long time, communism had held a stronghold on French cultural life, as it had in Italy. The events in Prague in 1968 had a stunning effect, however, and deeply affected the liberal left. The repression and the ideological rigidity of the Soviet Communist Party, compounded by the behavior of a still-Stalinist French PCF party, unleashed a hemorrhage among the ranks of its sympathizers.[6] In 1974 French public opinion was electrified by the appearance of Aleksandr Isayevich Solzhenitsyn on prime-time television; Soviet dissidents became *"des causes celèbres."*

The proclamation in Poland in December 1981 of martial law and the brutal repression of *Solidarnosc* added to the evolution of French public opinion. Traditional French sympathy for the Poles, reinforced by a large inflow of Polish workers from the 1930s, distant memories of French support for the Polish uprising of 1830, and the spontaneous rise of a wide network of supporters from Catholic and trade union associations, which clandestinely sent material help to Poland, made support of *Solidarnosc* a popular movement that could no longer be ignored by French politicians.

Mitterrand himself had been involved in those debates as a member of the Council of Europe. He had travelled extensively in Eastern

Europe as a participant in meetings of the Socialist International, a federation of European socialist parties where the German SPD had dominant influence. He supported Willy Brandt's *Ostpolitik*, much to the consternation of the French foreign policy establishment, which was aware that until Mitterrand's election in 1981 he had not yet distanced himself openly from Egon Bahr's 1963 proposals for a progressive evolution of Central Europe towards neutralization.

The idea had infuriated President Pompidou and Henry Kissinger, but at the time had been supported by several Central and Eastern European dissidents, including Václav Havel: the "Prague Appeal" of March 1985 called for the dissolution of the two Pacts and the withdrawal of American and soviet troops.

For President Mitterrand, who had in 1981 gambled on an electoral alliance with the French Communist party and included some members in the government, support for freedom in Eastern Europe and for the dissidents was therefore not only a matter of personal conviction but also a way to distance himself from his temporary communist and leftist political partners. Mitterrand did not hesitate to take diplomatic risks to support the dissidents openly.

In June 1984, during his first official dinner in the Kremlin Great Hall, Mitterrand stunned his Politburo hosts by not hesitating ask for the release of Andrei Sakharov. Later, on his first visit to Prague in December 1988, one year before the fall of the Berlin Wall, Mitterrand made his visit to President Gustáv Husák conditional on a guarantee that he could receive eight well-known dissidents, including Havel, at the French Embassy for a breakfast. Havel said that "he came to Palais Buquoy with his toothbrush," expecting to be arrested by the police when he left.

Moscow was well aware of Mitterrand's lack of sympathy vis-à-vis the USSR. He had campaigned against Giscard d'Estaing's attempts to keep open the dialogue with the Soviet Union after the Afghan invasion. At the beginning of his term, Mitterrand expelled as spies 46 members of the Soviet Embassy in Paris.[7] Therefore, there was never great confidence from either side in the Paris-Moscow dialogue, even if Moscow feigned appreciation for the French position on NATO enlargement, which, as Russians confided on many occasions to other interlocutors, including Americans, "was different from that of Washington."

In his Moscow meeting with Gorbachev on May 25, 1990, Mitter-rand tried to clarify his position: "I am perfectly aware that German reunification and its membership in NATO create very big problems for you. I am also experiencing difficulties in this regard but of a dif-ferent order. This is why I am stressing the need to create security conditions for you, as well as European security as a whole. This is one of my guiding goals, particularly when I proposed my idea of creating a European Confederation. It is similar to your concept of a common European home." He added, however, the question of reunified Ger-many included as a whole within NATO: "France cannot allow itself to end up somewhere on the sidelines of the North Atlantic Alliance."[8]

The CSCE Gambit

German reunification in 1990 came as a diplomatic surprise. It is important to recall, however, that for years the West had managed a successful policy towards the East. The principal instrument was the CSCE process, which had long involved the civil society and intellec-tuals of the new democracies that were now aspiring to NATO mem-bership. The history of EU and NATO enlargement cannot be totally disassociated from this context.

Before the fall of the Berlin Wall, there was already a large consen-sus, officialized in the Alliance's Harmel Report of 1967, that the West should try to "Finlandize" Eastern Europe, as Lord Carrington used to say, and to "set a policy of controlled, peaceful and piecemeal chang-es—one that would ultimately alter the face of Eastern Europe without triggering off the defence mechanism arising from the age-old Russian security complex," as Theo Sommer, editor of *Die Zeit*, put it.[9]

Indeed, from the first preliminary talks held in the Helsinki suburb of Dipoli in 1972 until the approval of the Charter of Paris in 1990, the CSCE process became one of the main themes of French diplomacy in East-West relations, for three reasons.[10]

First, notwithstanding the fact that the alliances remained a reality during the negotiations, the CSCE became the first practical experi-ment of a common European external policy, and a successful one at that.

Second, the CSCE was a daring experiment with a kind of modern "post-Westphalian diplomacy." Through pan-European circulation of persons and ideas the aim was to counter the prevailing incarnation, among Warsaw Pact countries, of the old principle of *cuius regio eius religio*.

Third, the CSCE process was not only about human rights, as has too often been presented. It also involved economic cooperation and security considerations. The latter aspect became the be main objective of French diplomacy at the Madrid Review Conference from 1980 to 1983.

In the United States, President Gerald Ford and Secretary of State Henry Kissinger, faced with Congressional opposition to "détente," were tempted to belittle the importance of the CSCE process, their priority at the time being negotiations to reduce strategic arms (SALT) and conventional forces (MBFR).[11]

The French, the Germans and other Europeans insisted on receiving precise commitments in the "Third Basket" of issues dealing with human rights, press and culture and freedoms. While Kissinger joked about the "swahili" of those detailed negotiations, the French were battling, among other measures, to secure the right to open "reading rooms" within French cultural institutes in East Central European countries that would be accessible to ordinary citizens. Before 1989, Havel himself valued his regular visits to the French cultural institute on Stepanska street in Prague. The widespread publication of the text of the Helsinki Act in "the principal journals" of all signatory countries, including those in the East, contributed to establish the creation of "Helsinki groups" of dissidents and encouraged contacts with civil society in those countries.

The Helsinki Final Act,[12] the result of long and patient diplomatic work, was thus considered in Paris as a great success that should not be abandoned because of NATO enlargement. For the French, the two processes did not collide and could be complementary, especially because the CSCE, in spite of its imperfections and the cumbersome way it functioned, was still at the time of German reunification the only Europe-wide framework available.

A few days after the Berlin Wall fall, Chancellor Kohl seized the political initiative by presenting to the Bundestag 10 points the German government intended to follow. Several of the points referenced an overall European process: (6) "the embedding of the future structure of Germany within the Pan-European process, for which the West has paved the way with its concept of a lasting and just order of peace;" (7) "openness and flexibility of the European Community with respect to all reformed countries in Central, Eastern and Southeastern Europe, naturally including the GDR;" (8) "energetic progress in the CSCE process using the forthcoming forums."

Most importantly, the Helsinki Final Act stated explicitly that each nation had the right to choose its own military alliance or remain neutral. At the crucial Bush-Gorbachev meeting in Washington on May 31, 1990, President Bush, referring to the Helsinki Final Act, cleverly advanced the argument that a new united Germany would have the right to choose its alliance. Gorbachev could not find a way to object, much to the consternation of his delegation.

When Boris Yeltsin visited Warsaw in August 1993, he would also acknowledge with Lech Wałęsa that the Helsinki Final Act recognized the right of all member countries to choose their alliance: it was immediately interpreted by Wałęsa as the "green light" for Poland to be allowed to join NATO, even if, soon afterward, Yeltsin retreated from his position.

During the 2+4 negotiations on German reunification, the Allies repeated that the "CSCE should be enhanced to ensure a significant role for the USSR in the new Europe." Gorbachev came back repeatedly to the idea that "the CSCE be the principal mechanism to developing a new security order in Europe." The London NATO summit in June 1990 echoed the intent of the Allies to diversify and "strengthen the role of the CSCE."

In the same vein, Yeltsin told Clinton at their Halifax meeting in June 1995 that "NATO is a factor too of course, but NATO should evolve into a political organization."[13] Moscow was never able to make precise proposals, however, beyond the reference to the need of using the CSCE forum to negotiate the reduction of conventional forces in Europe.

Negotiations to reduce Conventional Forces in Europe (CFE) originated from a French initiative at the second CSCE Review Conference in Madrid. In November 1980 a proposal had been endorsed by the Atlantic Alliance with the aim to prepare a mandate for opening an alternative to the deadlocked MBFR negotiations in Central Europe, which had been going on for about a decade. Paris had long been hostile to this pact-to-pact negotiation on troop reductions in a narrow band of territory in Central Europe. Paris became even more preoccupied when NATO introduced what it called "option 3" dealing with nuclear-deployed weapons in the zone. The idea to introduce a new approach of conventional arms control in the CSCE framework raised, at first, American opposition. The human rights specialists worried, in the words of the head of delegation at Madrid, Max Kampelman, that "putting the elephant of security in the bathtub of human rights" would unbalance the whole process.

There were also some reservations at NATO headquarters. The MBFR had been seen as an opportunity to establish contacts with the Warsaw Pact in Vienna and as a way to head off the Mansfield amendment in the U.S. Congress, which threatened to reduce U.S. troops in Europe. A French proposal aimed, in fact, to kill MBFR and to start the conventional negotiations over again with a wider framework of 23 countries, beginning with confidence-building measures, was therefore a priori eminently suspect.[14]

However, even if some NATO delegates went almost apoplectic during the intra-Alliance preparation of the negotiating package, which was further addressed at a Stockholm Conference in 1984, the approach succeeded and led to a complex agreement on conventional forces reductions and transparency measures. The CFE framework proved itself quite useful to settle the difficult issue of troops ceiling for reunified Germany. The adaptation of regional troop ceilings in CFE II would later take into account the massive conventional force reductions resulting from the end of the Warsaw Pact. Signed in November 1990 in Paris, the CFE treaty remained an element of the new European security architecture until Russia withdrew from it in 2008.[15]

The CSCE as a new pan-European security framework was also widely supported by the democratic opposition in Central and Eastern Europe. As the one institution to which they already belonged, and with its focus on an all-European approach, it was natural that such a political forum should be attractive for them and that it could possibly be institutionalized. In Prague, Havel and his foreign affairs minister Jiří Dienstbier therefore proposed in April 1990 a permanent OSCE-based "Security Commission," which would replace both NATO and the Warsaw Pact. It was obviously not acceptable for NATO and other East Central European countries. Havel demurred at a meeting of the Council of Europe in May.

The idea of semi-permanent structures for the CSCE reappeared in the "Paris Charter for a new Europe," signed at the Paris Summit of 1990. This CSCE Summit meeting was considered a French success, but Mitterrand didn't build on it. In the meantime, he had become wedded to his personal pet project: the "Confederation."

The Confederation: A Bridge Too Far?

At the end of December 1989, Mitterrand surprised everyone by introducing a proposal for a new East-West forum, which he called the "Confederation," whose link with the CSCE was ambiguous. The stated purpose was to develop concrete long-term cooperative projects in a flexible framework, allowing nations, firms, institutions to build bridges between the two sides. Those projects could be advanced with different combinations of participants ("variable geometry") so as to avoid institutional rigidities. Military and security issues were not to be addressed in the Confederation.

The subtext was that the Confederation would serve as a bridging mechanism between the present economic and social condition of aspirants to the EEC and the ultimate date of accession to the EC, which Mitterrand saw as a more distant objective. It had also the purpose of harmonizing the various agreements between the concerned candidates. Mitterrand had pointed out to Havel that accession to the EC (later EU) would require time; aspirants would need to meet the substantial conditions of the *acquis communautaires*. It was better to start with a series of practical cooperation initiatives, which could lead progressively to the required level of readiness to accession.

As soon as the details emerged, however, many began to question the very rational for this French proposal. The Germans started to distance themselves from an initiative that they saw as duplicating the Second Basket of the CSCE and possibly complicating the ambitious national policy they were about to implement in an area in which Germany historically had been present. While the inclusion of the already weakened USSR was mentioned (Mitterrand argued it was important "not to isolate them" just when the Soviet Union was being dismantled), U.S. participation was not anticipated, at least at the start: civil society representatives and economic actors would represent them. Washington was furious and began a campaign against the whole idea. The European Commission was also worried about potential competition in its own area of competence.

Havel, who at first applauded at the project and had agreed to host it in Prague, began to retract, not only because the United States would be absent, but also because of the negative reactions he was getting from around Europe. The legitimate suspicion that the Confederation was designed as a way station before enlarging the EC, or even worse, as a permanent holding pen, could only generate negative reactions. Mitterrand himself, to the utter dismay of his staff, bluntly confirmed these suspicions in a radio interview on June 12, 1991, on the very eve of the opening of the conference, and so, essentially, sank the whole idea.

The ensuing debates in Prague were considered as "useful" but, as Havel put it at the closing of the conference on June 14, somewhat "futurologistic." The small secretariat supposed to be created in Prague was forgotten and the follow-on anticipated for the conference attracted no takers. Two months later, the attempted putsch in Moscow diverted attention from the already- stillborn Mitterrand project.

The failure of the Confederation had no real political impact in France. By the end of the year the success of the Maastricht Treaty silenced the criticism of a bungled diplomatic venture. It could have been anticipated, but the personal involvement of the President and his close staff had made the forewarning of failure not an easy task for the diplomatic apparatus. It was a disaster for the influence of France in East Central Europe and had a lasting effect on Paris' credibility as far as the EU enlargement was concerned. It would be up to Mitterrand's successor, Jacques Chirac, to redress the negative impressions created, even at the price of a rather demagogic competition with Kohl for promising a fixed date for the accession of new candidates to the EU.

Some diplomats argued that the Confederation could have played a useful role, and that it was a "good idea too soon."[16] Paris had however misunderstood that Washington's policy toward the new Europe was not simply geared to preserving NATO and the U.S. military presence but to redefining American political influence on the continent. Trying to separate the two tracks was indeed consistent with the French view about the role of the EC, but was not acceptable to Washington.

Bosnia and the NATO 1997 Madrid Summit: Who Would Be Next?

The enlargement debate clearly could not be isolated from external crises. The Bosnian war, which began in 1991 after Slovenia and Croatia unilaterally declared independence from the Yugoslav Federation, was critical. As Ron Asmus wrote: "NATO enlargement would never have happened absent the U.S. and NATO's all-out and eventually successful effort to stop the war raging in Bosnia."[17]

Bosnia had a decisive impact on the Paris-Washington relationship and on the way the French would see the need for NATO to adapt its structures and missions. While the Americans supported in principle the goal of European integration, they were determined to prevent the emergence of European security arrangements they feared could undermine NATO and particularly arrangements related to the Alliance's integrated military structure. Persistent endeavors by the French to raise the profile of a European Security and Defense Identity (ESDI) within NATO were therefore not welcomed. Since France simultaneously was putting much needed troops on the ground in Bosnia and hinting at its rapprochement with NATO in military matters, Washington was also eager not to confront Paris directly.

The Balkans were a huge shock for the candidate countries, who discovered that the end of the Warsaw Pact was not the anticipated recipe for stability and democracy in Europe and that NATO and the EU, because of the Gulf War and then Bosnian crisis, were not prioritizing enlargement in the way they had first assumed. The Bosnian wars would in due course represent an opportunity for some candidates to show their contribution to NATO through the Partnership for Peace. A few of them sent small contingents to IFOR. Hungary distinguished itself by welcoming on its soil a useful logistical hub for NATO-led forces.

When Jacques Chirac was elected President of France in May 1995, he found the Bosnian crisis on the doorstep of his mandate when Serbian forces took hostage 300 UNPROFOR soldiers, including some from France. UNPROFOR, set up in 1992 at the level of 14,000 troops, had limited operational flexibility and few military powers, due to political constraints introduced by the U.N. Security Council. Chirac ordered immediately a strong military reaction by the French contingent, by-passing U.N. local representative Yashusi Akashi. He also began, with the help of London and of a new European "Contact Group," to develop plans for a Rapid Reaction Force to try to contain the growing ethnic conflict between Serbs and Muslims in the Balkans. Eventually the French would deploy up to 7,000 troops and suffer one-third of the casualties.

During President Chirac's first visit to Washington on June 14, 1995, he was able to convince the Clinton White House and the Congressional leadership that the credibility of the West and NATO was at stake in this first open military conflict in Europe since World War II. It led to an important shift in U.S. policy.[18]

In the wake of the Serb attacks on Sarajevo, widespread ethnic cleaning and the atrocities of Srebrenica on July 11, 1995, President Clinton decided upon greater American involvement, but still without any troops deployed on the ground (save some special forces in Croatia).

After the Dayton peace arrangement, when the conflict restarted in Kosovo, a massive NATO air operation began. For the first time since its creation, NATO was engaged into a real military operation. It proceeded with difficulties, especially regarding political control of the intervention by the North Atlantic Council. NATO's Supreme Allied Commander (SACEUR), General Wesley Clark, would later complain about "waging a war by committee," and objected to the way British General Michael Jackson disobeyed his orders to stop the rush of the Russian contingent towards Pristina airport; Clark was particularly incensed by Jackson's comment that he didn't "want to be the first to begin the Third World War."[19]

The Europeans, who bore the brunt of military actions on the ground while the American were deployed in the air, were unhappy with the whole affair and the new mood indirectly affected the debate about NATO enlargement.

It was unavoidable that the Balkans crisis would keep the French pushing the issue of the "European pillar" (ESDI) within NATO. Paris believed it had secured London's support (as would later be confirmed in the French-British bilateral declaration at their St. Malo Summit on December 4, 1998). In exchange, France signaled its readiness to move closer to full integration into NATO military structures. In Paris, the Elysée had been convinced that progress had been made through confidential Franco-American conversations throughout the spring and summer of 1996, including at a foreign ministers' meeting in Berlin in early June. Therefore, Paris was severely disappointed by Washington's negative reaction to new and ambitious French proposals to reorganize NATO military commands, including that France would assume command of AFSOUTH in Naples, one of the two major NATO commands in the Mediterranean area, from the United States.[20] On August 28 President Chirac made the tactical error to send a letter to President Clinton, detailing the proposals prepared by his staff, boxing himself into a hardline position. The letter would eventually leak.[21] The Pentagon, which was in no mood for any concessions to Paris, was infuriated. Chirac was extremely upset and made it a personal issue in his relationship with Clinton. Washington began to fear that the French would make enlargement hostage to the reform of NATO. It poisoned the atmosphere for preparation of the Madrid NATO Summit of 1997.

Meanwhile, the work within the Alliance on enlargement was continuing. In December 1994 the North Atlantic Council started a "process of examination" inside the Alliance to determine how NATO would deal with enlargement. By fall 1995, based on a set of criteria set forth by U.S. Secretary of Defense William Perry (which came to be known as the "Perry principles"), Allies had agreed that candidates had to make commitments to democracy and market economy precepts, recognize the sovereignty of other countries, agree to NATO's decision-making by consensus, develop interoperability, and to defend other Allies.

The Russians were cooperative enough at the time, while still opposing the enlargement of NATO. They agreed to send a military contingent to implement the Dayton Peace Accords, under the proviso that Russian forces would be under the "tactical command" of U.S. General George Joulwan in his U.S. role, rather than as Supreme Allied Commander of NATO.

The mood begun to harden, however, after the Russian Duma elections of December 1995, the reelection of Yeltsin in 1996 and his choice of the more conservative Yevgeny Primakov as Foreign Minister, replacing the Western-oriented Andrei Kozyrev.

As Moscow was again presenting alternative plans for postponing the enlargement, U.S. Secretary of State Warren Christopher responded by stating publicly in Prague the unwavering U.S. commitment. It was only after the Clinton–Yeltsin meeting in Helsinki on March 21, 1997 that the Russians began to yield.

Worried about the prospect that Yeltsin might not remain in power for long, and in order to consolidate this progress, Washington decided to accelerate the diplomatic processes, setting as the goal a NATO Summit in June 1997, in order to take into account the need not to weaken Yeltsin by the time of the Russian elections in 1996.

Chirac was, however, still pleading to slow down the process, seeking to reassure Moscow about the meaning of enlargement, now that fractures were appearing within the Russian leadership.

Many in Washington shared this view of a "double track"—pushing for enlargement while trying to appease Russia with carrots of special arrangements. It was thus proposed to Moscow, as a demonstration of good will, that a "new relationship to NATO" would be announced. After intense discussions in and among European capitals and with Moscow, the "NATO Russia Founding Act" was signed in Paris on May 27, 1997.

The Founding Act stated that NATO and Russia "do not consider each other as adversaries," and intended to develop "a strong, stable and enduring partnership." The Act went as far as to envision "goals and mechanisms of consultation, cooperation, joint decision-making and joint action," and developing a broad program.

A key provision, which still resonates in the public debate more than two decades later, was a unilateral statement by NATO members that they "have no intention, no plan, and no reason to deploy nuclear weapons on the territory of new members, nor any need to change any aspect of NATO's nuclear posture or nuclear policy—and do not foresee any future need to do so." The Act also called for an adaptation of the CFE agreement to consider further conventional reductions. As far as the conventional posture was concerned, "NATO reiterates that in the current and foreseeable security environment, the Alliance will carry out its collective defense and other missions by ensuring the necessary interoperability, integration and capability for reinforcement rather than by additional permanent stationing of substantial combat forces."

Having thought that they had placated Moscow, the Allies had to decide whether to select a broad number of candidates or only a privileged few, and in the latter case, what to do with those not accepted in the next membership wave.

At the May 29-30, 1997 meeting of NATO foreign ministers in Cintra, Portugal, differing views were expressed. The United States was steadfast in its support only for Poland, the Czech Republic and Hungary, excluding Meciar's Slovakia from the first round. Italy, France and some other Allies declared themselves also in favor of including Romania and Slovenia, given their internal political evolution and the need not to consider in the first round of enlargement only a "German security belt." The United States, in turn, was concerned that the larger the first round, the more difficult it would be not to consider at the same time the Baltic countries. No agreement was reached. As Ronald Asmus recalled, "the Cintra meeting was a public relations disaster" and U.S. behavior was denounced in Paris "as hegemonic."[22]

Chirac, still bristling from the rejection of the French proposal about AFSOUTH, proved himself unyielding on including Romania at a June meeting with Clinton in the margins of the G-8 in Denver.

The NATO Madrid Summit on July 7-9 1997 opened therefore on a split: France and Italy, supported by 7 other allies, opted for a broader first round while the United States and 6 allies favored a smaller group of new members. Considerations about easier Congressional support for a limited number of candidates, the willingness to guarantee a second round later for those excluded from Madrid, and strong ethnic lobbying by Polish and Czech minorities in the United States were important factors for Washington.

For Paris, close links with Romania and the wish to reestablish a balance between Central Europe and Southeast Europe was considered to be equally important. Italy was also keen to have Slovenia, a neighbor, on board.

During the Madrid meeting Clinton was able to rally German Chancellor Helmut Kohl to his side. After tense discussions, Clinton—who did not want to put Chirac into a difficult position (after he had recently lost parliamentary elections and was saddled with a "cohabitation" government largely hostile to a NATO rapprochement)—managed with the help of NATO Secretary General Javier Solana to obtain a presentational change of the final communique, which was a face saver for France and Italy.

The option for a limited first round enlargement to the 3 Visegrád countries (minus Slovakia) was therefore adopted. As a way to demonstrate that NATO was willing to keep "an open door," NATO agreed to intensify its individual dialogues with candidate countries. As Daniel Hamilton recounts in this volume, as a complementary effort Washington developed a Northern European Initiative and in January 1998 offered the three Baltic states a "Charter of Partnership."

The long battle of ratification in the U.S. Senate saw foreign policy establishment luminaries such a U.S. Senators Sam Nunn and John Warner, former defense secretary Robert McNamara, Ambassadors Paul Nitze and Jack Matlock, and Henry Kissinger criticize aspects of the Clinton Administration's approach to NATO enlargement. George Kennan denounced NATO enlargement as an error of historic dimensions. Eventually, however, as Jeremy Rosner recounts in this volume, the U.S. Senate voted 80 against 19 for the ratification on May 1, 1998. An amendment asking the candidates to first join the EU before joining NATO was defeated on the floor. Senator Warner's amendment to delay a second round of enlargement by three years received 44 votes, but was also defeated. At NATO's 50th Anniversary Summit in Washington on April 23-24 1999, Poland, the Czech Republic and Hungary made their official debut in NATO as full members.

In France, the three protocols of accession by Poland, the Czech Republic and Hungary were ratified on June 19, 1998. While debates focused on the implications for Russia, the Kosovo crisis and the costs involved (they were differences between NATO's estimates and those of the U.S. administration's General Accountability Office), they did not attract much attention. The French debate about further NATO enlargement also remained low key in ensuing years for the next few years, unlike those about the accession of the countries of Central and Eastern Europe to the EU.

Consequently, it was not surprising when the Prague Summit of November 21-22, 2002 formally endorsed the candidacy of a second group of candidates, including the three Baltic countries as well as Bulgaria, Romania, Slovakia, and Slovenia. Their accession was completed in May 2004. Albania and Croatia acceded in 2009 and Montenegro was admitted in June 2017.

Meanwhile, in the wake of the tragic events of September 11, 2001, NATO had shifted its principal mission to the fight against terrorism and begun preparations to intervene in Afghanistan, where some candidate countries were already ready to deploy troops alongside the Alliance. At the Prague Summit, the main issue for the French was no longer enlargement but the creation of a Rapid Reaction Force (RRF) of some 21,000 troops that could be rapidly deployed. President Chirac, now in his second term, decided to participate in this initiative. For the first time, French troops were included into a NATO military force on a permanently rotating basis. He also offered to deploy French forces as part of NATO's intervention in Afghanistan.

By 2002, the element of excitement and novelty that had surrounded the entry of the first group of Central European countries had evaporated. Each of the new candidates had gone through a long bureaucratic examination, often verging on the inconsequential.[23]

Soon, however, the problem of the Ukrainian and Georgian candidacies would split the Alliance and show that it was easier to speak about a "NATO Open Door policy" than it was to implement its implicit promise.

At the NATO Bucharest Summit in April 2008, President George W. Bush pushed Allies to offer a Membership Action Plan to Ukraine.

A majority, including France and Germany, was not convinced it was wise to go beyond the NATO-Ukrainian Charter of 1997. This was not just because of worries about Russia's probable reaction, but also because of divisions within Ukrainian public opinion at the time. The most important consideration, however, was that NATO was not, at that time, ready to provide a security commitment either to Ukraine or to Georgia.

The dynamism of NATO enlargement in Europe was losing steam. Priority attention was devoted to NATO's partnerships in the Mediterranean, the Middle East and the Gulf (the Istanbul Cooperation Initiative proposed at the Summit of June 2004), and in Asia. The very concept of membership and association with NATO was thus evolving. As shown in Iraq and Afghanistan, the new focus was consistent with U.S. Secretary of Defense Donald Rumsfeld's preference for "coalitions of the willing," given that the "mission determined the coalition" and not the reverse.

At the same time, tensions grew between France and the United States due to the progress of the EU's European Security and Defense Policy (ESDP) and of the severe rift over the 2003 Iraq war. The idea of Europe "whole and free" and NATO unity would be forgotten during this diplomatic crisis. In fact, by an ironic twist of history, the Bush Administration considered NATO enlargement to be a useful weapon against the stubborn French.

Rumsfeld was increasingly annoyed by what he saw as "French machinations" when it came to the intra-Alliance dispute over Iraq. He decided to take the offensive. In an interview with a Dutch journalist on January 22, 2003, he divided NATO into a cantankerous "Old Europe" and a "New Europe" that he characterized as more loyal to the United States:

> Now you are thinking of Europe as Germany and France. I don't. I think that it is old Europe. If you look at the entire NATO Europe today, the center of gravity is shifting to the east. And there are a lot of new members.[24]

On February 5, 2003 Rumsfeld's Assistant Secretary of Defense Peter Rodman wrote:

> It is now clear that that our counterstrategy (against the French)—bringing Central Europe and Eastern Europe in the game—is winning. Your reference to old Europe not only brought into public consciousness what has been evolving for some time. When Central and Eastern Europe get into not only NATO but also the EU, the French game is over![25]

On February 18, 2003, in a letter to President Bush, Rumsfeld asserted that "France is clearly trying to destroy NATO, in favor of the EU."

A few days later, Central and Eastern European ministers from the self-designated "New Europe" published a letter of support for the U.S. position on Iraq in the *Wall Street Journal*, resulting in a strong French reaction.

Richard Haass, then Director of Policy Planning at the State Department, observed that U.S. efforts to forge alliances with the "new" members could "break up an EU already diluted by its own eastward enlargement."[26]

It was up to President Barack Obama in Prague in 2009 to reverse this rhetoric and policy approach (which would however yet again be resurrected by his successor Donald Trump): "in my view there is no old Europe or new Europe. There is only a united Europe."

Some years thereafter, however, the Russian interventions in Georgia (2013) and Ukraine and Crimea (2014) were a wakeup call for NATO.

A new and much more fundamental debate opened up about the cohesion of the Alliance. It was reminiscent of Alliance discussions in the 1970s between the Central European front and the flanks, albeit in a changed geostrategic context. The Baltic countries, Poland, Romania and Bulgaria, with the support of Ukraine, were understandably demanding military "reassurance" and a new set of priorities for NATO.

While agreeing with the need to deal with those Allies' security concerns in Eastern and Central Europe, France and Southern European Allies called for renewed attention to the situation on the southern rim of the Alliance—the Mediterranean and the Sahel. In an era of global, regional and local instabilities, the growing issue was whether NATO should continue to deal primarily with threats stemming from Russia or those emanating from its southern and southeastern periphery.

Who Lost Russia?

In contrast to the years when the West and Russia sought to find a role for Moscow as a partner of NATO in a new European order built around a larger NATO and a larger EU, today we are faced with a complete turnaround in Moscow's position.

The shift was clearly expressed by Vladimir Putin in his speech at the 2007 Munich Security Conference, when, among other accusations, he lambasted the expansion of "NATO infrastructures" up to the borders of Russia. Putin claimed that the West had purposefully exploited post-Soviet Russia's state of weakness and that the Alliance's open-door policy vis-à-vis the East was in contradiction "with the assurances given at the time."

Putin's 2007 revisionist views—constantly repeated since, and apparently shared by a large segment of Russian society—represented a complete reversal of his proclaimed solidarity with America in the aftermath of the September 2001 attacks on the Twin Towers in New York City and on the Pentagon in Virginia, and his promises to join George W. Bush in his fight against terrorism, including offering logistical support for NATO's Afghanistan operations, opening its airspace, and granting Allies the use of Russia's Central Asian airbases.[27]

From today's perspective, it is perhaps hard to recall the positive atmosphere surrounding the first NATO-Russia Summit hosted by Italian Prime Minister Silvio Berlusconi at Pratica di Mare, near Rome, in May 2002. The Summit's joint declaration stated that "today we are opening a new page in our relations, aimed at enhancing our ability to work together in areas of common interest and to stand together against common threats and risks to our security."

Such cordiality was short-lived. Within 5 years, Putin had grown hostile. NATO became "the enemy"—justifying in Putin's mind a rebalancing of forces in Europe that, he hoped, would provide Russia with a new security zone and sphere of influence beyond its current post-1991 borders.

The Kremlin thus proved immune to the attempts of Obama Administration in March 2009 to achieve a "reset" of the Russian-American relationship. The Western decision to intervene in Libya worsened the relationship. Russia's military intervention in Georgia in 2008 and against Ukraine in 2014 deepened the break. Putin even justified Russian actions by suggesting they were equivalent to the NATO intervention in Kosovo in 1999. NATO-Russia Council meetings became largely irrelevant.

Did Moscow feel it was deceived by the West on enlargement? Or, more simply, did it believe, at the time, that it would never come? The answer to each question is no. Russia accepted the new larger NATO and even worked together with it.

The downward spiral in relations with the Kremlin since 2007 was triggered by a different series of events, including the planned deployment in Europe of missile defenses against a possible Iranian threat and, most certainly, U.S. and European support of the democratic movements in and around Russia. U.S. and EU help to the "Orange Revolution" and the later "Euromaidan" in Ukraine are the top items on Putin's long list of grievances, due to the Kremlin's fear of democratic contamination.

In sum, Moscow's change of course vis-a-vis the West, after 20 years of NATO enlargement and attempts to build a stable relationship with Russia, has led to a situation in which NATO has become both a proclaimed enemy and an alibi for the Kremlin's revisionist policy.

It also highlights the fact that for the Kremlin, NATO has been the security institution with the most far-reaching influence on the remaking of a post-Cold War order in Europe with which Russia has not yet resigned itself to live.

Notes

1. A very reliable source for this period is Frédéric Bozo, *Mitterand, la fin de la guerre froide et l'unification allemande, de Yalta à Maastricht* (Paris : Odile Jacob, 2005). See also G.H. Soutou, *La guerre de Cinquante ans Les relations Est Ouest 1943-1990* (Paris: Fayard, 2001) and Hubert Vedrine, *Les mondes de Francois Mitterrand A l'Elysée 1981-1995* (Paris: Fayard 1996). Beyond Ron Asmus' detailed memoir, *Opening NATO's Door: How the Alliance Remade Itself for a New Era* (New York: Columbia University Press, 2002), see also Frédéric Bozo, N. Piers Ludlow, Leopoldo Nuti, and Marie-Pierre Rey, eds., *Europe and the End of the Cold War: A Reappraisal* (London: Routledge, 2008).

2. On the issue of German reunification debates see Kristina Spohr, "Precluded or Precedent-Setting? The "NATO Enlargement Question" in the Triangular Bonn-Washington-Moscow Diplomacy of 1990–1991, *Journal of Cold War Studies*, Fall 2012, Vol. 14, No. 4, pp. 4–54.

3. The U.S. Embassy in Bonn's summary of the speech in a cable of February 9th (012107Z FEB 9) was that "Genscher warned that any attempt to extend "Nato military structures" to the territory of today's structures would block German unity. In his vision of Europe, Genscher sees the Alliance continuing but assuming role a political than a military role. Genscher also stressed the need to maintain NATO as a framework for a continuing-and necessary-US presence in Europe."

4. Mary Elise Sarotte, "Not One Inch Eastward?" in *Diplomatic History* 34.1 (2010) also by the same author, *1989: The Struggle to Create Post-Cold War in Europe* (Princeton: Princeton University Press, 2014).

5. Pierre Gremion, *Intelligence de l'anticommunisme* (Paris:Fayard, 1995).

6. Marie Pierre Rey, "Which socialism after the Cold War? Gorbachev's vision and its impact on the French left ," in Frédéric Bozo, Marie-Pierre Rey, N. Piers Ludlow and Bernd Rother, eds., *Visions of the End of the Cold War in Europe, 1945-1990* (New York: Berghahn, 2012).

7. On the basis of information given to Paris by a KGB defector, Vladimir Vetrov. A large batch of intelligence (the Farewell files) were shared by Mitterrand at his first meeting with Reagan as a demonstration of the continuing Western orientation of France, notwithstanding the inclusion of communists in the government.

8. Alexander Galdin and Anatoly Chernyaev, eds., *Mikhail Gorbachev I germanskii vopros* (Moscow: Ves Mir 2006), pp. 454-466.

9. IISS Adelphi Papers. Conference on the conduct of East West relations in the 1980s. 25th Conference of the IISS in Ottawa September 1983.

10. John J. Maresca, *To Helsinki: The Conference on Security and Cooperation in Europe, 1973-1975* (Durham: Duke University Press, 1985).

11. Moscow had made the signing of the Helsinki Act a precondition of the opening of the MBFR forces negotiations sought by Kissinger as a hedge against the Mansfield amendment on reduction of U.S. troops in Europe. The Europeans insisted on bringing the human rights element as a condition of the language of the Act on the "peaceful change of borders" (i.e. a reference to the eventual unification of Germany).

12. Approved on August 1, 1975.

13. National Security Archives, S.Savranskaya and Tom Blanton, December 2017.

14. Veronika Heyde, *Frankreich im KSZE Prozess: Diplomatie im Namen der europäischen Sicherheit 1969-1983* (Berlin, Boston: De Gruyter Oldenbourg, 2017).

15. Catherine McArdle Kelleher, Jane M.O. Sharp, Lawrence Freedman, *The Treaty on Conventional Armed Forces in Europe: The Politics of Post-Wall Arms Control* (Baden-Baden: Nomos Verlagsgesellschaft, 1996).

16. See Jean Musitelli, "François Mitterrand, architecte de la grande Europe : le projet de Confédération européenne (1990-1991), in *Revue Internationale et Stratégique*, 2011/2, No. 82, pp.18-28.

17. Asmus, op. cit., p.124.

18. Secretary Baker had proclaimed that the whole affair was a European responsibility," adding that "the United States didn't have a dog in this fight." Meanwhile European minister Jacques Poos had famously declared that "it was the "hour of Europe." The key issue was the protection of the European troops on the ground, who needed U.S. support.

19. Wesley K. Clark, *Waging Modern War: Bosnia, Kosovo and the Future of Combat* (New York: Public Affairs, 2001).

20. At the start there was a misunderstanding about the possibility of a European SACEUR, then the debate centered around AFSOUTH in Naples, possibly divided, and given to a French commander.

21. Thomas Friedman wrote that the "French want to control the 7th Fleet," which of course was out of the question.

22. Asmus, op. cit., p. 221.

23. For example, when it was Romania's to be examined before the North Atlantic Council, the United States insisted, under pressure of an adoption lobby, that Romania continue to propose visas for those children. The same morning, the EU had castigated Bucharest for the practice of this very same trade. The defense expenditures of each country were evaluated according to whether they reached 2% of their GDP—a meaningless benchmark, if only because the inheritance of

bloated Warsaw Pact military structures and manpower. Security services had also a free hand to denounce alleged former pro-Soviet officials and require for demotion experienced army officers (they even accused the King of Romania, and future Prime Minister of the country, to have benefited during his Madrid exile from KGB subsidies).

24. Forgetting that the negative reference to "Old Europe" comes from Karl Marx, *The Communist Manifesto*, 1848.

25. Rumsfeld Library. Feb 4 2003. (USDP Dep Sec I-03/001420)

26. See Jacques Rupnik, "From EU enlargement to European unification," *Pouvoirs* 2003/3, No. 108, Le Seuil.

27. The French Air Force flying into Afghanistan shared the same airport in Dushanbe with Russian planes.

Chapter 24

NATO Enlargement and Russia: A Military Perspective

Wesley K. Clark

While the work on NATO enlargement was rightly the business of policymakers and diplomats, the military was also involved, but always subordinate to civilian authority. And because the military goes into and out of policy positions, most officers have only an episodic understanding of the policy issues. That was certainly the case with me.

When I served at Supreme Headquarters, Allied Powers Europe (SHAPE) from February 1978 through June 1979 as Assistant Executive Officer to NATO Supreme Allied Commander (SACEUR) General Alexander M. Haig, Jr., I did have visibility into some of the most sensitive and pressing policy matters. I helped write much of his correspondence and speeches and traveled often with him. But it wasn't until 1994, fifteen years later, that I worked NATO policy in the Pentagon as the Director for Strategic Plans and Policy, J-5. What follows are my impressions of NATO enlargement and our relationship with Russia.

When I served at SHAPE in the late 1970s there was talk that at some point, NATO would perhaps take on new members. After West Germany had come Greece and Turkey. Spain was possible, also Sweden perhaps, or even Austria. Spain did in fact join NATO in 1982. Our primary focus, however, was on the problem of the new Soviet missile, the SS20, which was challenging NATO's deterrent, and the NATO strategy of flexible response.

For the bulk of the U.S. Army, even the so-called "heavy force," which consisted of tanks, mechanized infantry, and self-propelled artillery, and was in fact oriented to the NATO mission of deterring—or, if deterrence failed, defending—in assigned sectors in southern Germany, NATO and its issues were specialized problems that we occasionally studied in school. The U.S. Army was fully occupied recovering from the Vietnam War experience. We had become an Army of volunteers—no draftees. We were constantly upgrading outdated equipment, exchanging old tanks for new models, new trucks, new radios, and so on. We also brought in new training methods—everything from laser devices to explicit soldiering tasks to be tested by the units themselves. Though patriotic, we were non-ideological and non-political.

From the mid-1970s through the late 1980s, the U.S. Army slowly upgraded our deployments, our doctrine and our equipment to respond to what we viewed as the growing Soviet threat. We stationed a new, separate armored brigade in Northern Germany near Hamburg and prepositioned several brigades worth of ready-to-go equipment in Belgium so that reinforcements could be airlifted in and used to augment what was believed to be the sectors most vulnerable to a Soviet attack. We replaced our old doctrine of an active (elastic) defense with a concept of fighting in-depth to disrupt the second echelon of the enemy's attacking forces. We brought in the new Black Hawk and Apache Helicopters, M1 tanks, and M2 Infantry Fighting Vehicles. We struggled to provide the military backing for deterrence, and should that fail, to offer flexible defense in accordance with NATO doctrine. Never did I see any plan to initiate an attack, nor even, in the defense, to counterattack with ground forces into East Germany or Czechoslovakia. The Army was prepared for the Cold War to last indefinitely, with soldiers and their families rotating into Germany from assignments in the United States and back every two to three years.

By late 1987, however, even the officers in far-away Fort Carson, Colorado—where I was serving as Commander, 3rd Brigade, 4th Infantry Division—could sense strategic change. Soviet President Mikhail Gorbachev had visited Washington, DC, and while he was being driven in a motorcade from Congress to the White House, he got out of his car, and, walking among the bystanders, was greeted with warm applause. Observing this on the evening news, I was unsettled—here we were, training to go to war in case deterrence failed, while in Washington it seemed that Gorbachev was greeted as a kind of hero. We were training in a generations-long effort to fight a country whose leader was welcomed by our own citizens as a hero?

The American military was never anti-Soviet. Curious, respectful, in awe of the World War II experience would be the best way to describe our perspective. We studied what Soviet writings we could, historical and current, to understand Soviet military doctrine, and decision-making. We worried about Soviet technology—air-to-air missiles that could launch backwards, the incredibly maneuverable MiG 29, explosive reactive armor on tanks, with automatic loaders, tanks that could "squat" and dig themselves in to lower their silhouettes, and so on. We trained against what we believed to be their tactics, constituting "aggressor squadrons" for the Air Force at Red Flag, and a Soviet-styled "OpFor" at the Army's National Training Center in the Mojave Desert.

On a personal level, I had studied Russian at West Point and become somewhat fluent, read translations of Tolstoy, Dostoyevsky and Sholokhov, listened to Tchaikovsky, Prokofiev and Mussorgsky, and even travelled as a tourist in the summer of 1964 to the Soviet Union, along with three other West Point cadets. We met young Soviet officers, and verbally jousted over the Olympics, the space program and other matters. We spent hours visiting Kazanskiy Cathedral, the Hermitage, Red Square, and debating Communism with our Intourist guide and with the curator of the Lenin Museum in Kiev. We left impressed and concerned, but mostly with a warm feeling for the historic hardships and suffering of the people there.

The U.S. Army wasn't "politicized" in the way that, for example, the Soviet and Chinese armies were. There were no commissars governing our appreciation of world politics. We considered ourselves "professional," aiming for expertise in the use of weapons and forces, at the direction of the political leaders elected and appointed over us.

By the late 1980s the Cold War was clearly ending. Gorbachev was struggling to reform the entrenched Soviet bureaucracy, and the Communist idealism I had heard first hand in 1964 was long gone. The U.S. military was delighted with the end of the Cold War—we immediately got rid of the U.S. Army's tactical nuclear weapons. We respected Soviet Marshal Akhromeyev and his personal relationship with our chairmen of the Joint Chiefs of Staff, Admiral William Crowe and later General Colin Powell, and were saddened to learn that he had committed suicide. There was no sense of triumph expressed.

We were also distracted by the invasion of Panama, and subsequent actions in Kuwait and Iraq. In a personal meeting on a Friday afternoon in May, 1991, discussing Operation Desert Storm, the Undersecretary of Defense for Policy explained it to me this way: "…we learned we can intervene militarily in the Mideast with impunity—the Soviets won't do a thing to stop us." This wasn't anti-Soviet, but rather a recognition that the Soviet threat was a fading concern.

When I arrived in Washington to become the J-5 in April 1994, the United States was engaged in multiple crises—a total embargo of Haiti, a crisis with North Korea about their possible reprocessing of spent nuclear fuel, NATO operations Deny Flight and Display Determination in the Balkans, which were designed to smother the conflict in former Yugoslavia, an unfolding humanitarian crisis and genocide in Rwanda, a continuing commitment to the Kurds in Iraq, an airlift to Beirut from Cyprus, as well as a dozen other pressing issues. Worse, there was no prepared national security strategy. Without a Soviet force to face, what was the purpose of the U.S. Armed Forces, and how should they be sized and equipped, and with what level of resourcing?

In the midst of wrestling with these issues I was also charged with leading the first U.S.-Russian staff talks; someone previously had determined that they would be held in Moscow, in early August, 1994. There was no agenda, and no precedent.

Our Russian hosts from the Main Operations Directorate of the Russian General Staff were gracious but reserved. I met my counterpart, Colonel-General Barynkin, the Chief of the Main Operations Directorate, and his boss, General Kolesnikov, the Chief of the Russian General Staff. The Defense Ministry was less impressive on the inside than its façade would have implied—large, high-ceilinged offices, but sparsely furnished, with threadbare carpeting.

General Barynkin spoke no English, and my Russian had faded to little more than introductions and niceties. As we conversed through an interpreter, he stood by a five-foot-high globe in his office and slowly spun it around. "I can put my hand on any spot,' he said, "and I will know what is happening there. Can you?" It was a boast and a challenge, I sensed born more of insecurity rather than curiosity. Not much different than listening in 1964 as Soviet lieutenants over a lunch table boasted that they had the first astronaut and the best astronauts.

On a warm afternoon in early August 1994, sitting across the conference table and assisted by our defense attaché, we followed a loose agenda in the Staff talks, more of a get-acquainted than an effort directed at specific accomplishments. NATO was discussed, because NATO was seeking to engage all the former members of the Warsaw Pact in a Partnership for Peace, and of course, the Russians were curious about NATO operations to support the U.N. in the Balkans.

The United States had made no decision on NATO enlargement at that point, but all matters associated with NATO were met by the Russians with skepticism, resentment, and concern. In particular, I was asked, "When will your NATO ships be in our port of Riga?" I answered, "I don't know, but the more you ask that question, the sooner they will come." (I had already heard from East European attaches in Washington their concerns about the Russians.) I left Moscow with the impression that whatever the friendliness between Presidents Clinton and Yeltsin, these Russian military leaders would be difficult. But I would try to work it.

I invited Colonel-General Barynkin to visit me in Washington, and upon returning to DC, worked hard through the Russian Defense attaché to have him actually make the trip. He arrived in May 1995, protesting, "I have never been west of East Berlin." This, I thought, was precisely why it was important for him to visit us.

We hosted a dinner for him, inviting several of the staff from the Office of the Secretary of Defense (OSD), the State Department, and the National Security Council (NSC) who worked Russian issues. We saw the sights in Washington DC, visited the 82nd Airborne Division at Ft. Bragg, got a briefing in Russian and a demonstration of several aircraft from the Air Combat Command at Langley Air Force Base, and overflew the Atlantic Fleet at Norfolk on the way back to Washington. Barynkin looked enviously at the carriers and amphibs docked at the Navy base. Through the interpreter, he said, "I am in charge of nuclear weapons. Are you?" It was about insecurity, I felt. He departed with the Russian attaché to go to Brooklyn for a couple of days with the Russian community there. I later learned that he had been quite uncomfortable, even alleging that we had tried to entrap him with a beautiful Russian-speaking woman, OSD Russian expert Elizabeth Sherwood-Randall.

I was invited back to Russia by another Russian, the deputy Chief of Defense, Colonel General Bogdonov. It was a reciprocal visit—a welcoming dinner, a sauna, a tennis game, a chance to test weapons, and various discussions. All good natured. General Bogdonov explained that as a youngster he had almost starved in the postwar Soviet Union. At one point as a four year old they lived for a few weeks largely on green apples. We discussed a battle in Grozny, where he had played a part in the Russians' unsuccessful push into the city in 1994. We talked about families and life. It was the kind of relationship with the Russians that most American officers had always sought—military leaders serving great countries, sharing the special bonds and common interests of the military profession, despite our separate loyalties.

In October 1995, after the first few weeks of shuttle diplomacy with Ambassador Richard Holbrooke to end the conflict in the former Yugoslavia, I traveled with Deputy Secretary Strobe Talbott to Moscow to share with Russia details of our negotiations, and to pave the way for Russian participation in the NATO peacekeeping force. While Secretary Talbott visited the Foreign Ministry and Presidency, I went to my counterpart, Colonel General Barynkin. After I briefed the U.S. seven-point peace plan, Barynkin observed, "You Americans are coming into our part of Europe, and you say you will be gone in a year, but you will not be." I protested. "The Administration has testified before Congress that the troop presence will last only one year," I said, "and we intend to stick with that." Barynkin wasn't at all persuaded; he replied, "Please, we are Russians, we understand you." Then he added, "but if we were in your position, we would do the same thing." Nevertheless, we didn't get a "no" from the Russian military—just their continuing sense of ownership and privilege in Eastern Europe.

General George Joulwan, the NATO Supreme Allied Commander at the time, working under Secretary of Defense William Perry, finalized the details of Russian military participation within the peacekeeping force planned to enforce Dayton peace agreement. The Russians refused to serve under NATO—NATO was the old enemy, the survivor of the Cold War struggle, and the threat to Russia's future. In a meeting with Russian Defense Minister Pavel Grachev and Secretary Perry, Joulwan persuaded the Russians to serve only under U.S. command— exercised through Joulwan and by virtue of his dual responsibilities as U.S. Commander in Europe as well as NATO Supreme Allied Commander. It fit together nicely with other efforts of President Yeltsin and Foreign Minister Andrei Kozyrev to have Russia more engaged in Europe, while respecting the Russian institutional distaste for NATO.

Another factor was pressing in on our relationship with Russia, however—NATO enlargement. On Friday, before Labor Day weekend in 1994, a speech prepared for Vice President Gore to deliver on Sunday in Berlin came through my staff for clearance. As J-5, we acted on behalf of the Chairman, General Shalikashvili, in clearing and coordinating important statements and policies. In scanning the speech, I noted that it called for NATO to admit new member states from Eastern Europe. My staff had flagged this as a problem. While I had seen no interagency policy discussion of NATO enlargement, it was known that both Defense Secretary Perry and General Shalikashvili opposed such a policy. I lined out the offending sentences. That afternoon the speech came back through. Once again I struck the offending sentences. On Saturday morning the speech draft made a third trip through my office, and once more, the language on NATO enlargement had been reinserted. I struck it a third time and took the paper to General Shalikashvili. "I'll take care of it," he said. However, as delivered, the speech contained the offending commitment to expand NATO

Two weeks later incoming Assistant Secretary of State for European Affairs Richard Holbrooke assumed duties and called a meeting to announce the new U.S. policy. The United States would support NATO enlargement. It was a surprise to the Pentagon, and to me. Richard Holbrooke was at his dramatic best, explaining not only a strategic rationale but underscoring it this way: "After Yalta, Senator Barbara Mikulski's grandmother turned over the picture of FDR on her dresser and never looked at it again for her whole life. Is there anyone here who doesn't believe this is the policy of the United States?" Deputy Assistant Secretary of Defense Joe Kruzel raised his hand, and attempted to discuss the premises, but Holbrooke brushed his question away. I raised my hand, and bluntly said, "No, I don't think it is the policy..." I had expected some kind of a formal decision-making process, or at least a formal notification.

There was a moment of stunned silence.

"Anyone who questions this policy is disloyal to the President of the United States," thundered Holbrooke, looking at me. He was accusing me of disloyalty? I felt my ears turning red. Reflexively, I moved to unzip my jacket, pushed back my chair, and replied something like, "How dare you question my loyalty; this has nothing to do with loyalty to the President."

For a moment it was heated and personal—he knew he had gone too far. But Holbrooke backed away, explained in a more conversational tone that in fact a policy decision had been made, and he had chosen this way, rather than a memo, to announce the decision.

I returned to the Pentagon and reported the confrontation to General Shalikashvili, with some trepidation. But he was totally amused and smiling. "Wes, I have already heard from Brussels; they say you are a hero…" (presumably for standing up to Holbrooke).

A few hours later Holbrooke asked me and my staff to prepare the briefings for Allies on the why, how, and who of enlargement from the military perspective.

No doubt my Russian hosts, from 1995 onwards, were well aware of the change in U.S. policy, but however much they might have resented NATO, and the humiliation of the Soviet Union's demise, at the top, Russia's leaders seemed to sing a different tune. President Clinton and Russian President Boris Yeltsin seemed almost chummy. Overall, Russian policy simply didn't reflect the attitudes of the state institutions and especially the power ministries, and especially the Ministry of Defense and intelligence agencies. While I continued to repeat the U.S. position that NATO enlargement would help stabilize Europe, was therefore in Russia's interest, and in fact NATO hoped that someday Russia itself would join NATO, it was clear to me when I spoke with Russians—their military attaché in Washington, Generals Barynkin and Bogdonov—that this wasn't selling to my counterparts in Russia.

Nevertheless, extending stability eastwards was precisely what NATO was doing in Bosnia. Without the NATO commitment, and U.S. forces on the ground, there would have been no Dayton peace agreement. Without NATO, the U.N. was simply incapable of ending the war, and stabilizing the region. And despite all the dire predictions, there had not been a single incident of resistance, nor a single NATO casualty. Here was the proof of the value of NATO's expansion "out-of-area."

When I assumed General Joulwan's position as Supreme Allied Commander Europe in July 1997, the Russian peacekeeping mission in Bosnia-Herzegovina was established and performing well. But they had begun downgrading the cooperation, replacing a prominent Russian three-star with a two-star, and reducing the level of forces. Russian General Anatoliy Krivalopov, formerly a leader of Russia's strategic rocket forces (which were now downsized), was newly assigned as Deputy Commander in charge of Russian Forces. The Russian forces consisted of a Russian motorized rifle battalion under the operational control of the U.S. division deployed across northern Bosnia-Herzegovina. It seemed a remarkable transformation from the hostility of the Cold War—but the honeymoon ended just as I arrived.

The day of my change of command, British forces in their sector of Bosnia had conducted the first arrest of indicted Serb war criminals Milan Kovačević and Simo Drljača. Kovačević had been the Mayor of Priedor and Drljača his police chief. Both were accused of imprisoning and abusing Bosniak civilians in concentration camps where many of them died. Drljača resisted arrest, shot at the British troops and was killed in an exchange of fire. Kovačević was detained. It was a deft military operation, executed by British SAS following careful reconnaissance. Kovačević was swiftly helicoptered out and flown to the Hague. For NATO, and for British Prime Minister Tony Blair, the operation was a great success. But it stepped over the line that Serb President Slobodan Milošević had warned us about at Dayton: "Serb people do not like occupying power; NATO must not become occupying power." It was more than a warning—it was a veiled threat. Now, NATO was behaving exactly like an "occupying power."

NATO's action in arresting indicted war criminals broke with the understanding that senior U.S. generals had extracted from our political leaders—namely, that NATO wouldn't undertake "police-type actions." We would simply enforce the Dayton Agreement uniformly on all parties, and we had full legal authority to do that. But with the new leadership in the UK came a new resolve to do the right thing in supporting the International Criminal Tribunal on Yugoslavia. President Clinton didn't disagree, and, over reservations by the military commanders, action began. At this point there was a secret list of twenty-odd persons indicted for war crimes—and they were all Serbs.

From the beginning, the Russian peacekeeping force had been cleanly tucked in under command of the U.S. 1st Armored Division, and then, as units rotated, 1st Infantry Division. There was full transparency (so we believed) in all activities, with Russian liaison officers and the Russian commander attending all important meetings at the Division headquarters. The Russian battalion was located in the ethnically-cleansed Republika Srpska entity of Bosnia-Herzegovina, where it forged a warm and reassuring relationship with the local Serb authorities and population and stayed away from potentially hostile Bosnian Muslims.

When NATO, a few months into the mission in 1996, conducted a special operation targeting Iranian extremists in the Federation entity, there had been no problem with the Russians. These Iranians were "foreign forces," not permitted under the terms of the agreement. But now, the introduction of classified planning cells, secret reconnaissance, and "snatch operations" conducted by special forces and directed against indicted Serb war criminals—and carefully screened from the Russian forces—put the Russian mission under stress from the locals as well as from Moscow.

Within two days the Serbs struck back against NATO, with a series of less-than-lethal-force actions directed against NATO—broken windows, angry crowds, and so forth. It was clearly directed by Serb authorities.

A few weeks later there was a complete orchestrated, non-lethal attack—rocks, mobs, threats, beatings—on U.S. forces in the city of Brcko. This might have intimidated a U.N. force, operating under limited authorities, but the U.S. division commander, Major General Dave Grange, was ready. In a series of moves he disabled the Serb radio station that was instigating the action, blocked and dispersed the mob, rescued a cut-off U.S. unit, and occupied key terrain, including a hilltop on which a Serb microwave communications station was located. NATO proved it was not the U.N.—and this was a shot in the arm to the entire international community as they worked to implement the Dayton Agreement.

Then we received information that Milošević's Serb intelligence agents were going to assassinate a somewhat progressive rival to Serb leader Radovan Karadžić, Biljana Plavšić, at an election rally in Banja Luka. Their plan was that Karadžić's (and Milošević's) group would bus in several hundred thugs to contest the rally, cause a riot, and in the confusion gun-down Plavšić. U.S. and British forces set up a series of road blocks on the route to Banja Luka, repeatedly halting and searching the buses, until they arrived too late to impact the rally. Plavšić was saved, and Milošević and his Serb agents humiliated. A few weeks later, we confiscated the rifles and machine guns of the Bosnian Serb Special Police units and closed a few police stations, in a further demonstration of NATO power. The Russian battalion had no part to play in this.

In these ways, the NATO force in Bosnia became increasingly proactive in breaking the resistance to the implementation of the Dayton agreement. And as the alignment against Russian sympathies became clearer, so the pressures increased on my Russian deputy. We had cordial discussions, lunchtime meetings, and shared visits to Bosnia. On one visit, the new Russian Chief of Defense, Colonel General (soon to be General) Kvashnin hosted me at the Russian battalion, where we inspected troops and equipment, and reminisced about our respective military careers. He had commanded a Soviet division in Afghanistan: "We always air landed troops at the tops of the mountains, and then attacked the bandits from above, but once your Stinger missiles arrived, that tactic became impossible, and we were lost." I related my Vietnam experience—where I was hit by bullets from one of "his" AK-47 rifles. Olga, the Russian wife of a U.S. airman serving at SHAPE translated for us. It was the kind of military-to-military communication that could have fostered a strong and lasting professional military relationship.

As I traveled across Eastern Europe, however, I saw the fear that Eastern European governments had of Russia, and their determination to seek safety with NATO and the West. As the Foreign Minister of Bulgaria explained at a meeting in 1997, "Today Russia is weak, but someday it will be strong again, and before then, Bulgaria must be protected by NATO." The Romanian Defense Minister angrily recalled past Russian incidents of domination: "In 1878 we allowed Russian troops to pass through Romania, and they stole our province of Bessarabia." OK, the East Europeans had long memories, some Americans chuckled later. But he wasn't joking. Romania and Bulgaria, Estonia, Latvia, and Lithuania, and others, wanted NATO membership. They put their trust in the United States—our values, and our reputation as a reliable ally.

Meanwhile, the leadership in Moscow was also changing. Andrei Kozyrev had been replaced in early 1996 as foreign minister by Yevgeny Primakov. When Primakov became prime minister in September 1998 he was succeeded by Igor Ivanov, a man I had worked alongside at Dayton when he was the Russian representative to Ambassador Holbrooke's team. He was pushing back more against NATO: "Under the terms of this Conventional Forces in Europe (CFE) Treaty, NATO could declare a crisis and deploy a division into Slovakia, threatening Russia." Seriously? One little NATO division? I asked. Ivanov laughed; we had a personal relationship. And he knew better.

Control of the Russian Armed Forces was brought more under the control of the Russian intelligence agencies. My access to the Russian Chief of Defense was curtailed—no more spontaneous calls or friendly conversations. My Russian deputy, clearly under instruction, began to question NATO actions more vigorously. "Why does NATO take sides against Serbs?" "Why do you like these Albanians?" I knew we were jeopardizing him personally, and our relationship with the Russians, and I tried to provide the rationale and facts to justify our actions as they unfolded, even before he had to come in and challenge us. It was painful to see the old Cold War lines of stress reemerging in his questions.

Kosovo was a real dilemma for NATO. Although the region was 90 percent or more Albanian by ethnicity, the minority Serbs held the power and worked to crush Albanian culture, rights and opportunities. President Bush had warned the Serbs in December 1992 that if they used force against the Albanian inhabitants, they would feel the weight of U.S. airpower. Holbrooke had tried to bring the subject into the agreements at Dayton, only to have Milošević refuse again and again to discuss Kosovo, saying this was an internal matter.

The Albanian Kosovars themselves, however, had begun to organize into a militia force able to strike against the Serb police and military. Neighboring Albania, a member of Partnership for Peace, demanded consultations, and complained about Serb ethnic cleansing and Serb use of heavy weapons against civilians. NATO was fully occupied with its mission in Bosnia, but could it stand by and allow a repeat of the ethnic cleansing, and the waves of refugees again, only a hundred miles away in the region of southwestern Serbia known as Kosovo?

In late February, 1998, Serb forces had surrounded the farm belonging to the Jashari family, assaulted, and eventually murdered some 60 members of the family. Women and children were found lain out on the floor, shot in the head at close range. Macedonian President Gligorov asked me to visit, and warned that there would be a much wider war in Kosovo. "These Albanians will fight back," he said.

NATO was in the process of preparing for its 50th Anniversary Summit in Washington, which would be held in April, 1999. Based on success in Bosnia, NATO authorities, and especially the U.S. leadership, could see a bright new future for NATO, acting as a stabilizing force, even beyond the boundaries of NATO member nations. A new NATO Strategic Concept incorporating this purpose was being drafted for unveiling at the Summit. And yet, would that mean acting to halt Serb brutality and ethnic cleansing inside its own borders, in the region known as Kosovo?

The Albanian Chief of Defense visited me in May, 1998. "We can see Serb mortar rounds falling on our Albanian villages in Western Kosovo,' he said.

As NATO concerns began to focus on Kosovo, and Serb ethnic cleansing there, my Russian Deputy brought more issues. "This KLA – we know they are connected to Chechen terrorists." "These Albanians are mostly criminals." I'm sure these same kinds of arguments were made at the political level by Russia in NATO, where the Russians had privileged access to NATO representatives through the NATO-Russia Founding Act, negotiated in 1997 as a means of appealing to Russia.

Former KGB agent Yevgeny Primakov, a man who had masterminded support to Palestinian terrorists in the 1970s, returned to the scene, as head of Russian intelligence and Foreign Minister, then as Prime Minister. His remarks in NATO meetings in 1998, and elsewhere, were the stuff of the Cold War—a beleaguered Russia, surrounded by enemies, Russia with no permanent friends, only permanent interests. While he was known and personally charming to NATO diplomats, he bristled with resentment and hostility in his public remarks. He even threw me a few hostile glances at meetings.

"What can we do about Kosovo?" I was asked by NATO ambassadors and foreign ministers. They wanted the Serb ethnic cleansing stopped.

I consulted with the Pentagon and the State Department. Then, with permission from the Pentagon, I went to the White House to suggest the same general approach that had worked for Bosnia—NATO airpower and diplomacy. The Pentagon wasn't happy about this—for them, the objective was budget growth and prepping for possible action against Saddam Hussein. Nevertheless, the White House prevailed in internal discussions.

At the direction of NATO authorities, SHAPE was tasked with preparing "concept plans" for possible intervention. My British Deputy, acting on instructions from the Ministry of Defense in London, challenged me, asking, "What are you trying to do?" But it was obvious that NATO could not stand idly by.

On my visit to Moscow in the summer of 1998, General Kvashnin sat across the table, joined by someone from the Foreign Ministry and the intelligence services, as he argued, "You aim to take these countries in Eastern Europe away from us; they are our countries, and you want to sell them your weapons." And, "you aim is to take our minerals and make us poor." And the very charming Olga, the interpreter who accompanied me on the trip, divorced her American husband a few months later, when she was discovered to be a Russian spy planted in our headquarters.

By the autumn of 1998, some 400,000 Kosovars had fled their homes and were hiding in the rugged mountains to escape Serb special police efforts to arrest and eliminate the "troublemakers." NATO had warned Milošević the violence must stop, had flown aircraft around Serbia's northern and western periphery as a warning that NATO could repeat the types of airstrikes that had brought an end to the Serb siege of Sarajevo in 1995. And through the fall of 1998 NATO escalated the diplomatic pressure and threats. NATO Secretary General Solana, Chairman of the Military Committee Klaus Nauman and I traveled to Belgrade to dissuade Milošević.

NATO's statements and actions—my own headquarters was leading the planning effort—put my Russian deputy under severe pressure from Moscow. He delivered a GRU booklet purporting to prove that Albanians were really Chechens; it was so poorly done that even he couldn't defend it. He was recalled by Moscow, in late 1998, returned briefly for a couple of weeks in early 1999, and then departed for good.

According to reports, he was held under house arrest for some time, and stripped of his pension, before being eventually released.

The Serbs began their ethnic cleansing campaign anew in January 1999. French-led negotiations at Rambouillet between the Serbs and Albanians failed in early March, 1999. Serbia then deployed more of its military forces into Serbia and intensified its activities there.

By the time we admitted Poland Hungary, and the Czech Republic to NATO on March 16, 1999, and then, a week later, began the air campaign to stop Serb ethnic cleaning in Kosovo, the NATO-Russian relationship was in tatters, and the U.S.-Russian relationship was sustained only by President Clinton's friendliness with President Yeltsin and Vice President Gore's occasional collaboration on economic issues with Russian Vice President Chernomyrdin.

NATO conducted its first airstrikes on the evening of March 24, 1999. Political authorities were hoping that a day or two of strikes would convince Milošević to back down. But he didn't.

On Friday, March 26th, Hungarian Ambassador András Simonyi delivered a message from Hungary's Prime Minister, young Victor Orbán: "Twice before in this century Hungary has joined an Alliance and then gone straight to war; both times it lost and was dismembered; please do not allow this to happen again."

At one point during the air campaign, as hundreds of thousands of Kosovar Albanian fled their homes to escape the Serbs, and NATO escalated its series of strikes, Russia threatened to sally forth its Black Sea fleet to impede NATO air actions—but after stern warnings by Deputy Secretary Talbott, nothing came of this.

And in the midst of this was NATO's 50th Anniversary Summit in Washington, and the unveiling of the new Strategic Concept. For NATO political authorities, and for the heads of state, the air operation was more than embarrassing. It was a stark challenge to the new Strategic Concept, a severe threat to NATO itself and even a personal political threat to heads of state. Certainly NATO could not afford to fail, but would the air operation succeed? Why was the United States so dominant in this operation? And, if ground forces were necessary, would they be provided?

The air actions continued for 78 days, steadily escalating in scope and intensity. Bulgaria and Romania allowed their airspace to be used by NATO and completed the encirclement of Serbia. Heads of state agreed to do "whatever was necessary to succeed," thus authorizing planning to begin for ground operations. Eventually Russia agreed to participate with Finland in bringing to Serb President Milošević a proposal to halt NATO action and accept the NATO peacekeeping force which had been proposed earlier for Kosovo, in return for the withdrawal of all Serb military and police from Kosovo. On June 11, the day after the U.N. accepted the peace agreement and approved its implementation, the Russian military, in conjunction with the Serbs, made a belated effort to undercut the agreement. They deployed the Russian battalion by highway from Bosnia through Serbia to occupy the airfield in Pristina, Kosovo, in preparation for flying in reinforcing Russian airborne brigades. It was a well-televised crisis moment for NATO, and for me. But diplomatic and Presidential pressure on Russia blocked the reinforcing brigades, and the Russian battalion eventually moved out to a small sector of eastern Kosovo for peacekeeping duties in coordination with NATO.

Some two months after the Summit, Kosovo was a crisis resolved and a NATO success won by diplomacy, as well as by airpower and the threat of a ground invasion. 1.4 million Albanians returned to their homes. And to this day, it marks NATO's most successful action.

When new Russian Prime Minister Vladimir Putin visited Kyiv in November, 1999, for the inauguration of Ukrainian President Kuchma, he remarked in his speech, "Russia and Ukraine are more than brothers, we are in each other's souls." The Polish National Security Advisor came later to warn me that now Russia's aim was clear, to restore the Soviet space; already, he said, they have formed commercial companies to buy up electricity generating and transmission companies in Poland so they have control." The new Romanian Defense Chief warned me that the Russians were distributing fake Romanian passports in Moldova, attempting to instigate border riots and uncertainty, in an effort to block Romania's eventual accession to NATO.

In retrospect, NATO nations lacked the understanding, resources and will, to help transform Russia after the fall of the Soviet Union. While the top leaders in Russia formed certain relationships with the

West, the efforts of transformation were too difficult and complex to be accomplished without far deeper and much more extensive engagement by the West. And beneath the diplomatic exchanges and visits, the military and security services held the ultimate power in Russia. The historical legacy of antagonism to the West, resentment at the loss of Eastern Europe and the Soviet republics, and stubborn, deeply embedded nationalism, and their own stubborn self-interest became the dominant factors in regenerating hostility. The situation was an eerie echo of Weimar Germany's resentments after Versailles.

NATO enlargement was nothing more than the inevitable response to Eastern European fears, while Europe and the United States, overly optimistic in the aftermath of the Cold War, were pushed by the collapse of Yugoslavia to extend the zone of stability eastwards from the old Cold War boundaries. Had NATO failed to enlarge, it would have opened the door earlier to Russian efforts to restore Soviet space and Russian power in Eastern Europe. As it is, NATO enlargement has become a convenient excuse for the Russians to act out historic policies, and a whipping boy for disenchanted, overly idealistic Western strategists.

NATO did in fact extend stability eastwards and make possible an expansion of the European Union as well.

Today both NATO and the European Union are challenged by resurgent nationalism, a sometimes-faltering European economy, an unexpected security challenge in the form of migrants from the south, and increased Russian military and diplomatic pressure. In Afghanistan, NATO remains saddled with a military operation undertaken at U.S. urging without a plan or strategy for success. But if NATO and its partner organization, the European Union, can maintain their unity and resolve, and together manage the proper response to China's ascending power, the gradual transformation of Eastern Europe and even Russia itself is indeed possible. To use Gorbachev's phrase, "a common European home," and a Europe whole and free, Atlantic to the Urals, is not yet out of reach.

Chapter 25

Responsibilities of Alliance: Czech, Hungarian, and Polish Contributions During and After NATO's Kosovo Intervention

John-Michael Arnold

Introduction[1]

By joining NATO, the Czech Republic, Hungary, and Poland assumed new international responsibilities. As U.S. Secretary of State Madeleine Albright explained in December 1997:

> These nations are accepting a fundamental change in their national identities. For decades they looked to the free world for reassurance and support in their struggles for freedom and independence. Now, for the very first time, they are accepting responsibility for the freedom and security of others. We will be counting on them to stand by us in our future hours of need, and when other nations look for our reassurance and support.[2]

At the event formally admitting the three countries to the alliance, held on March 12, 1999, the new members' foreign ministers also remarked upon the duties that came with entering NATO. Jan Kavan of the Czech Republic emphasized that "we are prepared to fulfill our part of the responsibilities and the commitments of member states, and to meet all the obligations and duties which stem from this membership." Hungary's János Martonyi stressed that "Hungarians know that membership in NATO is a combination of advantages to enjoy and obligations to meet." The Polish foreign minister, Bronisław Geremek, assured that "Poland in the Alliance will be a good and credible ally for good and bad weather."[3]

The three new members confronted the realities of NATO membership immediately. Just 12 days after they joined, on March 24, 1999,

NATO launched Operation Allied Force, an air campaign against the Federal Republic of Yugoslavia (FRY), which by then comprised only Serbia and Montenegro. NATO aimed to compel Serbia's leader, Slobodan Milošević, to reach a political agreement with the Kosovo Albanians that would arrest an escalating conflict in Kosovo and prevent further humanitarian abuses there.

Examining how the three new NATO members contributed to the Alliance's Kosovo intervention, launched when the ink on their instruments of accession was barely dry, offers a way to reflect upon the responsibilities of NATO membership. All three new NATO members met their alliance obligations during Operation Allied Force and all of them contributed meaningfully to the Kosovo Force (KFOR) peacekeeping mission that followed.

Section I provides background to Operation Allied Force and gives an overview of the intervention and its results. Section II details the contributions made by Poland, Hungary, and the Czech Republic during the air campaign. Section III describes the contributions of the new allies to the aftermath of Operation Allied Force, both to KFOR and to the broader effort to integrate the Balkans into the Euro-Atlantic community. The concluding section, Section IV, makes three major points: (1) NATO membership comes with real responsibilities; (2) since NATO is an alliance of democracies, there will be political debates within members about what is required of them during military interventions; and (3) due to the complex nature of such interventions, allies can contribute to them, and thereby fulfill the responsibilities of alliance, in many ways.

I: Background to Operation Allied Force and Overview of the Intervention

By the late twentieth century, the Serbian province of Kosovo had a population of almost two million people, of whom 90 percent were ethnic Albanians.[4] In 1989, Serbia's leader, Slobodan Milošević, ended the political autonomy that Kosovo had long possessed.[5] By diminishing the status of the predominantly Muslim Kosovo Albanians, Milošević portrayed himself as the avenger of a historic defeat suffered by a Serb-led army in Kosovo in 1389 at the hands of the Ottomans.[6] In late

1989, a group of Kosovo Albanians established the Democratic League of Kosovo (LDK), a movement that pursued Kosovo's independence through a strategy of non-violence.[7]

In this era, Yugoslavia as a whole was entering a period of dramatic upheaval. In 1991, the republics of Slovenia, Croatia, and Macedonia all declared their independence, then Bosnia followed in 1992. While Macedonia was able to exit Yugoslavia peacefully and Slovenia's independence led to a very brief struggle, Croatia's move precipitated a war that cost 10,000 lives.[8] The greatest bloodshed, however, occurred in Bosnia. Lasting from 1992 until 1995, the conflict there killed 200,000 people. Muslim, Serb, and Croat military units were all guilty of abuses, but Serb forces were responsible for the overwhelming majority of atrocities.[9] In late August 1995, NATO began serious air strikes—Operation Deliberate Force—and, together with ground offensives by Croat and Bosnian Muslim forces, they pushed the Bosnian Serbs onto the back-foot militarily.[10] That convinced Slobodan Milošević, the patron of the Bosnian Serbs, that it was time to accept serious diplomatic negotiations. American diplomat Richard Holbrooke orchestrated the resulting peace talks, which culminated in the signing of the Dayton Accords in late 1995.

The old Yugoslavia had fragmented, but the Kosovo Albanians remained stuck within Serbia, which itself was now only in a federation with the much smaller republic of Montenegro. Madeleine Albright later summarized the situation of the Kosovo Albanians in the second half of the 1990s, writing that:

> Kosovo's Albanians looked around and saw that the Bosnians, Croats, Slovenes, and Macedonians had all left Yugoslavia to form independent states. The Albanians shared the same ambition but the Dayton Accords did nothing for them.[11]

With the Democratic League of Kosovo's efforts to achieve independence having made little headway, an alternative faction, the Kosovo Liberation Army (KLA), embarked upon a violent guerilla campaign. The conflict between the KLA and Serb forces intensified dramatically in late February 1998 when Serb forces attacked KLA strongholds and killed 85 people, including civilians, in one week.[12]

During the following months, the United States worked alongside international partners to encourage a political dialogue between the Serbian government and the Kosovo Albanians. On the ground, however, the violence got worse. In July 1998, the KLA embarked upon a major offensive and Serb forces responded by targeting both KLA fighters and civilians.[13] By October 1998, approximately 300,000 Kosovo Albanians were either internally displaced persons or refugees.[14]

In mid-January 1999, Serbian forces massacred forty-five civilians in Račak, which precipitated an intensification of diplomatic efforts to resolve the conflict. In February 1999, the United States—along with France, Germany, Italy, Russia, and the United Kingdom—convened a conference in Rambouillet, France, between the warring parties. Both the Serbs and Kosovo Albanians disliked elements of the political framework they were asked to consider and the negotiations dragged on for weeks. Ultimately, the Kosovo Albanians signed a political agreement on March 18, 1999. Following that, the Clinton Administration sent Richard Holbrooke to Belgrade in one last attempt to get Milošević to sign the agreement, but he refused to do so.[15]

On March 24, 1999, NATO resorted to armed force to compel Serbia to accept a settlement. Informed by events earlier in the 1990s, especially the West's extreme tardiness in halting the carnage in Bosnia and the failure to do anything to stop the Rwandan genocide, NATO leaders decided it was better to act sooner rather than later. As Secretary of State Albright said three weeks after the Račak massacre, "we learned in Bosnia that we can pay early, or we can pay much more later" and "the only reward for tolerating atrocities is more of the same."[16]

During the 78 days of Operation Allied Force, NATO aircraft flew over 38,000 sorties, of which 10,484 were strike sorties.[17] Alliance aircraft hit tactical targets, such as Serb forces in Kosovo, as well as strategic targets across the Yugoslav federation. Despite NATO's aim of preventing further outrages, the humanitarian situation on the ground actually got worse during the initial part of the campaign because Serb units intensified their expulsions of Kosovo Albanians.[18] At the end of the conflict, over 800,000 Kosovo Albanians were refugees, while an additional several hundred thousand were internally displaced.[19] NATO's demands for ending the air campaign included the withdrawal of all Serb forces from Kosovo, the deployment of a NATO-led peacekeeping force, and the ability for all refugees to return home.[20] The shorthand version of these aims was to get "Serbs out, NATO in, refugees back."[21]

Following NATO's late April 1999 summit in Washington D.C., several developments produced Milošević's capitulation. First, the Alliance escalated its air campaign.[22] Second, American and NATO military commanders began preparatory assessments of a ground invasion of Kosovo, signaling to Belgrade that NATO might be willing to escalate beyond airstrikes.[23] Third, President Yeltsin of Russia, which had a close relationship with Serbia, committed his country to working for a diplomatic end to the war.[24]

Yeltsin's eagerness to participate in the diplomacy of war termination set the stage for a series of meetings between Viktor Chernomyrdin, the Russian presidential envoy for Kosovo, U.S. Deputy Secretary of State Strobe Talbott (representing NATO), and Martti Ahtisaari, the president of Finland, who represented the European Union (EU). That diplomatic troika met several times and, after strenuous efforts, developed a commonly-agreed list of terms that Milošević would have to accept to end the airstrikes.[25] Those terms included all of the major objectives that NATO had established. On June 2, 1999 Viktor Chernomyrdin and Martti Ahtisaari conveyed the terms to Milošević, who formally accepted them the following day. After NATO and Yugoslavia finalized the technical arrangements for a settlement, NATO ended Operation Allied Force on June 10, 1999.[26] The U.N. Security Council passed resolution 1244, which authorized the deployment of a peacekeeping force to Kosovo and put civil administration in the hands of the United Nations Interim Administration Mission in Kosovo (UNMIK). The NATO-led Kosovo Force (KFOR) began its deployment on June 12, 1999.[27]

II: Contributions of Poland, Hungary, and the Czech Republic to Operation Allied Force

None of the new NATO members contributed combat aircraft to Operation Allied Force. That was hardly surprising because all were flying Soviet-made fighter and ground-attack aircraft—MiG-21s, MiG-23s, MiG-29s, and SU-22s—and the vast majority of those aircraft had not been modernized and were not interoperable with other NATO air forces.[28]

Milada Anna Vachudová, an expert on post-communist Europe, emphasizes that Poland's government was among the most politically supportive of the intervention within NATO.[29] Poland's prime minister at the time was Jerzy Buzek, who had been in office since 1997 and led a coalition government of his own bloc, Solidarity Electoral Action, and the Freedom Union party. Opinion polls reported that a majority of Poland's public approved of the air campaign.[30] Despite such support, NATO did not have a need to request the use of Polish airspace.[31] Jeffrey Simon, an American expert on Central European militaries, notes that Poland provided NATO with one of its transport aircraft to help with logistical demands.[32] Additionally, Poland sent 140 soldiers to the NATO-led Albania Force (AFOR), which provided humanitarian assistance to Kosovar refugees.[33]

Hungary was a cautious supporter of Allied Force. Public opinion polls showed similar levels of popular support for the campaign as existed in Poland, with 53 percent of Hungarian respondents indicating their approval of NATO's action in April 1999.[34] Hungary was the only NATO member at the time that bordered Serbia. András Simonyi, Hungary's first ambassador to NATO, recalls in this volume how the country's government was keenly aware that its involvement in the operation might cause Milošević to retaliate against ethnic Hungarians in Serbia.

On the opening day of NATO's air campaign, Hungary's parliament voted to make the country's airspace and airfields available to its fellow allies.[35] That same day, Prime Minister Viktor Orbán—who had entered office in 1998 and led the Fidesz party—assured the public that "NATO has so far not requested, nor will it in the future, armed participation from Hungary and, for that matter, our country could not fulfill such an expectation in view of its special situation."[36] In April 1999, Hungary sent 35 public health specialists to assist refugees in Albania.[37]

Although Hungary did not directly participate in air strikes, the Alliance's use of the country's airfields contributed to combat operations. By the time of the Kosovo intervention, Hungary's Taszár airbase, located in the south of the country and just 40 miles from the border with Serbia, had become a major logistical hub for American troops that were part of the peacekeeping forces in Bosnia.[38] In support of that same operation, the United States had deployed unarmed Predator drones to Taszár, from where they flew reconnaissance missions over Bosnia.[39] During Operation Allied Force, the United States used the Predators based in Hungary to conduct sorties over Serbia. The Predators provided intelligence that enabled strikes by manned aircraft against military targets.[40] NATO also deployed KC-135 tanker aircraft to Hungary and they provided refueling to combat aircraft.[41]

In May 1999, as NATO escalated its air campaign, Hungary's government assented to the basing of 24 U.S. Marine Corps F/A-18 Hornet aircraft—a multi-role aircraft with strike capabilities—at Taszár.[42] That precipitated some opposition among Hungary's public, with opinion polls finding that around two-thirds of the population opposed NATO's launching of strikes directly from Hungary's soil.[43] László Kovács, the parliamentary leader of the Hungarian Socialist Party, proposed prohibiting NATO strike sorties launched from Hungary, but the parliament failed to pass that measure.[44] By May 25, the American "Hornets" had arrived and Foreign Minister Martonyi defended the decision to accept them, remarking: "This is exactly the kind of NATO we wanted to join 10 years ago, one that stands for a certain set of values. Now, NATO is fighting to defend those values."[45]

The F/A-18s began flying combat missions several days later. As Benjamin Lambeth emphasizes in his study of the war, basing those aircraft in southern Hungary exacerbated the challenges faced by what remained of Yugoslavia's air defense units. Those units now confronted NATO aircraft attacking from yet another launching point, in addition to those that had already seen considerable use, such as airbases in Italy.[46] As one F/A-18 pilot deployed to Hungary commented at the time, "we'll make Milošević feel like he's in a box, with NATO staring at him from every side."[47] Of course, the strike missions flown from Taszár began just days before Milošević capitulated, but at the time the aircraft were moved there it was as yet unclear just so long Milošević would hold on. NATO's decision to fly bombing missions from Hungary was one element of the steadily intensifying military and diplomatic pressure that Milošević faced in late May 1999.

Of the three new NATO members, the Czech Republic experienced the most contentious political debate regarding Operation Allied Force.

Opinion polls found that only 35 percent of the Czech public approved of the campaign.[48] The year after the intervention, as part of a detailed study on Czech attitudes towards NATO, analysts Ivan Gabal, Lenka Helsusova, and Thomas Szayna asked Czech respondents whether "at the time we joined NATO, did you consider that by doing so we also took on such responsibilities as participation in Operation Allied Force?" Among the respondents, 34 percent reported that "I never considered something like that at all," while 30 percent stated that "I did not expect something as intensive."[49] In the same study, the authors also emphasized that "a lack of consensus at the highest levels of the Czech representative bodies persisted throughout the entire Operation."[50]

On March 16, 1999, representing the Czech Republic for the country's first time at NATO's North Atlantic Council, Prime Minister Miloš Zeman of the Social Democratic Party (ČSSD) stated that "the development in the Former Yugoslavia is particularly tragic" and added that "the international community must take a strong stand against aggression, violations of human rights and suppression of basic freedoms."[51] Notwithstanding those words, Prime Minister Zeman was unenthusiastic about the air campaign.[52] On the day the alliance's operations began, he remarked that "it is our obligation to proceed toward this nation [Yugoslavia] in such a way so as to comply with our commitments arising from NATO membership and not to assume the position of troglodytes who believe that bombs will solve everything." During the same statement, Zeman reminded the Czech public of the strong historical relations between the Czech people and Serbia, notably including Yugoslavia's opposition to the 1968 Soviet invasion of Czechoslovakia.[53] Within the Social Democratic Party government, Foreign Minister Jan Kavan offered public support for the air campaign, but there was considerable opposition within the government and the wider party.[54]

The second largest political party in the Czech parliament at the time was the center-right Civic Democratic Party (ODS). Its leader, Václav Klaus, also opposed NATO's air strikes.[55] Nevertheless, some of his party's leading members, as well as some of the party's local bodies, offered support for the military campaign.[56] In the Czech parliament, two other opposition parties—the Freedom Union and the Christian Democratic Union-Czech People's Party—also supported NATO's campaign.[57]

The most prominent supporter of NATO's intervention, within the Czech Republic, was President Václav Havel. In a statement issued on March 25, 1999, he recounted Milošević's mistreatment of the Kosovo Albanians and emphasized that Serbia had refused to sign the political agreement produced by the Rambouillet negotiations.[58] Just days after the end of the NATO summit in late April 1999, President Havel addressed Canada's parliament and offered a vigorous defense of NATO's intervention, arguing that the alliance was "fighting in the name of human interest for the fate of other human beings."[59]

Despite its political divisions over the issue, the Czech Republic still made limited contributions to the air campaign. The government approved NATO's use of the country's airspace and airfields on April 6, 1999, a step that was also approved by the Czech parliament.[60] Additionally, the Czech Republic deployed a field hospital and a transport aircraft to NATO's humanitarian assistance effort in Albania.[61]

Towards the close of May 1999, Foreign Minister Jan Kavan joined forces with his Greek counterpart, George Papandreou, to offer a diplomatic proposal aimed at ending the intervention. In Greece, only around 2 percent of the public approved of the air campaign.[62] The "Czech-Greek Peace Initiative" was unveiled on May 23, 1999 and, among its provisions, it called for a 48-hour bombing pause and provided that most, but not all, Serbian forces would have to leave Kosovo.[63]

Foreign Minister Kavan emphasized that the peace plan was not meant to undermine other diplomatic efforts.[64] Nevertheless, for the United States government, as well as for many others in NATO, the initiative was problematic because a bombing pause threatened to weaken the military and diplomatic pressure confronting Milošević. Furthermore, the very fact that two NATO members were putting forward their own diplomatic initiative threatened to signal serious cracks in the alliance's political unity, at a moment when NATO had a strategic interest in showing Milošević that he could not hope to outlast the alliance. As it happened, the Czech-Greek peace initiative did not do serious damage to the campaign of coercive diplomacy because, as a result of the discussions between Chernomyrdin, Ahtisaari, and Talbott, Serbia was presented with a combined NATO-Russia-EU position just 10 days after the Czech and Greek foreign ministers had proffered their own plan.

III: The New Allies' Contributions to the Aftermath of Operation Allied Force

On June 10, 1999, the day Allied Force ended, European Union foreign ministers, together with counterparts from the Balkans region, and other nations such as the United States and Russia, announced that they would establish the "Stability Pact for South Eastern Europe." Joining the ministers were representatives from a host of international organizations. All participants pledged to work on a collective strategy for achieving "lasting peace, prosperity and stability for South Eastern Europe."[65] The design of the Stability Pact was led by Germany, which held the EU Presidency for the first half of 1999, alongside the United States. For its part, the Clinton Administration helped to conceptualize the project, but deemed it appropriate for the European Union to take ownership of the initiative.

The Stability Pact was formally launched in late July 1999 in the capital of Bosnia, Sarajevo, at a meeting attended by leaders from almost 40 countries.[66] Launching the pact in Sarajevo, which had been besieged for the duration of the Bosnian war, underscored the goal of helping the region move beyond the horrors of its recent past. As Daniel Hamilton, one of the authors in this volume and a U.S. State Department official who worked on both the design and implementation of the initiative, said in congressional testimony:

> The guiding principle behind the Stability Pact is a bargain between integration and reform: the international community will work to stabilize, transform and integrate the countries of this region into the European and transatlantic mainstream; they, in turn, will work individually and together to create the political, economic and security conditions by which this can be possible.[67]

Hungary played a significant role in the Stability Pact. From the moment it joined NATO, Hungary had pledged that, because of its geographic location, it would try to help the nations of South Eastern Europe to follow in its own footsteps and to integrate into the Euro-Atlantic community.[68] Among its efforts as part of the Stability Pact, Hungary led an initiative known as the "Szeged Process." That project aimed to strengthen the independent press in Serbia and it also tried to improve governance in that country by connecting members of the Serbian opposition, specifically those in municipal government, with municipal leaders from other states in the region.[69] Additionally, in April 2000, Hungary and the United States convened a conference in Budapest regarding efforts to further economic reform in South Eastern Europe and enhance the region's integration into the global economy.[70]

In addition to Hungary's active and enthusiastic role in the Stability Pact, it contributed to the KFOR peacekeeping operation in Kosovo, along with both the Czech Republic and Poland. All three countries already had experience of peacekeeping in the Balkans, having contributed to the mission—known initially as the Implementation Force (IFOR), then subsequently the Stabilization Force (SFOR)—that deployed to Bosnia in the aftermath of the 1995 Dayton Peace Accords.[71] Poland began deploying troops to KFOR on June 23, 1999.[72] Its initial contribution was to send a 800-personnel unit, comprising Polish soldiers alongside troops from Ukraine and Lithuania.[73] Hungary's initial troop contribution to KFOR was 324 soldiers, who began deploying to Kosovo on July 15, 1999.[74] Also in July 1999, the Czech Republic sent 124 troops to KFOR, a contingent that grew to 175 personnel by the end of that year.[75]

The potential risks associated with participating in KFOR became apparent quickly. In December 1999, a Polish Captain was killed while handling a M-60 grenade rifle that had been confiscated during patrols near the Macedonian border.[76] In early April 2000, after U.S. military police and Polish troops seized weapons from a Serb house, they were surrounded by 150 Serbs who refused to let the American and Polish personnel leave. After eight hours the standoff was defused, having resulted in injuries to 11 American personnel and one Polish solider.[77]

KFOR remains deployed in Kosovo at the time of this writing. The overall size of the peacekeeping operation has been on a downward trend since 1999, with fluctuations based on conditions on the ground. Beginning in 2006, a United Nations-led diplomatic effort aimed to resolve Kosovo's political status, but by the end of 2007 that process had failed to produce an agreement that the Kosovo Albanians, Serbia, the EU, Russia, and the United States could all agree upon.[78] In February 2008, Kosovo declared its independence from Serbia and more than 100 states now recognize Kosovo as a sovereign state.[79] NATO decided that KFOR would continue to operate in Kosovo, in line with UNSCR

1244.[80] Since 2008, KFOR has been reduced from about 16,000 soldiers to roughly 3,600 troops at the time of writing.

The Czech Republic, Hungary, and Poland have each made sustained contributions to KFOR. Table 1 shows, year by year, the troops contributed by each country, as well as the approximate total size of KFOR. The table also shows what proportion of KFOR's overall force was represented by the collective contributions of the Czech Republic, Hungary, and Poland. Ever since 2003, the combined deployments of these three allies have exceeded 5 percent of KFOR's total force and for many years they have been significantly above that proportion.

IV: Reflections on the Responsibilities of NATO Membership

Considering the contributions of the Czech Republic, Hungary, and Poland to Operation Allied Force and its aftermath, I reach three major conclusions.

First, membership of NATO comes with real responsibilities. In his memoir, former Supreme Allied Commander Europe (SACEUR) General Wesley Clark recounted a phone conversation that he had with the Hungarian Chief of Defense, General Ferenc Vegh, early in the Kosovo campaign. Clark wrote the following about the conversation:

> I tried to imagine how he must feel; he and his wife had come for dinner just two weeks ago when we were celebrating Hungary's admission to the Alliance. Welcome to NATO; you're now at war![81]

On May 28, 1999, just 80 days after Hungary had joined NATO, American F-18s were taking off from Hungarian soil and bombing targets in a neighboring country. The United States and the other most powerful members of the Alliance are not the only ones who take on responsibilities to their fellow Allies through NATO.

Second, because NATO is an alliance of democracies, there is the potential for serious domestic political arguments within member states about what is required of them during military campaigns.

During the Kosovo intervention, there were significant debates in both the Czech Republic and Hungary. In the case of the Czech Republic, there were divisions about whether the Alliance should have

Table 1. Czech, Hungarian and Polish Contributions to KFOR

Year	Poland's Troops in KFOR	Hungary's Troops in KFOR	Czech Republic's Troops in KFOR	Total of Poland, Hungary, and Czech Republic Combined	Approx. Overall Troop Strength of KFOR	Poland, Hungary, and Czech Republic Troops Relative to KFOR (%)
2000	763	325	160	1248	50,000	2.50
2001	532	325	175	1032	50,000	2.06
2002	574	325	400	1299	39,000	3.33
2003	574	325	409	1308	26,000	5.03
2004	574	294	408	1276	20,000	6.38
2005	574	294	410	1278	17,500	7.30
2006	312	484	500	1296	17,000	7.62
2007	312	268	445-501	1025-1081	17,000	6.36
2008	312	484	500	1296	16,000	8.10
2009	271	317	400	988	15,000	6.59
2010	226	243	393	862	10,200	8.45
2011	152	242	103	497	5,000	9.94
2012	295	245	7	547	5,000	10.94
2013	160	194	7	361	5,000	7.22
2014	228	201	7	436	4,700	9.28
2015	254	336	9	599	4,700	12.74
2016	240	357	11	608	4,700	12.94
2017	253	366	12	631	4,352	14.50
2018	240	373	9	622	3,642	17.08

Sources: KFOR Website, https://jfcnaples.nato.int/kfor, IISS Military Balance, Years 2000-2018, *Reuters*, September 2, 2009, NATO to Cut Troops in Kosovo Despite Unrest.

been intervening against Serbia at all. In the case of Hungary, the most significant political debate concerned whether the country should allow alliance aircraft to launch bombing missions from Hungarian soil. The debates that occurred in these two new members did not make them exceptional; there were political debates and controversies within many members of the alliance regarding Kosovo. As noted above, polls found that only around 35 percent of the Czech Republic's population approved of NATO's air campaign. That was not that different from public opinion in a number of other allied states: only 42 percent of Belgium's population approved; 41 percent approved in Portugal; 39 percent approved in Spain; and only 2 percent of Greece's population supported the air campaign.[82]

Additionally, across NATO, there were various views about how the air war should be waged. For example, some allies had concerns about hitting certain targets within Yugoslavia. Meanwhile, in the United States, within both the administration and Congress, there were real concerns about whether to contemplate a ground invasion of Kosovo as a way to bring about Milošević's surrender. Even the call for a bombing pause that was central to the Czech-Greek peace initiative, although it had the potential to undercut the diplomatic pressure that was building on Milošević, mirrored an idea that a number of other allies had advocated previously.[83] Debates about how exactly to meet the responsibilities of alliance are something that comes with NATO's character as a club of democracies.

Third, what the new NATO members' contributions to the Kosovo intervention demonstrate is that there are many ways Allies can meet their responsibilities during military campaigns. After all, interventions are complex and multi-faceted undertakings, whose success does not depend merely upon contributions that enhance the "tip of the spear." In the case of Operation Allied Force, Hungary's airfields were an important piece of infrastructure in NATO's air campaign. Additionally, all three members contributed personnel to humanitarian assistance efforts for Kosovar refugees. Finally, and especially significantly, the Czech Republic, Hungary, and Poland each made sustained troop contributions to the KFOR peacekeeping mission.

To illustrate the benefits to the United States of the Czech Republic's, Hungary's, and Poland's involvement in KFOR, we can consider the year 2008, when the three Central European Allies collectively had 1,300 troops in KFOR, representing around 8 percent of the total force. That was close to the United States' commitment of troops to KFOR that year, which numbered 1,640.[84] That year was also one in which U.S. forces were carrying significant burdens around the world; there were 160,000 American troops in Iraq at the opening of that year, following the surge of 2007, and the United States had close to 25,000 troops in Afghanistan.[85] By sending 1,300 troops to KFOR, the Czech Republic, Hungary, and Poland were helping to secure and sustain the victory NATO attained in June 1999 and lessening the troop commitment that the United States had to make there. That same year, the Czech Republic, Hungary, and Poland collectively had 2,600 of their troops deployed in Afghanistan and Iraq as well.[86]

A recurring complaint heard during discussions about NATO in the United States is that America's European Allies often do not contribute a fair share to the Alliance and they "free-ride" on the efforts of the United States. Such criticisms of America's European allies are grounded in the fact that a minority of NATO's European members have met the alliance's pledge to spend 2 percent of their GDP on defense. Additionally, during military campaigns, the United States has contributed the majority of capabilities. During Operation Allied Force, for example, American aircraft flew 60 percent of the total sorties, 90 percent of the intelligence and reconnaissance sorties, and released 80 percent of the precision-guided bombs used.[87]

Even so, American criticisms about the scale of NATO Allies' contributions can sometimes be too harsh. As the experiences of the Czech Republic, Hungary, and Poland during and after the Kosovo intervention showed, all allies take on responsibilities as a result of NATO membership. The three new members contributed to Operation Allied Force and, in an even more pronounced way, they helped to bear the burdens associated with the KFOR peacekeeping operation that followed afterwards and that continues until this day.

Notes

1. I am grateful for the helpful comments I received on earlier drafts of this chapter from my colleagues at SAIS and from other contributors to this volume.

2. Madeleine Albright, "Statement during the North Atlantic Council Ministerial Meeting, NATO HQ, Brussels, Belgium," December 16, 1997, https://www.nato.int/docu/speech/1997/s971216aa.htm.

3. All of the quotes are from U.S. Department of State, Office of the Spokesman, "Secretary of State Madeleine K. Albright And Foreign Ministers of the Czech Republic, Hungary and Poland Remarks on Accession to the North Atlantic Treaty Organization, Truman Presidential Library, Independence, Missouri," March 12, 1999, https://1997-2001.state.gov/statements/1999/990312.html.

4. Samantha Power, *A Problem from Hell: America and the Age of Genocide*, 1st Harper Perennial ed. (New York: Harper Perennial, 2002), p. 445.

5. Strobe Talbott, *The Russia Hand: A Memoir of Presidential Diplomacy*, vol. 1st ed. (New York: Random House, 2002), p. 298.

6. Daniel Paul Serwer, *From War to Peace in the Balkans, the Middle East and Ukraine, Palgrave Critical Studies in Post-Conflct Recovery* (Basingstoke: Palgrave Macmillan, 2018), p. 72.

7. Ivo H. Daalder and Michael E. O'Hanlon, *Winning Ugly: NATO's War to Save Kosovo* (Washington, D.C.: Brookings Institution Press, 2000), p. 8.

8. Power, op cit., p. 247.

9. Ibid., pp. 251, 310.

10. Regarding the combined impact of the air strikes and the ground offensives, see Robert A. Pape, "The True Worth of Air Power," *Foreign Affairs*, March 1, 2004.

11. Madeleine Albright, *Madam Secretary: A Memoir* (New York: Miramax Books, 2003), p. 380.

12. Daalder and O'Hanlon, op cit., p. 27.

13. Albright, *Madam Secretary*, op. cit., pp. 386–87.

14. Daalder and O'Hanlon, op. cit., p. 41.

15. For a good overview of the problems both sides had with the Rambouillet framework, see Albright, *Madam Secretary*, op. cit., pp. 397–407.

16. Madeleine Albright, "Remarks and Q&A Session at the U.S. Institute of Peace, Washington, D.C.," February 4, 1999, https://1997-2001.state.gov/statements/1999/990204.html.

17. "Kosovo Air Campaign (Archived), Operation Allied Force," NATO, April 7, 2016, https://www.nato.int/cps/en/natohq/topics_49602.htm.

18. Serwer, op. cit., p. 75; Wesley K. Clark, *Waging Modern War* (New York: PublicAffairs, 2001), p. 234.

19. James Dobbins et al., *America's Role in Nation-Building: From Germany to Iraq* (Santa Monica: RAND Corporation, 2003), p. 113, https://www.rand.org/pubs/monograph_reports/MR1753.html.

20. Daalder and O'Hanlon, op. cit., p. 113; Talbott, op. cit., p. 309.

21. Albright, *Madam Secretary*, op. cit., p. 410.

22. Clark, op. cit., pp. 274–76.

23. Strobe Talbott, *The Great Experiment: The Story of Ancient Empires, Modern States, and the Quest for a Global Nation*, Simon & Schuster Paperback (New York, N.Y.: Simon & Schuster, 2009), p. 318; Clark, op. cit. pp. 281–86.

24. On the final day of NATO's Washington summit, April 25, Russian President Boris Yeltsin telephoned President Bill Clinton and made that commitment. See Memorandum of Telephone Conversation, Conversation with Russian President Boris Yeltsin, April 25, 1999, 10:35 - 11:58 a.m. EDT, Available from National Security Council and NSC Records Management System, 'Declassified Documents Concerning Russian President Boris Yeltsin,' Clinton Digital Library, https://clinton.presidentiallibraries.us/items/show/57569.

25. Daalder and O'Hanlon, op. cit., pp. 168–73.

26. Ibid., pp. 173-174.

27. Dobbins et al. op. cit., p. 115.

28. *The Military Balance 1999*, vol. 99 (International Institute for Strategic Studies, 1999), pp. 51, 61, and 68; Stefan Rutkowski (The Polish Air and Air Defense Forces), *Transformation of Polish Air Forces: What Is Required to Meet NATO Obligations* (Maxwell Air Force Base, Alabama: Air Command and Staff College, Air University, 2002); Jeffrey Simon, *Hungary and NATO: Problems in Civil-Military Relations* (Lanham: Rowman & Littlefield Publishers, 2003), pp. 61–62; Jeffrey Simon, *Poland and NATO: A Study in Civil-Military Relations* (Lanham: Rowman & Littlefield Publishers, 2004), p. 95.

29. Milada Anna Vachudová, "The Atlantic Alliance and the Kosovo Crisis: The Impact of Expansion and the Behavior of New Allies," in Pierre Martin and Mark R. Brawley, eds., *Alliance Politics, Kosovo, and NATO's War: Allied Force or Forced Allies?* (New York: Palgrave, 2000), p. 202.

30. Péter Tálas and László Valki, "The New Entrants: Hungary, Poland, and the Czech Republic," in Albrecht Schnabel and Ramesh Thakur, eds., *Kosovo and*

the Challenge of Humanitarian Intervention (United Nations University Press, 2000), pp. 206–9.

31. Ibid., p. 207.

32. Simon, *Poland and NATO*, op. cit., pp. 102–3.

33. Ibid., p. 103; "Operation Allied Harbour," NATO Allied Joint Force Command Naples, accessed February 8, 2019, https://jfcnaples.nato.int/page6322744/17-operation-allied-harbour-.

34. Tălas and Valki, op. cit., p. 201.

35. Ibid., p. 202; Simon, *Hungary and NATO*, op. cit., p. 62.

36. Ibid.

37. Ibid., pp. 62–63.

38. Jeffrey Simon, *NATO Expeditionary Operations: Impacts Upon New Members and Partners* (Washington, D.C.: National Defense University Press, 2005), p. 6.

39. Thomas P. Ehrhard, *Air Force UAVs: The Secret History* (Arlington, VA: Mitchell Institute, 2010), p. 51.

40. Daniel L. Haulman, "The U.S. Air Force in the Air War Over Serbia, 1999," *Air Power History* 62, no. 2 (Summer 2015): p. 12.

41. Simon, *Hungary and NATO*, op cit., p. 63.

42. Adam LeBor, "War in The Balkans: Baptism of NATO Fire for Hungary," The Independent, May 29, 1999, http://www.independent.co.uk/news/war-in-the-balkans-baptism-of-nato-fire-for-hungary-1096576.html.

43. Michael J. Jordan, "NATO Enlists a Reluctant Hungary into Kosovo War," *Christian Science Monitor*, June 2, 1999, https://www.csmonitor.com/1999/0602/p6s1.html.

44. Simon, *Hungary and NATO*, op. cit., p. 64; Tălas and Valki, op cit., p. 203.

45. Jordan, op. cit.

46. Benjamin S. Lambeth, *NATO's Air War for Kosovo: A Strategic and Operational Assessment* (Santa Monica, CA: RAND Corporation, 2001), pp. 50–51.

47. Jordan, op. cit.

48. William Drozdiak, "NATO's Newcomers Shaken by Airstrikes," *The Washington Post*, April 12, 1999, sec. A.

49. Ivan Gabal, Lenka Helsusova, and Thomas S. Szayna, *The Impact of NATO Membership in the Czech Republic: Changing Czech Views of Security, Military & De-*

fence (Royal Military Academy Sandhurst, United Kingdom: Conflict Studies Research Centre, 2002), p. 31.

50. Ibid., p. 4.

51. Miloš Zeman, "Speech at NATO's North Atlantic Council Meeting," March 16, 1999, https://www.nato.int/docu/speech/1999/s990316d.htm.

52. Milada Anna Vachudová, "The Atlantic Alliance and the Kosovo Crisis: The Impact of Expansion and the Behavior of New Allies," pp. 211–12.

53. Jeffrey Simon, *NATO and the Czech and Slovak Republics: A Comparative Study in Civil-Military Relations* (Lanham, MD: Rowman & Littlefield, 2004), p. 80.

54. Vachudová, op. cit., p. 212.

55. Ibid.

56. Jiří Pehe, "Kosovo Crisis Splits Czech Political Elite," *Reuters*, April 7, 1999, http://www.pehe.cz/clanky/1999/1999-Kosovocrisissplit.html.

57. Tälas and Valki, op. cit., p. 210.

58. Václav Havel, "Statement on the Situation in Kosovo," Prague, March 25, 1999, Available from Václav Havel Library, Digital Archive, https://archive.vaclavhavel-library.org/.

59. Václav Havel, "Address to the Senate and the House of Commons of the Parliament of Canada," Parliament Hill, Ottawa, 29 April 1999, Available from Václav Havel Library, Digital Archive, https://archive.vaclavhavel-library.org/.

60. Vachudová, op. cit., p. 212; Tälas and Valki, op. cit., p. 211.

61. Simon, *NATO Expeditionary Operations*, op. cit., pp. 11–12.

62. Daalder and O'Hanlon, *Winning Ugly*, op. cit., p. 161.

63. Simon, *NATO and the Czech and Slovak Republics*, op. cit., pp. 82–83.

64. Radio Prague, "Daily News Summary," May 26, 1999, http://www.radio.cz/en/section/bulletin/news-wednesday-may-26th-1999.

65. "Statement: Stability Pact for South Eastern Europe," Released at G8 Foreign and Finance Ministers' Meetings, Cologne, 10 June 1999, http://www.g8.utoronto.ca/summit/1999koln/pact.htm.

66. "Balkan Summit Leaders Endorse Stability Pact," CNN.com, July 30, 1999, http://www.cnn.com/WORLD/europe/9907/30/balkan.summit.04/.

67. "Statement of Daniel S. Hamilton, Special Coordinator for Implementation of the Stability Pact for Southeastern Europe and Associate Director of the Policy

Planning Staff, U.S. Department of State, March 8, 2000," Before House Committee on International Relations.

68. See the remarks by Foreign Minister Martonyi on March 12, 1999. U.S. Department of State, Office of the Spokesman, "Secretary of State Madeleine K. Albright And Foreign Ministers of the Czech Republic, Hungary and Poland Remarks on Accession to the North Atlantic Treaty Organization, Truman Presidential Library Independence, Missouri," March 12, 1999, https://1997-2001.state.gov/statements/1999/990312.html.

69. "Fact Sheet: The Stability Pact for Southeast Europe: One Year Later" (The White House, July 26, 2000), https://reliefweb.int/report/albania/fact-sheet-stability-pact-southeast-europe-one-year-later.

70. "Statement of Daniel S. Hamilton," op. cit.

71. Simon, *NATO Expeditionary Operations*, op. cit., pp. 5–9.

72. Simon, *Poland and NATO*, op .cit., p. 103.

73. Simon, *NATO Expeditionary Operations*, op. cit., p. 11.

74. Simon, *Hungary and NATO*, op. cit., p. 68.

75. Simon, *NATO and the Czech and Slovak Republics*, op cit., p. 84.

76. "KFOR Press Update by Major Roland Lavoie, KFOR Spokesman" (NATO Kosovo Force, December 12, 1999), https://www.nato.int/kosovo/press/1999/k991212a.htm.

77. Linda D. Kozaryn, "SHAPE Considers Troop Needs for Kosovo Force," American Forces Press Service, April 6, 2000, http://archive.defense.gov/news/newsarticle.aspx?id=45087.

78. "History," NATO Kosovo Force, accessed February 11, 2019; Serwer, op. cit., pp. 81–82.

79. Ibid, pp. 82–83.

80. "History," NATO Kosovo Force, accessed February 11, 2019.

81. Clark, op. cit., p. 217.

82. Daalder and O'Hanlon, op. cit., p. 161.

83. Clark, op. cit., pp. 177, 202, and 210.

84. *The Military Balance 2008*, vol. 108 (London: International Institute for Strategic Studies, 2008), p. 44.

85. Ibid., pp. 38 & 41.

86. Poland had 937 troops in Afghanistan and 900 in Iraq. Hungary had 225

troops in Afghanistan. The Czech Republic had 470 troops in Afghanistan and 99 in Iraq. Ibid., pp. 115, 131, and 144.

87. Daalder and O'Hanlon, op. cit., p. 150.

Chapter 26

Renewing the Vows: NATO @70

Mircea Geoană

"Et Si Tu N'Existais Pas?" (What If You Didn't Exist?)—this famous Joe Dassin song is a rhetorical question that we should ask ourselves about the present and future of NATO. A frantic conversation is under way in all possible formats and fora; time and energy are spent with the hope to find the miraculous cure to the current malaise and acrimony among key Allies, and to identify a miraculous solution to the current state of affairs in transatlantic relations. Reasons for concern abound from both sides of the Atlantic, rendering each of us weaker, to the satisfaction of our adversaries or competitors, who have been offered a "wild card" to re-enter the new Great Game.

NATO @70 should be more than just a celebration of past accomplishments. It should mainly be a realistic appraisal of the situation as it stands and of the few possible ways forward. We should not shy away from facing the reality: strong headwinds are facing our Alliance. If the hesitations to organize a proper NATO Summit on its 70th anniversary are any indication, imagine the difficulties to mobilize political energies for a new way forward. It is very good that London will host a special anniversary "Summit" at the end of 2019. But nice and well-scripted meetings cannot hide the truth: our Alliance is in crisis. Even the Munich Security Conference, the ultimate temple of transatlanticism, was engulfed in an exchange of jibes between American and German leaders, much to the sarcastic delight of the Russian foreign minister. We just cannot afford to continue to prepare for NATO summits fearing that Alliance leaders will fail to agree on the major challenges facing us.

Would it be too much to expect from our leaders to reconfirm in London the first paragraph of the Declaration adopted at the 60th NATO anniversary in Strasbourg and Kehl?

> We, the Heads of State and Government of the North Atlantic Treaty Organization, met today in Strasbourg and Kehl to celebrate the 60th anniversary of our Alliance. We have reaffirmed

> the values, objectives and obligations of the Washington Treaty which unite Europe with the United States and Canada, and have provided our transatlantic community with an unprecedented era of peace and stability.[1]

Or, to solemnly restate the (no longer so obvious) essence of our very existence?

> NATO continues to be the essential transatlantic forum for security consultations among Allies. Article 5 of the Washington Treaty and collective defense, based on the indivisibility of Allied security, are, and will remain, the cornerstone of our Alliance. Deterrence, based on an appropriate mix of nuclear and conventional capabilities, remains a core element of our overall strategy.[2]

NATO's Open Door policy has been a cornerstone of the transatlantic partnership. During the Cold War and after, the Alliance welcomed new Allies as different as Germany, Greece and Turkey, new members formerly belonging to the Warsaw Pact, and former Yugoslavia's new independent nations. 2019 is the 20th anniversary of NATO's enlargement to Poland, Hungary and the Czech Republic. It is the 15th anniversary of the enlargement to Bulgaria, Estonia, Latvia, Lithuania, Romania, Slovakia and Slovenia. And it is the 10th anniversary of the enlargement to Croatia and Albania. Accession of the Republic of Northern Macedonia, anticipated in 2019, may be considered as being part of the latter wave of enlargement, as the 2009 NATO Bucharest Summit extended invitations to the three countries, with the caveat that Greece and the Former Yugoslav Republic of Macedonia would resolved their dispute regarding the country's name, which they have now done.

Especially after the fall of communism, the rationale for the successive waves of enlargement was not as obvious as it appears today, mainly in the U.S. security, academic and political establishments. Each of these successive enlargements had a common thread, but also distinct conditions and significance.

The first wave of enlargement to Poland, Hungary and the Czech Republic was mainly about addressing the security architecture in Europe after German reunification and the demise of the Soviet Union.

The most ambitious enlargement to seven countries from the Baltic to the Black Sea in 2004 was possible also because terrorist attacks on the United States on September 11, 2001 dramatically transformed American threat perceptions. The first invocation of the North Atlantic Treaty's Article 5, used as a sign of European solidarity with the United States and implemented in Afghanistan, pushed the Alliance toward an "out-out of area" stance. The terrorist threat became a dominant factor in military planning and coalition-building in, and beyond, NATO's membership and contributions.

It is worth mentioning that the successful integration and smooth ratification in the U.S. Senate of the 1999 group of new Allies, as recounted by Jeremy Rosner in this volume, also played an important role in the "big-bang" approach to take in seven countries in 2004.

In addition, the Russia factor continued to play a role, especially with regard to including the three Baltic republics, as did the logic of "unfinished business" from the 1999 enlargement, when Romania and Slovenia were considered but not invited.

Over this time, European Allies have become more influential with regard to the decision-making process regarding enlargement. In the case of the 1999 wave, France pushed hard for Romania, yet failed in the face of U.S. and German opposition. By the time of the 2008 Bucharest Summit, it was the George W. Bush Administration that pushed hard, yet failed, to secure Alliance agreement to extend Membership Action Plans to Georgia and Ukraine in the face of strong German and French opposition.

The inclusion of Balkan states in the 2009 enlargement can also be interpreted as a continuation of the NATO pacification effort after its involvement in the wars in Bosnia in 1994 and Kosovo in 1999, but also as a response to Russia's resumption of a more aggressive stance in the region after its 2008 war on Georgia of 2008. That aggression has continued, marked by the 2014 annexation of Crimea, quasi-occupation of Eastern Ukraine, and military build-up in the Black Sea and the Eastern Mediterranean.

How may the situation develop? Three main scenarios may be envisaged: a further degradation of the situation; a buying-time, wait-and-see, muddling-through approach; or, preferably, a wake-up call for a new chapter of transatlantic ties, adapted to our time.

The Worst-Case Scenario

Let's take the worst-case scenario: what if NATO would cease to exist or to function properly? A crippled or dysfunctional Alliance is a remote possibility, but it cannot be completely ruled out. After all, nothing in life or history is inherently immune to changes that shifting circumstances may impose on any human, societal or political construct. Future generations will not necessarily receive a NATO certificate at birth, as our forefathers gave us. After all, the 30 years since the fall of communism have been more of an historical exception when it comes to the logic of Great Power confrontation, violence, and conflict.

A world without NATO? What if the United States decides to "go bilateral" by abandoning the multilateral framework that binds it to those some Americans consider to be ungrateful free riders? What would the impact be of such a huge vacuum on the world and on our interests? Is there a realistic and practical alternative?

I use such a dire and apocalyptic scenario as a pretext to force us to think and act differently and to rescue not only "the-most-success-ful-alliance-in-history." but our civilization, our way of life, our free-dom. Nature abhors a vacuum. What would replace NATO as the ul-timate security arrangement? The most likely answer is that a web of bilateral and regional security arrangements would begin to form, as so many times before in history. The United States would probably enter into a logic very much to the liking of the current Administration: concluding a series of bilateral defense deals that would link bilateral security guarantees to preferential economic and trade arrangements. The example at hand is the future of U.S.-UK commercial and security arrangements after Brexit.

Poland's proposal for "Fort Trump" and the defense deal recently signed by the United States and Hungary are improvisational exam-ples of a trend that could be consolidated and eventually become main-stream. Nordic cooperation will inevitably strengthen, with Norway, Finland, Sweden, Iceland and Denmark finding even more common ground. After Brexit the United Kingdom will try to leverage its newly-found freedom by proposing bilateral/regional arrangements not only to the United States, India and Japan but also to those EU and non-EU countries in Europe and around the world who share important strategic, military and intelligence with their British counterparts. The Visegrád 4 could coalesce around Poland's relatively robust defense posture and will try to lure other Central and Southeast European countries into variable geometry formats. The Polish Inter-Marum concept, resuscitated today in the Three Seas format, could conceivably become a framework in which countries between Russia and Germany come together in formalized security arrangements. Other European powers, large and small, could follow suit. European history is littered with similar efforts (Entente Cordiale, Little Entente), often with disastrous consequences.

Countries with strong transatlantic inclinations and interests like Romania or Poland will continue to consider the link to the United States as their primary security insurance. Others in the region will try to hedge their security risks, as may already be seen. Germany and France will try to boost European defense initiatives and industrial cooperation and attract as many current EU members as possible to join. A Franco–German "army" is not unthinkable after the signing of the Aachen/Aix-en-Provence new bilateral treaty.

The likely result of all this? The European security landscape would look more like Swiss cheese than a homogenous surface. Both the center and the peripheries would become weaker, with Russia and possibly China offered an undeserved "terrain de chasse." Turkey and possibly Greece would be more tempted to mitigate the political and economic risks and opportunities with closer ties to both Russia and China. The Western Balkans would re-enter the logic of Great Power competition, with complex consequences for the regional system of allegiances. Nuclear deterrence and anti-ballistic systems would continue to operate as a U.S. bilateral security anchor, with Romania and Poland in this category. The future of the Incirlik base in Turkey would come into question.

Not only would Europe become weaker in such a scenario, so would America. No one can anticipate the future of Russian-Chinese cooperation. A Russia-China "Kissinger" move, a tactical alliance to counter the dominant status of the United States, is not as unimaginable as some American pundits profess. A coordinated offensive towards Europe and the South China Sea could be an interesting war game to analyze.

A new OSCE-type arrangement with Germany and Russia at the core of a new pan-European security arrangement is a distinct possibility. After all, General de Gaulle was thinking of a Europe from the Atlantic to the Urals and some German leaders are again entertaining this idea. Speaking in favor of the Nord Stream II natural gas pipeline bypassing Ukraine, former Chancellor Gerhard Schröder has expressed the clear view, popular in many business and political circles, that Germany needs Russian resources to continue to expand its economic and export-oriented power house. After all, if America becomes mercantilist in its interpretation of international affairs, why shouldn't Germany?

The European Union itself would become the collateral victim of such a catastrophic series of events. Europe would return to its old habits. Old demons could resurface.

Muddling Through

This is the most likely scenario. Incremental change should be tried, as Nicholas Burns and Douglas Lute have proposed.[3] Buying time is sometimes the wise thing to do. Elections in America are looming large. Most of the Democratic hopefuls call for strengthening the Alliance—some of out of conviction, others because they believe President Trump's eclectic style of foreign policy and international affairs is vulnerable to Democratic pushback. Congress is and will continue to be active in this conversation a bipartisan way, including in the form of binding and non-binding legislation.

In this scenario, the Strategic Concept and other decisions adopted at previous NATO Summits would be carried out, if sometimes reluctantly. The 2024 target for all Allies to comply with the "Wales pledge" of 2% of GDP for defense would probably be met, with the caveat that some important European Allies will insist in introducing in the overall amount other budget items pertaining to cyber security (as Italy recently suggested) or peacekeeping or peace-building costs conducted outside NATO operations (as Germany insists). In terms of procurement, the 20% target for new equipment could be met but with a caveat: those European Allies who possess national/European defense industry capabilities are likely to insist on an implicit or explicit "buy European" clause. Countries without such industrial prowess would continue to navigate (and mitigate) the growing competition in procurement between the United States and core Europe for military and dual-use equipment.

Even in such circumstances, the NATO's 'vows" would require a solemn reaffirmation of the sanctity of the Article 5 mutual security guarantee. The perception that NATO was a "paper tiger" Alliance would be likely to grow. Lack of Allied unity would be likely to boost the probability of new quasi-Article V Russian provocations.

In such a scenario, NATO would probably continue to invest in deterrence measures against Russia's aggressive stance on the Eastern flank. Still, the Alliance would be marginally involved in the broader security and stability of the Southern neighborhood in Northern Africa and the broader Middle East. Terrorism would continue to be a menace to the transatlantic world and weak or accomplice states would continue to be targeted by ISIS and other radical Islamic movements. Russia, Pakistan and China would try to fill the void left by NATO's withdrawal from Afghanistan, with implications for the balance of power for the rest of Central Asia and Eurasia as a whole.

The situation in the Black Sea would continue to be tense as Russia proceeded to modernize its capabilities. Turkey's ambivalent stance on critical issues like Syria, and its flirtations with Russia and Iran, would also probably continue. The tensions between the United States and Germany, France and the UK over the Iran sanctions dossier would add to the mounting number of strategic uncertainties and security risks in the broader Black Sea, Caspian, Eastern Mediterranean and the Gulf areas.

In such a context, it would be more difficult to achieve a common NATO response to Russia's subversive measures in cyber defense, meddling in democratic processes, and use of energy as a political instrument. Bilateral support for Ukraine and Georgia would continue, but would most probably stop short of a more formalized relationship with the Alliance. In the Western Balkans, Northern Macedonia's accession to NATO will help maintain the credibility of the "Open Door" policy for the region.

NATO's partnerships around the world would continue to operate but be more resource-constrained. If Brexit becomes reality, the United Kingdom would use its influence in NATO to stay relevant in continental European affairs. Under this scenario, the currently incipient European defense institutions would gradually evolve. Suspicion over the final motives of the much proclaimed "strategic autonomy" of the EU from the United States would continue to corrode bonds of trust among the key Allies.

Lip service would be paid to streamlining Alliance decision-making processes, but with no measurable results. As long as Allies see eye to eye, NATO's consensus rule serves to unify. In more tense situations, however, it could also play the opposite role. European Allies are right in criticizing the fact they found out from open sources that the United States decided to withdraw from Syria or Afghanistan. Americans are right to criticize some European Allies for free riding on the U.S. security blanket.

Failure to adapt to a changing world is also a form of incipient irrelevance. The old saying "out-of-area or out-of-business" will come to haunt us, as the attention of the United States (rightly, in my view) is moving toward the competition for supremacy with China.

Back in Business: Ensuring Our Long-Term Security and Shaping the New World Order

The situation in NATO cannot be seen in isolation from the broader set of political, economic issues in transatlantic relations or from the overall state of world affairs. Neither Washington nor European capitals will invest new energy in their relations until and unless each once again realizes one simple truth: we thrive together, or we falter alone. There is no other logical solution. The United States or Europe must put their resources together if either is to have any hope of maintain influence and relevance in our turbulent times. We might differ on many tactical aspects, but a reality test should represent a wakeup call for the Western world: we simply cannot afford to continue to diverge. What is to be done?

Back to fundamentals: shared values and common interests

NATO is so much more than a mere security arrangement. It is the foundation of our free societies. The London anniversary Summit should solemnly reaffirm this indestructible foundation of our Alliance.

While America's vital role should be reaffirmed by all Europeans, Washington's Europe-bashing must stop. The United States and Europe are indispensable partners. This obvious reality is sometimes obscured by the raging conversation about the right balance between bilateralism and multilateralism, globalization and national interests. There is no possible way for the new or renewed world order to reflect and protect the interests of the West and of our democratic friends and allies around the world without America and Europe pulling together their still plentiful resources. The rise of authoritarianism, closed societies and state capitalism cannot be fought by America or by Europe alone. Any additional wedge between the two sides of the Atlantic not only weakens our own hand, it plays directly into the interests of our rivals and real competitors. Values and interests inside the Alliance should be realigned. Differences in risk and opportunity assessment among Allies should be recognized and dealt with punctually. The "strategic autonomy" of Europe should be seen as a sign of emancipation not from America but from our own strategic impotence. A more assertive Europe is an indispensable ingredient in our common success and relevance in decades to come.

Reviving American leadership of the Alliance should go hand-in-hand with reaffirming the sanctity of Article 5

We should not shy away from recognizing the damage that statements of President Trump have inflicted on Europe's trust in the resolve of the United States in fulfilling its Washington Treaty obligations. At the same time, we should also not exaggerate the significance of those statements, because if U.S. efforts to extract a better "deal" from other Allies works, this would not be such a bad proposition—maybe just the opposite. Meanwhile, Congress should pass legislation reconfirming unequivocally that there is bipartisan support for Article 5 and America's commitment to the Alliance as a whole. Congress should also continue to fund the "European Deterrence Initiative" against Russian aggression and expand it with new measures to counter the non-Article 5 threats Russia has so viciously employed in cyber warfare, hacking and election meddling. The next NATO Strategic Concept review should be started in London in December 2019. Alliance leaders should expressly demand a tight schedule to upgrade of NATO's strategic response to the deteriorating international security environment. This response should go beyond conversations about capabilities and burden-sharing. It should reconfirm and redefine the key role of NATO as the backbone of international security. New spending is critical to produce added NATO defense capabilities, including intelligence-surveillance-reconnaissance, cyber and digital technologies.

European Allies must step up their game

Procrastination on the 2% of GDP for defense targets should stop. It is our continent and our nations who are the most vulnerable to a multitude of traditional and non-traditional security threats. The 2024 deadline should be met by all Allies, from Germany to Canada and from the Netherlands to Italy and Spain.

The illusion that Russia is a threat only to Eastern flank countries should stop immediately. Russia's return to the Middle East, its flirtation with Turkey and Iran, its new assertiveness in the Arctic region, its ballistic posture in Crimea and Kaliningrad should be a strong incentive for all Allies to rouse themselves from strategic naivete, ambivalence or mere wishful thinking. Russia is a threat. We all should treat it as such, without giving up on efforts to engage and de-escalate the current situation.

Cold War rhetoric from Russia should not be reciprocated by the Alliance. But credible deterrence speaks more than a thousand communiques. Energy diversification in Europe must continue. This is more than the mercantilist interest of the United States to export its energy bounty to Europe. It is a security issue. The solution is not to stop doing business with Russia but to stop putting them in a dominant, monopolistic position. This not only would reduce the capacity that Moscow has in (ab)using energy as a strategic lever, but is an indispensable part of any strategy that envisages a more constructive relationship between NATO, Europe, and the Russian Federation.

After Brexit, 80% of NATO's defense spending will come from non-EU Allies. Only by investing more—appropriating more resources to

NATO, strengthening the Permanent Structured Cooperation (PES-CO), the European Defense Fund (EDF) and military mobility improvements—can Europe escape the strategic irrelevance it faces. Strategic prowess, strategic responsibility and specialization must become reality, and not just remain catchy phrases in speeches of European leaders.

NATO is so much more than Article 5 or the 2%...

Article 3 of the Washington Treaty stipulates that "The Parties to this Treaty (...) are determined to safeguard the freedom, common heritage and civilization of their peoples, founded on democracy, individual liberty and the rule of law." The erosion of democracy and of the rule of law is "the enemy from within," inevitably producing a severe breach in the very foundation of the edifice on which the Alliance is built. NATO should emulate the way in which the European Union deals with democratic slippages of its members under Article VII of the EU Treaty and introduce a similar mechanism of scrutiny and correction. This is a difficult change to be introduced but a mechanism (independent and/or with a peer review/Secretary General's assessment) should be crafted and formally put on the table.

...but new, bold, measures are badly needed in order to keep the Alliance relevant in the 21st century

Restoring European defense strength and credibility will take more than grudgingly upholding the Alliance's "Wales Pledge" for 2024. Here are a few suggestions.

• Implement an upgraded Quadrennial Defense Review, including a mechanism for peer and independent reviews. This should be announced on the occasion of the 70th anniversary and given as a task for the next NATO Summit. In addition to maintaining the commitment of appropriating 20% of defense spending for major new equipment and R&D of new capabilities, another 10% should be dedicated to countering the new array of threats. National cybersecurity and (military) intelligence efforts should be included in the calculation of the 2% benchmark of NATO-related expenditures, as some Allies suggest. European defense industry concerns related to access barriers to the U.S. market should also be addressed. More common ventures in traditional and new defense-related areas like A.I., robotics or outer space cooperation should be envisaged. The ultimate goal should be the creation of a transatlantic defense area, where cooperation and technology transfer should be the norm, not the exception. New spending is critical to produce added NATO defense capabilities, including intelligence-surveillance-reconnaissance, cyber and digital technologies. Transatlantic cooperation in these critical fields should be supported by the creation of a transatlantic R&D and Innovation Fund/Trust.

- Addressing vulnerabilities in the area of hybrid warfare should go hand-in-hand with active measures of deterrence of hybrid (sub-conventional) attacks short of the narrow Article 5 definition of an "armed attack." Adapt traditional deterrence principles to the cyber realm. Cyber offensive options to deter Russia and China have become a strategic necessity.

- Containing Russia on the Eastern flank should include additional deterrence measures in the Black Sea, including by adding one more Multinational Battlegroup to the 4 decided for the Baltics and Poland. The NATO Readiness Initiative, which aims to provide 30 ready battle groups, air squadrons and naval combatants in 30 days should be complemented by a comprehensive Porcupine Defense strategy as suggested by the Naval War College.

- NATO should be winning the technology competition in the Digital Age—by aggressively investing in the NextGen of Warfare and maintaining the lead in military and intelligence. The EU should emulate the U.S. system of R&D between military and civilian, business, academic actors.

- Establish an Eisenhower Fund for Military Mobility, Logistics and Resilience in Europe. Military mobility and logistics represent key components of NATO's capabilities to operate, fight and deter. The shift from the doctrine of conventional war to out-of-area operations led to a downgrade of NATO's overall military mobility in the European theatre. Moreover, recent military exercises in Eastern flank countries revealed severe weaknesses in transport, infrastructure, logistics and supply chains, underlying significant practical obstacles in readiness and easily deployable

NATO assets in the region. The truth is that the "fine weather" atmosphere in which the last three rounds of enlargement took place inhibited the need to also invest in the density and quality of dual-use infrastructures and organic transport capabilities in Central and Southeastern Europe similar to how Western Europe invested in established routes during the Cold War. The 2014 conflict in Ukraine was the turning point in military in contingency planning aimed at ensuring credible and effective Article 5-type operations not only for reinforcements but for proper combat operations.

- The meager quality of such infrastructure in the new member states represents a major liability, making military planners face the unpleasant reality of weak force sustainment, given untested supply lines and transport capabilities, all the way from the Baltic to the Black Sea. The situation is complicated by numerous other problems, such as the time needed to get national movement permits, the complexity of cross-border, multinational and EU regulations, and coordination of military transport with civilian transport routes. Vital infrastructure assets like bridges, tunnels, roads and railroads are antiquated and incapable of handling heavy military transports. The time has come to address this intolerable situation. A number of ideas have been tested, including in the Three Seas format, but the level of resource needs requires bolder moves.

- Resilience in our societies should go beyond protecting physical infrastructures and coordination. NATO should define common standards for national resilience and clarify shared responsibilities for deterring hybrid attacks, where information-sharing and investment are paramount.

- The creation of the Eisenhower Fund (recognizing the role of the President in the founding of the Alliance on 1949) would represent the military and security equivalent of the Juncker Plan, introduced after the financial and economic crisis of 2008-2009, with the European Investment Bank as the primary lender, in association with commercial banks and the private sector. The Eisenhower Fund would also focus its activities towards dual-use infrastructures and involve the private sector and a number of institutional investors like the European Investment Bank (EIB), EBRD and OPIC/IFC. A portion of the next European Financial Framework (the 2021-2028 EU budget) should be dedicated to such dual-use projects, including in the energy sector. The European Defense Fund should also be significantly beefed-up. EU-NATO cooperation on this direction will prove critical, beyond the 2016 NATO-EU Joint Declaration on strategic partnership and the EU and NATO Councils' 34 new actions for cooperation. The new European Commission should revisit the Joint Communication of the current Commission and further clarify cooperation between military and non-military activities, expedite military mobility, and ensure the necessary conditions for strategic pre-deployment of military forces and resources. The European Defense Agency should also play its part in ensuring the right synergies between military and non-military capabilities.

NATO is more than our military. It's about our people

Many in our young generations know nothing about the horrors that lead to the creation of the Alliance and of the array of global institutions at the end of World War II. Employees at Microsoft refuse to work for applications that could be used by the military. We speak more and more of American values or European values, but not that much of Western values. Surveys indicate a very low desire among publics in some European countries to come to the rescue of other Allies in case of foreign aggression. The perception of the United States in Europe is deteriorating, and Europe is beginning to be perceived more as a competitor than as an indispensable ally. Investing in a new generation of transatlantic leaders and in the trust of our citizenry represents a priority as important as any of the critical issues tormenting our ties across the Atlantic.

An ambitious Columbus Scholarship Program should be launched—a combination of Erasmus Plus (that allows exchanges of students and faculty) and the Fulbright/Rhodes Scholarship programs. Institutions like the German Marshall Fund of the United States should find a number of counterparts in Europe, with government and private sector support.

Renewing the Vows @70 should also mean strengthening the democratic nature of the Alliance and its democratic processes. The role and scope of the NATO Parliamentary Assembly should be enhanced. National parliaments should appoint to the NATO PA the most relevant politicians. Formalism in the relations between the NATO General Secretariat should be replaced by permanent exchange of information and enhanced role for democratic scrutiny of the Assembly on the activities and functions of the Alliance.

Out of area or out of business? NATO after Afghanistan

Ending the Afghan War is in sight and maintaining readiness of highly trained servicemen and women will be a challenge. A joint Spirit of NATO effort should be launched, using as a model the fantastic work of Spirit of America for U.S military personnel and diplomats. The entire southern neighborhood of NATO and Europe remains highly unstable. Further engagement of NATO in the Mediterranean Dialogue, established with seven of the partners in the region, should be broadened and deepened. Selectively, more of these partnerships should be brought up to the level of Individual Cooperation Programs (ICP) with Egypt and Israel, thus establishing long-term, structured and effective cooperation with these countries. Trust funds established for Jordan or Mauritania in previous years should be offered to all interested Mediterranean Dialogue partners. The NATO training cooperation initiative with partners in the Greater Middle East should be beefed up, with significant contributions from European allies and partners. A transatlantic stability and security toolbox for the Greater Middle East should be decided upon at the next NATO-EU Strategic Partnership meeting.

A NATO global partnership network?

The NATO Summit in 2008 welcomed the largest number of NATO partners to date. The Bucharest Declaration still stands and should be brought to the next level on the next appropriate occasion: "The Alliance places a high value on its expanding and varied relationships with other partners across the globe. Our objectives in these relationships include support for operations, security cooperation, and enhanced common understanding to advance shared security interests and democratic values. We have made substantial progress in building political dialogue and developing individual Tailored Cooperation Packages with a number of these countries." The significant contributions or support offered by Australia, Japan, New Zealand, Singapore or the Republic of Korea to NATO-led efforts in Afghanistan should not be wasted but used to step up a NATO global partnership network.

The rise of a more assertive China will call on much closer cooperation with democratic nations in the Indo-Pacific area. Competition to develop new technologies like A.I., cyber, robotics, quantum computing and biotechnology would mean a much closer cooperation between the United States and Europe. NATO should play its part in anticipating the next generation of warfare, not only in Europe but also in the Asia-Pacific.

Missile Defense

Ballistic missile proliferation and the Russian build-up in Kaliningrad, Crimea and Syria pose an increasing threat to Allies' forces, territory and populations. Especially after losing the INF Treaty and on the way to the renewal of the START Treaty in 2021, missile defense forms an indispensable part of the response to counter this threat. The substantial contribution to the protection of Allies from long-range ballistic missiles to be provided by European-based U.S. missile defense assets in Romania and Poland remains paramount, as an integral part of any future NATO-wide missile defense architecture. Bearing in mind the principle of the indivisibility of Allied security as well as NATO solidarity, options for a comprehensive missile defense architecture to extend coverage to all Allied territory and populations not otherwise covered by the United States system should become a priority.

Conclusion

Restoring trust in the transatlantic relationship seems like a daunting task. Some suggest we should wait for the next American president and recognize that NATO as we knew it is "dead." Others remind us that this is not the only difficult moment in the last 70 years of transatlantic relations and that we will eventually get over this one, too. Over time, even the most durable marriages lose some of the original magic and transform into a more pragmatic contract. If we were to renew the vows at our 70th anniversary, what should we say before the high priest of history? That in complicated times, we are stronger together or we just give up? That what unites us is more valuable and enduring or what separates us? And, more importantly, that we have an obligation to the next generations to do whatever it takes to make sure they also will live in peace, freedom and democracy or they will go through the tragedy and destruction we thought over forever?

And ask our current leaders to imagine the world without this formidable alliance of democracies: *Et Si Tu N'Existais Pas?*

Notes

1. Declaration on Alliance Security Issued by the Heads of State and Government participating in the meeting of the North Atlantic Council in Strasbourg / Kehl on April 4, 2009, https://www.nato.int/cps/en/natohq/news_52838.htm.

2. Ibid.

3. See the recent Harvard Kennedy School Belfer Center Report, "An Alliance in Crisis," conducted by Ambassadors Nicholas Burns and Douglas Lute.

About the Authors

Madeleine K. Albright is Chair of Albright Stonebridge Group, a global strategy firm, and Chair of Albright Capital Management LLC, an investment advisory firm focused on emerging markets. She was the 64th Secretary of State of the United States. Dr. Albright received the Presidential Medal of Freedom, the nation's highest civilian honor, from President Obama on May 29, 2012. In 1997 she was named the first female Secretary of State and became, at that time, the highest-ranking woman in the history of the U.S. government. As Secretary of State, Dr. Albright reinforced America's alliances, advocated for democracy and human rights, and promoted American trade, business, labor, and environmental standards abroad. From 1993 to 1997, she served as the U.S. Permanent Representative to the United Nations and was a member of the President's Cabinet. From 1989 to 1992, she served as President of the Center for National Policy. Previously, she was a member of President Jimmy Carter's National Security Council and White House staff and served as Chief Legislative Assistant to U.S. Senator Edmund S. Muskie. She is a Professor in the Practice of Diplomacy at the Georgetown University School of Foreign Service. She chairs the National Democratic Institute for International Affairs and serves as president of the Truman Scholarship Foundation. She also serves on the Board of the Aspen Institute. In 2009, Dr. Albright was asked by NATO Secretary General Anders Fogh Rasmussen to Chair a Group of Experts focused on developing NATO's New Strategic Concept. She received a B.A. with Honors from Wellesley College, and Master's and Doctorate degrees from Columbia University's Department of Public Law and Government, as well as a Certificate from its Russian Institute. Her most recent book is *Fascism: A Warning*.

John-Michael Arnold is a DAAD Post-Doctoral Fellow at the Johns Hopkins School of Advanced International Studies (SAIS). He holds a Ph.D from Princeton University's Woodrow Wilson School of Public and International Affairs and his research interests include U.S. foreign policy, strategic studies, transatlantic relations, and NATO. During his doctorate, he was a graduate fellow at Princeton's Center for International Security Studies (CISS) and he completed a pre-doctoral fellowship at the George Washington University's Institute for Security and Conflict Studies (ISCS). Prior to enrolling at Princeton, he worked as special assistant to the president of the Brookings Institution. He also has a master's degree in International Relations from Yale University and a BA in Philosophy, Politics, and Economics (PPE) from the University of Oxford.

Wesley K. Clark is a businessman, educator, writer and commentator who serves as Chairman and CEO of Wesley K. Clark & Associates, a strategic consulting firm. Clark retired as a four star general after 38 years in the United States Army, having served in his last assignments as Commander of U.S. Southern Command and then as Commander of U.S. European Command/Supreme Allied Commander, Europe. He graduated first in his class at West Point and completed degrees in Philosophy and Politics. He studied Economics at Oxford University as a Rhodes scholar. He worked with Ambassador Richard Holbrooke in the Dayton Peace Process, where he helped write and negotiate significant portions of the 1995 Dayton Peace Agreement. In his final assignment as Supreme Allied Commander Europe he led NATO forces to victory in Operation Allied Force, a 78-day air campaign, backed by ground invasion planning and a diplomatic process, saving 1.5 million Albanians from ethnic cleansing. His awards include the Presidential Medal of Freedom, Defense Distinguished Service Medal (five awards), Silver Star, Bronze Star, and Purple Heart.

Benoît d'Aboville is a career diplomat and former Ambassador. Between 2000 and 2005 he served as France's Permanent Representative to NATO. He is currently Vice President of the *Fondation pour les Études Stratégiques* in Paris and Associate Professor at Sciences-Po/Paris School of International Affairs. He is member of the board and vice president of the International Institute of Humanitarian Law in San Remo and Geneva. He serves as Chairman of the editorial committee of *Revue de Défense Nationale*. During his diplomatic career he was posted in Washington, Moscow, Geneva, Madrid (CSCE) and New York. He was Deputy Political Director at the Quai d'Orsay and senior auditor at the French *Cour des Comptes*. In 2018 he was appointed a member of the NATO Secretary General's Senior Advisory Board. He contributes to various publications on international and political military affairs.

Stephen J. Flanagan is a Senior Political Scientist at the RAND Corporation in Washington. His research interests include U.S. defense strategy, alliance and partnership relations in Europe/Eurasia, strategic deterrence, and outer space security. He served in several senior positions in the U.S. government over the past four decades including: at the National Security Council staff as Special Assistant to the President and Senior Director for Defense Policy (2013-15) and for Central and Eastern Europe (1997-99); National Intelligence Officer for Europe; Associate Director and Member of the State Department's Policy Planning Staff; and Professional Staff Member, Senate Select Committee on Intelligence. He also held senior research and faculty positions at the Center for Strategic and International Studies, National Defense University, the International Institute for Strategic Studies, and Harvard's Kennedy School of Government. He served as the lead advisor to former Secretary of State Madeleine Albright in her capacity as Chair of the Group of Experts that developed the foundation for NATO's Strategic Concept. He has published six books and many reports and journal articles and is a member of the Council on Foreign Relations. He earned an A.B. from Columbia Univ. and a Ph.D. from the Fletcher School, Tufts University.

Mircea Geoană is president of the Aspen Institute Romania and a preeminent international public figure. He ran for the Presidency of Romania in 2009. In an unprecedented narrow and contested election, he received 49.6% of the ballots cast. He served as the President of the Romanian Senate and as Ambassador of Romania to the United States of America. From 2000 to 2004, he served as Minister of Foreign Affairs of Romania. He also served as OSCE Chairman-in-Office in 2001. He is Chairman and Founder of MG International Strategic Consulting Group, a strategic advisory firm. An alumnus of the Polytechnic Institute and, respectively, the Law School at the University of Bucharest, he graduated in 1992 from the *Ecole Nationale d'Administration* in Paris, France. He graduated in 1999 from the World Bank Group Executive Development Program at the Harvard Business School. He holds a Ph.D from the Economic Studies Academy of Bucharest. He was decorated Commander of the National Order "The Star of Romania," awarded the "Legion d'Honneur" (France) and "Stella della Soliedarita" (Italy). He is married to Mihaela, an architect by training. They have two children, Ana Maria and Alexandru. He is fluent in English, French, Spanish and Italian.

Elias Götz is a DAAD Post-Doctoral Fellow at the Foreign Policy Institute of Johns Hopkins SAIS and researcher at the Institute for Russian and Eurasian Studies (IRES), Uppsala University. He holds a Ph.D in Political Science from Aarhus University (2013). His main areas of expertise are security studies, international relations theory, and Russian foreign policy. He has published on these topics in journals such as *International Studies Review*, *International Politics*, *Foreign Policy Analysis*, *Global Affairs*, and *Contemporary Politics*. He is currently working on a book project entitled *Russia's Quest for Regional Primacy*.

Daniel S. Hamilton is the Austrian Marshall Plan Foundation Professor and Senior Fellow at the Foreign Policy Institute of Johns Hopkins University's Paul H. Nitze School of Advanced International Studies (SAIS). From 2002 to 2010 he was the Richard von Weizsäcker Professor at SAIS, and is Richard von Weizsäcker Fellow at the Robert Bosch Academy in Berlin. He was the Founding Director of the School's Center for Transatlantic Relations, and for fifteen years served as Executive Director of the American Consortium for EU Studies. He has served as Deputy Assistant Secretary of State for European Affairs, responsible for NATO, OSCE and transatlantic security issues, U.S. relations with the Nordic-Baltic region, and stabilization of Southeastern Europe following the Kosovo conflict; U.S. Special Coordinator for Southeast European Stabilization; Associate Director of the Policy Planning Staff for U.S. Secretaries of State Madeleine K. Albright and Warren Christopher; Senior Policy Advisor to Assistant Secretary of State and U.S. Ambassador to Germany Richard C. Holbrooke. In 2008 he served as the first Robert Bosch Foundation Senior Diplomatic Fellow on the policy planning staff of German Foreign Minister Frank-Walter Steinmeier. His book *Rule-Makers or Rule-Takers: Exploring the Transatlantic Trade and Investment Partnership*, was named "#1 Global Policy Study of the Year" in 2016. Selected publications include *Advancing U.S-Nordic-Baltic Security Cooperation*; *The Eastern Question: Russia, the West and Europe's Grey Zone*; and *Alliance Revitalized: NATO for a New Era*. He has been presented with Germany's Federal Order of Merit (*Bundesver-dienstkreuz*); named a *Chevalier* of France's *Ordre des Palmes Académiques*; and awarded Sweden's Knighthood of the Royal Order of the Polar Star. He was presented the State Department's Superior Honor Award for his work to integrate the Baltic states into Euro-Atlantic structures.

Jan Havránek is the Policy Adviser at the Policy Planning Unit of the Office of the NATO Secretary General in Brussels. He previously served as the Head of Defense Section at the Czech Republic's Permanent Representation to NATO in Brussels (2014-2017); Assistant First Deputy Minister of Defense (2013-2014); and foreign policy advisor to Alexandr Vondra (2010-2012). In 2013, he was named to the *Diplomatic Courier*'s annual list of the "Top 99 Under 33 Foreign Policy Leaders." His other engagements have included a fellowship at Center for European Policy Analysis (CEPA, 2013-2014) and work for the Prague Security Studies Institute (PSSI, 2003-2006) and the Association for International Affairs (AMO, 2002-2007). He holds a master's degree in international security studies from the Fletcher School of Law and Diplomacy, Tufts University (2009).

Liviu Horovitz is a DAAD Post-Doctoral Fellow at the Foreign Policy Institute of Johns Hopkins SAIS. He is currently writing a book on the United States' desire for military preponderance within the current international system. He has served as a research fellow at Harvard University's Belfer Center for Science and International Affairs, a senior researcher on nuclear policy at the Center for Security Studies in Zurich, a consultant for the Preparatory Commission for the Comprehensive Nuclear-Test-Ban Treaty Organization in Vienna, and a research associate at the James Martin Center for Nonproliferation Studies in Monterey. His work has been published in, for instance, the *Journal of Strategic Studies, European Security, International Spectator, RUSI Journal, The Washington Quarterly, Nonproliferation Review*, and *Bulletin of the Atomic Scientists*. He holds a doctorate from ETH Zurich.

Robert E. Hunter was U.S. Ambassador to NATO from 1993 to 1998. He served on the National Security Council staff from 1977 to 1981 with lead responsibility for West European Affairs and then Middle East Affairs. He was Foreign Policy Advisor to Senator Edward M. Kennedy and worked on education issues as a member of the domestic staff in the White House for President Lyndon Johnson. He has been affiliated with many boards and institutions, including the Pentagon's Defense Policy Board and the State Department's International Security Advisory Board, the Center for Transatlantic Relations (Johns-Hopkins-SAIS), the Center for Transatlantic Security Studies at the National Defense University, the RAND Corporation, and the Center for Strategic and International Studies. He had a senior policy role in nine U.S. presidential campaigns and has been a speechwriter for more major candidates than anyone else in U.S. history (including 3 presidents and 4 vice-presidents). He is the author of over 1200 publications. Decorations include the Defense Distinguished Civilian Service Award (twice) and French Legion of Honor. He received a B.A. from Wesleyan University a Ph.D from the London School of Economics, where he was a Fulbright Scholar.

Géza Jeszenszky is a professor of history and a Hungarian diplomat. He served as Hungary's Minister for Foreign Affairs from 1990-1994, President of the Hungarian Atlantic Council from 1995-1998, Hungary's Ambassador to the United States from 1998-2002, and Hungary's Ambassador to Norway and Iceland from 2011-14.

Jan Jireš has been the Head of Defense Section at the Czech Republic's Permanent Representation to NATO in Brussels since August 2017. From March 2014 to July 2017 he served as the Defense Policy Director at the Ministry of Defense of the Czech Republic. From 2004 to 2014, he was a lecturer in international relations and security studies at Charles University in Prague. Between 2009 and 2013, he worked as director of the Prague Centre for Transatlantic Relations at the CEVRO Institute College. He has worked with a number of U.S. and European research institutes and think-tanks on various security policy-related projects (CTR SAIS Washington, CESS Groningen, DCAF Geneva, CEPI Bratislava, PISM Warsaw, SOWI Strausberg, PSSI Prague, SAC Bratislava, CEPA Washington). He holds an M.A. in Political Science and History from Charles University. In 2012, he received a Ph.D from Charles University for his dissertation on the evolution of U.S.-Central European relations in the post-Cold War era.

Stephan Kieninger is a DAAD Post-Doctoral Fellow at Johns Hopkins University SAIS. He received his Ph.D in Modern History from

Mannheim University in 2011. His current research looks into Western financial assistance for the Soviet Union and its impact on the peaceful end of the Cold War. He is the author *The Diplomacy of Détente. Cooperative Security Policies from Helmut Schmidt to George Shultz* (London: Routledge, 2018) which explains how East-West trade and the Helsinki process fostered cooperative security policies despite recurring crisis in international relations. His first book, *Dynamic Détente, The United States and Europe, 1964–1975* (Lanham: Rowman & Littlefield, 2016) investigates the emergence of détente and the origins of the Helsinki Final Act in 1975.

John Kornblum served for more than 35 years an American diplomat. As a specialist for Europe, he was posted in Germany, Austria, Belgium and Finland, in addition to numerous postings in the State Department in Washington, DC. His assignments included positions as Minister and Deputy Commandant in Berlin, Deputy U.S. Permanent Representative to NATO, U.S. Ambassador to the Organization for Security and Cooperation in Europe, Assistant Secretary of State for European and Canadian Affairs, Deputy head of the U.S. Delegation to the Dayton Balkan Peace Talks, Special Envoy to the Balkans and U.S. Ambassador to Germany. Ambassador Kornblum has worked in private industry on both sides of the Atlantic since retiring from the Foreign Service in 2001. He lives with his family in Berlin.

László Kovács is a Hungarian politician and diplomat. He served twice as Foreign Minister of Hungary, from 1994 to 1998 and from 2002 to 2004. He was a founder of the Hungarian Socialist Party (MSZP) in October 1989, becoming a member of the presidium of the National Board in May 1990. He was party spokesman on foreign affairs from November 1990. He also served as party chairman from 1998 to 2004. From 1994 to 2004 he was a Member of the Hungarian Parliament. From 2004 to 2010 he served as Member of the European Commission in Brussels, responsible for Taxation and the Customs Union. From 2010 to 2014 he was Deputy Chairman of the Foreign Affairs Committee in the Hungarian Parliament. Earlier in his career, between 1975 and 1986, he worked in the Foreign Affairs Department of the Central Committee of the Hungarian Socialist Workers Party, establishing relations with social democratic parties in Western Europe. From 1986 to 1987 he served as Deputy Foreign Minister and 1988-1989 as State Secretary in the Ministry of Foreign Affairs.

Andrei Kozyrev is the former Foreign Minister of the Russian Federation. In 1974 he graduated from the Moscow State Institute for International Relations and subsequently earned a degree in Historical Sciences. He joined the Ministry of Foreign Affairs in 1974 and served as head of the Department of International Organizations from 1989-1990. He became the Foreign Minister of the Russian Soviet Federative Socialist Republic in October 1990 and retained his position when the Russian Federation gained independence in 1991. He was an early proponent for increased cooperation between the United States and Russia and advocated for the end of the Cold War. He was a participant in the historic decision taken in December 1991 between the leaders of Russia, Belarus, and Ukraine to peacefully dissolve the Soviet Union. As Russia's first Foreign Minister, he promoted a policy of equal cooperation with the newly formed independent states of the former Soviet Union, as well as improved relations with Russia's immediate neighbors and the West. He left the post of Foreign Minister in January 1996, but continued in politics by representing the northern city of Murmansk in the Russian Duma for four years. Since 2000, Kozyrev has lectured on international affairs and served on the boards of a number of Russian and international companies.

Sir Malcolm Rifkind served as a UK Government Minister, under Margaret Thatcher and John Major, continuously from 1979-1997. Among other ministerial and Cabinet appointments, he was Minister responsible for the UK's relations with the Soviet Union from 1982-86. He was Secretary of State for Defense from 1992-1995 and Foreign Secretary from 1995-1997. He was Chairman of the Intelligence and Security Committee of Parliament, with responsibility for oversight of the UK's Intelligence Agencies, from 2010-2015. He was a member of the OSCE's Eminent Persons Panel which examined the crisis in Ukraine and Western relations with the Russian Federation. He is a Visiting Professor at the Department of War Studies of King's College, London University.

Jeremy Rosner is Managing Partner at Greenberg Quinlan Rosner, a Washington-based polling and strategy firm. He served as Senior Adviser to the President and Secretary of State for NATO Enlargement Ratification from 1997-1998. During 1993-1994 he was Special Assistant to the President, serving as Counselor and Senior Director for Legislative Affairs on the staff of the National Security Council. He has served as an adviser for an array of political leaders, organizations and private sector executives and is a frequent contributor to policy journals and media. From 1994-1997 he served as a Senior Associate at the Carnegie Endowment for International Peace and from 1991-1993 as Vice President for Domestic Affairs at the Progressive Policy Institute. He holds a Doctorate in Policy Studies from the University of Maryland School of Public Policy, a Master's degree in Public Policy from Harvard University's John F. Kennedy School of Government, and a BA in Politics, summa cum laude, from Brandeis University.

Volker Rühe served as the Minister of Defense of the Federal Republic of Germany from April 1, 1992 to October 27, 1998. As Germany's longest-serving defense minister, he oversaw the country's integration of the former East German army, expanded Germany's role within NATO, and played a central role in opening NATO's door to aspiring candidates from Central and Eastern Europe. Between September 11, 1989 to October 27, 1992 he served as Secretary General of Germany's Christian Democratic Union (CDU). He represented his constituency in Hamburg as a Member of the German Bundestag from December 14, 1976 to October 18, 2005, and served as Chair of the Foreign Affairs Committee from 2002 to 2005.

András Simonyi (Ph.D) is an economist by training. He was Hungary's first Ambassador to NATO (1995-1999) and his country's first Permanent Representative to the North Atlantic Council (1999-2001). He was Hungary's Ambassador to the United States (2002-2007). He is an independent foreign policy consultant living in Washington D.C.

Kristina Spohr is Helmut Schmidt Distinguished Professor at the Henry A. Kissinger Center for Global Affairs at Johns Hopkins University's School of Advanced International Studies (SAIS). Normally she is on the faculty of the London School of Economics and Political Science (LSE). She studied at the University of East Anglia, Sciences Po Paris, and Cambridge University, where she earned her Ph.D in History and then held a post-doctoral fellowship. She also worked as a Research Fellow in the Secretary General's Private Office at NATO headquarters in Brussels. She has authored several books, most recently *The Global Chancellor: Helmut Schmidt and the Reshaping of the International Order* (Oxford University Press, 2016) – also in extended German edition *Helmut Schmidt: Der Weltkanzler* (WGB/Theiss, 2016) – and co-edited *Transcending the Cold War: Summits, Statecraft, and the Dissolution of Bipolarity in Europe, 1970-1990* (Oxford UP, 2016). Her newest book, on the global exit from the Cold War, is *Post Wall, Post Square: Rebuilding the World after 1989* (HarperCollins/UK; Yale University Press/US)—German edition entitled *Wendezeit: Die Neuordnung der Welt nach 1989* (DVA 2019).

Strobe Talbott is a distinguished fellow in residence in the Foreign Policy program at the Brookings Institution. Previously he served as President of the Brookings Institution from July 2002 to October 2017, after a career in journalism, government, and academe. Prior to joining Brookings, he was founding director of the Yale Center for the Study of Globalization. Before that, he served in the State Department from 1993 to 2001, first as Ambassador-At-Large and Special Adviser to the Secretary of State for the New Independent States of the former Soviet Union, then as Deputy Secretary of State for seven years. He entered government service after 21 years with *Time* magazine. As a reporter, he covered Eastern Europe, the State Department, and the White House, then was Washington bureau chief, editor-at-large and foreign affairs columnist.

Alexander Vershbow is a Distinguished Fellow at the Atlantic Council in Washington, DC. He served as Director of the U.S. State Department's Office of Soviet Union Affairs (1988-91), U.S. Deputy Permanent Representative to NATO (1991-93), Special Assistant to President Clinton and Senior Director for European Affairs on the National Security Council staff (1994-97), U.S. Ambassador to NATO (1998-2001), U.S. Ambassador to the Russian Federations (2001-2005), U.S. Ambassador to the Republic of Korea (2005-08), Assistant Secretary of Defense for International Security Affairs (2009-2012) and Deputy Secretary General of NATO (2012-16).

Karsten D. Voigt is member of the board of Aspen Germany and Senior Associate fellow and member of the presidium of the German Council on Foreign Relations (DGAP). From 1976-1998 he was member of the German Bundestag. There he served als Foreign Policy Speaker of the Social Democratic party caucus (*Fraktion*) from 1983-1998. For many years he was chairman of the German–Soviet and later the German–Russian parliamentary group in the Bundestag. From 1992-1994 he was elected as Vice President and from 1994-1996 as President of the NATO Parliamentary Assembly. From 1999-2010 he served as the German-American Coordinator in the Federal Foreign Office.

Jenonne Walker served as Special Assistant to the President and Senior Director for Europe on the U.S. National Security Council staff in 1993-1994 and then as U.S. Ambassador to the Czech Republic 1995-1998. Earlier in her government career she had been an analyst of West European affairs at the Central Intelligence Agency, a member of the Policy Planning staffs of U.S. Secretaries of State Henry A. Kissinger and Cyrus R. Vance, Political Counselor at the U.S. Embassy in Stockholm, Sweden, and chair of the U.S. Government's interagency committees on the negotiations to eliminate Intermediate Range Nuclear Forces (INF) and to reduce and limit Conventional Forces in Europe (CFE) during the second term of U.S. President Ronald Reagan. During a period out of government (1990-1992) she was a Senior Associate at the Carnegie Endowment for International Peace and a Fellow at the Woodrow Wilson International Center for Scholars. From retiring in 1998 through 2000 she was Vice President for Europe of the World Monuments Fund.

Andrei Zagorski is Head of Disarmament and Conflict Resolution Studies at the Primakov Institute of Word Economy and International Relations (IMEMO) of the Russian Academy of Sciences. He is also Professor of international relations at the Moscow State Institute of International Relations (MGIMO-University) and member of the Russian International Affairs Council. Previously, he served as Vice-Rector of MGIMO; Senior Vice-President of the EastWest Institute; Faculty Member of the Geneva Center for Security Policy and Deputy Director of the Institute for Applied International Research, Moscow. His areas of expertise include European security, OSCE studies, arms control, post-Soviet studies, Arctic studies, Russian foreign and security policy, negotiations studies, and conflict resolution.

Ryszard Zięba is a full professor and the Head of the History & Theory of International Relations Department at the Faculty of Political Science and International Studies, University of Warsaw, where he teaches courses on Poland's foreign policy, International Politics, European Security, Theory of International Relations, and Foreign Policy Analysis. He was a member of the Steering Committee of the Standing Group on International Relations in the European Consortium for Political Research and the coordinator for Poland in the Central and East European International Studies Association. He has served in the National Security Strategic Review Commission appointed by the President of the Republic of Poland and prepared expertise for Polish Parliament, Ministry of Foreign Affairs, Ministry of Regional Development, National Security Bureau and for the European Commission as Jean Monnet Chair. He has published 26 books and about 400 papers, articles, reviews and expert opinions on international security, the foreign and security policies of Poland and other Central European states, and on the theory of security studies and international relations. Recent publications include *The Euro-Atlantic Security System in the 21st Century: From Cooperation to Crisis* (Cham, Switzerland: Springer International Publishing, 2018) and (in Polish) *International Security in the XXI Century* (Warsaw: Poltext, 2018).